PROFESSIONAL
SHAREPOINT® 2010 DEVELOPMENT

PROFESSIONAL

SharePoint® 2010 Development

PROFESSIONAL

SharePoint® 2010 Development

Tom Rizzo
Reza Alirezaei
Paul Swider
Jeff Fried
Scot Hillier
Kenneth Schaefer

Wiley Publishing, Inc.

Professional SharePoint® 2010 Development

Published by
Wiley Publishing, Inc.
10475 Crosspoint Boulevard
Indianapolis, IN 46256
www.wiley.com

Copyright © 2010 by Wiley Publishing, Inc., Indianapolis, Indiana

Published simultaneously in Canada

ISBN: 978-0-470-52942-3

Manufactured in the United States of America

10 9 8 7 6 5 4 3 2 1

For general information on our other products and services please contact our Customer Care Department within the United States at (877) 762-2974, outside the United States at (317) 572-3993 or fax (317) 572-4002.

Wiley also publishes its books in a variety of electronic formats. Some content that appears in print may not be available in electronic books.

Library of Congress Control Number: 2010923551

This book is dedicated to the memory of Dyana Eckstein who was a loved sister, aunt, and friend. She will always be loved and remembered in our thoughts. We miss and love you.

—Tom Rizzo

I would like to dedicate this book to S. Khatoon. Thank you for being the love of my life, my best friend, and my family!

—Reza Alirezaei

ABOUT THE AUTHORS

 TOM RIZZO is a senior director in the SharePoint team at Microsoft. This is Tom's second stint with SharePoint having worked in the SharePoint and Exchange Server teams back in the SharePoint 2001 timeframe. Before working in SharePoint, Tom worked in the SQL Server team and also as a technical specialist in the Microsoft field organization, where he evaluated and deployed Microsoft technologies for the United States Department of Defense. You can reach Tom, who authored chapters 1 through 4, 7, 14, and Appendix A, at thomriz@microsoft.com.

 REZA ALIREZAEI is an independent consultant and a five-time recipient of Microsoft's Most Valuable Professional (MVP) award for Microsoft SharePoint Portal Server & Microsoft Office SharePoint Server. He is focused on designing and implementing enterprise solutions for SharePoint, related .Net technologies, and Microsoft Business Intelligence stack. Reza can be reached at reza@devhorizon.com.

 PAUL J. SWIDER is a freelance consultant and the Enterprise SharePoint Strategist for OnClick Solutions. In addition, he is President of the Charleston SharePoint Users Group and an accomplished entrepreneur. Paul has trained and consulted thousands of SharePoint administrators, developers, and architects. In addition, he writes and teaches about enterprise collaboration concepts with demonstrated knowledge you can only get in "the trenches." His specialties include enterprise information architecture, SharePoint development patterns, and social media integration. When not working, Paul enjoys sailing and snowboarding. He wrote chapters 5 and 10.

 SCOT HILLIER is an independent consultant and Microsoft SharePoint Most Valuable Professional focused on creating solutions for Information Workers with SharePoint, Office, and related .NET technologies. He is the author/coauthor of 12 books on Microsoft technologies including "Inside SharePoint 2010." Scot splits his time between consulting on SharePoint projects and training for Critical Path Training (www.criticalpathtraining.com). Scot is a former U. S. Navy submarine officer and graduate of the Virginia Military Institute. Scot authored chapter 11 and can be reached at scot@shillier.com.

 JEFF FRIED is a senior product manager at Microsoft, specializing in strategic applications of search technology. Jeff is a frequent speaker and writer in the industry, holds 15 patents, has authored more than 50 technical papers, and has led the creation of pioneering offerings in next generation search engines, networks, and contact centers. He wrote chapter 6.

 KENNETH SCHAEFER is an independent developer and designer focusing on SharePoint and web-based solutions. Ken lives in the Chicago area with his daughter, Alexa. Ken, who authored chapter 8, can be reached at ken@kenschaefer.name.

ABOUT THE TECHNICAL EDITORS

MATT RANLETT, a SQL Server MVP, has been a fixture of the Atlanta .NET developer community for many years. A founding member of the Atlanta Dot Net Regular Guys (www.devcow.com), Matt has formed and leads several area user groups. Despite spending dozens of hours after work on local and national community activities such as the SharePoint 1, 2, 3! series (www.sharepoint123 .com), organizing three Atlanta Code Camps, working on the INETA Board of Directors as the Vice President of Technology, and appearing in several Pod Casts such as .Net Rocks and the ASP.Net Pod Cast, Matt recently found the time to get married to a wonderful woman named Kim, who he helps to raise three monstrous dogs. Matt currently works as a Senior Consultant with Intellinet and is part of the team committed to helping people succeed by delivering innovative solutions that create business value.

KANWAL KHIPPLE is an independent consultant and Microsoft SharePoint MVP working with enterprise clients in America and Canada. Kanwal strives to build SharePoint solutions that make life easier for Information Workers. His passion lies with Information Architecture, Governance, Business Process Automation, and Branding. Kanwal is an integral part of the global SharePoint Community, contributing through his blog www.sharepointbuzz.com. He can be reached at kanwal@khipple.com.

CREDITS

ACQUISITIONS EDITOR
Paul Reese

DEVELOPMENT EDITORS
Lori Cerreto

PROJECT EDITOR
Ami Frank Sullivan

TECHNICAL EDITORS
Matt Ranlett
Kanwal Khipple

PRODUCTION EDITOR
Rebecca Anderson

COPY EDITOR
Foxxe Editorial

EDITORIAL DIRECTOR
Robyn B. Siesky

EDITORIAL MANAGER
Mary Beth Wakefield

ASSOCIATE DIRECTOR OF MARKETING
David Mayhew

PRODUCTION MANAGER
Tim Tate

VICE PRESIDENT AND EXECUTIVE GROUP PUBLISHER
Richard Swadley

VICE PRESIDENT AND EXECUTIVE PUBLISHER
Barry Pruett

ASSOCIATE PUBLISHER
Jim Minatel

PROJECT COORDINATOR, COVER
Lynsey Stanford

PROOFREADER
Beth Prouty, Word One

INDEXER
Johnna VanHoose Dinse

COVER DESIGNER
Michael E. Trent

COVER IMAGE
© Stephen Strathdee/istockphoto

ACKNOWLEDGMENTS

I WOULD LIKE TO THANK Spencer Harbar and Robert Bogue who answered some of my technical questions during the process of writing my chapters. I also want to thank those at Microsoft who provided their kind support: Chris Keyser, Arpan Shah and Pej Javaheri. And, a special thanks goes to Vahid Haeri, a close friend who always made sure that I had access to my testing farms with the latest bits installed.

—REZA ALIREZEAI

CONTENTS

INTRODUCTION

THIS BOOK IS FOR ANYONE INTERESTED in developing applications on top of SharePoint 2010. While some knowledge is assumed about SharePoint, readers will find the examples comprehensive and easy to follow if they have previous knowledge of web development and development tools.

WHAT THIS BOOK COVERS

SharePoint 2010 is a big product and this book is a big, diverse book. So, before you dive into the book, we wanted to give you a little feel for what each chapter entails and what you can expect once you have read the chapter.

Introductory Chapters

The first couple of chapters provide an introduction to SharePoint 2010, since the 2010 release is a large release across all the many SharePoint workloads. In these chapters, you will develop an understanding of the features that 2010 provides, from creating collaboration sites to managing your content.

From there, you will explore the new developer tools in Visual Studio 2010 for SharePoint. With the 2010 release of Visual Studio, Microsoft has invested in making Visual Studio a first-class SharePoint development tool with new development, debugging, and testing tools targeted specifically at SharePoint 2010.

Finally, you will see the IT professional improvements for developers. These improvements make deploying and debugging with your IT counterparts faster and easier.

Platform Services

The next section of the book is about the base platform services and APIs provided by SharePoint. This is a big section since SharePoint is a big product with a lot of platform services. This section also serves as a basis for the rest of the book when it comes to the APIs and protocols that you will use to develop with SharePoint.

Workload Chapters

The majority of the book focuses on the workload services and platform provided by SharePoint. This includes social networking, content management, search, forms, and business intelligence. This section of the book is where you can learn to build applications that extend the built-in workloads of SharePoint and shape them to perform the functionality you need to solve your business problems.

Online Services

The last section introduces you to moving your applications to Microsoft's cloud services called Microsoft Online Services. Through these cloud services, specifically Microsoft SharePoint Online, you can start hosting and sharing your application in the cloud with either coworkers or business partners without having to run the IT infrastructure yourself.

HOW THIS BOOK IS STRUCTURED

This book is structured to build logically on the skills you learn as you progress through it. After the initial introduction and base platform chapters, the book moves into the more advanced part of the platform. Each chapter builds on knowledge acquired from earlier in the book, so you will want to read through the chapters in succession or at the very least read the introduction and platform chapters before reading later chapters in the book.

WHAT YOU NEED TO USE THIS BOOK

First, you will need a copy of SharePoint 2010. The book is written to the public beta of SharePoint 2010, so you will want to download the beta. We have done our best to also test against the released version of SharePoint, so please check the WROX site regularly to see if there are updated code samples available.

Besides SharePoint 2010, you will need Visual Studio 2010 and Office 2010. The easiest way to get all these products is to download the pre-build virtual machine, which includes these products that Microsoft will release after the RTM of SharePoint 2010.

CONVENTIONS

To help you get the most from the text and keep track of what's happening, we've used a number of conventions throughout the book.

Boxes like this one hold important, not-to-be forgotten information that is directly relevant to the surrounding text.

Notes, tips, hints, tricks, and asides to the current discussion are offset and placed in italics like this.

As for styles in the text:

> ➤ New terms and important words are *italicized* when introduced.

> ➤ Keyboard strokes are shown like this: Ctrl+A.

> ➤ File names, URLs, and code within the text looks like this: `persistence.properties`.

> ➤ Code is presented in two different ways:

```
We use a monofont type with no highlighting for most code examples.
We use bolded code to emphasize code that is of particular importance in the present
context.
```

SOURCE CODE

As you work through the examples in this book, you may choose either to type in all the code manually, or to use the source code files that accompany the book. All the source code used in this book is available for download at `http://www.wrox.com`. When at the site, simply locate the book's title (use the Search box or one of the title lists) and click the Download Code link on the book's detail page to obtain all the source code for the book. Code that is included on the Web site is highlighted by the following icon:

Available for download on Wrox.com

Listings include the filename in the title. If it is just a code snippet, you'll find the filename in a code note such as this:

code snippet filename

Because many books have similar titles, you may find it easiest to search by ISBN; this book's ISBN is 978-0-470-52942-3.

Once you download the code, just decompress it with your favorite compression tool. Alternately, you can go to the main Wrox code download page at `www.wrox.com/dynamic/books/download.aspx` to see the code available for this book and all other Wrox books.

ERRATA

Every effort is made to ensure that there are no errors in the text or in the code. However, no one is perfect, and mistakes do occur. If you find an error in one of our books, like a spelling mistake or faulty piece of code, your feedback is welcome. By sending in errata, you may save another reader hours of frustration and at the same time you will be helping us provide even higher quality information.

To find the errata page for this book, go to www.wrox.com and locate the title using the Search box or one of the title lists. Then, on the book's detail page, click the Book Errata link. On this page, you can view all errata that has been submitted for this book and posted by Wrox editors. A complete book list including links to each book's errata is also available at www.wrox.com/misc-pages/ booklist.shtml.

If you don't spot "your" error on the Book Errata page, go to www.wrox.com/contact/ techsupport.shtml and complete the form there to send us the error you have found. Once the information is checked, a message is posted to the book's errata page and the problem is fixed in subsequent editions of the book.

P2P.WROX.COM

For author and peer discussion, join the P2P forums at p2p.wrox.com. The forums are a Web-based system for you to post messages relating to Wrox books and related technologies, and interact with other readers and technology users. The forums offer a subscription feature to email you topics of interest of your choosing when new posts are made to the forums. Wrox authors, editors, other industry experts, and your fellow readers are present on these forums.

At http://p2p.wrox.com you will find a number of different forums that will help you not only as you read this book, but also as you develop your own applications. To join the forums, just follow these steps:

1. Go to p2p.wrox.com and click the Register link.

2. Read the terms of use and click Agree.

3. Complete the required information to join, as well as any optional information you wish to provide, and click Submit.

4. You will receive an email with information describing how to verify your account and complete the joining process.

 You can read messages in the forums without joining P2P, but in order to post your own messages, you must join.

Once you join, you can post new messages and respond to messages other users post. You can read messages at any time on the web. If you would like to have new messages from a particular forum emailed to you, click the Subscribe to this Forum icon by the forum name in the forum listing.

For more information about how to use the Wrox P2P, be sure to read the P2P FAQs for answers to questions about how the forum software works, as well as many common questions specific to P2P and Wrox books. To read the FAQs, click the FAQ link on any P2P page.

Introduction to SharePoint 2010

WHAT'S IN THIS CHAPTER?

➤ Information about tools to integrate with Silverlight, LINQ, and BCS

➤ New features in social computing

➤ New features in ECM

Microsoft SharePoint Server 2010 introduces a lot of new functionality that you need to understand in order to write better applications on the platform. Beyond increasing the new features in each of the SharePoint workloads, such as collaboration or portal, Microsoft has added entirely new products to the SharePoint family, including the acquired FAST technologies for Enterprise Search and the PerformancePoint services that enhance SharePoint's business intelligence (BI) capabilities. With these new additions, the surface area of SharePoint has doubled, so this chapter will quickly introduce the new set of features in both SharePoint and the Office client.

WHAT'S NEW IN THE SHAREPOINT PLATFORM AND TOOLS

SharePoint, as a development platform, has matured over time from server APIs to web services to now supporting the latest developer technologies, such as Silverlight, LINQ, and REST APIs. Developers who build on the SharePoint platform will find some very welcome additions to the platform, which users have been requesting for a number of years, such as the ability to develop and test on client operating systems, including Windows Vista and Windows 7. You no longer need to do remote development or run a virtual server OS on your client machine to develop on SharePoint. Let's look at the top new enhancements in the platform that you can build against.

Language Integrated Query (LINQ)

In the 2008 release of Visual Studio and .NET 3.5, Microsoft introduced new technology and semantics that allow developers to write against objects that map back to a number of different datasources, even if those datasources do not store the data using object storage. Effectively, LINQ is an object mapper with special operators in the .NET languages. Therefore, you can take a relational database table, use Visual Studio to map the database to your objects, and then write to your objects. For LINQ to work, you need a provider that takes the object calls and translates them into the correct native calls of the underlying datasource, such as SQL queries for databases. With SharePoint 2010, a new LINQ provider for SharePoint converts object operations into the correct SharePoint operations using the native CAML language that SharePoint understands.

List Enhancements

Lists are a critical part of the SharePoint platform. In fact, everything in SharePoint is powered by lists, whether it's a built-in application or your own custom application. With the 2010 release, lists have new, long-awaited functionality, including new scale limits, XSLT views for better customization, list relationships that allow cascade deletes and updates to work, and formula validation for columns in a list. There is also a new list type called the External Data List. This type of list allows you to surface external data, such as database or web service data, inside SharePoint with read/write capabilities. You'll learn more about this new type of list later in the book.

Business Connectivity Services

Business Connectivity Services (BCS) is the new name for the Business Data Catalog technologies from SharePoint 2007. BCS is greatly enhanced in the 2010 release with read/write capabilities, support for Windows Communication Foundation (WCF), and new client capabilities so that you have APIs both on the server and client, and can sync Line-of-Business (LOB) data from your backend systems to the client cache and work on that LOB data when offline. BCS will synchronize the data from the client with the server when you can reconnect. As part of the tooling, SharePoint Designer and Visual Studio include entity-modeling tools for BCS so that you can create business objects that connect to your LOB datasources from within these tools, and write your business logic for reading and writing your LOB data.

Silverlight Integration

If you are using SharePoint 2007, one of the biggest challenges is trying to get Silverlight to work in a SharePoint environment. You have to modify your `web.config`, hack around to deploy your Silverlight application to a content viewer web part, and then hope you don't need to debug the application. Silverlight shipped after SharePoint 2007, which made it difficult for the SharePoint team to foresee the requirements of being a great Silverlight host. With the 2010 release, SharePoint has become that great Silverlight host. Built into SharePoint is a Silverlight web part; you can drag and drop this web part onto your page, point it to your Silverlight application, and start using the Silverlight application in your SharePoint environment in minutes.

Client-Side OM

Frequently, developers want to write applications that need to talk to SharePoint from a client operating system and from client applications, such as the ones in the Office suite. With the addition of Silverlight integration to SharePoint, a client object model is critical because it makes it easier for developers to write applications against a full object model, rather than trying to call web services from within their client applications. Additionally, because Silverlight runs on the client rather than running server-side, the client Object Model (OM) makes it easier for developers to build rich Silverlight applications on SharePoint. SharePoint 2007 requires you to write against untyped web services for remoting your applications. The client object model provides a more productive development experience since it provides a typesafe environment that works with the Intellisense in Visual Studio.

Web 2.0 Protocols and New Standards

There are a number of new protocols and standards that SharePoint 2010 implements across its workloads. Some are considered "Web 2.0" protocols, such as Representational State Transfer (REST), Asynchronous JavaScript + XML (AJAX), JavaScript Object Notation (JSON) and ATOMSub/Pub, while others are going through standards validation, such as the Content Management Interoperability Services (CMIS). SharePoint still continues to support other standards such as WebDAV and web services. Adding these newer protocols and standards allows SharePoint to interoperate with other systems more easily, whether it is to create mash-ups between systems hosted in SharePoint or to allow data interoperability between systems.

Sandbox Solutions and Resource Governors

One of the biggest downsides to developing custom solutions in SharePoint 2007 is the requirement for the solution developer to be an administrator on the server. Often, IT administrators will not allow developers to access the server with the elevated privileges they need to deploy their solution, as custom web parts or other SharePoint solutions require that you place your code in the global assembly cache (GAC) or in the file system related to your SharePoint site. Plus, the administrator has no simple way to ensure that badly written code does not slow down the system, crash it, or perform malicious activities. You could implement code access security (CAS), but that requires the developer to write the code to implement it; in addition, managing CAS policies is not a simple task.

However, with SharePoint 2010, there is a new feature called Sandbox Solutions that allows for the deployment of SharePoint solutions inside a secure environment hosted in SharePoint. Because it is a secure environment, the IT administrator can control who can deploy solutions and how many resources these solutions receive through the new resource governors built into the system. For example, if a custom-developed solution is using too many CPU resources, SharePoint will automatically stop running the solution. That said, today the Sandbox Solution offers only a subset of the SharePoint object model, so while it might be a good solution for some custom applications, you will have to evaluate if there is enough functionality to meet your application needs.

SharePoint Designer

Besides making SharePoint Designer (SPD) free, Microsoft has invested in making SharePoint Designer better in the 2010 release. SPD has been redesigned to have more of a SharePoint-based view than the folder-based view it previously had. Now, you can browse by the types of items you are looking for rather than just through the site hierarchy. In addition, SPD introduces a new entity modeler to make it easier for you to build BCS connections to your backend systems and model the backend data inside of the SharePoint entity system. Finally, SPD has enhanced the workflow design capabilities that import Visio diagrams into SPD and allow you to add business logic to those diagrams using the SPD Workflow Designer, and then display the graphical status of your workflow overlaid on those diagrams as part of your workflow.

> *SPD 2010 will continue to be a free product, which makes it an invaluable tool for any SharePoint developer, even if you just use it as a simple web design or SharePoint debugging tool.*

Visio and Access Services

Two new web companions are available in SharePoint 2010, Visio Services and Access Services, in addition to the previous web companions — Excel Services and InfoPath Form Services. With Visio Services, you can design your Visio diagrams, connect those diagrams to backend systems for visualization of data, and then post those diagrams to SharePoint. SharePoint will render your diagram, with the data connectivity, through the SharePoint web experience.

> *Please note that the Visio web rendering is read-only, and to get the Visio Services functionality, you need a high-end version of Visio called Visio Ultimate. (Incidentally, this product is not part of the Office Ultimate suite.)*

With Access Services, you can convert your Access applications to web-based applications. With the previous version of Access, Access 2007, you could take certain Access databases that were compatible with SharePoint's logical data model and export that data to SharePoint but still manipulate it from within Access. With the new capabilities that Access Services provides, you can take your Access forms and move them over to web-based forms to complete the transformation of your application.

InfoPath (Forms, List Forms, Mobile Forms)

InfoPath Form Services has a number of new enhancements, including the ability to replace list item forms for activities such as editing properties on an item. This makes it easier to build richer forms with business logic and data connectivity that work in the rich client through the new SharePoint Workspace (formerly Groove), which is covered later in this chapter, and in the browser. In addition, InfoPath Forms Services adds new mobile form capabilities that let you create forms that run across mobile devices, browsers, and Office clients.

Visual Studio

With Visual Studio (VS) 2010, there is a major jump ahead for SharePoint developers. Previously, VS did not have much SharePoint development functionality and you had to download the community-supported Visual Studio Extensions for Windows SharePoint Services. With VS 2010, you can browse your SharePoint environment from the Server Explorer to quickly see your lists, libraries, content types, workflows, and other SharePoint artifacts. A visual Web Part Designer frees you from having to hand code HTML to add visual elements to your web parts. An entity modeling tool works with the BCS technologies that were discussed earlier so that you can model your business entities, write your business logic, and connect SharePoint to your backend systems. Finally, VS integrates SharePoint development into a team development environment with support for Team Foundation Server and easy deployment using the new Web Solution Package format, which is discussed next.

Web Solution Packages

To make it easier to package and deploy solutions, SharePoint 2010 improves the Web Solution Package (WSP) format so that it is supported across all tools, allowing you to export your site through the browser, SharePoint Designer, and Visual Studio. This means that you can quickly upgrade or downgrade your solutions between the tools, depending on the person working on the solution or the tool required to build the solution. In addition, SharePoint Online, the Microsoft-hosted version of SharePoint, supports this format so that you can move solutions from on-premises to the cloud without having to change formats or rework the package.

Developer Dashboard

One of most common culprits of poorly performing SharePoint sites is poorly performing code, whether the problem is bad .NET code, bad database calls the .NET code makes, or coding errors that cause excessive CPU, disk, or memory utilization. Tracking down and figuring out where the issues are in the code was a laborious process in the 2007 release. SharePoint 2010 introduces a new developer dashboard that allows you to see all the calls made on a page right inside of the user interface. Those calls can be ones that SharePoint is making or they can be your custom code. By looking at the call stack, response times, and utilization, you can quickly uncover where your code is performing poorly and try to fix it.

WHAT'S NEW IN COLLABORATION/SOCIAL COMPUTING

Collaboration and social computing are two of the fastest changing technologies in the industry. Looking back just a few years, you'll note a number of technologies in this space did not exist, such as social tagging, microblogging, and the APIs that support these technologies. SharePoint 2010 adds new capabilities in these areas, but this space is not done innovating, so at some point you may have to build your own social capabilities on top of SharePoint 2010 to take advantage of future technology advances in this area.

Enhanced Blogs and Wikis

SharePoint 2007 introduced blog and wiki capabilities to the SharePoint product. The most interesting piece of the blog and wiki capability was the integration with the rest of the SharePoint functionality for versioning and content approval. Unfortunately, blogs and wikis were a late addition to the 2007 product, so not all of the desired functionality made it into the final release. In the 2010 product, blogs and wikis are enhanced to add new capabilities to the core blog and wiki functionality. Also, these applications can take better advantage of new 2010 capabilities, such as content rating, tagging, and feeds. In addition, records management can now be applied to blogs and wikis just like any other content in SharePoint so that you can have compliance and governance on your blog and wiki content. Finally, SharePoint also introduces enterprise wikis, which combine the content publishing and social features to provide a more robust wiki solution that has capabilities such as ratings of wiki pages.

Social Tagging and Ratings

One phenomenon on the Internet is social tagging and content rating. If you have ever used Delicious or Digg, then you've used a social tagging technology where you can search, sort, and filter by tag, track what other people are tagging, and obtain feeds on your tags related to your areas of interest. Combined with tagging, ratings help you understand the value of the content and can help filter out poor content based on other people's ratings. Both of these features are implemented in the 2010 release so that you can tag anything in SharePoint, whether it's content or people. Plus, you can rate all of your content, so if you want to find all Word documents rated with four or more stars, you can quickly search your site to find this information. There is a blurring of the line between social and Enterprise Content Management (ECM) areas, as you will see throughout this book. The two areas are converging, with social being the bottom-up technology driven by users and ECM being the top-down technology that helps with compliance in your social environment. Many of the features are shared between the two technological areas, especially tagging, where the social tag infrastructure, called folksonomies, are actually open term sets in a corporate taxonomy. Finally, as everyone always asks about this in regard to 2007: yes, SharePoint 2010 does ship with a Tag Cloud web part.

Activity Feeds

If you have used Facebook or MySpace, then you know how powerful it is to have the ability to track what your circle of friends is doing. In a corporate environment, understanding what is happening in your social network is important so that if someone is working on a document that you may be interested in and that information appears in your social feed, you can quickly view the document. Another example is if there is a tag that you have been tracking as an interest area; you may want to get an activity feed on that tag as people tag other content or people with it.

Social Bookmarking

Often, there are interesting web bookmarks that people want to share with other members of their organizations. These bookmarks can be internal or external websites and can be rated, tagged, or shared using the other social features included in SharePoint.

Organization Browser

In both large and small organizations, browsing through an organizational chart is a good way to get an understanding of which people are in which groups and what they work on. While

SharePoint 2007 shipped a simple organizational tree view, many customers wanted something richer with which to look at their organizational hierarchy and the rich profile information stored in their organization. SharePoint 2010 ships a Silverlight-based organizational browser. The advantages of using Silverlight are a better navigation experience and the ability to quickly navigate the organizational hierarchy without postbacks to the server.

Outlook Social Newsfeeds and Expertise

No social solution would be complete without integrating into the most popular information management client that people leave open on their desktop all day — Outlook. While Outlook and SharePoint integrate today for working with tasks, discussions, and documents, Outlook 2010 now integrates with SharePoint and other social technologies, such as Facebook or MySpace, through its ability to surface richer information about people such as pictures, activity feeds, previous conversations, and even previous instant messaging sessions. By showing related information, you can quickly surmise the semantics around the conversation and the people involved.

Beyond social newsfeeds, Outlook supports expertise mining by discovering, surfacing, and allowing you to approve keywords associated with you based on your email communications. These keywords are stored with your profile, so they are searchable, which makes connecting to experts in an organization easier.

Microblogging and Mobile Client

One of the new developments on the Internet is microblogs — 140 character blogs — from services such as Twitter. With SharePoint, you are able to create microblogs and, with the new implementation of the SharePoint Mobile client, write those microblogs on your mobile device. The mobile client also supports browsing your SharePoint sites, synchronizing the content offline to your mobile device, and performing searches. By having a mobile client, you can quickly find information about people, including their status updates, tags, expertise, and other social information.

Social Search

Once you start using the new social features of SharePoint, finding information becomes easier because of the ability of the search engine to leverage the social information contained in other pieces of the product. Tags work with search queries, content rating can be used to refine results, and you get better social distance calculations and expertise results because of the enhanced people profiles. An improved search user interface makes finding the right information easier with a preview of Office documents, expertise location, and better navigators for filtering down to the right content or person.

WHAT'S NEW IN SEARCH

With the acquisition of FAST, Microsoft is making a lot of changes in search from the low-end to the high-end. With these changes come new challenges for the developer in understanding which technologies to use and how to write custom code. But, it also presents new opportunities to innovate in the applications you create that are powered by search.

New Core Search Query Capabilities

One criticism of the 2007 release was that search did not support wildcards, suffix matchings, grouping of query terms, or logical operators. Many of these deficiencies were not the result of the engine not supporting these options; it was that the search web parts did not expose these capabilities. So, developers had to write custom user interfaces to the search API if they wanted this functionality, which meant recreating all the functionality shipped in the web parts. With 2010, you no longer need to write this functionality yourself. In fact, the search web parts are also extensible in this release, unlike in 2007, in which they were sealed from developers.

Enhanced Core Search Results

There are a number of new capabilities in the visualization of search results. If you have seen search results for people in 2007, then you will be familiar with navigators which allow you to refine your results based on different properties, such as a person's title or department. This capability has been expanded to support not just people results but also core content results so that when you run a search, you can filter by author, document type, or other properties.

Beyond the navigators, search also provides rich previewing of content by leveraging the integrated FAST technologies. When an Office document is the search result, end users can preview that document. They do not have to open the document to see if it is the result they wanted. Instead, they can just preview the document, and then open it if they want to, which saves time hunting and pecking for the right content.

Enhanced People Search: Phonetics

Often when people are searching for another person, they don't know how to spell certain parts of the other person's name. They may know how it sounds phonetically but not the exact spelling. Normally, with search, if you don't spell the name correctly, the engine can't find it. However, with the 2010 release, the query engine has phonetic search capability for searching for people. As long as the spelling sounds like the name of the person (such as searching for Tom Risso when you are in fact looking for Tom Rizzo), the engine will sound out the search term and find the right person.

Enhanced People Search: Address Book Style Lookups

Most people are guilty of using the Outlook Address Book as a search engine or organizational browser. You need to find someone, so either you fire up a new message, type her name, and try to resolve it, or you open the address book and start typing. You may use the person's alias as a shortcut to looking up her name. However, if you tried the same thing in SharePoint, using partial names or putting in an alias, you would get different results or no results. With 2010, address-book-style lookups are supported to allow you to type an alias for someone and quickly find the person you are looking for.

Enhanced People Search Results

In 2010, the people results page is enhanced to show you more information about people, especially their expertise and place in the organizational hierarchy. The search results show inline the expertise that the person has, which allows you to find the person who has the expert skills that you are looking for. In addition, there is a quick link to the organizational browser so that you can quickly surf the organization to understand the hierarchy and reporting structures.

New Search Connector Framework

While SharePoint 2010 continues to support the protocol handler technologies for building search connectors to other systems, it ships with a new connector framework built on the business data connector. The BDC-style connectors are easier to write, can be written in managed code, and allow you to have a seamless experience from connecting the datasource to the end user, because the BCS is present throughout the product from search through surfacing in lists or content types.

FAST Integration

Microsoft has introduced a new piece of the SharePoint family, the FAST Search for SharePoint product. This new product brings the power of the acquired FAST technologies to the SharePoint environment, including integrated FAST web parts, an advanced indexing and query engine, and new search functionality. Some of the enhancements in FAST include more complex query support, entity extraction, sentiment analysis, and larger scale. With these new advanced capabilities, you can extend beyond what SharePoint search does out of the box and provide a seamless experience for your end users, while taking advantage of the new FAST capabilities.

WHAT'S NEW IN ECM

SharePoint 2010 introduces a number of new Enterprise Content Management features, such as taxonomy, better records management, and enhancements to existing ECM features such as document management. The usage of ECM in SharePoint solutions continues to be the highest of all the workloads, so understanding what is offered both from a new features and platform standpoint for ECM is important as you write your SharePoint applications.

What's New in ECM: Document Management

Document management has been a core part of SharePoint since SharePoint 2001. SharePoint 2010 innovates with a number of new features that round out the product and provide new platform services for developers.

Metadata Management and Navigation

SharePoint 2007 provided hierarchical folder-based navigation, which is very similar to a file share navigation that you would see in your Windows client or server infrastructure. While folder-based navigation is a good way to organize and browse files, sometimes you want to navigate not by location but by metadata in your content. You may have used the stacking feature in Windows Vista, where you can stack by author, type, or other metadata to help you navigate large collections of files. SharePoint 2010 provides a similar feature, called metadata views. With the metadata views, you can organize your navigation and also list views by using the metadata of your content. This way, even if the content is stored in a subfolder 50 folders away from the current folder, as long as the metadata matches the requested metadata in the view, that content will appear.

The new taxonomy service, which you'll learn about shortly, combined with metadata views, increases the power of SharePoint to store, manage, and visualize your data.

Location-Based Metadata

Unfortunately, people do not always fill out metadata. They either feel it's a burden or don't understand what the metadata should be. Without metadata, it's difficult for others to find the information and for SharePoint to crawl and index that data. SharePoint 2010 supports location-based metadata so that if a user posts a document into a specific location, metadata is automatically filled in for the user. Imagine that you have folders that are particular projects: a, b, and c. SharePoint can automatically fill out the metadata with the project name according to where users put content. Downstream, search can crawl that metadata and you can navigate your search results by project name, or you can use the metadata as properties in the documents.

Document Routing

If you have ever seen the records routing feature in SharePoint 2007, the document routing feature will be familiar to you. Based on content types and a set of rules, documents now can be routed to their correct location across your SharePoint infrastructure. Imagine a scenario in which your end user doesn't know where to save a particular file based on the corporate taxonomy. With document routing, the end user can submit it into SharePoint, and SharePoint will route the document to the right location.

Unique Document IDs

One big feature request for SharePoint 2007, that is now provided in 2010, is the ability to have unique document IDs so that users could search by document ID and quickly find the document that they were looking for. Plus, given the fragile nature of URL-based location, document IDs are a good replacement, because the ID never changes, even if a user moves a document. The ID can be used as metadata in the document, and lookups work with the search engine, so you can quickly find documents using IDs with search.

Taxonomy Services

One of the big advancements in 2010 is the addition of a taxonomy service. The taxonomy allows you to define different taxonomy hierarchies and apply them to your content. For example, you can create a taxonomy for products or a taxonomy for customers. The taxonomy service is an enterprise-wide service, so it can be shared across site collections. Plus, it works both as a top-down corporate taxonomy with locked terms and as a bottom-up folksonomy, which allows users to add new terms to the taxonomy. The term sets supported by the taxonomy service also support synonyms, so you can allow related terms in your set. Finally, the Office client ships with controls that understand the term sets you create, so in Office you can quickly tag your content with the terms and use features like synonyms or autocomplete.

Document Sets

Often when you are working with content, your project is made up of more than one piece of content. For example, if you are writing a sales proposal for a customer, you may have a Word document for the proposal, a PowerPoint presentation that walks the customer through your proposal, and an Excel document that contains the financials of your proposal. Together, this content is your proposal. With SharePoint, you can put all of this content in a document library, but you still must maintain each piece of content separately because you can't check out the set of content or perform a workflow on the entire set. This is solved by Document Sets in SharePoint 2010.

With 2010's new Document Sets feature, you can combine disparate content into a set and provide metadata, a user interface, a workflow, and document management on the individual content and the set. The easiest way to think about a document set is that it is just an enhanced folder type in SharePoint. With the set, you get a Welcome page that you can customize, metadata for the set and default metadata you can push into the content in the set, and even default content that can be created when the set is created. Document sets can be versioned independently of the versioning of the content in the set. Finally, you can export the set, and SharePoint will zip together all the content in the set for you.

Word Services

One of the biggest feature requests for Microsoft Word has been a server-side, programmable version of the Word engine to allow applications to convert documents or perform document assembly. Because the Word object model is not supported in a server environment, the only other choice is to write to the OpenXML format so that you can hand-generate a document to meet your needs. However, OpenXML is XML, which is not the easiest thing to create from scratch given its verbose nature. With SharePoint 2010's Word Services, you now have an API on the server that provides conversions and assembly without having to write to XML APIs. This is useful in many scenarios. For example, if you're working for an insurance company and you need to generate the insurance policy for your clients, which involves pulling information from your backend systems, emailing the policies to your agents, printing them, and mailing them to the end customer, Word Services can perform these steps on the server for you, giving you fast throughput document creation but in a format that is human-readable and editable.

CMIS Support

Content Management Interoperability Services (CMIS) is a new standard that allows for the interoperability between content management systems. The standard is sponsored by Microsoft, IBM, Oracle, Alfresco, OpenText, and a number of the other vendors in the content management industry. From a technology standpoint, CMIS is not just a create, read, update, and delete (CRUD) interface to the different systems that support the standard. It provides higher-level semantics that work across all systems such as check-in and check-out of the systems. The standard is built on other industry standards such as REST APIs for performing the operations against the different systems.

What's New in ECM: Records Management

Records management is a newer workload to SharePoint, first introduced in SharePoint 2007. With 2010, this workload gets some much needed features that make SharePoint 2010 a viable, enterprise-capable records management solution.

Multi-Stage Disposition

Often in records management, you want to be able to have multiple stages in your dispositions of documents, such as different points where you review the content, or be able to set different dispositions based on different rules. For example, you may want to have a 5-year destruction rule with a 1-year review rule to double-check the content and perhaps a 10-year destruction rule if the document is digitally signed. With 2010, multi-stage dispositions allow you to set different rules for your managed content based on your business requirements.

In-Place Records Management

In SharePoint 2007, you need to send your managed content to the Records Center to get certain features of the product to work. However, you may want to use records management with your content but leave it in place in your document libraries and lock it from editing. With the new in-place records management in 2010, you can apply records management policies to content, while retaining the content in its original location.

What's New in ECM: Web Content Management

Interest in building rich web sites is growing every day. If you look at both Internet and Intranet sites, design, rich media, and social interaction are all important features. To provide these, you need a good base web content management platform on which to build these solutions. With SharePoint 2010, WCM gets much more than just a facelift, and combined with the other enhancements in SharePoint that WCM can leverage, such as social or search, SharePoint WCM becomes an enterprise ready WCM solution.

Standards and Browser Support

To move away from the table layouts that cause issues in browsers other than Internet Explorer, SharePoint 2010 uses Cascading Style Sheets (CSS) and XHTML to provide layout information and strict HTML. In addition, to support accessibility, along with the changes to the HTML that SharePoint renders, SharePoint supports the Web Content Accessibility Guidelines (WCAG) accessibility standards. Finally, with the new rendering, support for non-IE browsers has been increased to fully support Firefox and Safari.

One-Click Page Layout

Many people have issues in SharePoint 2007 when trying to change their page layout after they create their page. With the 2010 release, creating and changing page layouts requires only a single click of the mouse. With this, you can quickly see how your content appears in different page layouts so that you can choose the best design for your site.

Enhanced Page Libraries

With 2010, you can have folders in your Pages library, which allows you to scale the number of items, to the millions, you can store there. SharePoint can automatically place the content into your subfolders using the content-routing engine discussed earlier. Not having folders in the Pages library was a major difficulty in the 2007 release.

Social Computing Crossover Features

With the convergence of ECM and collaboration/social areas, there are many crossover features that you can take advantage of on your intranet- or Internet-facing site that live in both worlds. For example, you can use the tagging and rating system built into SharePoint 2010 to build internal social communities or for external customer social communities. You can use social bookmarking internally or for external sites. The list goes on and on, but the key thing is that ECM and the social area are coming together, so the features you see in either area are applicable to the other, and they're all built on the common SharePoint platform.

What's New in ECM: Digital Asset Management

If you are using SharePoint 2007, you probably have run into the limitations around SharePoint's support for digital assets. Storing and streaming media from SharePoint 2007 is not efficient and SharePoint 2007 does not understand images or other rich media as deeply as you want. With 2010, much of this is remedied by the new support for digital asset management in the product.

Digital Asset Content Types

SharePoint 2010 supports content types out of the box for the most common digital assets, including video, audio, and images. As part of these content types, audio and video properties are supported, including data rates, frame height, width and rate, preview image URLs, and copyrights. By including a content type, you can leverage the rest of the SharePoint functionality to manage these types of data, including workflow and records management.

Bit Rate Throttling with IIS

To ensure that you stream the media out of the server, SharePoint 2010 supports bit rate throttling in Internet Information Server (IIS). The bit rate throttle reduces the bit rate of the media download to the correct speed based on the data rate of the source video. By doing this, media serving can scale better, and you get reduced cost for your bandwidth, because fewer users drop out after 20% of the video has played; you've throttled the usage rather than trying to deliver the entire video to the user at maximum speed. The easiest way to think about bit throttling is as just-in-time delivery of the content.

Content Rating

You will see many of the social computing features cross over into the ECM world, as there are requirements to manage social content just like any other digital content. With the Digital Asset Management (DAM) pieces of SharePoint, you can use content rating to rate the content so that only the highest-rated content is displayed or returned in search results.

Remote BLOB Storage

To support binary large object (BLOB) files, such as videos, SharePoint supports a remote BLOB storage provider model. This model requires drivers from your storage provider, and once configured, the provider allows you to move the BLOBs from SQL Server to the location that the provider supports. SharePoint will maintain transactional consistency between the metadata stored in SQL Server and the BLOB. With this capability, you can move the BLOB to cheaper storage than SQL or to a store that is optimized for the type of content that you're working with. SharePoint will support the FileStream provider in SQL Server 2008 and you can plug in your own remote BLOB storage providers if the FileStream provider does not meet your needs.

Image Property Promotion

To support rich metadata for the new media content types, SharePoint provides property promotion for images. The metadata for uploaded images will automatically be filled in based on the metadata of the image from the source such as size, date taken, and other properties.

Silverlight Web Part and Media Player

As mentioned earlier in the chapter, SharePoint supports Silverlight 2.0 out of the box through a Silverlight web part and a Silverlight media player web part. With the media player web part, you can just drag and drop the part onto your page and point it to your digital asset. This web part also supports theming, using XAML themes, so that you can change the user interface (UI) for the media buttons and skin the player. In addition, the player supports previewing images so that you can load a static preview image that appears before the user clicks the play button on the video.

What's New in ECM: Workflow

From simple task management to complex business processes, workflow is a critical part of many applications. With 2010, workflow gets a number of new features and better integration with a key workflow design tool: Visio. In addition, many of the challenges from Workflow in 2007 are addressed in the 2010 release.

OOB Modifiable Workflows

One of the biggest complaints about SharePoint 2007 workflows is that the out-of-the-box (OOB) workflows are not customizable. Therefore, if you want to tweak one step in the workflow and you can't do it through the properties or user interface of the OOB workflow, you must rewrite the entire workflow as a custom workflow. With 2010, all the OOB workflows are modifiable, so to change a step or add a step, you just fire up SharePoint Designer or Visual Studio and make your changes.

Site Workflows

With SharePoint 2007, your workflow had to run on an item. This limited your ability to be able to run workflows on folders or items that were external to SharePoint but surfaced through the Business Connectivity Services. With 2010, site workflows provide this capability. When you combine this with the external list capabilities, you can build some interesting applications that work with data not stored in SharePoint but stored in databases or Line-of-Business (LOB) systems.

Visio Services

Many business users create workflow diagrams in Visio. They drag and drop their process, draw lines between the boxes, and hope that IT can implement what they've drawn. With 2010, you can export the Visio diagram to SharePoint Designer (SPD), which will interpret the diagram and break it into workflow steps. Then, you can fill in the logic in SPD for the steps, such as the conditions and actions, and deploy your workflow. The nice thing is that the workflow's status will be displayed using the Visio diagram through the new Visio Services. Visio Services, like Excel Services, provides a web-based rendering of your Visio diagrams and even includes data connectivity so that you can have Visio Services refresh the diagram data from your backend systems. The back and forth between Visio and SPD can occur numerous times; it's not just a one-way export.

Forms Support in SharePoint Designer

SPD 2007 supported only ASP.NET forms for user initiation and modification of workflows. This limited the end-user-friendliness of both creating and consuming workflows. With 2010, SPD now fully supports InfoPath for creating workflow forms. This makes it easier for power users to create these forms, as InfoPath is easy to use, and it also makes the forms more powerful because you get the full InfoPath functionality, including data validation, connectivity, and customizability.

What's New in Forms

SharePoint 2007 provides good support for forms, either web-based or InfoPath-based forms. With 2010, many of the enhancements are to embed forms even deeper into the SharePoint platform so that InfoPath forms can replace many of the default functions for which you would normally have to write web-based forms. These enhancements make InfoPath a critical piece of technology that you should learn and understand.

Replacing Default Forms with InfoPath Forms

In SharePoint, there are default forms for creating and editing list items. You can override the controls on these forms, but it requires coding and numerous administrative tasks. With 2010, you can replace these forms with InfoPath forms, which will be rendered in the browser and on the client. With InfoPath, you can perform advanced logic and even data connectivity in these forms. Also, because InfoPath is both rich-client- and web-enabled, these forms will work offline if you have the InfoPath client installed and SharePoint Workspace, which is discussed next.

What's New in Groove (SharePoint Workspace)

The biggest new feature in the client for SharePoint is SharePoint Workspace (SPW). SharePoint Workspace is actually Groove renamed and rearchitected to be a rich SharePoint client. With SPW, you can synchronize your SharePoint lists, libraries, and forms, and work with these items offline. In fact, you can use BCS and InfoPath to synchronize LOB data to the client to work with that data and those forms offline and synchronize that data back to the LOB system. Outlook still supports synchronizing libraries offline, but with the new SPW, you'll find that you will use SPW as your primary client, especially if you're working over slow connections or there is latency to your server, as SPW can work in a primarily offline mode.

SUMMARY

This chapter covered a broad view of the new capabilities in SharePoint 2010. It provided a good overview to help level set the functionality in the product so as you write your code, you can understand which features may be the best to leverage to meet your application's needs. Throughout the rest of the book, more details will be provided on these new features and how to program against these features to build robust and very capable SharePoint 2010 applications.

2

Developer Tools for SharePoint 2010

WHAT'S IN THIS CHAPTER?

➤   Understand the different tools available to SharePoint developers

➤   Explore what's new in SharePoint Designer 2010

➤   Learn about the new SharePoint Tools in Visual Studio

➤   Understand how to get the most from these tools in your SharePoint development projects

While SharePoint 2007 has a decent set of tools, including out-of-the-box customizations, SharePoint Designer, and Visual Studio Extensions for WSS, the 2010 family enhances these tools and makes it easier for developers to design, develop, test, and deploy their solutions. The main enhancements come in SharePoint Designer (SPD) and Visual Studio (VS), both of which had major overhauls in the 2010 release. SPD now provides much more granular control of editing by end users so that they do not cause issues on your sites, a redesigned user interface to make the creation of SharePoint artifacts easier, and support for the Web Solution Package format so that you can upsize SPD projects to Visual Studio (VS). Visual Studio now has a completely revamped developer experience built into the VS environment. Unlike Visual Studio Extensions for WSS (VSeWSS), which was a separate download, many of the tools you need to quickly develop SharePoint applications are right in VS. Let's take a deeper look at each of these tools to understand what they can do for development with SharePoint.

OOB DEVELOPER EXPERIENCE

With SharePoint 2010, the out-of-the-box (OOB) experience has been enhanced in a number of ways for the developer customizing the SharePoint environment, including easier customization of sites, a new web part page design experience, and new web parts.

Customization of sites is one of the main actions that a developer needs to perform, whether that is modifying the master page, creating and designing the layout, or just working with web parts on the page. With 2010, all of these actions have become easier in a number of ways.

For example, you can now customize application pages with your master page so that the look and feel of the application pages are the same as the rest of your site, unlike in SharePoint 2007. In addition, SharePoint protects you from broken master pages by having some default application pages, such as the site administration page, fail back to a simple master page if your dynamic master page is broken.

In terms of creating and designing your layouts, SharePoint now has a much richer layout experience because of the new user interface. If you are working with publishing pages, you can quickly change the layout of your publishing pages with a single click. The Ribbon user interface makes it easier for you to work with your page design and web part properties by showing contextual tabs based on the web parts that you click on. Discoverability for both the developer and end user of web part properties is much better because of this new Ribbon interface, and with your custom web parts, you can perform the same steps as the Out of the Box (OOB) features and web parts to add your actions to the Ribbon. Figure 2-1 shows a custom Ribbon menu for OOB features.

FIGURE 2-1

Getting your web part onto the page and customizing it has changed in SharePoint 2010. The web part gallery, which appeared on the right-hand side of the page in 2007, has been replaced with a web part menu on the Ribbon for inserting your web parts. With this new user interface, you can select your web parts and insert them into the page as in the previous version. However, you can now also preview the web part before inserting it into the page to make sure it is the web part you are looking for. Figure 2-2 shows the new web part insert functionality with preview.

FIGURE 2-2

The modify web part settings have not changed from SharePoint 2007 to SharePoint 2010. They continue to appear on the right-side tool pane, allowing you to customize the properties for the web part, change its appearance, or modify its layout.

One of the nice things about SharePoint development is that you get a number of OOB web parts to speed your development so that you do not have to write everything from scratch. While the following isn't an exhaustive list of all the web parts in SharePoint, it includes a number of key new web parts that you should be aware of: Silverlight, Visio, Chart Viewer, the Chart web part, Web Analytics, the Tag Cloud, the InfoPath Form, the Media web part, and Profile Browser.

The Silverlight web part is exactly what its name sounds like — a generic Silverlight web part for you to add to your site. You point the web part to your Silverlight package, an XAP (XAP is the file extension for Silverlight applications) file, and then your Silverlight application is rendered in the site. In SharePoint 2007, you had to hack the web.config and adjust a number of other settings to get Silverlight to work, but with 2010, the Silverlight web part is baked right in with no configuration changes needed.

The Visio web part is used to graphically display Visio files. You use this in combination with Visio Services to display static or data-connected Visio diagrams. SharePoint uses the Visio web part as part of its workflow technology to graphically display the status of a workflow. Figure 2-3 shows the Visio web part used in an application.

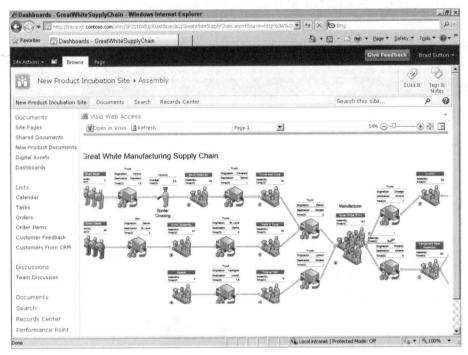

FIGURE 2-3

You may be wondering what the differences are among the Chart Viewer, Chart web part, and Excel Services. Before we talk about that, let's quickly discuss the business problem these web parts are trying to solve, which is graphically displaying data in an easy-to-consume format such as a chart. You could write your own web parts to do this, but having something available out of the box makes it easier and faster to build an application.

So, here's the difference. The Chart Viewer web part is a simple web part that allows you to chart data from a SharePoint list. It doesn't allow for complex scenarios, formulas, or the like. The Chart web part is a more general-purpose web part that provides a wizard-based user interface and can connect to more datasources, such as the business connectivity services, lists, web part connections, or even Excel Services. Excel Services is the ultimate tool, because it is Excel rendered through SharePoint. It has the most functionality, including spreadsheets, formulas, charts, and data connectivity. The only downside of Excel Services is that it can't connect to SharePoint data, so for charting data in SharePoint, you must use one of the other web parts.

The Web Analytics web part uses the web analytics engine in SharePoint to display the most popular content, search queries, or search results on the site. It is customizable so that you can filter by content type, show the popularity rank and trend, and also allow it to expose its data via an RSS feed. Whereas before you may have used the content query web part to try to figure this out, the Web Analytics web part makes it easier to display this information quickly and reliably in your site.

The Tag Cloud web part, another new feature in SharePoint 2010, allows you to graphically display the tags, in your environment and rank them according to the number of items tagged by making more frequently tagged items appear larger in the cloud than less frequently tagged items. You can specify the length of time to query the system from retrieving all tags regardless of date to tags created as recently as one month ago. In addition, you can specify how to filter the tags: by you, your colleagues, a particular group, or everyone. Finally, you can also show the number of times the tag is used in the user interface in addition to the scaling based on the count. Figure 2-4 shows the Tag Cloud web part.

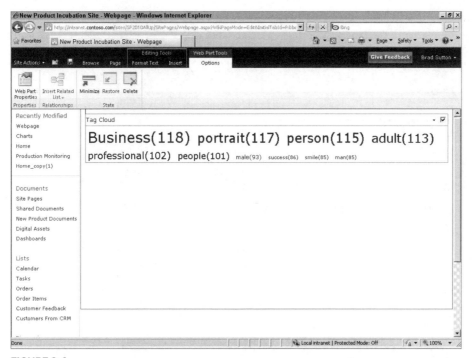

FIGURE 2-4

SHAREPOINT DESIGNER

Right about now, you might be thinking: How can a development book talk about SharePoint Designer? Isn't SPD the tool for the nonprofessional developer or end users, who break their site with it? Before you jump to conclusions about SPD, take a moment to understand how it can fit into your development tool continuum for SharePoint: SPD 2010 has a number of enhancements that you will want to take advantage of. You can extend SPD with Visual Studio so that it can be a tool you harness for others to use with your solution. And, because SPD has interoperability with Visual Studio, you can upsize your SPD projects to Visual Studio. All of these facts combined make SPD a tool that you definitely want to look at for certain scenarios.

New User Interface

The first thing you will notice in SPD is its new user interface. SPD now has the Ribbon UI, which makes it easier to discover the functionality you can perform in SPD against your SharePoint sites. In addition, the navigation of SPD has changed from a raw view of your SharePoint hierarchy to a more refined view of your SharePoint artifacts grouped in a logical way such as Site Pages, Master Pages, Page Layouts, Content Types, Workflows, and so forth. This new view makes navigation and discovery of your SharePoint sites and information architecture easier. Figure 2-5 shows the new user interface for SPD.

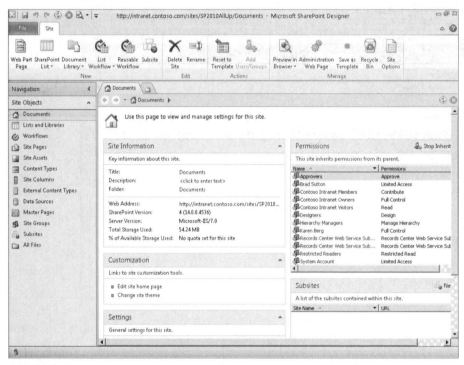

FIGURE 2-5

Top Ten New Features in SPD

Because this is a professional development book, you will not see deep coverage of SPD here, but you still should know the top features, beyond the new user interface, that SPD 2010 provides.

These include enhancements to workflow design, integration with Business Connectivity Services, and even lockdown capabilities.

Improved Workflow Design

One of the first things you will notice when designing workflows in SPD is that the Workflow Designer has been enhanced. The user interface has been streamlined by simplifying the wizard that you use to design the steps, allowing you to get more done with fewer clicks. Also, moving to the Ribbon user interface has resulted in the design steps being contained not in the Workflow Designer but in the Ribbon itself, which makes discoverability much better. Plus, you can now start typing your workflow items, and SPD will search for conditions or actions, based on what you're typing. It's a sort of IntelliSense built into SPD. Figure 2-6 shows the new user interface for the Workflow Designer.

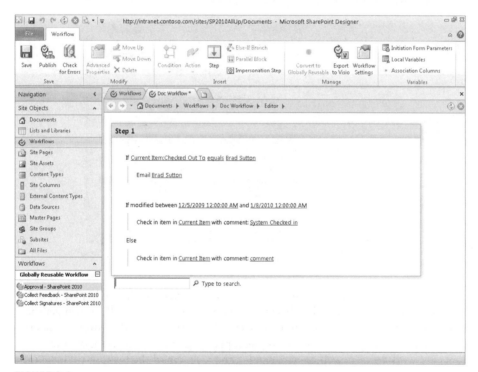

FIGURE 2-6

The other enhancement in workflow design is the support for parallel branches in your workflow. You can have particular blocks of your workflow run in parallel with the main parts of your workflow. This is useful if you want a particular action to occur while you are performing another action. In addition, SPD now supports nested actions so that you can nest your actions and show those actions in a simpler way through the user interface.

Another nice addition to SPD for workflow design is the new Task/Approval Designer. With an SPD workflow, you often want to be able to create a task or approval process. The previous version was very simplistic in the way you could assign a task to a user and have them complete that task. With SPD 2010, there is an entire new user interface for task creation and assignment, as shown in Figure 2-7.

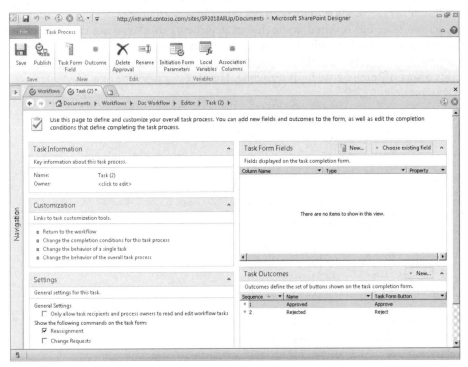

FIGURE 2-7

As you can see in the screenshot, you can design exit criteria for a task, such as what happens when someone approves or rejects the task. This exit criteria is a workflow itself, so you get the richness of the SPD workflow for your task subprocesses. With 2010, tasks also throw events that you can capture in SPD, such as when a task is assigned, pending, expired, deleted, or completed. All of these events are workflows as well, so you can log the task, email the task, or perform other workflow actions based on what your application requires.

Figure 2-8 shows the overall task process that you can modify in SPD. If you don't like the way the default task process is handled and want to add additional steps or change criteria, you can modify the approval process, which as stated earlier is just a workflow that you can modify. The main point to remember about the Task Process Designer is that it implements everything as workflows that you can modify.

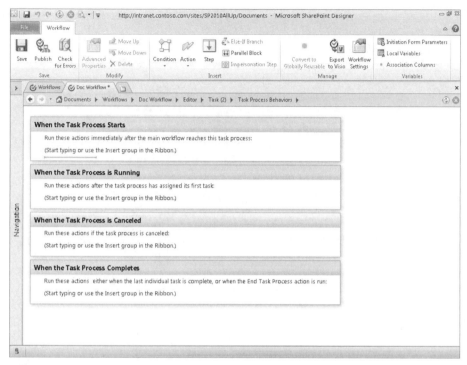

FIGURE 2-8

One of the other pieces of task design that you will see in the Task Designer is the ability to control the settings of a task in a richer way than in previous versions. A major new feature is the ability to have SPD automatically set the permissions of a task so that only the person to whom the task is assigned can read and edit it. Because SPD uses a SharePoint task list to just store tasks, people who access the task list cannot see the tasks assigned to others in the workflow and cannot approve or change the tasks.

The last piece for the task design is the forms used for your tasks. Because SPD is integrated with InfoPath, you can modify your task forms with InfoPath and use its power to perform database lookups or more complex logic. Figure 2-9 shows the customization of a workflow task form with InfoPath 2010. Make sure to publish the workflow, because SPD won't generate your forms before you do this step.

Another new capability of workflow design is the ability to take an entire step in a workflow and use impersonation to interact with it as the workflow's author. If you don't know the history here, it may not sound that impressive, but with the previous version, all workflows were run in the context of the user who initiated the workflow, not the workflow's author, so the workflow had permission to do only what the person who started the workflow could do. Previously, people hacked around this by making workflows start as the system account, which is bad for security, as the system account has access to everything. Therefore, users could see things that they were not intended to see by running particular workflows.

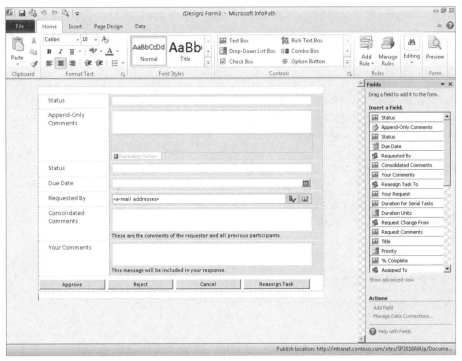

FIGURE 2-9

Impersonation of the workflow's author is a serious step, so you must consider what allowing someone to use impersonation means. The user will have access through your workflow actions to everything that you, as the workflow's author, have access to. Because you are writing the workflow, you can control what those actions do. It is useful to allow impersonation if you need users to perform actions in your workflow on items or lists that they normally wouldn't have access to. One example is when you want to be able update another list item from the workflow to which the user does not have permissions, such as a status update or having the approval of one item update the approval of another item to which they may not have access.

One challenge that still exists in workflow design is that SPD does not support looping. You still must go to the Visual Studio Workflow Designer to do this. Given all the enhancements to workflow, even without looping, SPD has taken a big step forward in workflow design.

New Workflow Actions

To complement the new workflow design, SPD has added a number of new workflow actions that resolve a lot of difficulties in the previous release. Remember that in SPD workflows, you can have conditions and actions. Actions perform the functions you want, and the workflows are customizable by writing custom actions. For many developers, the first task when working with SPD was to write their own lookup manager and permission-setting custom actions, because SPD didn't provide those capabilities. With 2010, both ship with SPD out of the box.

The lookup manager action is straightforward. You pass in the person whose manager you want to find, using the standard SPD lookup mechanics for the user, which could be a particular person, a user from your workflow context, or something from the item, such as the person who created the item or some other field. SPD will perform the lookup and pass back the value to you in a variable of your choosing. You can even specify the type for the variable returned — for example, you could return the name of the manager as a string or the user ID or email address of the manager. SPD can do all of this.

To assign permissions, you select the permissions you want to assign such as author, contributor, and so on, and then the item you want to assign the permissions to. SPD will always run this action in the context of the workflow's author even if you didn't explicitly create an impersonation step in your workflow. The reason for this is security. You can also remove permissions or inherit parent permissions as actions.

Another improvement in actions is the ability to work with document sets, a new feature in the SharePoint ECM technologies. You can capture a version of the document or route a document set for approval right from SPD actions.

Lastly, SPD includes new actions to work with SharePoint's records management capabilities. One new action allows you to declare the current item as a record. Depending on how you have records management configured, this could leave the item in place as a record or move it to the records center with a stub left in its place. This action is good to use if your workflow works with content that needs to be managed by the records system. If any approvals or changes happen to the item, you can quickly declare the item to the records management system.

Reusable Workflows

One of the new additions to workflow is the ability to reuse workflows rather than having to pin your workflows to a list. With SPD, you can now create global workflows, which are usable by any user in any site in the site collection you publish to. SPD will publish your workflow to a global workflow catalog, which SharePoint now has. This is useful if you want to share a global approval workflow or some other workflow that you think will be used by all your users.

If you don't want to publish your workflow globally, you can also associate your workflow with a content type. Previously, this could be done only with Visual Studio workflows, so this new capability makes your SharePoint workflow usable across multiple lists where your content type is used. Combine that with the new support for enterprise content types, which allow content types to be used across site collections, and you have a powerful way to create workflows that will work across your content types anywhere in your organization.

Site Workflows

Sometimes, when you are writing your workflows, you want to trigger your workflow not off of a list item but instead off of other artifacts or time. For example, you may want to start a workflow on a folder to perform actions on all the items in that folder or you might want to run a workflow on an external list where there are no real items stored in SharePoint, but they come from a backend SQL Server database. The last example is that you may want to run a workflow using the new permission actions to provision a user for your site and set his or her permissions. Site workflows can perform all of these capabilities and extend the reach of the workflows that you can create in SPD.

InfoPath Integration

There are many places where InfoPath integrates better with SharePoint in 2010 than it did in 2007. To design the experience and connect InfoPath to SharePoint, SPD does a good job of surfacing these integration points. For example, you can customize your workflow forms using InfoPath. In fact, SPD will automatically generate your InfoPath forms for your workflows, so you have a starting point from which to customize these forms later with the InfoPath Designer.

Integration with Visio

One of the biggest requests users had for SPD workflows was to improve the status page of the workflow so that users could quickly see visually what was happening with their workflow. Another request was to make it easier for end users to generate workflows using diagramming tools such as Visio. SharePoint 2010 fulfills both requests, using the new Visio integration with SPD to model workflows and using Visio Web Access to show a diagram of the status of the workflow to the end user.

Visio 2010 ships with OOB stencils for SharePoint workflow design. Right in the Visio client you can draw your workflow using SharePoint conditions and actions. You can also validate your workflow using SharePoint rules so that you will know if your workflow will import correctly into SPD. Figure 2-10 shows the new workflow design capabilities in Visio 2010 for SharePoint.

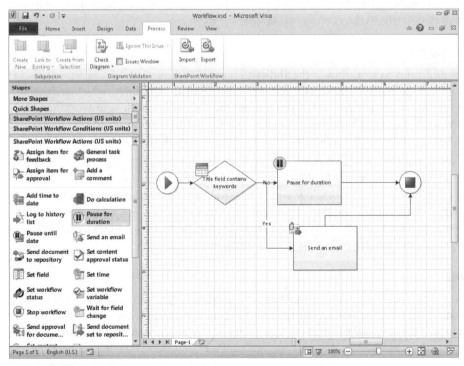

FIGURE 2-10

Once you have finished designing your workflow, you can export your workflow into SPD. You can also do the reverse and export existing workflows from SPD into Visio. Note that you cannot set the conditions or actions inside of Visio. You still must create your comparisons and action parameters inside of SPD. Once you have imported and set up your Visio workflow in SPD, you can then use the Visio diagram to display a graphical representation of the status of your workflow to your users by just checking a box on the setting for your workflow. Figure 2-11 shows what a user would see when viewing the status of his or her workflow in SharePoint.

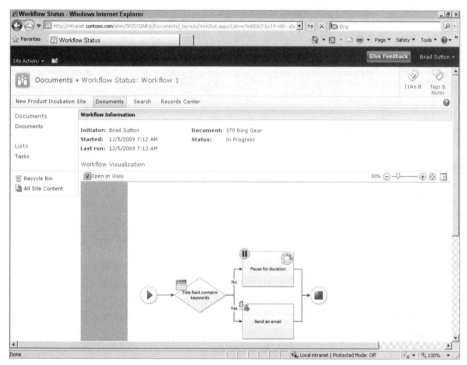

FIGURE 2-11

Task Process Designer

Often workflows are nothing more than a simple wrapper around a task assignment. Take for example a document approval workflow. Most times you want to route the document between a number of approvers and track their approval status. The overall process is pretty simple in that you need to collect the names of the approvers and when they need to approve by, and then create tasks for them to do that work. Most of the intelligence goes into the tasks you assign to the approvers rather than the wrapper process that sends the email to the approvers or tracks their status. Similarly, many workflows are task intensive and process light.

For this reason, SPD now includes a Task Process Designer to make it easier for you to design the tasks that go with your workflow. You might recall an introduction of this capability earlier in the chapter; this section provides more detail on what the Process Task Designer provides. It addresses conditions such as completion, behaviors for the overall task process, settings such as locking down the task items using permissions to allow only the assignee to see the items, and any task form fields and outcomes you want to associate with the task.

Having this designer makes it easier to build your tasks and workflows because all of these capabilities are accessed through one central user interface, as shown in Figure 2-12. As you can see in the screenshot, you can quickly navigate all the settings for your task design, and if you look under the covers, the way you design task processes is just workflows within workflows. The innovation here is improving the experience and tying this all together to make it easier to automate one of the most common operations in building workflows.

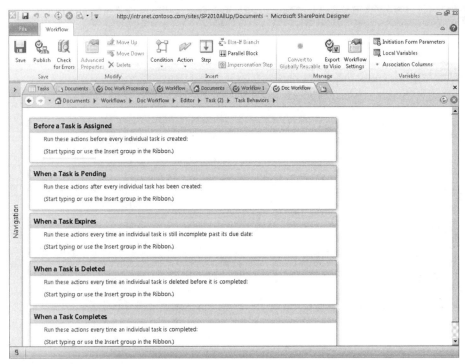

FIGURE 2-12

Editable OOB Workflows

Imagine the scenario in which the OOB workflows, such as the approval and collect feedback workflows, meet the needs of your application with one or two tweaks. Imagine your surprise when you discover that those OOB workflows are not editable and that you must rebuild them yourself to just add a single step to them. That's what happened to all developers in 2007. With 2010, all the OOB workflows are editable and appear in SPD for modification. Therefore, you can modify the flow, actions, conditions, and even forms, using SPD for the OOB workflows. All of the workflows use the new task process design features discussed earlier. Figure 2-13 shows editing of the approval workflow.

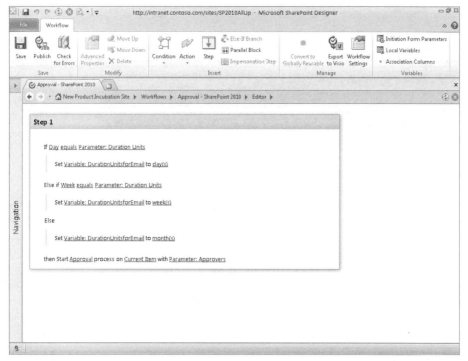

FIGURE 2-13

BCS Integration

One of the most exciting additions to SPD is the ability to create, design, and work with the Business Connectivity Services (BCS) in SharePoint 2010. SPD integrates with BCS through the new External Content Type feature in 2010. Figure 2-14 shows the user interface for external content types in SPD. As you can see in the screenshot, you can view your external content types and make new ones. The external content types can connect to databases, .NET types, or web services, and you can have SPD autogenerate the methods needed to perform your create, read, update, and delete (CRUD), and finder/query operations against these backends. Finally, you can create the external lists associated with your external content type in SPD.

You will learn more about BCS in Chapter 11 so jump ahead if this topic interests you. One interesting thing you can do with SPD and BCS is connect your external content type to Office so that the external data maps to either Word or Outlook, synchronizes offline with SharePoint Workspace, and is read/write. The most powerful way to see this in action is shown in Figure 2-15, which is a database surfaced in Outlook as a contact list. Right within Outlook, you can do all your normal contact activities, such as mapping the address, and you can edit all the properties in the contact as you would a normal contact. BCS will synchronize those changes to the backend datastore.

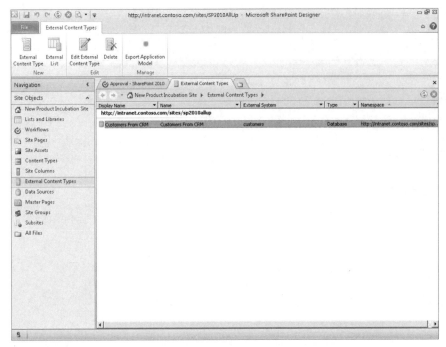

FIGURE 2-14

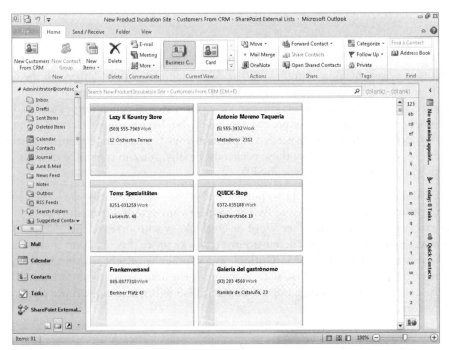

FIGURE 2-15

Browser to SPD

In SharePoint 2007, it was difficult for end users to quickly open a site in SPD and start editing. You had to open SPD and then find your site using the Open dialog box. SPD now supports an Edit Site in SharePoint Designer action directly off the Site Actions menu, which reduces the number of steps, making it easier to open and edit your site.

WSP Integration

To make integration easier between SPD and Visual Studio, SPD has moved to packaging solutions using the Web Solution Package (WSP) format. This allows you to build a workflow or other type of solution in SPD and uplevel it into Visual Studio to continue to work on that solution. Note that you may not be able to downlevel it from Visual Studio back to SPD, depending on what you create in the solution. Also, using WSPs makes the deployment easier, because you can deploy your WSP right into your SharePoint site and move it around, if you have a multi-tiered environment for development, test, QA, and production.

Locking Down SPD

Previously, one of the biggest complaints, at least from IT, not developers, was that because SPD was so powerful, end users could modify something to the point where it no longer worked and in the process break their site. A number of enhancements to both SharePoint and SPD have remedied this problem. First, you can completely turn off SPD access for the entire site collection through site collection settings. Previously, you would have had to modify the ONET.XML file, and it would stop all users from having access with SPD to the site collection, which is a binary on/off that you may not want.

Given that SPD is a valuable design tool for building sites, you may not want just the binary option, so there are some additional options other than just turning off SPD. For example, you can turn off the feature that allows the SPD user to detach pages from the site definition. In essence, this means that when a user customizes a page, her edits can cause the page to detach from the site definition and no longer be stored in the file system but instead be moved to the database. SPD, even in the previous version, would warn the user that she was going to detach the page, but now you can explicitly stop the user from doing this.

Another option is to disallow the customizing of Master and Page Layout pages. This allows you to stop end users from modifying these files, which control the site's default look and feel, and also the core operating files in the layouts directory, which control the site's functionality. SPD also has new editable regions support in which SPD will lock your pages down by default so that users can modify only content placeholders, unless you turn on the advanced edit mode in SPD. Combined, these options provide a powerful way to make sure that end users can use the tool to modify only the areas that they should modify.

Lastly, SPD allows you to turn off the feature that allows users to see the hidden URL structure, so the structure, such as _catalogs, will disappear from the users' sight, so they don't hunt around in the underpinnings of SharePoint trying to modify folders and files.

VISUAL STUDIO 2010

SharePoint developers will rejoice when they start Visual Studio 2010 for the first time. Rather than being a bolt-on or an afterthought, SharePoint development tools now are first-class citizens inside Visual Studio with VS shipping a number of new templates and tools that make SharePoint development easier. Before VS 2010, you would need an assortment of tools such as VseWSS, WSPBuilder, or STSDEV. Now you can just learn VS and quickly start developing applications for SharePoint.

> *Your previous tools will work against SharePoint 2010 so if you have invested in learning and customizing existing tools, you do not have to replace your tools. However, you may not be able to take advantage of new 2010 features depending on the tool.*

For those of you who have used VseWSS, you will be happy to discover that there is an upgrade capability from VseWSS to Visual Studio. As we all know, upgrades may not work 100%, so be sure to check the upgrade and fix any errors that are produced.

Before diving into the project types that Visual Studio supports for SharePoint, let's spend some time doing a quick walk around Visual Studio and the capabilities it provides for SharePoint regardless of the project type you select. These features include the ability to import web solution packages (WSPs) in the VS environment, a new SharePoint node in Server Explorer, integration with the Project Explorer, and finally a Package Designer that makes it easy for you to build your SharePoint web solution packages.

Importing WSPs

When working with SharePoint, you will want to export and import items, or even entire sites, to move the information around or modify it. With VS, you can import a web solution package (WSP), which could be your exported site or your workflow that you have exported from SPD to move over to VS. VS will import your lists, fields, content types, and other artifacts, so you can start working on them in VS. WSPs are now the recommended packaging format for all SharePoint development, so if you are unfamiliar with WSPs, you should learn more about them, as they provide valuable features that allow you to install and ship your SharePoint solutions to multiple environments.

SharePoint Server Explorer

The VS Server Explorer provides a powerful way to visualize different components of your server infrastructure, such as browsing through your data connections, services, event logs, and performance counters. When developing against SharePoint, you may want to browse your SharePoint site to understand what content types, fields, workflows, lists, and libraries are in your site. With the new SharePoint Server Explorer, you can see all of this information inside of the treeview and browse the properties about these items. Note that you cannot create new items in the Explorer, because it is a read-only experience. Having the Explorer saves you time from having to pop into the web browser to understand your site. Figure 2-16 shows the SharePoint Server Explorer.

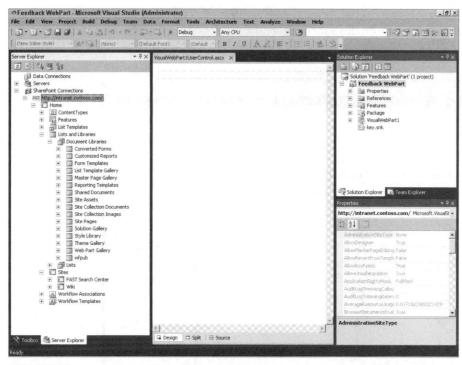

FIGURE 2-16

Solution Explorer Integration

As part of your general Visual Studio experience, the SharePoint tools for Visual Studio integrate with the Solution Explorer so that you can see the files that make up your solution. By default, when you select your project type, VS will create a number of files for your solution, such as the feature XML file, the package XML file, and a key to sign your feature, so you can deploy it. In addition, VS will logically lay out your solution so that you can quickly add new features or other projects to your solution.

Feature Designer

With SharePoint, the recommended way to deploy your applications is to use features and packages. A feature can have multiple items in it, such as a visual web part and a list definition. In addition, features can be dependent on the activation of other features. For example, Feature A may require that Feature B be activated. Features are also scoped to different levels in SharePoint, whether that is at the Farm level, which means that the feature will be available for the entire SharePoint farm, at the Site level, which means that it is available for all sites in a site collection, at the Web level, which means that it is available for a particular site, and finally at the Web Application level, which means that it is available for all websites in a web application. The Feature Designer allows you to configure your features with all this functionality. Figure 2-17 shows the Feature Designer.

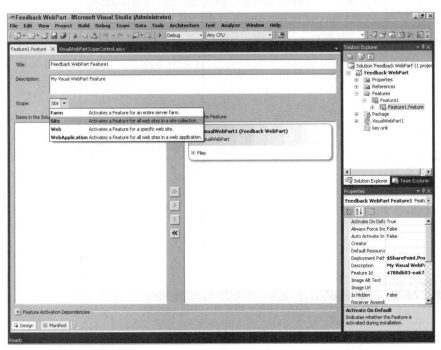

FIGURE 2-17

Beyond the graphical designer, you can also work with the XML that Visual Studio creates for your feature. You have two choices in working with the XML. First, you can add custom XML to the autogenerated XML that Visual Studio creates. Second, you can edit all the XML, even the autogenerated parts, which if you get wrong, could stop you from being able to work with your feature in Visual Studio. Editing all the XML is recommended only for advanced users who cannot meet their needs by inserting new XML into the VS autogenerated XML.

Package Designer and Packaging Explorer

Once you have created your features, you need to package them together and deploy them to your server. This is where the new Package Designer and Explorer come into play. If you have used SharePoint previously, you'll know that SharePoint supports a format called a Web Solution Package (WSP), which is just a CAB file that contains your solution files and a manifest or XML file that tells SharePoint what to do with your solution when deployed. You could write all the XML yourself and compile your CAB file, but Visual Studio makes this much easier. Figure 2-18 shows the Package Designer.

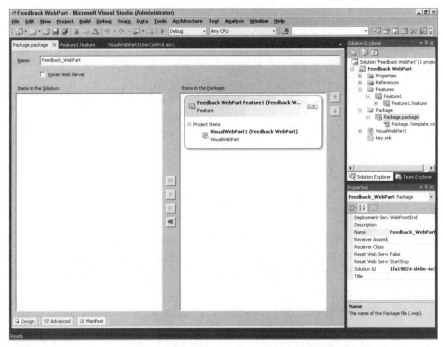

FIGURE 2-18

Some highlights of the Package Designer include the ability to add multiple items to the solution using a graphical interface, the ability to control whether the web server resets, the ability to add additional assemblies to your package, and, finally, the ability to write package rules that allow you to validate your package programmatically before deploying it to the server.

Project Type Templates

Besides all of the nice productivity tools found in VS for SharePoint, the heart of the new tools is the different SharePoint project-type templates that you can create with VS 2010. Combining both the project-type and project-item templates, there are over 20 new templates for you to take advantage of. Table 2-1 lists the different project-type templates, and Table 2-2 lists the item-type templates that you can use.

TABLE 2-1: SharePoint Project-Type Templates

NAME	DESCRIPTION
Business Data Connectivity Model	This template is used to build BCS models that allow you to connect SharePoint to your line-of-business systems, databases, or web services. VS includes a graphical designer for BCS models.
Content Type	Use this template to create a custom content type. While there is no graphical designer for content types, VS does support IntelliSense for creating the XML to define your content type.

continues

TABLE 2-1 *(continued)*

NAME	DESCRIPTION
Empty SharePoint Project	This template allows you to set up an empty project that has all the necessary elements for you to get started, such as folders for references, features, solutions, and a key to strong name your assembly.
Event Receiver	Use this template to start writing event receivers. Event receivers can be on a List, List Item, List Email, Web, or List Workflow event. VS will create the event receiver class for you, which you can customize for your application.
Import SharePoint Solution Package	This template allows you to import an existing WSP.
Import Reusable Workflow	This template allows you to import an existing reusable workflow that you created in SPD, which you can then customize and deploy from VS. Note that the import is one way, and once it is modified in VS, you cannot go back to SPD.
List Definition	You can create a list definition and list instance using this template. You can base your list on the Announcements, Calendar, Contacts, Custom List, Document Library, Links, or Tasks list types.
Module	A module type allows you to add additional files to your SharePoint projects. Included are an `Elements.xml` file and a `sample.txt` file that you can modify to meet your needs or you can add new files to the module.
Sequential Workflow	This template creates a new sequential workflow. The workflow can be a list or site workflow, and you can use the graphical workflow design tools to create your workflow in VS.
Site Definition	This template allows you to create a new site definition. Once it is created, you will see a number of files for this project type, including a default ASPX page; a `onet.xml` file, which defines the items in your site; a global resource file; local resource files; and a webtemp file used to tell SharePoint about your site.
State Machine Workflow	This template creates a new state machine workflow. You can use the graphical workflow design tools in VS to modify your workflow.
Visual Web Part	This template creates a new Visual web part, which allows you to drag and drop controls onto your web part for your user interface rather than having to write the user interface in code. It contains a web part and a User Control item.

TABLE 2-2: SharePoint Item-Type Templates (duplicates from previous table are not repeated)

NAME	DESCRIPTION
Application Page	Use this template to create an application page, which is just an ASP.NET page hosted in SharePoint.
Business Data Connectivity Resource Item	Use this template to create a resource file for your BCS model. A resource file allows you to localize the names in your model and apply permissions to objects.
Empty Element	This template creates an `elements.xml` file that allows you to define SharePoint artifacts using XML. The most common usage would be defining a field in your SharePoint project.
Global Resources File	Use this template to create a resource file, which will contain all the localized text strings for your project.
List Definition from Content Type	This template creates a list definition based on a content type in your project.
List Instance	This template creates an instance of a list by generating a new instance and an `elements.xml` file that describes the properties for the instance.
User Control	You can create a user control that you can use in an application page or web part with this template. You can design the control using the graphical designers in VS by dragging and dropping your controls onto the design surface.
Web Part	This template allows you to create a web part for your SharePoint environment.
Workflow Association Form	This template allows you to create a form that is displayed when a workflow is associated with its intended target, such as a list. The form will be an ASP.NET form, and the template creates two files, a Designer file and your code-behind file. You can use this form to collect any properties you need from the user for your workflow to create the workflow instance.
Workflow Initiation Form	This template creates a workflow initiation form, which is used when the workflow is activated. This template creates a Designer and a code-behind file for your ASPX form.

Mapping Folders

Previously, getting files into the SharePoint Hive (`%Program Files%\ Common Files\Microsoft Shared\web server extensions\14`), now called the SharePoint Root, was an exercise in file system navigation, as the Root is buried deep in the file system. You can use different techniques, such as creating Windows Explorer shortcuts, to get to the different folders quickly, but that doesn't help you in your Visual Studio projects, where you may want to place an image in or add something to the layouts folder.

With VS 2010, you can add mapped folders right into your project that will map to their SharePoint counterparts, such as the layouts folder in the SharePoint Root. To add a mapped folder, you simply right-click on your project in the Solution Explorer, and under the Add menu, you will see three commands: SharePoint Images "Mapped" Folder, SharePoint Layouts "Mapped" Folder, and SharePoint Mapped Folder. The last one will display a user interface for you to select the folder you want to map to. By using these capabilities, you can drag and drop items into your mapped folders, and VS will deploy your artifacts to the right location in SharePoint.

SETTING UP YOUR DEVELOPMENT ENVIRONMENT

Before you can start development, you need to set up your development environment. There are some new twists with SharePoint 2010 when it comes to the development environments that it supports. One of these twists is that SharePoint can run, for development purposes, on a desktop OS such as Vista or Windows 7. The other twist is that SharePoint, at the time of writing, supports only the .NET Framework 3.5, which will require some extra configuration on your part when you're building applications and could cause some gotchas if you forget to target the 3.5 framework.

System Requirements

There are a couple of system requirements you should be aware of when setting up your development workstation and also some choices that you need to make. First and foremost, SharePoint supports only 64-bit hardware. If you have a 32-bit desktop or server, then you're out of luck. You will need access to 64-bit hardware to get started with SharePoint 2010.

Operating System Requirements

Once you have 64-bit hardware, you can decide which operating system you want to run. SharePoint supports Windows Server 2008 with SP2 or above or Windows Server 2008 R2 for server operating systems and Windows Vista or Windows 7 for desktop operating systems. If you are using a desktop operating system, be aware that the prerequisite installer does not work with those operating systems. Instead, Microsoft will be shipping a script that will perform the operations that the prerequisite installer performs such as downloading and installing required DLLs.

Virtual or Physical?

Whether to install SharePoint virtually or physically on your machine is always a tough question. Most times, the answer will depend on the operating system you want to run for your guest OS and also whether you want to trade off performance for flexibility. Let's step through each issue in a little more detail.

In terms of the host OS, if you don't mind using Windows Server 2008 as your primary operating system, then you will have many options for installing SharePoint, whether that's physical or virtual, because Windows Server 2008 supports Hyper-V. Note that you need to make sure you have hardware that supports Hyper-V. Then, you can decide whether you want a physical or virtual deployment of SharePoint. If you're a developer, virtual is the better way to go, except when you want to do capacity planning or large-scale testing, if your production environment is physical.

If you prefer to run Vista or Windows 7 as your operating system, then your choices are more limited, because these desktop OSs don't support Hyper-V. This means that, if you want to virtualize, you need to use VMWare or Sun's Virtual Box, because Virtual PC and Virtual Server don't support 64-bit.

Once you have the right virtualization technology for your host OS, the question becomes whether or not to virtualize. Virtualization provides a lot of nice features, such as portability, ability to roll back changes, different environments on a single host OS, and so forth. There are many positives to virtualization. The only negative is the performance cost. To run a virtual environment, you need to give the guest OS and SharePoint a few GBs of memory, and you definitely need a fast disk, preferably 7200 RPM and above. If you don't, performance will be terrible. So, if you have the necessary hardware and you're developing solutions, then your first choice should be to virtualize. The new boot to VHD capabilities in Windows 7 and Windows Server 2008 R2 makes it easy to build a dual-boot system that is virtual.

An exception to the virtualization choice is if you don't mind running SharePoint on your client OS. You will need to make sure to turn off the services when not in use, as they can use a lot of memory and you do not want them hogging your machine when you're checking email or working on other projects.

SQL Server Version

SharePoint supports multiple versions of SQL Server, both 2005 and 2008. The main difference is in the SQL Server features, as most SharePoint features work across both versions. The only exception will be using the new Remote Blob Storage and SQL Server FileStream technology, which is supported only in SQL Server 2008. You can decide whether you want SQL Server Express or another version of SQL Server for your installation and development.

.NET Framework Support

As mentioned, one potential gotcha is that SharePoint supports only the .NET Framework 3.5. With VS 2010, you get the .NET Framework 4.0. Because the .NET Framework supports installing and running side-by-side, this shouldn't affect your SharePoint development installation. However, when you develop your solutions in VS, you must remember to target the 3.5 framework, because VS will usually target 4.0 by default if it is installed out of the box. If you don't target 3.5, then you will get errors that can be difficult to track down, as they can appear to be problems with your code rather than framework targeting problems.

> **SOME THINGS TO CHECK: CPU TYPE**
>
> When you change your targeting from .NET 4.0 to .NET 3.5, you may find that Visual Studio changes the CPU type from AnyCPU to x86. This will break your application if you are running a WinForms or Windows Presentation Framework (WPF) application that runs out of the SharePoint context. So, it's a good idea to check not only the framework version that you are targeting, but also whether the CPU is x64 or AnyCPU. Otherwise, you may get weird errors that are difficult to track down, for example, a return of null when trying to get the local farm from SPFarm.

TROUBLESHOOTING WITH DEBUGGING, AND TESTING

As a developer, you write perfect code the first time, right? No one does. This is why debugging, testing, and troubleshooting are critical components in any development lifecycle. With VS 2010, the tools and techniques for doing this against SharePoint are infinitely better than in its predecessor. Having capabilities like one-click deployment and debugging, the new developer dashboard, better logs, and customizable testing will make development and debugging a lot easier. Let's take a look at these new capabilities.

F5 Debugging

VS supports the ability to deploy and debug your SharePoint solutions by setting a breakpoint and starting the debugger. The first time you debug a SharePoint solution in VS, VS will ask you if you want it to automatically configure your `web.config` on your SharePoint server to support the debugging session. Allowing VS to do this will save you a number of steps and will remove the propensity to make mistakes setting this up. Note that you will need administrative permissions to your server, and that you should not do this, if you can avoid it, on your production systems.

VS will take three steps on your behalf. First, it will turn on the call stack in `web.config` by adding the line `CallStack=true`. Second, it will disable custom errors in ASP.NET so that you will receive detailed error information if there is an error, using `<customErrors mode="Off" />` in your `system.web` section. Lastly, VS will enable compilation debugging, which makes ASP.NET compile your binaries with additional information to make debugging easier using `<compilation debug = "true" />`.

Besides making these changes, VS performs a number of steps when you start the debugging session from deployment to attaching the debugger:

1. Runs your predeployment commands that you can customize.

2. Creates your WSP using MSBuild.

3. If you are deploying to the farm, it recycles the IIS application pool to free resources.

4. If you are deploying a new version of an existing solution, it will deactivate your feature, uninstall your existing solution, and delete the existing solution package on the server. If you have feature receivers, your code will be triggered.

5. Installs your new solution and features onto the server.

6. If you are building a workflow, it installs your workflow assemblies.

7. Activates your Site or Web features. For Web Application or Farm features, you need to activate these yourself. Again, your feature receivers will be triggered.

8. For workflows, it associates your workflow with the list or library you selected in the Workflow Wizard.

9. Runs your postdeployment commands.

10. Attaches the debugger to the SharePoint process (`w3wp.exe`) for Full Trust solutions and to `SPUCSPUWorkerProcess.exe` for Sandboxed Solutions.

11. If you are deploying to the farm, it starts the JavaScript debugger.

12. Launches your browser and displays the correct SharePoint site for your solution.

A few notes about these steps. First, if you are debugging a workflow, you need to trigger the workflow through the web browser, the client applications, or custom code that you have written. VS will not automatically trigger your workflow. In addition, for workflows, any additional assemblies you reference must be in the global assembly cache (GAC).

Second, if you are working with feature event receivers, don't have VS activate that feature event receiver for you. Instead, manually activate your feature event receiver so that it is in the same process as the debugger. You can disable activation in your deployment in your project settings.

Last, because SharePoint builds on many layers below it, such as Windows Communications Framework (WCF), you may want to enable advanced debugging in your VS environment. To do this, go into the registry editor, find `[HKEY_CURRENT_USER\Software\Microsoft\VisualStudio\10.0\SharePointTools]`, and change the `DWORD` value for `EnableDiagnostics` from 0 to 1. If the `DWORD` value does not exist, create it as a new `DWORD` value. When you set this value, you will see in the output window in VS all the information that VS is getting from SharePoint via the stack trace. Figure 2-19 shows debugging inside of Visual Studio.

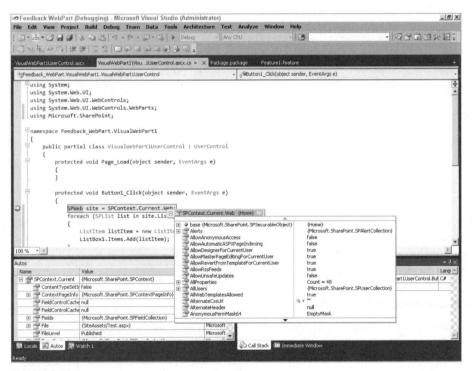

FIGURE 2-19

Debugging Using the Dev Dashboard

One of the new features in SharePoint 2010 is the developer dashboard. Often when you are writing code, you wish you could see what is happening with the system, for example whether it is SharePoint or your custom code that is causing the system to run slowly. With the developer dashboard, you get this view into your SharePoint environment and can understand what calls are being made and where the issues might be occurring. If you wrap your code correctly, you can also see your code and how it interacts in the SharePoint environment. Figure 2-20 shows the developer dashboard and its components.

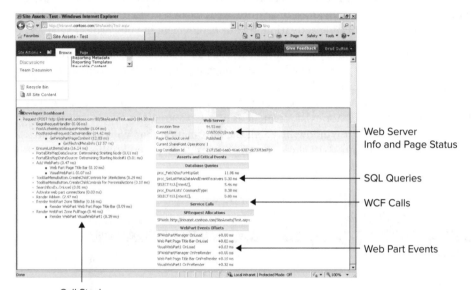

Web Server Info and Page Status

SQL Queries

WCF Calls

Web Part Events

Call Stack including SPMonitoredScope

FIGURE 2-20

Notice in the screenshot that the database calls are hyperlinked. You can click on the call, and SharePoint will display a dialog box that will tell you the SQL command that it called, with the call stack that triggered the call and the IO statistics. Figure 2-21 shows the database call dialog box.

Turning On the Developer Dashboard

By default, the developer dashboard is off. You have a couple of options when turning on the dashboard. First, you can make it available on demand, which will put an icon in the upper-right corner in your SharePoint site. When you click it, it will display the dashboard at the bottom of the screen. Your other option is to turn it on all the time so that the dashboard will always be

FIGURE 2-21

displayed on every page at the bottom of the screen. If you tire of clicking the icon, always on is a great option. Just remember to turn it off after you're done debugging.

There are a number of different ways to turn on the developer dashboard based on whether you want to use STSADM or PowerShellor write code. At the end of the day, they are all using the same calls to the APIs; it really is your preference which way you write your solution. The following PowerShell script turns on the developer dashboard all the time. You can also specify OnDemand or Off. To run the script, just use the following command line: `powershell.exe -noexit "c:\devdash.ps1"`

```
write-host
write-host "Loading PowerShell environment for SharePoint" -foregroundcolor Green
write-host
# unload & load the sharepoint powershell snapin
$snapin = Get-PSSnapin | where-object { $_.Name -eq
'Microsoft.SharePoint.PowerShell' }
if ($snapin -ne $null){
 write-host "Unloading SharePoint PowerShell Snapin..." -foregroundcolor Blue
 remove-pssnapin "Microsoft.SharePoint.PowerShell"
 write-host "SharePoint PowerShell Snapin unloaded." -foregroundcolor Green
}
$snapin = Get-PSSnapin | where-object { $_.Name -eq
'Microsoft.SharePoint.PowerShell' }
if ($snapin -eq $null){
 write-host "Loading SharePoint PowerShell Snapin..." -foregroundcolor Blue
 add-pssnapin "Microsoft.SharePoint.PowerShell"
 write-host "SharePoint PowerShell Snapin loaded." -foregroundcolor Green
}
write-host "Enabling the developer dashboard..." -foregroundcolor Blue
$contentService =
[Microsoft.SharePoint.Administration.SPWebService]::ContentService
$dashboardSetting = $contentService.DeveloperDashboardSettings
$dashboardSetting.DisplayLevel =
[Microsoft.SharePoint.Administration.SPDeveloperDashboardLevel]::On
$dashboardSetting.Update()
write-host "Developer dashboard enabled." -foregroundcolor Green
```

devdash1.ps

If you prefer to use STSADM, you can use the following command line with STSADM to turn on the developer dashboard: `stsadm -o setproperty -pn developer-dashboard -pv ondemand`.

Finally, if you want to write code, here's a little code snippet that will turn on the developer dashboard. Note that this code requires that you run it in a web part; you can use the new visual web part template in VS to create it. You will need a `using` reference to `Microsoft.SharePoint.Administration` in your code, and the web part must run in your Central Administration site, because the developer dashboard is a farmwide setting. If you attempt to run the code in a normal SharePoint site, then you will get a security exception, which is the correct default behavior.

```
SPWebService cs = SPWebService.ContentService;
cs.DeveloperDashboardSettings.DisplayLevel = SPDeveloperDashboardLevel.On;
cs.DeveloperDashboardSettings.Update();
```

Why Use the OnDemand Setting?

The best setting to use for your developer dashboard is the OnDemand setting, because it allows the site collection administrators to decide which sites they want to enable the developer dashboard for. Plus, the developer dashboard can be customized via permissions to allow only certain users with certain permissions to be able to see the dashboard. You will see how to do that later in this section. Finally, by making it OnDemand, you're not paying the price to bring up the trace every time you open a page.

Customizing the Developer Dashboard

One of the things you may want to do is customize the developer dashboard. The object model for the developer dashboard does provide some customizations, but don't expect a lot of control over what you can see in the user interface or the settings because the developer dashboard does a lot of the preconfiguration for you. To customize the developer dashboard, use the properties and methods of the SPDeveloperDashboardSettings class, which you can instantiate from the SPWebService's class DeveloperDashboardSettings property. Note that you need to call the Update method after you make any changes to the settings for your changes to be persisted back to SharePoint.

One of the customizations that you can do is to change the number of events to track. By default, SharePoint will track up to 50 critical events and up to 50 SQL queries. By using the MaximumCriticalEventsToTrack and MaximumSQLQueriesToTrack properties, you can modify both these values. By setting them to 0, you will turn off the tracking of these events.

The other customization you may want to perform is changing the permissions required for users to view the developer dashboard. By default, users who have the AddAndCustomizePages permission can view the dashboard. By using the RequiredPermissions property, you can modify the permissions of the user using a permissions mask from the SPBasePermissions enumeration such as requiring ManagePermissions or ManageWeb before they can see the developer dashboard.

One other method that makes using the developer dashboard easier is the EnableDiagnosticMode method. If you want to quickly turn on diagnostics on your system, just call this method, and the developer dashboard will be turned to the OnDemand setting. All users will have permissions to the dashboard, because the permissions mask will be EmptyMask. This method will turn on verbose tracing below the dashboard, which is normally off by default of the TraceEnabled property on your SPDeveloperDashboardSettings object. This is your nuclear option, so use it with care when you need to diagnose a problem, and when you need the most debugging information you can get.

Monitoring Your Own Code with the Dashboard

While seeing into what SharePoint is doing is a great diagnostic tool, looking at your own custom code in the context of the SharePoint calls is also important. You may find times when your code is slowing down SharePoint, and it is not the product itself causing issues. By default, the developer dashboard shows some information about custom code, but the information is about the calls the code is making, not the source code itself. For example, let's imagine that you've added a visual web part to the page, and you accidentally put in some bad code that takes a long time to render. If you looked at the developer dashboard, you would see the time it took to add your web part to the page and how long the pre-rendering or rendering for your web part took. However, you wouldn't see how long your code took to run, unless you calculated this off the total rendering time of the page and how long it took SharePoint to do its operations.

So, to add your own monitored code sections to the developer dashboard, you need to implement the SPMonitoredScope class in your custom code. As a best practice, wrap all your custom code that runs in SharePoint using the SPMonitoredScope class. Note that SPMonitoredScope will work only with full trust solutions, so even if you wrap your code that runs in a Sandbox solution, your sandbox code will not appear in the developer dashboard even though the sandbox executes your code. SPMonitoredScope is part of the Microsoft.SharePoint.Utilities namespace, so you need to add directives to your code to add this namespace.

As an example of using SPMonitoredScope, we're going to write some badly performing code that just sleeps the thread for 5 seconds so that you can see this time change in the developer dashboard. As you'll see in the code that follows, you can create an instance of the SPMonitoredScope in two different ways. One constructor allows you to just pass in a string, which is the name of your new scope. The other constructor takes a string with the name of the scope, an integer that is the maximum execution time for the monitored scope in milliseconds, and a parameter array of objects that implement the ISPScopedPerformanceMonitor class. When the maximum execution time is exceeded, the border around the developer dashboard user interface turns red, and SharePoint increases the trace level for the code. Table 2-3 lists the different classes that implement this interface that you can use.

TABLE 2-3: SharePoint Item-Type Templates (duplicates from the previous table are not repeated)

NAME	DESCRIPTION
SPCriticalTraceCounter	Traces critical events and asserts.
SPExecutionTimeCounter	Allows you to track execution time for your scope. You can use properties such as ElapsedTime, StartTime, EndTime, MaximumValue, and ValueIsExcessive to track usage and whether you are exceeding your allocated execution time.
SPRequestUsageCounter	Allows you to track the number of SPRequest objects your code uses. You can pass to the constructor for this object an integer that is the number of maximum SPRequest objects to use, and then you can check to see whether you have exceeded that value and the logging level is increased in the dashboard.
SPSqlQueryCounter	Tracks the number of SQL queries for your scope. The text, call stack, and duration are all tracked and accessible in your code.

```
using (new SPMonitoredScope("My Code"))
        {
            Thread.Sleep(5000);
        }

using (new SPMonitoredScope("My Scope Name",
            1000,
            new SPRequestUsageCounter(3),
```

```
            new SPSqlQueryCounter()))
    {
            Thread.Sleep(5000);
    }
```

Debugging Using SharePoint Logs

With the introduction of the developer dashboard, there are fewer times when you need to go to the logs than in 2007. The nice thing is, if you do need to go to the logs, the developer dashboard includes the Correlation ID, which will allow you to quickly look up events in the log that you saw in the developer dashboard user interface. While you could browse the Unified Logging System (ULS) logs yourself, using your favorite text editor, one great tool to check out is ULSViewer, which is a free download from MSDN: `http://code.msdn.microsoft.com/ULSViewer`. It is an unsupported tool, but it is good at parsing the ULS logs and provides real-time viewing, smart highlighting, in which it highlights similar log entries when you hover over them, and a number of other features. This tool works with both SharePoint 2007 and SharePoint 2010.

Debugging Silverlight Code

VS enables script debugging (and not Silverlight) by default. If you want to debug a Silverlight application that runs in SharePoint, you need to change the properties under your project in the SharePoint section to check the Enable Silverlight Debugging checkbox.

Keep in mind, also, that Silverlight does not allow cross-domain scripting by default. If you are making calls across domains, such as copying from one SharePoint site to another that may be in a different farm or use a different URL, then you need to become familiar with the `clientaccesspolicy.xml` file that you can use with Silverlight to override this policy. You would have to place this file in the root of your SharePoint web server in the file system so that Silverlight has access to the new policy file.

 MSDN has good resources to understand these restrictions - http://msdn. microsoft.com/en-us/library/cc645032(VS.95).aspx.

Unit, Capacity, and Load Testing

Once you've done some smoke testing on your dev machine, it is important to perform more formal testing of your code before deploying it. This is where unit, capacity, and load testing come into play. There are a couple of areas to look at with SharePoint related to these topics.

First, writing your code so that unit testing is easier starts with your development best practices. The Model-View-Controller (MVC) pattern is popular for ASP.NET development, and Microsoft does ship ASP.NET MVC. Unfortunately, ASP.NET MVC does not support SharePoint. You can hack together ASP.NET MVC to make it integrate with SharePoint, but instead you may want to look at the patterns and practices documentation from Microsoft, which implements a Model-View-Presenter (MVP) framework. We won't dive into a ton of detail on MVP and unit testing, because this is a major topic and is not that different between SharePoint 2007 and 2010. For more information on MVP and unit testing, check out http://msdn.microsoft.com/en-us/library/ dd206923.aspx. Separating data, data access, business logic and presentation layers is important, especially for making testing easier, and both models provide this pattern.

When it comes to capacity or load testing, it's a good idea to test your code to make sure that it can scale to meet the needs of your users. You do not want to be one of those developers who continually says that it worked on your machine! With capacity testing, you need to define up front what success looks like. Is it responses per second under a certain user load? Is it testing your custom code with a certain data size? Is it to test latency across a wide area network (WAN) for your code? Or is it all of the above? Once you decide why you are doing your testing, you can set up your test environment to make sure that you simulate your production environment and perform the right tests to get the results you want.

There are a couple of best practices and new tools when it comes to testing. Let's first look at the new tools, and then you can see the best practices for your environment.

Visual Studio 2010 Test Tools

All versions of Visual Studio include some test tools. Depending on which version you buy, you may get more than just unit testing. For example, the Ultimate edition of Visual Studio includes unit testing, code coverage, impact analysis, coded UI testing, web performance testing, and load testing.

When it comes to capacity and load testing, you will spend most of your time working on web tests, which allow you to record your keystrokes through a web browser, create validation rules and dynamic parameters, and create user loads from those tests that you can scale to multiple agents that simulate different connectivity speeds or multiple browser types.

While it is too big a topic to cover in this book, the test tools in Visual Studio, beyond the web tests, will help you write better code. One tool to look at immediately is the coded UI test. It will record your actions on the screen and then create code in VS that performs those actions. It allows you to automate tests that you would otherwise have to perform manually through the user interface.

Load Testing Kit

As part of the Administration Toolkit released for SharePoint 2010, Microsoft will be releasing a Load Testing Kit (LTK). This kit will contain pre-built web tests for the most common SharePoint scenarios, such as team collaboration, web content management, and social networking applications. The nice thing about these web and load tests is that you can customize them for your own needs. They are just Visual Studio tests. Using the LTK tests as a template will make the creation of your own tests much faster.

Another component of the LTK is a data generation utility. As you will see in the best practices section, trying to simulate your production environment is the best way to understand how your code will run in that environment under load and also with different users and different commands being sent to it. Many times, though, you can't get your production data into your testing environment, so you need to mimic that data in a reasonable way. Who wants to create 100,000 documents manually? That's where the data generation utility from the kit comes into play. It will automatically create for you usage pools that represent a subset of users with a particular load profile, create users in Active Directory (AD), create datasets on the farm, and create the run-tables for use with Visual Studio.

You can use the data generation utility to test new hardware configurations to see if they will withstand your needs. You can use it to test migrations, or you can use it to stress test your custom code.

The last area of the LTK is the log analysis tool. There may be times when you don't want to generate datasets, but instead you want to point the log analysis tool at your SharePoint farm and have the tool mine your Internet Information Service (IIS) logs for usage information. For example, you may want to mimic your real-world usage from your production systems in your tests. This means finding which sites people browse, the documents they use, and the operations they perform. The log analysis tool scans the IIS log and creates test loads using VS based on those logs so that you get real-world usage in your tests.

Best Practices for Capacity and Load Testing

There are a couple of best practices when it comes to your capacity- and load-testing efforts, such as mimicking your production environment and making sure that you're really validating the results in VS. Let's look at some of these ways you can make sure that you're getting the most out of your testing.

First, running tests in an environment where the data, user profiles, or user load is not similar to what you do in production is not always useful. Instead, try to mimic the production environment as best as you can. Now, if your production environment is a server farm of four servers with big hardware, it's going to be hard to mimic that environment unless you have a lot of money to spend on testing. But you can get as close to production as possible, by setting up Active Directory (AD) the same way in terms of hierarchy, security groups, and domain topology. The same goes for your network infrastructure in terms of load balancers, accelerators, and any other network topology that will be important for simulating your production environment.

Second, make sure that you are following best practices for SQL Server. You may generate your test data in your test farm and then immediately start running your tests. After inserting all that data, SQL may not have rebuilt the indexes or rerun statistics on your databases. So, you may get poor performance, but it's not because of your code; it's because the SQL Server hasn't been optimized in the way that SharePoint would optimize it. SharePoint does run a nightly timer job to rebuild indexes and update statistics, so be sure that you do that if you are not leaving your test dataset running overnight.

The other best practice for SQL Server is to pre-grow all your databases. It's an expensive operation for SQL Server to autogrow databases, and you should turn that on only as an insurance policy in your production environment. Be sure that you test hitting the autogrow in your tests.

Finally, there are a couple of best practices for web tests. First, set the Parse Dependent Requests property to False for your tests. VS will, by default, parse the HTML response for your web test and any dependent requests, such as images or style sheets that are automatically submitted. Because the SharePoint Web Front Ends (WFEs) and user machines will cache these resources, you may see a larger Requests Per Second (RPS) than your users will see when the WFE does not have these cached. Therefore, you should set up a separate web test to test having to go back to the content database when you miss on the WFE cache for a resource rather than relying on this capability inside of VS.

Another best practice is to design your tests to perform atomic operations versus user scenarios. The recommended approach is to make every web test an atomic operation, such as viewing a list or displaying an item, and then lash together your atomic web tests to perform a user scenario rather than doing one long user-scenario-based test that performs all those operations in a single recording. The reason for this is that, when simulating a user scenario, you may perform one step in your test that slows down the entire test, such as retrieving a large document. This may give you a false positive that your server is performing well, because you will starve the server for actions to perform.

Be sure to parameterize your server name, URLs, users, and Globally Unique Identifier (GUID)s. Otherwise, your web tests will fail because of encoded URLs, wrong GUIDs, and other factors. This is why the Load Testing Kit is so helpful, as it does include canned tests as well as utilities to help you parameterize your SharePoint tests.

Last, use validation rules in your web tests. With SharePoint, you will find that you receive a response saying that the test was a success, effectively a 200 status code from SharePoint, even though you may not have successfully performed the operation you thought your test was performing. The two primary examples of this are getting a general error, which returns `error.aspx` and getting an access denied response, which returns `accessdenied.aspx`. The web server will report success, because both are valid pages, yet you just errored out the request. To get around this, create three validation rules on your web requests: one to check for SharePoint returning `error.aspx` by finding the text `action="error.aspx"` and telling VS to fail the test, one to check for SharePoint returning "access denied" by finding the text `action="AccessDenied.aspx"` and telling VS to fail the test, and finally, one that finds the text of the page you expected to render, such as `mysite.aspx`, and tells VS to pass the test if that rule is met. Figure 2-22 shows the validation rules inside of VS.

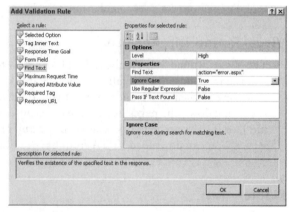

FIGURE 2-22

Other Useful Tools for Debugging and Testing

Beyond VS, there are other useful tools to help you with debugging and testing in SharePoint. Following are some recommended ones, but there are more on popular sites like codeplex - http://www.codeplex.com.

SPDisposeCheck

The SharePoint APIs allocate COM-based memory that the Common Language Runtime (CLR) garbage collector does not release. For this reason, you need to explicitly call the `Dispose()` method on certain objects such as the `SPSite` and `SPWeb` objects. If you don't, you will get memory leaks in your application, and it can be hard to track down which pieces of your code are causing the leaks.

For this reason, Microsoft released a tool called `SPDisposeCheck`, which will scan your code and tell you where you are not releasing this memory because of not calling the `Dispose()` method. This tool will save you a lot of time and heartache in tracking down memory leaks. You can download `SPDisposeCheck` from `http://code.msdn.microsoft.com/SPDisposeCheck`.

Internet Explorer 8 Developer Tools

Sometimes the best debugging tools are the ones built right into the product. Internet Explorer 8 includes the ability to browse your HTML, script, and Cascading Style Sheets (CSS) code right inside of its developer tools. To get to the developer tools, just press F12 in the browser. In fact, you can debug your HTML and CSS by using the treeview and editing both sources on the fly. It also has a built-in debugger for JavaScript, so that you can set a breakpoint and have the tools break when they hit your breakpoint. You get watch windows, local variables, call stacks, and an immediate window called the console. IE 8 also includes a JavaScript profiler that shows you the performance of your script code, including the number of times a function was used and the amount of time it took. With these tools, you can track down any issues in your client-side code.

FireFox and Firebug

If you use FireFox as your browser, you can use Firebug as your HTML development and debugging tool. Firebug provides very similar functionality to the IE8 developer tools in the FireFox environment.

Visual Round Trip Analyzer

The Visual Round Trip Analyzer (VRTA) sits on top of the network monitor tool from Microsoft and is a free add-on. It visualizes how long it takes a client to talk to a server — information that you can then use to understand if you are making excessive round trips, if your code is slowing down the pages (for example, because of loading many small JavaScript or CSS files), or if there are network issues causing any problems between your application and the server. You can download VRTA from `http://www.microsoft.com/downloads/details .aspx?FamilyID=119f3477-dced-41e3-a0e7-d8b5cae893a3&displaylang=en`.

Fiddler

No discussion of debugging tools would be complete without mentioning Fiddler. Fiddler is a web debugging proxy that logs all HTTP traffic between your computer and the Internet. Fiddler allows you to inspect all HTTP traffic, set breakpoints, and view your incoming and outgoing data. It is an essential tool to help you understand what server variables are coming back from your server, what the payload is, how many calls your client-side code took, and other factors that provide insight into your applications.

DEPLOYING AND MAINTAINING YOUR CODE

Once you develop and debug your code, you need to deploy and maintain it, because you probably will need to update it, for example, to fix bugs or add new enhancements. With the enhanced SharePoint VS tools in VS 2010, there are a lot more options for you to deploy and maintain your code in your environment. The areas we will look at include customizing the deployment actions in VS with the new VS tools, using the application lifecycle management tools in VS to do nightly builds or continuous integration, and debugging your production deployments where you can't run things like load tests or invasive debuggers.

Customizing Deployment in VS

In your project properties in VS 2010, you can customize how your project gets deployed to SharePoint, including any pre- and post-steps you want VS to perform when it deploys your package. You can also control whether your assemblies are deployed to the global assembly cache (GAC) or to your bin directory for your web application just by setting a single property. Figure 2-23 shows the default configuration for the deployment steps inside of Visual Studio.

As shown in the screenshot, VS performs several steps on your behalf, from deploying the solution to recycling the application pool. Using the user interface in VS, you can add or remove steps for your configuration. Note that, if you do create a new configuration, you need to set it as the active configuration, because VS does not do that by default. Otherwise, you will wonder why your new configuration may not be the one VS is using when you deploy.

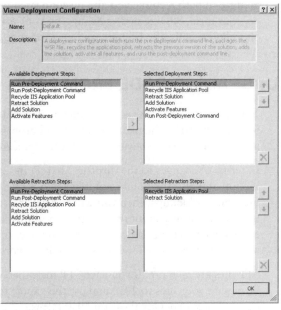

FIGURE 2-23

You can customize the pre- and postdeployment steps by adding command lines that direct VS to perform operations. These can be DOS or MSBuild command lines that copy files, run PowerShell scripts, or any other operations you need to perform for your SharePoint deployment.

ALM with VS 2010 and SharePoint

Application lifecycle management (ALM) and team development are important pieces in Visual Studio, and they now work with SharePoint because of the VS integration. As part of your SharePoint development, you can add your solution to your source control system just by checking the Add to source control checkbox when you create a new project. VS takes care of the rest in terms of checking your code in and out as you work on your project. You can also use the work management capabilities of VS to assign and track bugs and work items to the individuals on your team.

Moving from Test to Production

Once you have finished testing your code, you are ready to move from test to production. This means deploying your code to your production servers, which you can automate using a script or manually place into your SharePoint environment. Note that if you use continuous integration or a nightly build with SharePoint, many times your build server won't have SharePoint on it, so it can't compile the code that you want to build. You need to copy the SharePoint DLLs from your SharePoint Server to your build server into the GAC so that your builds will work.

SPDiag, which is part of the Administrative Toolkit for SharePoint 4.0, is a helpful tool when moving to a production environment. SPDiag will collect information on your farm that you can analyze in both a connected and disconnected way so that your analysis is not happening real time on your farm. SPDiag makes debugging your production system much easier, as it collects data from SharePoint, SQL, the IIS logs, and performance counters.

UPGRADING CODE FROM 2007

The last area is to cover is some gotchas to avoid when upgrading your code from SharePoint 2007 to SharePoint 2010. The main ones that will probably hit your upgrade are changes in the infrastructure around throttling, removal of STP files, deprecated APIs, and also the new user interface.

In terms of changes to the throttle, SharePoint 2010 limits the number of lists you can call in a lookup and also the number of items in a view. If your code is expecting to make a number of multiple list lookups, then you will receive an error from SharePoint. Be sure to test your code on upgrade to see if you hit the throttles, and turn them off to see if it fixes your code in your test environment. Then, you can either rearchitect or work with IT to make sure that the throttles are set to the appropriate level for your code to work.

STP files are no more. If you have STP files, then you will need to upgrade an existing SharePoint 2007 farm with your sites to 2010 and use the export functionality to export your sites to WSP files, so you can continue to deploy those on 2010 farms.

Some APIs are deprecated in SharePoint 2010. Most of them live under the `Microsoft` `.SharePoint.Portal` namespace, but check the documentation to see if the APIs you are using are deprecated. Also, make sure to recompile your code against the 2010 version of the DLLs in VS. The compiler will display warnings if you are using deprecated objects or methods so that you don't have to track this down yourself.

The other thing to take into consideration for your upgraded code is that SharePoint has the Ribbon UI and has refactored the CSS files. This may break code that relies on certain CSS styles from the 2007 CSS files or items in the 2007 Master Page. You can programmatically get the UI version that 2010 is running under, as 2010 does support visual upgrading, which means that you can keep the 2007 UI but run a 2010 server. Over time, you can visually upgrade that 2007 UI to the 2010 UI on a site-by-site basis. To get the UI version, you can use the `SPWeb.UIVersion` property, which will return 3 if the site is running in 2007 mode or 4 if it is using the new 2010 UI. Also, you can place in your ASP.NET code the ability to detect the UI version and make certain content render only if a certain version of the UI is running. The code puts a placeholder control and a content control on the page only if the 2010 UI is running. The `VersionedPlaceHolder` control is for post-execution so that your content will be placed on the page after rendering is finished.

```
<SharePoint:VersionedPlaceHolder ID="vph4" runat="server" UIVersion="4">
   <div>Your Content Here</div>
</SharePoint:VersionedPlaceHolder>

<SharePoint:UIVersionedContent ID="vc4" runat="server" UIVersion="4">
<ContentTemplate>
<div>Your Content Here</div>
</ContentTemplate>
<SharePoint:UIVersionedContent>
```

One of the new features that will make your life easier is the new binding redirect functionality. Sometimes you may want to redirect your existing code to new assemblies without having to recompile your code. Many developers avoided versioning their assemblies with 2007, because it led to other headaches that forced them to update all their files. With binding redirect, you can just tell SharePoint to redirect any references to a certain version of the assembly to another version you specify. The following snippet from a `manifest.xml` shows how to use the binding redirect feature.

```
<Assemblies>
   <Assembly DeploymentTarget="GlobalAssemblyCache" Location="CustomWebPart.dll">
      <BindingRedirects>
        <BindingRedirect OldVersion ="1.0.0.0" />
      </BindingRedirects>
      <SafeControls>
        <SafeControl Assembly="CustomWebPart, Version=2.0.0.0, Culture=neutral"
Namespace="CustomWebPart" TypeName="*" Safe="True" />
      </SafeControls>
   </Assembly>
</Assemblies>
```

Another nice enhancement to SharePoint 2010 is that it supports the ability to version your features and upgrade between feature versions. Part of the new feature set is the ability to require a minimum feature level so that, if your feature is dependent on another feature to be activated, you can make sure that the other feature is a particular minimum version.

Another new feature upgrade function is declarative feature upgrading. By specifying an XML block in your `feature.xml`, you can give a range of feature versions on which to perform the actions in that block, so you can say for version 1.0 to 2.0, perform action x and for 2.1 through 3.0 perform action y. A sample XML block is shown here:

```
<Feature …>
  <UpgradeActions>
     <VersionRange BeginVersion="1.0.0.0" EndVersion="2.0.0.0">
        . . .
     </VersionRange>
     <VersionRange BeginVersion="2.0.0.1" EndVersion="3.0.0.0">
        . . .
     </VersionRange>

  </UpgradeActions>
</Feature>
```

Sometimes when you want to update a feature, you just want to add another field to a content type or you want to change filepaths for your files. SharePoint 2010 supports this functionality through the AddContentTypeField and MapFile elements shown here:

```
<Feature>
  <UpgradeActions>
    <VersionRange BeginVersion="1.0.0.0" EndVersion="4.0.0.0">
      <AddContentTypeField ContentTypeId="" FieldId="" PushDown="True"/>
      <MapFile FromPath="OldPath\AppPage.aspx" ToPath="NewPath\AppPage2.aspx"/>
    </VersionRange>
  </UpgradeActions>
</Feature>
```

There may be scenarios where you want to add new elements to your elements.xml file on upgrading. To inject these elements, use the ApplyElementManifest XML block shown here:

```
<Feature>
  <UpgradeActions>
    <ApplyElementManifests>
      <ElementManifest Location ="CustomApp\Elements.xml"/>
    </ApplyElementManifests>
  </UpgradeActions>
</Feature>
```

There is also a new CustomUpgradeAction element that you can use with the new FeatureUpgrading event to give you even more flexibility in controlling what happens when your feature upgrades, because you can write code. The XML code shows how to specify a feature receiver event in your CustomUpgradeActionElement. You can specify the version range for the action to fire on. In addition, you can pass parameters to the event so that you can pass custom properties to your code. The code that follows shows the XML for the CustomUpgradeAction.

```
<CustomUpgradeAction>
<Feature>
  <UpgradeActions>
    <VersionRange BeginVersion="1.0.0.0" EndVersion="4.0.0.0">
      <CustomUpgradeAction Name ="MyCustomAddSiteColumnAction">
        <Parameters>
          <Parameter Name="ColumnName">MyCustomSiteColumnText</Parameter>
          <Parameter Name="ColumnType">Text</Parameter>
          <Parameter Name="ColumnDisplayName">My Custom Site Column
           Name</Parameter>
        </Parameters>
      </CustomUpgradeAction>
    </VersionRange>
  </UpgradeActions>
</Feature>
```

You then can implement your FeatureUpgrading event code inside of VS using your language of choice. As part of the event, you can check to see if the upgrade action is being performed, and you can read in the parameters passed to your event receiver. You can then write your code to perform whatever custom actions you need as part of your upgrade.

```
public override void FeatureUpgrading(SPFeatureReceiverProperties
properties,string upgradeActionName,
System.Collections.Generic.IDictionary<string, string> parameters)
        {
            // Check upgrade being performed
            if (upgradeActionName.Equals("MyCustomAddSiteColumnAction") == true)
            {
                // Read parameters
                String ColumnName = parameters["ColumnName"];
                String ColumnType = parameters["ColumnType"];
                String ColumnDisplayName = parameters["ColumnDisplayName"];
//Perform your actions
        }
        }
```

As part of the object model, there is a new `QueryFeatures` method that you can use to find all the features at a number of different scopes in SharePoint from your farm to your site. Once you have the features, you can figure out which ones you need to upgrade. Take a look at the Software Development Kit (SDK) for all the different overloaded versions of the `QueryFeatures` method.

SUMMARY

In this chapter, the new tools for SharePoint were introduced. One of those tools, SharePoint Designer, while not targeted at professional developers, is an invaluable tool for the professional developer because it can troubleshoot SharePoint deployments quickly. With the new SharePoint tools in Visual Studio 2010, developers can quickly build SharePoint applications, and use VS to deploy and debug these solutions. Finally, this chapter showed you some tips and tricks around testing your solutions to make sure they can scale as the application requirements grow.

3

IT Pro Enhancements for the Developer

WHAT'S IN THIS CHAPTER?

➤ An Introduction to IT Professional Features that affect developers

➤ Best practices for working with the SharePoint 2010 Infrastructure Enhancements

When it comes to developing with SharePoint, it's very helpful if developers are able to be good friends with the IT pro who set up the SharePoint infrastructure, because often developers do not control the final server configuration that the code they write runs on. For example, unless an administrator allows a full-trusted solution to run in his or her environment, a developer will have a smaller set of SharePoint platform technologies to choose from when writing code. With SharePoint 2010, the choices for both IT and developers have grown, and developers need to understand what IT improvements have been made in SharePoint that could affect their applications. These improvements fall into the categories of performance, high availability, security, and management. Each of these areas is covered in this chapter.

PERFORMANCE IMPROVEMENTS

The performance improvements in SharePoint 2010 are important for developers. These improvements will make your code run faster, but there are also some performance lockdowns that may affect your code, as SharePoint will protect the system from being overrun with bad queries or large amounts of data entering the system. In your code, you must be aware that you may run into certain limits and make sure that you have good error checking to fail gracefully if the error is hit. You will learn how to do this later in this chapter.

List Throttling

One of the main sources of performance problems in SharePoint is either users or developers writing too many items to a list and then requesting a view or a query that tries to return a large number of items. This causes locking on the database, and in a multiuser environment like SharePoint, this causes issues for other users who may be working in other SharePoint sites. To stop this, SharePoint 2010 has implemented list and library throttling so that the result sets are trimmed down regardless of the number of results requested. For example, SharePoint can store up to 50 million items in a list. Let's imagine you didn't have a list that large but had a list with a million items. A user creates a view that tries to return 50,000 items on a page. SharePoint 2010 will throttle that query and return either an error or the first set of results up to the number put in the throttle. Be aware that by default, SharePoint sets list throttles to 5,000 items.

One thing to realize is that, as a developer, you can trigger this throttle even when performing operations that seem as if they would not cause issues. For example, let's imagine that you have a list with 10,000 items in it and your throttle is 8,000. You're returning only 2,000 items in your views, and you try to sort on a nonindexed column to display those items. You will get an exception, because SharePoint will need to return all 10,000 items to sort and display your 2,000 items, which would exceed the throttle. Thankfully, SharePoint will throw a special exception if you hit the throttle in your operations, so you can catch this. This exception is `SPQueryThrottledException`.

The throttle can also be set on lookups in a list. You can limit the number of lookup columns in a list. If there are too many lookup columns, performance will suffer, so SharePoint can limit this for the administrator. As a developer, you must be aware of this limitation so that you do not hit it in your code, or if you do, you're able to fail gracefully. Figure 3-1 shows the different options you have when setting the throttle.

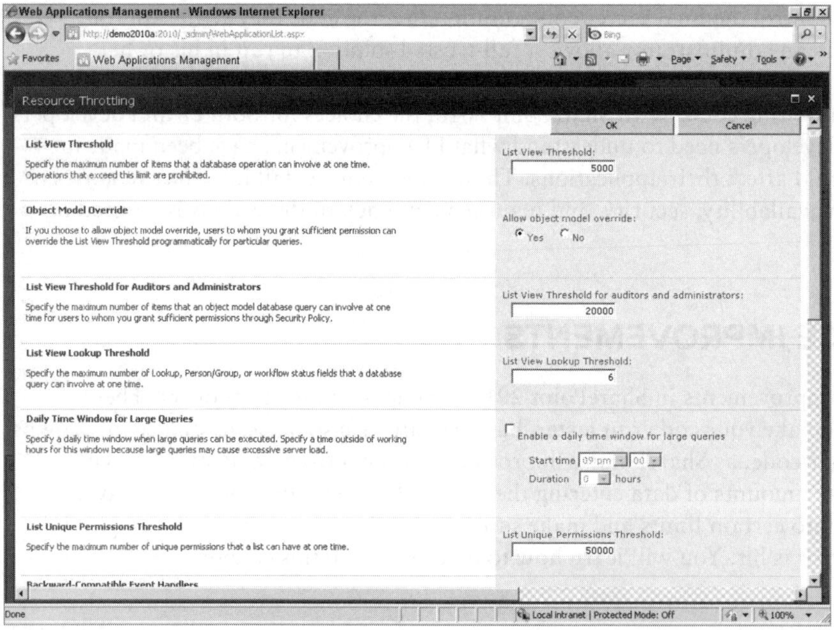

FIGURE 3-1

One of the settings you can configure for the throttle is the maximum number of items to be retrieved in a single request. You can also set an object model (OM) override that will be combined with the maximum number of items an auditor or administrator can retrieve via the object model. The administrator or auditor cannot see more items in the list view — only via the object model. To be an administrator or auditor, the farm administrator needs to grant you the correct permissions level to be a Site Collection Administrator or a Site Collection Auditor. When you look at the code to set the object model override, you will also see a Windows PowerShell override of the API override. In the end, administrators get the final say on whether an override can occur.

There is also a setting for something affectionately referred to as happy hours. This setting allows you to create a block of time, typically when usage is low, when you will allow large queries to run and not enforce the throttles.

One thing to note about the settings: they are not used if you are a SharePoint administrator and you execute a query. In that case, all of the results will be returned to you. This means that when you are testing your code, make sure that you use multiple different authentication methods so that you are not running as a super user all the time; otherwise, you will not catch throttling errors.

Working with the Throttle Programmatically

Through the SharePoint API, you can change or remove the throttle as long as the object model override was checked in the settings for the throttle. Before changing or removing the throttle, you need to check if the throttle is enabled. The following section demonstrates different ways to work with the throttle programmatically.

First, to check if the throttle is enabled, you will use a number of properties and methods of the `SPWebApplication` object that represents your web application. Table 3-1 shows the different properties and methods to detect the settings for the throttle with the `SPWebApplication` object; Table 3-2 shows the same thing for the `SPList` object.

TABLE 3-1: Detecting Throttle Properties and Methods on SPWebApplication

NAME	DESCRIPTION
`CurrentUserIgnoreThrottle`	This method returns a Boolean that tells you whether the throttle is ignored because the user has sufficient privileges, such as being an administrator, or if the throttle is not enforced at this particular time.
`IsUnthrottledPrivilegedOperationsAllowed`	This method returns a Boolean that specifies whether unthrottled operations are allowed.
`MaxItemsPerThrottledOperation`	This Integer property gets or sets the maximum number of items in your throttled operations.

continues

TABLE 3-1 *(continued)*

NAME	DESCRIPTION
MaxItemsPerThrottledOperationOverride	This Integer property gets or sets the maximum number of items to return when the throttle is overridden. Default is 20,000.
MaxItemsPerThrottledOperationWarningLevel	This integer gets or sets the maximum items allowed in the list before a warning is displayed in the UI and the farm admin receives email.
MaxQueryLookupFields	This integer property gets and sets the maximum lookup fields you can have in the list. The default is 6.
UnthrottledPrivilegedOperationWindowEnabled	This Boolean specifies whether the happy hour feature is enabled.
DailyStartUnthrottledPrivilegedOperationsHour	This gets or sets the hour to start allowing unthrottled operations.
DailyStartUnthrottledPrivilegedOperationsMinute	This gets or sets the minute to start allowing unthrottled operations.
DailyUnthrottledPrivilegedOperationsDuration	This gets or sets the number of hours to allow unthrottled operations. Note that if an operation goes beyond the duration, SharePoint will allow it to continue to run as long as it was started in the allowed time window.

TABLE 3-2: Detecting Throttle Properties and Methods on SPList

NAME	DESCRIPTION
IsThrottled	This method returns a Boolean that tells you whether the throttle is ignored because the user has sufficient privileges, such as being an administrator, or if the throttle is not enforced at this particular time.

Second, once you know whether the throttle is enabled, you can change your queries based on that knowledge to avoid hitting the throttle. However, there may be times when you fail to change your query and hit the throttle. This is where using the SPQueryThrottledException class in your code is helpful. The example that follows shows how to catch this exception, which tells you that you have exceeded the throttle on the list. Notice how even using the Count method on the Items object for a document library can trigger the throttle.

```
try
        {
                int ItemCount = doclib.Items.Count;

        }
        catch (SPQueryThrottledException)
        {
                //Retrieving all items can trigger the throttle
        }
```

Finally, once you know the throttle is there and can catch exceptions, you may want to override the throttle, using the object model. There are a couple of ways to do this. First, you can do it on an individual query, using the SPQuery or SPSiteDataQuery object's QueryThrottleMode property. Second, if you are a farm admin, you can use the SPList's EnableThrottling property to turn throttling off. Last, you can use the OM to set the time when the throttle is off. The most common approach is the SPQuery or SPSiteDataQuery object. The code that follows demonstrates how to use the SPQuery object and override the throttle. Please note that there is also a SPQueryThrottleOption, called Strict, if you want to apply the throttle regardless of permissions, even if an administrator is the logged in user.

```
using (SPSite site = new SPSite("http://intranet.contoso.com"))
        {
                using (SPWeb web = site.RootWeb)
                {
                    try
                    {

                        SPList list = web.Lists["Shared Documents"];

                        SPQuery qry = new SPQuery();
                        qry.QueryThrottleMode = SPQueryThrottleOption.Override;

                        //create your query
                        SPListItemCollection coll = list.GetItems(qry);
                    }

                    catch (SPQueryThrottledException)
                    {
                        //
                    }
                }
        }
}
```

External List Throttling

Beyond standard list throttling, SharePoint also supports External List throttling. External Lists are lists that are connected to other systems using Business Connectivity Services (BCS) and External

Content Types. Sometimes when connecting to these backend systems, the backend can take a long time to respond, or you might try to retrieve too many items, overloading the backend. To solve this problem, BCS implements a throttle per connection type whether that is a database or web service that you are connecting to.

There are four types of throttles in BCS. One is a rows per fetch against a database, which limits the number of rows BCS will retrieve from the database. The second is the typical timeout for your operations against the backend. The third is size of fetch, as it's hard to use rows against a web service because a web service may return XML, text, or binary data, which may not translate easily into a rows metaphor. Each of these throttles is per instance, so you can have multiple instances of a BCS application against a single backend, each with different throttles. The fourth type is a global, meaning that regardless of the type of connection throttle, you can throttle the number of connections to the backend system, so you don't overload the backend with a lot of connections. Table 3-3 describes the default throttles for BCS.

TABLE 3-3: External List Throttles

CONNECTION TYPE	TYPE OF THROTTLE	LIMIT
Database	Rows per fetch	2000
Database	Timeout	3 Minutes
Web Service/WCF	Size of fetch	30MB
Web Service/WCF	Timeout	3 Minutes
Global	Connections	100

The following PowerShell script demonstrates how to get and set the External List throttles:

```
$snapin = Get-PSSnapin | where-object { $_.Name -eq
'Microsoft.SharePoint.PowerShell' }
if ($snapin -eq $null){
 write-host "Loading SharePoint PowerShell Snapin..." -foregroundcolor Blue
 add-pssnapin "Microsoft.SharePoint.PowerShell"
 write-host "SharePoint PowerShell Snapin loaded." -foregroundcolor Green
}

$bdcAppProxy = Get-SPServiceApplicationProxy | where {$_ -match "Business
Data Connectivity"}

Get-SPBusinessDataCatalogThrottleConfig -Scope Database -ThrottleType Items -
ServiceApplicationProxy $bdcAppProxy

$throttleDb = Get-SPBusinessDataCatalogThrottleConfig -Scope Database -
ThrottleType Items -ServiceApplicationProxy $bdcAppProxy

#Alternative way to write out settings write-host $throttleDb.Default

#Uncomment to set your throttle limits
```

```
#Set-SPBusinessDataCatalogThrottleConfig -Identity $throttleDb -maximum 12000
-default 10000


$throttleWCF = Get-SPBusinessDataCatalogThrottleConfig -Scope WCF -
ThrottleType Size -ServiceApplicationProxy $bdcAppProxy

#Set-SPBusinessDataCatalogThrottleConfig -Identity $throttleWCF -maximum
100000000 -default 50000000


$throttleConn = Get-SPBusinessDataCatalogThrottleConfig -Scope Global -
ThrottleType Connections -ServiceApplicationProxy $bdcAppProxy

#Set-SPBusinessDataCatalogThrottleConfig -Identity $throttleConn -maximum 200
-default 150

write-host "Completed Run" -foregroundcolor Blue
```

HTTP Request Throttling

One other throttle to be aware of is the new HTTP request throttle. Previously, SharePoint would not throttle requests. Therefore, all requests coming in would have the same priority, so the server could be overloaded by many people trying to write to the server at the same time. As far as user activities, SharePoint is very similar to email in that users perform a lot of reads and deletes but not as many writes. For this reason, SharePoint 2010 optimizes for the read scenarios when it comes to HTTP throttling, rather than write scenarios.

HTTP throttling works by comparing the server resources to the levels configured every 5 seconds. By default, the Server CPU, Memory, Request in Queue, and Request wait times are monitored, and after three failed checks against acceptable parameters, the server will enter a throttling period. This throttling period will continue until a successful check is completed and the levels are below the configured levels. Requests generated prior to the server entering into the throttling mode will be completed, so that users do not lose their work. Any new HTTP GET and Search Robot request will generate a 503 error message and will be logged in the Event Viewer. For the user, they will see a Server Too Busy error and can refresh their browser to try again. Any new timer jobs will also not be started while in the throttling period. However, HTTP PUT operations will be allowed so that submitting forms and saving documents will work.

You can enable or disable throttling through Central Administration. You manage the throttle on a per web application basis, so some web applications can be throttled and others can be unthrottled. To enable throttling, look under the Application Management section and then Manage Web Applications. Click on a web application to select it, then click on the General Settings drop-down, and select the Resource Throttling menu. Find the section titled HTTP Request Monitoring and Throttling, where you will find a radio button option to turn it off or on. HTTP resource throttling is on by default. Figure 3-2 shows how to set HTTP resource throttling.

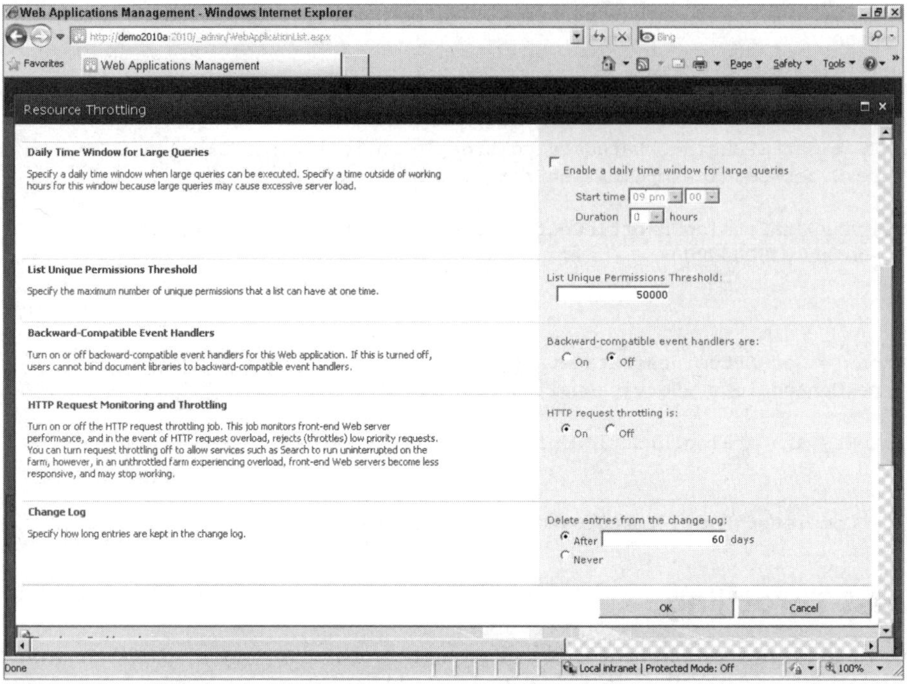

FIGURE 3-2

To get and set the parameters and see the values, you can use either PowerShell or the API. This is one instance in which using PowerShell as a developer might be easier than trying to use the API, because PowerShell has two commandlets that make viewing and editing the throttles easy. The first one is the `Get-SPWebApplicationHttpThrottlingMonitor` commandlet. This commandlet allows you to pass the URL to the web application you want to check using the `Identity` parameter. When you run this commandlet, you will get an output that looks similar to that here:

```
Category: Memory
Counter: Available Mbytes
Instance:
AssociatedHealthScoreCalculator : [1000.0,500.0,400.0,300.0,200.0,100.0,80.0,60
.0,40.0,20.0]

Category: ASP.NET
Counter: Requests Queued
Instance:
AssociatedHealthScoreCalculator : [0.0,1.0,2.0,4.0,8.0,16.0,32.0,64.0,82.0,100.
0]

Category: ASP.NET
Counter: Request Wait Time
Instance:
AssociatedHealthScoreCalculator : [10.0,50.0,100.0,200.0,400.0,800.0,1000.0,200
0.0,4000.0,15000.0]
```

To set the different throttles, use `Set-SPWebApplicationHttpThrottlingMonitor` and pass in the parameters for the category, counter, instance, minimum, and maximum. You can pull these from the Windows Performance Monitor if you don't know the categories or counters.

Remote Blob Storage

If you are familiar with the external blob storage (EBS) capabilities in SharePoint 2007, then remote blob storage (RBS) won't seem that different to you in SharePoint 2010. The main difference is that RBS takes advantage of the APIs from SQL Server 2008 and can use the new FILESTREAM capabilities in the SQL Server 2008 product. EBS was built on its own API, and the move to RBS moves the blob storage capabilities from SharePoint into the more mainstream API for blobs.

You may be wondering when you use blob storage. As a developer, the blob storage is pretty transparent to you, except if you're writing your own blob storage provider. IT pros are the ones who will make the decision and enable external blob storage in their environment. The main reason you will use external blob storage is if you want to move your blobs to more commodity-related hardware storage devices. You may be able to lower your cost a bit, because you don't have to store, manage, or maintain the blobs in SQL. Again, as a developer, it's transparent to you whether the blob is in SQL or another system.

There are a couple of things you need to remember about RBS. It does not get around the 2GB limit for file sizes in SharePoint. This is a hard limit. So as a developer, don't ask your IT administrator to implement RBS to get around this limit. Plus, RBS could lower your performance, especially if you write a poor provider. Therefore, as a developer, make sure that the benefits of using RBS and writing your own provider outweigh the cost, because if you write poor code, possibly every read or write operation on documents could call your code in SharePoint. SharePoint must block the user until it receives the blob back from your provider, because it wants to keep the metadata, which is still stored in SQL, and the blob consistent. Writing a storage provider is beyond the scope of this book. The SDK has some good documentation, but again, before you write one, make sure that you really need one and that, if you want RBS, the SQL Server FILESTREAM provider is not sufficient to meet your needs.

Streaming Media and Bit Rate Throttling

One of the other areas of enhancement that you can take advantage of in your applications is streaming and bit throttling. Given the explosion of digital media and its integration into applications, this is important. You do not want unhappy end users if the speed and performance of your sites that use video are such that it takes a long time to start playing or it plays inconsistently. SharePoint 2010 has many new digital asset management capabilities. When it comes to digital media, you have features such as the media player web part, support for video in the Content by Query web part, out-of-the-box (OOB) support for RSS/podcasting, and bit rate throttling support. If you are doing a lot of development with digital media, you need to understand the infrastructure that SharePoint provides for this asset type. Take a look at the Media Player web part API. It has a client-side API that allows you to customize the player to tell it to start, stop, pause, and set the source. Also, you can get the embed tag from the API so that others can embed a link right to the video. Finally, you can skin the player using Expression Blend, because it is just an XAML application.

HIGH AVAILABILITY IMPROVEMENTS

When it comes to high availability (HA), most developers don't concern themselves with what IT folks have implemented. This is a mistake because your application needs to be resilient if there is a failure. In addition, with SharePoint you may actually be running against a different database server than the one that you originally connected to in your application. For this reason, understanding the High Availability (HA) enhancements that affect developers is important. This chapter covers two primary HA enhancements. The first is database mirroring and clustering, which allow SQL Server to fail over to a backup server if the primary server fails. The second is read-only databases, which enable administrators to turn on read-only content databases to allow for scenarios where data can be shipped globally, but make it read-only to avoid write conflicts, or for upgrade and migration scenarios.

Database Mirroring and Clustering

No one wants their SharePoint deployments to experience downtime. To minimize this, IT administrators implement database mirroring, log shipping, or failover clustering in SQL Server so that when the primary SQL Server in the farm experiences issues, SQL Server will fail over to the secondary server and continue processing requests. As with any sort of interruption of service, transactions may have to be retried, depending on where they were when the failure occurred. You should always check the error codes returned in your applications to see if your transaction failed and then retry the transaction.

SharePoint 2010 supports the ability to specify a failover partner both through the Central Administration user interface and programmatically. Figure 3-3 shows the Central Administration interface for configuring database mirroring.

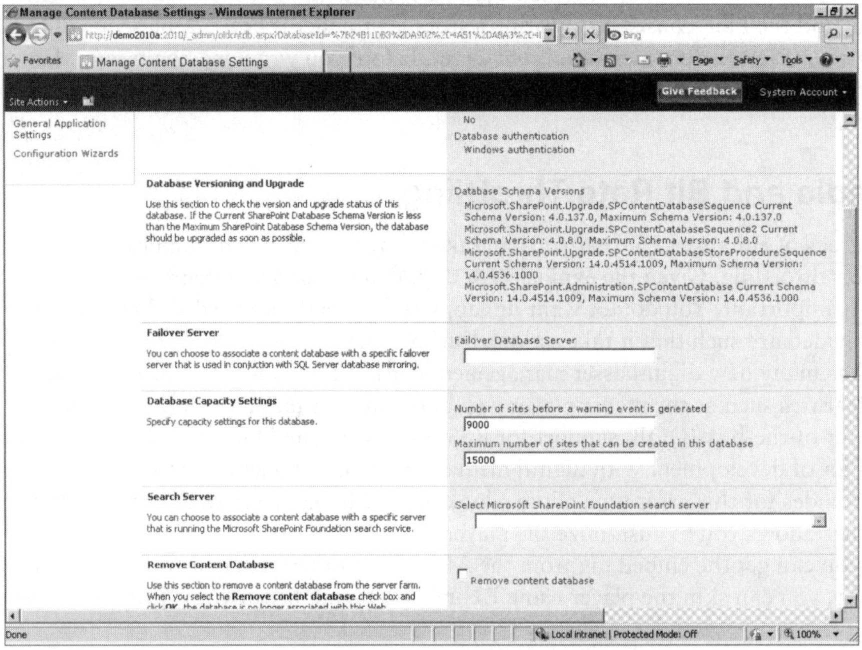

FIGURE 3-3

To work with this programmatically, use the SPDatabase class and the properties on this class, including FailoverServer, which will return the SPServer object that is the mirror, and FailoverServiceInstance, which returns an SPDatabaseServiceInstance that is the mirror. You can also use the method AddFailoverServiceInstance to specify a connection string to the failover partner SQL Server that you want the primary to work with. The code that follows shows these methods and properties in use.

```
SPDatabaseServiceInstance databaseServiceInstance = new
SPDatabaseServiceInstance();



            SPService service =
SPFarm.Local.Services.GetValue<SPDatabaseService>();
            foreach (SPDatabaseServiceInstance si in service.Instances)
            {
                if (si.TypeName == "Microsoft SharePoint Foundation Database"
                    || si.TypeName.Contains("Microsoft SharePoint Foundation"))
                {
                    databaseServiceInstance = si;
                    break;
                }
            }

            SPDatabase database = databaseServiceInstance.Databases["WSS_Content"];

            SPDatabaseServiceInstance siFail = database.FailoverServiceInstance;

            database.AddFailoverServiceInstance("Connection String");
        database.Update();
```

Read-Only Databases

One new edition to 2007, late in its product lifecycle, was the support for read-only databases. With 2010, this support continues and is improved. Read-only databases are useful when you want to perform maintenance or provide copies of your database globally but you don't want to allow users to write to the database. Having a read-only database can work with high-availability technologies, such as log shipping or database snapshots.

Note that the user interface will understand when the database is in a read-only state. The UI will attempt to disable any functionality that would trigger a write, such as changing properties or saving content, rather than give users error messages.

As a developer, you should follow good error-handling etiquette to catch an error if the database is in a read-only state. You can also use the object model to detect whether the site and database are in a read-only state, so that you can either continue to try to write to the database or wait for the read-only state to be removed. The Boolean ReadOnly properties on the SPSite and the SPDatabase objects make it easy to check the read-only state of your site collection and your database. There is also a Boolean ReadLocked property you can use to see if the site collection is also read-locked so that you can't retrieve data from it. The code that follows shows how to use these properties.

```
SPDatabaseServiceInstance databaseServiceInstance = new
SPDatabaseServiceInstance();

        SPService service =
SPFarm.Local.Services.GetValue<SPDatabaseService>();
        foreach (SPDatabaseServiceInstance si in service.Instances)
        {
            if (si.TypeName == "Microsoft SharePoint Foundation Database"
                || si.TypeName.Contains("Microsoft SharePoint Foundation"))
            {
                databaseServiceInstance = si;
                break;
            }
        }

        SPDatabase database = databaseServiceInstance.Databases["WSS_Content"];

        //Check to see if the database is read only
        bool isReadOnly = database.IsReadOnly;

        //Check to see if the site is read only
        SPSite site = new SPSite("http://intranet.contoso.com");

        bool readLocked = site.ReadLocked;

        bool readOnly = site.ReadOnly;

        site.Dispose();
```

SECURITY IMPROVEMENTS

Security is a major topic for developers. It often trips up developers because their code may be running in the wrong security context in order to perform operations, may not have the right identity, may be trying to perform multiple authentication hops, or may be attempting to perform cross-domain calls. All of these things can lead to errors or code that doesn't perform the way you expect it to. Security issues are also sometimes hard to track down. For this reason, understanding the security improvements in SharePoint 2010 will make you a better developer. There are a lot of improvements, and some will add more complexity rather than less, but they will give you the power to make your applications work in more environments than previously possible.

Claims-Based Authentication

Understanding claims-based authentication is a book unto itself. For this reason, this section will give just a quick primer on claims-based authentication and what it means to you as a developer. Claims-based authentication is based on identity and trust. Some systems may identify you as being 20 years old, and some may identify you as being 30 years old. With claims-based authentication, you decide which claim you want to trust, the 20-year-old or the 30-year-old claim. Claims-based authentication, in a way, is more complex that using Windows-based authentication from an IT standpoint but provides better functionality from an identity protection and platform standpoint.

What Is the Value of Claims?

To understand the value of claims, you need to forget for a moment all the other authentication methods that you are used to. If you box yourself into thinking about or comparing claims to those other methods, it will be hard to break out of the constraints of those authentication methods. For example, if you use Windows integrated authentication, you probably think of identity in terms of Windows user accounts and groups. For ASP.NET, membership and roles provider are your context, and for forms-based authentication, usernames, passwords, and roles are your context. If you abstract out from these authentication methods to the high-level concepts, you have a claim of some type of information, and you have an issuer or authority that verifies that claim. Because you have a trust relationship with the issuer, you trust the claim that comes from that issuer. Trust is explicit, which is different from the other authentication methods you may be used to.

The value of claims is flexibility. Because claims are extensible and standards-based, you can create different attributes on your identity, pass that around to different applications, create roles and even use standards-based tokens, such as Security Assertion Markup Language (SAML) tokens, to identify and make a claim against access to a resource or application. The other value of claims is that you can use almost any authentication method you want on the backend, but in your application, you do not have to recode if you want to switch from NTLM to Kerberos or to forms-based authentication. This gives you ultimate flexibility in the security and authorization part of your application.

When to Use Claims

Not every application needs claims. For example, if you can get by with Windows authentication, and you are reasonably confident that your identity needs won't change, stick with Windows authentication. Claims-based authentication is a good choice when you need flexibility and functionality and are willing to pay the price for those capabilities. If you are working in a hybrid identity and authentication environment, look at claims as a solution, so that you can practice writing all your applications as claims-aware applications, whether they are internal, external, or somewhere in-between. Having the flexibility of claims will make your application lifecycle management easier.

Claims-Based Authentication Simplifies Your Authentication Code

Almost every application has code that supports identity and authentication. It may not be explicit sometimes, but it is in the layers that make up your application, even if you did not write it yourself. If you are used to writing using Windows authentication, you probably haven't had to worry about authentication code as much as a web developer who uses forms-based authentication and must write the code to check the username and password and perform password resets and account lockouts has. Windows authentication developers have the power of the domain and domain controllers to help them with all the services surrounding identity and user management.

Even with Windows authentication, while authentication may be provided for you, there are limitations. Once you go beyond the domain limit to try to authenticate against other domains that you may not trust, the developer becomes responsible for making sure that the complexities of trusts and relationships are set up by IT. In addition, if you want more information than username and password for your application, then you must move away from your authentication code to write to directory services. This means that you will be maintaining two code paths, one for authentication and one to get additional identity attributes.

Claims can solve these issues because they can be more than just usernames and passwords, and can contain things like groups, manager, email, and other user profile attributes that you may need for your application. Again, you factor out the authentication provider in claims from your claims-aware application, so you do not care how the authentication was performed on the backend.

How Does Claims-Based Authentication Work?

This is the simplified version of how claims work. The easiest way to think about how claims work is to take a real-world example. Let's imagine that you need to board an airplane. First, you need to check in. That could be at the ticket counter or that could be online. Both require you to authenticate yourself but in different ways. The ticket counter requires you to show some form of ID and that ID comes from a trusted source. Online, you're forced to log in and that login must be trusted in order for you to print your boarding pass.

Your boarding pass contains a lot of extra information rather than just your name. It contains your destination, the gate you're leaving from, your flight number, and also your seat information. When you reach the gate, the gate agent checks your boarding pass. This agent doesn't really care whether your claim came from the ticketing agent or from your printer at home. The boarding pass is a trusted claim and you're allowed to get on your flight. If we translate this to software, that boarding pass is a signed security token from a trusted issuer. Your application would validate it and allow the user or application presenting that token to have access to the resource that was requested.

SharePoint Claims

How SharePoint implements claims is seamless to you as the developer. The IT administrator selects claims-based authentication when creating a web application, as shown in Figure 3-4.

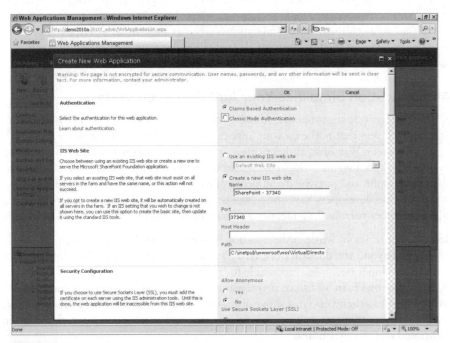

FIGURE 3-4

As a developer, you are shielded from the complexity of claims. You continue to use classes such as SPUser without caring whether the authentication was done by Windows, forms, or a SAML token. The only time you must get into the weeds on the claims classes that are in the `Microsoft` `.SharePoint.Administration` namespace is if you want to write your own claims provider, which is rare for the common developer.

Code Access Security

SharePoint continues to support code access security, in which you can specify your own code access security (CAS) policy for your web parts so that you can perform operations that are not normally allowed inside of your SharePoint application. SharePoint provides minimal permissions out of the box for your web parts, which usually meet your needs, so use custom CAS policies with caution. Instead, take a look at Sandbox Solutions, which we will discuss next, as a possible alternative to using CAS. Sandbox Solutions do not require changes to the configuration in SharePoint. They have resource throttling, and they can be deployed both on-premise or in the cloud in SharePoint Online. In addition, Sandbox Solutions leverage CAS under the covers, so you do not have to configure CAS policies yourself.

Sandbox Solutions

Sandbox Solutions are a new feature in SharePoint 2010. Frequently, developers have difficulty deploying solutions to SharePoint in their environments because IT does not allow them access to the server. For example, you need to be an administrator on the machine to add DLLs to the GAC. Most developers are not administrators on centrally managed SharePoint servers. This causes problems for IT and also for the developer.

Plus, IT may worry that custom code running on their servers, if written poorly, will severely affect performance. For example, if you write a web part that does an infinite loop or calls out to an external system and it maxes out the server resources, then every site running on that server will be slow, even if they aren't using your custom web part.

Out of these concerns, Sandbox Solutions were born. Sandbox Solutions are derivatives of your standard solution package that, when deployed to the server, SharePoint runs in a special process that has limited permissions. In your SharePoint Server, you will see three new processes running on the server for Sandbox Solutions. One is called `SPUCHostService.exe`, which decides whether the WFE on which this service is running will participate in the Sandbox Solutions. Because you can isolate or load balance your servers running Sandbox Solutions, not all the WFEs in your farm have to be running this service. You decide which servers are execution hosts for Sandbox Solutions.

Another process is called `SPUCWorkerProcess.exe`. This is the process where your code will run. As you can see, your code does not run in `w3wp.exe` but in this special process. Therefore, when you connect your debugger to a process, be sure to select the right process based on the type of solution you built for SharePoint.

Finally, there is `SPUCWorkerProcessProxy.exe`, which is part of the services application architecture for SharePoint. There are now proxies between web applications and service applications so that, when you call services from your Sandbox code, the proxy will make sure that you are calling the right services based on the permissions of your sandbox.

A picture is worth a thousand words, so Figure 3-5 shows the architecture for Sandbox Solutions.

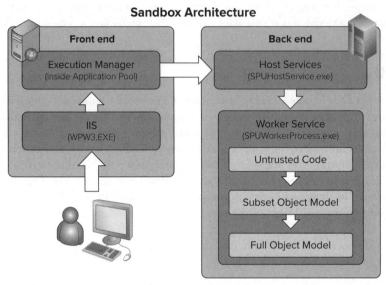

FIGURE 3-5

Sandbox Solutions are covered more in the following chapters, so view this as a primer in context of other IT changes of which you should be aware.

Cross-Site Scripting

To help secure SharePoint and the users who use SharePoint from malicious code, some changes were made in 2010 to prevent Cross-Site Scripting (XSS) attacks. Some of this will affect the way your applications may work. Part of these changes had to be made because of the new Client Object Model in SharePoint, where malicious users could possibly cut and paste code into properties in SharePoint and attempt to perform bad operations.

One example of a change relates to web parts. By default, contributors now are not allowed to view/edit custom web part properties. As a developer, you can override this default behavior either through an object model attribute — `RequiresDesignerPermissionAttribute` — or through a `SafeControl` attribute — `SafeAgainstScript`. The object model attribute wins over the `SafeControl` attribute, so if you set the OM attribute to false, then contributors would not be able to view/edit custom web part properties even if `SafeAgainstScript` were set to true. Note that this is true only for general web parts. If the user has personalized the web part either by making personal settings or by adding it as a personal web part, then these changes won't be implemented for those web parts. You will have to implement custom code to allow this customization.

Another change relates to how files are handled. SharePoint 2010 does not allow HTML files to be rendered in document libraries. Therefore, if your application has been posting HTML files to document libraries and your end users have been viewing them in the browser, this won't work in 2010. Instead, SharePoint will force the users to save the HTML files locally before viewing them. This is implemented using HTTP headers and is configurable at the List or Web Application level, or you can change the Safe List by Mime Type to allow this operation.

Another change is that the functionality that enabled contributors to upload ASPX files in 2007 is blocked in 2010. This is an important change to be aware of, because it may break the way your 2007 application works.

MANAGEMENT IMPROVEMENTS

As a developer, the management improvements in 2010 will help both you and your IT counterparts maintain and track SharePoint and your custom code that runs on top of SharePoint. IT will be able to see slow-running pages where your code may not be performing properly. You can help IT by writing additional health rules, helping surface your applications in their reports, and extending PowerShell with new commandlets for them to use. This section will cover some of the new enhancements for IT that developers will care about and want to understand to make their applications better.

Health Monitoring and Reports

Your application is only as reliable and can perform as well as the infrastructure you run the application on. If your SharePoint infrastructure is undersized, unreliable, or does not perform well, your application will be affected no matter how well written your code is. For this reason, understanding how the health monitoring and reporting in SharePoint works and how you can plug into this infrastructure is important.

In 2010, there is a new health analyzer that runs health rules to help IT uncover issues in their environment. IT can then have SharePoint attempt to automatically repair those problems. Figure 3-6 shows the new health analyzer in SharePoint 2010.

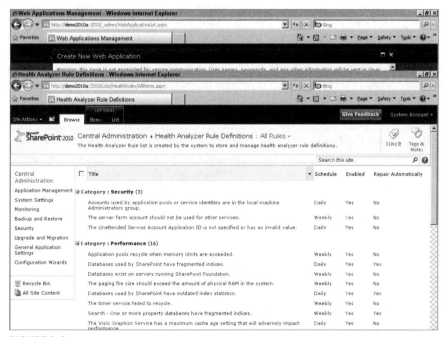

FIGURE 3-6

As a developer, the namespace that you will use to implement your health rules is the `Microsoft.SharePoint.Administration.Health` namespace. In particular, the class for your rules will inherit from the `SPHealthAnalysisRule` class. You implement the required members in your derived class, and you have a new health rule that IT can implement.

The SDK is a good resource for details on writing and deploying health rules. Note that you may want to write rules that monitor your applications for preventive maintenance. For example, if your application uses a custom SQL database or a timer job, you may want to proactively monitor the database and the timer job to make sure both are operational and configured correctly. If they are not, you can write code in your rule so that your application self-heals and repairs the issues.

Service Applications

SharePoint 2010 moves to a new architecture when it comes to application services. If you are used to the Shared Services Provider (SSP) in 2007, the SSP architecture is replaced with the new Service Applications. The best way to think about a Service Application is that it is a configured logical instance of a service that provides data or computing, such as user profiles or search. The Service Application provides an administrative interface and user resources, including an instance of a database in SQL Server and an Application Pool in IIS.

When it comes to usage, features such as web parts that run on a web application use the Service Application. This connection is made through a Service Application Proxy. The associations between web application and Service Application are set by the administrator and can be changed at any time. These associations can be managed individually or through a group called a Service Application Proxy Group.

So, why the change in architecture? With SSPs, everything was lumped together, even though some services offered very different capabilities. This made SSPs difficult to deploy and manage over the lifetime of your SharePoint deployment. Plus, because SSPs were effectively grouped together into a single database, scalability became difficult. In addition, allowing administration of a single service in the SSP, so that every administrator could administer any service, was next to impossible. Finally, you couldn't really share services across farms. There were many restrictions and the administrative and management overhead made administration difficult.

As a developer, you can write your own Service Applications that provide services to your features that run on the SharePoint WFEs. There are certain scenarios in which this makes sense. For example, if you need specialized computing and analytics; if you want to share data across sites, site collections, and farms; if you need to execute long-running operations; or if you want to scale out your application by taking advantage of the services infrastructure. You should not use Service Applications if your data or features are specific to a site, a site collection, or a site template. Instead, you should write code that runs within the boundaries of your site or site collection, such as an event receiver or web part.

Writing a complete Service Application is beyond the scope of this book, but to get you started, here are some steps to be aware of and also the APIs associated with Service Applications. To write a good Service Application, you should have a working knowledge of Windows Communication Foundation (WCF), because Service Applications use WCF extensively to communicate between the Service Application Proxy and the consumer.

The steps to write a Service Application at the high level are:

1. Create Service Application
2. Create Service Application endpoint using WCF
3. Create Service Application installers
4. Install and provision Service Application
5. Create Service Application Proxy
6. Create Service Application Proxy installers
7. Install and Provision the Service Application Proxy
8. Create Service Application consumers
9. Install, deploy, and test consumers

The APIs that you will use to create your service application are described in Table 3-4.

TABLE 3-4: Service Application APIs

API	DESCRIPTION
SPService	A service that provides the core business logic of the service. It usually has no UI. You can have multiple instances of your service running across multiple servers but only a single instance of your service on any one server. The SPService object has an Instances property that holds all the instances of the service that are running on various servers in the farm. Each instance is represented by an object of a class derived from SPServiceInstance.
SPServiceInstance	SPServiceInstance represents an instance of a service on a server in the farm. Just like Window Services, your service instances may be in different states such as started or stopped. An instance is the host process for the service application.
SPServiceApplication	A service application is usually created by an administrator by configuring and running your service. That service is then hosted by a service instance.
SPServiceProxy	An SPServiceProxy is the parent of the SPServiceApplicationProxy.
SPServiceApplicationProxy	Service application proxies are the public interface for your service application. Through the proxy, other services or programs can interface with your service application.

Recall the earlier section on read-only databases, and you will see SPService in use in the sample code.

PowerShell Support

The last area we will look at is PowerShell support. SharePoint 2010 ships a lot of PowerShell commandlets, so you will need to become familiar with the different cmdlets available to help you deploy your solutions or browse your service applications. STSADM is still functional, but over time may be deprecated, so it is important to start learning PowerShell now. There are times, though, when you will find STSADM to be faster from a productivity standpoint, because it requires only one command line command to perform certain operations versus PowerShell, which might require a more comprehensive script. If you remember that STSADM is not a long-term solution, but that you can use it tactically to achieve your goals faster and more easily, then definitely take advantage of it for the short term.

PowerShell is too large of a topic to fully cover all of the functionality it provides in this book. Instead, we will offer grounding in the basics of PowerShell here. Please look to other books by Wrox to learn more about the depths of PowerShell and what you can do with it.

PowerShell Tools

Before you write your first PowerShell script, you need to know the tool options. There are a ton of PowerShell tools on the Internet, so we will focus here on the OOB ones, as you can evaluate the ones on the Internet on your own.

The first tool is the PowerShell command line. If you are a hardcore scripter, this may be your tool of choice. It has no fancy UI, it has no overhead, it is just bare-metal DOS-style scripting through a text UI. If you are going to use the PowerShell command line, you will want to launch the SharePoint 2010 Management Shell to get to the command line, because this will register the SharePoint 2010 cmdlets so that you do not have to do that step yourself.

For the more GUI-style person, there is the Windows PowerShell Integrated Scripting Environment, as shown in Figure 3-7. This GUI provides the ability to write, execute, and debug your scripts. If you are a Visual Studio person, it will take some time to get used to the user interface, but once you learn it, you will be more productive with PowerShell.

PowerShell Basics

Again, SharePoint ships with hundreds of cmdlets, and covering them all is beyond the scope of this book. Instead, understanding the basic commands will help you navigate around. Plus, PowerShell works directly with the API, so if you learn a SharePoint API, the cmdlet that works with that section of SharePoint most likely will use the same methods and properties you learned in the API. Therefore, learning the SharePoint API is the first step to becoming a SharePoint PowerShell pro.

First, you may want to get a list of all the SharePoint cmdlets. To do this, use Get-Command "*sp*" -CommandType cmdlet.

Second, to get a count of all the SharePoint cmdlets grouped by verb, use Get-Command "*sp*" -CommandType cmdlet | Group-Object -Property Verb or, to get a nicely formatted set of tables,

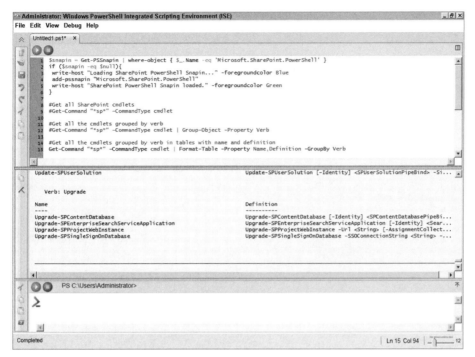

FIGURE 3-7

use `Get-Command "*sp*" -CommandType cmdlet | Format-Table -Property Name,Definition -GroupBy Verb`. Finally, to get help for any cmdlet, use `Get-Help <cmdlet> -Full`.

One trap that many new PowerShell programmers fall into is not referencing the SharePoint PowerShell snap-in. To do that, use the following code:

```
$snapin = Get-PSSnapin | where-object { $_.Name -eq
'Microsoft.SharePoint.PowerShell' }
if ($snapin -eq $null){
 write-host "Loading SharePoint PowerShell Snapin..." -foregroundcolor Blue
 add-pssnapin "Microsoft.SharePoint.PowerShell"
 write-host "SharePoint PowerShell Snapin loaded." -foregroundcolor Green
}
```

SUMMARY

In this chapter, you saw how the new IT improvements in SharePoint 2010 affect you as a developer. Some of these improvements affect your applications immediately, such as throttling, while others you need work with your IT counterparts to understand what the right settings are for IT and your applications. With SharePoint 2010, having a good relationship with IT and understanding the SharePoint deployment your application is running on in a deeper way will make you a better SharePoint developer.

SharePoint Platform

WHAT'S IN THIS CHAPTER?

➤ An overview of the SharePoint 2010 platform

➤ Programming using the new Ribbon user interface

➤ Working with new functionality: Event Receivers

➤ How to use the new object models, such as LINQ and the client object model

➤ Programming using the new Sandbox Solutions architecture

The SharePoint 2010 platform is a large platform. If you think about all the capabilities that SharePoint provides, you can see why it needs to be big. SharePoint provides a user interface, data query and modeling, data storage, and application services as part of the product. For the developer, this provides a sea of riches, but navigating the technologies and establishing when to use one versus the other can be difficult. This chapter presents an overview of these technologies so that you can understand which API or service makes sense for the problem you are trying to solve.

PLATFORM OVERVIEW

One of the best overviews of the developer ecosystem of SharePoint comes from Microsoft itself. Figure 4-1 shows a diagram from a Microsoft poster that covers the possibilities of the SharePoint platform, the surrounding tools and ecosystem, and the target applications.

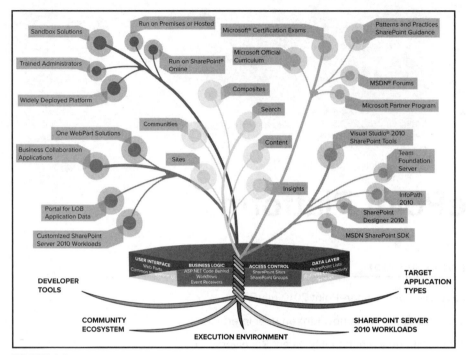

FIGURE 4-1

The SharePoint surface area is huge, since you not only have the SharePoint set of platform services to build on, but also the Office client integration functionality and APIs, ASP.NET, and web technology to learn, as well as the .NET Framework and its set of technologies. For this reason, being a great web or .NET developer is a good first step to becoming a great SharePoint developer, since both of those technologies are foundational technologies for SharePoint. One thing to note is that SharePoint does not support .NET 4.0, so while you can have it installed on your SharePoint Server, SharePoint or your SharePoint applications cannot take advantage of it.

NEW USER INTERFACE

The first new platform area to explore is the user interface. SharePoint has moved to using the Office Ribbon user interface as part of its web experience. You can turn off the Ribbon by changing the Master Page in your SharePoint environment if you want your own user interface, or want to use SharePoint on the Internet where a Ribbon might not be appropriate. Beyond the Ribbon, SharePoint also implements a new AJAX-style user interface so that multi-select list views, using no refreshes, and other streamlined user interface operations are possible without refreshing the page. In addition, your UI changes now can be applied not only to your application pages but also to the administration pages under the _layouts folder. There is a new dialog framework as well to make the SharePoint dialogs modal in the web experience. Plus, a new theming infrastructure makes it easy for end users or developers to customize the theme of the site. Lastly, the user interface implements a new status bar and notification area so that end users know what operations SharePoint or your application is performing on your behalf. Let's step through each of these areas and examine the changes.

General Platform Improvements

In terms of platform improvements, one of the biggest areas of investment in SharePoint 2010 was refactoring both Cascading Style Sheets (CSS) and JavaScript used in SharePoint. If you look at the CSS for 2007, it is a large CSS file that is hard to decipher and also is a big payload for the browser to download. With 2010, the CSS has been split into multiple files and supports on-demand downloading so that the CSS file will be downloaded and parsed only when the CSS class is needed for the particular HTML rendering.

Same thing goes for the JavaScript (JS) files in SharePoint. Before, you would have to download a large JavaScript file for your SharePoint site, but with 2010 the JavaScript files have been split apart and also support on-demand downloading. Plus, they have been *minified*, which means that all the spaces have been removed from the file. Minified files are harder to read for developers, which is why SharePoint ships a debug version of the JavaScript files. SharePoint initializes a ScriptManager control from ASP.NET AJAX to allow the new SharePoint UI to take advantage of the AJAX features in .NET.

Now, you may be wondering how you debug a minified version of the JS files. Navigate to `%ProgramFiles%\Common Files\Microsoft Shared\web server extensions\14\TEMPLATE\ LAYOUTS`, and you will find the debug versions of the JavaScript files in the same directory as the minified ones. The debug versions will have debug in their name — for example, `sp.debug.js` or `sp.core.debug.js`. You can browse through these JavaScript files to see the source code. In addition, you can force SharePoint to use these JavaScript files rather than the minified versions by modifying your `web.config`, located at `%inetpub%\wwwroot\wss\VirtualDirectories\80` and adding `<deployment retail="false"/>`, to the `system.web` section.

Beyond the size changes, the JavaScript has been refactored. A big change is the naming of the JavaScript code to try to delineate between public JavaScript and internal-use-only JavaScript. So, if you see a function called `SP.UI.UtilityInternal.CreateButton`, that is not supposed to be used by your code.

Master Pages and _Layouts

One of the biggest pain points in SharePoint 2007 was that you could skin the application pages in your site with your own Master Page, but the administration user interface and any pages under _Layouts would not use the applied Master Page. Rather, they would use the standard SharePoint Master Page affectionately known as "blue and white." With 2010, you can now set whether the pages under _Layouts use the same Master Page as the rest of your site. This will reduce the confusion for your end users when they go from the site to the administration pages for your site and the pages look different, as in 2007. Figure 4-2 shows the setting you need to check in order to enable or disable this functionality through the web application settings in Central Administration. It is on by default and that is probably the way you want to keep it, unless you want your application pages to look different than your site.

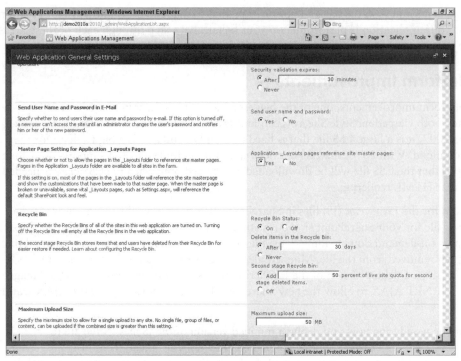

FIGURE 4-2

The _Layouts pages will use a dynamic Master Page based on the site they are being accessed from. You can use the tokens `~masterurl/default.master` or `~masterurl/custom.master` to reference System or Site Master Pages that you want to use for your pages. If you want to create your own application page, the page must derive from `Microsoft.SharePoint.WebControls.LayoutsPageBase`.

For security reasons, there are seven pages that do not reference your custom Master Page unless you explicitly change this through PowerShell or the SharePoint API. The seven pages are `accessdenied.aspx`, `confirmation.aspx`, `error.aspx`, `login.aspx`, `reqacc.aspx`, `signout.aspx`, and `webdeleted.aspx`.

To change the Master Page using code, you will want to use the `CustomMasterUrl` and `MasterUrl` properties on your SPWeb and set those to the Master Page that you want to put in place of the current Master Page. Also, remember to change any CSS that you may need to in order to support your Master Page by using the `AlernateCSSUrl` property.

```
using (SPSite siteCollection = new SPSite("http://intranet.contoso.com"))
    {
        using (SPWeb web = siteCollection.RootWeb)
        {
            MessageBox.Show(web.CustomMasterUrl.ToString());
            web.MasterUrl = "/_catalogs/masterpage/minimal.master";
            web.CustomMasterUrl = "/_catalogs/masterpage/minimal.master";
```

```
                    web.Update();
            }
    }
```

If SharePoint cannot find your referenced Master Page for any of your pages, it will default to the standard SharePoint Master Page so that the site does not break.

There are a few new Master Pages that you should be aware of with SharePoint 2010. Some were added to support the new user interface and some are added to support the older 2007 user interface running in SharePoint 2010. The first is V4.Master. This Master Page is the default Master Page for the 2010 user interface. It supports the Ribbon and all the new visuals in the 2010 product. One other reason to use V4.Master is that it implements the ability to display both the full chrome and also no chrome, depending on whether your page is displayed in context in the site with navigation and a Ribbon or as a dialog using the new dialog framework without chrome and without a Ribbon. There is nothing you have to do in order to get this functionality if you use V4.Master, since SharePoint automatically uses the right CSS classes on your behalf, based on the context your page is being called in. This allows you to use the same page for an application page as well as a dialog page, which is great for reusability.

The next is default.master. This Master Page is used to support the 2007 user interface and is used by visual upgrade to make your 2010 sites look like 2007 sites. This will make your site appear without a Ribbon and perform like a 2007 site.

One welcome addition is minimal.master. Every developer either downloads or builds their own minimal.master so that they can start with a simple Master Page and then build on top of it. Now, minimal.master ships in the SharePoint box, and you do not have to build it yourself. It is a very stripped Master Page that includes no navigation, so you will want to start adding pieces to the Master Page if you intend to use it in your site.

The last Master Page is simple.master. It is used on the seven pages that we talked about earlier, and it cannot be customized.

The Ribbon

One of the major changes you will have to get used to is the new Ribbon user interface. The Ribbon provides a contextual tab model and a fixed location at the top of the page so that it never scrolls out of view. In terms of controls, if you have worked with the Office client Ribbon, the SharePoint Ribbon has near parity with the client. The areas that are missing between the client and the server are controls that provide more complex functionality. The best example of a control that is on the client but not on the server is the in-Ribbon gallery control. It is used, for example, when you click on styles in Word and you can see all the styles, or in Excel, where you can select cell styles right from the gallery control.

The Ribbon does support the majority of controls that you will need, and the main unit of organization for these controls is tabs. You can build custom tabs that contain your custom controls. Even though the server can support up to 100 tabs, it is recommended that you try to limit the tabs to 4–7 in order not to confuse your users. Table 4-1 lists the different controls supported by SharePoint with a description of each.

TABLE 4-1: SharePoint Ribbon Controls

NAME	DESCRIPTION
Button	A simple button that can be pushed.
Checkbox	A checkbox that either can have a label or not.
ColorPicker	A grid of colors/styles that can be used to choose a color.
ComboBox	A menu of selections that can be typed or selected.
DropDown	A menu of selections that can be selected by clicking.
FlyoutAnchor	An anchor button that includes a button that triggers a fly-out menu.
InsertTable	A 10x10 grid of boxes used to specify dimensions for a table.
Label	A line of text.
Menu	A container for showing popups. It can be put inside of other controls that show menus, such as the FlyoutAnchor.
MenuSection	A section of a menu. It can have a title and controls.
MRUSplitButton	A split button control that remembers the last item that was chosen out of its submenu and bubbles it up into its "button" part.
Spinner	Allows the entering of values and "spinning" through them using the up and down arrows.
SplitButton	A control with a button and a menu.
Textbox	A box where text can be entered.
ToggleButton	A button with an on/off state.

If you look at the architecture for the Ribbon in SharePoint, you will find that SharePoint makes a lot of usage of AJAX, on-demand JavaScript, caching and CSS layout to implement the Ribbon. One thing you will find is that the Ribbon uses no tables, so it is all CSS styling and hover effects that make the Ribbon function. For this reason, you should investigate the CSS classes that the Ribbon uses, especially corev4.css. Look through the styles beginning with ms-cui, which is the namespace for the Ribbon in the CSS file.

Ribbon Extensibility

The Ribbon is completely extensible in that you can add new tabs or controls, or you can remove the out-of-the-box (OOB) controls on existing tabs. In fact, you can entirely replace the Ribbon just by using your own custom Master Page. The Ribbon does support backward compatibility in that any custom actions you created for 2007 toolbars will appear in a custom commands tab in the Ribbon.

To understand how to customize the Ribbon, look through the different actions you normally would want to perform and the way to achieve those actions. Before diving in, though, you need to get a little bit of grounding in how the architecture of the Ribbon works.

The architecture of the Ribbon allows you to perform your customizations by creating XML definition files. At runtime, the Ribbon runtime merges your XML definitions with its own to add your custom Ribbon elements and code to handle interactions. For more complex customizations, such as writing more complex code, you will want to look at using a JavaScript Page Component. The section below looks at both options.

If you want to understand how SharePoint implements its Ribbon XML elements, go to `%Program Files%\Common Files\Microsoft Shared\Web Server Extensions\14\TEMPLATE\GLOBAL\XML` on your SharePoint Server and find the file `cmdui.xml`. In that file, you will see the SharePoint default Ribbon implementation, and it is a good template to look at as you implement your own Ribbon controls, because it will help you to understand how certain controls work inside of the SharePoint environment.

If all the different types, elements, and attributes get confusing, take a look at the XSD for the Ribbon by browsing to `%Program Files%\Common Files\Microsoft Shared\Web Server Extensions\14\TEMPLATE\XML` and looking at `cui.xsd` and `wss.xsd`. These XSD files will help you understand what SharePoint is expecting in terms of structure and content to make your custom user interface.

XML-Only Operations

The first way you will look at customizing the Ribbon is by using only XML. When you write your custom XML to define your Ribbon, SharePoint combines your XML changes with its own definitions in `cmdui.xml` and the merged version is used to display the new Ribbon interface. Even though you are using XML, you want to deploy your custom Ribbon XML using a SharePoint feature. So, the easiest way to get started creating a feature is by using Visual Studio 2010. Make sure to create an Empty SharePoint Project and customize the feature name and deployment path. Ribbon extensions can be Sandbox Solutions, which you will learn about later, so they can run in a restricted environment.

Once you have created your Visual Studio project, you want to create a new feature. Add a new file to your project and create an empty elements file. This is where you will place the XML for your new Ribbon interface. To understand the XML, break it down piece by piece. The snippet that follows shows some XML from a custom Ribbon:

Available for download on Wrox.com

```xml
<?xml version="1.0" encoding="utf-8"?>

<Elements xmlns="http://schemas.microsoft.com/sharepoint/">

  <CustomAction

    Id="CustomRibbonTab"

    Location="CommandUI.Ribbon.ListView"

    RegistrationId="101"

    RegistrationType="List"
```

```
    Title="My Custom UI"

    Sequence="5"

>



  </CustomAction>

</Elements>
```

Elements.xml

First, all of your XML for the Ribbon will be wrapped in a `CustomAction` node. This tells SharePoint that you want to perform customization of the user interface. For the node, there are attributes that you can set to specify the specifics for your customization. One key one is the `Location` attribute. The `Location` attribute tells SharePoint where your customization should appear, such as on a list view, on a form, or everywhere. The pattern match for the `Location` attribute is `Ribbon.[Tab].[Group]` `.Controls._children`. Table 4-2 outlines the options for the `Location` attribute.

TABLE 4-2: Location Attribute Settings

NAME	DESCRIPTION
CommandUI.Ribbon	Customization appears everywhere.
CommandUI.Ribbon.ListView	Customization appears when ListView is available.
CommandUI.Ribbon.EditForm	Customization appears on the edit form.
CommandUI.Ribbon.NewForm	Customization appears on the new form.
CommandUI.Ribbon.DisplayForm	Customization appears on the display form.

One other piece to notice in the XML is the `RegistrationID`. Combined together, the registration ID and the registration type define what set of content you want your custom UI to appear for. The registration type can be a list, content type, file type, or a progID. The registration ID is mostly used with the content type registration type, and it's where you specify the name of your content type. This allows you to customize even further when your custom UI will appear, depending on what is displayed in SharePoint.

The `Sequence` attribute, which is optional, allows extensions to be placed in a particular order within a set of subnodes of a node. The built-in tab controls use a sequence of 100, so you want to avoid using any multiples of 100 for your sequence in tabs, and groups use a sequence in multiples of 10, so avoid multiples of 10. For example, if there is a Ribbon tab with the following groups: Clipboard, Font, Paragraph, then their sequence attributes could be set to 10, 20, and 30, respectively. Then, a new group could be inserted between the Clipboard and the Font groups via the feature framework by setting its sequence attribute to 15. A node without a `Sequence` attribute is sorted last.

Let's expand the XML a bit more, since the current XML does nothing because you haven't added any new commands to the user interface. To add commands, you want to create a `CommandUIExtension` element. This `CommandUIExtension` is a wrapper for a `CommandUIDefinitions` element, which is a container for a `CommandUIDefinition`.

The `CommandUIDefinition` element has an attribute that allows you to set the location for your UI. In the example, you're adding a new button to the new set of controls in a document library. You can see `_children` as part of the location that tells SharePoint to not replace a control, but instead add this as a child control on that user interface element.

The `CommandUIDefinition` element is where you create your user interface elements, whether they are tabs, groups, or individual controls. In this simple example, you create a button that has the label Click me!, has two images for use depending on whether it's rendered in 16x16 or 32x32, and calls some JavaScript code to perform the action when the button is pressed. The attributes are self-explanatory, except for `1 - TemplateAlias`. `TemplateAlias` controls whether your control is displayed in 16x16 or 32x32. If you set it to `o1`, you will get a 32x32 icon, and `o2` makes it 16x16. You can define your own template, but most times you will use the built-in values of `o1` or `o2`.

So, how do you call code from your Ribbon code? You will want to wrap your code in a `CommandUIHandler`, where you can put in the `CommandAction` attribute, which is inline JavaScript that will handle the action for your button. If you do not want to place your JavaScript inline, you can instead use the `ScriptSrc` attribute and pass a URL to your JavaScript file. Figure 4-3 shows our new custom button.

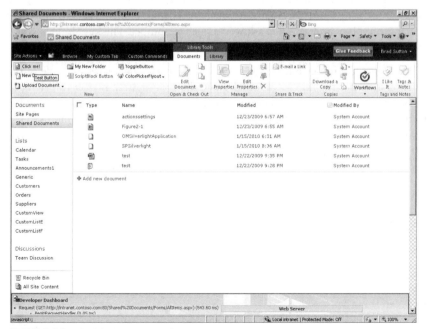

FIGURE 4-3

```
<CommandUIExtension>
    <CommandUIDefinitions>
        <CommandUIDefinition Location="Ribbon.Documents.New.Controls._children">
            <Button
                Id="Ribbon.Documents.New.RibbonTest"
                Alt="Test Button"
                Sequence="5"
                Command="Test_Button"
                LabelText="Click me!"
                Image32by32="/_layouts/images/ribbon_blog_32.png"
                Image16by16="/_layouts/images/ribbon_blog_16.png"
                TemplateAlias="o1" />
        </CommandUIDefinition>
    </CommandUIDefinitions>

    <CommandUIHandlers>
      <CommandUIHandler
        Command="Test_Button"
        CommandAction="javascript:alert('I am a test!');" />
    </CommandUIHandlers>

</CommandUIExtension>
```

Elements.xml

Replacing Existing Controls

There may be times when you want to replace existing, built-in controls from your SharePoint deployment and put your own control in its place. In fact, you can replace the entire Ribbon if you want. The way to replace an existing control is to insert your own custom control that overwrites the ID of the control you want to replace and also has a lower sequence number. The key thing is you have to get the Location attribute set to the exact same ID as the control ID you want to replace.

The following code replaces the new folder button for a document library. There are a couple of things to highlight in this code. First, notice the Location attribute in the CommandUIDefinition element. It maps exactly to an ID in the cmdUI.XML file. SharePoint will parse both files and if the same ID is found, the one with the lower sequence will be put into the final XML that is parsed and used to create the Ribbon layout. Also, notice the use of the $Resources for globalization and pulling from a compressed image. If you look at the formatmap on your server, you will see that it contains lots of icons and the XML code contains the coordinates to pull the new folder icon from the larger image.

```
<CustomAction Id="Ribbon.Documents.New.NewFolder.ReplaceButton"
        Location="CommandUI.Ribbon"
        RegistrationId="101"
        RegistrationType="List"
        Title="Replace Ribbon Button"
    >
    <CommandUIExtension>
      <CommandUIDefinitions>
        <CommandUIDefinition
          Location="Ribbon.Documents.New.NewFolder">
          <Button Id="Ribbon.Documents.New.NewFolder.ReplacementButton"
```

```
                        Command="MyNewButtonCommand"
                        Image16by16="/_layouts/$Resources:core,Language;/images/
                        formatmap16x16.png?vk=4536"
                        Image16by16Top="-240" Image16by16Left="-80"
                        Image32by32="/_layouts/$Resources:core,Language;/images/
                        formatmap32x32.png?vk=4536"
                        Image32by32Top="-352" Image32by32Left="-448"
                        ToolTipTitle="Create a New Folder"
                        ToolTipDescription="Replaced by XML Custom Action"
                        LabelText="My New Folder"
                        TemplateAlias="o1" />
                </CommandUIDefinition>
            </CommandUIDefinitions>
            <CommandUIHandlers>
                <CommandUIHandler
                    Command="MyNewButtonCommand"
                    CommandAction="javascript:alert('New Folder Replaced.');" />
            </CommandUIHandlers>
        </CommandUIExtension>
    </CustomAction>
```

Elements.xml

Figure 4-4 shows our replaced button. Even though the icon image is the same, the action performed when the user clicks on the icon is our custom code.

FIGURE 4-4

Using URL Actions

You may be wondering how you use just URLs with token replacements, rather than having to write JavaScript as the payload for your controls. To do this, you will use the URLAction node in your CustomAction node. Your URL actions can be simple URLs or you can use token replacement, such as ListID or ItemID. You can also place inline JavaScript if you want. When you use URL actions, you can make a simple CustomAction node to handle your changes, as shown in the following listing, which adds a new toolbar item to the new announcements form:

```
<CustomAction
      Id="SimpleAction"
      RegistrationType="List"
      RegistrationId="104"
      ImageUrl="/_layouts/images/saveas32.png"
      Location="NewFormToolbar"
      Sequence="10"
      Title="Custom Button"
      Description="This is an announcement button."
                        >
    <UrlAction Url="javascript:alert('Itemid={ItemId} and Listid={ListId}');"/>

</CustomAction>
```

Elements.xml

Why Doesn't My Button Show Up?

Troubleshooting your custom Ribbon user interface is not as easy as you would think. If you get something wrong, your customizations just do not appear. Even though this can be frustrating, there are a couple of places to start looking to troubleshoot your issues.

First, fire up your JavaScript debugger and set a breakpoint. Since the Ribbon is implemented in JavaScript, you can set breakpoints in the code in SP.Ribbon.debug.js. Also, make sure to look at the XML in cmdui.xml to see if there is a pattern your code resembles so you can model your code on that pattern.

The second thing to check is that the sequence is set correctly and does not collide with other controls. SharePoint uses sequences in multiples of 10 or 100, so make sure that you are not using those multiples.

Make sure to check that the name for your function is the same for your command attribute on your control definition and your CommandUIHandler. If you get the name wrong, even with the same spelling but different cases, your commands will not fire.

Check the registration for your CustomAction. Did you register your UI on a document library? When you test your code, are you in a document library? Or did you register on an edit form for announcements? This ties in with the next tip, which applies when you are wondering why your user interface does not appear if you select your list instance as a web part in another page. For example, suppose that you are on your home page and you added in your Shared Documents library as a web part on that page. When you select the document library as the web part, your button does not appear on the menu. The culprit behind this is the toolbar type property for the web part under web part properties. By default, it is set to summary toolbar and you want it to be set to full toolbar, since the summary toolbar will not load any of the customizations for the toolbar.

Rights and Site Administrators

As part of the definition of your CustomAction, you can also specify the rights required to view your custom interface. You can specify a Rights attribute, which takes a permissions mask that SharePoint will logically AND together, so the user must have all the permissions to view the new user interface. Permissions can be any permission from SPBasePermissions, such as ViewListItems or ManageLists.

Beyond permissions, you can also specify whether a person has to be a site administrator to view the new user interface. To do this, create a Boolean RequireSiteAdministrator attribute and set it to true to require the user to be a site administrator. This is useful for an administration-style UI that you do not want every user to see.

Hiding Existing Controls

There may be times when you want to hide controls rather than replace them. For example, the control may not make sense in the context of your application. To hide UI, use the HideCustomAction element and set the attributes to the nodes you want to hide as shown in the following code:

```
<HideCustomAction
    Id="HideNewMenu"
    Location="Microsoft.SharePoint.StandardMenu"
    GroupId="NewMenu"
    HideActionId="NewMenu">
</HideCustomAction>
```

Writing Code to Control Menu Commands

If you prefer to write code instead of XML, you can use the SharePoint object model to make changes to menu items. This hasn't changed from the EditControlBlock (ECB) technologies in 2007 and is shown here for completeness.

```
using (SPSite site = new SPSite("http://intranet.contoso.com"))
    {
    using (SPWeb web = site.RootWeb)
        {
        SPUserCustomAction action = web.UserCustomActions.Add();
        action.Location = "EditControlBlock";
        action.RegistrationType =
        SPUserCustomActionRegistrationType.FileType;
        action.RegistrationId = "docx";
        action.Title = "Custom Edit Command For Documents";
        action.Description = "Custom Edit Command for Documents";
        action.Url = "{ListUrlDir}/forms/editform.aspx?Source={Source}";
        action.Update();
        web.Update();
        site.Close();
        }
    }
```

Creating New Tabs and Groups

Beyond just creating buttons, you may want to add new tabs and groups. To do this, you just need to create `Tab` and `Group` elements in your code. The process is close to the same as adding a button with some minor tweaks, as you will see. Figure 4-5 shows a custom tab and group with three controls: two buttons and a combobox.

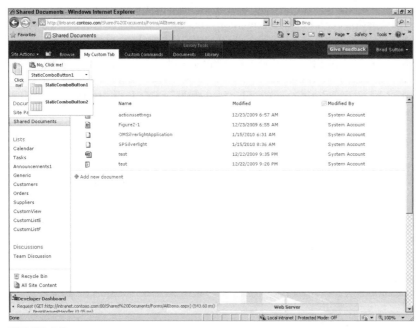

FIGURE 4-5

The code below shows the beginning of the new tab and group. As you can see, the XML looks very similar to earlier XML in creating a button. There is a tab defined that you will learn more about.

```
<!--Create new Tab and Group-->
  <CustomAction
  Id="MyCustomRibbonTab"
  Location="CommandUI.Ribbon.ListView"
  RegistrationId="101"
  RegistrationType="List">
    <CommandUIExtension>
      <CommandUIDefinitions>
        <CommandUIDefinition
          Location="Ribbon.Tabs._children">
          <Tab
            Id="Ribbon.CustomTabExample"
            Title="My Custom Tab"
            Description="This holds my custom commands!"
            Sequence="501">
            <Scaling
              Id="Ribbon.CustomTabExample.Scaling">
              <MaxSize
```

```
        Id="Ribbon.CustomTabExample.MaxSize"
        GroupId="Ribbon.CustomTabExample.CustomGroupExample"
        Size="OneLargeTwoMedium"/>
      <Scale
        Id="Ribbon.CustomTabExample.Scaling.CustomTabScaling"
        GroupId="Ribbon.CustomTabExample.CustomGroupExample"
        Size="OneLargeTwoMedium" />
    </Scaling>
    ...
```

First, tabs support scaling, so if the page is resized, you can control how your buttons look. Scaling has a `MaxSize` node that is the maximum size your buttons will be and a `Scaling` node that will be used if the page is resized. A couple of things about the `Scaling` node. It has a `GroupID` attribute, which should point to the group that the scaling will affect. Second, it has a `Size` attribute, which has a descriptor of the style of your group. For example, you can have `LargeLarge` if you have two buttons and want both to be large buttons, or `LargeMedium` if you want a large and a medium button.

After creating the tab, the code then creates the group, as you can see below. A group can have commands, descriptions, and all the standard attributes that other controls have. A group is a logical container for your controls and will physically lay out the controls in your group with your description at the bottom of the group user interface. Your `Group` node will contain the definition for your controls that live within that group.

```
<Groups Id="Ribbon.CustomTabExample.Groups">
            <Group
              Id="Ribbon.CustomTabExample.CustomGroupExample"
              Description="This is a custom group!"
              Title="Custom Group"
              Sequence="52"
              Template="Ribbon.Templates.CustomTemplateExample">
            <Controls>
    ...
```

Once you have your tab and group, you create your controls just as you would if the control were an extension of an existing group. The code earlier showed how to create a button, so the code below shows you how to create a combobox as a control in your group.

A combobox has more commands than a button, since users can interact more with a combobox by selecting options from its list. Also, either you can populate a combobox box statically, as the code does, by creating menu options in the XML, or you can pass a function that SharePoint will call to populate the combobox dynamically. Look at the `PopulateDynamically`, `PopulateOnlyOnce`, and `PopulateQueryCommand` sections of the code, since these combined operate the combobox options.

In addition, you can set attributes, such as `AllowFreeForm` and `InitialItem`, to control whether users can type values into the combobox and select the initial item in the combobox.

```
<ComboBox
  Id="Ribbon.CustomTabExample.CustomGroupExample.
  Combobox"  Sequence="18"
  Alt="Ribbon.CustomTabExample.CustomGroupExample.
  Combobox_Alt"
  Command="Ribbon.CustomTabExample.CustomGroupExample.
```

```
    Combobox_CMD"
  CommandMenuOpen="Ribbon.CustomTabExample.
   CustomGroupExample.Combobox_Open_CMD"
  CommandMenuClose="Ribbon.CustomTabExample.
   CustomGroupExample.Combobox_MenuClose_CMD"
  CommandPreview="Ribbon.CustomTabExample.
   CustomGroupExample.Combobox_Preview_CMD"
 CommandPreviewRevert="Ribbon.CustomTabExample.
  CustomGroupExample.Combobox_PreviewRevert_CMD"
                               InitialItem="StaticComboButton1"
                               AllowFreeForm="true"
                               PopulateDynamically="false"
                               PopulateOnlyOnce="true"
                               PopulateQueryCommand="Ribbon.CustomTabExample.
                               CustomGroupExample.Combobox_PopQuery_CMD"
                               Width="125px"
                               TemplateAlias="cust3">
                  <Menu Id="Ribbon.CustomTabExample.CustomGroupExample.
                   Combobox.Menu">
                    <MenuSection
                      Id="Ribbon.CustomTabExample.CustomGroupExample.Combobox.
                       Menu.MenuSection"
                      Sequence="10"
DisplayMode="Menu32">
                        <Controls Id="Ribbon.CustomTabExample.CustomGroupExample.
                          Combobox.Menu.MenuSection.Controls">
                        <Button
                          Id="Ribbon.CustomTabExample.CustomGroupExample.
                          Combobox.Menu.MenuSection.Button1"
                          Sequence="10"
                          Command="Ribbon.CustomTabExample.CustomGroupExample.
                           Combobox.Menu.MenuSection.Button1_CMD"
                          CommandType="OptionSelection"
                          Image16by16="/_layouts/$Resources:core,Language;
                          /images/formatmap16x16.png?vk=4536"
                          Image16by16Top="-48" Image16by16Left="-112"
                          Image32by32="/_layouts/$Resources:core,Language;
                          /images/formatmap32x32.png?vk=4536"
                          Image32by32Top="-192" Image32by32Left="-32"
                          LabelText="StaticComboButton1"
                          MenuItemId="StaticComboButton1"/>
                        <Button
                          Id="Ribbon.CustomTabExample.CustomGroupExample.
                          Combobox.Menu.MenuSection.Button2"
                          Sequence="20"
                          Command="Ribbon.CustomTabExample.CustomGroupExample.
                          Combobox.Menu.MenuSection.Button2_CMD"
                          CommandType="OptionSelection"
                          Image16by16="/_layouts/$Resources:core,Language;
                         /images/formatmap16x16.png?vk=4536"
                         Image16by16Top="-32" Image16by16Left="-112"
                          Image32by32="/_layouts/$Resources:core,Language;
                          /images/formatmap32x32.png?vk=4536"
                          Image32by32Top="-384" Image32by32Left="-352"
                          LabelText="StaticComboButton2"
                          MenuItemId="StaticComboButton2"/>
```

```
        </Controls>
      </MenuSection>
    </Menu>
  </ComboBox>
```

Elements.xml

After your controls, you can handle the commands that your controls need to respond to in your `CommandUIHandlers` node. For the complete listing for all the code for the commands, the tab, and the group, please refer to the sample code for this chapter.

ToolTips and Help

With your user interface, you should help guide the user on the usage of your controls. To aid in this, the Ribbon supports ToolTips and also linking out to help topics. Both of these are set using the `ToolTip*` set of commands such as `ToolTipTitle` and `ToolTipDescription`. The following code sets the title, description, and help topic, and shows the keyboard shortcut for your control:

```
ToolTipTitle="Tooltip Title"

ToolTipDescription="Tooltip Description"

ToolTipShortcutKey="Ctr-V, P"

ToolTipImage32by32="/_layouts/images/PasteHH.png"

ToolTipHelpKeyWord="WSSEndUser"
```

Writing a Page Component

So far, you have seen writing code inline in your XML in order to handle your control commands. However, SharePoint does allow you to write more complex handlers for your user interface if you need to. You should default to trying to keep your code in the XML definition if you are creating simple buttons with simple code. However, if you are creating Ribbon extensions that are dynamically populated via code; your Ribbon requires variables beyond the default ones you can get with {SiteUrl}, {ItemId}, or other similar placeholders; or your code is so long that it may make sense from a manageability standpoint to break it out separately, then you will want to look at creating a page component.

A page component is a set of JavaScript code that can handle commands from your user interface customizations. Your JavaScript has to derive from the `CUI.Page.PageComponent` and implement the functions in the prototype definition of the `RibbonAppPageComponent`. As part of this code, you can define the global commands that your page component works with. These are the tabs, groups, and commands, such as buttons, that you will handle in your page component. Additionally, you can define whether your global commands should be enabled or not through the `canHandleCommand` function. This is the function you want to use to enable or disable your control. For example, you may want to only enable your control if the context is correct for your control to work, such as an item being selected in the user interface or the right variables are set. If you return false to this function, your user interface will be grayed out.

Lastly, the page component allows you to handle the command so if someone clicks on your button, you can run code to handle that click.

Once you have defined all this JavaScript, you need to register your script with the `PageManager` that SharePoint creates so that SharePoint knows to call the script when actions are performed on the user interface.

A couple of points about the following code. First, notice how to get the selected items by using the `SP.ListOperation.Selection.getSelectedItems()` method. This is a good way to determine if any items are selected in the user interface so that you can enable or disable your control. You can go a step further and look for particular properties or item types by writing some more code.

Second, you could write more functions to do things like populate your drop-downs dynamically or change the buttons on your user interface. In fact, you can write your Ribbon component to perform a postback to the server that a custom .NET program can handle, so that you can avoid writing JavaScript. If you do this, you will want the command action be a postback command such as `CommandAction="javascript:__doPostBack('CustomButton', '{ItemUrl}')"`. Then, on the backend that captures the postback, you can handle the postback in two different ways. First, you can look at the `__EVENTTARGET` variable in the page request variables to see if your custom command caused the postback. The other way is to spin up a Ribbon object — make sure to reference `Microsoft.SharePoint.WebControls` — and implement the `IPostBackHandler` interface. Then, you can check to see if your custom button generated the postback by deserializing the postback event using the `SPRibbonPostBackCommand.DeserializePostBackEvent` method, and then checking the ID of the control that generated the event to the ID of the control you were looking for. If they match, handle the event. The first method is simpler and requires less code than the second method.

Figure 4-6 shows the custom button on the Ribbon. Also, notice that there are a custom color picker and other buttons in the figure. You can see the code to implement these other buttons in the sample code for this chapter.

FIGURE 4-6

```xml
<CustomAction
  Id="SharedDocAction"
  RegistrationType="List"
  RegistrationId="101"
  Location="CommandUI.Ribbon.ListView">
    <CommandUIExtension>
      <CommandUIDefinitions>
        <CommandUIDefinition
         Location="Ribbon.Documents.New.Controls._children">
          <Button
            Id="CustomContextualButton"
            Alt="MyDocumentsNew Alt"
            Command="MyDocumentsNewButton"
            LabelText="ScriptBlock Button"
            ToolTipTitle="Tooltip Title"
            Image16by16="/_layouts/$Resources:core,Language;
            /images/formatmap16x16.png?vk=4536" Image16by16Top="-80"
            Image16by16Left="0"
            Image32by32="/_layouts/$Resources:core,Language;
            /images/formatmap32x32.png?vk=4536"
            Image32by32Top="-96" Image32by32Left="-64"
            ToolTipDescription="Tooltip Description"
            TemplateAlias="o1"/>
        </CommandUIDefinition>
      </CommandUIDefinitions>
    </CommandUIExtension>
  </CustomAction>

  <CustomAction
   Id="MyScriptBlock"
   Location="ScriptLink"
   ScriptBlock="
ExecuteOrDelayUntilScriptLoaded(_registerMyScriptBlockPageComponent,
 'sp.ribbon.js');

function _registerMyScriptBlockPageComponent()
{
    Type.registerNamespace('MyScriptBlock');

    MyScriptBlock.MyScriptBlockPageComponent =
function MyScriptBlockPageComponent_Ctr() {
        MyScriptBlock.MyScriptBlockPageComponent.initializeBase(this);
    };

    MyScriptBlock.MyScriptBlockPageComponent.prototype = {

        init: function MyScriptBlockPageComponent_init() {
        },

        _globalCommands: null,


        buildGlobalCommands:
function MyScriptBlockPageComponent_buildGlobalCommands() {
```

```
        if (SP.ScriptUtility.isNullOrUndefined(this._globalCommands)) {
            this._globalCommands = [];
            this._globalCommands[this._globalCommands.length] = 'DocumentTab';
            this._globalCommands[this._globalCommands.length]
              = 'DocumentNewGroup';
            this._globalCommands[this._globalCommands.length]
              = 'MyDocumentsNewButton';
        }
        return this._globalCommands;
    },

    getGlobalCommands: function MyScriptBlockPageComponent_getGlobalCommands()
    {
        return this.buildGlobalCommands();
    },

    canHandleCommand: function
MyScriptBlockPageComponent_canHandleCommand(commandId) {
        var items = SP.ListOperation.Selection.getSelectedItems();
        if (SP.ScriptUtility.isNullOrUndefined(items))
            return false;
        if (0 == items.length)
            return false;
        if (commandId === 'DocumentNewTab'){
            return true;
        }
        if (commandId === 'DocumentNewGroup'){
            return true;
        }
        if (commandId === 'MyDocumentsNewButton'){
            return true;
        }
        return false;
    },

    handleCommand: function
    MyScriptBlockPageComponent_handleCommand(commandId, properties, sequence) {
        alert('You hit my button!');
        return true;
    }
}

MyScriptBlock.MyScriptBlockPageComponent.get_instance =
  function MyScriptBlockPageComponent_get_instance() {
    if (SP.ScriptUtility.isNullOrUndefined(MyScriptBlock.
      MyScriptBlockPageComponent._singletonPageComponent)) {
        MyScriptBlock.MyScriptBlockPageComponent._singletonPageComponent
          = new MyScriptBlock.MyScriptBlockPageComponent();
    }
    return MyScriptBlock.MyScriptBlockPageComponent._singletonPageComponent;
}
MyScriptBlock.MyScriptBlockPageComponent.registerWithPageManager
    = function MyScriptBlockPageComponent_registerWithPageManager() {
    SP.Ribbon.PageManager.get_instance().addPageComponent
```

```
                (MyScriptBlock.MyScriptBlockPageComponent.get_instance());
    }
    MyScriptBlock.MyScriptBlockPageComponent.unregisterWithPageManager =
    function MyScriptBlockPageComponent_unregisterWithPageManager() {
        if (false == SP.ScriptUtility.isNullOrUndefined(
        MyScriptBlock.MyScriptBlockPageComponent._singletonPageComponent)) {
            SP.Ribbon.PageManager.get_instance().removePageComponent(
        MyScriptBlock.MyScriptBlockPageComponent.get_instance());
        }
    }

    MyScriptBlock.MyScriptBlockPageComponent.registerClass(
    'MyScriptBlock.MyScriptBlockPageComponent', CUI.Page.PageComponent);
    MyScriptBlock.MyScriptBlockPageComponent.registerWithPageManager();
}">
  </CustomAction>
```

Elements.xml

Adding Buttons with SPD

The easiest way to add a button to the Ribbon or your items is to use SharePoint Designer. Built right into SPD is the ability to add custom actions to your list. SPD can create these actions on the Ribbon forms, such as the display, edit, or new form for a list item, and also on a list item drop-down menu. You can customize the action performed by the button, for example, navigating to a form such as the edit form for the item, initiating a workflow, or launching a URL. In addition, you can use SPD to assign graphics to your icons, set your sequence number, and even set your Ribbon location in the same way you set the `Location` attribute in the Ribbon XML you saw earlier. Figure 4-7 shows the form used to tell SPD how to customize the Ribbon for your list.

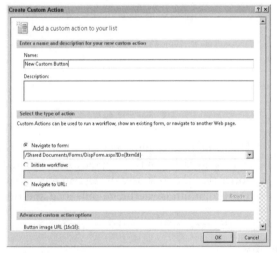

FIGURE 4-7

Contextual Tabs and Groups with Web Parts

There may be times when you want to build a ribbon user interface and have it automatically appear when a user selects a web part. This is the way the media player web part works where it displays a new tab in the ribbon when you select the web part in the user interface. To perform this functionality, you need to add a contextual tab and contextual group to the ribbon interface through code. You do not use the declarative XML file, but instead place the XML in code and add it programmatically to the ribbon.

In order to build a contextual web part, you create your web part as you normally do, but you want your web part to inherit from the `IWebPartPageComponentProvider` interface. You need to implement the `WebPartContextualInfo` method of the interface. This method tells the ribbon which group and tab to activate when the web part is selected.

```csharp
public WebPartContextualInfo WebPartContextualInfo
    {
        get
        {
            WebPartContextualInfo info = new WebPartContextualInfo();
            info.ContextualGroups.Add(
                new WebPartRibbonContextualGroup
                {
                    Id = "Ribbon.MyContextualGroup",
                    VisibilityContext = "WebPartSelectionTest",
                    Command = "MyContextualGroupCMD"
                }
            );
            info.Tabs.Add(
                new WebPartRibbonTab
                {
                    Id = "Ribbon.MyContextualGroup.MyTab",
                    VisibilityContext = "WebPartSelectionTest"
                }
            );

            info.PageComponentId = SPRibbon.GetWebPartPageComponentId(this);
            return info;
        }
    }
```

CustomWebPart.cs

Then, you need to implement a custom page component using JavaScript. This is very similar to the code from earlier in the chapter where you add and register the custom page component. You will notice that the code uses the `executeOrDelayUntilScriptLoaded` command, which is part of the SharePoint infrastructure to only load and run script on demand.

```csharp
private string DelayScript
    {
        get
        {
            string wppPcId = SPRibbon.GetWebPartPageComponentId(this);
            return @"
<script type=""text/javascript"">
//<![CDATA[

        function _addCustomPageComponent()
        {
            SP.Ribbon.PageManager.get_instance().addPageComponent(new
CustomPageComponent.TestPageComponent(" + wppPcId + @"));
        }

        function _registerCustomPageComponent()
```

```
                {
                    RegisterSod(""testpagecomponent.js"",
""\/_layouts\/TestPageComponent.js"");
                    var isDefined = ""undefined"";
                    try
                    {
                        isDefined = typeof(CustomPageComponent.TestPageComponent);
                    }
                    catch(e)
                    {
                    }
                    EnsureScript(""testpagecomponent.js"",isDefined,
_addCustomPageComponent);
                }
            ExecuteOrDelayUntilScriptLoaded(_registerCustomPageComponent,
""sp.ribbon.js"");
//]]>
</script>";
                }
        }
```

Contextual tabs actually always exist in the Ribbon, but are hidden. To add your tabs and groups to the Ribbon, you need to use the server-side Ribbon API to get the Ribbon and add your custom Ribbon elements as shown here.

```
private void AddCustomTab()
        {

            Microsoft.Web.CommandUI.Ribbon ribbon = SPRibbon.GetCurrent(this.Page);
            XmlDocument xmlDoc = new XmlDocument();

            //Contextual Tab
            xmlDoc.LoadXml(this.CuiDefinitionCtxTab);
            ribbon.RegisterDataExtension(xmlDoc.FirstChild,
"Ribbon.ContextualTabs._children");
            xmlDoc.LoadXml(this.CuiDefinitionScaling);
            ribbon.RegisterDataExtension(xmlDoc.FirstChild,
"Ribbon.Templates._children");
            exists = true;

        }
```

To tie it all together, you need to implement the `OnPreRender` method, which allows the code to add the new Ribbon elements to the page before the page renders. The following code calls the `AddCustomTab` method that does this, and also registers the script block that implements the custom page component with the SharePoint client script manager.

```
protected override void OnPreRender(EventArgs e)
      {
            base.OnPreRender(e);

            //RegisterDataExtensions; add Ribbon XML for buttons
            this.AddCustomTab();

            ClientScriptManager csm = this.Page.ClientScript;
            csm.RegisterClientScriptBlock(this.GetType(),
"custompagecomponent", this.DelayScript);
      }
```

The last piece to look at is the custom page component, which implements the functionality to tell SharePoint which commands the page component implements, and also when to focus on the contextual tab and when to yield focus depending on whether the web part is selected or not.

```
Type.registerNamespace('CustomPageComponent');

////////////////////////////////////////////////////////////////////////////////
// CustomPageComponent.TestPageComponent
var _myWpPcId;
CustomPageComponent.TestPageComponent = function
CustomPageComponent_TestPageComponent(webPartPcId) {
    this._myWpPcId = webPartPcId.innerText;
    CustomPageComponent.TestPageComponent.initializeBase(this);
}
CustomPageComponent.TestPageComponent.prototype = {

    init: function CustomPageComponent_TestPageComponent$init() {
    },

    getFocusedCommands: function
CustomPageComponent_TestPageComponent$getFocusedCommands() {
        return ['MyTabCMD', 'MyGroupCMD', 'CommandMyJscriptButton'];
    },

    getGlobalCommands: function
CustomPageComponent_TestPageComponent$getGlobalCommands() {
        return [];
    },

    isFocusable: function CustomPageComponent_TestPageComponent$isFocusable() {
        return true;
    },

    receiveFocus: function CustomPageComponent_TestPageComponent$receiveFocus() {
        return true;
    },

    yieldFocus: function CustomPageComponent_TestPageComponent$yieldFocus() {
        return true;
    },

    canHandleCommand: function
CustomPageComponent_TestPageComponent$canHandleCommand(commandId) {
```

```
        //Contextual Tab commands
        if ((commandId === 'MyTabCMD') || (commandId === 'MyGroupCMD') ||
(commandId === 'CommandMyButton') ||
        (commandId === 'CommandMyJscriptButton')) {
            return true;
        }
    },

    handleCommand: function CustomPageComponent_TestPageComponent$handleCommand
(commandId, properties, sequence) {

        if (commandId === 'CommandMyJscriptButton') {
            alert('Event: CommandMyJscriptButton');
        }
    },

    getId: function CustomPageComponent_TestPageComponent$getId() {
        return this._myWpPcId;
    }
}


CustomPageComponent.TestPageComponent.registerClass(
'CustomPageComponent.TestPageComponent', CUI.Page.PageComponent);
if(typeof(NotifyScriptLoadedAndExecuteWaitingJobs)!="undefined")
NotifyScriptLoadedAndExecuteWaitingJobs("testpagecomponent.js");
```

CustomWebPart.cs

Status Bar and Notification Area

Two new additions to the user interface for 2010 are the status bar, which appears right below the Ribbon tab, and the notification area, which appears below the Ribbon tab and to the right and is transient in nature. Both should be used to give the user contextual information without being distracting. For example, if you are editing a page and have not checked it in or published it, the status bar will tell you that only you can see the page. The status bar is for more permanent information, while the notification area is similar to instant message popups or Windows system tray notifications, in that notifications pop up and then disappear after a certain amount of time. Notification area messages are inherently more transient in nature than status bar messages.

Customizing the Status Bar

The status bar is extensible through both client- or server-side code. The message you can deliver in the bar is HTML, so it can be styled and contain links and images. In addition, the bar can have four different preset colors, depending on the importance of the message. To work with the status bar, you want to use the SP.UI.Status class. It is a pretty simple client-side API, since it contains only five methods, and you can find their definitions in SP.debug.js. On the server side, you will want to use the SPPageStatusSetter class, which is part of the Microsoft.SharePoint.WebControls namespace. That API is even simpler in that you call one method — AddStatus. You can also use the SPPageStateControl class to work with the status bar on the server side. Table 4-3 outlines the five methods for the client side.

TABLE 4-3: SP.UI.Status

NAME	DESCRIPTION
addStatus	Method that allows you to pass a title, the HTML payload, and a Boolean specifying whether to render the message at the beginning of the status bar. This function returns a status ID that you can use with other methods.
appendStatus	Method that appends status to an existing status. You need to pass the status ID, title, and HTML you want the new status appended to.
updateStatus	Updates an existing status message. You need to pass the status ID and the HTML payload for the new status message.
setStatusPriColor	Allows you to set the priority color to give a user a visual indication of the status messages' meaning, such as green for good or red for bad. You need to pass the status ID of the status you want to change color and one of four color choices: red, blue, green, or yellow.
removeStatus	Removes the status specified by the status ID you pass to this method from the status bar.
removeAllStatus	Removes all status messages from the status bar. You can pass a Boolean that specifies whether to hide the bar or not. Most times, you will want this Boolean to be true.

Programming the status bar is straightforward. The sample code with this chapter includes a snippet that you can add to the HTML source for a content editor web part. Once you do this, you will see what appears in Figure 4-8.

FIGURE 4-8

```javascript
<script type="text/javascript">

var sid;
var color="";

function AppendStatusMethod()
{
    SP.UI.Status.appendStatus(sid, "Appended:", "<HTML><i>My Status Append to "
+ sid + " using appendStatus</i></HTML>");
}

function UpdateStatus()
{
    SP.UI.Status.updateStatus(sid, "Updated: HTML updated for " + sid +
" using updateStatus");
}

function RemoveStatus()
{
    SP.UI.Status.removeStatus(sid);
}

function RemoveAllStatus()
{
    SP.UI.Status.removeAllStatus(true);
}


function SetStatusColor()
{
   if (color=="")
   {
     color="red";
   }
   else if (color=="red")
   {
     color="green";
   }
   else if (color=="green")
   {
     color="yellow";
   }
   else if (color=="yellow")
   {
     color="blue";
   }
   else if (color=="blue")
   {
     color="red";
   }

   SP.UI.Status.setStatusPriColor(sid, color);
}

function AppendStatus()
{
```

```
    SP.UI.Status.addStatus("Appended:", "<HTML><i>
My Status Message Append using atBeginning</i></HTML>", false);
}


function CreateStatus()
{
    return SP.UI.Status.addStatus(SP.Utilities.HttpUtility.htmlEncode(
"My Status Bar Title"), "<HTML><i>My Status Message</i></HTML>", true);
}


}
</script>
<input onclick="sid=CreateStatus();alert(sid);" type="button" value="
Create Status"/> <br/>
<input onclick="AppendStatus()" type="button"
value="Append Status using atBeginning"/> <br/>
<input onclick="AppendStatusMethod()" type="button"
value="Append Status using appendStatus"/> <br/>
<input onclick="UpdateStatus()" type="button"
value="Update Status using updateStatus"/> <br/>
<input onclick="SetStatusColor()" type="button" value="Cycle Colors"/> <br/>
<input onclick="RemoveStatus()" type="button" value="Remove Single Status"/> <br/>
<input onclick="RemoveAllStatus()" type="button" value="Remove All Status"/> <br/>
```

CustomDialogandNotifications.txt

Customizing the Notification Area

Beyond working with status information, you can also customize the notification area on the upper-right side of the screen below the Ribbon. Given that SharePoint is now leveraging a lot of AJAX, there was a need to give users feedback that their pages and actions were completed. The notification area does this by telling the user that the page is loading or that a save was successful, which used to be indicated by a postback and page refresh.

The notification API is limited in that you can just create and remove notifications. Table 4-4 describes the methods for SP.UI.Notify that work with notifications, with sample code below the table.

TABLE 4-4: SP.UI.Notify

NAME	DESCRIPTION
addNotification	Method that allows you to pass your HTML payload, whether the notification is sticky or not (which when set to false means the notification disappears after 5 seconds), your tooltip text, and the name of a function to handle the onclick event. The last two parameters are optional. This function returns an ID that you can use with the removeNotification method to remove your notification.
removeNotification	Removes the notification specified by the notification ID that you pass to this method.

```
<script type="text/javascript">

var notifyid;
function CreateNotification()
{
    notifyid = SP.UI.Notify.addNotification("My HTML Notification", true,
"My Tooltip", "HelloWorld");
    alert("Notification id: " + notifyid);
}

function RemoveNotification()
{
    SP.UI.Notify.removeNotification(notifyid);
}
</script>
<input onclick="CreateNotification()" type="button"
value="Create Notification"/><br/>
<input onclick="RemoveNotification()" type="button" value="Remove Notification"/>
```

CustomDialogandNotifications.txt

Working with Dialogs

Beyond working with notifications and status bars, SharePoint now also offers a dialog framework that you can write code to. The purpose of the new dialog framework is to keep the user in context and focus the user on the dialog rather than all the surrounding user interface elements. With the new dialog framework, dialogs are modal and gray out the screen, except for the dialog that is displayed. Figure 4-9 shows a custom dialog in SharePoint 2010.

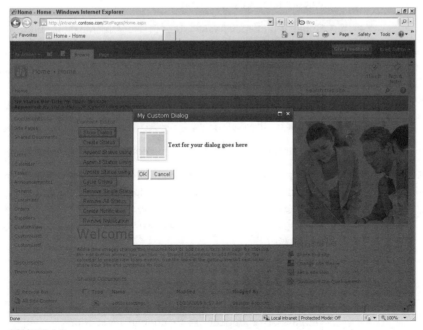

FIGURE 4-9

The implementation of the dialog is that your contents are loaded in an iframe in a floating div. The dialog is modal, so the user can't get to other parts of SharePoint from the dialog. Plus, the dialog can be dragged to other parts of the browser window and can be maximized to the size of the browser window.

Programming the Dialog Framework

If you look in `SP.UI.Dialog.debug.js`, you will see the implementation for the dialog framework. The framework has a JavaScript API that you can program against to have SharePoint launch and load your own dialogs. The way you do this is by calling the `SP.UI.showModalDialog` method and passing in the options you want for your dialog, such as height, width, page to load, and other options. You can see the full set of options in Table 4-5.

TABLE 4-5: Parameters for the SP.UI.showModalDialog method

NAME	DESCRIPTION
width	The width of the dialog box as an integer. If you don't specify a width, SharePoint will autosize the dialog.
Height	The height of the dialog box as an integer. If you don't specify a height, SharePoint will autosize the dialog.
autoSize	Boolean that specifies whether to have SharePoint autosize the dialog.
X	x coordinate for your dialog.
Y	y coordinate for your dialog
allowMaximize	Boolean that specifies whether to allow the Maximize button in your dialog.
showMaximized	Boolean that specifies whether to show your dialog maximized by default.
showClose	Boolean to specify whether to show the Close button in the toolbar for the dialog.
url	URL for SharePoint to load as the contents for your dialog.
Html	A DOMElement, which contains the HTML you want SharePoint to load as the contents for your dialog. Please note that this DOMElement is destroyed after use, so make a copy before passing it to SharePoint if you need it after the dialog is destroyed.
Title	Title of your dialog.
dialogReturnValueCallback	The function SharePoint will call back to when the dialog is closed. You create a delegate to this function for this option with the createDelegate function in JavaScript.

Now that you know the options you can pass to the showModalDialog function, programming a dialog is straightforward. A couple of tips before you look at the code. First, if you are going to use URLs, take a look at the SP.Utilities.Utility namespace. This namespace has a number of utilities to help you find the right places from which to grab your URLs no matter where your code is running. One utility you will see used in the code is SP.Utilities.Utility.getLayoutsPage Url('customdialog.htm'), which gets the URL to the _layouts folder so that the custom dialog HTML file can be retrieved.

Another tip is that dialogs support the Source=url querystring variable like the rest of SharePoint. So, if you want to have SharePoint redirect to another page, you can specify the source along the query string and SharePoint will respect that.

Looking at the following code, you will see the function OpenDialog. As part of this function, a variable called options is created, which uses the SP.UI.$create_DialogOptions method. This method returns a DialogOptions object that you can use to specify your options. In the code, all the options are specified, including the creation of the delegate that points to the function — CloseCallback — that will be called after the dialog is called. Then, the code calls the SP.UI.ModalDialog.showModalDialog with the options object that contains the specified options for the dialog.

If you look at the CloseCallback function, you will see that it gets the result and any return value. The result will be the button the user clicked. SharePoint has an enumeration for the common buttons OK and Cancel that you can check against with the result value — for example, SP.UI.DialogResult.OK or SP.UI.DialogResult.cancel.

```
function OpenDialog()
{
   var options = SP.UI.$create_DialogOptions();

   options.url = SP.Utilities.Utility.getLayoutsPageUrl('customdialog.htm');
   options.url += "?Source=" + document.URL;
   alert('Navigating to dialog at: ' + options.url);
   options.width = 400;
   options.height = 300;
   options.title = "My Custom Dialog";

   options.dialogReturnValueCallback = Function.createDelegate(null, CloseCallback);
   SP.UI.ModalDialog.showModalDialog(options);
}

function CloseCallback(result, returnValue)
{
   alert('Result from dialog was: '+ result);
   if(result === SP.UI.DialogResult.OK)
   {
     alert('You clicked OK');
   }
   else if (result == SP.UI.DialogResult.cancel)
   {
     alert('You clicked Cancel');
   }
}
```

Now that you have seen the code for calling the dialog and evaluating the result, look at what the HTML for the dialog body looks like. The code that follows is the code for the dialog loaded by SharePoint. A couple of things to note in the code: First, there are two buttons for OK and Cancel, respectively. If you look at the `onclick` event handlers for the button, you will notice that they use methods from the `window.frameElement` object. By using this object, you can get methods from the dialog framework. As you can see, `commitPopup` will return OK, and `cancelPopUp` will return Cancel as the result of your dialog. Table 4-6 shows the methods you want to use from the `frameElement`.

Available for download on Wrox.com

```
<p>
<img src="/_layouts/1033/images/DefaultPageLayout.gif" alt="Default Page"
style="vertical-align: middle"/>
<B>Text for your dialog goes here</B>
</p>

<input type="button" name="OK" value="OK"
onclick="window.frameElement.commitPopup();
return false;" accesskey="O" class="ms-ButtonHeightWidth" target="_self" />

<input type="button" name="Cancel" value="Cancel"
onclick="window.frameElement.cancelPopUp();
return false;" accesskey="C" class="ms-ButtonHeightWidth" target="_self" />
```

CustomDialogandNotifications.txt

TABLE 4-6: Methods for frameElement for Dialogs

NAME	DESCRIPTION
commitPopup	Returns OK as the result of your dialog
cancelPopUp	Returns Cancel as a result of your dialog
navigateParent	Will navigate to the parent of the dialog

Theming Infrastructure

One of the advancements in 2010 is a new theming infrastructure. With 2007, if you wanted to change the user interface, you had to do a mixture of changes from Master Pages to CSS to trying to hack inline styles contained in the product. With 2010, this is all simplified, since all styles are moved out into CSS files and certain styles are replaceable using the new theming infrastructure. Plus, rather than creating themes by hand, you can create themes using Office applications, such as PowerPoint, which makes it easy for end users to create new themes to apply to their sites.

Much of the SharePoint user interface supports theming. Supported elements include:

➤ Ribbon

➤ Site title, icon, and description

- ➤ Secondary title, description, and view name
- ➤ List item selection and bulk editing highlighting
- ➤ ECB menu
- ➤ Quick Launch
- ➤ Tree control
- ➤ Top navigation bar
- ➤ Site Actions menu
- ➤ Welcome menu
- ➤ Breadcrumb control
- ➤ Layout pages (Site Settings Menu)
- ➤ Popup dialogs
- ➤ Error messages/pages
- ➤ Web part chrome/Tool pane
- ➤ RTE Editor
- ➤ Search control
- ➤ Forms

In order to support theming, SharePoint processes the CSS and supporting images that you create. For example, SharePoint can add effects to your images, such as a gradient and rounded corners, if you provide the special theming markup to your elements. This special markup to support theming needs to be placed in your CSS file, and your CSS file has to be placed in a themable location, which is the content database or, more frequently for custom solutions, in the `%Program Files%\Common Files\Microsoft Shared\Web Server Extensions\14\TEMPLATE\LAYOUTS\1033\STYLES\Themable` folder.

The CSS processor works by looking for particular markups using CSS comments and then performing the actions specified by that markup to replace the CSS style with whatever theme is applied to the site. For example, suppose that you had a CSS declaration such as:

```
.major-font
{
    /* [ReplaceFont(themeFont: "MajorFont")] */
    font-family: Verdana, MS Sans Serif, Sans-Serif;
}

.minor-font
{
    /* [ReplaceFont(themeFont: "MinorFont")] */
    font-family: cursive;
}

.bg-image1-lt1dk1
```

```
{
    /* [RecolorImage(lightThemeColor: "Light1", darkThemeColor: "Dark1")] */
    background-image: url("../images/bl_Navbar_Gd_Default.jpg");
}

.class
{
    /*[ReplaceColor(BackgroundColor1)]*/
    Color:#FFFFFF;
}
```

Notice the markup before each of the CSS declarations. Because of these markups, SharePoint would replace the fonts, recolor the image, and change background color if a new theme was selected that used different elements than the ones specified.

To support theming, SharePoint has enhanced the site theme user interface so that you can preview your changes before you actually make them. Figure 4-10 shows the new site theme administration interface.

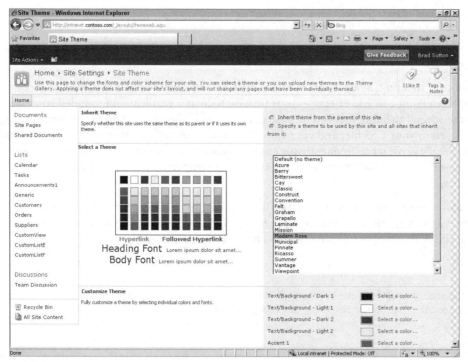

FIGURE 4-10

The three commands that you can perform are `ReplaceColor`, `ReplaceFont`, and `RecolorImage`. Each of these commands has parameters you can specify to customize the command. Table 4-7 describes these commands.

TABLE 4-7: Theme Commands

NAME	DESCRIPTION
`ReplaceColor(string themeColor)`	Replaces the color of the CSS rule with the specified color. You can specify advanced parameters, such as making colors lighter or darker by a certain percentage. For example, `/* [ReplaceColor(themeColor:" Light2" {lighter: 0.2})] */ background-color:#f5f6f7;`
`ReplaceFont(string themeFont)`	Replaces the `font-family` with the specified `font-family`. For example, `/* [ReplaceFont(themeFont: "MajorFont")] */ font-family: Verdana, MS Sans Serif, Sans-Serif;`
`RecolorImage(string startThemeColor, string endThemeColor, optional string grayscaleImageUrl, optional method: string method)`	Recolors the image. This only works for `background-image`. The `grayscaleImageURL` specifies a grayscale image that needs to be colorized. For example, `/* [RecolorImage(lightThemeColor: "Light1", darkThemeColor: "Dark1")] */ background-image: url("../images/bl_Navbar_Gd_Default.jpg");` If you want to recolor the image by blending, filling, or tinting it, you can use the optional method parameter, such as: `/* [RecolorImage(themeColor:"Light2",method:"Filling" )] */ background:url("/_layouts/images/qlbgfade.png") repeat-x left top;` Or `/* [RecolorImage(themeColor:"Light2",method:"Tinting")] */ background-image:url("/_layouts/images/bgximg.png");`

Because a lot of elements support themes, including web parts, you will want to make sure that when you design SharePoint applications, you keep theming in mind. This means that you should move away from using CSS inline styles, since these will not be themable by the engine. Instead, if you use CSS files and appropriately mark up those CSS styles using the theme attributes, then your custom applications will be themable using the built-in SharePoint infrastructure. The extra work of marking up your CSS is worth it for the time savings of not having to write your own theming interface for your applications, plus you will get better user interface integration by not having your application ignore the theme when it changes in the SharePoint product.

Programming Using the Theme API

To work with themes, there is a new class in the `Microsoft.SharePoint.Utilities` namespace, called `ThmxTheme`, that provides methods and properties that make programming with themes easier. This class allows you to create new themes and query existing themes in the system. Table 4-8 outlines the important methods and properties of the ThmxTheme class with supporting sample code below the table to show you how to use this class.

TABLE 4-8: ThmxTheme Class

NAME	DESCRIPTION
EnforceThemedStylesForWeb(SPWeb web)	Forces the styles for the theme to be applied to the SPWeb specified.
GetManagedThemes(SPSite site)	Returns a collection of themes as Theme objects for the specified site.
GetThemeUrlForWeb(SPWeb web)	Gets the Theme URL for the specified SPWeb object.
SetThemeUrlForWeb(SPWeb web, string themeUrl)	Sets the theme URL for the SPWeb specified to the string in the second parameter.
Open(Multiple Overloads)	Opens the theme either using a stream or using an SPFile object, which are the most common overloaded versions of this method.
Save	Saves the theme back to the stream.
AccentColor1	Property that specifies the accent color for the theme. You set it by setting the DefaultColor property and then saving the theme. Please note that there are many other similar properties such as AccentColor2, DarkColor1, HyperlinkColor, and LightColor1 that behave the same way and just change different styles.

```
using (SPSite site = new SPSite("http://intranet.contoso.com"))
        {
            //Get all the themes for the site

            foreach (ThmxTheme theme in ThmxTheme.GetManagedThemes(site))
            {
                //Get Azure hyperlink color
                if (theme.Name == "Azure")
                {
                    MessageBox.Show(theme.HyperlinkColor.DefaultColor.Name +
    " " + theme.HyperlinkColor.DefaultColor.ToString());
                }
            }
```

```
                    //Upload a new theme from the file system
                    FileStream fs = File.Open(
"c:\\users\\administrator\\desktop\\test.thmx",FileMode.Open);


                    ThmxTheme newtheme = ThmxTheme.Open(
fs,FileMode.Open, FileAccess.ReadWrite);
                    newtheme.Name = "My Test Theme";
                    newtheme.HyperlinkColor.DefaultColor = Color.Black;

                    newtheme.Save();
    }
```

LIST, VIEW, AND EVENT ENHANCEMENTS

There are a number of new list, view, and event enhancements in SharePoint 2010. For example, there is support for referential integrity and formula validation in lists. In addition, all views of lists are now based on the `XsltListViewWebPart`, which makes customization easier. Finally, there are new events that you can take advantage of with SharePoint 2010 — for example, when new sites and lists are added. Let's dive into these new enhancements.

List Enhancements

Lists are the backbone of SharePoint. They're where you create your data models and your data instances. They're what your users understand are their documents or tasks. Without lists, your SharePoint site would cease to function, since SharePoint uses lists itself for its own functionality and ability to run. With 2010, there are new list enhancements and even new tools that you can take advantage of to work with your custom lists.

 One enhancement, support for large lists and list throttling, already has been discussed in Chapter 3, so refer to that chapter to understand that enhancement.

SharePoint Designer and Visual Studio Support

Before diving into the new enhancements in lists, you need to first look at the tools used to create your lists. The tools of choice are SharePoint Designer (SPD) and Visual Studio (VS). Both are good choices, depending on what you are trying to do. If you want barebones, down to the metal, XML-style creation of lists, then Visual Studio will be your choice. If you would rather work with a GUI, SPD provides a nice interface to work with your lists, whether it is creating columns or views, or customizing your list settings. Of course, you can use the built-in list settings in SharePoint to work with your lists, but SPD would be a better choice if you are interested in a GUI editor.

Diving into SPD, SPD makes it easy to work with your lists, whether it's creating new lists or modifying your existing lists. SPD can make quick work of your columns, views, forms, content types, workflows, and even custom actions for your list. If you need to rapidly create a list or list definition, SPD is going to be the fastest and easiest way to work with your SharePoint lists. You will have to give up some control, since SPD does not allow you to get down to the same level of customization that Visual Studio does, but you trade customizability for speed when you work with SPD. Figure 4-11 shows the List Settings user interface for SPD.

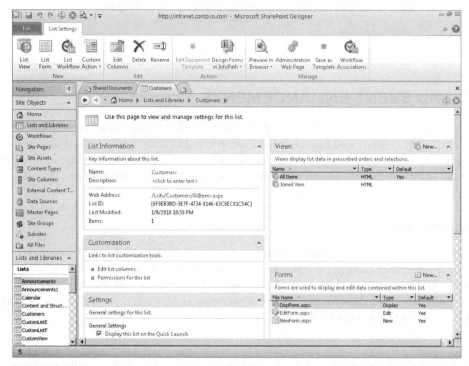

FIGURE 4-11

With Visual Studio, you can create list definitions and list instances. List definitions are a built-in project type for Visual Studio.

One word of warning, don't expect nice designers when you create a list definition. Instead, get ready to work with some XML. The nice thing about the list definition project in Visual Studio is that it allows you to create a list instance at the same time. Plus, your application is deployed as a feature, so you can reuse the list definition and instance in many different sites. If you need the ultimate in flexibility, VS is your tool of choice for creating list definitions and customizing lists.

List Relationships with Cascade or Block

One common complaint about SharePoint is how it does not behave like a relational database. For example, if you have a lookup between two lists and you want to have some referential integrity, SharePoint previously would not block or cascade your deletes between your lists. With 2010, SharePoint now can block or cascade your deletes between lists automatically. Now, don't think SharePoint is going to become your replacement for SQL Server with this functionality. It is implemented more to make simple relationships work, and if you have a very complex data model, you will want to use SQL Server and surface SQL Server through SharePoint, using Business Connectivity Services (BCS) and external lists.

The way that list relationships work is you create a lookup between your lists. One new thing about lookups in a list is that you can retrieve more than just the identifier and can retrieve additional properties from the list such as built-in or custom fields. On the list where you create your lookup, you can enforce the relationship behavior to either restrict deleting parent list items if items exist in the list that are related to the parent item, or cascade the delete from the parent list to the child list. Figure 4-12 shows the user interface for setting the properties of the lookup column to enforce relationship behaviors.

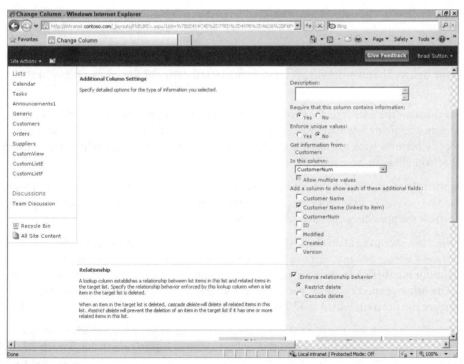

FIGURE 4-12

If you restrict the delete, SharePoint will throw an error telling the user that there is an item in the related list that exists and will cancel deleting the error, as shown in Figure 4-13.

FIGURE 4-13

If you cascade the delete, SharePoint will perform a transacted delete of the related items in the related list.

Please note that through the user interface you cannot create cross-web lookups, but through the object model and by using Site Columns, you can. Cross-web lookups will not support the referential integrity features such as cascading delete. Also, referential integrity will not be enforced for a lookup that you allow to have multiple values.

When working with the object model, you want to use the `RelationshipDeleteBehavior` property on your `SPFieldLookup object`. This property takes a value from the `SPRelationshipDeleteBehavior` enumerator of which the possible values are `None`, `Cascade`, or `Restrict`.

If you look at the `SPWebApplication` class, you will see two properties that affect relationships. The first property is `CascadeDeleteMaximumItemLimit`, which allows you to specify as an integer the maximum number of cascaded items that SharePoint will delete. By default, this value is 1000 items. The other property is `CascadeDeleteTimeoutMultiplier`, which allows you to specify as an integer the timeout, which is 120 seconds by default.

To find lookup fields, you can use the `GetRelatedFields` method of your list, which returns a `SPRelatedFieldCollection` collection. From this collection, you can iterate through each related field. From there, you can retrieve properties, such as the `LookupList` that the field is related to, the `ListID`, the `FieldID`, or the relationship behavior when something is deleted from the list.

```
using (SPSite site = new SPSite("http://intranet.contoso.com"))
{


    SPList list = site.AllWebs[""].Lists["Orders"];
    SPRelatedFieldCollection relatedFields = list.GetRelatedFields();
    foreach (SPRelatedField relatedField in relatedFields)
    {
        //Lookup the list for each

        SPList relatedList = relatedField.LookupList;
        MessageBox.Show(relatedField.ListId + " " +
relatedField.FieldId);
            //MessageBox.Show("List Name: " +
relatedList.Title + " Relationship Behavior: " +
relatedField.RelationshipDeleteBehavior.ToString());


    }
}
```

Validation with Excel-Like Formulas

Another new list feature is the ability to do list validation using formulas. This is more of an end user or power user feature, but for simple validation scenarios, developers will find this feature easy to use, and quick to write formulas rather than writing code. You can write validation at either the list level or the column level, depending on your needs. SharePoint also supports this approach for site columns that you add to your content types. Figure 4-14 shows setting the formula, and Figure 4-15 shows the custom error message that appears when the formula does not validate.

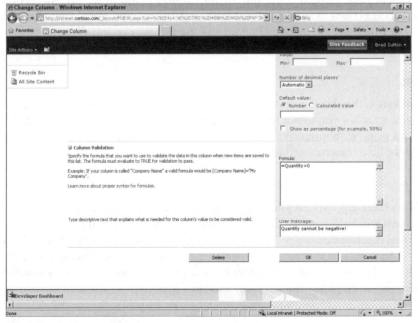

FIGURE 4-14

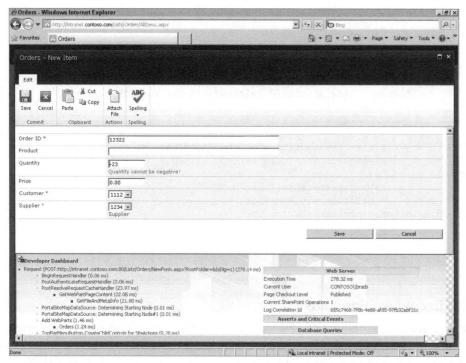

FIGURE 4-15

One of the easiest ways to understand what formulas you can enter into the validation rules is to connect Microsoft Access to your SharePoint list and use the formula editor in Access. SharePoint supports the same formula functions as Access, so you can use string manipulation, logic, financial, conversion, and date/time functionality. In the API, you will use the `SPList.ValidationFormula` and `SPField.ValidationFormula` properties to get and set your formulas.

Ensuring Uniqueness

Another new feature of lists is the ability to ensure uniqueness for the values in your columns. SharePoint would previously allow you to not require unique values so that multiple items could have the same value for a field. With uniqueness, SharePoint can use the field as an index to make lookups faster because the field is guaranteed to have a unique value.

List Joins

Just like a database, SharePoint supports list joins. Again, SharePoint won't provide as much functionality as a relational database, since its data model sits above the bare-metal database, but compared to 2007 the join functionality is a welcome addition. SharePoint can perform left and inner joins but not right joins. An inner join is where you combine the values from the datasources based on the join predicate, such as "show me all employees who are in a particular department based on their department ID," which joins an employee list and a department list, both of which have department

IDs in them. A left join or left outer join just means that anything that appears in the leftmost list, even if it does not exist in the other list, will be returned in the result set.

The code below performs a join across two lists on a lookup field. You need to set the `Joins` property on your `SPQuery` object with the join you want to perform. In the code, you are joining on the Customers list, where the customer is the same as the Customer in the Orders list.

Beyond setting the Joins property, you must specify a value for the `ProjectedFields` property. This property gets fields from the lookup list. You can alias the field by using the `Name` attribute and tell SharePoint the field name by using the `ShowField` attribute. Once you get back your results, you will have to use the `SPFieldLookupValue` object to display the values for your projected fields.

```
SPList OrderList = web.Lists["Orders"];
        SPQuery CustomerQuery = new SPQuery();
        CustomerQuery.Joins =
            "<Join Type='INNER' ListAlias='Customers'>" +
                "<Eq>" +
                    "<FieldRef Name='Customer' RefType='Id' />" +
                    "<FieldRef List='Customers' Name='ID' />" +
                "</Eq>" +
            "</Join>";
        StringBuilder ProjectedFields = new StringBuilder();
        ProjectedFields.Append("<Field Name='CustomerTitle'
Type='Lookup' List='Customers' ShowField='Title' />");
        ProjectedFields.Append("<Field Name='CustomerAddress'
Type='Lookup' List='Customers' ShowField='CustomerNum' />");
        CustomerQuery.ProjectedFields = ProjectedFields.ToString();
        SPListItemCollection Results = OrderList.GetItems(CustomerQuery);
        foreach (SPListItem Result in Results)
            {
            SPFieldLookupValue CustomerTitle = new
  SPFieldLookupValue(Result["CustomerTitle"].ToString());
            SPFieldLookupValue CustomerAddress = new
  SPFieldLookupValue(Result["CustomerAddress"].ToString());

            MessageBox.Show(Result.Title + " " + CustomerTitle.LookupValue + "
  " + CustomerAddress.LookupValue);

            }
```

Customize Default Forms Using Web Parts or InfoPath

One of the new features for lists is the ability to customize the default forms for your list items. SharePoint 2010 moves to using web part pages for the default forms, so your customization can be as easy as adding new web parts to the existing default forms, or you can even replace the default forms with your own custom InfoPath forms. With 2010, you can modify the New, Display, and Edit forms. For more on forms, take a read through Chapter 9.

When you use the Ribbon option to edit the form in InfoPath, InfoPath will automatically be launched, connect to your list, and display your form as shown in Figure 4-16.

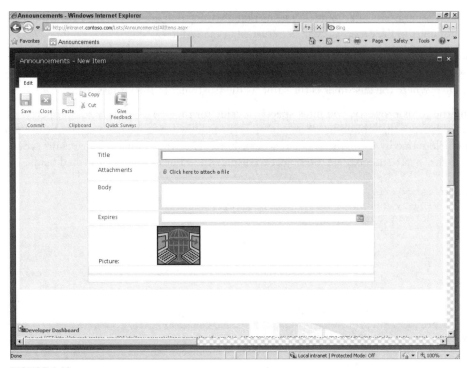

FIGURE 4-16

View Enhancements

The biggest change with views in 2010 is the change of the technology used to display views. 2010 uses the SharePoint Designer XsltListViewWebPart as the default view web part for viewing lists. There are a number of reasons why this is much better than 2007. First, XSLT views allow you to replace your use of CAML to create views, and can move to using standards-based XSLT to define your view. Second, performance is better than 2007 with the new XSLT view. Third, editing with SPD is easier, since the XSLT view technology is an SPD technology. Lastly, the same view technology is used for all SharePoint lists, including standard SharePoint lists and external lists.

The easiest way to understand, prototype. and get sample code is to use SPD to design your views and then view the code that SPD creates to work with your XSLT views. For example, you may want to create a view that makes any numbers that meet or exceed a limit turn red, yellow, or green and implements a custom mouseover event. With SPD, this is as easy as using the conditional formatting functionality and the IntelliSense built in to modify the view. Figure 4-17 shows the editing of the view in SPD.

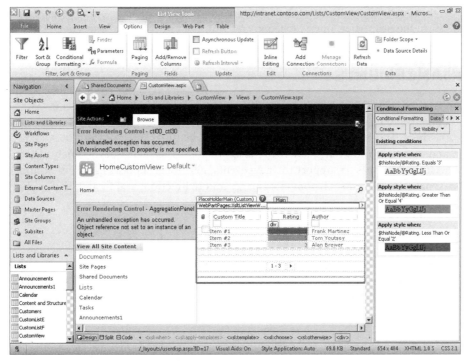

FIGURE 4-17

The following code shows the conditional formatting XSLT that SPD generates for you:

```
<div align="right" onmouseover="javascript:alert('You moused over!');">
            <xsl:attribute name="style">
                    <xsl:if test="$thisNode/@Rating. = 3"
                            xmlns:ddwrt="http://schemas.microsoft.com
/WebParts/v2/DataView/runtime" ddwrt:cf_explicit="1">background-color:
#FFFF00;</xsl:if>
                        <xsl:if test="$thisNode/@Rating. &gt;= 4"
xmlsn:ddwrt="http://schemas.microsoft.
com/WebParts/v2/DataView/runtime" ddwrt:cf_explicit="1">background-color:
#71B84F;</xsl:if>
                            <xsl:if test="$thisNode/@Rating. &lt;= 2"
                            ddwrt:cf_explicit="1" xmlns:ddwrt="
http://schemas.microsoft.com/WebParts/v2/DataView/runtime">background-color:
#FF0000;</xsl:if>

            </xsl:attribute>
```

To work with views programmatically, you will use the SPView object and SPViewCollection. You can add new views, modify existing views, or delete views. There are a few properties that you will be interested in. One is the DefaultView off the SPList object; this property returns an SPView object, which is the default view for your list. From there, you can use the RenderAsHTML method, which will return the HTML that your view will render. You can also use `PropertiesXml`, `Query`, `SchemaXml`, and `Xsl`, which return the properties, query, schema, and XSL used in your list, respectively.

EVENTS ENHANCEMENTS

With 2010, there are six new events that you can take advantage of, including `WebAdding`, `WebProvisioned`, `ListAdding`, `ListAdded`, `ListDeleting`, and `ListDeleted`. This is in addition to the existing events that were introduced in SharePoint 2007, such as the `ItemAdding`, `ItemUpdating`, and `ItemUpdated` events. There are also other enhancements beyond new events, including new registration scopes to support the new events, new tools support in Visual Studio, support for post-synchronous events, custom error pages and redirection, and finally, impersonation enhancements.

New Events

As part of SharePoint 2010, there are six new events that you can take advantage of. These events allow you to capture creation and provisioning of new webs and the creation and deletion of lists. Table 4-9 goes through each of the events and what you can use them for.

TABLE 4-9: New 2010 Events

NAME	DESCRIPTION
`WebAdding`	A synchronous event that happens before the web is added. Some URL properties may not exist yet for the new site, since the new site does not exist yet.
`WebProvisioned`	A synchronous or asynchronous after-event that occurs after the web is created. You make the event synchronous or asynchronous by using the `Synchronization` property and setting it to `Asynchronous` or `Synchronous`. This is located under the `Receiver` node in the `elements.xml` file for your feature.
`ListAdding`	A synchronous event that happens before a list is created.
`ListAdded`	A synchronous or asynchronous after-event that happens after a list is created but before being it is presented to the user.
`ListDeleting`	A synchronous event that happens before a list is deleted.
`ListDeleted`	A synchronous or asynchronous after-event that happens after a list is deleted.

Using these events is the same as writing event receivers for any other types of events in SharePoint. The nice thing about writing event receivers with SharePoint 2010 is that you have Visual Studio 2010 support for writing and deploying your event receivers. Figure 4-18 shows the new event receiver template in Visual Studio, where you can select the type of event receiver you want to create and the events you want to listen for in your receiver. Once you finish the wizard inside of Visual Studio, you can modify your feature definition or your code using the standard Visual Studio SharePoint tools. Plus, with on-click deployment and debugging, it's a lot easier to get your receiver deployed and start debugging it.

The code that follows shows you how to use the new web events in SharePoint. The code writes to the event log the properties for the event. The sample applications with this book include the same sample for the new list

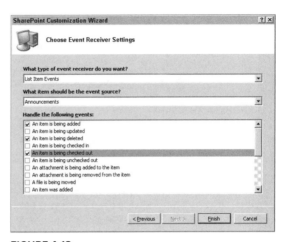

FIGURE 4-18

events, but for brevity only the web event sample code is shown. If you wanted to, you could cancel the before-events, such as `WebAdding`, `ListDeleting`, or `ListAdding`, by using the `Cancel` property and setting it to false. These events will fire even in the Recycle Bin, so if you restore a list or delete a list, you will get an event for those actions.

```
namespace WebEventReceiver.EventReceiver1
{
    /// <summary>
    /// Web Events
    /// </summary>
    public class EventReceiver1 : SPWebEventReceiver
    {
        /// <summary>
        /// A site is being provisioned.
        /// </summary>
        public override void WebAdding(SPWebEventProperties properties)
        {
            LogWebEventProperties(properties);

            base.WebAdding(properties);
        }

        /// <summary>
        /// A site was provisioned.
        /// </summary>
        public override void WebProvisioned(SPWebEventProperties properties)
        {
            LogWebEventProperties(properties);
            base.WebProvisioned(properties);
        }


        private void LogWebEventProperties(SPWebEventProperties properties)
```

```
        {
            StringBuilder sb = new StringBuilder();

            try
            {
                sb.AppendFormat("{0} at {1}\n\n", properties.EventType,
 DateTime.Now);
                sb.AppendFormat("Cancel: {0}\n", properties.Cancel);
                sb.AppendFormat("ErrorMessage: {0}\n", properties.ErrorMessage);
                sb.AppendFormat("EventType: {0}\n", properties.EventType);
                sb.AppendFormat("FullUrl: {0}\n", properties.FullUrl);
                sb.AppendFormat("NewServerRelativeUrl: {0}\n",
properties.NewServerRelativeUrl);
                sb.AppendFormat("ParentWebId: {0}\n", properties.ParentWebId);
                sb.AppendFormat("ReceiverData: {0}\n", properties.ReceiverData);
                sb.AppendFormat("RedirectUrl: {0}\n", properties.RedirectUrl);
                sb.AppendFormat("ServerRelativeUrl: {0}\n",
properties.ServerRelativeUrl);
                sb.AppendFormat("SiteId: {0}\n", properties.SiteId);
                sb.AppendFormat("Status: {0}\n", properties.Status);
                sb.AppendFormat("UserDisplayName: {0}\n",
properties.UserDisplayName);
                sb.AppendFormat("UserLoginName: {0}\n", properties.UserLoginName);
                sb.AppendFormat("Web: {0}\n", properties.Web);
                sb.AppendFormat("WebId: {0}\n", properties.WebId);
            }
            catch (Exception e)
            {
                sb.AppendFormat("Exception accessing Web Event Properties: {0}\n",
e);

            }


            //Log out to the event log
            string source = "WebEventCustomLog";
            string logName = "Application";

            if (!EventLog.SourceExists(source))
            {
                EventLog.CreateEventSource(source, logName);
            }

            try
            {
                EventLog.WriteEntry(source, sb.ToString());
            }
            catch (Exception e)
            { }

        }

    }
}
```

WebEventReceiver/Receiver1.cs

New Event Registration Feature

To support the new events, SharePoint has added a new registration capability for registering your event receivers, using the <Receivers> XML block. The new capability includes registering your event receiver at the site collection level by using the new Scope attribute and setting it either to Site or Web, depending on the scope that you want for your event receiver. If you set it to Web, your event receiver will work across all sites in your site collection, as long as your feature is registered across all these sites as well. You can tell SharePoint to just have the receiver work on the root site by using the RootWebOnly attribute on the <Receivers> node. The last new enhancement is the ListUrl attribute, which allows you to scope your receiver to a particular list by passing in the relative URL.

Post-Synchronous Events

With 2007, all your after-events were asynchronous, so if you wanted to perform some operations after the target, such as an item, was created but before it was presented to the user, you couldn't. Your event receiver would fire asynchronously, so the user might already see the target, and then if you modified properties or added values, the user experience might be not ideal. With 2010, there is support for synchronous after-events, such as listadded, itemadded, or webprovisioned. To make the events synchronous, you need to set the Synchronization property either through the SPEventReceiverDefinition object model if you are registering your events programmatically or by creating a node in your <Receiver> XML that sets the value to Synchronous or Asynchronous. That's it.

Custom Error Pages

With 2007, you can cancel events and return an error message to the user, but that provides limited interactivity and not much help to the user beyond what your error message says. With 2010 events, you can cancel the event on your synchronous events and redirect the user to a custom error page that you create. This allows you to have more control of what the users see, and you can try to help them figure out why their action is failing. The custom error pages and redirection will only work for pre-synchronous events, so you cannot do this for post-synchronous events such as ListAdded. Plus, this will only work with browser clients. Office will just put up an error message if you cancel the event.

The way to implement custom error pages is to set the Status property on your property bag for your event receiver to SPEventReceiverStatus.CancelWithRedirectUrl, set the RedirectUrl property to a relative URL for your error page, and set the Cancel property to true.

```
properties.Cancel = true;
properties.Status = SPEventReceiverStatus.CancelWithRedirectUrl;
properties.RedirectUrl = "/_layouts/mycustomerror.aspx";
```

Impersonation Enhancements

The last area of enhancement for events is in the impersonation that events support. SharePoint runs your events in the context of the user who triggered the event. Generally, this is okay, but there may be certain times when you want to let a user perform actions on lists, libraries, or the system that the current user does not have permissions to do. In most cases, you would use SPSecurity's RunwithElevatedPrivileges method. However, you may want to revert to the originating user on some operations. With 2010, the event property bag contains the OriginatingUserToken, UserDisplayName, and UserLoginName, which you can use to revert to the original user. The following code shows how, in a ListAdding event, you can elevate some code to the system account and then revert some code to the original user by using these properties.

```
public override void ListAdding(SPListEventProperties properties)
        {
            LogListEventProperties(properties);
            StringBuilder sb = new StringBuilder();

            SPSecurity.RunWithElevatedPrivileges(delegate()
            {

                using (SPSite site = new SPSite(properties.SiteId))
                {
                    // Running under the "system account" now
                    // Perform operations
                    sb.AppendLine("SiteURL: " + site.Url);
                    sb.AppendLine("Impersonating: " + site.Impersonating.ToString());
                    //Get the web to get the current user
                    using (SPWeb web = site.OpenWeb())
                    {
                        sb.AppendLine("Name and LoginName: " +
web.CurrentUser.Name.ToString() + " " + web.CurrentUser.LoginName.ToString());
                    }
                    LogImpersonation(sb.ToString());


                }
            });

            //Clear our stringbuilder
            sb.Length = 0;
            sb.Capacity = 0;


            //Now access the site with the original user token
            using (SPSite originalsite = new SPSite(properties.SiteId,
properties.OriginatingUserToken))
                {
                    //Running under the original user account that generated the event
                    //Perform operations
                    sb.AppendLine("SiteURL: " + originalsite.Url);
                    sb.AppendLine("Impersonating: " +
originalsite.Impersonating.ToString());
                    //Get the web to get the current user
                    using (SPWeb web = originalsite.OpenWeb())
                    {
```

```
                sb.AppendLine("Name and LoginName: " +
web.CurrentUser.Name.ToString() + " " + web.CurrentUser.LoginName.ToString());
            }

        LogImpersonation(sb.ToString());

    }

    base.ListAdding(properties);
}

private void LogImpersonation(string valueToLog)
{

    string source = "ListEventCustomLog";
    string logName = "Application";

    if (!EventLog.SourceExists(source))
    {
        EventLog.CreateEventSource(source, logName);
    }

    try
    {
        EventLog.WriteEntry(source, valueToLog);
    }
    catch (Exception e)
    { }
}
```

ListEventReceiver/EventReceiver1.cs

OVERVIEW OF DATA TECHNOLOGIES

When it comes to SharePoint, working with, manipulating, and displaying data is one of the most important tasks you do as a developer. If you break SharePoint down to its simplest form, it is just an application that sits on top of a database. Since SharePoint can surface its data in so many different ways, whether that is through the browser, inside of Office, in applications running on the SharePoint server, or in applications running off the SharePoint server, there are a number of different data technologies you can take advantage of when working with SharePoint. Which one you use depends on your comfort level with the technology required and also whether you are writing your application to run on or off the SharePoint server. Your choices in 2010 are: LINQ, Server OM, Client OM, or REST. Of course, you can continue to use the web services APIs of SharePoint, but you will want to look at moving to the client OM rather than using that technology. Table 4-10 goes through the pros and cons of each data access technology.

TABLE 4-10: Data Access Technologies

NAME	PROS	CONS
LINQ	Entity-based programming Strongly typed Supports joins and projections Good tools support and IntelliSense	Server-side only New API, so new skills required Pre-processing of list structure required, so changing list could break application
Server OM	Familiar API Works with more than just list data	Server-side only Strongly typed
Client OM	Works off the server Easier than web services API Works in Silverlight, JavaScript and .NET More than just list data	New API Weakly Typed
REST	Standards-based URL-based commands Strongly typed	Only works with lists and Excel

SharePoint LINQ Support

With SharePoint 2007, you had to use CAML queries to write queries against the server, using the `SPQuery` or `SPSiteDataQuery` objects. You would write your CAML as a string and pass it to those objects, so there were no strongly typed objects or syntax checking as part of the API. Instead, you would either have to cross your fingers that you got the query right or use a third-party tool to try to generate your CAML queries. To make this easier, SharePoint 2010 introduces SharePoint LINQ (SPLINQ). By having a LINQ provider, 2010 allows you to use LINQ to write your queries against SharePoint in a strongly typed way with IntelliSense and compile-time checking. Under the covers, the SharePoint LINQ provider translates your LINQ query into a CAML query and executes it against the server. As you will see, you can retrieve the CAML query that the LINQ provider generated to understand what is being passed back to the server.

Getting Started with SharePoint LINQ: SPMetal

The first step in getting starting with SPLINQ is generating the entity classes and properties for your lists. Rather than writing these by hand, you can use the command-line tool that ships with SharePoint, called SPMetal. SPMetal will parse your lists and generate the necessary classes for you that you can import into your Visual Studio projects. You can find SPMetal at `%ProgramFiles%\ Common Files\Microsoft Shared\web server extensions\14\ BIN`. You can run SPMetal from the command prompt, but if you prefer, you can write a batch file that you have Visual Studio run as part of your pre-build for your project so that the latest version of your entity classes are always included.

Using SPMetal is straightforward for the common scenarios that you will want to do. It does support XML customization, but most of the time you will find that you do not need to customize the default code generation. Table 4-11 shows the SPMetal command-line parameters that you can pass.

TABLE 4-11: SPMetal Command-Line Parameters

NAME	DESCRIPTION
web	Absolute URL of the website you want SPMetal to generate entity classes for.
code	The relative or absolute path of the location where you want the outputted code to be placed.
language	The programming language you want generated. The value for this can be either csharp or vb. SPMetal can look at your code parameter and infer the language you want by the extension.
namespace	The namespace you want used for the generated code. If you do not specify this property, SPMetal will use the default namespace of your VS project.
useremoteapi	SPMetal will use the client object model if you specify this parameter.
user	Allows you to specify *DOMAIN\username* such as */user:DOMAIN\username* that SPMetal will run as.
password	The password that SPMetal will use to log on as the user specified in the /user parameter.
serialization	Specifies whether you want your objects to be serializable or not. By default, this parameter is none, so they are not. If you specify unidirectional, then SPMetal will put in the appropriate markup to make the objects serializable.
parameters	Specifies the XML file used to override the parameters for your SPMetal settings. This is for advanced changes.

The following code snippet shows you some of the generated code, but to give you an idea of the work SPMetal does for you, the complete code for even a simple SharePoint site is over 3000 lines long! You will definitely want to use SPMetal to generate this code and tweak SPMetal as you need to in order to meet your requirements.

```
/// <summary>
/// Use the Announcements list to post messages on the home page of your site.
/// </summary>
[Microsoft.SharePoint.Linq.ListAttribute(Name="Announcements")]
public Microsoft.SharePoint.Linq.
EntityList<AnnouncementsAnnouncement> Announcements {
        get {
                return this.GetList<AnnouncementsAnnouncement>("Announcements");
```

```
                }
            }

/// <summary>
/// Create a new news item, status or other short piece of information.
/// </summary>
[Microsoft.SharePoint.Linq.ContentTypeAttribute(Name="Announcement", Id="0x0104")]
[Microsoft.SharePoint.Linq.DerivedEntityClassAttribute
(Type=typeof(AnnouncementsAnnouncement))]
public partial class Announcement : Item {

        private string _body;

         private System.Nullable<System.DateTime> _expires;

        #region Extensibility Method Definitions
        partial void OnLoaded();
        partial void OnValidate();
        partial void OnCreated();
        #endregion

        public Announcement() {
                this.OnCreated();
         }

        [Microsoft.SharePoint.Linq.ColumnAttribute(Name="Body",
Storage="_body", FieldType="Note")]
        public string Body {
                get {
                        return this._body;
                }
                set {
                        if ((value != this._body)) {
                                this.OnPropertyChanging("Body", this._body);
                                this._body = value;
                                this.OnPropertyChanged("Body");
                        }
                }
        }

        [Microsoft.SharePoint.Linq.ColumnAttribute(Name="Expires", Storage="_expires",
FieldType="DateTime")]
        public System.Nullable<System.DateTime> Expires {
                get {
                        return this._expires;
                }
                set {
                        if ((value != this._expires)) {
                                this.OnPropertyChanging("Expires", this._expires);
                                this._expires = value;
                                this.OnPropertyChanged("Expires");
                        }
                }
        }
}
```

What about Default Fields?

One thing you may realize is that SPMetal, by default, does not generate all the fields for your content types. So, you may find that fields such as `Created` or `ModifiedBy` do not appear in the types created by SPMetal. To add these fields, you can specify them in a `Parameters.XML`. The example that follows adds some new fields to the contact content type.

```xml
<?xml version="1.0" encoding="utf-8"?>
<Web xmlns="http://schemas.microsoft.com/SharePoint/2009/spmetal">
  <ContentType Name="Contact" >
    <Column Name="CreatedBy" />
    <Column Name="ModifiedBy"/>
  </ContentType>
</Web>
```

Adding References in VS

Once you have your generated SPMetal code imported into VS, it's time to make sure you have the right references set up to use that code. You will want to add two references at a minimum. The first is a reference to `Microsoft.SharePoint`, which is the general SharePoint namespace. The second is a reference to the specific SharePoint LINQ assembly using `Microsoft.SharePoint.Linq`. This will add all the necessary dependent LINQ assemblies to your project.

Working with DataContext Object

The `DataContext` object is the object that provides the heart of your LINQ programming. Your `DataContext` object will be named whatever you named the beginning of your generated file from SPMetal. For example, if you had SPMetal create a `LINQDemo.cs` file for your outputted code, your `DataContext` object will be `LINQDemoDataContext`. To create your `DataContext` object, you can pass along the URL of the SharePoint site to which you want to connect.

Once you have your `DataContext` object, you can start working with the methods and properties of that object. The `DataContext` will contain all your lists and libraries as `EntityList` properties. You can retrieve these lists and libraries and then work with them. Table 4-12 lists the other methods and properties you will use from the `DataContext` object.

TABLE 4-12: Common Methods and Properties on DataContext Object

NAME	DESCRIPTION
`GetList<T>`	Returns the list of the specified type, for example, `GetList<AnnouncementsItems>("Announcements")`
`Refresh`	Refreshes the datasource.
`RegisterList`	Allows you to register a list by registering a new name and new URL (if needed) as a replacement for the old name. This is helpful if a list has been renamed or moved and you do not want to rewrite your code.

continues

TABLE 4-12 *(continued)*

NAME	DESCRIPTION
ChangeConflicts	Returns a `ChangeConflictCollection`, which is a list of conflicts from your transactions.
DeferredLoadingEnabled	Boolean that gets or sets whether LINQ should defer loading your objects until they are needed.
Log	Gets or sets the CAML query generated by LINQ. This is a good way to view what LINQ is generating on your behalf.
ObjectTrackingEnabled	Gets or sets whether changes to objects are tracked. If you are just querying your site, for performance reasons, you should set this to false.
Web	Gets the full URL of the SharePoint website the `DataContext` object is connected to.

Typed Data Classes and Relationships

As part of SPMetal, you will get autogenerated typed data classes and relationships using the `Association` attribute. This allows you to use strongly typed objects for your lists and also to do queries across multiple lists that are related by lookup fields. As you will see in the examples, this makes programming much cleaner and also allows you catch compile-time errors when working with your objects, rather than runtime errors.

Querying Data, Enumerating, and Inefficient Queries

To query and enumerate your data, you need to write LINQ queries. When you write your queries, you need to understand that LINQ translates the query into CAML, so if you try to perform LINQ queries that cannot be translated into CAML, SharePoint will throw an error. SharePoint considers these inefficient queries, and the only way to work around them is to use LINQ to Objects and perform the work yourself. The following is a list of the unsupported operators that SharePoint will error on:

- ➤ Aggregate
- ➤ All
- ➤ Any
- ➤ Average
- ➤ Distinct
- ➤ ElementAt
- ➤ ElementAtOrDefault
- ➤ Except

- Intersect
- Join (in complex instances)
- Max
- Min
- Reverse
- SequenceEqual
- Skip
- SkipWhile
- Sum

The simplest query you can write is a `select` from your list. The following code performs a `select` from a list and then enumerates the results:

```
var context = new LinqDemoDataContext("http://intranet.contoso.com");
var orderresults = from orders in context.Orders
                        select orders;

foreach (var order in orderresults)
{
    MessageBox.Show(order.Title + " " + order.Customer);
}
```

As you can see in the code, you first need to get your `DataContext` object. From there, you define your LINQ query as you do against any other datasource. Once you have the results, you can enumerate them using a `foreach` loop. If you want, you can also use the `ToList` method to return a generic list that you can perform LINQ to Object operations on.

You can add `where` clauses to your queries to perform selection. For example, if in the query above you wanted to select only orders that were more than $1000 dollars, you would change the query to the following one:

```
var orderresults = from orders in context.Orders
                        where orders.Total > 1000
                        select orders;
```

For the next example, the query will perform a simple INNER join between two lists that share a lookup field. Since CAML now supports joins, this is supported in LINQ as well. A couple of things to note. First, you'll notice that you get the `EntityList` objects for the two lists that you will join, so you can use them in the query. Then, in the query, you just use the join operator to join the two lists together on a lookup field. From there, the code uses the `ToList` method on the query results so that you can get back a LINQ to Object collection that you can iterate over.

```
var context = new LinqDemoDataContext("http://intranet.contoso.com");


EntityList<OrdersItem> Orders = context.GetList<OrdersItem>("Orders");
```

```
            EntityList<CustomersItem> Customers = context.GetList<CustomersItem>
("Customers");

            var QueryResults = from Order in Orders
                               join Customer in Customers on Order.Customer.Id
equals Customer.Id
                               select new { CustomerName = Customer.Title,
Order.Title, Order.Product };

            var Results = QueryResults.ToList();
            if (Results.Count > 0)
            {

                Results.ForEach(result => MessageBox.Show(result.Title + " " +
result.CustomerName + " " + result.Product));
            }
            else
            {
                MessageBox.Show("No results");
            }


            }
```

Adding, Updating, and Deleting Data and Dealing with Conflicts

LINQ allows you to add, delete, and update your data in SharePoint. Since LINQ is strongly typed, you can just create new objects that map to the type of the new objects you want to add. Once the new object is created, you can call the InsertOnSubmit method and pass the new object or the InsertAllOnSubmit method and pass a collection of new objects. Since LINQ works asynchronously from the server with a local cache, you need to call SubmitChanges after all modifications to data through LINQ.

To update items, it's a matter of updating the properties on your objects and then calling SubmitChanges. For deleting, you need to call DeleteOnSubmit or DeleteAllOnSubmit, passing either the object or a collection of objects, and then call SubmitChanges.

Since LINQ does not directly work against the SharePoint store, changes could be made to the backend while your code is running. To handle this, SharePoint LINQ provides the ability to catch exceptions if duplicates are present, if conflicts are detected, or general exceptions. The code that follows shows how to code for all of these cases. One thing to note is that the code uses the ChangeConflict exception and then enumerates all the ObjectChangeConflict objects. Then, it looks through the MemberConflict objects, which contain the differences between the database fields and the LINQ object fields. Once you decide what to do about the discrepancies, you can resolve the changes with the ResolveAll method. The ResolveAll method takes a RefreshMode enumeration, which can contain one of three values: KeepChanges, KeepCurrentValues, or OverwriteCurrentValues. KeepChanges keeps the new values since retrieval, even if they are different than the database values, and keeps other values the same as the database. Another choice is KeepCurrentValues, which keeps the new values since retrieval, even if they are different from the database values and keeps other values the same as they were retrieved, even if they conflict with the database values. OverwriteCurrentValues keeps the values from the database and discards any changes since retrieval. You need to call `SubmitChanges` after resolving any conflicts to save changes.

```csharp
try
        {
                EntityList<OrdersItem> Orders =
    context.GetList<OrdersItem>("Orders");
                OrdersItem order = new OrdersItem();
                order.Title = "My LINQ new Order";
                order.Product = "Chai";

                //Add a lookup to Customers
                EntityList<CustomersItem> Customers =
    context.GetList<CustomersItem>("Customers");
                var CustomerTempItem = from Customer in Customers
                            where Customer.Title == "Contoso"
                            select Customer;

                CustomersItem CustomerItem = null;
                foreach (var Cust in CustomerTempItem)
                    CustomerItem = Cust;

                order.Customer = CustomerItem;

                Orders.InsertOnSubmit(order);
                context.SubmitChanges();

                //Delete the item
                Orders.DeleteOnSubmit(order);
                context.SubmitChanges();

        }
        catch (ChangeConflictException conflictException)
        {
                MessageBox.Show("A conflict occurred: " +
    conflictException.Message);
                foreach (ObjectChangeConflict Items in context.ChangeConflicts)
                {
                    foreach (MemberChangeConflict Fields in Items.MemberConflicts)
                    {
                        StringBuilder sb = new StringBuilder();
                        sb.AppendLine("Item Name: " + Fields.Member.Name);
                        sb.AppendLine("Original Value: " + Fields.OriginalValue);
                        sb.AppendLine("Database Value: " + Fields.DatabaseValue);
                        sb.AppendLine("Current Value: " + Fields.CurrentValue);
                        MessageBox.Show(sb.ToString());
                    }
                }

                //Force all changes
                context.ChangeConflicts.ResolveAll(RefreshMode.KeepChanges);
                context.SubmitChanges();

        }
```

```
        catch (SPDuplicateValuesFoundException duplicateException)
        {
            MessageBox.Show("Duplicate value found: " +
duplicateException.Message);
        }
        catch (SPException SharePointException)
        {
            MessageBox.Show("SharePoint Exception: " +
SharePointException.Message);
        }
        catch (Exception ex)
        {
            MessageBox.Show("Exception: " + ex.Message);
        }

    }
```

Inspecting the CAML Query

If you want to inspect the CAML query that LINQ is generating for you, you can use the Log property and set that to a TextWriter or an object that derives from the TextWriter object, such as a StreamWriter object. If you are writing a console application, the easiest way to set the Log property is to set it to the Console.Out property. From there, you can retrieve the CAML query that SharePoint LINQ would execute on your behalf. The following code shows how to write a log file for your LINQ query using the Log property, and then shows the CAML query that is generated by LINQ.

```
var context = new LinqDemoDataContext("http://intranet.contoso.com");

        context.Log = new StreamWriter(File.Open("C:\\SPLINQLog.txt",
FileMode.Create));


        EntityList<OrdersItem> Orders = context.GetList<OrdersItem>("Orders");
        EntityList<CustomersItem> Customers =
context.GetList<CustomersItem>("Customers");

        var QueryResults = from Order in Orders
                            join Customer in Customers on Order.Customer.Id
 equals Customer.Id
                            select new { CustomerName = Customer.Title,
 Order.Title, Order.Product };

        context.Log.WriteLine("Results :");

        var Results = QueryResults.ToList();
        if (Results.Count > 0)
        {

            Results.ForEach(result => context.Log.WriteLine(result.Title
```

```
             + " " + result.CustomerName + " " + result.Product));
                    }
                    else
                    {
                        context.Log.WriteLine("No results");
                    }

                    context.Log.Close();
                    context.Log = null;
```

OUTPUT:

```
<View><Query><Where><And><BeginsWith><FieldRef Name="ContentTypeId" /><Value
Type="ContentTypeId">0x0100</Value></BeginsWith><BeginsWith><FieldRef
Name="CustomerContentTypeId" /><Value
Type="Lookup">0x0100</Value></BeginsWith></And></Where><OrderBy
Override="TRUE" /></Query><ViewFields><FieldRef Name="CustomerTitle"
 /><FieldRef Name="Title" /><FieldRef Name="Product"
/></ViewFields><ProjectedFields><Field Name="CustomerTitle" Type="Lookup"
List="Customer" ShowField="Title" /><Field Name="CustomerContentTypeId"
Type="Lookup" List="Customer" ShowField="ContentTypeId"
/></ProjectedFields><Joins><Join Type="INNER" ListAlias="Customer"><!--List
Name: Customers--><Eq><FieldRef Name="Customer" RefType="ID" /><FieldRef
List="Customer" Name="ID" /></Eq></Join></Joins><RowLimit
Paged="TRUE">2147483647</RowLimit></View>
```

Best Practice: Turning off Object Change Tracking

One best practice is to turn off object tracking if you are just querying the list and are not planning to add, delete, or update items in the list. This will make your queries perform better, since LINQ will not have the overhead of trying to track changes to the SharePoint objects. The way to turn off object tracking is to set the ObjectTrackingEnabled property to false on your DataContext object.

If you do need to make changes to the list, you can open another DataContext object to the same list with object change tracking enabled. LINQ allows two DataContext objects to point at the same website and list, so you can have one DataContext object for querying and another for writing to the list.

When to Use CAML and LINQ

There are still definite times when you should revert to using CAML directly. One scenario is where performance is paramount. LINQ makes CAML programming much easier, but no matter how LINQ is optimized, it will add some overhead to your code. Another example is if you have large amounts of adds, deletes, or updates that you need to perform. CAML will provide better performance in this scenario.

Managed Client OM

If you wanted to program on the client side in SharePoint 2007, you had in reality one choice of API, which was the web services API. While functional, the web services API was not the easiest API to program against, and while it was easy to program the web services API from Windows

Forms, programming it from JavaScript or Silverlight was difficult at best. With the growth of client-side technologies, such as .NET CLR–based clients (e.g., Windows Presentation Framework (WPF) or Silverlight); new technologies for programming in JavaScript, such as JSON; and the introduction of REST, moving from the web services API to a richer API was sorely needed in SharePoint. Welcome the managed client object model, which this chapter refers to as the client object model.

The client OM is really two object models. One works with .NET-based clients, such as Windows Forms, WPF, or Silverlight, since these clients can handle the results in .NET objects, while ECMAScript/JavaScript will get back the JSON response. Figure 4-19 shows the way the client object model works.

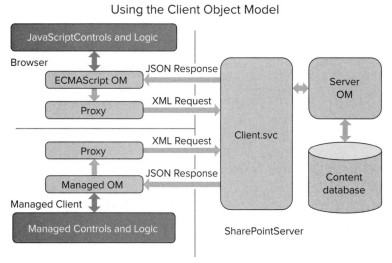

FIGURE 4-19

One principal of the client object model is to minimize network chatter. When working with the client OM, Fiddler will be a key tool to help you troubleshoot any issues, since the client OM batches together its commands and sends them all at once to the server at your request. This minimizes the round trips and network bandwidth used by the object model and will make your application perform better. In addition, you will want to write asynchronous code with callbacks when working with the client OM so that your user interface doesn't block when users perform actions, which is what they are used to when working with web-based applications.

In terms of API support, the client OM supports a subset of the server object model, so you will find access to lists, libraries, views, content types, web parts, and users/groups as part of the object model, but it does not have coverage of all features, such as the taxonomy store or BI. Figure 4-20 shows the major objects in the client OM.

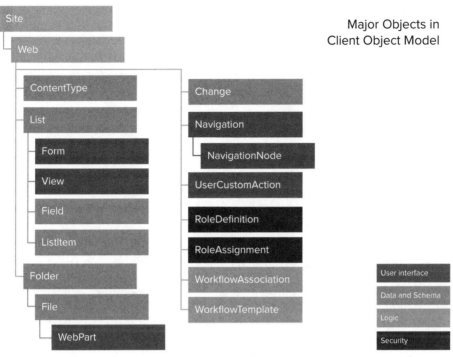

Major Objects in
Client Object Model

FIGURE 4-20

There is also a difference in the namespaces provided by the .NET and ECMAScript object models. Since you will extend the Ribbon using script, the ECMAScript OM has a Ribbon namespace, while the managed client OM does not. Plus, there is a difference in naming conventions for the foundational part of the namespaces. For example, if you wanted to access a site, in the .NET API you would use the `Microsoft.SharePoint.Client.Site` object, but in ECMAScript you would use `SP.Site`. Table 4-13 shows the different namespaces for the two client OMs.

TABLE 4-13: Supported Namespaces in Client OMs

.NET MANAGED	ECMASCRIPT
`Microsoft.SharePoint.Client.Application`	N/A
N/A	`SP.Application.UI`
N/A	`SP.Ribbon`
N/A	`SP.Ribbon.PageState`
N/A	`SP.Ribbon.TenantAdmin`
N/A	`SP.UI`

continues

TABLE 4-13 *(continued)*

.NET MANAGED	ECMASCRIPT
N/A	SP.UI.ApplicationPages
N/A	SP.UI.ApplicationPages.Calendar
Microosft.SharePoint.Client.Utilities	SP.Utilities
Microsoft.SharePoint.Client.WebParts	SP.WebParts
Microsoft.SharePoint.Client.Workflow	SP.Workflow

To show you how to map your understanding of server objects to the client, Table 4-14 shows how server objects would be named in the client OMs.

TABLE 4-14: Equivalent Objects in Server and Client OMs

SERVER OM	.NET MANAGED	ECMASCRIPT
Microsoft.SharePoint.SPContext	Microsoft.SharePoint.Client.ClientContext	SP.ClientContext
Microsoft.SharePoint.SPSite	Microsoft.SharePoint.Client.Site	SP.Site
Microsoft.SharePoint.SPWeb	Microsoft.SharePoint.Client.Web	SP.Web
Microsoft.SharePoint.SPList	Microsoft.SharePoint.Client.List	SP.List
Microsoft.SharePoint.SPListItem	Microsoft.SharePoint.Client.ListItem	SP.ListItem
Microsoft.SharePoint.SPField	Microsoft.SharePoint.Client.Field	SP.Field

Which DLLs Implement the Client OM

Before diving into writing code with the client OM and adding references in VS, you first need to understand where these DLLs are located and some of the advantages of the DLLs, especially size. As with other SharePoint .NET DLLs, you will find the .NET DLLs for the client OM located under `%Program Files%\Common Files\Microsoft Shared\Web Server Extensions\14\ISAPI`. There are two DLLs for the managed OM, `Microsoft.SharePoint.Client` and `Microsoft.SharePoint.Client.Runtime`. If you look at these DLLs in terms of size, combined they are under 1MB. Compare that with `Microsoft.SharePoint`, which weighs in at over a hefty 15MB.

Since the ECMAScript implementation is different from the .NET one and needs to live closer to the web-based code for SharePoint, this DLL is located in `%Program Files%\Common Files\ Microsoft Shared\Web Server Extensions\14\TEMPLATE\LAYOUTS`. There, you will find three relevant JS files, `SP.js`, `SP.Core.js`, `SP.Ribbon.js`, and `SP.Runtime.js`. Of course, when you are debugging your code, you will want to use the debug versions of these files, such as `SP.debug.js`, since the main versions are crunched to save on size and bandwidth. Also, you can set your SharePoint deployment to use the debug versions of these files automatically by changing the `web.config` file for your deployment located at `%inetpub%\wwwroot\wss\VirtualDirectories\80` and adding to the `system.web` section the following line `<deployment retail="false" />`. Again, these files are less than 1MB.

Lastly, Silverlight is a little bit different in that it has its own implementation of the client OM for Silverlight specifically. You can find the Silverlight DLLs at `%Program Files%\Common Files\ Microsoft Shared\Web Server Extensions \14\TEMPLATE\LAYOUTS\ClientBin`. You will find two files, `Microsoft.SharePoint.Client.Silverlight` and `Microsoft.SharePoint.Client .Silverlight.Runtime`. Combined the files also come under 1MB in size.

Microsoft is finalizing the distribution of these files, since on client machines you may need to be able to distribute the files, depending on whether the machine has the required DLLs already installed from other applications, such as Microsoft Office 2010. Until this is finalized, for your development machines, you can either develop on your server or copy the correct files to your development machine.

Adding References Inside VS

Depending on the type of application you are writing, the way you reference the different client OMs will vary. With WPF or WinForms, you use the VS Add Reference user interface to add a reference to the DLLs discussed earlier. From there, you can use the proper statements to leverage the namespaces in your code. The same process is true for Silverlight. Figure 4-21 shows adding a reference inside of Visual Studio.

When it comes to the ECMAScript object model, the way you will reference this is by using the `ScriptLink` control, which is part of the `Microsoft.SharePoint.WebControls` namespace, to add a reference to the ECMAScript files. The following code snippet shows you how to do this:

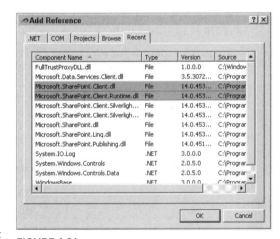

FIGURE 4-21

```
<SharePoint:ScriptLink ID="ScriptLinkSPDebug" Name="sp.debug.js"
LoadAfterUI="true" Localizable="false" runat="server" />
```

Authentication

Before you write your first line of code, you need to understand the context your code will run in. With the client OM, by default, your code will run in the context of the Windows authenticated user. Since many web applications support forms-based authentication, the client OM supports this as well. You will have to provide the username and password for the client OM to use and also set the authentication mode to forms-based authentication on your `ClientContext` object. The following code shows you how to set the client OM to use forms-based authentication and set the correct properties to send a username and password:

```
clientContext.AuthenticationMode = ClientAuthenticationMode.FormsAuthentication;
 FormsAuthenticationLoginInfo formsAuthInfo = new
FormsAuthenticationLoginInfo("User", "Password");
clientContext.FormsAuthenticationLoginInfo = formsAuthInfo;
```

ClientContext Object

At the heart of all your code is the `ClientContext` object. This is the object that you will instantiate first to tell SharePoint what site you want to connect to in order to perform your operations. With the .NET API, you must pass an absolute URL to the client context in order to open your site, but with the ECMAScript API, you can pass a relative or blank URL in your constructor and SharePoint will either find the relative site or use the current site as the site you want to open.

One quick note on `ClientContext` is that, if you look at the implementation, you will notice that it inherits from `IDisposable`. This means that you will want to properly dispose of your `ClientContext` objects either by wrapping your code with using statements or by calling `Dispose` explicitly. If you don't dispose correctly, you may run into memory leaks and issues.

Looking at the constructor for the `ClientContext`, you can pass in either a string that is the URL to your site or a URI object that contains the URL to your site.

Table 4-15 shows the important methods and properties for the `ClientContext` class.

TABLE 4-15: Methods and Properties for the ClientContext Class

NAME	DESCRIPTION
Dispose	Call this method to dispose of your object after you are done using it.
ExecuteQuery	After loading all the operations for your site, such as queries, call this method to send the commands to the server.
executeQueryAsync	Available in the ECMAScript object model, this allows you to call a query and pass two delegates to call back to. One is for when the query succeeds and the other is used when the query fails.

NAME	DESCRIPTION
Load	Allows you to load your query using the method syntax of LINQ and will fill the object you pass. You can also just pass an object without a query to return just the object, such as `Site`.
LoadQuery	Use this to return a collection of objects as an `IQueryable` collection. This supports both the method and query syntax for LINQ.
AuthenticationMode	Gets or sets the authentication mode for your object. The values can be `Default`, `FormsAutentication`, or `Anonymous`.
FormsAuthenticationLoginInfo	Use this property to set the username and password for your forms authentication to authenticate against your site.
RequestTimeout	Get or set the timeout for your requests.
Site	Gets the site collection associated with the `ClientContext`.
URL	Gets the URL of the site that the `ClientContext` is associated with.
Web	Gets the website that the `ClientContext` is associated with.

As you will see in the sample code throughout this section, you will use the `Load` or `LoadQuery` method on the `ClientContext` object and then call the `ExecuteQuery` or `executeQueryAsync` method to execute your query. The rest of this section goes through the different programming tasks you will want to perform with the client OM, to show you how to use it.

Retrieving Items from SharePoint

To retrieve items from SharePoint, the easiest way to get back your list is to just use the `Load` method to load the object into the client OM. For example, if you wanted to load a `Web` object into the client OM and then access the properties from it, you would use the following code.

```
ClientContext context = new Microsoft.SharePoint.Client.ClientContext(
        "http://intranet.contoso.com");
            Web site = context.Web;
            context.Load(site);
            context.ExecuteQuery();
            MessageBox.Show("Title: " + site.Title + " Relative URL: " +
  site.ServerRelativeUrl);
context.Dispose();
```

One thing to note is that if you try to use any of the other objects below the requested site, you will get an error saying that the collection is not initialized. For example, if you try to retrieve the lists in the site, you will get an error. With the client OM, you need to be explicit about what you want to load. The following modified sample shows you how to load the list collection and then iterate over the objects in the collection:

```
//Load the List Collection
            ListCollection lists = context.Web.Lists;
            context.Load(lists);
            context.ExecuteQuery();

            MessageBox.Show(lists.Count.ToString());

            foreach (Microsoft.SharePoint.Client.List list in lists)
            {
                MessageBox.Show("List: " + list.Title);
            }
```

Properties Returned and Requesting Properties

By default, SharePoint will return a large set of properties and hydrate your objects with these properties. For performance reasons, you may not want to have it do that if you are only using a subset of the properties. Plus, certain properties are not returned by default, such as permission properties for your objects. As a best practice, you should request the properties that you need rather than letting SharePoint retrieve all properties for you. This is similar to the best practice of not doing a SELECT * in SQL Server.

The way to request properties is in your load method. As part of this method, you need to request the properties you want to use in your LINQ code. The following example changes the previous site request code to retrieve only the Title and ServerRelativeURL properties, and for our lists only the Title property, since that is all we use in the code.

```
ClientContext context = new Microsoft.SharePoint.Client.ClientContext(
"http://intranet.contoso.com");

            Web site = context.Web;
            context.Load(site, s => s.Title, s => s.ServerRelativeUrl);
            ListCollection lists = site.Lists;
            context.Load(lists, ls => ls.Include(l => l.Title));

            context.ExecuteQuery();



            MessageBox.Show("Title: " + site.Title + " Relative URL: " +
        site.ServerRelativeUrl);



            MessageBox.Show(lists.Count.ToString());
```

```
foreach (Microsoft.SharePoint.Client.List list in lists)
{
    MessageBox.Show("List: " + list.Title);
}


context.Dispose();
```

Load vs. LoadQuery

You may be wondering what the difference is between Load and LoadQuery. Load hydrates the objects in-context, so if you pass a Web object to your Load method, SharePoint will fill in that object with the properties of your SharePoint web. LoadQuery does not fill in the objects in-context, so it returns an entirely new collection. The LoadQuery method is more complex, but it also is more flexible. In certain cases, it allows the server to be more effective in processing your queries. Plus, you can query the same object collection multiple times and have different result sets for each query. For example, you can have one query that returns all lists with a certain title, while another collection returns lists with a certain number of items. You can destroy these objects also out of context. With the Load method, the objects are tied to the client context, so they are only destroyed and are eligible for garbage collection when the client context is destroyed.

The LoadQuery method is very similar to the Load method, except that it returns a new collection. The other key difference is that the properties for objects off the client context are not populated with LoadQuery after your LoadQuery call. You need to call Load method to populate these. The following code shows you a good example of this:

```
ClientContext context = new Microsoft.SharePoint.Client.ClientContext(
"http://intranet.contoso.com");

Web site = context.Web;
ListCollection lists = site.Lists;


IEnumerable<List> newLists = context.LoadQuery(lists.Include(
 list => list.Title));
context.ExecuteQuery();

foreach (List list in newLists)
{
    MessageBox.Show("Title: " + list.Title);
}

//This will error out because lists is not populated
MessageBox.Show(lists.Count.ToString());

context.Dispose();
```

Nesting Includes in your LoadQuery

In your `LoadQuery` calls, you can nest `Include` statements so that you can load fields from multiple objects in the hierarchy without making multiple calls to the server. The following code shows how to do this:

```
ClientContext context = new Microsoft.SharePoint.Client.ClientContext(
  "http://intranet.contoso.com");

            Web site = context.Web;
            ListCollection lists = site.Lists;


            IEnumerable<List> newLists = context.LoadQuery(lists.Include(
        list => list.Title, list => list.Fields.Include(Field => Field.Title)));
            context.ExecuteQuery();

            foreach (List list in newLists)
            {
                MessageBox.Show(" List Title: " + list.Title);
                foreach (Field field in list.Fields)
                {
                    MessageBox.Show("Field Title: " + field.Title);
                }
            }

            context.Dispose();
```

Using CAML to Query Lists

In the client OM, you can use CAML to query the server as part of the `GetItems` method. As you see in the code that follows, you create a new `CamlQuery` object and pass into the `ViewXml` property the CAML query that you want to perform. From there, you call the `GetItems` on your `ListCollection` object and pass in your `CamlQuery` object. You still need to call the `Load` and `ExecuteQuery` methods to have the client object model perform your query. Also, CAML does support row limits, so you can also pass a `<RowLimit>` element in your CAML query and page over your results. In the OM, on the `ListItemCollection` object, there is a property `ListItemCollectionPosition`. You need to set your `CAMLQuery` object's `ListItemCollectionPosition` to your own `ListItemCollectionPosition` object to keep track of your paging and then you can position your query starting point before querying the list, and iterate through the pages until there are no pages of content left, as shown here:

```
        ClientContext context = new Microsoft.SharePoint.Client.ClientContext(
    "http://intranet.contoso.com");


        List list = context.Web.Lists.GetByTitle("Announcements");

        ListItemCollectionPosition itemPosition = null;
        while (true)
        {
```

```
CamlQuery camlQuery = new CamlQuery();
camlQuery.ListItemCollectionPosition = itemPosition;
camlQuery.ViewXml = @"
    <View>
        <Query>
            <Where>
                <IsNotNull>
                    <FieldRef Name='Title' />
                </IsNotNull>
            </Where>
        </Query>
        <RowLimit>1000</RowLimit>
    </View>";
ListItemCollection listItems = list.GetItems(camlQuery);
context.Load(listItems);
context.ExecuteQuery();

itemPosition = listItems.ListItemCollectionPosition;

foreach (ListItem listItem in listItems.ToList())
{
    MessageBox.Show("Title: " + listItem["Title"]);
}


if (itemPosition == null)
{
    break;
}

MessageBox.Show("Position: " + itemPosition.PagingInfo);

}
```

Using LINQ with Queries

If you don't want to use CAML to query your lists, you can also use LINQ to query your lists. To do this, you create your query and put it in a variable. Next, using the LoadQuery method you pass your LINQ query. Then, you can call the ExecuteQuery method to execute your query and iterate through the results.

```
ClientContext context = new Microsoft.SharePoint.Client.ClientContext(
"http://intranet.contoso.com");

var query = from list
            in context.Web.Lists
            where list.Title != null
            select list;

var result = context.LoadQuery(query);
context.ExecuteQuery();

foreach (List list in result)
```

```
{
    MessageBox.Show("Title: " + list.Title);
}

context.Dispose();
```

Creating Lists, Fields, and Items

Using the client OM, you can create lists and items. To do this, you need to use the ListCreationInformation object and set the properties for your list, such as the title and the type. Your ListCollection object has an Add method that you can call and pass your ListCreationInformation object to in order to create your list.

To create a field, use the Fields collection for your list and define the XML in the AddFieldAsXml property. This property takes your XML, a Boolean that specifies whether to add the field to the default view, and AddFieldOptions, such as adding the field to the default content type.

Once you have added your field, you can create list items by first creating a ListItemCreation Information object, and pass that to the AddItem method, which will return a ListItem object representing your new item. Using this object, you can set the properties for your item. Make sure to call the Update method when you are done modifying your properties.

When you are done with all your changes, make sure to call the ExecuteQuery method to have the client OM send your changes back to the server.

```
ClientContext context = new Microsoft.SharePoint.Client.ClientContext
("http://intranet.contoso.com");
        Web site = context.Web;

        ListCreationInformation listCreationInfo = new
ListCreationInformation();

        listCreationInfo.Title = "New List";
        listCreationInfo.TemplateType = (int)ListTemplateType.GenericList;
        List list = site.Lists.Add(listCreationInfo);

        Field newField = list.Fields.AddFieldAsXml(@"
            <Field Type='Text'
                DisplayName='NewTextField'>
            </Field>", true, AddFieldOptions.AddToDefaultContentType);

        ListItemCreationInformation itemCreationinfo = new
ListItemCreationInformation();
        ListItem item = list.AddItem(itemCreationinfo);
        item["Title"] = "My New Item";
        item["NewTextField"] = "My Text";
        item.Update();


        context.ExecuteQuery();

        context.Dispose();
```

Deleting Lists and Items

To delete lists and items, you can use the `DeleteObject` method. One caveat is that when you are deleting items from a collection, you will want to materialize your collection into a `List<T>` object, using the `ToList` method, so you can iterate through the list and delete without errors.

```
ClientContext context = new Microsoft.SharePoint.Client.ClientContext(
"http://intranet.contoso.com");

List list = context.Web.Lists.GetByTitle("New List");

CamlQuery camlQuery = new CamlQuery();

camlQuery.ViewXml = @"
    <View>
        <Query>
            <Where>
                <IsNotNull>
                    <FieldRef Name='Title' />
                </IsNotNull>
            </Where>
        </Query>
    </View>";
ListItemCollection listItems = list.GetItems(camlQuery);

context.Load(listItems, items => items.Include(item => item["Title"]));
context.ExecuteQuery();
foreach (ListItem listItem in listItems.ToList())
{
    listItem.DeleteObject();
}

context.ExecuteQuery();
context.Dispose();
```

Working with Users and Groups

Another feature of the client OM, beyond working with lists, libraries, and items, is the ability to work with users and groups. The client OM includes the `GroupCollection`, `Group`, `UserCollection`, and `User` objects to make working with users and groups easier. Just as you iterate on lists and items, you can iterate on users and groups using these collections. The client OM also has access to built-in groups such as the owners, members, and visitors groups. You can access these off your context object using the `AssociatedOwnerGroup`, `AssociatedMemberGroup`, and `AssociatedVisitorGroup` properties, which return a `Group` object. Remember to hydrate these objects before trying to access properties or `User` collections on the objects.

To add a user to a group, you use the `UserCreationInformation` object and set the properties on that object, such as `Title`, `LoginName`, and other properties. Then, you call the `Add` method on your `UserCollection` object to add the user, and `ExecuteQuery` to submit the changes. Since this is very similar to the steps to create items, the sample code that follows shows you how to query users and groups but not create users.

```
ClientContext context = new Microsoft.SharePoint.Client.ClientContext(
"http://intranet.contoso.com");

            GroupCollection groupCollection = context.Web.SiteGroups;

            context.Load(groupCollection,
                groups => groups.Include(
                    group => group.Users));

            context.ExecuteQuery();

            foreach (Group group in groupCollection)
            {

                UserCollection userCollection = group.Users;

                foreach (User user in userCollection)
                {
                    MessageBox.Show("User Name: " + user.Title + " Email: " +
    user.Email + " Login: " + user.LoginName);


                }
            }
            //Iterate the owners group
            Group ownerGroup = context.Web.AssociatedOwnerGroup;

            context.Load(ownerGroup);
            context.Load(ownerGroup.Users);
            context.ExecuteQuery();
            foreach (User ownerUser in ownerGroup.Users)
            {
                MessageBox.Show("User Name: " + ownerUser.Title + " Email: " +
    ownerUser.Email + " Login: " + ownerUser.LoginName);
            }

            context.Dispose();
```

Working Asynchronously

All of the code so far that we have looked at is synchronous code running in a .NET client, such as a WPF, console, or Windows Forms application. You may not want to write synchronous code, even in your .NET clients, so your application can be more responsive to your users, rather than having them wait for operations to complete before continuing to use your application. ECMAScript and Silverlight are asynchronous by default, so you will see how to program them separately, but for .NET clients, you need to do a little bit of work to make your code asynchronous. The main change is that you need to use the `BeginInvoke` method to execute your code and pass a delegate to that method, which .NET will call back on when your code is done executing asynchronously. Then, you can do other work while you are polling to see if the asynchronous call is complete. Once it's complete, you call the `EndInvoke` method to get back the result.

```
public delegate string AsyncDelegate();

    public string TestMethod()
    {
        string titleReturn = "";
        using (ClientContext context = new
Microsoft.SharePoint.Client.ClientContext("http://intranet.contoso.com"))
        {
            List list = context.Web.Lists.GetByTitle("Announcements");
            context.Load(list);
            context.ExecuteQuery();
            titleReturn = list.Title;
        }
        return titleReturn;
    }

    private void button1_Click(object sender, EventArgs e)
    {

        // Create the delegate.
        AsyncDelegate dlgt = new AsyncDelegate(TestMethod);

        // Initiate the asychronous call.
        IAsyncResult ar = dlgt.BeginInvoke(null, null);

        // Poll while simulating work.
        while (ar.IsCompleted == false)
        {
            //Do work
        }

        // Call EndInvoke to retrieve the results.
        string listTitle = dlgt.EndInvoke(ar);

        //Print out the title of the list
        MessageBox.Show(listTitle);
```

Working with ECMAScript

Using ECMAScript with the client object model is very similar to the .NET object model. The main differences are that you use server-relative URLs for your ClientContext constructor and the ECMAScript object model does not accept LINQ syntax for retrieving items from SharePoint. Instead, you will use string expressions to define your basic queries. Also, ECMAScript is always asynchronous, so you have to use delegates and create callback functions for the success and failure of your call into the client OM. The final piece, as you see in the code that follows, is that you need to reference the WebControls namespace from the Microsoft.SharePoint assembly, reference the ECMAScript client OM in SP.js or SP.debug.js, using a SharePoint:ScriptLink control, and finally put a SharePoint:FormDigest on your page for security reasons, if you want to be able to write or update to the SharePoint database.

```
<%@ Page Language="C#" %>
<%@ Register Tagprefix="SharePoint"
    Namespace="Microsoft.SharePoint.WebControls"
    Assembly="Microsoft.SharePoint, Version=14.0.0.0, Culture=neutral,
PublicKeyToken=71e9bce111e9429c" %>

<!DOCTYPE html PUBLIC "-//W3C//DTD XHTML 1.0 Transitional//EN"
"http://www.w3.org/TR/xhtml1/DTD/xhtml1-transitional.dtd">
<html xmlns="http://www.w3.org/1999/xhtml">
  <head>
    <title>ECMAScript Client OM</title>
      <script type="text/javascript">


            function CallClientOM() {
                var context = new SP.ClientContext.get_current();
                this.website = context.get_web();
                this.listCollection = website.get_lists();

                context.load(this.listCollection, 'Include(Title, Id)');
                context.executeQueryAsync(Function.createDelegate(this,
    this.onQuerySucceeded), Function.createDelegate(this, this.onQueryFailed));
            }


            function onQuerySucceeded(sender, args) {

            var listInfo = '';

            var listEnumerator = listCollection.getEnumerator();

            while (listEnumerator.moveNext())
            {
                var list = listEnumerator.get_current();
                listInfo += 'List Title: ' + list.get_title() + ' ID: ' +
    list.get_id() + '\n';
            }
        alert(listInfo);


            }

            function onQueryFailed(sender, args) {
                alert('request failed ' + args.get_message() + '\n' +
    args.get_stackTrace());
            }

        </script>
  </head>
  <body>
    <form id="form1" runat="server">
      <SharePoint:ScriptLink ID="ScriptLink1" Name="sp.debug.js" LoadAfterUI="true"
```

```
    Localizable="false" runat="server" />

<a href="#" onclick="CallClientOM()">Click here to Execute</a>

        <SharePoint:FormDigest runat="server" />
    </form>
  </body>
</html>
```

ClientOM.aspx

Working in Silverlight

Working with Silverlight is also similar to working with the .NET client, except for two major differences. First is that you will want to perform all your operations asynchronously, so this requires you to create delegates and program success and failure methods. Second, since your code runs on a background thread, you will need to get on the user interface thread before you attempt to write to the UI. The easiest way to do this is to wrap your code with the BeginInvoke method of the Dispatcher object. This method guarantees that your code will run on the Silverlight UI thread. If you do not do this, you will receive a threading error. One other thing to remember is to use the right client OM DLLs. Silverlight has special DLLs in the %Program Files%\Common Files\ Microsoft Shared\Web Server Extensions\14\TEMPLATE\LAYOUTS\ClientBin directory for the core OM and the runtime.

The last bit you need to know about Silverlight is how to get your applications deployed. They need to run in a trusted area of SharePoint, which could be in a SharePoint library or in the ClientBin directory. For the ClientBin, the easiest way to get your code there is to make the output of your project go to this directory. For deploying to SharePoint document libraries, you could manually upload your XAP file to SharePoint and point the Silverlight Web Part at your manually uploaded XAP. Another way is to use a Sandbox Solution, which you will learn about later, to create a feature that copies the file up to your SharePoint site using a Module with a File reference in your Elements manifest.

One thing to watch out for is caching of your Silverlight application while you are developing it. Make sure that an old version is not loaded by updating the AssemblyVersion and FileVersion in your AssemblyInfo file in VS. You may also have to clear your browser cache. Another recommendation is to change something in the UI to make sure that your application is the latest; this allows you to tell visually.

Also, if you are working across domains, you will need to understand how to create cross-domain policies using a ClientAccessPolicy.XML file that you host at the root of your website. If you are working in the same domain, you do not have to write this policy file, but if you go across domains (for example, if your Silverlight application runs in your domain but calls a service in another domain) you will have to use the ClientAccessPolicy.XML file to allow those calls. Figure 4-22 shows the Silverlight application in action.

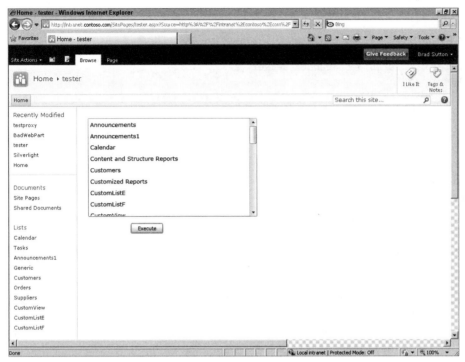

FIGURE 4-22

```
using SP = Microsoft.SharePoint.Client;

namespace SPSilverlight
{
    public partial class MainPage : UserControl
    {

        IEnumerable<SP.List> listItems = null;
        public MainPage()
        {
            InitializeComponent();
        }

        private void getItemsSucceeded(object sender,
    Microsoft.SharePoint.Client.ClientRequestSucceededEventArgs e)
        {
            Dispatcher.BeginInvoke(() =>
            {
                //Code to display items
                //Databind the List of Lists to the listbox

                listBox1.ItemsSource = listItems;
                listBox1.DisplayMemberPath = "Title";
            });
```

```
        }

        private void getItemsRequestFailed(object sender,
Microsoft.SharePoint.Client.ClientRequestFailedEventArgs e)
        {
            Dispatcher.BeginInvoke(() =>
            {
                MessageBox.Show("Error:  " + e.ErrorCode + " " + e.ErrorDetails + "
" + e.Message + " " + e.StackTrace.ToString());
            });
        }

        private void button1_Click(object sender, RoutedEventArgs e)
        {

            ClientContext context = null;

            if (App.Current.IsRunningOutOfBrowser)
            {
                context = new ClientContext(
                    "http://intranet.contoso.com");
            }
            else
            {
                context = ClientContext.Current;
            }

            var query = from listCollection
        in context.Web.Lists
                        where listCollection.Title != null
                        select listCollection;

            listItems = context.LoadQuery(query);


            ClientRequestSucceededEventHandler success = new
ClientRequestSucceededEventHandler(getItemsSucceeded);
            ClientRequestFailedEventHandler failure = new
ClientRequestFailedEventHandler(getItemsRequestFailed);
            context.ExecuteQueryAsync(success, failure);


        }

    }
}
```

MainPage.xaml.cs

Programming Using REST

With SharePoint 2010, you can program against SharePoint and Excel Services using
Representational State Transfer (REST). This section covers the core SharePoint REST Services.

SharePoint REST services are implemented using the ADO.NET Data Services, formerly known as Astoria. If you don't know what REST is, the easiest way to think about REST is that it provides URL-accessible functionality, so you can query, create, and delete lists and items using just the standard HTTP protocol.

Here are a couple of best practices before getting started with REST in SharePoint 2010. First, you will want to make sure you install the ADO.NET data services on the SharePoint 2010 Server where you are developing using REST. REST is implemented in your `_vti_bin` directory by accessing `http://yourserver/_vti_bin/ListData.svc`, so if you connect to that URL and get a 404 error, you do not have the ADO.NET Data Services technologies installed. Second, if you are connecting to your REST services for SharePoint from Internet Explorer (IE), you will want to turn off Feed Reading View in IE so that you get the raw XML returned from SharePoint. You can find this under Tools ➪ Internet Options ➪ Content ➪ Feeds and Web Slices.

The easiest way to get started with REST in SharePoint is to look at what is returned when you connect to `http://yourserver/yoursite/_vti_bin/ListData.svc`, as shown in Figure 4-23. You will see the XML returned for all your lists in your site.

FIGURE 4-23

If you have never worked with REST before, there are two ways in SharePoint that you can return your data. First, there is ATOM, which returns XML and is a standard. Then, there is JavaScript Object Notation (JSON), which returns your data using JSON markup so that you can parse that data using JavaScript objects. JSON is good if you want to turn the returned data into Javascript objects. You can specify the type of data you want returned by using the `Content-Type` header in your request. The tools that work with REST, such as Visual Studio, use ATOM, not JSON, so you need to request JSON specifically if you want your results in that format.

Since REST uses a standard URL-addressable format and uses standard HTTP methods, such as `GET`, `POST`, `PUT`, and `DELETE`, you get a predictable way to retrieve or write items in your SharePoint deployment. Table 4-16 lists some examples of URL addresses.

TABLE 4-16: Methods and Properties for the ClientContext Class

TYPE	EXAMPLE
List of Lists	`../_vti_bin/listdata.svc`
List	`listdata.svc/Listname`
Item	`listdata.svc/Listname(ItemID)`
Single Column	`listdata.svc/Listname(ItemID)/Column`
Lookup Traversal	`listdata.svc/Listname(ItemID)/LookupColumn`
Raw Value Access (no markup)	`listdata.svc/Listname(ItemID)/Column/$value`
Sorting	`listdata.svc/Listname?$orderby=Column`
Filtering	`listdata.svc/Listname?$filter=Title eq 'Value'`
Projection	`listdata.svc/Listname?$select=Title,Created`
Paging	`listdata.svc/Listname?$top=10&$skip=30`
Inline Expansion (Lookups)	`listdata.svc/Listname?$expand=Item`

Using REST in Visual Studio

Since Visual Studio has built-in support for using ADO.NET Data Services, programming with REST starts with adding a service reference in your code. In this reference, point to your `ListData.svc` URL in `_vti_bin`. Please note that in the beta, you will have to change the reference VS adds from `System.Data.Service.Client` to `Microsoft.Data.Services.Client` by removing the reference and adding a new reference to `%Program Files (x86)\ADO.NET Data Services V1.5 CTP2\bin`. Then, you will have to create new proxy classes by running in a command prompt `DataSvcUtil.exe /uri:"http://URL/_vti_bin/ListData.svc" /out:Reference.cs`. This will create a C# file that you will use to replace the existing `Reference.cs` in your project, which you will find in the file directory for your project, not in the user interface, unless you turn on Show All Files in Solution Explorer.

From there, you should see your lists in the Data Source window inside of Visual Studio, as shown in Figure 4-24. If you do not see your datasource in the window, right-click your service reference and select Update Service Reference. You will have to go back and change the `System.Data` `.Services.Client` reference again to `Microsoft.Data.Services.Client`.

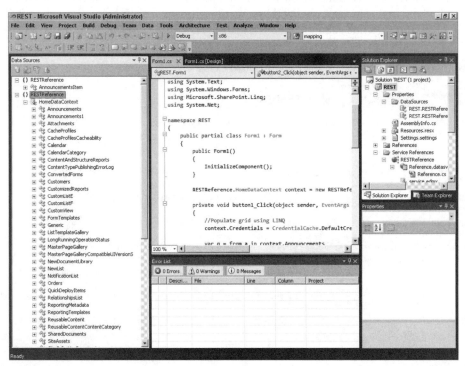

FIGURE 4-24

From there, you can add a new `Object` datasource to your project, so you can work with a subset of the lists, such as binding the datasource to a datagrid in your code. You can do this by creating a new `Object` datasource and selecting the lists you are interested in, as shown in Figure 4-25.

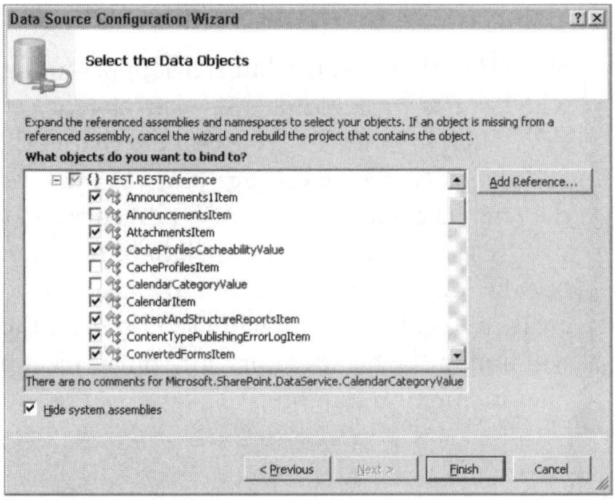

You can drag and drop your datasource onto your form, and Visual Studio will create and bind a grid to your datasource. You can also use LINQ to program against your REST datasource. Figure 4-26 shows a databound grid against a SharePoint REST datasource.

FIGURE 4-25

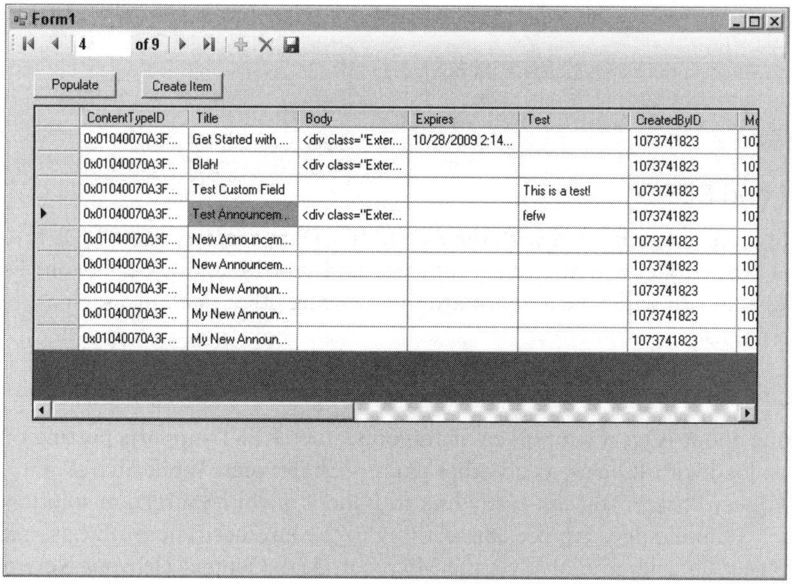

FIGURE 4-26

Since the code for programming using REST is very similar to programming using the rest of the client OM, there is a quick example below of adding an item to your SharePoint list using REST. You will notice a call to generate a context for the rest of your calls to leverage so that you can batch commands and send them to server when you need to. For adding, you call the specific `AddTo` method for your list, such as `AddToAnnouncements`. For updating and deleting, you use the `UpdateObject` and `DeleteObject` methods and pass in the object you want to delete, which is derived from your item type, such as `AnnouncementItem`.

```
RESTReference.HomeDataContext context = new RESTReference.HomeDataContext(
new Uri("http://intranet.contoso.com/_vti_bin/listdata.svc"));

        private void button1_Click(object sender, EventArgs e)
        {
            //Populate grid using LINQ
            context.Credentials = CredentialCache.DefaultCredentials;

            var q = from a in context.Announcements
                    select a;

            this.announcementsItemBindingSource.DataSource = q;
        }

        private void button2_Click(object sender, EventArgs e)
        {
            //Add a new Announcement
            RESTReference.AnnouncementsItem newAnnounce = new
    RESTReference.AnnouncementsItem();
```

```
        newAnnounce.Title = "My New Announcement! " + DateTime.Now.ToString();

        context.AddToAnnouncements(newAnnounce);
        context.SaveChanges();
    }
```

External List Support and REST

Unfortunately, external lists are not supported with the ADO.NET Data Services and REST. If you look at your lists using REST, you will find that your external lists will not appear in your list results. This is a deficiency that you will have to work around by using other methods, such as the client OM, to access external lists.

JQuery and SharePoint

You may also be wondering about JQuery support in SharePoint, since REST supports putting out JSON objects that you can load with JQuery, as do other parts of SharePoint. While SharePoint itself does not include a JQuery library, you can easily link to JQuery in your SharePoint solutions. One thing to note is that this linking does require connectivity to the Internet. Microsoft has made JQuery and a number of other libraries available via the Microsoft Ajax Content Delivery Network. To get the JQuery library from the CDN use the following statement in your code:

```
<script src="http://ajax.microsoft.com/ajax/jquery/jquery-1.3.2.js"
type="text/javascript"></script>
```

SANDBOX SOLUTIONS

Often developers who want to build solutions on SharePoint can't, because they require administrator access to SharePoint and their solutions must be deployed as a full-trust solution, which could affect the stability of the server if they write bad code. For these reasons, IT administrators do not allow developers to write code against SharePoint 2007. With Sandbox Solutions in SharePoint 2010, the server administrator can allow site administrators to deploy code and developers to write code and still protect the integrity of the server. Sandbox Solutions are self-regulating, since there are quotas for resource usage and the server will shut down any solutions that exceed their quota.

Types of Solutions You Can Build

With Sandbox Solutions, you can build a subset of all the solutions you can build in SharePoint. Solutions that require extensive privileges are not allowed in the sandbox because of the limited nature of the sandbox. The following list gives you the types of solutions you can build with Sandbox Solutions.

➤ Content Types

➤ Site Columns

➤ Custom Actions

➤ Declarative Workflows

➤ Event Receivers

➤ Feature Receivers

➤ InfoPath Forms Services (not admin-approved, that is, without codebehind)

➤ JavaScript, AJAX, jQuery, REST, or Silverlight Applications

➤ List Definitions

➤ Site Pages (but no application pages with code behind)

➤ Web parts (but not visual web parts)

Executing Code in the Sandbox

Before a Sandbox Solution can be run, a site administrator must upload the solution and activate it in the site. When you upload a Sandbox Solution, you upload it to the Solution gallery.

The Solution gallery contains all your Sandbox Solutions and displays the resource quota that your solutions are taking both for the current day and averaged over the past 14 days. The Solution gallery is located in _catalogs/solutions.

If you look at the architecture for Sandbox Solutions, there are three main components when executing your solution. First, there is the User Code Service (SPUCHostService.exe). This service decides whether the server where this service is running will participate in Sandbox Solutions. SharePoint has a modular architecture for Sandbox Solutions where you can run them on your WFEs or you can dedicate separate servers for executing your Sandbox code. If the User Code Service is running on a machine, Sandbox Solutions can run on that machine. When you troubleshoot your Sandbox Solutions, the first thing to check is to make sure that this service is running on a SharePoint server in your farm.

From an architecture standpoint, SharePoint allows you to pin the execution of the Sandbox Solution to the server that received the web request. This means that the User Code Service must run on all your Web Front Ends (WFEs) in your farm. While this provides easy administration, since you do not have to create separate servers for Sandbox Solutions or remember which servers the service runs on, it does limit your scalability because the WFEs have to process other web requests while running the Sandbox Solutions.

Your other option is to run requests by solution affinity. You set up application servers in your SharePoint farm that run the User Code Service and are not processing web requests. SharePoint will route Sandbox Solutions to these servers rather than have the solution run on your WFE.

The second component and next process is the Sandbox Worker Process (SPUCWorkerProcess.exe). This is the process where your code executes. As you can tell, it is not part of w3wp.exe, which is one reason why you don't have to reset your entire site when you deploy a Sandbox Solution. If debugging does not work for your sandbox, you can always manually attach the debugger to this process, but be forewarned that SharePoint may kill your debugging session in the middle if you take too long or exceed one of the quotas that is set on the sandbox.

The last component and process is the Sandbox Worker Proxy (`SPUCWorkerProcessProxy.exe`). Given that SharePoint has the service application architecture, this proxy allows Sandbox Solutions to tie into that infrastructure.

Subset Object Model

Sandbox does implement a subset of the `Microsoft.SharePoint` namespace. Sandbox Solutions do allow you to use full trust proxies to access other APIs or capabilities, for example, accessing network resources, but OOB the following capabilities from the `Microsoft.SharePoint` namespace are supported:

- ➤ `Microsoft.SharePoint`, **except**
  - ➤ `SPSite` constructor
  - ➤ `SPSecurity` object
  - ➤ `SPWorkItem` and `SPWorkItemCollection` objects
  - ➤ `SPAlertCollection.Add` method
  - ➤ `SPAlertTemplateCollection.Add` method
  - ➤ `SPUserSolution` and `SPUserSolutionCollection` objects
  - ➤ `SPTransformUtilities`
- ➤ `Microsoft.SharePoint.Navigation`
- ➤ `Microsoft.SharePoint.Utilities`, **except**
  - ➤ `SPUtility.SendEmail` method
  - ➤ `SPUtility.GetNTFullNameandEmailFromLogin` method
- ➤ `Microsoft.SharePoint.Workflow`
- ➤ `Microsoft.SharePoint.WebPartPages`, **except**
  - ➤ `SPWebPartManager` object
  - ➤ `SPWebPartConnection` object
  - ➤ `WebPartZone` object
  - ➤ `WebPartPage` object
  - ➤ `ToolPane` object
  - ➤ `ToolPart` object

What about Accessing External Data?

One common question you may be asking yourself is "If I can't access local resources such the hard drive on the server or network resources except for SharePoint, how do I get at external data like a database or Twitter or some other external datasource?" Well, you can use external lists and BCS in SharePoint to access external data, since Sandbox Solutions can access external lists. Of course, you need to have permissions to set up BCS and external lists, but if there are already BCS solutions set up with access to the external datasources that you need, you can quickly use the external lists in your Sandbox Solutions to read and write to that external data.

What about Iframes?

Sandbox Solutions do support iframes, so you can add a literal control to your nonvisual web part and make the text the iframe that you want to display in the control. This allows you to connect to many solutions on the Internet, such as Silverlight or web pages that expose information that you want to display in your environment. Using Sandbox Solutions for this, rather than content editor web parts, makes the control reusable and easier to distribute.

Code Access Security (CAS)

You can find a lot of information about Sandbox Solutions under the `UserCode` folder in your SharePoint root. If you look at the `web.config` file located there, you will see that Sandbox Solutions are restricted by an OOB CAS policy. By default, you cannot access anything outside of the SharePoint object model. You should not modify these permission levels and instead should use full trust proxies to allow your sandbox code to perform allowed operations that it does not have by default. The exact permission levels are:

➤ `SharePointPermission.ObjectModel`

➤ `SecurityPermission.Execution`

➤ `AspNetHostingPermission.Level=Minimal`

API Block List

Beyond the default CAS policy, SharePoint also implements an API block list. Imagine the scenario where you find some code exploiting your sandbox using a particular API from SharePoint. You may want to block API across your environment. This is where the API block list comes in. A new object was added to `SPWebService` called `RestrictedObjectModel`. This object contains a collection of restricted types that implements an add method, so you can add new API methods to block. For the add method, you need to pass in the type and method you want to block. For example, if you wanted to block the `Update` method of the `SPWeb` object you would call `SPWebService.RestrictedObjectModel.RestrictedTypes.Add(typeof(SPWeb), "Update")`. By default, nothing is blocked.

Visual Studio Support

One of the nice features of VS 2010 is that it supports Sandbox Solutions. When you create a new SharePoint project, for projects that support Sandbox Solutions, VS will give you the option of deploying your solution as a Sandbox Solution, as shown in Figure 4-27. In addition, VS will limit the API set in IntelliSense to just the APIs that work for Sandbox Solutions. VS does not do a compile-time check if you are using restricted APIs, since you program against the full SharePoint namespace and at runtime, your code is limited. So, if you ignore IntelliSense and write to APIs that are not supported in the sandbox, you will not get a compile-time error but instead will get a runtime error. One trick around this is to reference the `Microsoft.SharePoint.dll` under the

Assemblies folder under the UserCode folder in the SharePoint hive. That will limit the APIs you can use. You MUST change back the reference to the full `Microsoft.SharePoint.dll` before deployment. This may be fixed in the released version of Visual Studio 2010.

Solution Monitoring

One of the powerful features of the sandbox is the monitoring. There are site collection quotas that administrators can set up for all Sandbox Solutions running in that site collection. These quotas stop the Sandbox Solutions from overloading the server, such as maxing out the CPU or pegging the database.

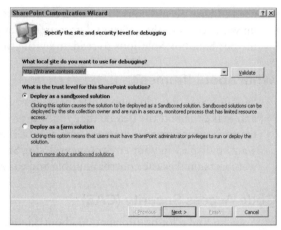

FIGURE 4-27

Resource calculations are not instantaneous so that you may have to wait a bit during development to see the quota usage change. In addition, there is a daily timer job that aggregates server resource usage, resets any solutions that have exceeded their quota so that they can run again, and deletes old resource usage records.

Farm administrators decide how many resource points a site collection receives in Central Administration. If you look at the Configure Quota and Locks under Application Management in the section called User Solutions Resource Quota, you will see where a farm administrator can set the resource quota for Sandbox Solutions. This is shown in Figure 4-28.

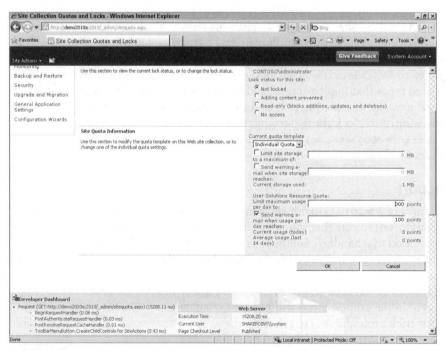

FIGURE 4-28

Since the resource quota is for the site collection's Sandbox Solutions, one bad apple ruins the bunch. If Sandbox Solutions eat up all the resources, no Sandbox Solutions will run on that site collection for the rest of the day. So, it's a good idea to make sure that you're writing good code; otherwise, you could use all the resources, even those for other developers running in the same site collection.

What Is Monitored?

In terms of monitoring, SharePoint tracks 14 different counters and tries to normalize across them. For example, how many points should be a millisecond of CPU execution time as compared to the number of SharePoint database queries you make? How do you normalize across different counters to make an aggregate that makes sense? Well, it's easy to see how SharePoint attempts to do it. You can look at using PowerShell by using the SPUserCodeService object. The following PowerShell code returns all the counters measured by Sandbox Solutions:

```
$snapin = Get-PSSnapin | where-object { $_.Name -eq
 'Microsoft.SharePoint.PowerShell' }
if ($snapin -eq $null){
 write-host "Loading SharePoint PowerShell Snapin..." -foregroundcolor Blue
 add-pssnapin "Microsoft.SharePoint.PowerShell"
 write-host "SharePoint PowerShell Snapin loaded." -foregroundcolor Green
}

[Microsoft.SharePoint.Administration.SPUserCodeService]::Local.ResourceMeasures

# The ReadKey functionality is only supported at the console (not is the ISE)

if (!$psISE)

{

    Write-Host -NoNewLine "Press any key to continue. . . "

    $null = $Host.UI.RawUI.ReadKey("NoEcho,IncludeKeyDown")

    Write-Host ""

}

write-host "Completed Run" -foregroundcolor Blue
```

Sandbox Resource Measures.ps1

If you bubble up this list, you get the counters and metrics in the bulleted list below. The way to read the list is as the type of counter and then how many counts must occur or the time to count as a single resource point. For example, if you make 20 SharePoint database calls through your calls to different SharePoint APIs, that counts as one resource point.

➤ **AbnormalProcessTerminationCount:** 1

➤ **CPUExecutionTime:** 3600

- ➤ CriticalExceptionCount: 3600

- ➤ InvocationCount: 100

- ➤ PercentProcessorTime: 85

- ➤ ProcessCPUCycles: 100000000000

- ➤ ProcessHandleCount:10000

- ➤ ProcessIOBytes: 10000000

- ➤ ProcessThreadCount: 10000

- ➤ ProcessVirtualBytes: 100000000

- ➤ SharePointDatabaseQueryCount: 20

- ➤ SharePointDatabaseQueryTime: 120

- ➤ UnhandledExceptionCount: 50

- ➤ UnresponsiveprocessCount: 2

The counters are customizable in that you could bump them up or down using the object model any of the counters. For example, if you wanted to allow 40 database calls, you could change that by using the SharePoint object model. However, it's a little like changing search relevancy algorithms yourself; it may cause unintended consequences, so try the default restrictions to see if they meet your needs before you modify them.

Also, there are absolute limits. Absolute limits will terminate a solution even if the resource limits have not been hit. For example, `UnresponsiveprocessCount` has an absolute limit of 1. This means that, if your Sandbox Solution is not responding, it will be terminated immediately. Then, two points will be added to the aggregate. The solution could try to run again, but it will be terminated if it becomes unresponsive and again two resource points will be added to the aggregate.

If there are solutions that just keep breaking, administrators can block them from running either by using the object model or, more easily, by selecting the solution by browsing for it and putting in a message that tells the user why the solution can't run.

Managing Solutions

When it comes to managing your solutions, there are two key areas to take a look at beyond monitoring. One is solution validation, which allows you to be proactive in validating solutions. You decide what to check on the solution and, if it fails validation, it is not allowed to be activated in the site collection. The second is full-trust proxies. These proxies allow Sandbox Solutions to call more functionality than what the sandbox provides, but in a managed way.

Solution Validation

To work with solution validation, you just need to inherit from the `SPSolutionValidator` class. Once you write your code for this class, you add it to the `SPUserCodeService SolutionValidators` collection using either the API or PowerShell. Following is sample code for the solution validator:

```csharp
using System;
using System.Collections.Generic;
using System.Linq;
using System.Text;
using System.Runtime.InteropServices;
using Microsoft.SharePoint;
using Microsoft.SharePoint.Administration;
using Microsoft.SharePoint.UserCode;
using System.IO;


namespace SolutionValidation
{
    [Guid("7158c574-9881-42b3-9116-2575485af534")]
    public class SolutionValidator : SPSolutionValidator
    {

        //Create constant to pass to constructor
        private const string solutionValidatorName = "Solution Validator";
        //Create constant for Validator Signature
        private const int sigValue = 1;


        public SolutionValidator()
        {
            //Blank Constructor
        }


         public SolutionValidator(SPUserCodeService userCodeService)
            :base(solutionValidatorName, userCodeService)
        {
            this.Signature = sigValue;

        }

         public override void ValidateSolution(
SPSolutionValidationProperties properties)
        {
            //Validate your solution such as checking the code files in
the solution
            foreach (SPSolutionFile solutionFile in properties.Files.Where(
               f => String.Equals(
                     Path.GetExtension(f.Location), ".dll",
                        StringComparison.InvariantCultureIgnoreCase)))
            {
                //Perform Validation of files
            }

            base.ValidateSolution(properties);

            properties.Valid = false;
```

```
            properties.ValidationErrorMessage = "Illegal Solution";
            properties.ValidationErrorUrl =
"/_layouts/SolutionValidation/SolutionValidationError.aspx";

        }

        public override void ValidateAssembly(
SPSolutionValidationProperties properties, SPSolutionFile assembly)
        {
            //You can open the assembly using OpenBinary
            base.ValidateAssembly(properties, assembly);
            properties.Valid = true;
        }
    }
}
```

SolutionValidator.cs

A couple of things in the code: First, you can see where the code inherits from the SPSolutionValidator class. In addition, you need to create your own GUID to assign to your class, since you will use that GUID when you remove the solution validator from SharePoint in your feature deployment.

From there, you can see the blank constructor and another constructor that overloads the base constructor to assign a signature value to your validator. If you update the validator, you will want to update the signature number.

For the implementation, the code has ValidateSolution and ValidateAssembly methods. The ValidateSolution method gets passed a SPSolutionValidationProperties collection, which contains a number of properties for your SharePoint solutions, such as the files in the solution. You can perform validation in this method and, if the solution is valid, set the Boolean Valid property to True. If the solution is not valid, set the Valid property to False. You can also specify the ValidationErrorMessage and ValidationErrorUrl, which is the message to display and, if you want, the URL of the error message page. You can use the mapped folder feature in Visual Studio to add a custom ASP.NET page to your Layouts folder to display your error message.

For the ValidateAssembly method, you can validate individual assemblies in the solution. You get the assembly, and you can open it using the OpenBinary method, write all the bytes, and look at the bits contained in it. If the assembly is valid, set the Valid property to True.

Once you have your implemented class, you need to create a feature that deploys your solution validator. It must be a farm-level solution, since you want to validate all solutions in your farm. As part of the feature, you will want to write code for your feature event receiver to turn on your solution validator and turn it off when the feature is activated. The following code does this. Note how the same GUID is used in the FeatureDeactivating event that you used to mark up your class. Figure 4-29 shows the solution validator in action, denying a solution the right to activate.

```
    public override void FeatureActivated(SPFeatureReceiverProperties properties)
        {
            //Add solution Validator using our class name
            SPUserCodeService.Local.SolutionValidators.Add(
```

```
new SolutionValidator(SPUserCodeService.Local));

    }



    public override void FeatureDeactivating(
SPFeatureReceiverProperties properties)
    {
        //Remove our solution validator using our GUID
        SPUserCodeService.Local.SolutionValidators.Remove(new Guid(
"7158c574-9881-42b3-9116-2575485af534"));

    }
```

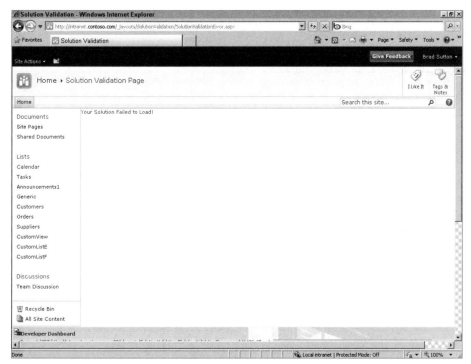

FIGURE 4-29

Full-Trust Proxy

The last area we will look at is creating full-trust proxies. Full-trust proxies allow you to extend
Sandbox Solutions without throwing everything out of the sandbox. For example, you may
need to access a network resource to get at data but not want to make the full solution a fully
trusted solution; instead you want to provide a limited proxy to just that network resource. With
full-trust proxies, you can provide an API just to the network resource and allow your Sandbox
Solutions to call through that API to your resource.

To create a full-trust proxy, you need to implement a class that inherits from the `SPProxyOperation` class. Then, you need to figure out the arguments that you want passed to your proxy by creating a serializable class that inherits from the `SPProxyOperationsArgs` class. Once you have done this, generate the DLL and put this DLL into the global assembly cache (GAC). Then, you can register the DLL with SharePoint and call it using the `SPUtility.ExecuteRegisteredProxyOperation` method.

The following code creates a class that mimics accessing a network resource. It passes a fake username and password, and the full-trust proxy returns an array of data. You could imagine that you make a call to ADO.NET or other data access technologies to perform a real database call. Notice in the code that you need to create a serializable class that implements the proxy arguments. The calling Sandbox Solution then displays the data from the datasource that is accessed by using the full-trust proxy.

```
using System;
using System.Collections.Generic;
using System.Linq;
using System.Text;
using Microsoft.SharePoint.UserCode;

namespace FullTrustProxyDLL
{
    public class AccessDatabase : SPProxyOperation
    {
        public override object Execute(SPProxyOperationArgs args)
        {
            if (args != null)
            {

                ProxyArgs proxyArgs = args as ProxyArgs;

                //Get the user name
                string userName = proxyArgs.userName;

                //Get the password
                string password = proxyArgs.password;

                //Access the datasource here
                string[] results = { "A", "B", "C" };


                return results;
            }
            else return null;

        }

    }

    [Serializable]
    public class ProxyArgs : SPProxyOperationArgs
```

```
    {
        public string userName { get; set; }

        public string password { get; set; }

    }
}
```

In order to make your proxy callable from partially trusted code applications, you need to add a line to your `AssemblyInfo.cs`, as shown here:

```
//Allow partially trusted callers
[assembly: System.Security.AllowPartiallyTrustedCallers]
```

Once you have compiled your proxy DLL, you need to register it in the GAC. Once that is done, you can register it with SharePoint. The following PowerShell script performs this step:

```
$snapin = Get-PSSnapin | where-object { $_.Name -eq
 'Microsoft.SharePoint.PowerShell' }
if ($snapin -eq $null){
 write-host "Loading SharePoint PowerShell Snapin..." -foregroundcolor Blue
 add-pssnapin "Microsoft.SharePoint.PowerShell"
 write-host "SharePoint PowerShell Snapin loaded." -foregroundcolor Green
}


$userCodeService = [Microsoft.SharePoint.Administration.SPUserCodeService]::Local
$assemblyName = "FullTrustProxyDLL, Version=1.0.0.0, Culture=neutral,
PublicKeyToken=3098f04d94800e33"
$typeName = "FullTrustProxyDLL.AccessDatabase"
$proxyOperationType = new-object -typename
 Microsoft.SharePoint.UserCode.SPProxyOperationType -argumentlist
$assemblyName, $typeName
userCodeService.ProxyOperationTypes.Add($proxyOperationType)
$userCodeService.Update()
```

Now you can use the proxy in your Sandbox Solution. The following code and Figure 4-30 below shows the full trust proxy being used and how to call the proxy class from your sandbox code:

```
ProxyArgs proxyA = new ProxyArgs();
          proxyA.userName = "TestUser";
          proxyA.password = "Password";

          string assemblyName = "FullTrustProxyDLL, Version=1.0.0.0,
Culture=neutral, PublicKeyToken=3098f04d94800e33";
          string typeName = "FullTrustProxyDLL.AccessDatabase";

          accessDatabaseButton.Click += (object sender, EventArgs e) =>
          {
              string[] results;
              results = (string
[])SPUtility.ExecuteRegisteredProxyOperation(assemblyName, typeName, proxyA);
```

```
                lbl.Text = "First result: " + results[0];
            };

            Controls.Add(accessDatabaseButton);
            Controls.Add(lbl);
```

FIGURE 4-30

SUMMARY

In this chapter, you have seen how you can use the base services in SharePoint to integrate your applications into the new Ribbon user interface, write event receivers, and even work with the new client OM in your various applications. The SharePoint 2010 platform is a large one with many APIs, so it will take some time for you to absorb all the new APIs. Experimenting with the new APIs is the key to understanding how they work and what their limitations and trade-offs are.

5

Collaboration and Social Computing

WHAT'S IN THIS CHAPTER?

➤ Details about the new social computing features available in SharePoint 2010

➤ Managing profiles using the User Profile Service Application

➤ Examples of how the object model and web services can be used to access social data

➤ My Site enhancements

➤ What's new in blog and wiki sites

The term "social computing" can be defined as the use of technology to allow people to connect with each other, usually online. Examples include blogs with responses, wikis, and social networks like Twitter, Facebook, and LinkedIn. In addition, there are new rating applications, web applications, and social technologies being developed, allowing users to connect to and benefit from the strength and knowledge of a community.

Today, your business users are more socially aware, and social applications can be easily adopted. One of the reasons for the quick adoption of SharePoint Portal Server 2003 and Microsoft Office SharePoint Server 2007 was that people needed to connect as a group to collaborate efficiently. When the 2003 version of the product was released, users had fast PCs, quick Internet connections and the software tools needed to be productive as individuals. The next logical step was learning to use software and creating new applications, which facilitated being productive as groups and organizations instead of as individuals.

Microsoft has been experimenting with social technology since before the term "social computing" was adopted to define the online efforts to bring social concepts to the Internet. Several releases of Internet Explorer contained electronic Post-it-style notes, which could be left on websites. As other users who shared the same note server browsed the sites, your notes would be visible and those users could respond with comments of their own.

A decade ago, when team sites were first introduced, the technology allowed users to connect online via a website and collaborate on documents, enter into discussions forums, and communicate with team members. Microsoft Office SharePoint Portal Server 2003 is a collaborative portal solution that connected people, teams, and information.

Enhanced online communication features, including blogs and wiki technology, were introduced in SharePoint 2007. The marriage of wiki and blog technology with an enterprise content management system was ahead of its time. Since the initial release of SharePoint Server 2007, the use of social computing technology has grown significantly, in part because of the popularity of Internet sites like Facebook, Twitter, and LinkedIn. Concepts like micro-blogging and tagging have proven to be effective ways to stay connected and find information.

The new release of SharePoint Server 2010 is designed from the ground up to support a user-centric model, and brings forth new ways to collaborate using both social and enterprise computing tenets. Traditionally, enterprise software defines a user as an identity, which can be assigned access and privileges to data and applications. This is not the case with SharePoint 2010. The product aligns software and services in such a way that the user is at the center of the experience, allowing a mix of social and enterprise computing.

Social networking tools are now "first-class citizens" in SharePoint; an example is the enhanced Content tab in My Sites. Having the ability to add many types of enterprise content to your My Site allows navigation of content based on a person and social properties, rather than a folder or site hierarchy. Other examples include social tagging, ratings, networks, activity feeds, and the new organization browser. But the main feature is the improvement in the My Site. The My Site is now a personal portal for users to consume information from colleagues and those with the same interests.

PEOPLE-CENTRICITY

The people-centric model in SharePoint 2010 begins with the user profile store and the User Profile Service Application. The core of any social application is the user profile. User profiles allow searching for and connecting to colleagues, in addition to leveraging existing organizational relationships and knowledge. The more you know about your users, the more (cool) things you can do with your software. Of course, today this includes enabling the types of social computing features and social connections users have embraced using the Internet.

User Profile Service Application

You manage user profiles, connections to directories, imports, and settings using the new User Profiles Service Application (UPA) shown in Figure 5-1. Like many of the services available in SharePoint, the architecture uses a service model. A farm administrator must grant you permissions before you can access the UPA through Central Administration (CA).

FIGURE 5-1

As a developer, it is important to understand how user profiles are created, modified, and managed using CA, as well as the object model. All the information SharePoint stores to track users, tags, ratings, and other social data is stored in the user profile and social database. This information is managed using UPA and is exposed to you through the `Microsoft.Office.Server.UserProfiles` namespace.

Use PowerShell to Automate Creating a UPA in Your Development Environments

Using the PowerShell command prompt, enter the following:

```
$app_UPA = New-SPProfileServiceApplication -Name UPA -PartitionMode
-ApplicationPool $appPool
```

To provision the UPA on your development server, you need to have the required permission levels. Use the following list to avoid issues with services not starting or synchronization failures. These account settings should not be used in a production environment.

1. Your account is a member of Farm Administrator group within Central Administration.

2. Your account is added to local administrator group.

3. Your account is added to the Sysadmin role on SQL server.

4. Your account is allowed by policy to log on locally to the server where profile synchronization will be deployed.

5. Your account is at least a member of the domain's Pre–Windows 2000 Compatible Access group.

6. If your user is a domain administrator, membership in this group isn't required.

7. The user account specified to perform a profile import requires Replicate Directory Changes permission.

Once the UPA is created, you can use the object model to create profiles. Listing 5-1 illustrates using the `UserProfileManager` class to create a new profile.

LISTING 5-1: Create a User Profile Using the Object Model

```
public void CreateUserProfile()
{
//We have to get current context of the service application
strUrl = "http://site";
SPSite site = new SPSite(strUrl);
SPServiceContext serviceContext = SPServiceContext.GetContext(site);

//UserProfileManager class contains members for profiles
UserProfileManager upmanager = new UserProfileManager(serviceContext);

//create a new user profile
string strAccount = "domain\\user";
if (!upmanager.UserExists(strAccount))
upmanager.CreateUserProfile(strAccount);
}
```

createuserprof.cs

The UPA administration screen in CA is divided into four sections. The functionality found in each section is outlined below.

1. People

   ➤ **Manage User Properties:** Existing properties can be viewed and new properties added. You can map properties to existing Active Directory attributes.

   ➤ **Mange User Profiles:** Existing user profiles can be viewed and managed. New profiles can be added manually without importing from a directory.

   ➤ **Manage User Sub-types:** Create subtypes of user profiles. Examples of subtypes include contractors and students. Subtypes allow you to track different profile properties based on a type of user. You can create and manage subtypes using this link.

   ➤ **Manage Audiences:** Audiences can be created and managed using this link. Audiences are created using properties and group-based rules. Audience features allow you to provide in-context information to users.

➤ **Compile Audiences**: When an audience is compiled, the rules are processed to determine what users belong in the audience. This compiling needs to happen on a regular basis for your audience to be up to date.

➤ **Schedule Audience Compilation**: Using this link you, can schedule when an audience is compiled.

➤ **Manage User Permissions**: Permissions can be set to control which users can create My Sites, and use personal features and social features. Removing the Create Personal Site permission eliminates the My Site link for that user.

➤ **Profile services policies**: Use this link to manage the policy for Profile Services. There are settings that control how individual properties will be displayed in My Site, as well as who can view the properties. You can control colleagues, memberships, and Links and their visibility in My Site.

2. Synchronization

➤ **Configure Synchronization Settings**: Create a connection to import user information from Active Directory, IBM Directory, Novell eDirectory, or Sun ONE Directory Server. Imports can also be created using Business Connectivity Service applications.

➤ **Configure Synchronization Time Job**: Use this section to modify the schedule specifying when the timer job will run. Daily, weekly, and monthly schedules also include a window of execution. The timer service will pick a random time within this interval to begin executing the job on each applicable server.

➤ **Configure Synchronization Settings**: Use this page to manage the settings for profile synchronization of users and groups. You can use an external identity manager for Profile Synchronization; to do this, select Enable External Identity Manager.

➤ **Start Profile Synchronization**: Use this link to start a full or incremental Synchronization.

3. Organizations

➤ **Manage Organization Properties**: Use this page to add, edit, organize, delete, or map organization profile properties. Organizations are a new feature, managed much like user profiles; however, they allow you to treat organizations you work with as individuals with profiles and social data.

➤ **Manage Organization Profiles**: Just like you can manage profiles for users, you can also manage profiles for organizations. Using this screen, you can create Organization Profiles, Organization Sub-types, and filters based on the Sub-types. The options are the same ones you use for user profiles; however, they are in the context of an organization rather than a user.

➤ **Manage Organization Sub-types**: Using this section, you can create and manage the Sub-types described previously.

4. My Site Settings

➤ **Setup My Sites:** Use this link to manage My Site settings. You can set a My Site host, personal site location, and other My Site options.

➤ **Configure Trusted Host Locations:** You can specify trusted My Site locations, which can exist in other UPAs. You will have to apply audiences to identify users with sites hosted in the trusted location.

➤ **Configure Personalization Site:** This feature is very useful for developers wishing to create role-based dashboards. You can configure links to applications and dashboards and publish based on audience membership. You can see in Figure 5-2 the dashboards and application links will appear in the My Site on the navigation bar after the My Personal Content link.

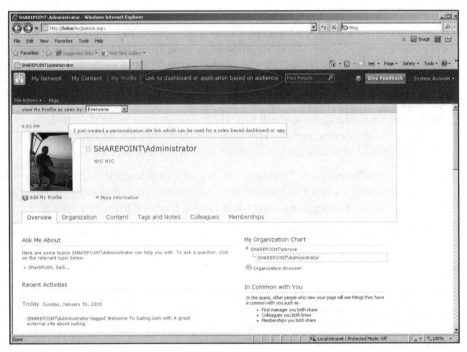

FIGURE 5-2

➤ **Published Links to Office Applications:** These settings allow you to publish links that will show up in your users' Office applications when you select the option to save files. Office will retrieve a list of published locations once a day from the server. Links can be published to users based on audience membership.

➤ **Manage Social Tags and Notes:** You can use this page to manage users' social items such as tags and notes. You can find and delete tags.

Profile Synchronization

After your farm administrator has created a User Profile Service Application, a designated administrator of the User Profile Service Application can manage the following (the synchronization process). Once the synchronization process occurs, you can begin to use the user profile and social data from your applications with the object model and web services.

As a developer, you should note that properties can be configured to write back to the import source. This is a big change from previous versions, where the profile synchronization was a one-way import and never updated the source directory. The user profile store has properties that, by default, are mapped to Active Directory and imported during synchronization. You can create custom properties in SharePoint and then map the properties to attributes that exist in Active Directory. Table 5-1 lists the properties that are mapped to Active Directory attributes by default.

TABLE 5-1: The Default Profile Properties and Mappings

ACTIVE DIRECTORY ATTRIBUTE	USER PROFILE STORE PROPERTY
<dn>	SPS-DistinguishedName
objectSid	SID
Manager	Manager
displayName	PreferredName
givenName	FirstName
Sn	LastName
PhoneticDisplayName	PhoneticDisplayName
PhoneticFirstName	PhoneticFirstName
PhoneticLastName	PhoneticLastName
telephoneNumber	WorkPhone
Mail	WorkEmail
physicalDeliveryOfficeName	Office
Title	Title
Department	Department
sAMAccontName	UserName
wWWHomePage	PublicSiteRedirect
SIP Address	proxyAddresses

Microsoft TechNet

User Subtypes

A subtype is a type of user. SharePoint 2010 allows you to define different types of users. Examples include contractors and consultants. These different types of users may have different properties associated with them. Subtypes help you resolve the issues that arise because you need to identify different profiles for different types of users. After a subtype is created, you can create new profile properties that are targeted at these types of users. User profiles can be filtered based on subtypes. These subtype features are new in SharePoint 2010.

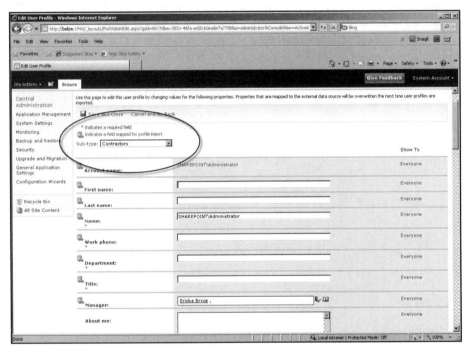

FIGURE 5-3

User Profile Customization and Code

Developers can use the object model to create, modify, and delete user profiles. Using the object model, properties can be added and modified as well. When you use the object model from Visual Studio, you must add references to a new assembly found in the ISAPI directory under the SharePoint root. The name of the new assembly is `Microsoft.Office.Server.UserProfiles`; Table 5-2 lists the commonly used namespaces.

Once the reference is added, you will have access to the following namespaces from your code:

➤ `Microsoft.Office.Server.UserProfiles`

➤ `Microsoft.Office.Server.Audience`

➤ `Microsoft.Office.Server.ActivityFeed`

➤ `Microsoft.Office.Server.SocialData`

TABLE 5-2: Namespace Definitions and Descriptions Defined in the SharePoint SDK

NAMESPACE	DESCRIPTION
`Microsoft.Office.Server.ActivityFeed`	Contains classes that create, gather, and publish newsfeeds. Some of the most commonly used types in this namespace are `ActivityManager`, `ActivityEvent`, `ActivityType`, `ActivityTemplate`, and `ActivityTemplateVariable`.
`Microsoft.Office.Server.Audience`	Contains classes that create audiences and target data to a specific audience. A commonly used type in this namespace is `AudienceManager`.
`Microsoft.Office.Server.SocialData`	Contains classes that create and manipulate pieces of social data. Some of the most commonly used types in this namespace are `SocialCommentManager`, `SocialRatingManager`, and `SocialTagManager`.
`Microsoft.Office.Server.UserProfiles`	Contains classes that create and manipulate user profiles. Some of the most commonly used types in this namespace are `UserProfileManager`, `OrganizationProfileManager`, `MemberGroupManager`, and `ProfileSubtypePropertyManager`.

SharePoint Server SDK, MSDN

The following code demonstrates how you can use the object model and namespaces in Table 5-2 to update properties of an existing profile. You will set references defined above. The output is depicted in Figure 5-4.

```
using System;
using System.Collections.Generic;
using System.Linq;
using System.Text;
using Microsoft.SharePoint;
using Microsoft.Office.Server.UserProfiles;
using Microsoft.Office.Server;

namespace UserProfileStoreOM
{
    class Program
    {
        static void Main(string[] args)
        {
            using (SPSite site = new SPSite("http://belize:777"))
            {
//Get service context
                SPServiceContext context = SPServiceContext.GetContext(site);
                UserProfileManager
//Get profile
uprofileManager =
```

```
newUserProfileManager(context);
                string strAccount = "sharepoint\\administrator";
                UserProfile up = uprofileManager.GetUserProfile(strAccount);

//Update values                up[PropertyConstants.Office].Value = "NYC";
                up[PropertyConstants.Manager].Value = "SharePoint\\Ebryce";
                up[PropertyConstants.CellPhone].Value = "333-333-3333";

                up.Commit();
                Console.WriteLine("Office has been updated to: " +
up[PropertyConstants.Office].Value);
                Console.WriteLine("Manager has been updated to: " +
up[PropertyConstants.Manager].Value);
                Console.WriteLine("Cell Phone has been updated to: " +
up[PropertyConstants.CellPhone].Value);
                site.Dispose();
            }
            Console.Read();

        }
    }
}
```

Userprofile.cs

The following section illustrates how you can begin to leverage the user profile store using web parts and web services. A web part project will be created using Visual Studio. The web part will use the object model to retrieve user profile property names and display names. This technique can be used to update or control user properties. To get detailed information regarding web part development and deployment, refer to the section on web parts in Chapter 2.

FIGURE 5-4

To set up the project, you need to create a blank team site that can be used for debugging. Next, create a blank SharePoint 2010 project using C# and name the project `SocialWebParts`. When starting Visual Studio, run the application as administrator by right-clicking on the start menu shortcut and select the Run as Administrator option. When the SharePoint Customization Wizard prompts you for a debugging site, enter the URL of the blank debugging site created above. Be sure to select the .NET Framework 3.5 and the Deploy as a full-trust solution option when prompted.

Using the following steps, you will create a visual web part project that consumes the user profile web service.

1. Right-click on the SocialWebParts project and add a new Visual Web Part project template. Name the new web part UserProfileData.

2. Open the file named `UserProfileData.webpart`, and change the title and description as shown in the code.

Available for download on Wrox.com

```
<?xml version="1.0" encoding="utf-8"?>
<webParts>
  <webPart xmlns="http://schemas.microsoft.com/WebPart/v3">
    <metaData>
      <type name="SocialWebParts.UserProfileData.UserProfileData,
        $SharePoint.Project.AssemblyFullName$" />
      <importErrorMessage>$Resources:core,ImportErrorMessage;</
        importErrorMessage>
    </metaData>
    <data>
      <properties>
        <property name="Title" type="string">User Profile Data Web Part</
          property>
        <property name="Description" type="string">
        This web part demonstrates consuming data from
        userprofile.asmx</property>
      </properties>
    </data>
  </webPart>
</webParts>
```

UserProfiledata.webpart

3. Open the `elements.xml` file and change the URL attribute by appending `SocialWebParts_` to the beginning of the property. While the file is open, change the group name to Social Web Parts as shown below.

Available for download on Wrox.com

```
<?xml version="1.0" encoding="utf-8"?>
<Elements xmlns="http://schemas.microsoft.com/sharepoint/" >
  <Module Name="UserProfileData" List="113" Url="_catalogs/wp">
      <File Path="UserProfileData\UserProfileData.webpart"
      Url="SocialWebParts_UserProfileData.webpart"
          Type="GhostableInLibrary" >
          <Property Name="Social web Parts" Value="Custom" />
      </File>
  </Module>
</Elements>
```

elements.xml

4. Drag a data grid from the toolbox to the design surface of the visual web part.

Available for download on Wrox.com

```
<%@ Assembly Name="$SharePoint.Project.AssemblyFullName$" %>
<%@ Assembly Name="Microsoft.Web.CommandUI, Version=14.0.0.0,
Culture=neutral, PublicKeyToken=71e9bce111e9429c" %>
<%@ Register Tagprefix="SharePoint" Namespace="Microsoft.SharePoint.
WebControls" Assembly="Microsoft.SharePoint, Version=14.0.0.0,
Culture=neutral, PublicKeyToken=71e9bce111e9429c" %>
<%@ Register Tagprefix="Utilities" Namespace="Microsoft.SharePoint.Utilities"
Assembly="Microsoft.SharePoint, Version=14.0.0.0,
Culture=neutral, PublicKeyToken=71e9bce111e9429c" %>
<%@ Register Tagprefix="asp" Namespace="System.Web.UI"
Assembly="System.Web.Extensions, Version=3.5.0.0,
Culture=neutral, PublicKeyToken=31bf3856ad364e35" %>
```

```
<%@ Import Namespace="Microsoft.SharePoint" %>
<%@ Register Tagprefix="WebPartPages"
Namespace="Microsoft.SharePoint.WebPartPages"
Assembly="Microsoft.SharePoint, Version=14.0.0.0, Culture=neutral,
PublicKeyToken=71e9bce111e9429c" %>
<%@ Control Language="C#" AutoEventWireup="true" CodeBehind=
"UserProfileDataUserControl.ascx.cs" Inherits=
"SocialWebParts.UserProfileData.UserProfileDataUserControl" %>


<asp:GridView ID="GridView1" runat="server" AutoGenerateColumns="false">
<Columns>
<asp:BoundField DataField="Key"/>
<asp:BoundField DataField="Value"/>
</Columns>
</asp:GridView>
```

UserProfileDataUserControl.ascx

5. Open the `UserProfileDataUserControl.asx.cs` file, and add an `OnPreRender` method.

Available for download on Wrox.com

```
using System;
using System.Collections.Generic;
using System.Web.UI;
using System.Web.UI.WebControls;
using System.Web.UI.WebControls.WebParts;
using Microsoft.Office.Server;
using Microsoft.Office.Server.Administration;
using Microsoft.Office.Server.UserProfiles;
using Microsoft.SharePoint;


namespace SocialWebParts.UserProfileData
{
    public partial class UserProfileDataUserControl : UserControl
    {
        protected void Page_Load(object sender, EventArgs e)
        {
        }
        protected override void OnPreRender(EventArgs e)
        {
            using (SPSite site = new SPSite("http://BELIZE:333"))
            {
                SPServiceContext context =
                    SPServiceContext.GetContext(site);
                UserProfileManager m_mngr = new UserProfileManager(context);

                //Get the properties
                PropertyCollection props = m_mngr.Properties;

                //Create a Dictionary to store property data.
                Dictionary<string, string>
UserProps = new Dictionary<string, string>();

                foreach (Property prop in props)
```

```
                    {
                        UserProps.Add(prop.Name, prop.DisplayName);
                    }
                    //Bind the Dictionary to a GridView control.
                    GridView1.DataSource = UserProps;
                    GridView1.Columns[0].HeaderText = "Property Name";
                    GridView1.Columns[1].HeaderText = "Display Name";
                    GridView1.DataBind();

                }
            }
        }
    }
```

UserProfileDataUserControl.ascx.cs

Now it is time to add an instance of the web part to the debugging site you created earlier. Navigate to the home page, `default.aspx`, of the debugging site. Click on the Edit tab on the ribbon at the top of the page and then select the command from the edit Page button. Make sure that a Web Part zone is selected so that the contextual Page Tools ribbon tab is displayed. Click the Insert tab on the ribbon and click on the Web Part button. Add the User Profile Web Part instance to the page. The web part should look the one shown in Figure 5-5.

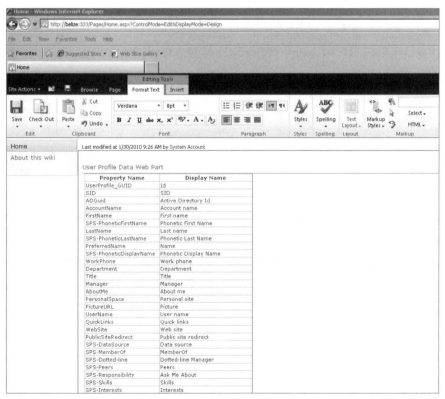

FIGURE 5-5

In addition to using the object model to create and modify user profiles, you can use the `userprofile.asmx` web service. Listing 5-2 shows how to retrieve memberships for a user.

LISTING 5-2: Program.cs

```csharp
using System;
using System.Collections.Generic;
using System.Linq;
using System.Text;
using GetMembershipData.WSUserProf;

namespace GetMembershipData
{
    class Program
    {
        static void Main(string[] args)
        {
            WSUserProf.UserProfileService myUserProfServ = new
WSUserProf.UserProfileService();
            myUserProfServ.Credentials =
System.Net.CredentialCache.DefaultCredentials;

            GetMembershipData.WSUserProf.MembershipData[]
                memberships =
 myUserProfServ.GetUserMemberships("domainname\\username");
            for (int i = 0; i < memberships.Length; i++)
            {
                Console.WriteLine(memberships[i].DisplayName);
            }
            Console.Read();

        }
    }
}
```

program.cs

SOCIAL NETWORKING AND MY SITE

Many of the social computing features in SharePoint are accessed and managed using My Sites. Since its introduction in SharePoint Portal 2003, My Sites have been enhanced to become the social networking hub for individuals in organizations. A My Site is a personal site that provides users in your organization with a comprehensive set of social computing features. In addition, My Sites contain personal information about your users as well as personal and public views of information, documents, and other content. My Sites host personal blogs, lists, and web parts. You can add colleagues and organize them into logical groupings. By using activity feeds, you can keep track of the activities that you or your colleagues create.

There are several significant additions to My Sites in the new release of SharePoint. These additions include a My Networks page for managing colleagues, interests, and newsfeed settings; a My Content page for managing documents and photos; and a My Profile page for managing things like user profile information and social tags and notes.

Other enhancements you will notice in the new My Sites include the new Fluent UI and user profile. My Sites have been designed to give you quick access to your content, profile, and social network. You can still customize, target, and personalize pages to the needs of different roles and users in your organization. The activity feed infrastructure helps track interests and colleagues.

A My Site is divided into three sections using tabs, My Network, My Content, and My Profile. A My Site with tabs, newsfeed, and activity preferences is illustrated in Figure 5-6 and 5-7.

FIGURE 5-6

➤ **My Network:** Displays a list of recent updates from your colleagues. Your settings for interests and newsfeeds (see Figure 5-7) can be managed.

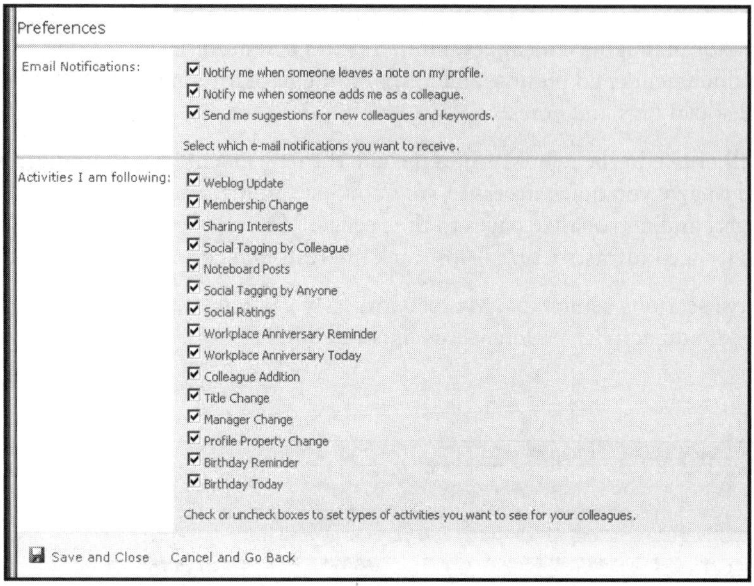

FIGURE 5-7

➤ **My Content:** Contains the default views of Shared Document and Personal Documents.

➤ **My Profile:** The default view of My Site. You can modify properties stored in the user profile database as well as view the activity feed.

In addition to the three tabs at the top of My Site, the following six tabs are used to navigate personal and social data:

➤ **Overview:** Contains web parts for Organization Chart and In Common with You. Also displays the activity feed, which helps keep track of your recent activities.

➤ **Organization:** Displays the Silverlight Organizational Browser, which contains your organization hierarchy.

➤ **Content:** Displays blog posts, documents, and pictures. Blogs and lists can be secured or shared openly.

➤ **Tags and Notes:** Displays all the tags and notes you create throughout SharePoint.

➤ **Colleagues:** Displays all the people added as colleagues.

➤ **Memberships:** Displays details about the sites of you are a member of.

A My Site can be provisioned using the object model, as shown in Listing 5-3.

LISTING 5-3: Using the Object Model to Create a My Site

```
public void CreateMYSite()
{
SPServiceContext serviceContext = SPServiceContext.Current;

UserProfileManager up = new UserProfileManager(serviceContext);
string sAccount = "domain\\user";
UserProfile uprof = up.GetUserProfile(sAccount);
uprof.CreatePersonalSite();
SPSite newmysite = uprof.PersonalSite;
}
```

createmysite.cs

Social Tagging and Ratings

The `Microsoft.Office.server.SocialData` namespace contains classes that are used to access social data. The following classes are defined in the SharePoint developers SDK, and updated members and descriptions can be found on the MSDN website.

TABLE 5-3: Classes in the SocialData Namespace

CLASS	DESCRIPTION
DeletedSocialComment	Represents a social comment whose information has been deleted from the database
DeletedSocialData	Abstract base class representing a piece of social data whose information has been deleted from the database
DeletedSocialRating	Represents a social rating whose information has been deleted from the database
DeletedSocialTag	Represents a social tag whose information has been deleted from the database
FeedbackData	Contains a set of properties that are logged as analysis data whenever a `SocialRating` is set
PluggableSocialSecurity TrimmerManager	Instantiates registered security trimmers for social data
SocialComment	Contains properties that represent a social comment
SocialCommentManager	Contains methods and properties that allow you to add, delete, retrieve, and manage social comments

continues

TABLE 5-3 *(continued)*

CLASS	DESCRIPTION
SocialData	Represents an abstract class that contains properties composing a piece of social data
SocialDataManager	Represents an abstract base class that contains methods and properties that enable you to add, delete, retrieve, and manage social data
SocialRating	Contains properties representing a social rating, which is a specific piece of social data that ranks an entity on a scale of 0–5
SocialRatingAverage	Represents the average rating for a specific URL
SocialRatingManager	Contains methods and properties used to manipulate social rating data
SocialTag	Represents a social tag, consisting of a URI and a term from the taxonomy term store
SocialTagManager	Contains methods and properties used to manipulate social tag data
SocialTerm	Represents a term that has been made available for social tagging
SocialUrl	Represents a URL that has been tagged at least one time with a SocialTag

MSDN SharePoint SDK

Social Data Web Service

SharePoint has several web services that can be used to access data in the user profile and social database. The web services provide a convenient way to integrate existing applications with SharePoint, as your code does not need to execute on the SharePoint server. The web services are located in the ISAPI directory found in the SharePoint root. References can be added using the _vti_bin mapped path from Visual Studio.

For example, if you had an existing web application on a server named Belize using port 777, the URL used to locate the service would be `http://belize:777/_vti_bin/socialdataservice.asmx`. You can enter the URL into your browser and see the members of the web service as shown in Figure 5-8.

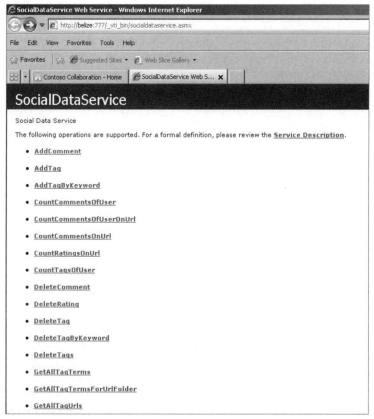

FIGURE 5-8

The Social Data web service can be used to access social data stored in SharePoint. As you explore all the methods available in the web service, you will see there is a lot of functionality exposed. An example of this functionality is shown in the following code listing. In Listing 5-4, the web service is used to retrieve ratings for a URL, which can represent a page or a document.

Available for download on Wrox.com

LISTING 5-4: Using SocialdataService.asmx to Retrieve Ratings

```
using System;
using System.Collections.Generic;
using System.ComponentModel;
using System.Data;
using System.Linq;
using SocialWebService.ServiceReference1;

namespace SocialWebService
{
```

continues

LISTING 5-4 *(continued)*

```
    class Program
    {
        static void Main(string[] args)
        {
            string GetRatingForThisURL = "http://belize:333/Pages/Home.aspx";
            ServiceReference1.SocialDataService mySocialDataService =
new ServiceReference1.SocialDataService();
            mySocialDataService.Credentials =
System.Net.CredentialCache.DefaultCredentials;
            mySocialDataService.Url =
 "http://localhost:777/_vti_bin/socialdataservice.asmx";
            SocialRatingDetail details =
 mySocialDataService.GetRatingOnUrl(GetRatingForThisURL);
            Console.Write("The rating for " + GetRatingForThisURL + " is " +
 details.Rating.ToString());
            Console.Read();
        }
    }
}
```

Activity Feeds

Twitter and the status updates on Facebook have made the concept of microblogging popular with Internet users. SharePoint implements this capability using status updates, which can be updated by your users. As you browse content and apply tags and notes, your activity feed can be updated with the tag and note data. One business use of the activity feed is to allow other community members to keep track of work in progress, presence awareness, and progress. *Presence awareness* technology allows you to determine where your colleagues are at any given time. An example is an instant message application that signals when users are online, offline, or available via mobile device or other communication device. You can build a vast array of applications using social computing technologies with the classes defined in Table 5-3. The documentation and samples in the SDK will be extended when SharePoint is released.

Tags and Notes

The act of tagging content is the assignment of metadata or categories to that content. There are two types of tagging: social tagging and structured tagging. Structured tagging refers to content and adds metadata to content to describe what it is, what it contains, or what it does. Social tagging is related to a person and describes the person, such as what they do, which projects they work on, or what skills they have.

You can also tag and create notes on external sites. All of the tag, notes, and rating data is stored in the social database and can be accessed from your My Site or programmatically using the object model. A farm administrator can manage tags using the UPA as shown in Figure 5-9. The aggregation of tags and notes in the activity feed might prove useful when your users are working with many pages, lists, and documents throughout many sites.

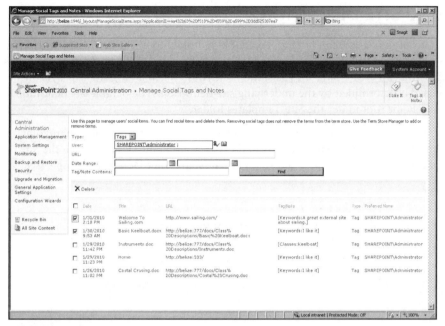

FIGURE 5-9

TABLE 5-4: Artifacts That Can Be Tagged, Noted, and Rated

DESCRIPTION	TAGS	NOTES	RATINGS
Web part/control	No	Yes	Yes
Discover content by colleague or keyword	Both	Colleagues	Colleagues
Web pages, list items, documents	Yes	Yes	Yes
Doc library/list sort and filter	Yes (doc authors only, requires enterprise keywords field)	No	Yes
Indexed by Search	Yes	No	Yes
Bookmark-let for external or non-SharePoint pages	Yes	Yes	No
Enterprise taxonomy management	Yes	No	No
In Office 2010 client	Yes (doc authors only, requires enterprise keywords field)	Yes	No?
In Office web apps	Yes	Yes	No

SharePoint Product Team Slide

BLOGS AND WIKI SITE DEFINITIONS

Each user within your organization can have a personal blog linked to his or her My Site, making it easy for other people to find. New blog posts are added to the Recent Activity section of the user's My Site home page. You can create blog sites as standalone sites. When a blog site is provisioned, the configuration used is determined by the underlying site definition. The default site definition can be found in the SharePoint root under the Site Templates folder.

You will find it refreshing to develop and extend the functionality of your blog using SharePoint Designer. Simply browse to your blog site and select Edit with SharePoint Designer from the Site Actions menu. Working with the blog, lists, and web parts in SharePoint Designer is simple (see Figure 5-10).

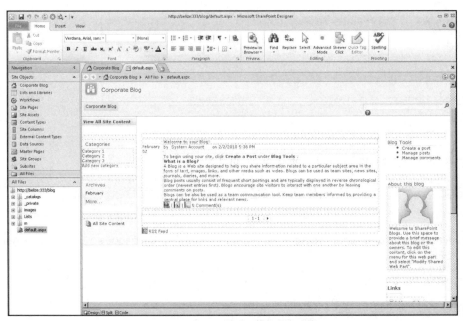

FIGURE 5-10

Like any other SharePoint site, a blog site can be branded using Master Pages, style sheets, and SharePoint Designer. In addition, you can save an existing blog site as a web template, import it into Visual Studio, and customize the site definition. The customized site definition can be deployed to the SharePoint root as a new site definition and used when your blog sites are provisioned. As with any other site definition, you can staple features to the custom blog definition to add functionality. The onet.xml file shown in Listing 5-5 can be customized to change the configuration of blog sites created using the custom site definition.

LISTING 5-5: Adding Lists and Web Parts to the onet.xml file Using Visual Studio

```xml
<View List="303" BaseViewID="0" WebPartZoneID="BlogNavigator" WebPartOrder="1">
<![CDATA[
                          <webParts>
                              <webPart
xmlsn="http://schemas.microsoft.com/WebPart/v3">
                                  <metaData>
                                      <type name=
"Microsoft.SharePoint.WebPartPages.XsltListViewWebPart,Microsoft.SharePoint,Version
=14.0.0.0,Culture=neutral,PublicKeyToken=71e9bce111e9429c" />
                <importErrorMessage>Cannot import this Web Part.</importErrorMessage>
                                  </metaData>
                                  <data>
                                      <properties>
<property name="AllowConnect" type="bool">True</property>
<property name="ChromeType" type="chrometype">None</property>
                                      </properties>
                                  </data>
                              </webPart>
                          </webParts>
                      ]]></View>
        <AllUsersWebPart List="301" WebPartZoneID="BlogNavigator" WebPartOrder="2">
<![CDATA[
                      <WebPart xmlns="http://schemas.microsoft.com/WebPart/v2">

      <Assembly>Microsoft.SharePoint, Version=14.0.0.0, Culture=neutral,
PublicKeyToken=71e9bce111e9429c</Assembly>
                      <TypeName>Microsoft.SharePoint.WebPartPages.
BlogMonthQuickLaunch
</TypeName>
                      <Title>$Resources:core,months_schema_blg_title;</Title>
                      <Description>$Resources:core,blog_month_quick_launch;
</Description>
                      <FrameType>None</FrameType>
                      <FrameState>Normal</FrameState>
                      <IsVisible>true</IsVisible>
                      </WebPart>
                  ]]></AllUsersWebPart>
        <AllUsersWebPart List="301" WebPartZoneID="Right" WebPartOrder="1">
<![CDATA[
                      <WebPart xmlns="http://schemas.microsoft.com/WebPart/v2">
                      <Assembly>Microsoft.SharePoint, Version=14.0.0.0, Culture=
neutral,
PublicKeyToken=71e9bce111e9429c</Assembly>

<TypeName>Microsoft.SharePoint.WebPartPages.BlogAdminWebPart
</TypeName>

<Title>$Resources:core,adminlinks_schema_blg_title;</Title>

<Description>$Resources:core,blog_admin_links;</Description>
                      <FrameType>Default</FrameType>
```

continues

LISTING 5-5 *(continued)*

```
                            <FrameState>Normal</FrameState>
                            <IsVisible>true</IsVisible>
                            </WebPart>
                    ]]></AllUsersWebPart>
        </File>
```

Enterprise Wiki Sites

The Collaboration Portal in SharePoint 2007 has been deprecated and the functionality replaced with the Enterprise Wiki (EW) site definition, shown in Figure 5-11. The EW is a publishing site with all of the publishing features enabled at the site collection level. Wiki pages are stored in a pages library and can benefit from output caching and other Web Content Management features enabled for the page library.

When you create an EW you must first create and configure the following:

➤   Managed Metadata Service Application

➤   User Profiles Service (required for My Site)

➤   Publishing features

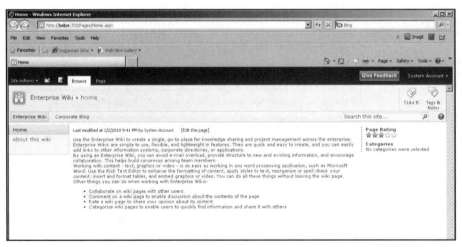

FIGURE 5-11

The Wiki page content type has a Wiki Category column, which you use to categorize individual wiki pages. The category column is a managed metadata field that allows the categories to be managed using a term set in the term store. When you edit a wiki page, you have the option to select a category for the page based on the defined term set linked to the category column.

When editing a wiki page, you can add web parts. Unlike web parts added to web part pages, the wiki web parts do not have to be added to a Web Part zone. Web parts are added to wiki pages using the same Ribbon you use when adding them to any other page. The wiki page has a hidden Web Part zone named WP Zone, which allows for the inline adding of web parts. Another nice feature is that, when a wiki page version is restored, the web part properties are also restored.

 The WikiEditPage *class can be found in the* Microsoft.SharePoint .WebPartPages *namespace. The class includes a method* InsertWebPartIntoWik iPage*, which handles adding your web parts to the wiki pages. Additional members can be used to extend the wiki page publishing infrastructure.*

SUMMARY

This chapter covered the new people-centric features available to you as you deploy and develop solutions using SharePoint. Microsoft is investing a lot in the social and community capabilities of SharePoint. SharePoint has a vast object model, which can be used by developers to track and modify social data. Understanding the differences between business-centric, enterprise computing, and social computing is important as you deploy people-centric solutions using SharePoint. Tags, ratings, and notes are ubiquitous in SharePoint and allow you to share tacit and structured social information with your organization. The keystone to any social application is the user profile store; remember, the more you know about your users the more cool things you can do with your software.

Search

WHAT'S IN THIS CHAPTER?

➤ Overview of the new Enterprise Search product line with guidance on which product to use for a given situation

➤ Tour of new architecture and user experience features

➤ Common patterns for developing extensions and applications with Enterprise Search

➤ Details on customizing all aspects of search, from user experience and social search to federation, connectors, and content processing

➤ Examples you can use to get started on custom search projects

Microsoft has been in the Enterprise Search business for a long time. The last two years have seen an increased focus in this area, including the introduction of Search Server 2008 and the acquisition of FAST Search and Transfer. Search is becoming strategic to many businesses, and Microsoft's investments reflect this.

Enterprise Search delivers content for the benefit of the employees, customers, partners, or affiliates of a single company or organization. Companies, government agencies, and other organizations maintain huge amounts of information in electronic form, including spreadsheets, policy manuals, and web pages, just to name a few. Contemporary private datasets can now exceed the size of the entire Internet in the 1990s — running into petabytes or even exabytes of information. This content may be stored in file shares, websites, content management systems, or databases, but without the ability to find this corporate knowledge, managing even a small company would be difficult.

Enterprise Search applications are found throughout most enterprises — both in obvious places (like intranet search) and in less visible ways (search-driven applications often don't look like "search"). Search supports all of these applications, and also complements all of the other workloads within SharePoint 2010 — Insights, Social, Composites, and the like — in powerful ways.

Learning to develop great applications, including search, will serve you and your organization very well. You can build more flexible, more powerful applications that bridge different information silos while providing a natural, simple user experience.

This chapter provides an introduction to developing with search in SharePoint 2010. First, it covers the options, capabilities, and architecture of search. A section on the most common search customizations gives you a sense of what kind of development you are likely to run into. Next, you run through different areas of search: social search, indexing connectors, federation, content processing, ranking and relevance, the UI, and administration. In each of these areas, this chapter provides a deeper look at the capabilities and how a developer can work with them, as well as an example. Finally, the summary gives an overview of the power of search and offers some ways to combine it with other workloads in SharePoint 2010.

SEARCH OPTIONS WITH SHAREPOINT 2010

With the 2010 wave, Microsoft has added new Enterprise Search products and updated existing ones — bringing in a *lot* of new capabilities. Some of these are brand new, some are evolutions of the SharePoint 2007 search capabilities, and some are capabilities brought from FAST. The result is a set of options that lets you solve any search problem, but because of the number of options, it can also be confusing.

Figure 6-1 shows the Enterprise Search products in the 2010 wave. There are many options; in fact, there are 9 offerings for Enterprise Search. This is evidence of the emphasis Microsoft is putting on search, and also a byproduct of the ongoing integration of the FAST acquisition.

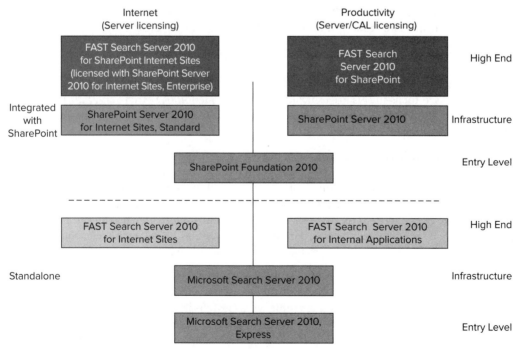

FIGURE 6-1

This lineup might seem confusing at first, and the sheer number of options is a bit daunting. As you will see, there is some method to this madness. For most purposes, you will be considering only one or two of these options.

Looking at the lineup from different perspectives helps in understanding it. There are three main dimensions to consider:

➤ **Tier** (labeled along the right side of Figure 6-1): Microsoft adopted a three-tier approach in 2008 when it introduced Search Server 2008 Express and acquired FAST. These tiers are entry level, infrastructure, and high end. Search Server 2010 Express and the search in SharePoint Foundation 2010 are entry level; SharePoint Server and Search Server 2010 comprise the infrastructure tier, and any option labeled "FAST" is high end.

➤ **Integration** (labeled along the left side of Figure 6-1): Search options integrated with SharePoint have features, such as social search, that are built on other parts of SharePoint. Standalone search options don't require SharePoint, but they lack these features.

➤ **Application** (labeled across the top of Figure 6-1): Applications are divided into Internet applications or Productivity applications. For the most part, the distinction between search applications inside the firewall (Productivity) and outside the firewall (Internet) is a pure licensing distinction. Inside the firewall, products are licensed by server and by client access license (CAL). Outside the firewall, it isn't possible to license clients, so products are licensed by server. The media, documentation, support, and architecture are the same across these applications (e.g., horizontally across Figure 6-1). There are a few minor feature differences, which are called out in this chapter where relevant.

There is another perspective useful in understanding this lineup: codebase. The acquisition of FAST brought a large codebase of high-end search code, different from the SharePoint search codebase. As the integration of FAST proceeds, ultimately all Enterprise Search options will be derived from a single common codebase.

At the moment, there are three separate codebases from which Enterprise Search products are derived. The first is the SharePoint 2010 search codebase, an evolution from the MOSS 2007 search code. Search options derived from this codebase are in medium gray boxes, as shown in Figure 6-1. The second is the FAST standalone codebase, a continuation of the code from FAST ESP, the flagship product provided by FAST up to this time. Search options derived from this codebase are shown in light gray boxes in Figure 6-1. The third is the FAST integrated codebase, a new one resulting from reworking the ESP code, integrating it with the SharePoint search architecture, and adding in new elements. Search options derived from this codebase are shown in dark gray boxes in Figure 6-1.

The codebase perspective is useful for developers, as it provides a sense of what to expect with APIs and system behavior. The FAST integrated codebase uses the same APIs as the SharePoint search codebase, but extends those APIs to expose additional capabilities. The FAST standalone codebase uses different APIs. Note that search products from the FAST standalone codebase are in a special status — licensed through FAST as a subsidiary and under different support programs. This book doesn't cover products from the FAST standalone codebase or the APIs specific to them.

If you consider the search options across application areas as the same, and disregard the FAST standalone codebase, you are left with five options in the Enterprise Search lineup, rather than nine. Look at each of these options and see where you might use each one. This chapter will also introduce some shorter names and acronyms for each option to make the discussion simpler.

SharePoint Foundation

Microsoft SharePoint Foundation (also called SharePoint Foundation, or SPF) is a free, downloadable platform that includes search capabilities. The search is pretty basic — limited to content within SharePoint, no search scopes, and no refinement. SPF is in the entry-level tier and is integrated with SharePoint.

If you are using SharePoint Foundation and care about search (which is likely, because you are reading this chapter!), you should forget about the built-in search capability and use one of the other options. Most likely this will be Search Server Express, as it is also free.

Search Server 2010 Express

Microsoft Search Server 2010 Express (also called Search Server Express or MSSX) is a free, downloadable standalone search offering. It is intended for tactical, small-scale search applications (such as departmental sites), requiring little or no cost and IT effort. Microsoft Search Server 2008 Express was a very popular product — Microsoft reports that there have been over 100,000 downloads. There is a lot added with the 2010 wave — better connectivity, refinement, improved relevance, and much more.

Search Server Express is an entry-level standalone product. It is limited to one server with up to 300,000 documents. It lacks many of the capabilities of SharePoint Server, such as taxonomy, or people and expertise search, not to mention the capabilities of FAST. It can, however, be a good enough option for many departments that require a straightforward site search.

If you have little or no budget and an immediate, simple, tactical search need, use Search Server Express. It is quick to deploy, easy to manage, and free. You can always move to one of the other options later.

Search Server 2010

Microsoft Search Server 2010 (also called Search Server or MSS) has the same functional capabilities as MSS Express, with full scale — up to about 10 million items per server and 100 million items in a system using multiple servers. It isn't free, but the per server license cost is low. MSS is a great way to scale up for applications that start with MSS Express and grow (as they often do).

MSS is an infrastructure-tier standalone product. Both MSS and MSS Express lack some search capabilities that are available in SharePoint Server 2010, such as taxonomy support, people and expertise search, social tagging, and social search (where search results improve because of social behavior), to name a few. And, of course, MSS does not have any of the other SharePoint Server capabilities (BI, workflow, etc.) that are often mixed together with search in applications.

If you have no other applications for SharePoint Server, and need general intranet search or site search, MSS can be a good choice. But in most cases, it makes more sense to use SharePoint Server 2010.

SharePoint Server 2010

Microsoft SharePoint Server 2010 (also called SharePoint Server or SP) includes a complete intranet search solution that provides a robust search capability out of the box. It has many significant improvements over its predecessor, *Microsoft Office SharePoint Server 2007* (also called MOSS 2007) search. New capabilities include refinement, people and expertise search with phonetic matching, social tagging, social search, query suggestions, editing directly in a browser, and many more. Connectivity is much broader and simpler, both for indexing and federation. SharePoint Server 2010 also has markedly improved its scale-out architecture, providing flexibility for different performance, scale, and availability needs.

SharePoint Server has three license variants in the 2010 wave — all with precisely the same search functionality. With all of them, Enterprise Search is a component or "workload," not a separate license. SharePoint Server 2010 is licensed in a typical Microsoft server/CAL model. Each server needs a server license, and each user needs a client access license (CAL). For applications where CALs don't apply (typically outside the firewall in customer-facing sites), there is SharePoint Server 2010 for Internet Sites, Standard (*FIS-S*) and SharePoint Server 2010 for Internet Sites, and Enterprise (*FIS-E*).

For the rest of this chapter, these licensing variants will be ignored, and we will refer to all of them as SharePoint Server 2010 or SP. All of them are infrastructure-tier, integrated offerings.

SharePoint Server 2010 is a good choice for general intranet search, people search, and site search applications. It is a fully functional search solution and should cover the scale and connectivity needs of most organizations. However, it is no longer the best search offered with SharePoint, given the integration of FAST in this wave.

FAST Search Server 2010 for SharePoint

Microsoft FAST Search Server 2010 for SharePoint (also called FAST Search for SharePoint or FS4SP) is a brand-new product. It is a high-end Enterprise Search product, providing an excellent search experience out of the box and the flexibility to customize search for very diverse needs at essentially unlimited scale. FS4SP is notably simpler to deploy and operate than other high-end search offerings. It provides high-end search, integrated with SharePoint.

The frameworks and tools used by IT professionals and developers are common across the SharePoint search codebase and the FAST integrated codebase. FAST Search for SharePoint builds on SharePoint Server, and integrates into the SharePoint 2010 architecture using some of the new elements, such as the enhanced connector framework and the federation framework. This means that FAST Search for SharePoint shares the same object models and APIs for connectors, queries, and system management. In addition, administrative and frontend frameworks are common — basically the same management console and the same Search Center web parts.

Figure 6-2 shows how FAST adds on to SharePoint Server. In operation, both SharePoint servers and FAST Search for SharePoint servers are used. SharePoint servers handle crawling, accept and federate queries, and serve up people search. FAST Search for SharePoint servers handle all content processing and core search. The result is a combination of SharePoint search and FAST search technology in a hybrid form, plus several new elements and capabilities.

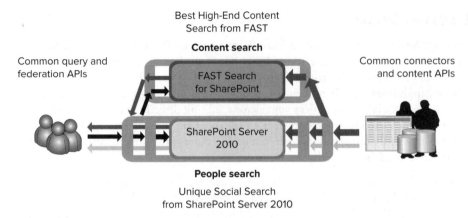

Best High-End Content
Search from FAST

Content search

Common query and
federation APIs

FAST Search
for SharePoint

Common connectors
and content APIs

SharePoint Server
2010

People search

Unique Social Search
from SharePoint Server 2010

Common IT pro and developer experience

FIGURE 6-2

FAST Search for SharePoint provides significant enhancements to SharePoint's Enterprise Search capabilities. This means that there are capabilities and extensions to APIs that are specific to FAST Search for SharePoint. For example, there are extensions to the Query Object Model (OM), to accommodate the additional capabilities of FAST such as FAST Query Language (FQL). The biggest differences are in the functionality available: a visual and "contextual" search experience; advanced content processing, including metadata extraction; multiple relevance profiles and sorting options available to users; more control of the user experience; and extreme scale capabilities.

FAST LICENSING VARIANTS

Just like SharePoint Server, FS4SP has licensing variants for internal and external use. FS4SP is licensed per server, requires Enterprise CALs (e-CALs) for each user, and needs SharePoint Server 2010 as a prerequisite. FAST Search Server 2010 for SharePoint Internet Sites (FS4SP-IS) is for situations where CALs don't apply, typically Internet-facing sites with various search applications. In these situations, SP-FIS-E (enterprise) is a prerequisite, and SP-FIS-E server licenses can be used for either SP-FIS-E servers or FS4SP-IS servers. FS4SP and FS4SP-IS have essentially the same search functionality with a few exceptions. We will largely ignore these variants for the remainder of this chapter and refer to them both as FAST Search for SharePoint or FS4SP.

FAST Search for SharePoint handles general intranet search, people search, and site search applications, providing more capability than SharePoint Server does, including the ability to give different groups using the same site different experiences via user context. FS4SP is particularly well suited for high-value search applications such as those described below.

Choosing the Right Search Product

Most often, organizations implementing a Microsoft Enterprise Search product will choose between SharePoint Server 2010's search capabilities and FAST Search for SharePoint. SharePoint Server's search has improved significantly since 2007, so it is worth a close look, especially if you are already running SharePoint 2007's search. FAST Search for SharePoint has many capabilities beyond SharePoint Server 2010's search, but it also carries additional licensing costs. By understanding the differences in features and the applications that can be addressed by each feature, you can determine whether you need the additional capabilities offered by FAST.

With Enterprise Search inside the firewall, there are two distinct types of search applications:

➤ *General-purpose* search applications increase employee efficiency by connecting "everyone to everything." These search solutions increase employee efficiency by connecting a broad set of people to a broad set of information. Intranet search is the most common example of this type of search application.

➤ *Special-purpose* search applications help a specific set of people make the most of a specific set of information. Common examples include product support applications, research portals ranging from market research to competitive analysis, knowledge centers, and customer-oriented sales and service applications. This kind of application is found in many places, with variants for essentially every role in an enterprise. These applications typically are the highest-value search applications, as they are tailored to a specific task that is usually essential to the users they serve. They are also typically the most rewarding for developers.

SharePoint Server 2010's built-in search is targeted at general-purpose search applications, and can be tailored to provide specific intranet search experiences for different organizations and situations. FAST Search for SharePoint can be used for general-purpose search applications, and can be an "upgrade" from SharePoint search to provide superior search in those applications. However, it is designed with special-purpose search applications in mind. So applications you identify as fitting the "special-purpose" category should be addressed with FAST Search for SharePoint.

Because SP and FS4SP share the connector framework (with a few exceptions covered later), you won't find big differences in connectors or security, which traditionally are areas where search engines have differentiated themselves. Instead, you see big differences in content processing, user experience, and advanced query capabilities. Examples of capabilities specific to FAST Search for SharePoint are:

➤ Content-processing pipeline

➤ Metadata extraction

➤ Structured data search

➤ Deep refinement

➤ Visual search

➤ Advanced linguistics

➤ Visual best bets

➤ Development platform flexibility

➤ Ease of creating custom search experiences

➤ Extreme scale and performance

Common Platform and APIs

There are more aspects in common between SharePoint Server 2010 Search and FAST Search for SharePoint than there are differences. The frameworks and tools for use by IT pros and developers are kept as common as possible across the product line, given the additional capabilities in FAST Search Server 2010 for SharePoint. In particular, the object models for content, queries, and federation are all the same, and the web parts are largely common. All of the products described above provide a unified Query Object Model. The result is that if you develop a custom solution that uses the Query Object Model for SharePoint Foundation 2010, for example, then it will continue to work if you upgrade to SharePoint Server 2010, or if you migrate your code to FAST Search Server 2010 for SharePoint.

Figure 6-3 shows the "stack" involved with Enterprise Search, from the client down to the search cores.

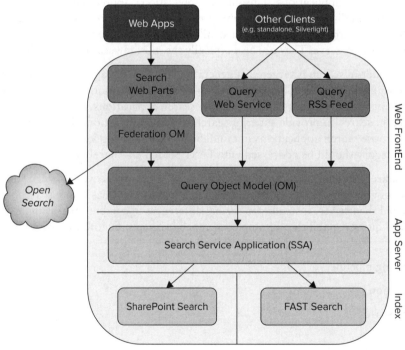

FIGURE 6-3

For the rest of this chapter, we will describe one set of capabilities and OMs and call out any specific differences within the product line where relevant.

SEARCH USER EXPERIENCE

Information workers typically start searches either from the Simple Search box or by browsing to a site based on a Search Center site template. Figure 6-4 shows the Simple Search box that is available by default on all site pages. By default, this search box issues queries that are scoped to the current site, because users often navigate to sites that they know contain the information they want before they perform a search.

Navigation to Search Center   Simple Search Box

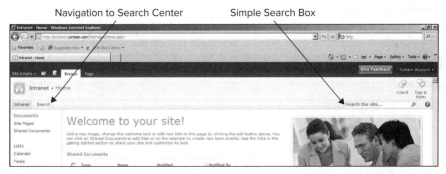

FIGURE 6-4

Search Center

Figure 6-5 shows a search site based on the Enterprise Search Center template. Information workers use Search Center sites to search across all crawled and federated content.

FIGURE 6-5

By default, the Search Center includes two search tabs: "All Sites" and "People". The Search Center includes an Advanced Search Box that provides links to the current user's search preferences and advanced search options.

Figure 6-6 shows the default view for performing an advanced search, with access to phrase search features, language filters, result type filters, and property filters.

FIGURE 6-6

All of the search user interfaces are intuitive and easy to use, so information workers can start searches in a straightforward way. When an information worker performs a search, the results are displayed on a results page, as shown in Figure 6-7. The SharePoint Sever 2010 Search core results page offers a user-friendly and intuitive user interface. People can use simple and familiar keyword queries, and get results in a rich and easy-to-navigate layout.

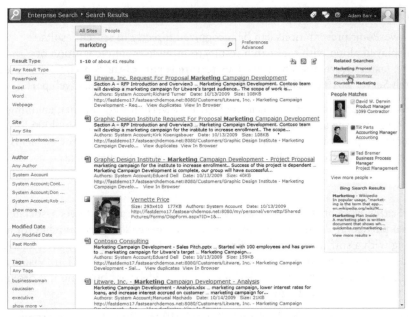

FIGURE 6-7

Visual Cues in Search Results with FAST

FAST Search for SharePoint adds visual cues into the search experience. These provide an engaging, useful, and efficient way for information workers to interact with search results. People find information faster when they recognize documents visually. A search result from FAST Search for SharePoint is shown in Figure 6-8.

FIGURE 6-8

Thumbnails and Previews

Word documents and PowerPoint presentations can be recognized directly in search results. A thumbnail image is displayed along with the search results to provide rapid recognition of information and, thereby, faster information finding. This feature is part of the Search Core Results web part for FAST Search Server 2010 for SharePoint, and can be configured in that web part.

In addition to the thumbnail, a scrolling preview is available for PowerPoint documents, enabling an information worker to browse the actual slides in a presentation. People are often looking for a particular slide, or remember a presentation on the basis of a couple of slides. This preview helps them recognize what they're looking for quickly, without having to open the document.

Visual Best Bets

SharePoint Server 2010 Search keywords can have definitions, synonyms, and Best Bets associated with them. A Best Bet is a particular document set up to appear whenever someone searches for a keyword. It appears along with a star icon and the definition of that keyword. FAST Search Server 2010 for SharePoint adds the ability for you to define Visual Best Bets for keywords. This Visual Best Bet may be anything you can identify with a URI — an image, video, or application. It provides a simple, powerful, and very effective way to guide people's search experiences.

These visual search elements are unique to FAST Search Server 2010 for SharePoint and are not provided in SharePoint Server 2010 Search.

Exploration and Refinement

SharePoint Server 2010 also provides a new way to explore information — via search refinements, as shown on the left of Figure 6-9. These refinements are displayed down the left-hand side of the page in the core search results. They provide self-service drill-down capabilities for filtering the search results returned. The refinements are automatically determined by SharePoint Server 2010, using tags and metadata in the search results. Such refinements include searching by the type of content (web page, document, spreadsheet, presentation, and so on), location, author, last modified date, and metadata tags. Administrators can extend the refinement panel easily to include refinements based on any managed property.

Refinement with FAST Search Server 2010 for SharePoint is considerably more powerful than refinement in SharePoint Server 2010. SharePoint Server 2010 automatically generates *shallow* refinement for search results that enable a user to apply additional filters to search results based on the values returned by the query. Shallow refinement is based on the managed properties returned from the first 50 results by the original query.

In contrast, FAST Search Server 2010 for SharePoint offers the option of deep refinement, which is based on aggregation of managed property values within the entire result set. These are shown in Figure 6-9 both in out-of-the-box form and as custom visual refiners.

Using deep refinement, you can find the "needle in the haystack," such as a person who has written a document about a specific subject, even if this document would otherwise appear farther down the result list. Deep refinement can also display counts and lets the user see the number of results in each refinement category. You can also use the statistical data returned for numeric refinements in other types of analysis.

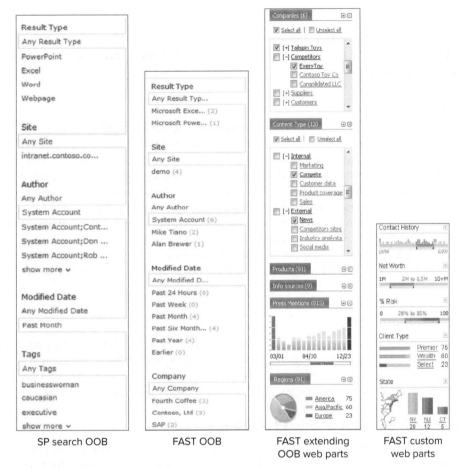

SP search OOB   FAST OOB   FAST extending   FAST custom
                               OOB web parts   web parts

FIGURE 6-9

"Conversational" Search

Search is more than "find"; it is also "explore." In many situations, the quickest and most effective way to find *or* explore is through a dialogue with the machine — a "conversation" allowing the user to respond to results and steer to the answer or insight. The conversational search capabilities in FAST Search for SharePoint provide ways for information workers to interact with and refine their search results, so that they can quickly find the information they require.

Sort Results on Managed Properties

By default, SharePoint Server 2010 sorts results on each document's relevance rank. Information workers can re-sort the results by date modified, but these are the only two sort options in SharePoint Server 2010. With FAST Search Server 2010 for SharePoint, users can sort results on any managed properties, such as sorting by Author, Document Size, or Title. Relevance ranking profiles can also be surfaced as sorting criteria, allowing end users to pick different relevance rankings as desired.

This sorting is considerably more powerful than sorting in SharePoint Server 2010 Search.

Similar Results

With FAST Search Server 2010 for SharePoint, results returned by a query include links to "Similar Results." When a user clicks on the link, the search is redefined and rerun to include documents that are similar to the result in question.

Result Collapsing

FAST Search Server 2010 for SharePoint provides a result collapsing capability which can be used for de-duplication and also for result roll-up. Documents that have the same value stored in a field in the index will be collapsed as one document in the search result. If that field is a managed property such as "author", all documents matching a given query with the same author can be rolled up in the result, and expanded by the user as desired. If that field is a checksum or other unique signature of the document's content, collapsing provides duplicate detection. This means that documents stored in multiple locations in a source system will be displayed only once during a search using the collapse search parameter. The collapsed results include links to "Duplicates." When a user clicks on the link, the search result displays all versions of that document. Similar results and result collapsing are unique to FAST Search Server 2010 for SharePoint and are not provided in SharePoint Server 2010 Search.

Contextual Search Capabilities

FAST Search Server 2010 for SharePoint allows you to associate Best Bets, Visual Best Bets, document promotions, document demotions, site promotions, and site demotions with defined user contexts in order to personalize the experience for information workers. You can use the FAST Search User Context link in the Site Collection Settings pages to define user contexts for these associations.

Relevancy Tuning by Document or Site Promotions

SharePoint Server 2010 enables you to identify varying levels of authoritative pages that help you tune relevancy ranking by site. FAST Search Server 2010 for SharePoint adds the ability for you to specify individual documents within a site for promotion or demotion and, furthermore, enables you to associate each promotion or demotion with user contexts.

Synonyms

SharePoint Server 2010 keywords can have one-way synonyms associated with them. FAST Search Server 2010 for SharePoint extends this concept by enabling you to implement both two-way and one-way synonyms. With a two-way synonym set of, for example, {auto car}, a search for "auto" would be translated into a search for "auto OR car," and a search for "car" would be translated into a search for "car OR auto." With a one-way synonym set of, for example, {car coupe}, a search for "car" would translate into a search for "car OR coupe," but a search for "coupe" would remain just "coupe."

People Search

SharePoint Server 2010 provides an address-book-style name lookup experience with name and expertise matching, making it easy to find people by name, title, expertise, and organizational structure. This includes phonetic name matching that will return names that sound similar to what the user has typed in a query. It will also return all variations of common names, including nicknames.

The refiners provided for the core search results are also provided with people search results — exploring results via name, title, and various fields in a user's profile enables quick browsing and selection of people. People search results also include real-time presence through Office Communication Server, making it easy to immediately connect with people once they are found through search. Figure 6-10 shows a people search results page.

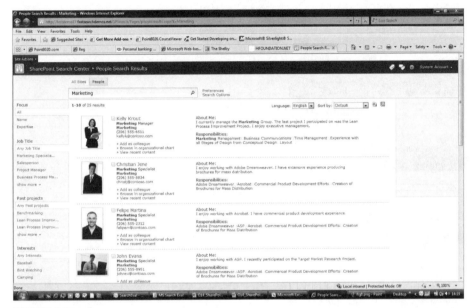

FIGURE 6-10

The people and expertise finding capabilities with SharePoint Server 2010 are a dramatic enhancement over MOSS 2007. They are remarkably innovative and effective, and tie in nicely to the social computing capabilities covered in Chapter 5. The exact same capabilities are available with FAST Search for SharePoint.

SEARCH ARCHITECTURE AND TOPOLOGIES

The search architecture has been significantly enhanced with SharePoint Server 2010. The new architecture provides fault-tolerance options and scaling well beyond the limits of MOSS 2007 search (to 100M documents). Adding FAST provides even more flexibility and scale. Of course, these capabilities and flexibility add complexity. Understanding how search fits together architecturally will help you build applications that scale well and perform quickly.

SharePoint Search Key Components

Figure 6-11 provides an overview of the logical architecture for the Enterprise Search components in SharePoint Server 2010.

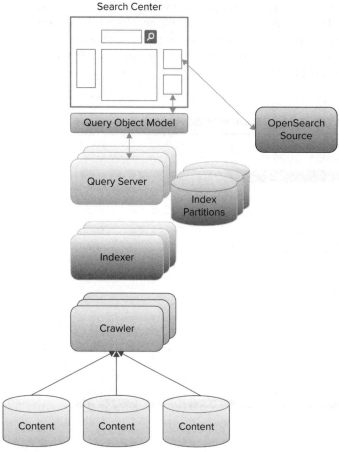

Search Center

FIGURE 6-11

As shown in Figure 6-11, there are four main components that deliver the Enterprise Search features of SharePoint Server 2010:

➤ **Crawler:** This component invokes connectors that are capable of communicating with content sources. Because SharePoint Server 2010 can crawl different types of content sources (such as SharePoint sites, other websites, file shares, Lotus Notes databases, and data exposed by Business Connectivity Services), a specific connector is used to communicate with each type of source. The crawler then uses the connectors to connect to and traverse the content sources, according to crawl rules that an administrator can define. For example, the crawler uses the file connector to connect to file shares by using the FILE:// protocol, and then traverses the folder structure in that content source to retrieve file content and metadata. Similarly, the crawler uses the web connector to connect to external websites by using the HTTP:// or HTTPS:// protocols and then traverses the web pages in that content source by following hyperlinks to retrieve web page content and metadata. Connectors load specific IFilters to read the actual data contained in files. Refer to the "Connector Framework" section later in this document for more information about connectors.

➤ **Indexer:** This component receives streams of data from the crawler and determines how to store that information in a physical, file-based index. For example, the indexer optimizes the storage space requirements for words that have already been indexed, manages word breaking and stemming in certain circumstances, removes noise words, and determines how to store data in specific index partitions if you have multiple query servers and partitioned indexes. Together with the crawler and its connectors, the indexing engine meets the business requirement of ensuring that enterprise data from multiple systems can be indexed. This includes collaborative data stored in SharePoint sites, files in file shares, and data in custom business solutions, such as customer relationship management (CRM) databases, enterprises resource planning (ERP) solutions, and so on.

➤ **Query Server:** Indexed data that is generated by the indexing engine is propagated to query servers in the SharePoint farm, where it is stored in one or more index files. This process is known as "continuous propagation"; that is, while indexed data is being generated or updated during the crawl process, the changes are propagated to query servers, where they are applied to the index file (or files). In this way, the data in the indexes on query servers experience a very short latency. In essence, when new data has been indexed (or existing data in the index has been updated), those changes will be applied to the index files on query servers in just a few seconds. A server that is performing the query server role responds to searches from users by searching its own index files, so it is important that latency be kept to a minimum. SharePoint Server 2010 ensures this automatically. The query server is responsible for retrieving results from the index in response to a query received via the Query Object Model. The query sever is also responsible for the word breaking, noise-word removal, and stemming (if stemming is enabled) for the search terms provided by the Query Object Model.

➤ **Query Object Model:** As mentioned earlier, searches are formed and issued to query servers by the Query Object Model. This is typically done in response to a user performing a search from the user interface in a SharePoint site, but it may also be in response to a search from a custom solution (hosted either in or out of SharePoint Server 2010). Furthermore, the search might have been issued by custom code, for example, from a workflow or from a custom navigation component. In any case, the Query Object Model parses the search terms and issues the query to a query server in the SharePoint farm. The results of the query are returned from the query server to the Query Object Model, and the object model provides those results to the user interface components (or other components that may have issued the query).

Figure 6-12 shows a process view of SharePoint Server Search. The Shared Service Application (SSA), new to SharePoint 2010, is used to provide a shareable and scalable service. A search SSA can work across multiple SharePoint farms, and is administered on a service level.

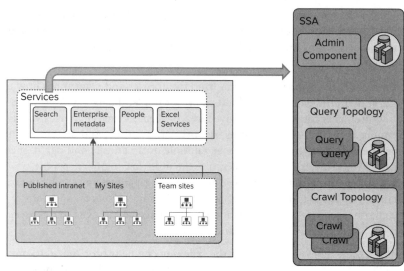

FIGURE 6-12

Search Topologies, Scaling, and High Availability

SharePoint Server 2010 enables you to add multiple instances of each of the crawler, indexing, and query components. This level of flexibility means that you can scale your SharePoint farms. (Previous versions of SharePoint Server did not allow you to scale the indexing components.)

The Enterprise Search in SharePoint Server 2010 is designed to provide subsecond query latencies for all queries, regardless of the size of your farm, and to remove bottlenecks that were present in previous versions of SharePoint Server. SharePoint Server 2010 lets you scale out every logical component in your search architecture, unlike previous versions.

As shown in Figure 6-13, the architecture provides scaling at multiple levels. You can add multiple crawlers to your farm to provide availability and to scale to achieve high performance for the indexing process. You can also add multiple query servers to provide availability and to scale to achieve high query performance. All components, including administration, can be fault tolerant and can take advantage of the mirroring capabilities of the underlying databases.

The crawlers handle indexing as well. Each crawler can crawl a discrete set of content sources, so not all indexers need to index the entire corpus. This

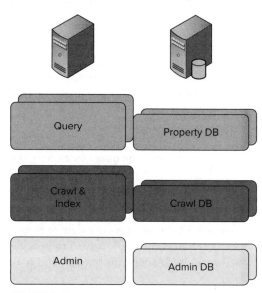

FIGURE 6-13

is a new capability for SharePoint Server 2010. Crawlers are now stateless, so that one can take over the activity of another if it fails, and they use the crawl database to coordinate the activity of multiple crawlers. Indexers no longer store full copies of the index; they simply propagate the indexes to query servers. Crawling and indexing are I/O and CPU intensive; adding more machines increases the crawl/index throughput linearly. Since content freshness is determined by crawl frequency, adding resources to crawling can provide fresher content, too.

When you add multiple query servers, you are really implementing index partitioning; each query server maintains a subset of the entire logical index and, therefore, does not need to query the entire index (which could be a very large file) for every query. The partitions are maintained automatically by SharePoint Server 2010, which uses a hash of each crawled document's ID to determine in which partition a document belongs. The indexed data is then propagated to the appropriate query server.

Another new feature is that property databases are also propagated to query servers so that retrieving managed properties and security descriptors is much more efficient than in Microsoft Office SharePoint Server 2007.

High Availability and Resiliency

Each search component fulfills high-availability requirements by supporting mirroring. Figure 6-14 shows a scaled-out and mirrored architecture, sized for 100M documents. SQL Server mirroring is used to keep multiple instances synchronized across geographic boundaries. In this example, each of the six query processing servers serves results from a partition of the index and also acts as a failover for another partition. The two crawler servers provide throughput (multiple crawlers) as well as high availability — if either crawler server fails, the crawls continue.

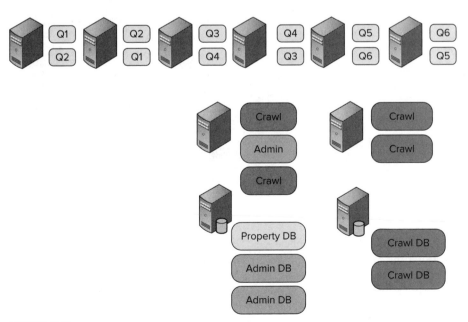

FIGURE 6-14

As with any multi-tier system, understanding the level of performance resiliency you need is the starting point. You can then engineer for as much capacity and safety as you need.

FAST Architecture and Topology

FAST Search for SharePoint shares many architectural features of SharePoint Server 2010 search. It uses the same basic layers (crawl, index, query) architecturally. It uses the same crawler and query handlers, and the same people and expertise search. It uses the same OMs and the same administrative framework.

However, there are some major differences. FAST Search for SharePoint adds on to SharePoint server in a hybrid architecture (see Figure 6-2). This means that processing from multiple farms is used to make a single system. Understanding what processing happens in what farm can be confusing; remembering the hybrid approach, with common crawlers and Query OM but separate people and content search, is key to understanding the system configuration. Figure 6-15 shows a high-level mapping of processing to farms. Light grey represents the SharePoint farm, medium grey represents the FAST backend farm, and dark grey represents other systems, such as the System Center Operations Manager (SCOM).

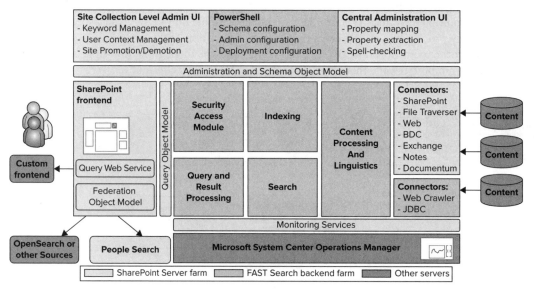

FIGURE 6-15

SharePoint 2010 provides shared service applications (SSAs) to serve common functions across multiple site collections and farms. SharePoint Server 2010 search uses one SSA (see Figure 6-12). FAST Search for SharePoint uses two SSAs: the **FAST Query SSA** and the **FAST Content SSA**. This is a result of the hybrid architecture (shown in Figure 6-2) with SharePoint servers providing people search and FAST servers providing content search. Both SSAs run on SharePoint farms and are administered from the SharePoint 2010 central administration console.

The FAST Query SSA handles all queries and also serves people search. If the queries are for content search, it routes them to a FAST Query Service (which resides on a FAST farm). Routing uses the default service provider property — or overrides this if you explicitly set a provider on the query request. The FAST Query SSA also handles crawling for people search content.

The FAST Content SSA (also called the FAST Connector SSA) handles all the content crawling that goes through the SharePoint connectors or connector framework. It feeds all content as crawled properties through to the FAST farm (specifically a FAST content distributor), using extended connector properties. The FAST Content SSA includes indexing connectors that can retrieve content from any source, including SharePoint farms, internal/external web servers, Exchange public folders, line-of-business data, and file shares.

The FAST farm (also called the FAST backend) includes a Query Service, document processors that provide advanced content processing, and FAST-specific indexing connectors used for advanced content retrieval. Configuration of the additional indexing connectors is performed via XML files and through Windows PowerShell cmdlets or command-line operations, and are not visible via SharePoint Central Administration. Figure 6-16 gives an overview of where the SSAs fit in the search architecture.

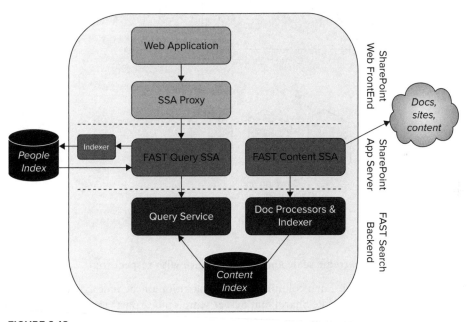

FIGURE 6-16

The use of multiple SSAs to provide for one FAST Search for SharePoint system is probably the most awkward aspect of FAST Search for SharePoint and the area of the most confusion. In practice, this is pretty straightforward, but you need to get your mind around the hybrid architecture and keep this in mind when you are architecting or administering a system. As a developer, you also have to remember this when you are using the Administrative OM.

Scale-Out with FAST

FAST Search for SharePoint is built on a highly modular architecture where the services can be scaled individually to achieve the desired performance. The architecture of FAST Search for SharePoint uses a row and column approach for core system scaling, as shown in Figure 6-17.

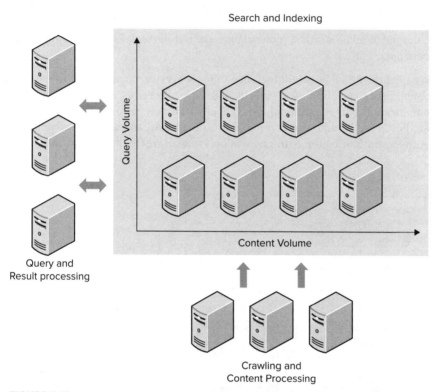

FIGURE 6-17

This architecture provides both extreme scale and fault tolerance with respect to:

➤ **Amount of indexed content:** Each column handles a partition of the index, which is kept as a file on the file system (unlike SharePoint Server search index partitions, which are held in a database). By adding columns, the system can scale linearly to extreme scale — billions of documents.

➤ **Query load:** Each row handles a set of queries; multiple rows provide both fault tolerance and capacity. An extra row provides full fault tolerance, so if an application required four rows for query handling, a fifth row would provide fault tolerance. (For most inside-the-firewall implementations, a single row provides plenty of query capacity.)

➤ **Freshness (indexing latency):** FAST Search for SharePoint enables you to optimize for low latency from the moment a document is changed in the source repository to the moment it is searchable. This can be done by proper dimensioning of the crawling, item processing, and indexing to fulfill your requirements. These three parts of the system can be scaled independently through the modular architecture.

Figure 6-18 shows an example of a FAST Search for SharePoint topology, with full fault tolerance, sized for roughly sixty million documents.

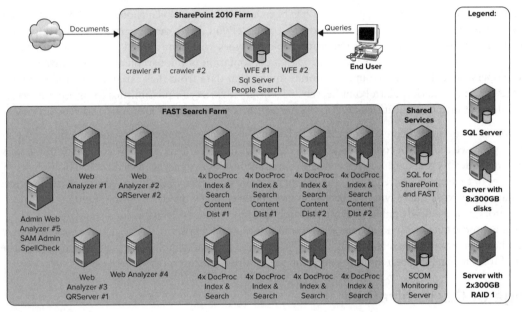

FIGURE 6-18

This example includes both the SharePoint Server farm and the FAST Search backend farm. Because the connector framework is the same, crawling scale out and redundancy are the same as with SharePoint Server 2010 Search — unless FAST-specific connectors are in use. The query-mirroring approach is the same as with SharePoint Server Search, except that content queries are processed very lightly before handing off to FAST — so query capacity per machine or VM is much higher for the SharePoint servers. The center layer is a farm of FAST Search servers, in a row-column architecture — which provides both scaling and fault tolerance.

How Architecture Meets Applications

Capacity planning, scaling, and sizing are usually the domain of the IT pro; as a developer, you need only be aware that the architecture supports a much broader range of performance and availability than MOSS 2007. You can tackle the largest, most demanding applications without worrying that your application won't be available at extreme scale.

Architecture is also important for applications that control configuration and performance. You may want to set up a specific recommended configuration — or implement self-adjusting performance based on the current topology, load, and performance. The architecture supports adding new processing on the fly — in fact, the central administration console makes it easy to do so. This means that your applications can scale broadly, ensure good performance, and meet a broad range of market needs.

DEVELOPING WITH ENTERPRISE SEARCH

Developing search-powered applications has been a difficult task. Even though search is simple on the outside, it is complicated on the inside. With SharePoint 2010, developers have a development platform that is *much* more powerful and simpler to work with than MOSS 2007. That fact extends to search-based applications as well. Through a combination of improvements to the ways in which developers can collect data from repositories, query that data from the search index, and display the results of those queries, SharePoint Server 2010 offers a variety of possibilities for more powerful and flexible search applications that access data from a wide array of locations and repositories.

There are many areas where development has become simpler — where you can cover with configuration what you used to do with code, or where you can do more with search. The new connector framework provides a flexible standard for connecting to data repositories through managed code. This reduces the amount of time and work required to build and maintain code that connects to various content sources. Enhanced keyword query syntax makes it easier to build complex queries by using standard logical operators, and the newly public Federated Search runtime object model provides a standard way of invoking those queries across all relevant search locations and repositories. The changes enable a large number of more complex interactions among Search web parts and applications, and ultimately a richer set of tools for building search result pages and search-driven features.

Range of Customization

Customization of search falls into three main categories, as shown in Figure 6-19:

➤ **Configure:** Using configuration parameters alone, you can set up a tailored search system. Usually, you are working with web part configuration, XML, and PowerShell. Most of the operations are similar to what IT pros use in administering search — but packaged ahead of time by you as a developer.

➤ **Extend:** Using the SharePoint Designer, XSLT, and other "light" development, you can create vertical and role-specific search applications. Tooling built into SPD lets you build new UIs and new connectors without code.

➤ **Create:** Search can do amazing things in countless scenarios when controlled and integrated using custom code. Visual Studio 2010 has tooling built in, which makes developing applications with SharePoint much easier. In many of these scenarios, search is one of many components in the overall application.

There are no hard rules here — general-purpose search applications, such as intranet search, can benefit from custom code and might be highly customized in some situations, even though intranet search works with no customization at all. However, most customization tends to be done on special-purpose applications with a well-identified set of users and a specific set of tasks they are trying to accomplish. Usually, these are the most valuable applications as well. Customization is well worth it for these cases.

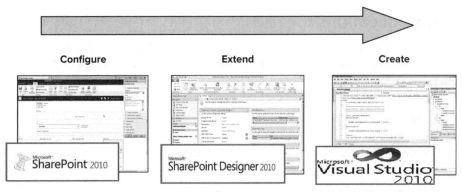

Configure **Extend** **Create**

FIGURE 6-19

Top Customization Scenarios

Although there are no hard rules, there are common patterns found when customizing Enterprise Search. The most common customization scenarios are:

> ➤ **Modify the end user experience:** To create a specific experience and/or surface specific information. Examples: add new refinement category, show results from federated location, modify the look and feel of the OOB end user experience, enable sorting by custom metadata, add a visual Best Bet for upcoming sales event, configure different rankings for the human resources and engineering departments.

> ➤ **Create a new vertical search application:** For a specific industry or role. Examples: reaching and indexing specific new content, designing a custom search experience, adding Audio/Video/Image search.

> ➤ **Create new visual elements:** Add to the standard search. Examples: show location refinement on charts/maps, show tags in a tag cloud, enable "export results to a spreadsheet," summarize financial information from customers in graphs.

> ➤ **Query and Result pipeline plug-ins:** Used to process questions and answers in more sophisticated ways. Example: create a new "single view of the customer" application that includes customer contact details, customer project details, customer correspondence, internal experts, and customer-related documents.

> ➤ **Query and Indexing shims:** Add terms and custom information to the search experience. Examples: expand query terms based on synonyms defined in the term store, augment customer results with project information, show popular people inline with search results, or show people results from other sources. Both the Query OM and the connector framework provide a way to write "shims" — simple extensions of the .NET assembly where a developer can easily add custom data sources and/or do data mash-ups.

➤ **Create new search-driven sites and applications:** Create customized content exploration experiences. Examples: show email results from personal mailbox on Exchange Server through Exchange Web Services (**EWS**), index content from custom repositories like Siebel, create content-processing plug-ins to generate new metadata.

Search-Driven Applications

Search is generally not well understood or fully used by developers building significant applications. SharePoint 2010 will, hopefully, change all that. By making it easier to own and use high-end search capabilities, and by including tooling and hooks specifically for application development, Microsoft has taken a big step forward in helping developers do more with search.

Figure 6-20 lists some examples of search-driven applications, and shows a screenshot of one of them. These are applications like any other, except that they take advantage of search technology, in addition to other elements of SharePoint, to create flexible and powerful user experiences.

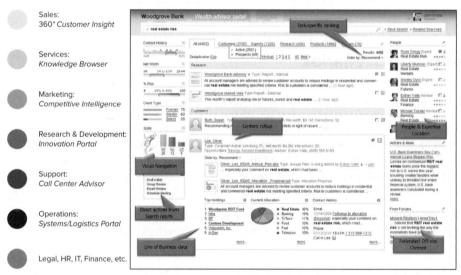

FIGURE 6-20

The rest of this chapter covers different aspects of search with SharePoint 2010, highlighting how you can customize them and how you can include them in search-driven applications.

CUSTOMIZING THE SEARCH USER EXPERIENCE

While the out-of-the-box user interface is very intuitive and useful for information workers, power users can create their own search experiences. SharePoint Server 2010 includes many search-related web parts for power users to create customized search experiences, including Best Bets, refinement panel extensions, featured content, and predefined queries. Figure 6-21 shows the standard Search web parts.

IT pros or developers can configure the built-in search web parts to tailor the search experience. As a developer, you can also extend the web parts, to change the behavior of built-in web parts on search results pages. Instead of building new web parts, developers can build onto the functionality of existing ones.

In addition, query logging is now available from customized search web parts, and from any use of the Query object to query the Search Service.

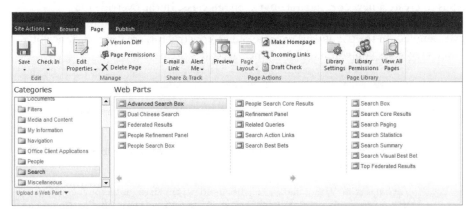

FIGURE 6-21

Example: New Core Results Web Part

Let's walk you through the creation of a new search web part in Visual Studio 2010. (The full code is included with Code Project 6-P-1, and is courtesy of Steve Peschka.) This web part inherits from the CoreResultsWebPart class and displays data from a custom source. The standard CoreResultsWebPart part includes a constructor and then two methods that we will modify in this example.

The first step is to create a new WebPart class. Create a new web part project that inherits from the CoreResultsWebPart class. Override CreateChildControls to add any controls necessary for your interface, and then override CreateDataSource. This is where you get access to the "guts" of the query. In the override, you will create an instance of a custom datasource class you will build.

```
class MSDNSample : CoreResultsWebPart
    {

        public MSDNSample()
        {
            //default constructor;        }

        protected override void CreateChildControls()
        {
            base.CreateChildControls();
```

```
            //add any additional controls needed for your UI here
        }

        protected override void CreateDataSource()
        {
            //base.CreateDataSource();
            this.DataSource = new MyCoreResultsDataSource(this);
        }
```

The second step is to create a new `CoreResultsDatasource` class. In the override for `CreateDataSource`, set the `DataSource` property to a new class that inherits from `CoreResultsDataSource`. In the `CoreResultsDataSource` constructor, create an instance of a custom datasource view class you will build. No other overrides are necessary.

```
    public class MyCoreResultsDataSource : CoreResultsDatasource
        {
            public MyCoreResultsDataSource(CoreResultsWebPart ParentWebpart)
                : base(ParentWebpart)
            {
                //to reference the properties or methods of the web part
                //use the ParentWebPart parameter

                //create the View that will be used with this datasource
                this.View = new MyCoreResultsDataSourceView(this,"MyCoreResults");
            }
        }
```

The third step is to create a new `CoreResultsDatasourceView` class. Set the `View` property for your `CoreResultsDatasource` to a new class that inherits from `CoreResultsDatasourceView`. In the `CoreResultsDatasourceView` constructor, get a reference to the `CoreResultsDatasource` so that you can refer back to the web part. Then, set the `QueryManager` property to the shared query manager used in the page.

```
    public class MyCoreResultsDataSourceView : CoreResultsDatasourceView
            {

            public MyCoreResultsDataSourceView
                (SearchResultsBaseDatasource DataSourceOwner, string ViewName)
                    : base(DataSourceOwner, ViewName)
            {
                //make sure we have a value for the datasource
                if (DataSourceOwner == null)
                {
                    throw new ArgumentNullException("DataSourceOwner");
                }

                //get a typed reference to our datasource
                MyCoreResultsDataSource ds =
                    this.DataSourceOwner as MyCoreResultsDataSource;

                //configure the query manager for this View
```

```
              this.QueryManager = SharedQueryManager.GetInstance
                  (ds.ParentWebpart.Page).QueryManager;
      }
```

You now have a functional custom web part displaying data from your custom source. In the next example, we take things one step further to provide some custom query processing.

Example: Adding Sorting to Your New Web Part

The `CoreResultsDataSourceView` class lets you modify virtually any aspect of the query. The primary way to do that is in an override of `AddSortOrder`. This class provides access to `SharePointSearchRuntime` class, which includes: `KeywordQueryObject`, `Location`, and `RefinementManager`.

The code example below adds sorting by overriding `AddSortOrder`. (The full code is included with Code Project 6-P-1, courtesy of Steve Peschka.)

```
public override void AddSortOrder(SharePointSearchRuntime runtime)
        {
            #region Ensure Runtime
            //make sure our runtime has been properly instantiated
            if (runtime.KeywordQueryObject == null)
            {
                return;
            }
            #endregion

            //remove any other sorted fields we might have had
            runtime.KeywordQueryObject.SortList.Clear();

            //get the datasource so we can get to the web part
            //and retrieve the sort fields the user selected
            SearchResultsPart wp =
                this.DataSourceOwner.ParentWebpart as SearchResultsPart;
            string sortField = wp.SortFields;

            //check to see if any sort fields have been provided
            if (!string.IsNullOrEmpty(sortField))
            {
                //if posting back, then use the value from the sort drop-down
                if (wp.Page.IsPostBack)
                {
                    //get the sort direction that was selected
                    SortDirection dir =
                        (wp.Page.Request.Form
                        [SearchResultsPart.mFormSortDirection] == "ASC" ?
                        SortDirection.Ascending : SortDirection.Descending);

                    //configure the sort list with sort field and direction
                    runtime.KeywordQueryObject.SortList.Add
                        (wp.Page.Request.Form[SearchResultsPart.mFormSortField],
                        dir);
                }
```

```
            else
            {
                //split the value out from its delimiter and
                //take the first item in descending order
                string[] values = sortField.Split(";".ToCharArray(),
                    StringSplitOptions.RemoveEmptyEntries);
                runtime.KeywordQueryObject.SortList.Add(values[0],
                    SortDirection.Descending);
            }
        }
        else  //no sort fields provided so use the default sort order
            base.AddSortOrder(runtime);
```

The `KeywordQueryObject` class is what's used in this scenario. It provides access to key query properties like:

EnableFQL	RowLimit
EnableNicknames	SearchTerms
EnablePhonetic	SelectProperties
EnableStemming	SortList
Filter	StartRow
QueryInfo	SummaryLength
QueryText	TrimDuplicates
Refiners	. . . and many more

To change the sort order in your web part, first remove the default sort order. Get a reference to the web part, as it has a property that has the sort fields. If the page has been posted back, then get the sort field the user selected. Otherwise, use the first sort field the user selected. Finally, add the sort field to the `SortList` property.

To allow sorting, you also need to provide fields on which to sort. Ordering can be done with DateTime fields, Numeric fields, or Text fields where: `HasMultipleValues = false`, `IsInDocProps = true`, and `MaxCharactersInPropertyStoreIndex > 0`.

You can limit the user to only selected fields by creating a custom web part property editor. This uses the same process as in SharePoint 2007: inherit from `EditorPart` and implement `IWebEditable`. The custom version of `EditorPart` in this example web part uses a standard LINQ query against the search schema to find properties.

Web Parts with FAST

SharePoint search and FAST Search for SharePoint share the same UI framework. When you install FAST Search for SharePoint, the same Search Centers and Small Search Box web parts apply; the main Result web part and Refiner web part are replaced with FAST-specific versions, and a Search

Visual Best Bets web part is added. Otherwise, the web parts (like the Related Queries web part or Federated Results web part) remain the same.

Because of the added capabilities of FAST, there are some additional configuration options. For example, the core results web part allows for configuration of thumbnails and scrolling previews — whether to show them or not, how many to render, and so forth. The search Action Links web part provides configuration of the sorting pulldown (which can also be used to expose multiple ranking profiles to the user). The Refinement web part has additional options, and counts are returned with refiners (since they are deep refiners — over the whole result set).

The different web parts provided with FAST Search for SharePoint and the additional configuration options are fairly self-evident when you look at the web parts and their documentation. Since most web parts are now public with SharePoint 2010, you can look at them directly and see the available configuration options within Visual Studio.

SEARCH CONNECTORS AND SEARCHING LOB SYSTEMS

Acquiring content is essential for search: if it's not crawled, you can't find it! Typical enterprises have hundreds of repositories of dozens of different types. Bridging content silos in an intuitive UI is one of the primary values of search applications. SharePoint 2010 supports this through a set of pre-created connectors, plus a framework and set of tools that make it much easier to create and administer connectivity to whatever source you like. There is already a rich set of partner-built connectors to choose from, and as a developer, you can easily leverage these or add to them.

SharePoint Server 2010 will support existing protocol handlers (custom interfaces written in unmanaged C++ code) used with MOSS 2003 and MOSS 2007. However, indexing connectors are now the primary way to create interfaces to data repositories. The Connector Framework uses .NET assemblies, and supports the Business Connectivity Services (BCS) declarative methodology for creating and expressing connections. It also enables connector authoring by means of managed code. This increased flexibility, with enhanced APIs and a seamless end-to-end experience for creating, deploying, and managing connectors, makes the job of collecting and indexing data considerably easier.

A number of productized connectors included with SharePoint Server 2010 provide built-in access to some of the most popular types of data repositories (including SharePoint sites, websites, file shares, Exchange public folders, Documentum instances, and Lotus Notes databases). The same connectors can be configured to work with a wide range of custom databases and web services (via BCS). For complex repositories, custom code lets you access line-of-business data and make it searchable.

Search leverages Business Connectivity Services (BCS) heavily in this wave. (See Chapter 11 for more information about BCS.) BCS is a set of services and features that provide a way to connect SharePoint solutions to sources of external data and to define External Content Types that are based on that external data. External Content Types allow the presentation of and interaction with external data in SharePoint lists (known as external lists), web parts, Microsoft Outlook 2010, Microsoft SharePoint Workspace 2010, and Microsoft Word 2010 clients. External systems that Microsoft Business Connectivity Services can connect to include SQL Server databases, SAP applications, web services (including Windows Communication Foundation web services), custom applications, and websites based on SharePoint. By using Microsoft Business Connectivity Services, you can design and build solutions that extend SharePoint collaboration capabilities and the Office user experience to include external business data and the processes that are associated with that data.

Microsoft Business Connectivity Services solutions use a set of standardized interfaces to provide access to business data. As a result, developers of solutions do not have to learn programming practices that apply to a specific system or adapter for each external datasource. Microsoft Business Connectivity Services also provide the runtime environment in which solutions that include external data are loaded, integrated, and executed in supported Office client applications and on the web server. Enterprise Search uses these same practices and framework — and connectors can surface information in SharePoint that is synchronized with the external line-of-business system, including writing back any changes. Search connectors can use other BCS features, such as external lists.

New Connector Framework Features

The connector framework, shown in Figure 6-22, provides improvements over the protocol handlers in previous versions of SharePoint Server. For example, connectors can now crawl attachments, as well as the content, in email messages. Also, item-level security descriptors can now be retrieved for external data exposed by Business Connectivity Services. Furthermore, when crawling a Business Connectivity Services entity, additional entities can be crawled via its entity relationships. Connectors also perform better than previous versions of protocol handlers, by implementing concepts such as inline caching and batching.

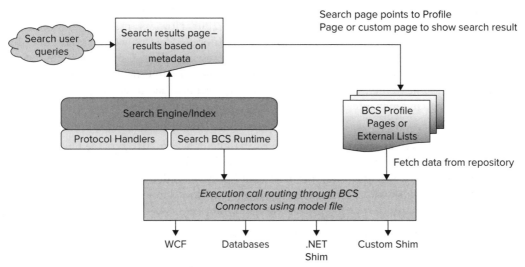

FIGURE 6-22

Connectors support richer crawl options than the protocol handlers in previous versions of SharePoint Server. For example, they support the full crawl mode that was implemented in previous versions, and they support timestamp-based incremental crawls. However, they also support change log crawls that can remove items that have been deleted since the last crawl.

Creating Indexing Connectors

In previous versions of SharePoint Server, it was very difficult to create protocol handlers for new types of external systems. Protocol handlers were required to be coded in unmanaged C++ code and typically took a long time to test and stabilize.

With SharePoint Server 2010, you have many more options for crawling external systems. You can choose to:

➤ Use SharePoint Designer 2010 to create external content types and entities for databases or web services and then simply crawl those entities

➤ Use Visual Studio 2010 to create external content types and entities for databases or web services, and then simply crawl those entities

➤ Use Visual Studio 2010 to create .NET types for Business Connectivity Services (typically for backend systems that implement dynamic data models, such as document management systems), and then use either SharePoint Designer 2010 or Visual Studio 2010 to create external content types and entities for the .NET type.

 You can still create protocol handlers (as in previous versions of SharePoint Server) if you want to. However, it's better to use the new connector framework instead.

Model Files

Every indexing connector needs a model file (also called an application definition file) to express connection information and the structure of the backend, and a BCS connector for code to execute when accessing the backend (also called a "shim"). The model file tells the search indexer what information from the repository to index and any custom-managed code that developers determine they must write (after consulting with their IT and database architects). The connector might require, for example, special methods for authenticating to a given repository and other methods for periodically picking up changes to the repository.

You can use OOB shims with the model file or write a custom shim. Either way, the deployment and connector management framework makes it easy — crawling content is no longer an obscure art. SharePoint 2010 also has great tooling support for connectors.

Tooling in SPD and VS2010

Both SharePoint Designer 2010 and Visual Studio 2010 have tooling that manages authoring connectors. You can use SharePoint Designer to create model files for out-of-box BCS connectors (such as a database), to import and export model files between BCS services applications, and to enable other SharePoint workloads, such as External Lists. Use Visual Studio 2010 to implement methods for the .NET shim or to write custom shims for your repository.

When you create a model file through SharePoint Designer, it is automatically configured for full-fidelity performance crawling. This takes advantage of features of the new connector framework, including inline caching for better citizenship, and timestamp-based incremental crawling. You can specify the search click-through URL to go to the profile page, so that content includes writeback, integrated security, and other benefits of BCS. Crawl management is automatically enabled through the Search Management console.

Figure 6-23 shows the relationships between the elements that are most commonly changed when creating a new connector using SharePoint Designer and OOB shims. Figure 6-24 shows the Configuration panel within SharePoint Designer.

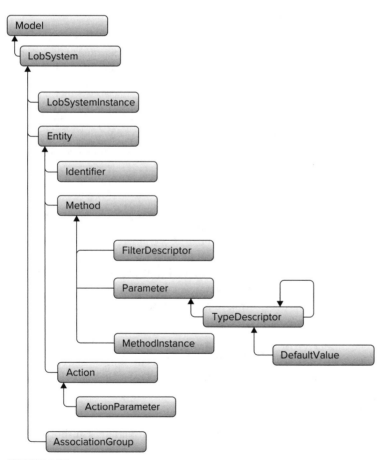

FIGURE 6-23

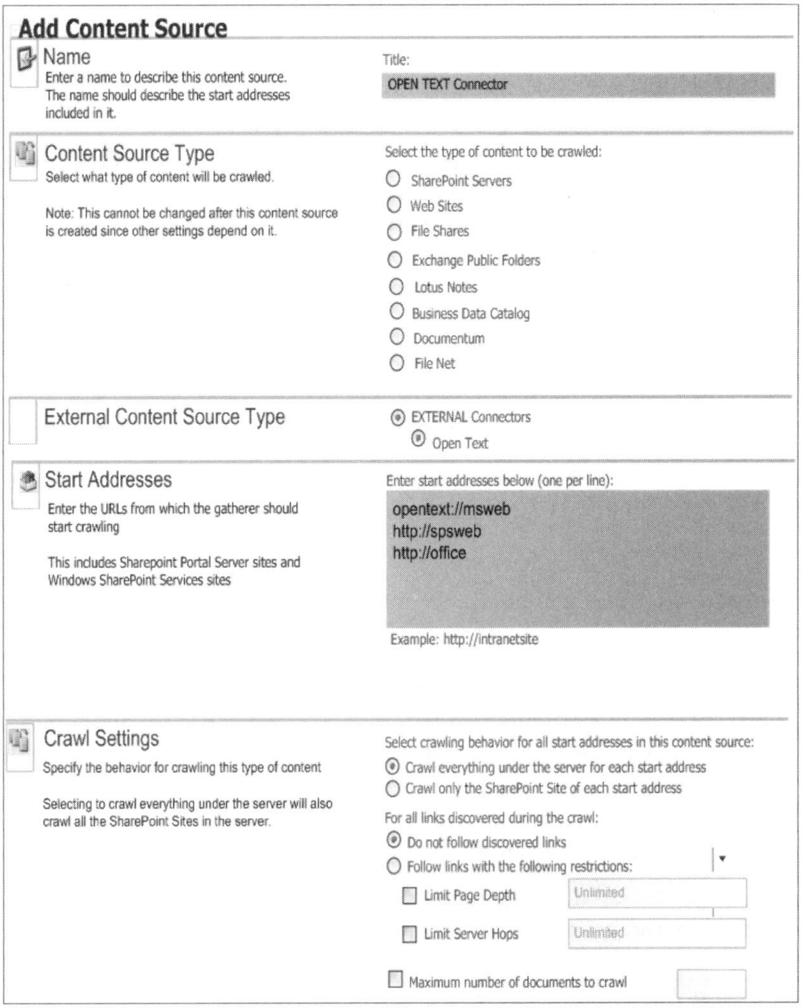

Add Content Source

Name
Enter a name to describe this content source. The name should describe the start addresses included in it.

Title:
OPEN TEXT Connector

Content Source Type
Select what type of content will be crawled.

Note: This cannot be changed after this content source is created since other settings depend on it.

Select the type of content to be crawled:
- ○ SharePoint Servers
- ○ Web Sites
- ○ File Shares
- ○ Exchange Public Folders
- ○ Lotus Notes
- ○ Business Data Catalog
- ○ Documentum
- ○ File Net

External Content Source Type

- ◉ EXTERNAL Connectors
  - ◉ Open Text

Start Addresses
Enter the URLs from which the gatherer should start crawling

This includes Sharepoint Portal Server sites and Windows SharePoint Services sites

Enter start addresses below (one per line):

```
opentext://msweb
http://spsweb
http://office
```

Example: http://intranetsite

Crawl Settings
Specify the behavior for crawling this type of content

Selecting to crawl everything under the server will also crawl all the SharePoint Sites in the server.

Select crawling behavior for all start addresses in this content source:
- ◉ Crawl everything under the server for each start address
- ○ Crawl only the SharePoint Site of each start address

For all links discovered during the crawl:
- ◉ Do not follow discovered links
- ○ Follow links with the following restrictions:

  - ☐ Limit Page Depth   Unlimited
  - ☐ Limit Server Hops   Unlimited

- ☐ Maximum number of documents to crawl

FIGURE 6-24

Writing Custom Connectors

Now let's walk through creating an example of a connector with a custom shim. Assume that you have a product catalog in an external system and want to make it searchable. Code Project 6-P-2 shows the catalog schema and walks through this example step by step.

There are two types of custom connectors: a managed .NET Assembly BCS connector and a custom BCS connector. In this case, we use the .NET BCS connector approach. We need to create only two things: the URL parsing classes, and a model file.

The code is written with .NET classes and compiled into a Dynamic Link Library (DLL). Each entity maps to a class in the DLL, and each BDC operation in that entity maps to a method inside that class. Once the code is done and the model file is uploaded, you can register the new connector either by adding DLLs to the global assembly cache (GAC) or by using PowerShell cmdlets to register the BCS connector + model file. Configuration of the connector is then available through the standard UI; the content sources, crawl rules, managed properties, crawl schedule, and crawl logs work as they do in any other repository.

If you chose to build a custom BCS connector, you implement the `ISystemUtility` interface for connectivity. For URL mapping, you implement the `ILobUri` and `INamingContainer` interfaces. Compile the code into a DLL and add DLL to the GAC, author a model file for the custom backend, register the connector using PowerShell, and you are done! The SharePoint Crawler invokes the `Execute()` method in the `ISystemUtility` class (as implemented by the custom shim), so you can put your special magic into this method.

A Few More Tips

The new connector framework takes care of a lot of things for you. There are a couple more new capabilities you might want to take advantage of:

➤ **To create item-level security:** Implement the `GetSecurityDescriptor()` method. For each entity, add a method instance property:

```
<Property Name = "WindowsSecurityDescriptorField" Type ="System.Byte[]">
Field name </Property>
```

➤ **To crawl through entity associations:** For association navigators (foreign key relationships), add the following property:

```
<Property Name="DirectoryLink"  Type="System.String"> NotUsed </Property>
```

Deploying Connectors

Developers and administrators use the Windows SharePoint Services 3.0 solutions framework to deploy connectors. After authoring a solution, the developer creates a CAB (`.cab`) file that combines the application's definition file and the solution code. An administrator or a developer then creates a Windows SharePoint Services 3.0 solutions management consumable package — a manifest file that contains the CAB file, connection information, and other resources. When the CAB file is available, the administrator uses the Windows SharePoint Services `Stsadm` command-line tool to upload the file, placing the CAB file into the configuration database of the server farm. Then, the administrator deploys the solution in the Windows SharePoint Services solutions management interface. This step also registers the solution and puts its DLLs in the global assembly cache of all the index servers.

After the connector is installed, the associated repository can be managed and crawled via the Content Source type list in the administration UI.

FAST-Specific Indexing Connectors

The connector framework and all of the productized connectors work with FAST Search for SharePoint as well as SharePoint Server search. FAST also has two additional connectors.

The Enterprise crawler provides web crawling at high performance with more sophisticated capabilities than the default web crawler. It is good for large-scale crawling across multiple nodes and supports dynamic data, including JavaScript.

The Java Database Connectivity (JDBC) connector brings in content from any JDBC-compliant source. This connector supports simple configuration using SQL commands (joins, selects, etc.) inline. It supports push-based crawling, so that a source can force an item to be indexed immediately. The JDBC connector also supports change detection through checksums, and high-throughput performance.

These two connectors don't use the connector framework and cannot be used with SharePoint Server 2010 Search. They are FAST-specific and provide high-end capabilities. You don't have to use them if you are creating applications for FAST Search for SharePoint, but it is worth seeing if they apply to your situation.

Customizing Connectivity in Summary

Using OOB shims (`Database`/`WCF`/`.NET`) is very straightforward with SharePoint 2010. This is recommended if the backend structure is static.

➤ Create/deploy the model file using SPD and use the search UI to configure crawls.

➤ Create/deploy .NET classes using Visual Studio and use the search UI to configure crawls.

Writing a custom shim and a Model file is the best approach for cases with dynamic backend structures. One example of this is the Exchange public folders. This approach also provides a cleaner integration with search user interface.

WORKING WITH FEDERATION

In addition to indexing information, search can present information to the user via federation. This is a "scatter-gather" approach: the same query is sent to a variety of different places, and the results are displayed together on the same page. Federation is not a replacement for indexing, but it is an essential tool for situations in which indexing is impossible (web search engines have the whole web covered; you don't have the storage or computer power to keep up with that) or impractical (you have an existing vertical search application that you don't want to touch). Federation can also be a great mechanism for migration. Figure 6-25 shows some of the situations where you might use indexing and federation. Microsoft has embraced federation wholeheartedly, in particular the OpenSearch standard.

When to Use Indexing

- If there is no way to search a repository.
- You want common relevance ranking.
- You want to extract full text and metadata.
- You want to be able to scope to an arbitrary subset of content.
- The source search performance/reliability is insufficient.

When to Use Federation

- You need a quick, powerful way to bring together results across multiple search systems.
- Data is distributed across multiple repositories.
- Search already exists in the repository.
- Crawling is not feasible...
  - Cost or integration difficulty
  - Geo-distribution of systems
  - Proprietary/Legal restrictions on source content access

FIGURE 6-25

Microsoft began supporting OpenSearch in 2008 with the introduction of Search Server 2008. Now all of Microsoft's Enterprise Search products support OpenSearch, and all of them have implemented comprehensive support for federation with out-of-the-box federation connectors to a range of search interfaces. Federation is built to be easy to set up, taking less than five minutes for an administrator to add a federated connector and see federated results appear in search queries. Further flexibility and control over the use of federated connectors come from triggering, presentation, and security features. Enterprise Search offerings can act as OpenSearch providers, OpenSearch clients, or both.

OpenSearch is a standard for search federation, originally developed by Amazon.com for syndicating and aggregating search queries and results. The operation of OpenSearch is shown in Figure 6-26. It is a standard used throughout the industry. The basic operation involves a search Client — which could be a desktop (Windows 7), a browser (Internet Explorer 8), or a server (SharePoint 2010). It also involves a Search Provider — which is any server with a searchable RSS feed, meaning that it accepts a query as a URL parameter and returns results in RSS/Atom.

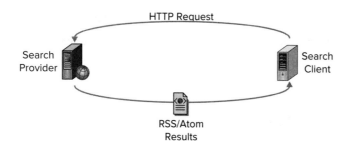

- • HTTP Request with query in the URL:
  - – http://www.site.com/srchrss.aspx?q={searchTerms}
- • RSS/Atom results:
  - – RSS results with <title>, <link>, <description>
  - – Best sources also include:
    <pubdate>, <author>, <category>, <media:thumbnail>
  - – Optionally include custom metadata:
    <recordid>, <projectname>, <contactnumber>

FIGURE 6-26

OpenSearch is now supported by a broad community (see Opensearch.org) and is in common use among online information service providers (such as Bing, Yahoo!, Wikipedia, and Dow Jones-Factiva). It is becoming more and more common in business applications. Following Microsoft's introduction of OpenSearch into its Enterprise Search products, partners built OpenSearch connectors to applications such as EMC Documentum, IBM FileNet, and OpenText Hummingbird.

Microsoft Search Server 2008 supported OpenSearch and Local Index Federation. It included a federation administration UI and several Federation web parts, but federation was a bit of a side capability. The main Results web part, for example, couldn't be configured to work with federation.

With SharePoint Server 2010, all web parts are built on the Federation OM. Connections to Windows 7, Bing, IE8, and third-party clients are built in. FAST Search for SharePoint supports federation in the same way, and the Federation OM is now public — so you can create your own type of federated connector!

Customization Examples Using Federation

The Code example below shows a custom OpenSearch provider (the full code is included with Code Project 6-P-2). This code creates a simple RSS feed from the result of a database query.

```
resultsXML.Append("<rss version=\"2.0\"
  xmlns:advworks=\"http://schemas.adventureworks.com/Products/Search/RSS\"
  xmlns:media=\"http://search.yahoo.com/mrss/\">");
resultsXML.Append("<channel>");
resultsXML.AppendFormat("<title>Adventure Works: {0}</title>", queryTerm);
resultsXML.AppendFormat("<link>{1}?q={0}</link>", queryTerm, RSSPage);
resultsXML.Append("<description>Searches Products in the Adventure Works database.
</description>");
while (sqlReader.Read())
{
    ...
    resultsXML.Append("<item>");
    resultsXML.AppendFormat("<title>{0}</title>", sqlReader[0]);
    resultsXML.AppendFormat("<link>{1}?v={0}&amp;q={2}</link>", sqlReader[1],
      RSSPage, query);
    resultsXML.AppendFormat("<description>{0}
      ({1}) has {2} units of inventory and will need to order more at {3} units.
      </description>", sqlReader[0],
    sqlReader[1], sqlReader[2], sqlReader[4]);
    ...
    resultsXML.Append("</item>");
}
resultsXML.Append("</channel></rss>");
```

The behavior of this is described in an OSDX file, which is shown below. An OSDX file is simple XML, and clients like Windows 7 can incorporate this with one click. Of course, SharePoint 2010 also acts as an OpenSearch client (as well as an OpenSearch provider).

```
<?xml version="1.0" encoding="UTF-8"?>
<OpenSearchDescription
xmlsn:ms-ose="http://schemas.microsoft.com/opensearchext/2009/"
  xmlns="http://a9.com/-/spec/opensearch/1.1/">
  <ShortName>ProductsSearch</ShortName>
  <Description>Searches the Adventure Works Products database.</Description>
  <Url type="text/html" template=
    "http://demo/sites/advsearch-prod/Pages/productresults.aspx?k={searchTerms} "/>
  <Url type="application/rss+xml" template=
    "http://demo/_layouts/adventureworks/productsearch.aspx?q={searchTerms}"/>
</OpenSearchDescription>
```

Further Considerations in Federation

There are a number of additional things to remember when using federation. First, ranking is up to the provider, so mixing results is not as dependable as you might think. Simple mixers that use round-robin results presentation are okay for situations in which all the sources are of the same type and strong overall relevance ranking is not crucial. Second, OpenSearch does not support refinement OOB — use custom runtime code and OpenSearch extensions to pass refiners if you need to. You may want to translate the query syntax to match a given source system — use a custom web part or runtime code for that. Security also needs special handling with federation — there is nothing built into OpenSearch. Microsoft has provided extensions to OpenSearch and a framework that handles security on a wide range of authentication protocols. Implementing this, however, requires you to be aware of the security environments your application will run in.

When designing an application using federation, plan out synchronous and asynchronous federation approaches. If the federation is synchronous, it is only as strong as its weakest link — results will be returned only when the slowest system comes back, and relevance ranking will be worse than the worst system involved. If federation is asynchronous, pay careful attention to the number of different result sets and how they are laid out on the UI. If you want to make your solution available via desktop search, this is easy with Windows 7 — and it works out of the box with standard SharePoint or FAST Search. You do this by creating an OpenSearch Description (.osdx) file, which can then be deployed to Windows 7 via Group Policy if you like.

We have noted a few common federation design patterns. The federation-based search vertical application would focus on using federation with core results to provide a complete results experience. A lightweight preview of results, in contrast, would show a few (~three) results to preview a source. "Instant answer across multiple sources" is supported by the top Federated Results web part, which is useful for finding an exact match or quick factoid. Last, a custom application using the Federation OM might use query alteration, refinement, and query steering across multiple sources.

Federation is a powerful tool in your arsenal, and SharePoint 2010 has made it easy to use it. It is not a panacea — if you can pragmatically index content, this is nearly always better. However, using the Federation OM and building OpenSearch providers can help in many situations.

WORKING WITH THE QUERY OM

Query processing is an essential part of search. Since effective search depends on getting good queries from the user, query processing is often used to improve the queries, by adding context or doing pre-processing. An example is location-aware searches, where the user is looking for results within a preferred distance of a particular location, and the location might be taken from the user's context (such as a GPS coordinate in a mobile phone). Query-side processing can be used to examine search results as they return and trigger more searches based on their contents. There is a huge range of things you can do using the SharePoint Query OM, and some very exciting applications you can build with it.

Query-Side APIs and OMs

Figures 6-27 and 6-28 show the "stack" with query-side APIs and OMs, for SharePoint search and for FAST Search for SharePoint, respectively. In these figures, light grey components are on

SharePoint Server or FAST Search backend farms, and dark grey components are on other servers. Content flow is also shown in these figures, so that you can see how the whole system fits together.

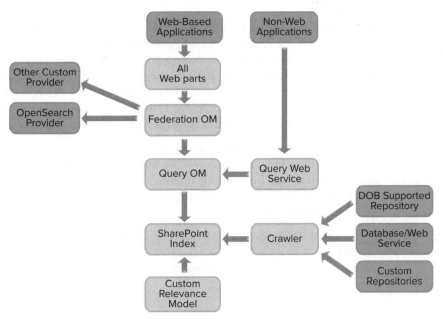

FIGURE 6-27

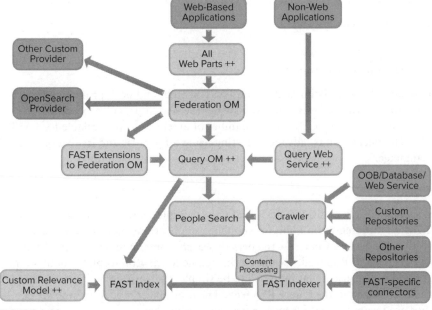

FIGURE 6-28

It's important to understand the different ways you can access queries and results, so these next sections go through each of the query-side OMs.

The Federation Object Model (OM)

This is a new search object model in SharePoint 2010. It provides a unified interface for querying against different locations (search providers) and giving developers of search-driven web parts a way to implement end-user experiences that are independent of the underlying search engine. The object model also allows for combining and merging results from different search providers. Out-of-box web parts in SharePoint 2010 are based on this OM, and SharePoint 2010 ships with three different types of locations: SharePoint Search, FAST Search, and OpenSearch. The Federation OM is also extensible, should you want or need to implement a custom search location outside of the supported types.

The Federated Search runtime object model is now public, enabling developers to build custom web parts that search any federated location. This change, combined with richer keyword query syntax, provides a common and flexible interface for querying internal and external locations. The Federated Search Object Model now provides a consistent way to perform all queries from custom code, making it easier to write clean, reusable code.

An important enhancement of the Federated Search Object Model is the public `QueryManager` class, which makes it possible to customize the query pipeline. For example, developers can build a web part that passes search results from a given location or repository to other web parts. A single query can, therefore, serve multiple web parts.

The Query Web Service

This is the integration point for applications outside your SharePoint environment, such as standalone, non-web-based applications or Silverlight applications running in a browser. The Query web service is a SOAP-based web service and supports a number of operations, including:

➤ Querying and getting search results

➤ Getting query suggestions

➤ Getting metadata (managed properties)

The same schema is shared by SharePoint Search and FAST Search, and both products support the same operations. For querying, clients can easily switch the search provider by setting a `ResultsProvider` element in the request XML. A number of extensions are available for FAST Search, for example, refinement results, advanced sorting using a formula, and issuing queries using the FAST Query Language.

The Query RSS Feed

Certain scenarios, such as simple mash-ups, may need only a simple search result list. The RSS feed is an alternative, lightweight integration point for supplying applications outside of SharePoint with a simple RSS result list. The Search Center — the default search frontend in SharePoint 2010 — includes a link to a query-based RSS feed. Switching the engine to the RSS format is done simply by setting a URL provider. Because it was designed to be simple, there are some limitations to what can be returned and customized in the Query RSS feed. The user object models or web service integration scenarios are recommended for more advanced applications.

The Query Object Model

This is the lowest-level object model, used by the Federation Object Model, the Query web service, and the Query RSS feed. Both SharePoint Search and FAST Search support the `KeywordQuery` object in this object model. While the Federation OM returns XML (to web parts), the Query OM returns data types.

Figure 6-29 shows the newly customizable pipeline for queries that originate from SharePoint Server 2010. All objects in the figure can be customized with the exception of the rightmost one, Query Processing, which cannot be customized.

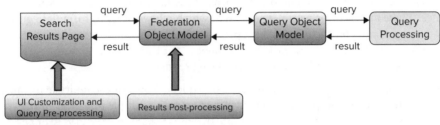

FIGURE 6-29

Query Syntax

The federation and Query OM are the methods for submitting queries. The queries themselves are strings that you construct and pass to the Search Service. A query request from a query client normally contains the following main parts:

➤ **The user query:** This consists of the query terms that the user types into a query box found on the user interface. In most cases, the user simply types one or more words, but the user query may also include special characters like "+" and "-". The user query will normally be treated as a string that is passed transparently by the query client on the interface.

➤ **Property filters:** These are additional constraints on the query that are added by the query client to limit the result set. These may include filters limiting the results by creation date, file type, written language, or any other metadata associated with the indexed items.

➤ **Query features and options:** These are additional query parameters that specify how a query is executed and how the query result is to be returned. This includes linguistic options, refinement options, and relevancy options.

Search in SharePoint supports four types of search syntax for building search queries:

➤ KQL (Keyword Query Language) syntax (search terms are passed directly to the Search Service)

➤ SQL syntax (extension of SQL syntax for querying databases), for SharePoint search only

➤ FQL (FAST-specific Query Language syntax), for FAST only

➤ URL syntax (search parameters are encoded in URL and posted directly to the search page)

KQL is the only syntax that end users would typically see. As a developer, this syntax is simpler to use than the SQL search syntax because you do not have to parse search terms to build a SQL statement; you pass the search terms directly to the Search Service. You also have the advantage that KQL works across both SharePoint and FAST, whereas SQL and FQL are codebase-specific. You can pass two types of terms in a Windows SharePoint Services Search keyword query: keywords (the actual query words for the search request) and property filters (the property constraints for the search request). KQL has been enhanced with SharePoint 2010 to include parametric search, so there should be very little need for SQL.

Keywords can be a word, a phrase, or a prefix. These can be simple (contributes to the search as an OR), included (must be present — for example, AND, denoted by "+"), or excluded (must not be present — for example, AND NOT, denoted by "-").

Property filters provide you with a way to narrow the focus of the keyword search based on managed properties. These are used for parametric search, which allows users to formulate queries by specifying a set of constraints on the managed property values. For example, searching for a wine with parameters of {Varietal: Red, Region: France, Rating: ⩾90, Price: ⩽$10} is easy to achieve with property filters, and easy to explore using refiners.

KQL supports using multiple property filters within the same query. You can use multiple instances of the same property filter or different property filters. When you use multiple instances of the same filter, it means OR; for example, `author:"Charles Dickens" author:"Emily Bronte"` will return results with either author. When you use different property filters, it means AND; for example, `author:"Isaac Asimov" title:"Foundation*"` will only return results that match both. Property filters also allow you to collapse duplicates; for example, `duplicate:http://` `<displayUrl>` requests duplicate items for the specified URL (which would otherwise be collapsed).

With SharePoint Server 2010, enhancements to keyword query syntax enable more complex search queries that in the past were supported only by the SQL query syntax. These enhancements include support for wildcard suffix matching, grouping of query terms, parentheses, and logical operators, such as AND, OR, NOT, and NEAR. Improved operators now support regular expressions, case-sensitivity, and content source prioritization. KQL can express essentially anything you can say with SQL. The Advanced Search page, for example, now creates KQL rather than SQL.

FAST Query Language (FQL)

FAST Search has a number of extensions beyond the standard SharePoint search that are available on both the Federation and Query Object Models, and also on the Query web service. Some examples are:

➤ The FAST Query Language, which supports advanced query operators, such as XRANK for dynamic (query-time) term weighting and ranking

➤ Deep refiners over the whole results set and the possibility of adding refiners over any managed property

➤ Advanced sorting using managed properties or a query-time sort formula

➤ Advanced duplicate trimming, with the ability to specify a custom property on which to base duplicate comparisons

➤ "Similar documents" matching

➤ The FAST Search Admin Object Model for promoting documents or assigning visual Best Bets to query keywords/phrases

The FAST Query Language (FQL) is intended for programmatic creation of queries. It is a structured language and not intended to be exposed to the end users. The FAST Query Language can be used only with FAST Search for SharePoint. Certain FAST Search for SharePoint features may only be accessed using this query language, such as:

➤ Detailed control of ranking at query time, using RANK/XRANK operators, query term weighting, and switching on/off ranking for parts of a query

➤ Advanced proximity operators (ordered/unordered NEAR operators)

➤ Advanced sorting, using SORT/SORTFORMULA operators

➤ Complex combinations of query operators, such as nesting of Boolean operators

FQL opens a whole world of search operations to the developer. The full set of capabilities is too long to cover in this book, but the reference documentation is available on MSDN.

Examples Using Query Customization

Now let's see how all of this works together, using some examples. First, imagine that you are building an application that helps users research information about companies. Perhaps you want to bring back additional information about a company whenever it is mentioned. If a query uses a company name of a publicly listed company, let's bring back stock information; if a query uses a ticker symbol, let's put that information on top. Finally, if a query brings back information that is tagged with companies, let's show the current stock price as metadata in the main Results web part.

Code Project 6-P-4 walks through this example. It processes the query and adds synonyms and parameters, in addition to using federation, if there is a ticker symbol to be found. On the content side, it uses ticker symbol metadata to look up the current price for the top results returned.

Another example is location-aware search. Now we will use a FAST-specific operator, SORTFORMULA, to sort results in order of distance. We can also cut out results beyond a threshold. Figure 6-30 shows how this works, and Code Project 6-P-5 walks through how to do this.

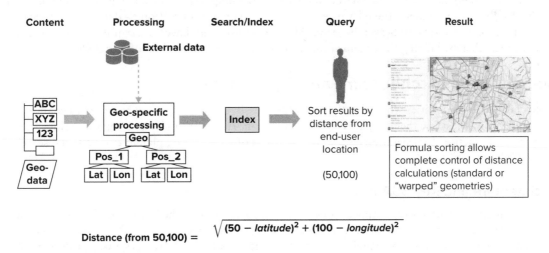

$$\text{Distance (from 50,100)} = \sqrt{(50 - latitude)^2 + (100 - longitude)^2}$$

```
query=hotel&sortby=+[formula:sqrt(pow(50-latitude,2)+pow(100-longitude,2))]
```

FIGURE 6-30

SOCIAL SEARCH

A significant aspect to an individual's work in an organization is interacting with other people and finding the right people to connect with who have specific skills and talents. This can be a daunting challenge in a large organization. SharePoint Server 2010 addresses this challenge through search, and connects this search to the social capabilities in SharePoint Server 2010. A People Search Center provides specific capabilities for connecting with people.

End-User-Visible Functionality

We touched on the people search function at the beginning of this chapter (see Figure 6-10). Now let's run through a few other aspects of social search that are visible to the end user, so that you can see how to use this in your application.

Mining and Discovering Expertise

Users can manually submit or automatically generate a list of colleagues mined from Outlook. Using automatically generated lists of colleagues is a way of rapidly inferring social relationships throughout the organization, which speeds the adoption and usefulness of people search results. SharePoint Server 2010 also infers expertise by automatically suggesting topics mined from the user's Outlook inbox and suggesting additions to her expertise profile in her My Site. This makes it easy to populate My Site profiles and means that more people have well-populated profiles and get the benefits of this in both search and communities.

Improving Search Based on Social Behavior

For many organizations, SharePoint sites have become gathering places where people create, share, and interact with information. Social behavior is taken into account in order to provide high-quality search results in several ways. First, the relevance ranking for people search takes social distance into account: a direct colleague will appear before someone three degrees removed (e.g., a friend-of-a-friend-of-a-friend). Second, SharePoint Server 2010 supports the social tagging of content, and this feedback can influence the relevance of content in search results. People's day-to-day usage of information in SharePoint Server 2010 and Microsoft Office can have a measurable effect on search relevance, thereby helping the organization harness the collective wisdom of its people.

Social Search Architecture and Operations

Social search capabilities work directly out of the box. In most cases, you won't need to change them; you can just use them as part of your application. However, understanding the architecture and good practices for operations is useful, regardless of whether you plan to extend social search capabilities.

Architecture and Key SSAs

There are three Shared Service Applications (SSAs) that are critical to the SharePoint 2010 farm tuned for social search. The user profile SSA is the datasource, which can draw from AD, LDAP, or other repositories storing data about employees. The managed metadata SSA provides a way of storing relationships between metadata values and allowing admins some control over the health of the data in the profile store. The Search SSA features tune results, refinement, and ranking to take advantage of the data coming from the user profile application and the managed metadata application.

Figure 6-31 shows these components and how they relate to each other in SharePoint 2010.

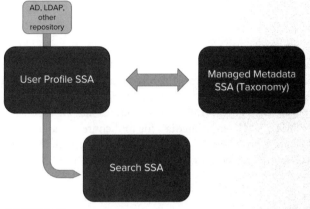

FIGURE 6-31

Managing User Profiles

Because social search is based in large part on user profiles, there are some basic techniques organizations should use to help keep these profiles fresh and high quality. These include encouraging users to use photos and update profile information. Turning on "knowledge mining" and encouraging users to publish suggested keywords are also possible techniques. All of these use out-of-the-box features, without any extensions.

SharePoint 2010 provides out-of-the-box properties such as Responsibilities, Interest, Skills, and Schools, but as a developer, you may want to add new properties. This involves setting up a connection to Managed Metadata SSA, adding custom profile properties, and then adding the new property to the profile store.

You may also want to extend user profiles and social search in other ways, for example, by bringing in external profile information, generating and normalizing profile information, and so forth. You can also extend the colleague and expertise suggestion capabilities.

Social Tags

Social tags are indexed as part of the people content source. The tag is stored with the person, not the item, until it gets to the search system. This is important because it means that end users can tag external content, and anything with a URL. Tagging is useful for many purposes, including content management and social computing.

Social tags affect the ranking of search results for SharePoint Server 2010 Search but not for FAST Search for SharePoint. To provide this for FAST, you would extend the standard crawl and/or provide application logic to collect and pre-process social tags.

EXTENDING SOCIAL SEARCH

People search can be extended in the same ways that we described for content search: customized web parts, federation, and query processing. It can also be extended via user profiles as described earlier.

CONTENT ENHANCEMENT

The old adage "garbage in, garbage out" springs to mind when considering content quality. Content preparation means selecting the right content, appropriately transforming and tagging it, cleansing or normalizing the content (making content regular and consistent, using appropriate spelling or style), and reducing the complexity of disparate data types. Information sources may include everything under the sun: web/intranet (HTML, XML, multimedia), file and content management systems (Doc, XLS, PDF, text, XML, CAD, etc.), email (email text, attachments), and databases (structured records). Findability is enhanced significantly by content enhancements and linguistic techniques.

Metadata, Linguistics, and Search

Metadata and linguistics are essential to search. Understanding how they work and how you can extend them enables you to build great search-driven applications.

Crawled Properties, Managed Properties, and Schemas

Search is performed on managed properties. Managed properties contain the content that will be indexed, including metadata associated with the items. Mapping from crawled properties to managed properties is controlled as part of the search configuration. A typical approach is to first perform a crawled property discovery based on an initial set of crawled items. Based on the results, you can change the mapping to managed properties.

Managed properties can be used for ranking, sorting, and navigation (refiners). Assessing which managed properties to use as metadata in your application is one of the most important aspects of creating great findability — search will find information anywhere via a full-text search on the body of documents, but using metadata makes the search quality better, as well as enables sorting and navigation. You can add additional managed properties at any point in the development and deployment process, but having a good core set to start makes development and testing much easier.

Multilingual Search

In the search world, linguistics is defined as the use of information about the structure and variation of languages so that users can more easily find relevant information. This is important for properly using search tools in various "natural" languages; think of the structural differences between English and Chinese. It is also important to industry-specific language usage — for instance, the English used in an American pharmaceutical company versus that used in a Hong Kong–based investment bank.

As you plan your application, get a sense of the number of languages involved — both in the content and among the user population. Find out what vocabularies exist in the organization — these may be formal taxonomies, dictionaries purchased from specialist firms, or informal lists from glossaries and team sites.

The Problem of Missing Metadata

Missing or incorrect metadata is a significant problem. An anecdotal example illustrates this point: A census performed on one company's PowerPoint presentations a year ago showed that nearly a quarter were authored by the CEO himself. This result was, doubtless, because, as the founder, he created early presentations that have since been edited, copied, and modified many times over. As the saying goes: "This is my grandfather's axe; my father changed the blade, and I changed the handle." Lacking automatic systems that update metadata, the "history" of the document can incorrectly categorize the current version.

Advanced Content Processing with FAST

FAST Search for SharePoint includes a scalable, fault-tolerant, and extensible content-processing pipeline, based on technology from FAST. Figure 6-32 shows the high-level structure of the content-processing pipeline.

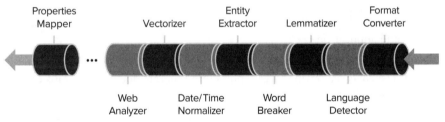

FIGURE 6-32

The content-processing pipeline is a framework for refining content and preparing it for indexing, with the following characteristics:

➤ A content-processing pipeline is composed of small simple stages, each of which does one thing. Stages identify attributes such as language, parse the structure of the document encodings (document format, language morphology, and syntax), extract metadata, manipulate properties and attributes, and so forth.

➤ A wide range of file formats (over 400) are understood and made available for indexing by the pipeline.

➤ A wide range of human languages are detected and supported by the pipeline (82 languages detected, 45 languages with advanced linguistics features. This includes spell-checking and synonyms (which improves the search experience) and lemmatization (which provides higher precision and recall than standard techniques like stemming).

➤ Property extraction creates and improves metadata by identifying words and phrases of particular types. Pre-built extractors include Person, Location, Company, E-mail, Date, and Time. A unique offensive-content-filtering capability is also included.

Content Pipeline Configuration

The content-processing pipeline in FAST Search for SharePoint can be configured and extended. This is made available in a structured fashion — simpler, more robust, and less error prone than with FAST ESP. Configuration of each stage is done via GUI or XML configuration, and is available via PowerShell. In the pipeline, content is mapped into "crawled properties" (whatever is found in the content) and then into "managed properties" (mapped into a schema and made available for searching, sorting, and navigation). This schema is accessible via GUI or PowerShell.

Content Pipeline Extensibility

There are several ways for developers and partners to add value in content processing:

➤ Configure connectors, pipeline configurations, and the index schema to support specific search applications.

➤ Apply optional pipeline stages such as using the XML properties mapper, the Offensive Content Filter, and field collapsing (which allows grouping or folding results together).

➤ Create custom verbatim extractors (dictionary-driven identification terms and phrases; for example, to ID all product names or project names and extract these as managed properties for each document.

➤ Create custom connectors, using BCS (or other APIs) to bring in and index data from specific systems and applications.

➤ Process content prior to crawling — for some applications pre-processing content prior to crawling is useful (such as separating large reports into separate documents). This can be done externally to search or within a connector shim.

➤ Extend the pipeline — by creating code that is called right before the `PropertiesMapper` stage, you can apply specialized classifiers, entity extractors, or other processing elements to support specialized scenarios.

Multilingual Search

If your organization is truly global, then the need for multilingual search is clear. But even if you initially think that all of your organization's search needs are English only, it is fairly common to discover that some percentage of users and content are non-English.

You should think carefully about the language-specific features of your search function. If people search only for content in their own language, or if there is wide variation in the language types used (English, Polish, and Chinese, for example), then it will help to have users specify their language in the query interface. Where there are common linguistic roots — on an e-commerce site featuring English and Dutch content, say — it may be easier to handle everything in the most common language, in this case, English.

A full description of linguistics and how you can use them to improve search is beyond the scope of this book. But there are a few things you should know about linguistics:

➤ Better use of linguistics will improve precision and recall

➤ Industry and user knowledge are needed to optimize search systems

➤ Linguistic choices can affect hardware and performance

➤ Some sites should favor language independence

➤ Bad queries can be turned into good queries with the proper linguistic tools

For many search applications, the out-of-the-box search configuration is all you need. User language choices are set in the Preferences panel of the Search Center and, by default, are determined from the browser. But be aware that linguistic processing can provide a lot of power in multilingual situations or in situations that demand particularly tuned recall and precision.

EXTENDING SEARCH USING THE ADMINISTRATIVE OM

SharePoint Server 2010 provides an extensible Search Health Monitoring Object Model. This object model enables administrators and developers to customize the administrative dashboards and pages that provide snapshots of the overall health of the search system, and to provide ways to troubleshoot and identify the underlying causes of any problems. The Search Health Monitoring user interface provides tools for monitoring the health of functional search subsystems (for example, crawling and indexing), search content sources, and key components (for example, databases) of the search system's topology.

Authentication and Security

Security in search is both a simple and a deep subject. Simply put, search uses the user's credentials and the entitlements on any content that has been indexed to ensure that users can see only content they are entitled to read. For OOB connectors and straightforward security environments, this just works. As you build custom connectors and work in heterogeneous and complex security environments, you also have the responsibility to extend security for search.

There are two major new security enhancements with SharePoint 2010. First, item-level security descriptors can now be retrieved for external data exposed by Business Connectivity Services. This means that search security is straightforward when building new connectors with BCS. Second, claims authentication (see Chapter 11) provides a wide range of security options for heterogeneous environments. Search benefits from these significantly, because search is often used as a "bridge" to look across information from many different systems.

Search Reports

The object model supports a reporting system that you can easily customize and extend. You can modify default alert rules and thresholds, for example, by changing the alert rules XML file. You can also upload new reporting applications developed by third parties to a standard search administration document library. The reports generated by these reporting applications are XML files in the standard Report Definition Language Client-Side (RDLC) format. For more information, see the Report Definition Language Specification, which is available on Microsoft TechNet.

SUMMARY: CUSTOMIZING SEARCH WITH SHAREPOINT 2010

Building powerful search applications is easier than ever in SharePoint 2010. You can create a wide range of applications based on search, at various levels of customization. You can also combine search with other parts of SharePoint (Insights, Social, Composites, Sites, and Content) to create compelling solutions.

FAST Search is now integrated into the SharePoint platform, and developers of search-driven solutions and applications can leverage a common platform and common APIs for both SharePoint Server 2010 search and FAST Search for SharePoint. This means you can build applications to support both search engines and then extend them if and when desired to take advantage of the more advanced features available with FAST Search, such as dynamic ranking, flexible sort formulae, or deep refiners for insight into the full result set. FAST Search for SharePoint web parts use the same unified object model as SharePoint Server 2010 search. The result is that if you develop a custom solution that uses the Query Object Model for SharePoint Server 2010, for example, then it will continue to work if you migrate your code to FAST Search Server 2010 for SharePoint.

7

ECM: Records Management

WHAT'S IN THIS CHAPTER?

➤ An overview of SharePoint 2010 records management

➤ Programming using the Records Management APIs in SharePoint 2010

With the explosion of digital information and the requirements of keeping this information compliant with government and industry regulations, records management (RM) has become a critical component of any SharePoint deployment. If you haven't heard of records management, you will. RM is the process of classifying, securing, discovering, and managing your information from creation to destruction. With SharePoint 2010, there are a number of new enhancements, as well as enhancements to previous features such as the records center, that allow end users, developers, and IT pros to make their applications and information compliant.

While this chapter will not be the end all, be all introduction to RM, there are a number of Internet resources that will help give you a good introduction to RM. For cross-product RM topics, check out Association for Information and Image Management International (AIIM) at www.aiim.org. For SharePoint specific RM information, look at the SharePoint ECM blog at http://blogs.msdn.com/ecm. Lastly, check out the SharePoint dev wiki at www.sharepointdevwiki.com.

SHAREPOINT 2010 RECORDS MANAGEMENT OVERVIEW

In SharePoint 2010, there are four feature areas in records management:

➤ Recordization

➤ eDiscovery and Legal Holds

➤ Auditing and Reporting

➤ Retention and Expiration

Recordization is the process of formally managing your information by making it an official record. As part of making it an official record, you specify a retention schedule, any auditing requirements, and also how to dispose of the information.

eDiscovery and legal holds work together in that eDiscovery allows you to uncover your information assets using search no matter where they live, and legal holds allow you to break this retention based on legal actions that require longer retention. eDiscovery is very tied to search so if you are interested in eDiscovery, you will want to evaluate the Microsoft FAST technologies.

Auditing and Reporting allows you to audit, down to an item level, the changes made to an item such as when and who modified the content. Combined with reporting, you can get a report out to Excel that shows you the information about your information across your site and also which content is following your information policies across your site.

Retention and Expiration is the ability to set policies for retention and expiration of your information. You can control this at the individual piece of content level or force policies based on the location the content lives in SharePoint. Expiration is the process of archiving or destroying your content either when the content is no longer needed, or, for compliance reasons, you want to remove the content from your system.

These four areas, when combined, provide you a very robust records management application and platform to control the flow of information assets in your organization.

Recordization

Recordization is the turning of information assets into declared records. Becoming a declared record has implications for activities such as managing the lifecycle of the asset, making it discoverable, and archiving the record for longer-term storage. With SharePoint 2010, there are a number of new features in recordization. The first is support for in-place records management. With SharePoint 2007, you need to move the information from its location, such as a document library, into the SharePoint Records Center in order to manage the information as a record. With 2010, you can leave the asset in place in the library and manage the information as a record. Figure 7-1 illustrates declaring a record in place in a document library.

Another new feature of SharePoint 2010 is the ability to declare new types of information as records. With 2007, you could not use the records management features with social networking types, such as blogs and wikis. This was a major limitation, because this type of content is increasingly becoming a major source of new information in organizations. With 2010, all content can be used in records management.

Multi-stage disposition is a key new feature in records management. In SharePoint 2007, you have a single-stage disposition in that, when the timeframe set by the records manager is met, a single action is performed. That action could be complex, such as kicking off a workflow, but it still is a single stage. With 2010, you can have multiple stages based on different timeframes and criteria. This lets you set up policies, such as "check legal documents every year to see if they have expired or if the conditions on the contracts have been met," while also having a policy that deletes a contract seven years after the document is approved. Also of note is that this technology can work with non-records, so think about the scenarios where you can use this technology even outside of records management. Figure 7-2 shows multi-stage disposition.

FIGURE 7-1

FIGURE 7-2

With 2010, there is a new Records Center template, which allows easier access for users submitting documents and records managers searching for documents based on document ID. The Records Center also uses some of the other Enterprise Content Management (ECM) features, such as metadata-driven navigation, to make it easier to browse the Record center by metadata rather than by folder hierarchy. The last point about the new Records Center template is that you can have multiple Records Centers in a single site collection. Rather than forcing you to use a single Records Center, SharePoint 2010 allows you to have multiple Records Centers to which you can point different sets of users or content.

You may be wondering when to use the Records Center versus in-place records management. The real difference will be policy and preference. For example, if your company would rather manage active content separate from record content, using the Records Center makes sense. In addition, if you have a records manager for your organization and want centralized management of your records, rather than relying on individual groups to manage their policies, you will want to deploy the Records Center. If your users need access to their content after they declare it as a record, you will want to use in-place records management.

Figure 7-3 shows the new Records Center template.

FIGURE 7-3

As part of organizing your records, SharePoint 2010 supports a Content Organizer and Content Organizer rules. These rules allow you to specify where content should go based on a number of criteria, including properties such as content type. By having these rules, end users or applications can submit their documents to the Records Center; and the Records Center, or any SharePoint site where the Content Organizer is running, can route the content to the right location. Figure 7-4 shows the Content Organizer settings and you can see in the image that you can create customized content routing rules, both in the user interface and using the API.

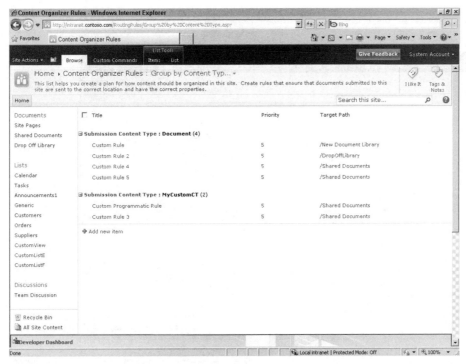

FIGURE 7-4

Records management is also supported across many of the features of SharePoint. For example, workflows have records management built-in so when you design a SharePoint Designer workflow, "declare as record" is one of the actions you can perform on your content.

The last feature is the hierarchical, metadata-driven file plan in the archive. Having the ability to set file plans through the metadata contained in the content makes administration easier. File plans allow different records actions according to location or content type.

eDiscovery and Holds

With the growing push towards compliance, eDiscovery is becoming a critical component of SharePoint deployments. eDiscovery allows you to find information and, if need be, put a legal hold on that information, which will break the retention policies on that content until the legal hold is removed. With 2010, you can search across all SharePoint sites (not just the Records Center, as in SharePoint 2007) for records to add to your holds. Figure 7-5 shows how a records manager can configure a search and hold in SharePoint 2010.

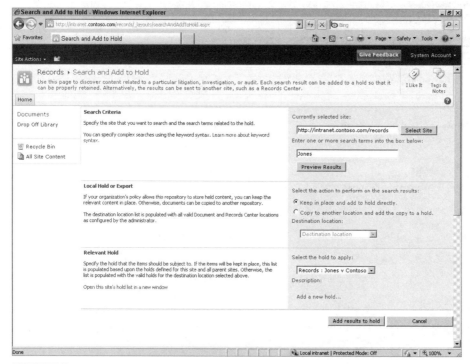

FIGURE 7-5

Auditing and Reporting

With any records management solution, good auditing and reporting are critical. Auditing allows you to track what users are doing with the content, whether they are accessing, deleting, or moving it. SharePoint supports per item reporting, so you can see the actions performed on content at an individual item level. SharePoint 2010 also supports reporting using the file plan, so you can understand the compliance details for your content. By providing a simple user interface similar to the Properties interface, SharePoint 2010 makes it very easy to understand the compliance details for your documents. Figure 7-6 shows the compliance details dialog box.

FIGURE 7-6

PROGRAMMING RM IN SHAREPOINT

Programming RM in SharePoint is familiar if you already know the SharePoint Server object model. Most of your programming will involve accessing content, declaring records, creating new information management policies, performing discovery and holds, and generating reports. Most of the object model sits in two key DLLs: `Microsoft.Office.DocumentManagement` and `Microsoft.Office` `.Policy`. Both of these DLLs reside in the location where all other SharePoint DLLs reside: `%Program` `Files%\Common Files\Microsoft Shared\Web Server Extensions\14\ISAPI`. The following sections will step you through performing actions using the different object models when working with records in SharePoint 2010. Please note that you need SharePoint Server 2010 and not just SharePoint Foundation 2010 to work with these capabilities, since Foundation does not support Records Management. In addition, these APIs are only available from full-trust SharePoint solutions, and are not available from Sandbox Solutions.

Declaring and Undeclaring a Record

One of the most common operations you will perform with RM in SharePoint 2010 will be declaring and undeclaring records. Please note that if you want to declare records in place, you will need to turn on the In Place Records Management feature for your site collection, and then the Record declaration settings option will appear in your site collection administration web page, as shown in Figure 7-7.

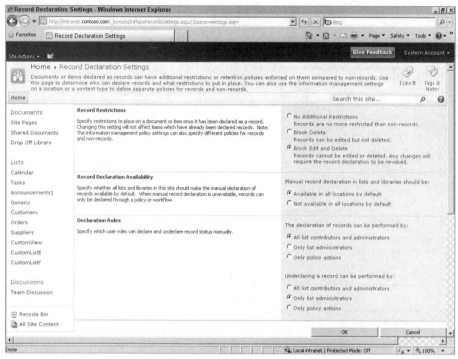

FIGURE 7-7

With SharePoint 2010, declaring records is straightforward. The methods you want to use are located in the `Microsoft.Office.RecordsManagement.RecordsRepository` namespace. The primary methods are `DeclareItemAsRecord` and `UndeclareItemAsRecord`. Both these methods take an `SPListItem` object and will declare or undeclare the item as a record.

The following code uploads a file to a document library. It uses the `IsInPlaceRecordsEnabled` method to check to see if in-place records management is enabled. Then it calls `DeclareItemAsRecord` to declare the new document as a record. To make sure that the record is declared, you have two options. You can check the expiration time to make sure that it was set to the right date, or you can use the `IsRecord` method, which takes an `SPListItem` object and returns a Boolean indicating whether the item is a record or not.

```
private const string SharePointURL = "http://intranet.contoso.com";
    private const string filePath = "c:\\test.docx";
    private const string SharePointListURL = "http://intranet.contoso.com/
shared%20documents/";
    private const string fileSharePointURL = "http://intranet.contoso.com/
shared%20documents/test.docx";


        using (SPSite site = new SPSite(SharePointURL))
        {
            SPWeb web = site.RootWeb;
```

```
            SPList list = web.GetList(SharePointListURL);


            Stream fileStream = File.Open(filePath, FileMode.Open);

            SPFile file = list.RootFolder.Files.Add(
fileSharePointURL, fileStream);

            SPListItem item = file.Item;

            file.Update();

            MessageBox.Show("In Place Records enabled: " +
Records.IsInPlaceRecordsEnabled(site).ToString());

            //Declare the item as a record
            Records.DeclareItemAsRecord(item);

            bool currentStageRecurs = false;
            DateTime? ExpireDT = Expiration.
              GetExpirationDateForItem(item, out currentStageRecurs);

            //Make sure it declared

            if (ExpireDT == null)
            {
                MessageBox.Show("Not declared!");
            }
            else
            {
                MessageBox.Show("Declared Expiration Date: " +
ExpireDT.ToString());                //Also show if Record using IsRecord
                MessageBox.Show("IsRecord: " + Records.IsRecord(item);
                //Could also use OnHold to check if on hold
            }

            //Undeclare the object
            Records.UndeclareItemAsRecord(item);



        }
```

CodeSnippetChap9.cs

Creating Retention Schedules

Another common operation you will perform is creating retention schedules. Retention schedules are created by using XML. Once you understand the pattern of the XML, generating and applying retention is a couple of codes. The hardest part is programmatically creating the XML using the XML Document Object Model (DOM). If you look at the easiest retention schedule, one that deletes content after six years, this would be the XML you would need to generate:

```
<Schedules nextStageId="2">
<Schedule type="Default">
<stages>
<data stageId="1">
<formula id="Microsoft.Office.RecordsManagement.PolicyFeatures.Expiration.Formula.
BuiltIn">
<number>6</number>
<property>Created</property>
<period>years</period>
</formula>
<action type="action"
id="Microsoft.Office.RecordsManagement.PolicyFeatures.
Expiration.Action.Delete" />
</data>
</stages>
</Schedule>
</Schedules>
```

CodeSnippetChap9.cs

In the XML, there is a top-level `Schedules` node that contains a property that is the ID of the next stage, even if that next stage does not exist. Below that, the `Schedule` node contains the multiple stages you want to occur on your content. To have multiple stages, you add multiple data nodes, each with a unique, incrementing integer in your `stageID` property. You can specify the type, which can be `Default` or `Record`. `Default` allows you specify custom actions to occur on any items, while `Record` will only perform the actions on declared records.

From the `data` node, you see the formula node. The `id` of the formula node is the ID of one of the built-in formulas in SharePoint. You could point at your own custom class to implement your own formulas by specifying the class name in the `id` attribute. The built-in formulas allow you to add days, months, or years to the column you specify in the `property` node. In the example, the formula is calculated from the `Created` property and six years are added to that property for the action to be triggered. The possible values for the `period` node are days, weeks, or years.

Next comes the action you want to perform if the formula's criterion is met. In the sample, this means six years from the creation date has expired. To specify the action you want to perform, you specify the action in the `id` attribute for the `action` node. Again, you can use a custom action here by specifying your custom action class implementation for the `id` value. In the example, `Microsoft.Office.RecordsManagement.PolicyFeatures.Expiration.Action.Delete` is specified, which is a delete action. Table 7-1 gives you the possible built-in action values. For brevity, `Microsoft.Office.RecordsManagement.PolicyFeatures.Expiration.Action` has been removed from all of them, so make sure to add this back before using the actions in your XML.

TABLE 7-1: Records Management Actions

NAME	DESCRIPTION
Custom	Specifies the use of a custom action.
Delete	Deletes the content.
DeletePreviousDrafts	Deletes all drafts of the content except for the most recent.

NAME	DESCRIPTION
DeletePreviousVersions	Deletes all previous versions except for the most recent.
MoveToRecycleBin	Moves the content to the recycle bin.
Record	Declares the content an in-place record.
Skip	Skips the step.
SubmitFileCopy	Submits the content to the records repository as a copy.
SubmitFileLink	Submits the content to the records repository and retains a link in the library.
SubmitFileMove	Submits the content to the records repository as a move that deletes the content from its current location.
Workflow	Triggers a workflow. You need to specify the GUID for the workflow in the `id` attribute for this action node. Please note that this action node does not need to be prefaced with `Microsoft.*` but instead should just be `<action type="workflow" id="GUID of workflow" />`

Now that you understand how to create a simple retention schedules, creating more complex retention schedules is a matter of building new XML nodes onto the simple example from earlier. The following XML sets three stages. The first stage recurs every six months and deletes the previous versions of the content. The second occurs six months from the modified date of the content and declares the content as a record. The last occurs five years from the created date and deletes the content.

```
<Schedules nextStageId="4" default="false">
  <Schedule type="Default">
    <stages>
      <data stageId="1" recur="True" offset="6" unit="months">
        <formula id="Microsoft.Office.RecordsManagement.PolicyFeatures.Expiration.
Formula.BuiltIn">
          <number>6</number>
          <property>
            Created</property><period>months</period>
        </formula>
        <action type="action" id="Microsoft.Office.RecordsManagement.
PolicyFeatures.Expiration.A
ction.DeletePreviousVersions" />
      </data>
      <data stageId="2">
        <formula id="Microsoft.Office.RecordsManagement.PolicyFeatures.Expiration
.Formula.BuiltIn">
          <number>6</number>
          <property>Modified</property>
```

```xml
            <period>months</period>
          </formula>
          <action type="action" id="Micros
oft.Office.RecordsManagement.PolicyFeatures.Expiration.Action.Record" />
        </data>
      </stages>
    </Schedule>
    <Schedule type="Record">
      <stages>
        <data stageId="3">
          <formula id="Microsoft.Office.RecordsManagement.PolicyFeatures.Expiration.
Formula.BuiltIn">
            <number>5</number>
            <property>
              Created</property><period>years</period>
          </formula>
          <action type="action" id="Microsoft.Office.RecordsManagement.
PolicyFeatures.Expiration.Action.Delete" />
        </data>
      </stages>
    </Schedule>
  </Schedules>
```

When it comes to applying your retention schedule to your content, you have two choices. You can attach the retention schedule to the content type or you can attach it to the list. When attached to the content type, the retention schedule will be followed regardless of where the content type is created. With the new content type syndication functionality in 2010, your retention schedule can travel wherever a content type travels.

If you associate the retention schedule with a list, then the schedule will work on content just in that list. Normally, you will want to use the content type option so that your retention schedule works everywhere.

To check to see if you have a custom list policy, you can use the ListHasPolicy property on the Microsoft.Office.RecordsManagement.InformationPolicy.ListPolicySettings object. This Boolean property returns whether the list has a custom policy. To set the list to use a custom policy, set the UseListPolicy Boolean to True and then call Update on your ListPolicySettings object. Set this to False to use the content type retention policy. The constructor for your ListPolicySettings object takes a SPList object, which is the list you want to investigate. The following code shows how to use these objects and properties:

```csharp
SPWeb web = site.RootWeb;
            SPList list = web.GetList(SharePointListURL);

            Microsoft.Office.RecordsManagement.InformationPolicy.
ListPolicySettings policy = new
Microsoft.Office.RecordsManagement.InformationPolicy.ListPolicySettings(list);

            if (!policy.ListHasPolicy)
            {
                //make the list use a custom list policy
```

```
                    policy.UseListPolicy = true;
                    policy.Update();
                }

                //Check to see if setting was successful
                MessageBox.Show("List Policy Set: " +
    policy.ListHasPolicy.ToString());
```

CodeSnippetChap9.cs

To set a custom retention policy on the list, use the following:

```
    private const string SharePointURL = "http://intranet.contoso.com";
        private const string SharePointListURL =
    "http://intranet.contoso.com/shared%20documents/";
            private const string fileSharePointURL =
    "http://intranet.contoso.com/shared%20documents/test.docx";
```

```
                using (SPSite site = new SPSite(SharePointURL))
                {
                    SPWeb web = site.RootWeb;
                    SPList list = web.GetList(SharePointListURL);
                    SPFolder folder = web.Folders[SharePointListURL];
                    SPWeb parentWeb = list.ParentWeb;


                    SPList parentList = parentWeb.Lists[folder.ParentListId];
                    Microsoft.Office.RecordsManagement.InformationPolicy.
                    ListPolicySettings listPolicySettings =
                    new Microsoft.Office.RecordsManagement.InformationPolicy.
                    ListPolicySettings(parentList);


                    string policyXml = @"
                    <Schedules nextStageId=""4"" default=""false"">
                    <Schedule type=""Default""><stages><data stageId=""1""
                    recur=""True"" offset=""6"" unit=""months"">
                    <formula id=""Microsoft.Office.RecordsManagement.PolicyFeatures.
                    Expiration.Formula.BuiltIn"">
                    <number>6</number><property>Created</property>
                    <period>months</period></formula>
                    <action type=""action""
    id=""Microsoft.Office.RecordsManagement.PolicyFeatures.Expiration.Action.
    DeletePreviousVersions"" />
                    </data><data stageId=""2""><formula
    id=""Microsoft.Office.RecordsManagement.PolicyFeatures.Expiration.
    Formula.BuiltIn"">
                    <number>6</number><property>Modified</property>
                    <period>months</period></formula>
                    <action type=""action""
    id=""Microsoft.Office.RecordsManagement.PolicyFeatures.Expiration.Action.Record"" />
    </data></stages></Schedule>
                    <Schedule type=""Record""><stages><data stageId=""3""><formula
```

```
id=""Microsoft.Office.RecordsManagement.PolicyFeatures.Expiration.
 Formula.BuiltIn"">
                    <number>3</number><property>Created</property5
                    <period>years</period></formula>
                    <action type=""action""
id=""Microsoft.Office.RecordsManagement.PolicyFeatures.Expiration.Action.
Delete"" />
                    </data></stages></Schedule></Schedules>";

            if (!listPolicySettings.UseListPolicy)
            {
                //Enable Location Based Policy if it isn't enabled
                listPolicySettings.UseListPolicy = true;
                listPolicySettings.Update();


                //Refresh to get the updated ListPolicySettings
                listPolicySettings = new
Microsoft.Office.RecordsManagement.InformationPolicy.ListPolicySettings
 (parentList);
            }

            listPolicySettings.SetRetentionSchedule(folder.ServerRelativeUrl,
                    policyXml, "My Custom Retention");
            listPolicySettings.Update();

            MessageBox.Show(listPolicySettings.
            GetRetentionSchedule(folder.ServerRelativeUrl));
    }
```

CodeSnippetChap9.cs

To create the same policy on a content type requires a bit more code, but the process is very similar. The code that follows is the same as the previous sample from the beginning of the chapter, but instead of getting the list policies, the code retrieves the content types in SharePoint, in particular the document content type. The code then uses the `GetPolicy` method to retrieve the Expiration policy for the content type. If that policy does not exist, it creates the policy. Then, it sets the `CustomData` property for that policy and calls the `Update` method to set the retention policy for the content type.

```
using (SPSite site = new SPSite(SharePointURL))
        {
            SPWeb web = site.RootWeb;
            SPList list = web.GetList(SharePointListURL);
            SPFolder folder = web.Folders[SharePointListURL];
            SPWeb parentWeb = list.ParentWeb;


            SPList parentList = parentWeb.Lists[folder.ParentListId];
            Microsoft.Office.RecordsManagement.InformationPolicy.
            ListPolicySettings listPolicySettings =
            new Microsoft.Office.RecordsManagement.InformationPolicy.
            ListPolicySettings(parentList);



            string policyXml = @"
```

```
                <Schedules nextStageId=""4"" default=""false"">
                <Schedule type=""Default""><stages><data stageId=""1""
                recur=""True"" offset=""6"" unit=""months"">
                <formula
id=""Microsoft.Office.RecordsManagement.PolicyFeatures.Expiration.
Formula.BuiltIn"">
                <number>6</number><property>Created</property>
                <period>months</period></formula>
                <action type=""action""
id=""Microsoft.Office.RecordsManagement.PolicyFeatures.Expiration.Action.
DeletePreviousVersions"" />
                </data><data stageId=""2""><formula
id=""Microsoft.Office.RecordsManagement.PolicyFeatures.Expiration.
 Formula.BuiltIn"">
                <number>6</number><property>Modified</property>
                <period>months</period></formula>
                <action type=""action""
id=""Microsoft.Office.RecordsManagement.PolicyFeatures.Expiration.Action.Record"" />
</data></stages></Schedule>
                <Schedule type=""Record""><stages><data stageId=""3""><formula
id=""Microsoft.Office.RecordsManagement.PolicyFeatures.Expiration.Formula.BuiltIn"">
                <number>3</number><property>Created</property>
                <period>years</period></formula>
                <action type=""action""
id=""Microsoft.Office.RecordsManagement.PolicyFeatures.Expiration.Action.
Delete"" />
                </data></stages></Schedule></Schedules>";

                SPContentType contentType = web.ContentTypes["Document"];

                Policy policy = Policy.GetPolicy(contentType);

                //Check to see if it exists, if not create it
                if (policy == null)
                {
                    Policy.CreatePolicy(contentType, null);
                    policy = Policy.GetPolicy(contentType);
                }



                PolicyItem retentionPolicy = policy.Items[Expiration.PolicyId];
                //See if a policy already exists, if not create one
                if (retentionPolicy == null)
                {
                    policy.Items.Add(Expiration.PolicyId, policyXml);
                    policy.Update();
                }
                else
                {
                    retentionPolicy.CustomData = policyXml;
                    retentionPolicy.Update();
                }

                //Return back policy XML to make sure it worked
```

```
                    retentionPolicy = policy.Items[Expiration.PolicyId];
                    MessageBox.Show("Policy XML: " +
        retentionPolicy.CustomData.ToString());
```

CodeSnippetChap9.cs

Creating Organizer Rules

SharePoint 2010 supports a new Content Organizer feature that allows SharePoint to route documents based on the rules you specify. While you can create these rules through the user interface, as shown in Figure 7-8, you can also create rules through the object model. The object model offers a class called `Microsoft.Office.RecordsManagement.RecordsRepository.EcmDocumentRoutingWeb`. This class is the base class that you will start working with, using the object model (OM). From this class, you can access the rules contained for the Content Organizer feature. One thing to remember is that you must activate the Content Organizer feature in your site feature settings. If you do not, you will not see any of the user interface for creating rules, and the object model won't work.

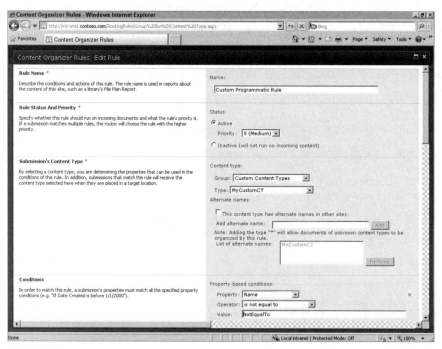

FIGURE 7-8

From the routing web object, you can access the `RoutingRuleCollection` that contains your `EcmDocumentRouterRule`. With the rule object, you can access the properties of an existing rule. To create a new rule, you create a new `ECMDocumentRouterRule` and pass the `SPWeb` object, which represents the SharePoint location where you want to create the rule.

Since content rules require XML conditions, the easiest way to create a content rule is by using the user interface and then copying the XML from the rule. Table 7-2 lists the properties you need to set to create a rule.

TABLE 7-2: Properties to Create a Rule

NAME	DESCRIPTION
Name	Name of the rule.
Description	Description for the rule.
Priority	String that is the priority of the rule compared to other rules. 1 is highest, 9 is lowest.
ContentTypeString	Content type string used to specify your content type. The format has to be ID|Name.
TargetPath	Relative path to the target folder such as /Shared Documents.
ConditionString	XML fragment that contains the conditions that you want met before the rule fires. Table 7-3 shows the different Operator options for this property, but the general format is <Conditions><Condition Column="Column ID|Column Internal Name|Column Title" Operator="Operator" Value="Value" /></Conditions>.
Enabled	Boolean that specifies whether the rule is enabled or not.

TABLE 7-3: Operators for Content Organizer Rules

NAME	DESCRIPTION
IsEqual	Checks to see if the value of the column is equal to the value specified.
IsNotEqual	Checks to see if the value of the column is not equal to the value specified.
GreaterThan	Checks to see if the value of the column is greater than the value specified.
LessThan	Checks to see if the value of the column is less than the value specified.
GreaterThanOrEqual	Checks to see if the value of the column is greater than or equal to the value specified.
LessThanOrEqual	Checks to see if the value of the column is less than or equal to the value specified.
BeginsWith	Checks to see if the value of the column begins with the value specified.
NotBeginsWith	Checks to see if the value of the column does not begin with the value specified.
EndsWith	Checks to see if the value of the column ends with the value specified.
NotEndsWith	Checks to see if the value of the column does not end with the value specified.

continues

TABLE 7-3 *(continued)*

NAME	DESCRIPTION
Contains	Checks to see if the value of the column contains the value specified.
NotContains	Checks to see if the value of the column does not contain the value specified.
IsEmpty	Checks to see if the value of the column is empty. You specify a blank string for the value.
IsNotEmpty	Checks to see if the value of the column is not empty. You specify a blank string for the value.

If you want to enable autofoldering based on a unique property, you use the `DocumentRouter` `AutoFolderSettings` class. This class contains a number of properties you need to set in order to make autofoldering work. Table 7-4 shows the properties for the `DocumentRouterAuto` `FolderSettings` class. The code below the table shows how to set these properties and use them in your code.

TABLE 7-4: DocumentRouterAutoFolderSettings Properties

NAME	DESCRIPTION
Enabled	Boolean that specifies whether these settings are enabled.
AutoFolderPropertyInternalName	The internal name of the field to use for autofoldering.
AutoFolderPropertyId	The property ID of the field to use for autofoldering.
AutoFolderPropertyName	The property name of the field to use for autofoldering.
AutoFolderPropertyTypeAsString	The property type as a string of the field to use for autofoldering.
AutoFolderFolderNameFormat	The name format to use for the folder. By default, this will be %1 - %2. %1 will be replaced by the name of the property. %2 will be replaced with the unique value for the property.

```
SPWeb web = site.RootWeb;
SPList list = web.GetList(SharePointListURL);
SPFolder folder = web.Folders[SharePointListURL];
SPWeb parentWeb = list.ParentWeb;

EcmDocumentRoutingWeb router = new EcmDocumentRoutingWeb(web);
foreach (EcmDocumentRouterRule rule in router.RoutingRuleCollection)
{
```

```
                        string s = "Alias: " + rule.Aliases + " AFP:" +
rule.AutoFolderPropertyName + " Cond:" + rule.ConditionsString + " CTS:" +
rule.ContentTypeString + " CR: " + rule.CustomRouter + " pri:" +
rule.Priority + " TP:" + rule.TargetPath + " Name:" + rule.Name +
" Desc:" + rule.Description;


                    try
                    {
                        DocumentRouterAutoFolderSettings autoFolder =
rule.AutoFolderSettings;

                        s = "name Format: "
                        + autoFolder.AutoFolderFolderNameFormat + " PropID:" +
autoFolder.AutoFolderPropertyId.ToString() + " InternalName:" +
autoFolder.AutoFolderPropertyInternalName + " PropName:" +
autoFolder.AutoFolderPropertyName + " TypeasString:" +
autoFolder.AutoFolderPropertyTypeAsString + " MaxItem:" +
autoFolder.MaxFolderItems.ToString() + " Term:" +
autoFolder.TaxTermStoreId.ToString();
                    }
                    catch { }


                }

                //Create a new rule

                //Can use helpers to get Content Type Info and Field Info

                SPContentType contentType = web.ContentTypes["MyCustomCT"];

                string contentTypeString = contentType.Id.ToString() + "|"
                + contentType.Name;

                //Field Internal Name
                SPField fieldName = contentType.Fields["Name"];

                string fieldNameString = fieldName.Id.ToString() + "|" +
fieldName.InternalName + "|" + fieldName.Title;



                EcmDocumentRouterRule newRule = new EcmDocumentRouterRule(web);
                newRule.Name = "Custom Programmatic Rule";
                newRule.Description = "Created by OM";
                newRule.Priority = "5";
                //Can be the content type ID and any aliases separated by |
                newRule.ContentTypeString = contentTypeString;
                //Relative path to target
                newRule.TargetPath = "/Shared Documents";
                newRule.ConditionsString = @"<Conditions>
                    <Condition
Column=""8553196d-ec8d-4564-9861-3dbe931050c8|FileLeafRef|Name""Operator=""IsNotEqual""
                    Value=""NotEqualTo"" />
                    <Condition
```

```
Column=""8553196d-ec8d-4564-9861-3dbe931050c8|FileLeafRef|Name""
Operator=""GreaterThan""
                        Value=""GreaterThan"" />
                        <Condition
Column=""8553196d-ec8d-4564-9861-3dbe931050c8|FileLeafRef|Name""
Operator=""LessThan""
                        Value=""LessThan"" />
                        <Condition
Column=""8553196d-ec8d-4564-9861-3dbe931050c8|FileLeafRef|Name""
Operator=""GreaterThanOrEqual""
                        Value=""GreaterThanEqual"" />
                        <Condition
Column=""8553196d-ec8d-4564-9861-3dbe931050c8|FileLeafRef|Name""
Operator=""LessThanOrEqual""
                        Value=""LessThanOrEqual"" />
                        <Condition
Column=""8553196d-ec8d-4564-9861-3dbe931050c8|FileLeafRef|Name""
Operator=""BeginsWith""
                        Value=""BeginsWith"" />
                        </Conditions>";

                //Create autofolder settings
                //Get Field Properties (must be required and single value property
                SPField customField = contentType.Fields["MyCustomString"];


                DocumentRouterAutoFolderSettings aFolder =
newRule.AutoFolderSettings;
                aFolder.Enabled = true;
                aFolder.AutoFolderPropertyInternalName = customField.InternalName;
                aFolder.AutoFolderPropertyId = customField.Id;
                aFolder.AutoFolderPropertyName = customField.Title;
                aFolder.AutoFolderPropertyTypeAsString = customField.TypeAsString;
                aFolder.AutoFolderFolderNameFormat = "%1 - %2";


                newRule.Enabled = true;


                router.RoutingRuleCollection.Add(newRule);
```

CodeSnippetChap9.cs

Creating Workflows That Use RM

One of the exciting additions for RM is the addition of workflow actions that take advantage of RM. With SharePoint Designer and Visio, RM has a number of actions you can perform on your content. The first is special to document sets, in that as an action in SPD, you can send the document set to the records repository. For RM in particular, there are two actions and they are opposites: Declare Record and Undeclare Record. As the names imply, these actions will declare or undeclare the current item as a record. Figure 7-9 shows using these actions in an SPD workflow. Figure 7-10 shows an example with the same actions in a SharePoint workflow using Visio.

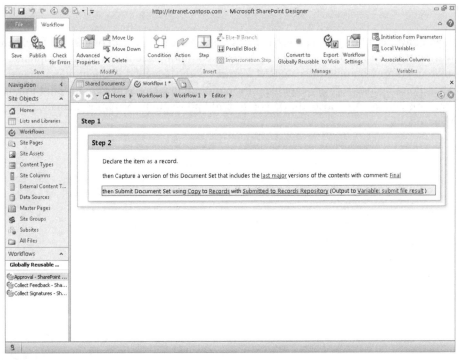

FIGURE 7-9

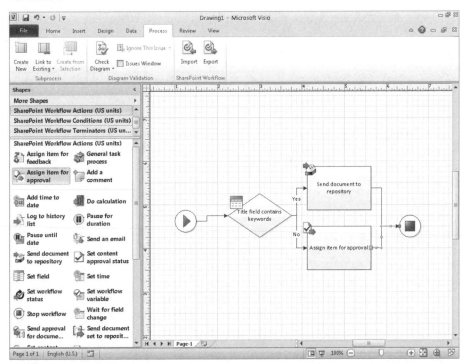

FIGURE 7-10

SUMMARY

In this chapter, you have seen how you can use records management in SharePoint 2010. Declaring records and creating Content Organizer rules will become commonplace if you build compliance applications on SharePoint. Combine the new RM features with the new document management features, and SharePoint becomes a very capable information management system for handling large amounts of data. This combination also allows you to build powerful information management solutions with SharePoint.

Web Content Management

WHAT'S IN THIS CHAPTER?

➤ Understand how the Publishing Framework supports web content management

➤ Develop site columns and content types for Publishing content

➤ Develop Page Layouts and Master Pages for Publishing sites

➤ Configure Navigation for Publishing sites

➤ Customize the Content by Query Web Part

➤ Setup and Use Content Conversion in Publishing sites

Web Content Management is a subset of Enterprise Content Management in SharePoint 2010. The conceptual models that we use for defining, administering, and managing enterprise content are equally relevant to web content systems. Whereas Enterprise Content Management systems typically focus on Document and Records management functions, Web Content Management tends to focus on Page management functions. Fundamentally, the approaches between the two are differentiated only in the artifacts that you process.

THE CONTENT LIFECYCLE IN WEB CONTENT MANAGEMENT

Understanding the conceptual models for content management begins with a clear definition of the content lifecycle. The content lifecycle defines the process by which content is created/captured, managed, distributed, and retained. It is a process model that is familiar to most developers because it is related to and mirrors the Software Development Lifecycle that is typically employed in projects.

In SharePoint 2010, creating and capturing content encompasses many different roles and forms. Developers are concerned with the creation of taxonomies in the form of site collections and sites, Information Architecture in the form of site columns and content types, templates in the form of master pages and page layouts, and content retention in the form of lists and libraries. Designers are concerned with the creation of branding, the user experience, and navigation artifacts. Business content owners are concerned with the creation of content, using templates to create the pages that end users view on the sites, and the creation of reusable content artifacts such as text, HTML, and images. Finally, site visitors and members are concerned with the creation of social content through comments, personalization, and rating systems.

Considering the variety of mechanisms that SharePoint 2010 provides to create and capture content in its Web Content Management system, it is important to understand the procedures for managing all of the content channels that are available. In the past, content management was handled by the developers who were the sole gatekeepers of the static pages. Later, management of the content was handed over to the content owners, who used web-based technologies to manage the content that appeared on the pages, while the developers continued to be the gatekeepers of the templates. SharePoint 2010's content management procedures add to the existing model by modularizing the locations of content in the system, allowing each role to manage its own content in the system.

Controlling distribution over a large variety of content sources and management processes is very important. Distribution policies provide a mechanism for determining who will see content, where content is deployed, and when content is available. It is the function of the Web Content Management system to provide mechanisms that allow the content creators to indicate whom content is intended for and when content is valid in the system. The web content system also allows the business to encapsulate all new content within a framework of workflows and governance that manages the variety of content inputs into the system.

Retention policies govern the final phase in the content's lifecycle; as content ages and becomes obsolete in the system, or is no longer published for general consumption because of the dictates of the distribution policy, the retention policies define how content is disposed of in the system. This may include the removal of content from the system, the storage of content in specified libraries or repository locations, or even the movement of content into durable archive systems.

For the SharePoint developer, the content lifecycle is an important conceptual model. This model assists the developer in identifying and using the capabilities that SharePoint offers in support of the content lifecycle. It also assists the developer in defining the components necessary to support the four phases of content life: 1) content types, site columns, and page layouts provide the means to create and capture content in the system; 2) workflows and information policies attached to content types provide the means to manage content as it is created in the SharePoint site; 3) workflows and policies also provide the means to distribute content; and 4) Record Management policies and custom code provide the means to manage the retention of content and pages as they leave the system.

Finally, the content lifecycle helps the developer to identify the taxonomy needed to support each phase of the content lifecycle. The taxonomy represents the logical categorization of content, lists, libraries, and pages in a SharePoint site, which is normally represented in a site model. SharePoint provides the Pages library and reusable content libraries that support the capture/creation of content in the system, but the developer will need to consider other lists and libraries to handle the movement of content through the system at its various stages. Having a view of content as a living entity that is conceptually modeled in a lifecycle helps the developer to understand the system as it grows.

Separation of Content and Development

Web Content Management in SharePoint 2010 includes technologies that allow you to separate the design and development of the website from the content that makes up the website. These technologies give greater control to both IT and business users over the parts of the website that they are most concerned about.

Before the creation of web content systems, websites consisted of static web pages. These pages included styling, layout, and content mingled together. This mingling later included client programming and server programming as technologies advanced and added more capabilities to the systems. In these systems, the pages were developed and deployed to the web by designers and developers.

The challenge of static systems is that the creation of sites and pages is a burdensome process whereby business stakeholders provide content to the developers, who in turn integrate the content into the design and programming of individual pages. Testing and approval of sites and pages was equally burdensome because it included an additional step of getting business sign-off on the content. In some organizations, this included the involvement of legal departments.

SharePoint 2010 addresses the issues of static site development by separating the three main roles of actors in website creation: Designers, Authors, and Approvers. SharePoint allows Designers/Developers to leverage the software development techniques and lifecycle that they are familiar with to create web assets and templates that are independent of business content. Authors are able to use these assets and templates to create sites and pages, focusing only on the content of the pages. Finally, the deployment of designed assets and content is managed by version control mechanisms and approval workflows that allow Approvers to review assets and content independent of the creation process.

The Important Role of Information Architecture

Information Architecture provides the conceptual models that facilitate Web Content Management and mediates the activities and roles of the Designers, Authors, and Approvers. It is the information architectural model that informs the development of templates and workflows, and the creation of lists and libraries; and provides an overall framework for user interaction within the system.

The development of Information Architecture in SharePoint tends to begin with the development of the site's hierarchy. The hierarchy provides a common model that is understandable by designers, developers, content authors, and business stakeholders. When developed visually with a tool such as Microsoft Visio, the hierarchy is solidified in the minds of the team and provides a basis from which to develop the remaining assets in the taxonomy.

Working with a model of the site's hierarchy, the designers and content authors begin to separate the components of the site's Information Architecture into asset categories, such as site columns and content types, that can be subjected to detailed design. This will result in design documents or models that identify page layouts needed for content authoring; content types and site columns needed to support the layouts; Master Pages, style sheets, and images needed for branding; lists and libraries to store content; and web parts to display content aggregations.

As well as identifying the necessary assets that make up the web content system, the hierarchical model will demonstrate the important distinction between the physical hierarchy and the user experience through navigational constructs. Using SharePoint's built-in navigational components and web parts, designers can achieve an effective navigational structure that is independent of the physical location of lists, libraries, sites, and pages.

Time spent developing complete Information Architecture models for a SharePoint web content system will ensure a robust and effective implementation. Poor planning will result in unanticipated changes to underlying components of the system, which will often lead to excessive refactoring in the site, such as changes to content types that are in use requiring additional effort to deploy, or changes to the data types of site columns that affect code in the page layouts. More than anything else, a solid Information Architecture will spare you many headaches.

FOUNDATIONS OF WEB CONTENT MANAGEMENT

SharePoint Server 2010 implements Web Content Management using the Publishing Site features. These features, when activated, add SharePoint components that enable Web Content Management on the site. These components include Master Pages, layout pages, content types, reusable content lists, and custom actions.

Activating the Publishing Features

SharePoint Server 2010 provides two site templates that activate the Publishing features during site provisioning: Publishing Portal and Enterprise Wiki. The Publishing Portal template is a generic template that you can use as a foundation for both internal and public-facing publishing sites. The template provisions a site that contains a single home page with a few instructional notes included in the Page Content field and the Publishing features activated. The Enterprise Wiki site is a specialized intranet site that implements wiki-based publishing.

The Publishing features are not limited to the two templates that are available during site creation; they can be activated on any existing site. To enable the Publishing features on an existing site, activate the Office SharePoint Server Publishing Infrastructure feature in the site collection features list (Site Actions ⇨ Site Settings ⇨ Manage site collection features) and activate the Office SharePoint Server Publishing in the site features list of each site that you want to have Publishing features. (Site Actions ⇨ Site Settings ⇨ Manage site features).

When enabling the Publishing feature manually, the Site Collection feature must be activated before the Site feature, because the Site feature has a registered dependency on hidden features that are activated by the Site Collection Publishing feature.

Publishing Feature Components

Activating the Publishing features in your site provisions a number of components, which include site columns, content types, layouts, Master Pages, and lists. It also makes a number of changes to the way in which the sites work by applying workflows, limiting provisioning, and adding publishing-specific permission groups. Taken together, these components implement Enterprise Content Management methodologies.

The Pages library is the document library that provides the document management functionality for all web pages in the managed site. As authors create pages using the Page Layouts, the completed pages are saved to this library. The library manages the publishing process by implementing two key components of content management. First, the pages in the library are subject to versioning with check-in/check-out support. Authors check out web pages to collaborate on the content of the web page and check in changes as they are completed. The checked-in changes are saved as minor versions of the web page that are not visible to the public until the page is published as a major version and approved by a content approver.

The second key component implemented in the Pages library is the application of an optional approval workflow that is automatically launched when a content author publishes a major version of a web page. When the author clicks the Publish button on the Ribbon or uses the actions menu in the Pages library, the workflow will launch the Start Workflow page, which prompts the author to enter some basic workflow information. This is a parallel approval workflow that ensures controlled publication of content to the site.

Besides adding document management capability to the web pages in the site, the Publishing features also provide controls over the look and feel of the site using Master Pages, Page Layouts, and Cascading Style Sheets, which allow designers to manage branding of the site as well as the templates that are available to content authors. Using the Page Layout and Site Template settings page (Site Actions ➪ Site Settings ➪ Page layouts and site templates), the designer can select which site templates authors may use when creating subsites within their content areas.

The Publishing framework differentiates content authors, content approvers, and designers/developers by implementing an Approvers group and a Designers group; it leverages the Members group for authors. The Publishing features implement these groups in the libraries and workflows that are created during the provisioning process.

Page Processing Model

When a site visitor requests a page, SharePoint combines content and templates from the site to render the final page. SharePoint begins by retrieving the requested page from the Page library. This provides SharePoint with the metadata that identifies the web page, as well as the content that the author entered into the page. Next, SharePoint retrieves the Master Page and the Layout page from the Master Pages and Page Layouts gallery. SharePoint determines the correct page layout by examining the content type of the requested web page. Finally, SharePoint combines the Master Page, Layout page, and content into a rendered HTML page that it sends back to the end user's browser as shown in Figure 8-1.

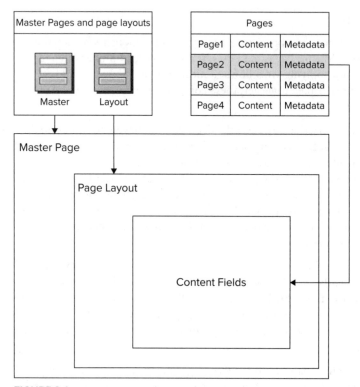

FIGURE 8-1

There is an important relationship between the templates and content that is defined by content types, as shown in Figure 8-2. The content type is a container for the site columns that define the content and metadata for the web pages. As the container for this information, the content type acts as the glue between the content and the templates. The content type is assigned to both the template and the Pages library. This allows the template to use placeholders that align to the site columns, and it allows the author to use the template within the site.

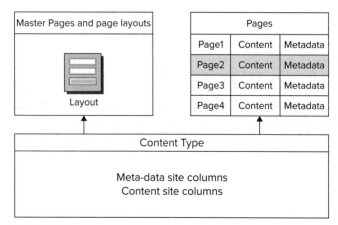

FIGURE 8-2

Site Columns

Site columns are an important part of the Publishing framework because they represent content and metadata in the site's web pages. Site columns do not actually contain the content of the web page — that is the function of the list or library that houses the site column. Rather, the site column defines the data format of the content contained in the list or library.

Site columns are used in two distinct ways in a Publishing site. First, the Pages library uses the site column definition to store content and metadata about the page. In this way, the Pages library uses site columns consistently with all other lists in SharePoint. The second way in which site columns are used is as placeholders for content in layout pages. Authors enter content into content locations specified by the designer. The designer makes these content placeholders available by associating the placeholder with the site column. It is this match between the field placeholder and the site column in the Page library that allows SharePoint to save content to the library as well as to retrieve it for page rendering.

The challenge to working with site columns in a Publishing site is differentiating between site columns that define content storage fields in a list from site columns that define metadata content that helps to identify the content container. For example, the Scheduled Start Date field of a Publishing Article page is a metadata field that describes when the page should be published. The Page Image field is a content storage field that holds the URL to an image that will appear with the article text on the rendered web page. Some fields represent a gray area between content and metadata, in particular the Title field, which is metadata for the page but is also the HTML title tag content that appears in the browser's window caption.

As a developer, creating site columns that will represent metadata and site columns that will represent web page content is identical; SharePoint makes no differentiation between the usage models for the site columns. The differentiation becomes important when you begin developing layout pages that provide the input fields to the author. Considering the difference at this stage will save you time and debugging later in the development process.

Browser-Based Site Column Development

SharePoint 2010 allows designers to define site columns from the browser-based site settings interface (Site Actions ➪ Site Settings ➪ Site columns). The Site Columns gallery lists all site columns defined for the site by group.

To create a site column, execute the following steps:

1. Click the Create button at the top of the Site Column Gallery listing.

2. Enter the Name, Type, Group, and Additional Column Settings for the site column.

3. Optionally, SharePoint 2010 adds the ability to include validation logic for each site column.

Browser-based site column development presents three substantial problems for the developer. The first is limited portability of the site column definition. When created by the browser interface, the site column is added directly to the site's content database. In cases where it is necessary to define a site column across many site collections, the designer will need to define the site column in each site collection. For enterprises that use multi-staged environments, this means that the site column will need to be created many times, which is an error-prone approach. Finally, site columns defined in the browser limit the ability to upgrade solutions that rely on the browser-created column, such as content type definitions and list definitions.

The second substantial problem with the browser-based approach to site column development is the lack of source control that is typical in most development shops. This makes differentiating custom site columns from SharePoint-defined site columns difficult. It is equally difficult to track changes over time, a task that is normally managed using a source control system such as Team Foundation Server.

Finally, the site column definition page does not differentiate between the internal name of the site column and the display name; rather, it presents only the display name and uses that value as the internal name. This results in what is known as the "space problem." The internal name for a site column cannot contain space characters; therefore, when SharePoint saves the site column in the browser interface, it will replace each space in the name field with the value _x0020_. This creates problems later when you reference the name in a Content Query web part or in your source code. The workaround in the browser interface is to create the site column with no spaces in the name, save it, and then edit the site column to add the spaces back into the name. This will cause SharePoint to save an internal name without spaces and then update the display name with spaces.

Feature-Based Site Column Development

Using a SharePoint Feature is the most common approach to developing site columns for a solution when the developer wants a source control-manageable code file. The developer uses Collaborative Application Markup Language (CAML) to define `Field` elements in the Feature's Elements file. When the Feature is activated within a site collection, all of the fields defined in the Elements file are deployed to the site collection as site columns.

Visual Studio 2010 includes improved integration and tools for SharePoint development that makes the process of creating a SharePoint Solution and Feature to hold site columns easier than in the past. Although Visual Studio 2010 does not include a specific template to create site columns, it does include a blank template that will allow you to add site columns to the Feature's Elements file.

To develop a CAML-based site column in Visual Studio, create a new project (File ➪ New ➪ Project). In the New Projects dialog shown in Figure 8-3, expand the SharePoint Installed Templates node for SharePoint and select the 2010 node. Select the Empty SharePoint Project template. Enter a project name and click OK to create a SharePoint Feature and solution.

When you create a SharePoint project in Visual Studio 2010, it will change your Framework target for you. You can see this if you open the project properties dialog and look in the Target framework selection. It will read 3.5 even if you had 4 selected in the New Project dialog. I also noticed that if you select 2.0 or 3.0 in the New Project dialog, all of the SharePoint project templates disappear.

The following example presents a web content management solution for a Human Resources department. The purpose of the solution is to allow Human Resources personnel to add web pages to the site that provide benefits information to employees. The following site columns provide metadata and content for page instances in the Human Resources site. Later the sample will add Content Types that will be tied into the Page Layouts.

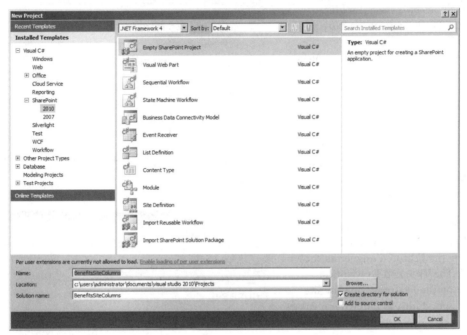

FIGURE 8-3

SharePoint 2010 introduces the concept of Sandboxed Solutions. These are solutions that can be deployed to a specific site collection as a user solution and are managed in the Solutions gallery (Site Actions ➪ Site Settings ➪ Solutions). This allows for the deployment of solutions to a testing environment where server resets are not necessary. When you create a project based on the SharePoint project templates, Visual Studio will ask you whether the project should be sandboxed or server-based, as shown in Figure 8-4. Because most development occurs on dedicated development virtual machines or in a development environment where you will have administrator privileges, it is more efficient to deploy as a farm solution. The examples in this chapter assume that you are deploying to the farm.

 If you opt to deploy as a sandboxed solution and would like to change to a farm solution later, you may do so by selecting the project in the Visual Studio Solution Explorer, then change the Sandboxed Solution property in the Properties pane to False.

Visual Studio 2010 creates a new project that includes references to `Microsoft.SharePoint.dll` and `Microsoft.SharePoint.Security.dll`. It is strongly named and includes two special folders specific to SharePoint projects: Feature and Package. The Feature folder represents the SharePoint Features included in this project. The Package folder represents the SharePoint Solution which is compiled into a WSP file that will deploy the Features to the designated solution store.

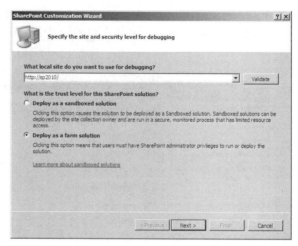

FIGURE 8-4

The Empty SharePoint Project template does not include any Features in the Features folder. To add a new Feature to this project, right-click the Features folder, and click Add Feature. This adds a new Feature component to the folder; double-click the Feature1 icon in Solution Explorer to modify the Feature's metadata using the Feature designer as shown in Figure 8-5. The Title and Description values appear on the Features pages in Site Settings. It is a good idea to make these values

FIGURE 8-5

descriptive so that administrators will know what they are adding to the site when they activate the feature.

The feature's scope determines where the feature can be activated within SharePoint. There are four possible scopes that you may select for a feature:

1. **Farm:** Activates a feature for the entire SharePoint farm and is available in Central Administration.

2. **WebApplication:** Activates a feature for all sites in a web application and is available in Central Administration.

3. **Site:** Activates a feature for all sites in a site collection and is available in Site Collection Features in the site collection root site's site settings.

4. **Web:** Activates a feature for a web site and is available in Site Features in the web's site settings.

Certain components, such as site columns, content types, Master pages, and Page Layouts, are installed at the site collection level and made available to all sites within the collection. These components require that the scope for the feature be set to "Site."

Next, add a new item to the project (Right-click project name ⇨ Add ⇨ New Item) and select the Empty Element template from the Add New Item dialog box, as shown in Figure 8-6.

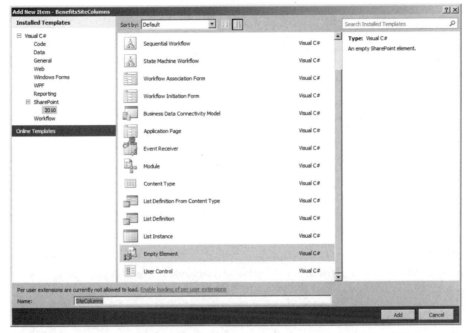

FIGURE 8-6

The Empty Element template is an XML file where you can enter CAML Field definitions. The following example shows the CAML definition for site columns. The DisplayName, Description, and Group attributes define the values that display in many of the browser-based interfaces including the site column gallery, and site column pickers in List properties. The type attribute indicates the data type of the site column; the available data type values are documented in the CAML section of the MSDN library.

Available for
download on
Wrox.com

```xml
<Elements xmlns="http://schemas.microsoft.com/sharepoint/">
   <Field ID="{76C140E1-D827-433B-AD38-257F9594B846}"
          Name="BenefitProvider"
          DisplayName="Provider Name"
          Group="Human Resources"
          Type="Text"
          Required="FALSE"/>
   <Field ID="{A1758D70-B479-469C-90BB-C3038ED42B15}"
          Name="BenefitProviderLogo"
          DisplayName="Provider Logo"
          Group="Human Resources"
          Type="Image"
          Required="FALSE"/>
   <Field ID="{5F516D92-969C-4661-81B9-C9210E2A2FDC}"
          Name="BenefitType"
          DisplayName="Benefit Category"
          Group="Human Resources"
          Type="Choice"
          Required="FALSE">
```

```
    <CHOICES>
      <CHOICE>Medical</CHOICE>
      <CHOICE>Dental</CHOICE>
      <CHOICE>Vision</CHOICE>
      <CHOICE>Insurance</CHOICE>
    </CHOICES>
  </Field>
  <Field ID="{521D5F12-16BC-4E82-997C-F28933ABE59E}"
        Name="BenefitDescription"
        DisplayName="Benefit Description"
        Group="Human Resources"
        Type="HTML" RichText="TRUE" RichTextMode="FullHtml"
        Required="FALSE"/>
</Elements>
```

BenefitsInformation\ Site Columns\ Elements.xml

Because CAML provides attributes for both the DisplayName and Name, you avoid the "spaces problem" that the browser-based interface presents. Using CAML, you can define a Name field that does not contain spaces; however, if you place spaces in the Name attribute, then SharePoint will save the name with the _x0020_ string as it does with the browser-based approach.

To deploy the Site Columns defined in the Elements file, right-click the project name in the Visual Studio Solution Explorer, and select Deploy. This will deploy the solution file to the solution store and activate the Feature in the targeted site collection. You can validate the installation of your site columns in SharePoint Designer or by viewing the Site Columns gallery in the Site Settings of the target Site Collection.

Feature-based site column development also avoids the problems of portability and synchronization of browser-based development. Using a SharePoint Solution for deployment, a feature can be installed across multi-stage environments with minimal effort. Portability becomes a matter of site administration and feature management. Features also ensure that site columns across environments remain synchronized in their metadata, eliminating the possibility of misspellings.

Object Model-Based Site Column Development

Using the SharePoint object model is a very powerful method for implementing site columns in SharePoint, as well as other SharePoint customizations. The object model is also a more familiar model to seasoned .NET developers who prefer to work with code rather than CAML. Finally, the object model provides additional flexibility for the developer, because it allows the creation of assets from entry points other than SharePoint Features, such as Application pages and .NET applications.

The most significant problem with developing site columns in CAML occurs when you are modifying or enhancing a Feature that has already deployed site columns into the site collection. In this situation, site columns are often assigned to content types and/or lists and may have data in place. Because the CAML feature does not validate the contents of the site, it may experience problems or cause exceptions when you attempt to upgrade the Feature.

Using object model code in a feature Receiver will allow you to perform validation on your site and additional data-massaging work before upgrading your Feature. Also, you have the option to include the definition and creation of the site columns in object model code rather than in CAML, in which case your Feature may consist solely of a receiver with no elements file attached.

Creating Site Columns in code using a Feature Receiver in Visual Studio 2010 is very similar to creating a CAML feature to create site columns. Create a new project (File ⇨ New ⇨ Project) and select an Empty SharePoint Project template to build the foundation of the project. Right-click the Features folder in Solution Explorer, and add a Feature to the project. You will set the properties of the Feature in the Feature Designer, but you will not add an Empty Elements file to the project as you did with the CAML approach.

Rather than add the Empty Elements, right-click on the Feature in the Features folder and select "Add Event Receiver" from the drop-down. This will add a class under the .Features folder in Solution Explorer as shown in Figure 8-7.

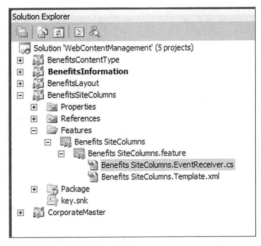

FIGURE 8-7

The Visual Studio–generated class contains commented override methods for each of the Feature's events. Uncomment the methods you wish to add code to and add the code. In this example, the FeatureActivated method will create two site columns and add them to the site collection.

```
public override void FeatureActivated(SPFeatureReceiverProperties properties)
{
  using (SPSite site = (SPSite)properties.Feature.Parent)
  {
    using (SPWeb web = site.RootWeb)
    {
      try
      {
        string benefitsDescription = web.Fields.Add(
          "Benefits_Description", SPFieldType.Note, false);
        string benefitsYear = web.Fields.Add(
          "Benefits_Year", SPFieldType.DateTime, false);
        web.Update();

        SPField benefitsDescriptionField = web.Fields[benefitsDescription];
        benefitsDescriptionField.Title = "Description";
        benefitsDescriptionField.Description = "Describe the benefits document";
        benefitsDescriptionField.Group = "Human Resources";
        benefitsDescriptionField.Update();

        SPField benefitsYearField = web.Fields[benefitsYear];
        benefitsYearField.Title = "Year";
```

```
          benefitsYearField.Description = "Year the benefits document is valid";
          benefitsYearField.Group = "Human Resources";
          benefitsYearField.Update();
        }
        catch (Exception ex)
        {
          Console.Write(ex.ToString());
        }
      }
    }
  }
```

Benefits SiteColumns.EventReceiver.cs

The code begins by connecting to the site collection using the properties of the Feature rather than using the SPContext class. The SPContext class will return a reference to a site collection only when the code is running within a SharePoint site; otherwise, no context exists. In the case of a Feature, a system administrator may not be using the Site Settings pages to activate Features; rather, she may be using a command-line script to activate the feature, in which case there is no SharePoint context. Therefore, FeatureActivating methods should use the Feature's properties to get the site collection.

The root web of the site collection contains the collection of SPFields (site columns) defined in the site collection. To create a site column in code, simply use the collection's Add method to define a new site column. The first argument is the name of the site column, the second is the data type, and the last flags whether the site column is required. A call to the SPWeb's Update method saves the site column to the site collection.

To configure additional attributes of the site columns, you need to reference each one, modify its properties, and update it. If this code is in the same method that you created the site column, getting the reference is easy because the field collection's Add method returns the internal name of the site column as a string. Using this string, you can instantiate an SPField object with a reference to the internal name. Finally, modify the site column's properties and call the Update method to save the completed site column.

Unlike site columns defined using CAML, when this Feature is deactivated, it does not remove the site columns from the site collection. To add this behavior, you need to override the FeatureDeactivating method and add code to remove the site columns that you created in code.

Available for
download on
Wrox.com

```
public override void FeatureDeactivating(SPFeatureReceiverProperties properties)
{
  if(properties.Feature.FeatureDefinitionScope != SPFeatureDefinitionScope.Site)
  {
    throw new Exception("This feature must be a 'Site' feature");
  }
  using (SPSite site = (SPSite)properties.Feature.Parent)
  {
    using (SPWeb web = site.RootWeb)
    {
      try
      {
```

```
        web.Fields["Benefits_Description"].Delete();
        web.Fields["Benefits_Year"].Delete();
      }
      catch (Exception ex)
      {
        Console.WriteLine(ex.ToString());
      }
    }
  }
}
```

Benefits SiteColumns.EventReceiver.cs

This simple example replicates the behavior demonstrated in the CAML code; however, it could easily include code that iterates through the lists in the site collection and that cleans up existing data that might be using these site columns. The code could also create lists, content types, or other related assets that are necessary to the web content solution.

Content Types

Content types are a conceptual container for content and processes in the system. They encapsulate metadata in the form of site columns, and functionality in the form of information policies and workflow. In a publishing site, content types are a bridge between the content-holding site columns and the template-oriented Page Layouts. Without a defined content type, SharePoint has no way of associating a page layout with the content contained in the Pages library.

 It is important to remember that you will both assign the content type to the Page Layout and add the content type to the Pages library.

Understanding Content Type Ids

Before you can develop a content type for any use in SharePoint, you must understand how Content Type IDs work. Unlike all other elements in SharePoint where the ID value is a GUID that identifies the element to SharePoint, the Content Type Id also contains hierarchical logic that identifies where the content type exists within the system.

Every content type in SharePoint must inherit from a parent content type. Similar to object inheritance in code, content types inherit all site columns, workflows, and information policies from their parent content type.

There are two approaches to defining Content Type Ids: the Hex approach and the GUID approach. The Hex approach defines a Content Type Id by adding a two-digit Hex value other than "00" to the end of the Parent's Content Type Id. The GUID approach adds the value "00" followed by a GUID (with all special characters stripped out) to the Parent's Content Type Id.

Hex: [Parent Content Type Id] + [2-digit Hex value]

GUID: [Parent Content Type Id] + 00 + [GUID with no {} or - characters]

For example, suppose you create a content type for an HR Benefits Document that inherits from the Document content type. Using the Hex approach would result in a Content Type Id that begins with the Document Content Type Id "0x0101" followed by a two-digit hex value "03."

```
Hex: 0x010103
```

Using the GUID approach for the same content type would also begin with the Document Content Type Id "0x0101" but it would be followed by "00" and then a GUID that is stripped of special characters "24CB1116BE6D49e9B482D492532921F2."

```
GUID: 0x01010024CB1116BE6D49e9B482D492532921F2
```

 There are three approaches to finding the Content Type Id of a parent content type. First, you can open the content type properties page from the Content Types gallery and then look in the page URL for the ctype *attribute. Second, you can go into the Features folder of the SharePoint Root in Windows Explorer and open the Elements file, where the content type is defined. Finally, if you have SharePoint Designer 2010, it contains a Content Type section that will show the properties of every content type in your site, including the ID.*

The best practice recommended by Microsoft is to use the GUID approach to define all custom content types in the system. The GUID approach avoids collisions between Content Type Ids that can occur with the Hex approach if the Hex values are not carefully managed by designers of the system. For example, the Hex value provided in the above example "03" for the Benefits Document is acceptable because it is not one of the out-of-the-box Ids; however, a quick look at the SDK documentation in the "Base Content Type Hierarchy" shows that there are a number of out-of-the-box types using neighboring hex values. It would be easy to collide with some of the Microsoft defined content type Ids.

Despite the recommendation, Content Type Ids are limited to a 1024 character size. Given a deep content type hierarchy, you can quickly run out of space for defining a Content Type Id. In these situations, you will need to use an approach that mixes both methods. You will begin with the GUID approach to inherit from the Parent Content Type, which results in a "base" content type that acts similarly to a namespace in code. Then, you will switch to a Hex approach to define internal children types.

Browser-Based Content Type Development

SharePoint provides a browser-based approach to creating content types that is similar to creating site columns in the browser (Site Actions ➪ Site Settings ➪ Site content types). The process by which the content type is created in the site works somewhat differently from that for other elements in SharePoint. The initial content type definition establishes the name, parent, and group of the content type.

After SharePoint creates the content type, it will display the Content Type properties page rather than redirect you back to the Content Type gallery. The Content Type property page provides the links and capabilities to add additional site columns to the content type, as well as to add, modify, or delete workflows and information policies.

Browser-based content type development suffers from the same portability and source management issues that browser-based site column development presents. SharePoint 2010 introduces a content management capability called Enterprise Content Types that will automatically publish content types across site collection boundaries within a SharePoint farm. This is a very powerful feature that merits close examination in your solutions; however, it does not work across multi-environment settings. Likewise, Enterprise Content Types do not provide any form of source control for content type definitions in your development lifecycle. Even when you use Enterprise Content Types, you should still define the content type with either the Feature or object model approaches.

Feature-Based Content Type Development

Feature-based content type development works within the SharePoint Solution and Feature framework in exactly the same way that feature-based site column development works. The content type is defined in the Feature's Elements file using CAML. Because content types are containers for custom site columns, it is a common practice to define the custom site columns at the top of the elements file and then define the custom content types at the bottom. This enables you to deploy both the site columns and their containers in one SharePoint Feature.

Visual Studio 2010's SharePoint tools include a template for content types that provides the basic framework for defining a content type in CAML. To begin creating a content type, create a new project (File ➪ New ➪ Project) and select the Content Type SharePoint Project template to build the foundation of the project, as shown in Figure 8-8.

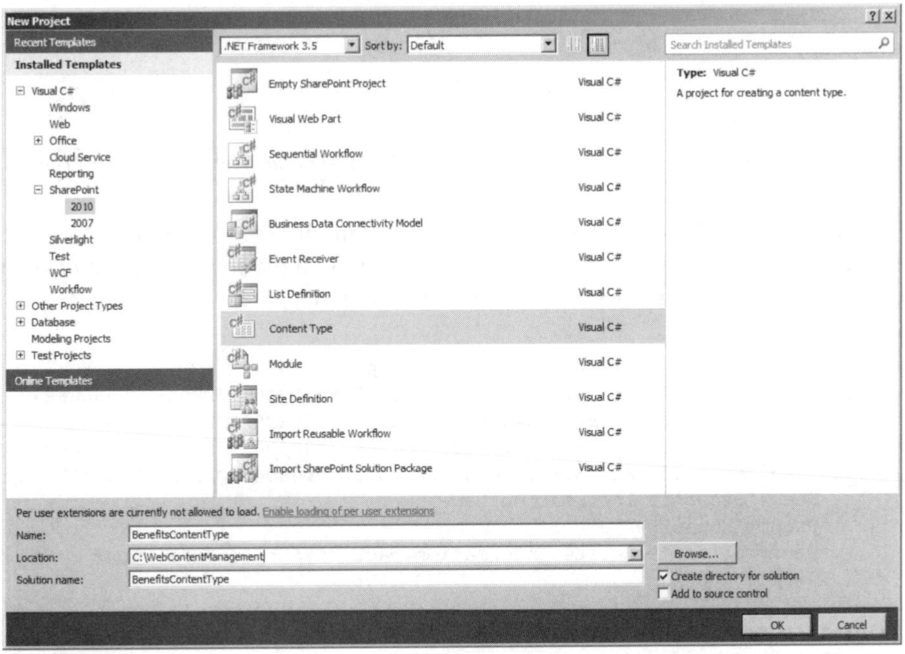

FIGURE 8-8

Next, Visual Studio will ask you to select the Parent Content Type. When creating a content type to use with a page layout, you must inherit from one of the page layouts, as shown in Figure 8-9.

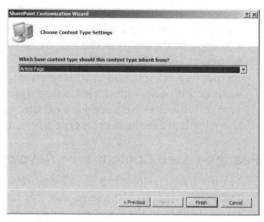

Visual Studio 2010 creates a CAML-based definition for the content type, including a Content Type Id that uses the GUID method. An added benefit is that it includes the parent's ID as a comment for easy reference. In most cases, you will want to modify the generated metadata values to content that is more fitting to your Information Architecture.

FIGURE 8-9

```xml
<?xml version="1.0" encoding="utf-8"?>
<Elements xmlns="http://schemas.microsoft.com/sharepoint/">
  <!-- Parent ContentType: Article Page (0x010100C568DB52D9D0A14D9B2FDCC96666E9F200
7948130EC3DB064584E219954237AF3900242457EFB8B24247815D688C526CD44D) -->
  <ContentType ID="0x010100C568DB52D9D0A14D9B2FDCC96666E9F2007948130EC3DB064584E219
954237AF3900242457EFB8B24247815D688C526CD44D007b07c2cdb6004430bfd2fe7a3eff5ecb"
                Name="Benefits Information Page"
                Group="Human Resources"
                Description="Benefits Information page layout content type"
                Version="0">
    <FieldRefs>
    </FieldRefs>
  </ContentType>
</Elements>
```

BenefitsInformation\ContentTypes\Elements.xml

To complete the content type definition, add field references within the `<FieldRefs></FieldRefs>` element. Each field reference element will associate a site column with the content type. Note that it is not necessary to include field references for fields inherited from the parent content type.

```xml
<?xml version="1.0" encoding="utf-8"?>
<Elements xmlns="http://schemas.microsoft.com/sharepoint/">
  <!-- Parent ContentType: Article Page (0x010100C568DB52D9D0A14D9B2FDCC96666E9F200
7948130EC3DB064584E219954237AF3900242457EFB8B24247815D688C526CD44D) -->
  <ContentType ID="0x010100C568DB52D9D0A14D9B2FDCC96666E9F2007948130EC3DB064584E219
954237AF3900242457EFB8B24247815D688C526CD44D007b07c2cdb6004430bfd2fe7a3eff5ecb"
                Name="Benefits Information Page"
                Group="Human Resources"
                Description="Benefits Information page layout content type"
                Version="0">
    <FieldRefs>
      <FieldRef ID="{76C140E1-D827-433B-AD38-257F9594B846}"
        Name="BenefitProvider"/>
```

```
<FieldRef ID="{A1758D70-B479-469C-90BB-C3038ED42B15}"
    Name="BenefitProviderLogo"/>
<FieldRef ID="{5F516D92-969C-4661-81B9-C9210E2A2FDC}"
    Name="BenefitType"/>
<FieldRef ID="{521D5F12-16BC-4E82-997C-F28933ABE59E}"
    Name="BenefitDescription"/>
    </FieldRefs>
  </ContentType>
</Elements>
```

BenefitsInformation\ContentTypes\Elements.xml

The challenge presented with this example is that the content type definition references site columns that are defined in a separate Feature. If the other Feature is not activated first, SharePoint will display an error page when you attempt to run this project. There are two ways to deal with this challenge. The first is to modify the Feature definition to add a Feature dependency between the two Features.

In Visual Studio 2010, adding a Feature dependency is very easy, especially if the Feature is already installed on your targeted SharePoint site. To add the dependency, open the Feature Designer by double-clicking the Feature in Visual Studio's Solution Explorer. At the bottom of the Designer, expand the section at the bottom labeled "Feature Activation Dependencies," then click the Add button to add the dependency. Visual Studio shows a list of the Features installed in the target SharePoint site as shown in Figure 8-10.

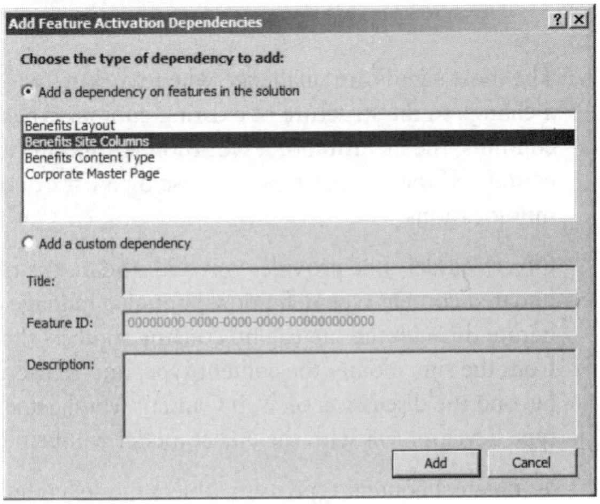

FIGURE 8-10

You can select one or more of the installed Features to make this Feature dependent. You also have the option to enter the Feature information for dependencies that you have not installed on the target SharePoint site. After you click Add, the Feature will be updated to include the dependencies as shown in Figure 8-11.

FIGURE 8-11

The second way to deal with the dependency created by this content type definition is to refactor the Features so that the site columns are included in the same Feature as the content type. This is a matter of either cutting and pasting the Site Column CAML into the content type's Elements file or adding the Site Column Elements file to the current project.

Object Model-Based Content Type Development

As with site columns, you can create content types using the SharePoint object model. The object model provides the flexibility to develop content types with .NET applications, application pages, web parts, and Feature Receivers using a code-based approach.

> **A NOTE ABOUT TERMINOLOGY**
>
> In MOSS 2007, everything was just 'object model' because there was only one option. Now there are two options: the new client, and the old server (which was referred to as the 'object model' for the past three years). I think many developers will continue to refer to the server object model by the generic term 'Object Model' but will differentiate when speaking about the Client Object Model, and that's what's done here.

The most significant challenge when working with content type occurs when business needs necessitate a change to the structure of existing content types. This may be the addition or subtraction of site columns, the inclusion of a workflow, or modification of other elements that content types may contain. If the content type is in use by a list or content, then you will not be able to deploy your modifications.

Object model code provides you with the means to develop mechanisms that will not only deploy updated content type definitions, but also manage existing content. In these cases, a Feature Receiver can iterate through the site to find content and lists that are using a content type, extract those components from the site, modify the content type, and reinsert the content. These procedures are code-intensive and beyond the discussion of Web Content Management, but understanding the basic concept of content type development with the object model will help you deal with upgrade situations when they arise.

To create a content type using object model code and a Feature Receiver, create a new Visual Studio project (File ➪ New ➪ Project) and select an empty SharePoint project template. Right-click the Features folder in Solution Explorer, and add a Feature to the project. You will set the properties of the Feature in the Feature Designer, but you will not add an empty element or a content type element to the Feature; rather, right-click the Feature and select Add Event Receiver from the drop-down menu.

In this example, uncomment the `FeatureActivated` and `FeatureDeactivating` methods to include code that will create a content type and remove it when the Feature is activated and deactivated, respectively. Creating a content type in object model code takes three distinct steps that mirror the three steps we followed in the CAML approach: define the parent, create the content type, and add additional components.

```
public override void FeatureActivated(SPFeatureReceiverProperties properties)
{
    using (SPSite site = (SPSite)properties.Feature.Parent)
    {
        using (SPWeb web = site.RootWeb)
        {
            try
            {
```

```
            SPContentType parentType = web.AvailableContentTypes["Document"];

            SPContentType contentType =
               new SPContentType(parentType, web.ContentTypes, "Benefits Document");
            contentType.Group = "Human Resources";
            contentType.Description = "Benefits documentation and forms";

            web.ContentTypes.Add(contentType);
            web.Update();

            SPField descriptionField = web.AvailableFields["Benefits_Description"];
            contentType.FieldLinks.Add(new SPFieldLink(descriptionField));
            SPField yearField = web.AvailableFields["Benefits_Year"];
            contentType.FieldLinks.Add(new SPFieldLink(yearField));

            contentType.Update();
          }
          catch (Exception ex)
          {
            Console.WriteLine(ex.ToString());
          }
        }
      }
    }
    public override void FeatureDeactivating(SPFeatureReceiverProperties properties)
    {
      using (SPSite site = (SPSite)properties.Feature.Parent)
      {
        using (SPWeb web = site.RootWeb)
        {
          try
          {
            SPContentType contentType = web.AvailableContentTypes["Benefits Document"];
            contentType.Delete();
            web.Update();
          }
          catch (Exception ex)
          {
            Console.WriteLine(ex.ToString());
          }
        }
      }
    }
  }
```

Benefits ContentType.EventReceiver.cs

This example begins by getting a reference to the Parent content type, using the AvailableContent Types collection. In this case, the content type will inherit from the document type. The next section of the code creates an instance of SPContentType, passing in the parent content type, the collection that the content type will be added to, and the name of the content type. You can set other properties of the content type such as Group and Description in the next few lines. Finally, the content type is added to the ContentTypes collection of the root web, and the web is updated to save the content type.

The last step in the process is to add the associated site columns to the content type and update it with those changes. The code retrieves each site column from the AvailableSiteColumns collection in the root web. The site columns are added to the content type as `SPFieldLink` objects that are added to the `FieldLink` collection in the content type. Finally, the `Update` method saves the changes to the content type.

As with the CAML-based approach, using existing site columns sets up a Feature dependency that can be handled in the same way as in the previous example, by setting a dependency in the Feature or by including the site column code in this receiver. An additional option available to object model code is to include validation methods that will look for the site columns in the site collection and either activate their Features from code or create them from code.

Client Object Model-Based Content Type Development

SharePoint 2010 includes a client object model that will allow your code to run on a separate server or workstation. This model supports building .NET forms and console applications, as well as WPF, Silverlight, and EMCA script applications. Client object model code operates through a set of classes that represent objects on the SharePoint server rather than interacting directly with the concrete objects as the object model does. This means that you need to establish a connection to the SharePoint server and load the objects that you need into the client application in order to access them.

Initially, this may appear to be more cumbersome than necessary to accomplish the same task as the server object model; however, the client object model opens up some interesting possibilities for Web Content Management. Because the client application does not need to run on the SharePoint server, the designer/developer can set up an authoring environment that is separate from content authoring environments, adding more modularization to the topology.

To create a content type using the client object model in Visual Studio 2010, create a new project (File ➪ New ➪ Project) and select a Console project template, as shown in Figure 8-12.

FIGURE 8-12

After the project starts, you will add references to the `Microsoft.SharePoint.Client.dll` and `Microsoft.SharePoint.Client.Runtime.dll` assemblies located in the 14\ISAPI folder (also listed under the .NET component listing in the Add References dialog box. Next, you will add code to the Main program that will make the connection to the site collection. Because client object model code can run externally to the SharePoint application server, it works through a `ClientContext` object. The `ClientContext` object provides access to objects in the site collection, but they must be explicitly loaded into the context in order to code against them.

```csharp
static void Main(string[] args)
{
    // Get a reference to the site collection
    ClientContext clientContext = new ClientContext("http://sp2010");
    Web web = clientContext.Web;

    // Load reference to content type collection
    ContentTypeCollection contentTypes = web.ContentTypes;
    clientContext.Load(contentTypes);
    clientContext.ExecuteQuery();
}
```

Program.cs

Unlike server object model code, in which you can create an instance of the `SPContentType` class and add it to the `ContentTypes` collection, client object model makes use of an `Information` class that contains the template of the content type. The information class works in a similar manner to the `SPContentType` class with the exception of the parent's reference; rather than pass in a reference to the parent's content type, client object model code gets the parent's ID.

```csharp
static void Main(string[] args)
{
    // Get a reference to the site collection
    ClientContext clientContext = new ClientContext("http://sp2010");
    Web web = clientContext.Web;

    // Load reference to content type collection
    ContentTypeCollection contentTypes = web.ContentTypes;
    clientContext.Load(contentTypes);
    clientContext.ExecuteQuery();

    // Create a Content Type Information object
    ContentTypeCreationInformation benefitArticleInfo =
      new ContentTypeCreationInformation();
    benefitArticleInfo.Name = "Benefits Article";
    benefitArticleInfo.ParentContentType = contentTypes.GetById(
    "0x010100C568DB52D9D0A14D9B2FDCC96666E9F2007948130EC3DB064584E219954237AF3900242457
    EFB8B24247815D688C526CD44D");
    benefitArticleInfo.Group = "Human Resources";

    // Create the content type
    ContentType benefitArticle = contentTypes.Add(benefitArticleInfo);
    clientContext.ExecuteQuery();
}
```

Program.cs

After the `Information` object is completed, a `ContentType` object is added to the `ContentTypes` collection that you loaded with the `ClientContext` using the `Information` object. Although this adds the content type, the type does not exist in the site collection until the `ClientContext` executes the query.

Working with content types is central to Web Content Management development. Understanding all of the `ContentType` creation objects will give you a greater ability to develop flexible and powerful solutions for your web content systems.

Page Layouts

In its most basic form, a page layout is a template that is used to author content in the web content solution. In this way, it is very similar to an input form. What makes the page layout unique is that it represents a WYSIWYG (what you see is what you get) input form for a web page. The author enters content into the layout pages at the locations on the page where the content will be rendered in response to visitor requests.

The page layout does not implement the overall branding for the site, so an individual layout page will need to implement specific styles and elements that will keep the page consistent with the branding strategy of the site. SharePoint combines the page layout with the Master Page to render the page to the browser. This means that your page layout will consist of content placeholder elements that will instruct SharePoint where to place elements of the page layout inside the Master Page.

From a content-authoring perspective, the page layout dictates how the authoring experience will function. It accomplishes this in two ways. First, every page layout must be associated with a content type that is available in the Pages library and inherits from the Page content type. Second, the page layout implements editable fields that provide authoring areas on the page. These fields match up with the site columns defined in the content type.

Although each page layout can be associated with only one content type, content types are not limited to one page layout. This offers designers a lot of flexibility when designing page layouts for web content solutions. A good example of this flexibility is the Article pages that are included in the Publishing framework. There is a page layout that shows the page image on the left, one with the image on the right, and one with only the body content.

Finally, because the page layout is a template for authoring and rendering content, the Designer may make changes to the page layout without affecting the underlying content.

Developing Page Layouts

The development process for creating page layout consists of two distinct steps. The first is the development of the Page Layout template that SharePoint uses for authoring and rendering content. This step consists of developing an `.aspx` file with content placeholders that leverage the Master Page's branding, and fields for accepting authored input, as well as other web page elements necessary to achieve the desired functional and design effects.

The second step of the process is the deployment of the page layout in SharePoint, where the content type association is made and the template becomes available for use. Page layouts are uploaded to the Master Pages and Page Layouts gallery (Site Actions ➪ Site Settings ➪ Master Pages and page layouts) in the SharePoint site collection.

Create a Page Layout with SharePoint Designer

SharePoint Designer 2010 makes the process of developing templates and deploying them to SharePoint easier by connecting directly to the target website and its associated content database. With SharePoint Designer 2010, you create a Layout page directly in the Master Pages and Page Layouts gallery, thereby allowing SharePoint Designer to save the page layout directly in the gallery.

SharePoint Designer 2010's site navigation pane, shown in Figure 8-13, includes a link to view the page layouts that are loaded in the Master Pages and Page Layouts gallery. When the Page Layouts item is selected in the navigation pane, SharePoint Designer also displays a custom Ribbon which contains actions specific to Layout pages in SharePoint. These include check-in/check-out of existing page layouts, importing and exporting of page layouts, and access to the Master Pages and Page Layouts gallery's list settings.

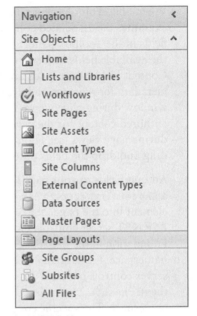

FIGURE 8-13

To create a new Layout page using SharePoint Designer, click the New Layout Page button in the SharePoint Designer Ribbon. As shown in Figure 8-14, the new action will show a dialog box that asks for the basic information necessary to create a page layout, notably the Content Type Group and Content Type Name of the associated content type that defines the authored content fields for the layout, and the file name and Title of the Layout page.

After SharePoint Designer gets the necessary information to create the page layout, it will instantiate the page in the Master Pages and Page Layouts gallery and open it in the Code View window. This is an important point because the deployment is essentially completed. If you open the Master Pages and Page Layouts gallery from within the Site Settings of the SharePoint site, you will see the new Page Layout in the gallery in a draft mode. This means that anyone with the appropriate permissions can see and use the page layout in your site.

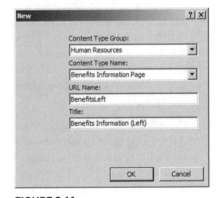

FIGURE 8-14

SharePoint Designer provides both a Code View and a Design View. The Design Editor is integrated into SharePoint so that it will load the branding that is defined by the Master Page into the Designer, giving you a complete view of the page layout as you develop its design. In Design View, you build the content of the page layout in the area designated by a box containing the label PlaceHolderMain (Custom), as shown in Figure 8-15.

FIGURE 8-15

When SharePoint Designer loads the page into the Editor, it examines the associated content type and lists the available fields in the Toolbox pane. SharePoint Designer also separates the available fields into two categories: Page Fields and Content Fields. Page fields are authored fields that indicate metadata for the page and are not rendered to the browser window during page views. Content fields contain the authored content for the page that is rendered to the browser during page views (see Figure 8-16). Using the toolbox, you drag and drop the fields onto the Layout page.

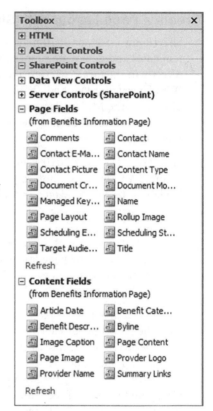

FIGURE 8-16

Adding Fields to your page layout in design mode inserts either a `SharePointWebControls` or `PublishingWebControls` element into the page. `SharePointWebControls` are the ASP.NET server controls included as part of the SharePoint Foundation in the `Microsoft.SharePoint.WebControls` namespace. `PublishingWebControls` are the ASP.NET server controls included as part of SharePoint Server in the `Microsoft.SharePoint.Publishing.WebControls` namespace. The specific control depends on the site column and content type associated with the Layout page; most site columns will be rendered with `SharePointWebControls`, but any publishing field will be rendered with the `PublishingWebControls`. The connection between the site column and the web control is made with the `FieldName` attribute of the web control. The value of this attribute is the internal name of the site column that defines the storage model for the field.

SharePoint 2010 is designed to make the migration from SharePoint 2007 easy. It accomplishes this by supporting assets created in SharePoint 2007. In a page layout, SharePoint adds a new web control, `UIVersionedContent`. The `UIVersionedContent` control is a container control that holds a `ContentTemplate`. The template contains the ASP.NET and HTML that renders for the contained section. The `UIVersion` attribute of the `UIVersionedControl` informs SharePoint which version the contained code supports: 3 for SharePoint 2007 and 4 for SharePoint 2010. The out-of-the-box Article pages make heavy use of the `UIVersionedContent` control and merit close examination if you are developing page layouts that may be rendered as a SharePoint 2007 or 2010 Master Pages.

The disadvantage of using SharePoint Designer is that, when it instantiates a new page layout, it is doing so inside the content database. This means that the page layout is limited to the site in which it was created. In scenarios where a multi-stage environment is used, or you are developing locally and then deploying to a SharePoint server, additional steps are necessary to export the page out of SharePoint Designer and to package it into a Feature. This is the subject of the next section.

Create a Page Layout with Visual Studio

Developing a page layout with Visual Studio 2010 requires that you consider the deployment path for the layout. Normally, page layouts are deployed using the Module element in a Feature. The

Feature is then packaged into a SharePoint Solution for deployment. Visual Studio 2010 includes SharePoint tools that simplify the development effort required to build the deployment packages.

Visual Studio 2010 does not include a project template for a page layout; rather, it includes a project template for a module. This template creates all of the necessary Feature artifacts and a Solution package. The purpose of a Module element is to provide a mechanism for provisioning assets into the content database. In this case, the module will provision the page layout into the Master Pages and Page Layouts gallery.

To create a Layout page in Visual Studio, create a new project (File ⇨ New ⇨ Project) and select the Module template. Visual Studio creates a Module folder that contains the SharePoint Elements file and a Sample text file. The Elements file contains the instructions that provision files into SharePoint when the Feature is activated.

There are two approaches to creating the page layout. The first approach is to manually add a Web Form page to the module by right-clicking the Module1 folder and selecting Add ⇨ New Item from the popup menu. Because the SharePoint project template is not an ASP.NET web application, the Web Form (`.aspx`) page template is not available in the Add New Item dialog box. To work around this, select the Text File template and give the file an ⸻ extension. This will add a blank file to the module and will create an entry in the Module's ⸻ for the page layout.

To build the page layout, start by adding the min⸻ ⸻tent placeholders. This serves as the foundation for the layout.

```
<%@ Page language="C#" Inherits="Mic                           ing.PublishingLayout
Page,Microsoft.SharePoint.Publishin                            e=neutral,PublicKeyT
oken=71e9bce111e9429c" meta:webpar                            a:progid="SharePoint
.WebPartPage.Document" %>
<%@ Register Tagprefix="SharePointWebCo                         "Microsoft.SharePoint.
WebControls" Assembly="Microsoft.SharePoint,        0.0.0, Culture=neutral, Publ
icKeyToken=71e9bce111e9429c" %>
<%@ Register Tagprefix="WebPartPages" Namespace="Microsoft.SharePoint.WebPartPages"
Assembly="Microsoft.SharePoint, Version=14.0.0.0, Culture=neutral, PublicKeyToken=71
e9bce111e9429c" %>
<%@ Register Tagprefix="PublishingWebControls" Namespace="Microsoft.SharePoint.
Publishing.WebControls" Assembly="Microsoft.SharePoint.Publishing, Version=14.0.0.0,
Culture=neutral, PublicKeyToken=71e9bce111e9429c" %>
<%@ Register Tagprefix="PublishingNavigation" Namespace="Microsoft.SharePoint.
Publishing.Navigation" Assembly="Microsoft.SharePoint.Publishing, Version=14.0.0.0,
Culture=neutral, PublicKeyToken=71e9bce111e9429c" %>
<asp:Content ContentPlaceholderID="PlaceHolderPageTitle" runat="server">
        <SharePointWebControls:FieldValue id="PageTitle" FieldName="Title"
        runat="server"/>
</asp:Content>
<asp:Content ContentPlaceholderID="PlaceHolderMain" runat="server">

</asp:Content>
```

BenefitsInformation.aspx

Next, add the web content, styles, and layouts necessary for the branding of the page layout. Finally, use SharePointWebControls to identify the locations for Page and Content Fields in the layout.

```
<%@ Page language="C#" Inherits="Microsoft.SharePoint.Publishing.PublishingLayoutPag
e,Microsoft.SharePoint.Publishing,Version=14.0.0.0,Culture=neutral,PublicKeyToken=71
e9bce111e9429c" %>
<%@ Register Tagprefix="SharePointWebControls" Namespace="Microsoft.SharePoint.
WebControls" Assembly="Microsoft.SharePoint, Version=14.0.0.0, Culture=neutral, Publ
icKeyToken=71e9bce111e9429c" %>
<%@ Register Tagprefix="WebPartPages" Namespace="Microsoft.SharePoint.WebPartPages"
Assembly="Microsoft.SharePoint, Version=14.0.0.0, Culture=neutral, PublicKeyToken=71
e9bce111e9429c" %>
<%@ Register Tagprefix="PublishingWebControls" Namespace="Microsoft.SharePoint.
Publishing.WebControls" Assembly="Microsoft.SharePoint.Publishing, Version=14.0.0.0,
Culture=neutral, PublicKeyToken=71e9bce111e9429c" %>
<%@ Register Tagprefix="PublishingNavigation" Namespace="Microsoft.SharePoint.
Publishing.Navigation" Assembly="Microsoft.SharePoint.Publishing, Version=14.0.0.0,
Culture=neutral, PublicKeyToken=71e9bce111e9429c" %>
<asp:Content ContentPlaceholderID="PlaceHolderPageTitle" runat="server">
  <SharePointWebControls:FieldValue id="PageTitle" FieldName="Title" runat="server" />
</asp:Content>
<asp:Content ContentPlaceholderID="PlaceHolderMain" runat="server">
  <div class="article article-left">
   <div class="captioned-image">
    <div class="image">
      <PublishingWebControls:RichImageField id="ImageField" FieldName=
      "PublishingPageImage" runat="server"/>
    </div>
    <div class="caption">
      <PublishingWebControls:RichHtmlField id="Caption" FieldName=
      "PublishingImageCaption"  AllowTextMarkup="false" AllowTables="false"
      AllowFonts="false" PreviewValueSize="Small" runat="server"/>
    </div>
    <div class="image">
      <PublishingWebControls:RichImageField id="ProviderImageField" FieldName=
      "ProviderImage" runat="server"/>
    </div>
   </div>
   <div class="article-header">
    <div class="date-line">
      <SharePointWebControls:DateTimeField id="datetimefield3" FieldName=
      "ArticleStartDate" runat="server"/>
    </div>
    <div class="by-line">
      <SharePointWebControls:TextField FieldName="ArticleByLine" runat="server"/>
    </div>
   </div>
    <div class="article-content">
      <PublishingWebControls:RichHtmlField id="Content" FieldName=
      "PublishingPageContent" runat="server"/>
   </div>
      <PublishingWebControls:EditModePanel runat="server" id="editmodepanel1"
      CssClass="edit-mode-panel">
        <!-- Add field controls here to bind custom metadata viewable and editable
        in edit mode only.-->
        <PublishingWebControls:RichImageField id="ContentQueryImage" FieldName=
        "PublishingRollupImage" AllowHyperLinks="false" runat="server" />
```

```
        <asp:Label text="<%$Resources:cms,Article_rollup_image_text%>"
        runat="server" />
    </PublishingWebControls:EditModePanel>
  </div>
</asp:Content>
```

BenefitsInformation.aspx

The second way to create a page layout is to first create the page in SharePoint Designer with all placeholders, content, styling, and fields in place. Then, use the export button on the Ribbon to save a copy of the page layout to a local folder: right-click on the Module folder in the Visual Studio Solution Explorer, and select Add ➪ Existing Item to add the exported page layout to the project. As with adding a new file, this will automatically create an entry in the Module's elements file.

The last step in the page layout development process is to modify the module's elements file so that it will provision the page layout into the Master Pages and Page Layouts folder. It is also a good idea to rename the module and Feature folders with more descriptive names and to set the properties of the Feature and package to better indicate what the Module Feature deploys to SharePoint.

In Visual Studio, open the Elements file located in the Module folder. If the `sample.txt` file is listed in the Elements file, delete the file from the Solution Explorer. To get the Page Layout into the Master Pages and Page Layouts gallery, modify both the Module element and the File element.

The Module element determines where files are provisioned in a SharePoint site collection. Visual Studio 2010 creates a Module element that has no attribute settings that will provision the files into the root of the site collection's root web. You will need to add the `Url` and `RootWebOnly` attributes to ensure that the Page Layout is provisioned to the Master Pages and Page Layouts gallery.

```
<?xml version="1.0" encoding="utf-8"?>
<Elements xmlns="http://schemas.microsoft.com/sharepoint/">
  <Module Name="BenefitsLayout"  Url="_catalogs/masterpage" RootWebOnly="TRUE">
    <File Path="BenefitsLayout\BenefitsInformation.aspx" />
  </Module>
</Elements>
```

Elements.xml

Although the Module element will now provision the layout file into the proper location in SharePoint, you cannot use it as a page layout template. The Layout page needs to be assigned a content type for the page and a publishing content type for the content. This is done by adding Property elements to the File element.

```
<?xml version="1.0" encoding="utf-8"?>
<Elements xmlns="http://schemas.microsoft.com/sharepoint/">
  <Module Name="BenefitsLayout"  Url="_catalogs/masterpage" RootWebOnly="TRUE">
    <File Path="BenefitsLayout\BenefitsInformation.aspx"
          Url="BenefitsInformation.aspx"
          Type="GhostableInLibrary">
      <Property Name="Title"
      Value="Benefits Information Page" />
```

```
        <Property Name="MasterPageDescription"
        Value="Use benefits page to publish content related to benefits information" />
        <Property Name="ContentType"
        Value="$Resources:cmscore,contenttype_pagelayout_name;" />
        <Property Name="PublishingAssociatedContentType"
        Value=";#Benefits Information Page;#0x010100C568DB52D9D0A14D9B2FDCC96666E9F200
        7948130EC3DB064584E219954237AF3900242457EFB8B24247815D688C526CD44D007b07c2cdb600
        4430bfd2fe7a3eff5ecb;#" />
    </File>
</Module>
</Elements>
```

Elements.xml

The ContentType property assigns a content type to the page layout itself. This is the content type that contains metadata and processing logic for the layout page within the gallery. Normally, this is the page layout content type that provides metadata for Title, Description, Contact, Preview Image, and a few other fields that are relevant to the page layout's .aspx file. These properties are viewable and editable from the item menu in the Master Page and Page Layouts gallery.

The PublishingAssociatedContentType is the content type that is added to the Pages library to inform the storage of Authored content using the page layout. This content type provides the fields that the author enters content into when creating a new page using this layout.

Although this example and the Visual Studio 2010 template demonstrate a single file, you may add as many File elements as you have page layouts. Remember that it is the Module element that determines where the files will be provisioned into the site; therefore, if you add File elements for files that should be provisioned elsewhere, you need to create new Module elements for those files.

At this point, the Layout pages are completed and the Feature contains the necessary information to provision the layout page into the site collection. Run or deploy the project into the target SharePoint site. To test the deployment of the page layout, create a new page in the SharePoint browser interface. After SharePoint creates the new page, click the Page Layout drop-down button in the Ribbon. The new page layout will appear in the list. Click the page layout, and SharePoint will reload the page, using the defined layout page. Verify that the expected fields are available and that the layout page appears correctly in SharePoint.

Master Pages

Most Web Content Management solutions include a design specification that dictates the graphic and communication designs for the website. These designs include not only the look and feel of the sites, but also the navigational elements and user experience presented by the design of the site. Taken together, these designed schemes make up the branding of the sites and pages in SharePoint.

Master Pages provide an entry point for branding a site according to a design specification. Master Pages consist of references to Cascading Style Sheets (CSS), navigation control definitions, search control definitions, and content placeholder definitions that provide areas for layout pages to place content in the final rendered page.

In SharePoint, Master Pages are defined within the Site Settings (Site Actions ⇨ Site Settings ⇨ Master page) of each website, and the ability to set or change the assigned Master Page is a permission that may be granted or revoked based on the governance plan for the site. This approach to setting the Master Page at a more global level, where it can be governed, addresses a common concern of designers, which is how to control the branding of the sites when other SharePoint capabilities, such as self-service site creation and content authoring, are enabled.

Within the Publishing framework, there are two Master Pages that you set: Site Master and System Master. The Site Master Page provides the branding for all authored pages on the site, meaning any page created from a page layout. The System Master Page provides branding to the list and library pages, forms, and administrative pages for the site.

Master Pages are deployed to the same Master Pages and Page Layouts gallery as page layouts. This means that the procedures for developing and deploying Master Pages are very similar to those outlined in the previous section for page layouts. The chief difference lies within the construction of the Master Page. Whereas a page layout has an associated content type that provides fields that are placed into the layout, the Master Page provides ASP.NET *content placeholders* where page layouts are rendered as well as other SharePoint components.

Create a Master Page with SharePoint Designer

Before developing a Master Page, it is important to understand that every Master Page has an assigned content type that describes the Master Page file itself. The assigned content type provides metadata and processes to the Master Page, which can be set or modified within the Master Pages and Page Layouts gallery.

In SharePoint, there are two Master Page content types installed with the Publishing framework. The first is a hidden content type called System Master Page and inherits from the Document content type. This is the Master Page content type that is typically assigned to Master Pages for nonpublishing sites and for System Master Pages. The second content type is called Publishing Master Page and inherits from System Master Page. This content type is typically assigned to Site Master Pages in the Publishing framework.

SharePoint Designer 2010's navigation pane includes a section specifically for Master Pages. This section displays the Master Pages and Page Layouts gallery filtered to show only the Master Pages. The Master Pages Ribbon provides three create options: two for Master Pages and one to create a web page from an existing Master Page. The Blank Master Page button creates a System Master Page that contains a single content placeholder and no other information. The From Content Type button allows you to create a Site Master Page from the Publishing Master Page or other specific content type.

To create a Site Master Page in SharePoint Designer 2010, click on the From Content Type drop-down list and select Publishing Master Page. SharePoint Designer adds an Untitled master page to the Master Pages gallery and sets the file name to rename mode so that you can enter in the name of the Master Page. At this point, a customized Master Page exists within your site and is checked out as a Draft. If you check in and publish this Master Page, it will be available to set in the site; no additional deployment steps are necessary.

The Publishing Master Page that SharePoint Designer creates is a bare minimum Master Page. The bare minimum includes all of the content placeholders expected by the Publishing framework for Site Master Pages, references to SharePoint's core style sheets for the site and the Ribbon, and other declarations and script necessary for the page to work within a Publishing site collection. The result is a Master Page that renders with no styling or layout; it simply renders everything in order from top to bottom.

In SharePoint 2010, pages are standards-compliant; they do not use tables to layout content. Rather, the bare minimum Master Page includes `<div></div>` elements that mark the major sections of the Master Page with assigned CSS classes that are semantic. This means that you may use the latest styling techniques to achieve nearly any visual effect that is possible on the web today.

As with everything in SharePoint Designer, the greatest limitation is that it saves the Master Page directly to the content database in customized form. This limits your ability to work with the Master Page in multi-stage environments; however, you can export the completed Master Page to a local file system and package it into a Visual Studio created SharePoint project that will deploy the Master Page to other environments in an uncustomized form.

Create a Master Page with Visual Studio

To develop a Master Page in Visual Studio 2010 you follow the same approach that you use for a page layout. You will include the Master Page in a Module project that will provision the Master Page into the Master Pages and Page Layouts gallery when the Feature is activated.

To create a Master Page in Visual Studio, create a new project (File ➪ New ➪ Project), and select the Module template. Visual Studio creates a Module folder that contains the SharePoint Elements file and a Sample text file. The Elements file contains the instructions that provision files into SharePoint when the Feature is activated.

Master Pages are substantially more difficult to develop than page layouts. For example, a missed field control in a page layout has no more ill effect on the page than providing no data entry field for the author to use; however, a missed content placeholder in a Master Page throws an exception when a page is rendered with the incomplete Master Page which makes any page that attempts to use the missing content placeholder unbrowsable. Because of the complexity and risks involved in developing Master Pages, it is best to import a bare minimum Master Page or a base Master Page from which to work rather than begin with a blank text file.

Using the procedures outlined in the previous section on developing Master Pages with SharePoint Designer 2010, you can create a bare minimum Master Page and export it using the Ribbon's Export File button, or develop a completed Master Page and export it. SharePoint Designer 2010's functionality and design-time workflow is sufficiently advanced and intuitive that there is no reason not to completely develop the Master Page in SharePoint Designer and use Visual Studio only to package and deploy the Master Page in a noncustomized form.

After completing the Master Page in SharePoint Designer and exporting it to your file system, import it into the Module folder in Solution Explorer: right-click the Module folder and select Add ➪ Existing Item. If you have not done so, delete the `sample.txt` file from the Module folder.

The Module element provisions files into a SharePoint site collection. The module created by Visual Studio provides a definition that will provision the listed Files into the root of the root web in a site collection. To get the Master Page into the Master Pages and Page Layouts gallery, you need to add the `Url` attribute to the Module element. The `Url` attribute instructs SharePoint where to provision the files contained in the module. In this case, the Master Page gallery is located at `_catalogs/masterpage`.

```xml
<?xml version="1.0" encoding="utf-8"?>
<Elements xmlns="http://schemas.microsoft.com/sharepoint/">
    <Module Name="CorporateMaster"
            Url="_catalogs/masterpage"
            Path="CorporateMaster"
            RootWebOnly="TRUE">
      <File Path="Corporate.master" Url="Corporate.master" />
    </Module>
</Elements>
```

Elements.xml

If you deploy the module at this point, it will provision the Master Page into the Master Pages and Page Layouts gallery, but you will not see the Master Page in the gallery. To make the Master Page available to the gallery, you need to add the Type attribute to the File element. The Master Page must be `GhostableInLibrary` so that it can be customized using SharePoint Designer. Is some cases, it is possible that the master page may already exist in the Master Pages gallery. In cases where you want to preserve any existing Master Page, add the `IgnoreIfAlreadyExists` attribute and give it a value of FALSE. If you do set this value to FALSE, you must keep in mind that any upgrade to this feature will not provision updates to the Master Page that you may make in your IDE.

```xml
<?xml version="1.0" encoding="utf-8"?>
<Elements xmlns="http://schemas.microsoft.com/sharepoint/">
    <Module Name="CorporateMaster"
            Url="_catalogs/masterpage"
            Path="CorporateMaster"
            RootWebOnly="TRUE">
      <File Path="Corporate.master"
            Url="Corporate.master"
            Type="GhostableInLibrary" />
    </Module>
</Elements>
```

Elements.xml

Finally, you need to add properties to the Master Page to set its Master Page content type and UI version. The `ContentType` property sets the system or site content type for this Master Page, as discussed in the previous section. In SharePoint 2010, Microsoft has made the migration path from SharePoint 2007 easier by adding support for SharePoint 2007 assets. This allows organizations to upgrade the SharePoint servers without forcing the organization to completely rebuild all custom development. The `UIVersion` property tells SharePoint what version of SharePoint this Master Page is compatible with; a value of 4 indicates SharePoint 2010 site content and a value of 3 indicates SharePoint 2007 site content. Notice that these values are consistent with the UIVersionedContent control introduced in the Page Layouts section.

```xml
<?xml version="1.0" encoding="utf-8"?>
<Elements xmlns="http://schemas.microsoft.com/sharepoint/">
    <Module Name="CorporateMaster"
            Url="_catalogs/masterpage"
```

```
            Path="CorporateMaster"
            RootWebOnly="TRUE">
    <File Path="Corporate.master"
          Url="Corporate.master"
          Type="GhostableInLibrary">
      <Property Name="ContentType"
                Value="$Resources:cmscore,contenttype_masterpage_name;" />
      <Property Name="UIVersion"
                Value="4" />
    </File>
  </Module>
</Elements>
```

Elements.xml

Once you have modified the Module and File elements and added the properties for the Master Page file, deploy the solution to your target SharePoint site. The Master Page will be provisioned to the Master Page and Page Layouts gallery. To test the Master Page, use Site Settings (Site Actions ⇨ Site Settings ⇨ Master Page) to set it as either the Site or System Master Page according to its purpose.

Setting the Master Page in Code

In many cases, you will want to not only deploy a Master Page to the site collection, but also set the Master Page automatically, without the additional step of going into Site Settings. Using a Feature Receiver and object model code, you can easily set the Master Page.

To add a Feature Receiver to the Master Page project from the previous section, right-click on the Feature and select Add Event Receiver from the drop-down menu; uncomment the `FeatureActivated` and `FeatureDeactivating` methods in the receiver's class.

The `SPWeb` class contains two properties that correspond to the Site and System Master Pages: `CustomMasterUrl` represents the Site Master Page, and `MasterUrl` represents the System Master Page. Provide the `Url` for each Master Page and call the `SPWeb`'s `Update` method to save your changes.

```
public override void FeatureActivated(SPFeatureReceiverProperties properties)
{
  using (SPSite site = (SPSite)properties.Feature.Parent)
  {
    using (SPWeb web = site.RootWeb)
    {
      try
      {
        web.CustomMasterUrl = "/_catalogs/masterpage/Corporate.master";
        web.MasterUrl = "/_catalogs/masterpage/v4.master";
        web.Update();
      }
      catch (Exception ex)
      {
        Console.WriteLine(ex.ToString());
      }
    }
  }
}
```

```
    }

    public override void FeatureDeactivating(SPFeatureReceiverProperties properties)
    {
      using (SPSite site = (SPSite)properties.Feature.Parent)
      {
        using (SPWeb web = site.RootWeb)
        {
          try
          {
            web.CustomMasterUrl = "/_catalogs/masterpage/nightandday.master";
            web.MasterUrl = "/_catalogs/masterpage/v4.master";
            web.Update();
          }
          catch (Exception ex)
          {
            Console.WriteLine(ex.ToString());
          }
        }
      }
    }
}
```

CorporateMasterPage.EventReceiver.cs

Navigation

Up to this point, this chapter has focused on the physical structure of the Publishing framework: how to provide templates for authored content and branding. These topics are relevant to the designers and content authors of the site, but the site's visitors will interact with the rendered output of these files. Visitors of your website will be more concerned with the presentation of content and the site's navigation.

Navigation in SharePoint 2010 is based on the ASP.NET Provider Model. This model provides an interface between a datasource that contains the navigational structure and the rendering components that display the structure in the web page. The site's Master Page sets up the structure by declaring the menu and providers, which are integrated into the overall branding strategy.

The specific rendering of navigational components is handled in a site-centric manner. Each site's settings allow configuration of navigational components that may inherit settings from the parent site or begin with a new navigational structure based on the site's hierarchy.

SharePoint offers a wide variety of customization mechanisms for sites. Taken together, SharePoint's navigation is flexible and capable of achieving nearly any Information Architecture.

Customizing Navigation with Site Settings

Out of the box, SharePoint 2010 sites provide dynamic navigation in the form of a top navigation tab bar, a left navigation Quick Launch toolbar, and breadcrumbs. By default, the top navigation bar displays a tab for each site and page contained within the root site of the site collection. Additionally, the tabs will form drop-down menus to display the sites and pages contained within each tab. The Quick Launch toolbar will show the same information, but is usually limited to showing only sites and pages that are below the current page.

In many cases, project requirements will necessitate modification of the default navigational behavior. The out-of-the-box navigation settings are changed in the Site Settings (Site Actions ⇨ Modify Navigation) of each site within site collection. Within the root site of the site collection, some options are disabled because they set inheritance parameters; these options are available at the subsite level. The Site Navigation Settings are divided into three sections that provide settings for Global Navigation (top navigation tabs), Current Navigation (Quick Launch toolbar), and Navigation Editing and Sorting.

The Global Navigation settings allow you to set what items show in the top navigation bar. Selecting the options to show subsites and/or pages, instructs SharePoint to display the sites or pages as additional tabs across the top navigation bar. The number of dynamic items to show determines the maximum number of tabs that will be displayed in the top navigation. This setting does not affect the number of items that appear in drop-down menus when a tabbed site contains pages and subsites. To set the maximum number of items in the menu, you set the number on the subsite's Navigation Settings page.

At the root site level the only display option is to show the sites and pages below the root as shown in Figure 8-17, but at the subsite level you have the option to use the parent's global navigation or to reset the top navigation to begin with the subsite's content. Most users, through their interactions with other websites, have come to expect the top navigation of a site to remain static across the site, thus the term "Global" navigation. Changing the inheritance pattern for the top navigation may create confusion for your end users.

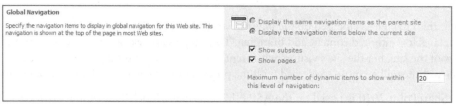

FIGURE 8-17

The Current Navigation settings are nearly identical to the Global Navigation settings, offering the same options to show subsites and pages, as well as to determine the number of items that appear in the Quick Launch toolbar. Where the Current Navigation settings differ is in the display options available to the subsites.

Whereas users expect the top navigation to remain static across a site, most users expect sidebar navigation to dynamically change based on the selected page or subsite. SharePoint provides the option to display the parent's sidebar navigation; at second-level sites, this setting will probably create a confusing experience for the end user, but at the lower levels this may be a valid setting. For example, if you have a benefits site under a Human Resources department site, it may be desirable to show the Human Resources navigation rather than a benefits-specific navigation.

The other two display options begin at the selected site's level when presenting navigation items, but they differ in determining whether to show all of the sibling sites, as shown in Figure 8-18. At the second level of the hierarchy, showing the siblings may replicate links that are available on the top navigation, but at lower levels, showing siblings may make a more effective navigation experience.

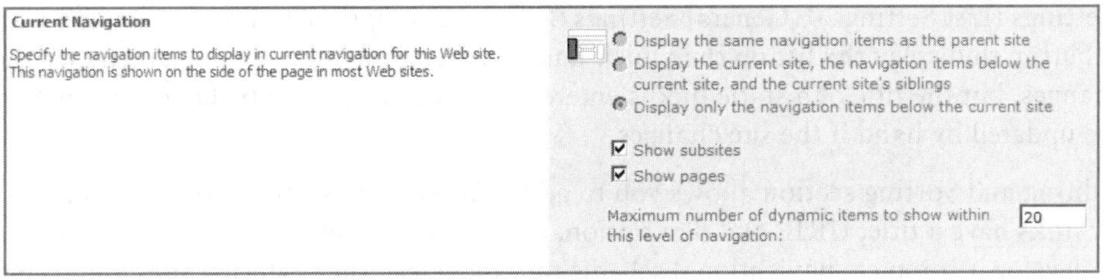

FIGURE 8-18

The Editing and Sorting section is a powerful configuration component that allows you to go beyond the out-of-the-box dynamic navigation. Editing and Sorting allows you to control where and whether dynamic components appear on the navigation bars. At the root site level, the Editing and Sorting section shows the links for both the Global Navigation and Current Navigation bars; at the subsite level, only Current Navigation is available.

In most cases, you will want to sort the navigation manually rather than automatically. An effective user experience is governed by an Information Architecture that outlines in what order links will appear in the top and sidebar navigation schemes, rather than an alphabetical arrangement. When manual sorting is selected, as shown in Figure 8-19, you have the ability to move pages and sites up and down within the Global and Current Navigation nodes.

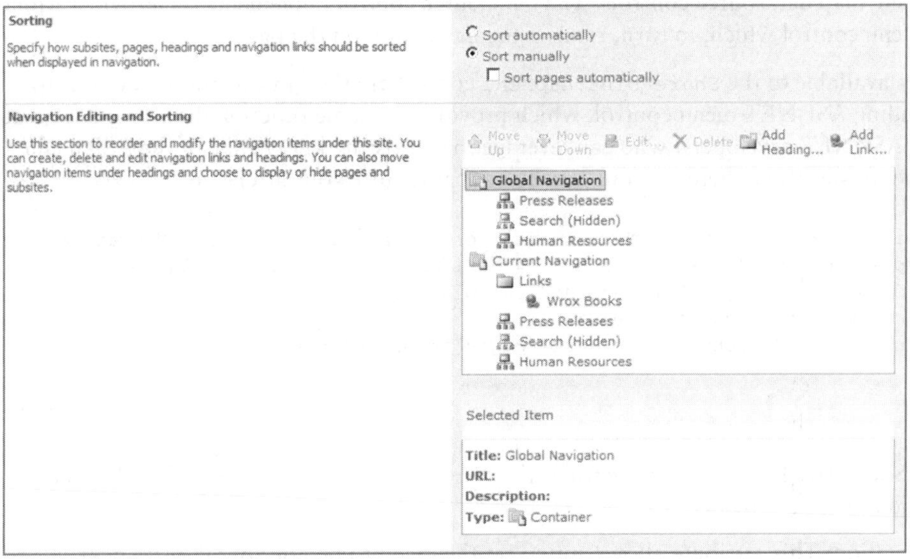

FIGURE 8-19

You also have the option to delete or hide pages and subsites. While the user experience for both options is the same — no link — there is a substantial operational difference. When a site or page is deleted from the navigation, it is removed from the dynamic navigation scheme. If you change your mind later and wish to have the item back in the navigation, you will need to go into the List or Library's settings (List Settings ➪ General Settings ➪ Title, description and navigation) and select the Yes radio button to display the list on the Quick Launch. Dynamic links will be updated if the site's name changes, but the title of a static link is entered into the navigation by hand, which means that it must be updated by hand if the site changes.

Finally, the Editing and Sorting section allows you to add headings and static links to the navigation scheme. Static links have a title, URL, and description, and can be targeted to an audience. This allows you to develop a complete navigational scheme that includes other external sites and pages that are relevant to the Global or Current Navigation. One thing to keep in mind is that the difference between a heading and a link is presentational only; headings may have a URL.

While the Navigational Settings in SharePoint 2010 are powerful and offer a lot of flexibility for configuring navigation in a site, they are cumbersome and not portable. If you have a very large site collection with complex Information Architecture, configuring navigation at each site may be too time-consuming. Also, if you are developing in a multi-stage environment, your only deployment options are to migrate the site from one environment to another or to reenter the navigation in each environment. Before exploring the programmatic methods for dealing with navigation, it is important to understand how SharePoint implements navigation.

Implementing Navigation in the Master Page

How and where navigational elements appear in the site is determined by the Master Page as part of the site's branding strategy. In the Master Page, the navigational elements leverage ASP.NET menu controls and site map datasource controls. The datasource control implements the Provider Model to the ASP Menu control which, in turn, renders the navigation on the page.

The attributes available to the `SharePoint:AspMenu` control are the same as those available to the corresponding ASP.NET menu control, which provides the same functionality. This is a great advantage to ASP.NET developers, who can leverage their existing knowledge of the ASP menu control. In the Master Page, there are four attributes that require your attention.

Available for download on Wrox.com

```
<SharePoint:AspMenu ID="GlobalNav" runat="server" DataSourceID="SiteMapDataSource1"
  UseSimpleRendering="true" Orientation="Horizontal" EncodeTitle="false"
  StaticDisplayLevels="1" MaximumDynamicDisplayLevels="1"
  CssClass="top-nav-menu band-menu"
  SkipLinkText="<%$Resources:cms,masterpages_skiplinktext%>"/>
```

Corporate.master

➤ **DataSourceID:** This attribute identifies the `PortalSiteMapDataSource` that the menu should use as its provider.

➤ **Orientation:** This attribute allows you to set the menu to be horizontal or vertical.

➤ **StaticDisplayLevels:** This attribute sets the default number of hierarchical levels to show in the menu.

➤ **MaximumDynamicDisplayLevels:** This attribute sets the default number of menu items to show in the fly-out menus.

The `PublishingNavigation:PortalSiteMapDataSource` control sets the provider that the menu control will use for rendering menu items. Whereas the menu control determines how the menu items are rendered, the datasource determines what is available to the menu control. The attributes of this control provide instructions to the provider that determines what nodes are provided to the menu.

```
<PublishingNavigation:PortalSiteMapDataSource ID="siteMapDataSource1" runat="server"
    SiteMapProvider="GlobalNavigation" EnableViewState="true"
    StartFromCurrentNode="true" StartingNodeOffset="0" ShowStartingNode="false"
    TreatStartingNodeAsCurrent="true" TrimNonCurrentTypes="Heading"/>
```

Corporate.master

➤ **SiteMapProvider:** This sets the provider that retrieves nodes from SharePoint.

➤ **ShowStartingNode:** When this is set to true, the menu will receive a node that represents the starting node. For example, the Global Navigation begins at the root site. If this is set to true, the menu will receive a node representing the root site.

➤ **StartFromCurrentNode:** When this is set to true, the `DataSource` object uses a set of rules for determining where it is in the navigational scheme and uses that as a starting location.

➤ **StartingNodeOffset:** This property works in conjunction with the `StartFromCurrentNode` property to determine the starting location of the dataset. The value can be positive or negative, depending on whether you want to start lower in the hierarchy or higher.

Out of the box, SharePoint 2010 includes a number of `SiteMapProviders`. `SiteMapProviders` are configured in the `web.config` file in the `sitemap` section. As with the other components of navigation in SharePoint, you can leverage your knowledge of ASP.NET's Provider Model to create your own providers and add them to SharePoint.

The two most important providers in publishing sites are the `CombinedNavSiteMapProvider` and the `CurrentNavSiteMapProvider`, which are associated with the Global Navigation menu and Current Navigation menu, respectively.

Customizing Navigation Using the Object Model

As noted earlier, customizing navigation from within the Navigation Settings page for each site is both cumbersome and not portable. These limitations are easily overcome by using the SharePoint object. Likewise, the object model provides the ability to create static navigational structures and modify the existing structure similarly to the way you perform customizations in the Editing and Sorting section of the Navigation Settings.

To customize navigation in Visual Studio, create a new Visual Studio project (File ➪ New ➪ Project) and select an Empty SharePoint Project template. Right-click the Features folder in Solution Explorer and add a Feature to the project. You will set the properties of the Feature in the Feature Designer, but you will not add an Empty Element or a Content Type element to the Feature; rather, right-click the Feature and select Add Event Receiver from the drop-down menu.

Adding static navigational structures using the object model is a matter of getting a reference to the navigational component that you want to modify and adding nodes to it. The `SPNavigation` object in each website includes properties for `TopNavigationBar` and `QuickLaunch`, which are both `SPNavigationNodeCollections`.

```
public override void FeatureActivated(SPFeatureReceiverProperties properties)
{
  using (SPSite site = (SPSite)properties.Feature.Parent)
  {
    // Add a static link to the root site's quick launch bar
    using (SPWeb web = site.RootWeb)
    {
      try
      {
        // Get reference to the left navigation
        SPNavigationNodeCollection leftNav = web.Navigation.QuickLaunch;
      }
      catch (Exception ex)
      {
        Console.WriteLine(ex.ToString());
      }
    }
  }
}
```

SiteNavigation.EventReceiver.cs

When adding items to the Node Collections, there is no difference between a heading node and a link node other than a heading node will contain children. To create a node, instantiate an `SPNavigationNode` and pass in the `Title`, `Url`, and a flag to indicate whether the link is internal or external to the site collection. The `SPNavigationNodeCollection` provides methods to add a node as the First element, Last element, or at a specific location in the collection.

```
public override void FeatureActivated(SPFeatureReceiverProperties properties)
{
  using (SPSite site = (SPSite)properties.Feature.Parent)
  {
    // Add a static link to the root site's quick launch bar
    using (SPWeb web = site.RootWeb)
    {
      try
      {
        // Get reference to the left navigation
        SPNavigationNodeCollection leftNav = web.Navigation.QuickLaunch;

        // Create a heading node to hold links
        SPNavigationNode heading = new SPNavigationNode("Links", web.Url,
        true);
        leftNav.AddAsFirst(heading);

        web.Update();
      }
```

```
        catch (Exception ex)
        {
          Console.WriteLine(ex.ToString());
        }
      }
    }
  }
}
```

The SPNavigationNode class has a Children property that returns an SPNavigationNodeCollection. To create a heading node, simply add nodes to an existing node's Children rather than to the Navigation Node collection.

```
public override void FeatureActivated(SPFeatureReceiverProperties properties)
{
  using (SPSite site = (SPSite)properties.Feature.Parent)
  {
    // Add a static link to the root site's quick launch bar
    using (SPWeb web = site.RootWeb)
    {
      try
      {
        // Get reference to the left navigation
        SPNavigationNodeCollection leftNav = web.Navigation.QuickLaunch;

        // Create a heading node to hold links
        SPNavigationNode heading = new SPNavigationNode("Links", web.Url, true);
        leftNav.AddAsFirst(heading);

        // Create a new node and add it to the end of the navbar
        SPNavigationNode wroxLink = new SPNavigationNode(
          "Wrox Books", "http://www.wrox.com", true);
        wroxLink.IsVisible = true;
        leftNav[0].Children.AddAsFirst(wroxLink);

        web.Update();
      }
      catch (Exception ex)
      {
        Console.WriteLine(ex.ToString());
      }
    }
  }
}
```

Using the object model, you can move beyond simply adding static links to the navigation bars to iterating through external site collections or a SharePoint list to provide additional navigation options that are not readily available out of the box.

Customizing Navigation with Web Parts

In SharePoint 2010, there is no shortage of navigational options. SharePoint includes two web parts that expand your ability to provide an effective navigational scheme: the Summary Links web part and the Table of Contents web part.

The Table of Contents web part provides an additional level of navigation from a more localized perspective than the top navigation and Quick Launch toolbar, which are included in the Master Page. It is the perfect tool when an additional sidebar navigational element is called for in the Information Architecture, but cannot be included the Master Page.

From a configuration perspective, the Table of Contents web part provides many of the same dynamic options as Global and Current Navigation. In the Content Settings of the web part, shown in Figure 8-20, you establish where the web part will begin listing content, the number of levels to show, and whether to show the starting location. An interesting option that the Table of Contents web part provides is to show hidden pages and sites. Recall from the "Navigation Settings" section that the Editing and Sorting section allows you to hide sites and pages from Global and Current Navigation — the Table of Contents can display those items that are not shown at a global level.

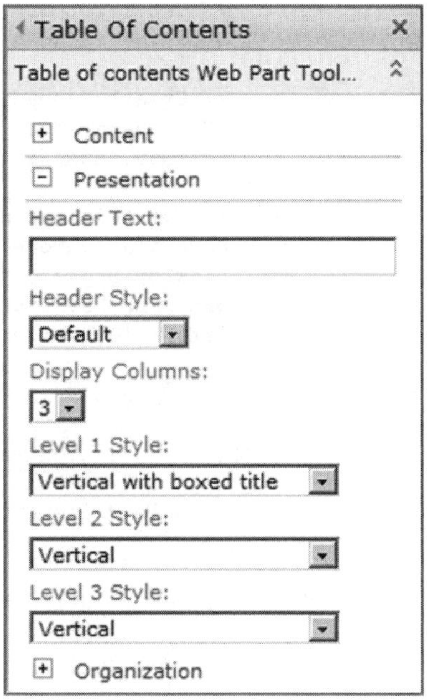

The Presentation Settings, shown in Figure 8-21, allow you to set the styles for headers and items in the Table of Contents. These style settings are defined in XSL files located in the Styles library. You can extend or replace the referenced XSL by exporting and reimporting the Table of Contents web part. This technique for modifying XSL is discussed in the Content by Query web part.

Finally, the Organization section, shown in Figure 8-22, provides sorting options to sort according to SharePoint's navigation settings or according to specific metadata for the items. The ability to change the sorting in the Table of Contents is not as rich as it is in the Editing and Sorting section of Navigation Settings, but it will generally fit most situations.

The Summary Links web part complements the Table of Contents in that it provides the capability to create a static navigational structure. The Summary Links web part adds options for links that are more flexible and extensive than those available when adding static links in the Editing and Sorting section of the Navigation Settings. You can create not only static links to internal and external sites and pages, but also links to People.

FIGURE 8-20

FIGURE 8-21

The Summary Links web part adds properties to the link, as you see in Figure 8-23, that allow you to display a description with the link, an image with alternative text, and a tooltip. These settings provide a very flexible mechanism for links that you can use to construct static directories of people, pages, documents, or other related links that have a unique styling and a user experience that has an appealing design.

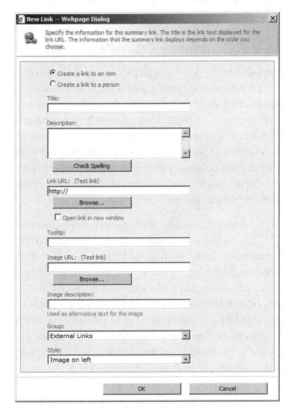

FIGURE 8-22

FIGURE 8-23

Like the Table of Contents web part, the Summary Links web part gets style information from an XSL file located in the Styles library. The out-of-the-box styles provide different user experiences for the link content that range from displaying a simple list of links to displaying a digest of information for the links.

The number of options that SharePoint provides for defining and customizing navigation in a site is evidence of the importance of constructing a positive user experience for the visitor. Although search capabilities have improved dramatically in the past few years, browsing through the structure of a website remains the primary model for user interaction.

Content by Query Web Part

The Content by Query web part is one of the most important development tools available in SharePoint. Out of the box, the Content by Query web part provides a lot of very powerful configuration options. Content authors are able to configure the web part to roll up and present content across the site collection. From a development point of view, understanding how to configure the Content by Query web part is important when more advanced customizations are necessary for the project. Developers are able to export the XML of the Content by Query web part to achieve more advanced configurations. Rather than exporting an empty Content by Query web part to configure, it is much more effective for the developer to configure the Content by Query web part using the web UI to get the closest possible configuration and then export it. This will save a lot of development time when customizing.

Using the Content by Query Web Part

The Content by Query web part divides the properties into two major categories and a number of more manageable sections, allowing the content author or developer a more organized approach to configuring the part. The two major sections are Query and Presentation: Query provides the web part with the information necessary to perform the content query, and Presentation provides the information to render the query results in the web part.

The first step to configure the Content by Query web part is to define the source that contains the content to execute a query against, as shown in Figure 8-24. This can be the entire site collection, a specific branch of the site collection's hierarchy, or a specific list. The selection of the source is a more global selection that is narrowed by the other settings in the web part. These settings allow the content author to narrow the larger site collection and branch sources down to a specific type of list/library, as well as to narrow down the query by a content type.

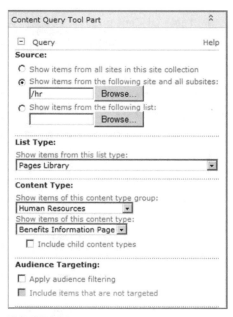

FIGURE 8-24

In SharePoint 2010, the Content by Query web part allows the content author to apply multiple filters to the query results, as shown in figure 8-25. The filters allow the author to select fields from the specified content type to filter the query results based on comparison criteria. What makes the filtering noteworthy for the developer is that it supports the use of a page field value and a query string value as the input to the comparison value. In the example that follows, the web part is using the Title field on the page layout to filter the query results where the category is equal to the text entered into the Title field. It is also using the Category variable in the query string to filter the results.

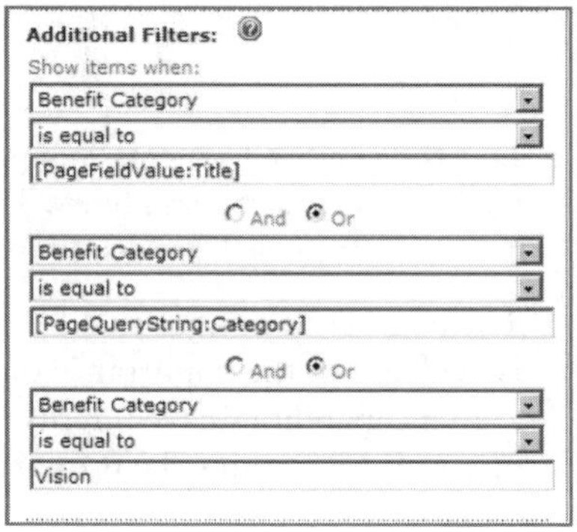

FIGURE 8-25

The use of these special tokens allow the developer or author to create a single configuration for the web part that can be added to multiple pages that will present different results. The developer need only to configure the web part one time, export it, and upload it to each page.

Once the author has configured the results that the Content by Query web part will return, the Presentation section allows configuration of the results. The grouping and sorting sections, shown in Figure 8-26, work as one would expect; the author selects the field to group by or sort by, the direction, and a dimensional limit. Although these settings are fundamental, an author or developer can achieve a number of different layouts with these settings alone.

Behind the scenes, the Content by Query web part stores the query results as XML. It uses a set of XSL files that are contained in the site collection's Style library to perform the rendering of the content in the part. The Styles section of the web part properties, shown in Figure 8-27, displays the definitions that appear in these XSL files. The group style selection displays the XSL logic that is stored in the `Header.xsl` file, and the Item style selection displays the XSL that is stored in the `ItemStyle.xsl` file. Lastly, the media player style comes from an XSL file that must be developed separately and selected for the web part.

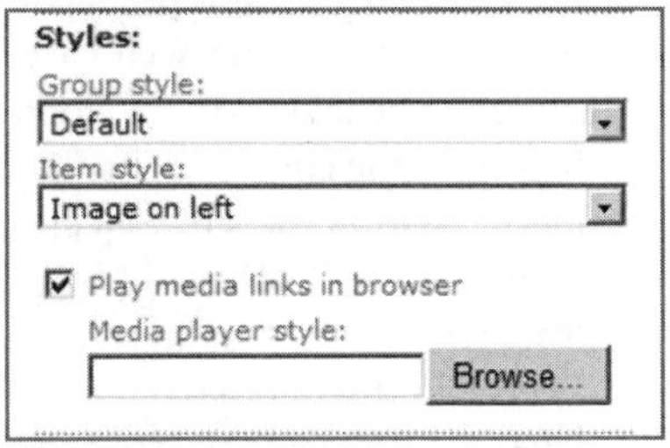

The "fields to display" section defines what site columns in the query results will be displayed for each of the four main fields of the Content by Query web part, as shown in Figure 8-28. Each field can contain more than one site column, and the columns are evaluated in the order of appearance: if the first site column contains no content, then the next column will be checked and so forth until a site column contains content.

Finally, a powerful function of the Content by Query web part is that it supports publication of query results using RSS, as shown in Figure 8-29.

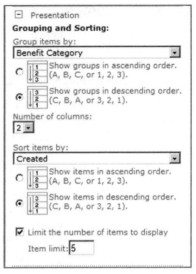

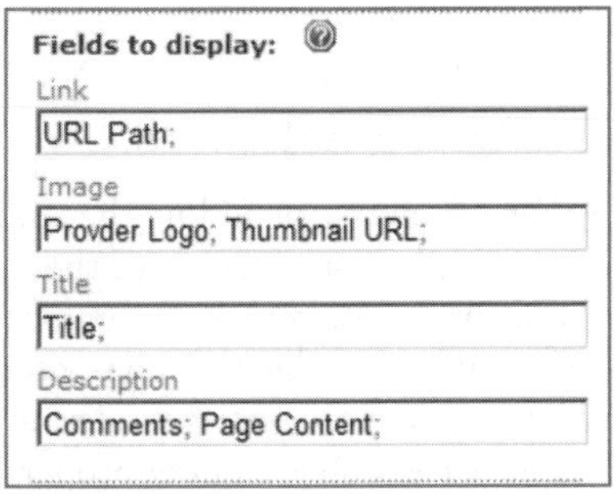

FIGURE 8-26

Styles:

FIGURE 8-27

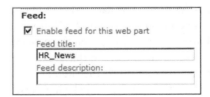

FIGURE 8-28

FIGURE 8-29

Customize Content by Query Web Part in XML

The Content by Query web part properties available in the SharePoint UI may seem extensive, but these are not the complete set of customizations that can be made to the web part. Developers can customize both the querying behavior and presentation logic in ways that go beyond those provided in the Web Part Properties Pane.

When a content author or developer adds a web part to a Web Part zone in a page, SharePoint inserts an XML document that contains a reference to the web part's assembly and all of the property values that apply to the web part. SharePoint allows the author or developer to export the XML to a local .webpart file. When exporting a .webpart file, SharePoint will save the XML, along with the property settings that are currently active in the Web Part Property Pane.

Although the additional properties in the .webpart file are available to a developer using SharePoint Designer 2010, the more common scenario is to export the .webpart file to a local folder and make modifications using Visual Studio. Visual Studio provides two advantages over all other methods. First, the .webpart code may be entered into a version control system like Team Foundation Server; and second, the .webpart file can be packaged into a SharePoint Feature and Solution for more controlled deployments.

The two categories of properties that are available in the .webpart file tend to match up with the two categories in the Web Part Properties Pane: Query and Presentation. The Query properties affect the behavior of the Content by Query web part and the Presentation properties affect the display of the content. The Query properties provide a great deal more flexibility in defining what is queried within the site collection. When developing these properties in the XML file, the properties defined in the XML will "trump" any settings entered by authors or developers in the Web Part Properties Pane. The Presentation properties also provide more flexibility in defining the display of content in the web part, but unlike the query properties settings made in the Web Part Properties Pane, the Presentation properties will "trump" the XML file.

There are five properties that support the most common developer customizations to the Content by Query Web Part.

> **QueryOverride:** Replaces the content source with a CAML-based query that allows for more control over query operation

> **WebsOverride:** Dictates whether the query will recurse over subsites

> **ListsOverride:** Allows you to query any kind of list, even those that are not defined in the Web Part Property Pane, such as custom lists that you develop

> **ViewFieldsOverride:** Requests a specific set of fields from the query

> **DataColumnRenames:** Renames column names before the data is passed to the XSL

For many of the properties in the .webpart file, configuring a value is a matter of adding the value to the XML element as you would with any XML document. For example, you can change the Title property by changing the text between the property's opening and closing tags. On one hand, if the element is a closed element, meaning that it is a single tag that ends with the "/>" characters, then make it an open element and insert the value. On the other hand, some properties require a CAML statement between the opening and closing tags, which is the case with the query properties.

Because CAML statements are themselves XML statements, you cannot simply enter them inside the property tags. The CAML must be enclosed in a CDATA section within the property tags. This is done by placing the CAML statement between the "`<![CDATA[`" and "`]]>`" characters. For example: `<![CDATA[ <Lists ServerTemplate="101"></Lists> ]]>`.

The `QueryOverride` property allows you to insert a custom-developed CAML query into the Content by Query web part. This allows you to build a set of data that can apply filtering and sorting before the web part's presentation categories conduct their operations. Taking into consideration all of the possibilities, the query override offers a more granular solution than the basic settings provided in the Web Part Properties Pane.

```xml
<property name="QueryOverride" type="string">
  <![CDATA[
    <Where>
      <Or>
        <Eq>
          <FieldRef Name="BenefitType" />
          <Value Type="Choice">Medical</Value>
        </Eq>
        <Eq>
          <FieldRef Name="BenefitProvider" />
          <Value Type="Text">United Medical </Value>
        </Eq>
      </Or>
    </Where>
    <OrderBy>
      <FieldRef Name="Created" Ascending="False" />
    </OrderBy>
  ]]>
</property>
```

The `WebsOverride` property simply tells the Content by Query web part whether to run the query against the current site only or to recursively search through all subsites under the current site. The implementation of this property is a closed XML tag that either has the `Recursive` attribute or does not; however, the tag is contained in a CDATA section in the property tag, which may appear somewhat unusual to some developers.

```xml
<![CDATA[
  <Webs Recursive="True"/>
]]>
 <![CDATA[
  <Webs/>
]]>
```

The `ListsOverride` property allows the developer to define the type of list that the query is executed against. The CAML data in this property defines whether the query executes against a specific list or a list type. Locating a listing of all `ServerTemplate` options can be a bit tricky. This attribute is based on the `SPListTemplateType` enumeration in the SharePoint object model. The enumeration values are listed in the SharePoint Foundation 2010 Class Library Reference (Server Class Library Reference ➪ Core Class Library Reference ➪ Microsoft.SharePoint Namespace ➪ PListTemplateType Enumeration).

```
<property name="ListsOverride" type="string">
  <![CDATA[
    <Lists ServerTemplate="850"></Lists>
  ]]>
</property>
```

The `ViewFieldsOverride` retrieves data of the specified type from the fields included in the CAML query. If the `nullable` attribute is included in the declaration, then the query will return items that do not have this column.

```
<property name="ViewFieldsOverride" type="string">
  <![CDATA[
    <FieldRef Name="Title" Nullable="True" Type="Text"/>
    <FieldRef Name="PublishingPageContent" Nullable="True" Type="HTML"/>
  ]]>
</property>
```

`DataColumnRenames` is a handy property for making XSL easier. This property maps the column name to a different name in the XSL. An example would be a set of properties that will have the same XSL transformation applied. Rather than define the transformation for each property name, the DataColumnRenames allows you to map all of the properties to a single XSL name.

```
<![CDATA[<property name="DataColumnRenames" type="string">BenefitsProvider,HR</
property>]]
```

Use Custom XSL to Modify the Presentation of Content

SharePoint 2010 uses XSL files to transform the query result's XML content into rendered HTML. These XSL files are located in the Publishing framework's Style library in a folder called XSL Style Sheets. Out of the box, this folder contains seven XSL files that are used for rendering the content of all three publishing web parts: Summary Links, Table of Contents, and Content by Query. All three web parts share the `Header.xsl` and `ItemStyle.xsl` files; the remaining XSL files are specific to each web part.

Although a developer or author may edit these files directly using SharePoint Designer or another editing tool, it is more common to create a separate custom XSL file for rendering customizations that may be necessary for the Content by Query web part. The customized XSL sheet can then be provisioned into the Style library using a Feature and associated with the Content by Query web part by customizing the `.webpart` file.

> *Do not let the name of the Style Library folder, "XSL Style Sheets," distract you from what the XSL files accomplish. They provide the logic to render XML data in an HTML format. Conceptually, it may be easier to think of these as layout sheets. The graphical style, or appearance, of the content in the browser remains the province of the Cascading Style Sheets.*

The most effective method for creating a custom XSL file is to download one of the existing XSL files from the Style library and add it to a Module element in Visual Studio, then remove all template elements that you do not need. This gives you an abridged version of the XSL that you can then add your own custom templates to.

The styles that each XSL sheet defines and that you will customize are the two selections that appear in the Styles section of the Web Part Properties Pane. The XSL templates defined in the `Header.xsl` file populate the drop-down selection for the *Group style* entry in Styles, and each template defined in the `ItemStyle.xsl` file populates the *Item style* drop-down selection.

Each XSL template that you define consists of two distinct sections: variables and div. The variables section processes the XML data that is running through the XSL file. SharePoint 2010 includes a number of functions that will help you process the data that is coming in through the query. Table 8-1 includes some of the more common functions.

TABLE 8-1: Table XSL Variable Functions

FUNCTION	DESCRIPTION
`OuterTemplate.GetSafeLink`	This function returns a safe URL that is derived from the `UrlColumnName` value. If the URL is not safe, this method returns a blank string.
`OuterTemplate.GetSafeStaticUrl`	Similarly to `GetSafeLink`, this function returns a safe URL from an item's `UrlColumnName`; otherwise, it returns a blank string.
`OuterTemplate.GetTitle`	This function returns the data in the Title column.

http://msdn.microsoft.com/en-us/library/bb447557(office.14,classic).aspx

The div section of the XSL template defines the HTML formatting of the rendered output. This section uses a combination of HTML and XSL to provide the layout instructions for SharePoint. Keep in mind that SharePoint 2010 is standards-compliant; therefore, you should use semantic HTML with div tags in your layout. Rely on your Cascading Style Sheets to provide the formatting and branding of your output.

After you have completed your custom XSL file, you will need to associate the file with the Content by Query web part that will be using the styles defined in the file. This is done by modifying the `.webpart` file; if you have not exported the Content by Query web part, then you will need to follow the steps in the previous section to export your web part.

There are two properties that you will modify to associate your custom style sheet. The first property is the `ItemXslLink` property. This is the property that points your web part to your custom XSL file. This element expects a string, not a CDATA section; simply add the location of the file.

```
<property name="ItemXslLink" type="string">
  /Style Library/XSL Style Sheets/HrItemStyle.xsl
</property>
```

The second property that you will modify is the `ItemStyle` or `GroupStyle` property, which sets the selected style in the Style section of the Web Part Property Pane. While changing or setting this property in your `.webpart` file is not required, it is generally a good idea to make sure that the property value matches an available XSL template in your custom XSL file. At the very least, your custom XSL should include the definition for the `default` template, and these two properties could be set to the default value. Keep in mind that the settings you provide to these two properties are the initial values that are used when the web part is added to the page. If the content author changes these values, then the web part will use the manually set values.

```
<property name="ItemStyle" type="string">ImageRight</property>
```

Before developing custom XSL for your Content by Query web part implementations, it is wise to become familiar with the out-of-the-box XSL files. Microsoft has provided XSL layouts that cover many situations that you will encounter. The underlying XSL files provide ample examples of source code for customizing your own XSL files.

Redeploy the Content by Query Web Part Using Visual Studio

Your customized Content by Query web part can be uploaded manually into SharePoint using the Ribbon, and your customized XSL files can be manually uploaded into the Style library and published. The manual approach suffers from the same portability issues as the SharePoint Designer approach, and it is much more time-consuming. Therefore, in most cases, you will package your customized part and XSL files into a Feature using Module elements that can then be deployed with SharePoint solutions across farms.

To deploy customized web parts using Visual Studio, create a new project (File ➪ New ➪ Project) and select the Module template. Visual Studio creates a Module folder that contains the SharePoint Elements file and a Sample text file. The Elements file contains the instructions that provision files into SharePoint when the Feature is activated.

Delete the `sample.txt` file from the Module element, and add the customized `.webpart` file by right-clicking on the Module folder and selecting Add ➪ Existing item from the popup menu. Next, open the `Elements.xml` file, which you will need to modify. Web parts, whether customized or custom-coded, are provisioned in the Web Parts gallery. Add a `Url` attribute to the Module element, and enter in `_catalogs/wp` for the location to provision to the gallery.

```
<Elements xmlns="http://schemas.microsoft.com/sharepoint/">
  <Module Name="WebParts"
          Url="_catalogs/wp"
          RootWebOnly="TRUE">
    <File Path="WebParts\Modified_HR_Benefits_Articles.webpart"
          Url="WebParts\Modified_HR_Benefits_Articles.webpart" />
  </Module>
</Elements>
```

Elements.xml

When you add a file to the Modules folder, Visual Studio will automatically create a File element in the Element file. The URL for the file will match the folder structure that Visual Studio maintains for the project. You will need to change the `Url` attribute of the File element so that the `.webpart` file is provisioned to the root of the gallery; also, add the `Type` attribute with a value of `GhostableInLibrary`. It is generally a good idea to provide the `Group` property to the file. This will create a group in the Web Part Picker that will contain your web part; otherwise, your provisioned web part will appear in the same group as the Content by Query web part, which may cause some confusion for content authors.

Available for download on Wrox.com

```xml
<Elements xmlns="http://schemas.microsoft.com/sharepoint/">
    <Module Name="WebParts"
            Url="_catalogs/wp"
            RootWebOnly="TRUE">
        <File Path="WebParts\Modified_HR_Benefits_Articles.webpart"
              Url="Modified_HR_Benefits_Articles.webpart"
              Type="GhostableInLibrary">
        <Property Name="Group"
                  Value="Human Resources"/>
        </File>
    </Module>
</Elements>
```

Elements.xml

If you are deploying both a customized web part and an XSL file, you will need to add a second Module element to the project. Each Module element dictates where its child files will be provisioned in SharePoint; therefore, you will need one module to provision into the Web Parts gallery, and one module to provision into the Style library. The only code difference between the two modules is the `Url` attribute of the Module element.

Available for download on Wrox.com

```xml
<Elements xmlns="http://schemas.microsoft.com/sharepoint/">
    <Module Name="StyleSheets"
            Url="Style Library/XSL Style Sheets"
            RootWebOnly="TRUE">
        <File Path="StyleSheets\HrItemStyle.xsl"
              Url="HrItemStyle.xsl"
              Type="GhostableInLibrary" />
    </Module>
</Elements>
```

Elements.xml

Once you have completed the module files, right-click on the project in the Visual Studio Solution Explorer and click Deploy. In your target SharePoint environment, you will be able to add the customized web part as you would any other web part: place the page in edit mode, select a Web Part zone, and click Add Web Part. If you have provided values for any of the override properties in your `.webpart` file, then you will see a notification in the Web Part Property Pane that indicates that a content author or developer is no longer able to edit the Query properties of the web part. If you have included a custom XSL file, then the Style section drop-down menus will include entries for the XSL templates defined in your files.

Learning how to customize the Content by Query Web Part and its associated XSL files is an essential skill for all Web Content Management developers. Mastering this one area of SharePoint development will often save you a lot of time and effort when fulfilling a variety of presentation and content roll-up requirements.

Content Conversion

SharePoint 2010 introduces the use of the Ribbon as an authoring and administration component that mirrors the authoring experience of Office applications. The addition of the Ribbon makes authoring content from within a SharePoint site substantially easier, more configurable, and more familiar to the content author. The Ribbon makes SharePoint's browser interface a capable and perhaps desirable authoring environment.

Despite the addition of the Ribbon and its functionality, there will be many situations in which a different authoring environment or offline authoring is desirable or necessary. SharePoint includes the capability to convert a document authored with an external tool into a SharePoint web page. Out of the box, SharePoint includes converters that will convert Word (both .docx and .docm), InfoPath, and XML documents to web pages in SharePoint. Using the object model, developers can add new document converters to SharePoint that allow conversion from other formats.

Setup Document Conversion

To use document converters in your SharePoint site, you will need to first activate the conversion services and then configure your site to use them. Enabling document conversion begins with the Services on the Server (Central Administration ⇨ System Settings ⇨ Services on Server). The Document Conversions Load Balancer Service must be started first, followed by the Document Conversions Launcher Service.

Document conversions must be explicitly enabled for each web application, as shown in Figure 8-30. To enable the conversions, access the Configure Document Conversions settings in Central Administration (General Application Settings ⇨ External Service Connections ⇨ Configure document conversions). This page includes options for customizing the settings of each converter installed in the web application.

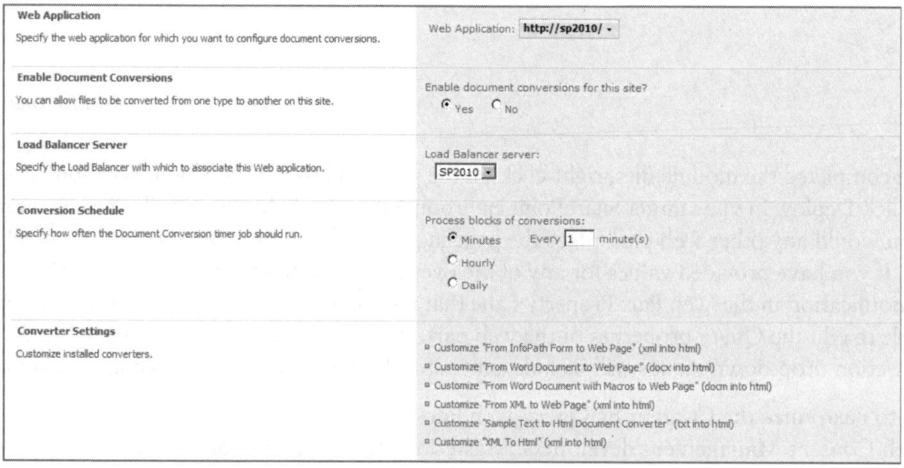

FIGURE 8-30

Document conversions are made available within the site collection by adding them to content types, as shown in Figure 8-31. The Manage document conversion for this content type link is available in the Content Type Properties page. This provides a great deal of control not only over what content types can be converted, but also over which converters can be used for each content type.

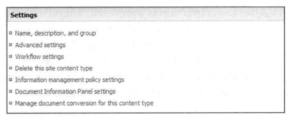

FIGURE 8-31

Using Document Conversion

Using document conversion to create a page from a document is a straightforward experience for the content author. Because the converter is associated with the content type, the content author is not limited to a particular document library. Rather, the content author loads the document into a library, assigns the content type to the uploaded document, and then right-clicks and selects Convert Document from the actions menu, as shown in Figure 8-32.

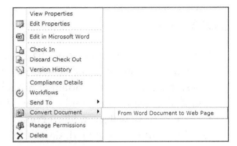

FIGURE 8-32

The author also has the flexibility to select the target location where the converter-generated page will be saved by SharePoint, as shown in Figure 8-33. In some cases, the document conversion process can be very resource-intensive. For this reason, the content author has the choice to set the processing in either synchronous or asynchronous modes in the Processing options. The remainder of the properties and options are specific to each converter.

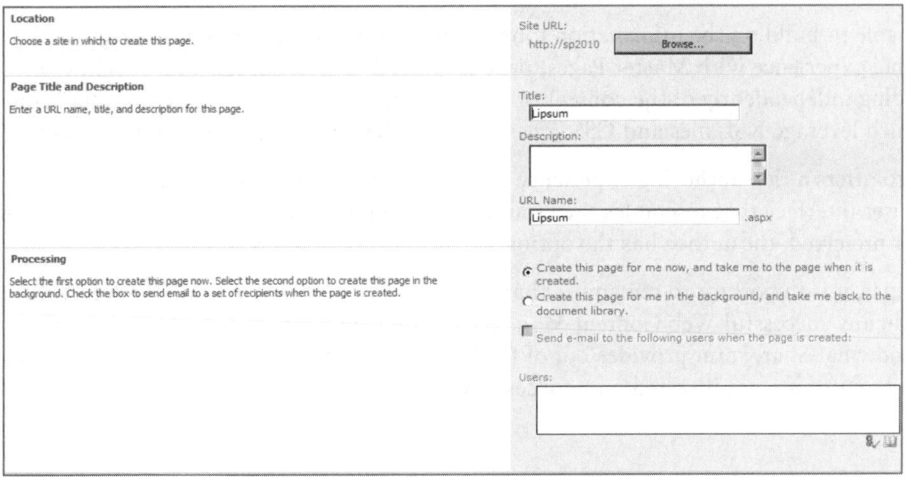

FIGURE 8-33

After the conversion is completed, SharePoint maintains a linkage between the original document and the generated page. This two-way linkage allows the content author to run conversions again when the document is updated. SharePoint allows the content author to generate multiple conversions on a document. This can take the form of a single converter being run repeatedly to generate additional pages, or multiple converters being run on a single originating document. In any case, it is only the last conversion that is maintained for the update linkage. All other conversions must be repeated manually.

For the developer, understanding document conversions and how they work in SharePoint will save custom development time when looking at offline or external authoring scenarios.

SUMMARY

Web Content Management in SharePoint 2010 brings together a variety of roles that traditionally were always present in the design and development of web pages, but were often channeled through a design team. The traditional approach had a tendency to make the development of content and design a slow and cumbersome effort that detracted from the dynamism that is necessary for competitive websites. SharePoint addresses the limitations of traditional web design and development by allowing designers to brand sites, developers to build components, and content authors to generate and maintain content independently of each other, yet within a controlled environment.

Building on solid Information Architecture, developers are able to build the site structure, content types, templates, and components that the authors need to build the content that makes up the site. Visual Studio 2010's integration with SharePoint 2010 and the variety of templates available to developers make the development effort easier and more intuitive. The templates in Visual Studio ultimately generate SharePoint Features and Solutions that enhance the portability of the development effort from one environment to another.

Designers are able to build on the information foundation built by the developers to create a unique branding experience with Master Pages, page layouts, and style sheets. The flexibility of defining branding independently of the content or functionality of the site extends to the built-in web parts, which leverage XSL files and CSS styles to define the rendering of web part contents.

SharePoint also offers a rich authoring experience in which content authors can interact with a SharePoint user interface that resembles the familiar Office interface. Yet, when working in Office is necessary or preferred, the author has the option to use converters to create new pages.

For the developer, it is important to remember that content types and Information Architecture take a central role in any successful Web Content Management implementation. Second in importance is to understand what SharePoint provides out of the box in all areas of web management so that costly time and money are not invested on unnecessary solutions.

Electronic Forms

WHAT'S IN THIS CHAPTER?

➤ Designing InfoPath Forms

➤ New features in InfoPath and InfoPath Forms Services 2010

➤ InfoPath Best Practices

➤ Sandboxing Your InfoPath Forms

➤ Form Development Tools

In today's world, most business processes rely on capturing information from the end users and translating it into appropriate and timely actions. A majority of these business processes simply start with a form and may use other forms throughout their lifecycle. Unfortunately, in many cases forms are received with inaccurate information, which leads to bad decision making, significant cost, and damage to organizations.

SharePoint ships with a great object model that can be used to build sophisticated forms for gathering data and feeding it to the enterprise business processes, such as workflow sequences and composite applications. The vision behind the product as an application development platform, however, has always been based on its ability to build powerful enterprise applications quickly and easily. The emphasis on the words *easy* and *quickly* in the product's vision statement means that there should be an easier way to create, distribute, and manage electronic forms with little or no code.

InfoPath 2003 was Microsoft's first attempt to uniquely position this product to handle the problems in business data collection and presentation needs. The main feature of InfoPath 2003 was the ability to author and render XML-based electronic forms with support for custom-defined schema. InfoPath 2003's native support for XML made it a compelling solution for integration with many backend systems that can understand and communicate in XML.

In SharePoint 2003, a form library and its form template were designed to glue the two products together. Collectively, the form library and its template allowed customers to create new instances of a single form template and translate the field values into column values upon saving the form, all done within the context of a SharePoint site but filled out via the InfoPath 2003 client.

Because of some architectural and deployment limitations in InfoPath 2003, this product never achieved adoption beyond simple departmental solutions that allowed members of small teams to collect, route, and store data within their own little collaborative sandboxes. But, how about the Enterprise?

Not all users who interact with business processes have access to the InfoPath client application; neither do they use one particular device, such as their computer, all the time! For example, sales agents need to take the forms offline and use their PDAs and smart phones to fill them out, partners use only their browser to interact with forms, and internal employees may use a combination of the InfoPath client and browsers to participate in various business processes across the enterprise.

When the Office 2007 suite hit the streets, Microsoft introduced a very exciting feature: Forms Services 2007 — included in the enterprise version of Microsoft Office SharePoint Server 2007.

 If you are interested in learning about electronic forms integration with Microsoft Office SharePoint 2007, Chapter 14 (by John Holliday) in the book Professional SharePoint 2007 Development *(Wrox, 2007), is a great resource.*

In a nutshell, Forms Services was all about allowing end users to use their browsers to fill out InfoPath forms and allowing administrators to manage those forms. Form Services 2007 was a great move to help extend the reach of electronic forms by ensuring that electronic forms can render content for a wide range of users using various client applications and different devices. The concept of content types and their association with form templates, two-way synching between form data fields and columns, and a better deployment model were all among major improvements Microsoft made to the product at that time.

With the power of the SharePoint Server 2010 platform, InfoPath 2010 and Forms Services 2010 represent even more significant improvements over their predecessors. Some of the improvements came from the core platform itself and some were made available in each product.

InfoPath 2010, available in the Professional Plus volume license SKU, is a form creation and data-gathering tool that ships with the Microsoft Office 2010 package. If we consider InfoPath 2003 Service Pack 1 as a major iteration in the product's lifecycle, then InfoPath, in its fourth iteration with the 2010 release, has evolved way beyond the product that was released back in August 2003. InfoPath 2010 is the most compelling release to date and is the quickest way to have a common form rendition in the browser, as well as in rich and offline clients.

Once you install InfoPath 2010, the first thing that you may notice is that InfoPath 2010 comes with two flavors: InfoPath Designer and InfoPath Filler. InfoPath Designer 2010 is the primary tool used by designers to create and design the forms with easy-to-use features based on pre-built templates and baked-in functionalities. As the name implies, InfoPath Filler 2010 comes with a Fluent UI, which provides a much improved and yet simpler end user experience for filling out forms. The following list provides a sneak peek of some of the new features introduced in InfoPath 2010 and InfoPath Form Services 2010:

➤ Richer browser forms with shorter load time.

➤ The capability to handle more requests per second.

➤ The capability to customize SharePoint list forms.

➤ A brand-new InfoPath Form web part.

➤ Equal rendition across the major browsers. Compliant browser forms (WCAG 2.0, XHTML 1.0, and strict CSS).

➤ Integration with Business Connectivity Services (BCS).

➤ Ability to query REST web services.

➤ Native offline integration with SharePoint through SharePoint Workspace 2010 client.

➤ New controls like the People/Group Picker, Date Time Picker, and Picture button.

➤ On-premises or multi-tenant hosting support (i.e., SharePoint online).

➤ Ability to script various operations using PowerShell, backup, and restore.

➤ Seamless integration with new Health Rule Definitions.

Enterprise forms is a broad topic that could make up several chapters, if not its own book. However, after reading this chapter, you will have a good understanding of how to leverage InfoPath in SharePoint to rapidly design and create forms used in enterprise management processes across your organization.

And with that, it is time to get started.

INTRODUCING THE TRAINING MANAGEMENT APPLICATION

In this chapter, you'll use an example of a Training Management application at a fictitious company, Adventure Works, which illustrates some of the new capabilities of InfoPath 2010 and Forms Services 2010. First, take a look at how this application works from the user's perspective.

The Human Resources (HR) department at Adventure Works uses SharePoint and InfoPath to implement a training-course system. You can think of the Training Management application as a set of three use cases as follows:

➤ New training creation use case

➤ Training registration use case

➤ Increment stat counter use case

As illustrated in Figure 9-1, Adventure Works staff can perform various activities in this application. For example, the training coordinator can create trainings and add them to a SharePoint list named Trainings. This list will be customized and enhanced by InfoPath 2010 to facilitate the training creation use case.

Also, the Human Resources department at Adventure Works allows its employees to register for a training opportunity. The training registration form is designed in InfoPath and hosted inside the new InfoPath Form web part on a web part page named Trainings Dashboard. The training registration form must be rendered in a typical desktop web browser and in browsers on handheld or mobile devices.

Once a training request is filled out and saved, the result is stored in a form library named Registrations, and an event handler associated with the Registrations form library fires and updates a counter in another custom SharePoint list, named Stats. The Stats list is hidden from employees so that its content can't be modified and it does not clutter navigation. At the end, the registration form is connected to the Stats list through the web part connections framework in SharePoint to demonstrate a simple form-driven mashup scenario.

As you may notice, the primary forms in driving the business process just described are all electronic forms and implemented in InfoPath 2010. The following diagram demonstrates a high level overview of the Training Management application.

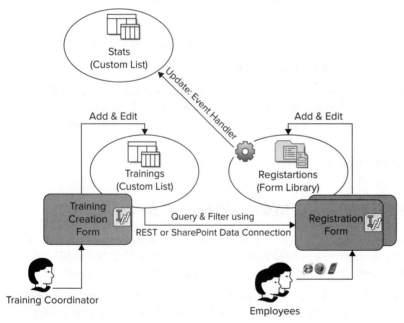

FIGURE 9-1

CUSTOMIZING SHAREPOINT LIST FORMS

In Windows SharePoint Services 3.0, list forms were regular ASP.NET pages serving as the visual interfaces to add an item to, or edit or display an item in, that list. Typically, list forms were defined in the list template and instantiated upon the creation of a new list instance. Although there are several ways to replace the out-of-the-box list forms (`DispForm.aspx`, `EditForm.aspx`, and `NewForm.aspx`) with custom ASPX pages, as described in the following list, each approach introduces its own challenges:

1. **SharePoint Designer Customization:** In this approach, you use SharePoint Designer 2007 to modify the layout of list forms and add custom business logic. For example, you could create a new `NewForm.aspx` form from scratch. This approach introduces a very limited customizability that limits you to using HTML, JavaScript, and Extensible Stylesheet Language (XSL) only. Additionally, customizing list forms using SharePoint Designer 2007 results in inserting a fairly big chunk of XSL into the HTML markup of the form, which makes it even harder to maintain!

2. **Customizing List Forms via a Browser:** You can add web parts to the Display, Edit, and New forms via a browser to add business logic for the inserting and editing of list item data. The problem with this approach is that Microsoft clearly states that it is not supported, meaning that if something breaks you'll have to remove the web part and leave the default List Form web part as the only web part on the page. This is certainly not a solution that you can always rely on either.

3. **Using Custom Content Types with Associated Custom Forms:** This is a better approach than the other two, because you can use all your ASP.NET coding skill sets and deploy the list forms in a much cleaner way. However, you cannot leverage this approach for the existing content types or lists that are not yours. Additionally, you need to write extra code to handle exceptions related to the CRUD operations (Create, Add, Update, and Delete). For instance, your code must handle concurrency violation when calling the `SPListItem` `.Update()` method.

One of the exciting features in InfoPath 2010 is the ability to extend or enhance the forms used by SharePoint lists for creating, editing, or showing list items. Today, you can modify list forms layouts, set validation rules, or create additional views using little or no code. When you are finished modifying the list forms, reflecting your changes back to SharePoint is just a matter of using the one-click publishing capability that comes out of the box with the list form.

In this section, you will explore some of the new functionalities of InfoPath 2010 used to customize SharePoint list forms in the context of a Training Management application, which you will build throughout the chapter.

Creating the Trainings List

Before diving into customizing the Trainings list forms using InfoPath, you need to create the SharePoint list and add the required fields to it. Business requirements of the Training Management application dictate that the training coordinator be able to create new training opportunities by selecting Add New Item in the Trainings list. This list resides on the Human Resources website and requires the following information:

➤ **Title:** A title for the training opportunity

➤ **Code:** A code that uniquely identifies the training (unique eight-character fixed)

➤ **Description:** The description of the training

➤ **Start Date:** The training's start date

➤ **End Date:** The training's end date

➤ **Cost:** The cost of the training (American dollars)

➤ **Level:** The difficulty level associated with the training (a number from one to five)

➤ **Enrollment Deadline:** The date that enrollment ends

➤ **Address:** The address of the training facility (multiple lines of text)

➤ **Additional Information:** Optional information about the training itself (enhanced rich text with pictures, tables, and hyperlinks)

Figure 9-2 illustrates all the fields of the new Trainings list, their types, and whether they are required when submitting to the list.

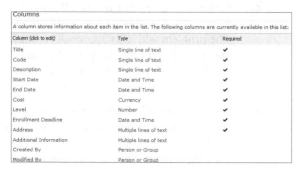

Customizing SharePoint List Forms

To customize the list forms in the Trainings list, navigate to the list and click Customize Form on the List tab that appears on the Ribbon, as shown in Figure 9-3.

FIGURE 9-2

FIGURE 9-3

This will launch InfoPath Designer in SharePoint list mode, and a basic form will be autocreated from the fields specified in the list's schema. You can see the fields in the Fields task pane on the right side of the design canvas in which mandatory fields are designated with a red asterisk.

Before going further, look at the controls that have been placed on the form (See Figure 9-4). For each Date and Time column in the Trainings list, a Date and Time Picker control has been generated by InfoPath. The Date and Time Picker is a new control in InfoPath 2010 that allows you to type a date and time or select a date from a calendar display.

Also notice that, when you click on one of the existing form fields (for example, Level), the control tools' contextual Ribbon appears on the top and gives you the ability to interact with the list columns inside the InfoPath Designer. Any changes at this point will be persisted later to the SharePoint list when the form is published. For example, if you change a control's binding to a new field, that field will be automatically added to the list's schema when the form template is published to SharePoint.

Control Tools Contextual Ribbon

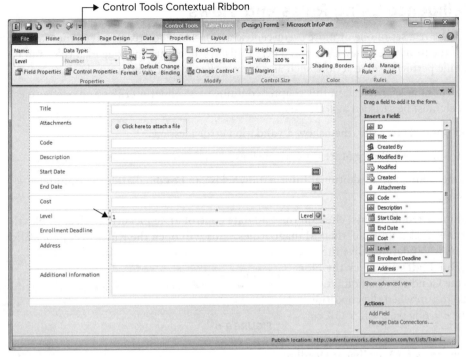

FIGURE 9-4

In addition to autogenerating the form through the Fluent UI interface, you can launch InfoPath Designer by going to the New tab in the Backstage and choosing SharePoint List as the template. You then enter the URL of the Trainings list, and the same InfoPath form will be autogenerated for you.

To save some real estate on the form, let's create an optional section that the training coordinator can use to insert or remove additional information about the training if necessary. Right-click on the autogenerated Additional Information rich textbox on the form and delete it. In the Fields task pane, switch to Show advanced view, then click on the drop-down menu next to the Additional Information field and choose Optional Section with Controls. This adds an optional section, and the same rich textbox bound to the Additional Information field is inserted into the form, as shown in Figure 9-5.

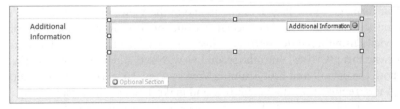

FIGURE 9-5

Adding Intelligence Using Rules and Views

Rules in InfoPath are a set of one or more event-centric actions used to create a dynamic experience for the users of the form when they fill it out. There is always an event that triggers a rule, and in response, the rule performs some action, such as a format change or a validation check.

The training form sample provided in this chapter contains two validation rules and one business logic rule, which must be satisfied as follows:

1. If End Date < Start Date, then show a validation error message.

2. If Enrollment Deadline > Start Date, then show a validation error message.

3. Only the Address and Additional Information fields can be edited after the training is created.

To implement these requirements, click on the End date control (date picker) to select it. Next, on the Home tab, click Add Rule, then Manage Rules. This will open the Rules task pane. Click New button, then Validation. Give the rule a name (e.g., RuleEndDate). Click the None hyperlink in the Condition section, and define the rule to run when the condition shown in Figure 9-6 is true. Click OK to save the rule.

FIGURE 9-6

Repeat the same steps for Enrollment Deadline.

> **BEST PRACTICE #1**
>
> InfoPath rules and formulas (collectively referred to as declarative logic) are powerful ways of adding intelligence to your electronic forms. It's not a best practice to write custom code where declarative logic can do the job!

As stated in Rule 3, you need to make sure that, when the training is created, there is no way someone can make changes in any fields except the address and additional information fields. To implement Rule 3, you need to leverage another powerful feature of InfoPath, called views. Views are a great way to present your form differently to the users based on different states that the form is in. In the case of the training creation form, you need to set a different view when a training is being edited than what it is when the training coordinator creates a new training. (This view is referred to as insert mode.)

To add the Edit View to your form, go to the Page Design tab and in the Views group, click New. Call the new view Edit Training, and click OK. One special attribute of views is that you can display the same fields on multiple views using separate controls — just copy (Ctrl+C) the layout and controls from the default view and paste them (Ctrl+V) onto the second view. Next, add a meaningful title to the top of the form for both the default and Edit Training Views — say, New Training and Edit Training. In Edit Training View, remove the attachment row and make Title, Code, Description, Cost, and Level controls read-only (Right-click ➪ Text box properties ➪ Display tab ➪ Read-only).

Because you can't make the Start Date, End Date, and Enrollment Deadline controls read-only (they're Date Picker controls), let's just delete them all and replace them with three textbox controls instead (Home Tab ➪ Control section ➪ Text box). At this point, right-click on each textbox control and choose Change Binding to bind it to the appropriate date field, as shown in Figure 9-7.

It's very important that you delete the field1, field2, and field3 fields that InfoPath automatically added to the Fields pane as a result of adding the new textboxes. Otherwise, the new fields will be promoted as list columns when you publish your form to SharePoint.

FIGURE 9-7

At this point, your Edit Training View should look like Figure 9-8.

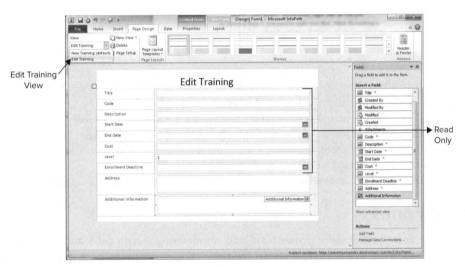

FIGURE 9-8

To glue everything back together, you need to set something up that flips the view between the new and edit modes based on a condition. Navigate to the Data tab and go to the section called Form Load. Click on the New button, select Action, and then type an appropriate name for the rule, such as RuleSwitchToEditView. Essentially this sets up a rule and runs when the form loads. Now, you need to specify under which condition this rule runs.

The condition is clear: you want to switch the view when users edit an existing training. Because Code is a mandatory field, it cannot be blank when training is created. Therefore, you can use this field to handle this particular situation, as shown in Figure 9-9.

FIGURE 9-9

After the condition is set, it's time to define the action that needs to kick in. Click on the Add button just below where you defined condition and select Switch Views. In the View drop-down box specify Edit Training View, if it's not already selected (see Figure 9-10). That's it!

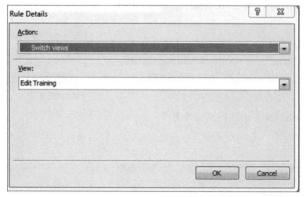

FIGURE 9-10

 Because external lists are just like lists with some extra hooks added to the backend Business Connectivity Services data source, they can be treated like typical lists in InfoPath. However, the steps you need to take to customize external list forms are different from those for typical list forms. External list form customization is mostly done in SharePoint Designer 2010.

Publishing List Forms

At this point, you are done with designing your form and empowering it with rules and views. Now, go ahead and publish the form to the SharePoint list from which it came. In the Backstage, go to the Info tab.

In Figure 9-11, a nice screenshot of the current state of the form is shown on the right side. Also, InfoPath already knows which list this form belongs to, meaning that there is no additional configuration required on your side to publish the form to SharePoint. Just click on the button that says Quick Publish, and you are done.

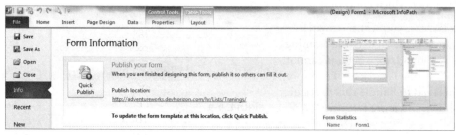

FIGURE 9-11

After the form is published to the Trainings list, do not close the form. Instead, click on Save As and save the template somewhere on your local drive. The important point to remember here is that saving a form template locally or on a network share is a totally different process from publishing it. Publishing versus saving a form template will be covered in greater detail later in this chapter, but for now just accept these as two different terms in the InfoPath lexicon.

Once the form has been successfully published and its template is locally saved, return to the Trainings list in the HR site and create a new training item. Sure enough, the default ASPX page is replaced with the default view of the form template you just customized and published. After filling out the form (see Figure 9-12), you can submit it by clicking Save on the top Ribbon. At this point, the form applies the appropriate rules to validate your input and adds a new list item to the Trainings list.

While you are still on the form, notice that the Additional Information field is partially invisible on the form because it is hosted in an optional section.

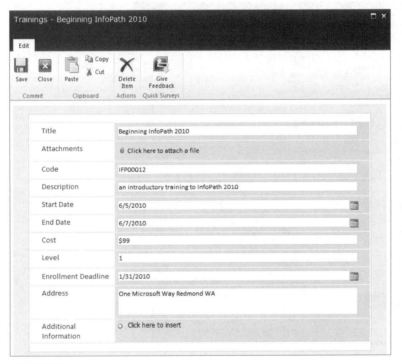

FIGURE 9-12

If you click anywhere on the rendered form and get a property of the page, you will see that the form, unlike uncustomized list forms, is not loaded by the `NewForm.aspx` page. Instead, it is loaded by another out-of-the-box web part page called `newifs.aspx`.

The `newifs.aspx`, `displayinf.aspx`, and `editifs.aspx` pages are new additions to the list's infrastructure in SharePoint 2010. They are all web part pages that can be customized via browser. All three pages are accessible from the List Ribbon ⇨ Form Web Part drop-down, as shown in Figure 9-13. Each page hosts an instance of the InfoPath Form web part that knows how to locate and load the form template associated with the Trainings list.

FIGURE 9-13

When editing an existing training, you will see that the rule you placed in Load event of the form kicks in and switches the view from New Training to Edit Training, where you can edit the last two fields of the form only, as illustrated in Figure 9-14.

FIGURE 9-14

 This form template (Trainings.xsn) can be found in the code download for this book.

If, at some point during the customization process, you decide to undo everything and revert to the out-of-the-box ASPX forms, it's easy. Browse to the list's List Settings page, click Form Settings, select Use the default SharePoint form, and click OK. Optionally, if you leave the Delete the InfoPath Form from the server unchecked, the InfoPath form you customized will remain on the server. Thus, the next time you click Customize Form, the saved InfoPath form will be used in InfoPath Designer, instead of a new one being autogenerated from scratch.

There are two things about SharePoint list forms to consider. First, custom code is not supported in customized list forms using InfoPath 2010. Right-click on the form template you just saved in your local drive, and select Design to launch InfoPath Designer 2010. There is no Developer tab on the Ribbon to launch Visual Studio Tools for Applications (VSTA) for writing custom code (see Label 1 in Figure 9-15). Second, you can only publish a list form to the list it belongs to (see Label 2 in Figure 9-15). This also means that converting your list form to a form library is not possible.

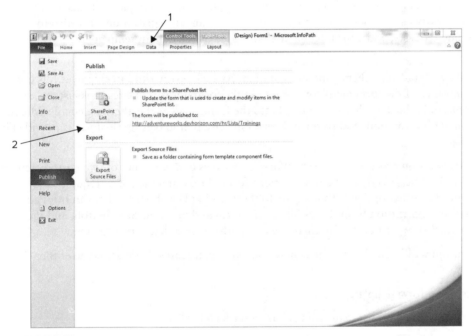

FIGURE 9-15

Distributing the Trainings List

To distribute the InfoPath forms attached to the Trainings list, you need to export the Trainings list as a template and make the template available for use in other sites by uploading it to their List Template gallery, as shown in Figure 9-16.

 For creating custom list definitions that use InfoPath Forms, see my blog post at `http://www.devhorizon.com/go/13.`

FIGURE 9-16

DESIGNING INFOPATH FORM TEMPLATES

The second use case to implement is the registration use case, which demonstrates how Adventure Works employees can register for a training opportunity. To implement this use case, Adventure Works has decided to create a form library named Registrations in which to store the training requests, and a form template that is used as the default template for the form library.

InfoPath separates data from schema and presentation. As such, every time an employee fills out the form, an instance of the form template is stored in the form library. The result is just an `.xml` file that contains only the data that was entered into the form, such as the alternate email address, emergency contact information, and so forth. Everything else that makes up the form is provided by its form template.

To begin the registration process, Adventure Works employees can use either of two custom actions. One option is to browse directly to the Registrations form library and file a new request for a specific training. The other option is to navigate to the Training Dashboard, where an InfoPath form web part hosts the registration form. Users fill out the form and press the Save button, and the result is saved in the Registrations library. So, there are two paths to complete a registration.

In this section, you will learn about various new and existing features. Here are some of the takeaways:

> ➤ Designing a form template
> ➤ Querying SharePoint list items using SharePoint REST APIs
> ➤ Writing custom managed code in forms
> ➤ Publishing form templates
> ➤ Form security
> ➤ Deploying forms as Sandbox Solutions

What Is a Form Library?

In nutshell, a form library is just a special document library that includes an InfoPath form as its primary template and easily allows users to fill out a new InfoPath form or edit an existing one.

Although InfoPath Designer 2010 allows you to create a form library on a SharePoint site when you publish your form template, there are situations in which you may want to create the form library beforehand. For example, you may want to create the form library, change its settings such as versioning, and set up permissions to it before publishing the form template, simply because people who publish may not have enough permissions to complete such a task. Follow these steps to create a form library to host registration forms:

1. Click Site Settings ⇨ More Options.

2. In Filter By category, select Library, and then click Form Library.

3. In the Name box, type **Registrations**. If you plan to enable the Registrations library to receive registrations by email, then click on More Options and type the email address of the Registrations library in the description textbox, so that Adventure Works employees can easily find it.

4. If you want to add a link to this library on the SharePoint Quick Launch menu, Select Yes in the Navigation section.

5. In the Document Version History section, click Yes only if you think that creating a version (minor or major) each time a request is checked into the form library is necessary.

6. Click Create.

Once the form library is created, you can specify how its form templates should be opened. Browse to the Registrations form library ⇨ Form Library Settings, and select Advanced Settings. These settings are listed under Opening Documents in the Browser, as shown in Figure 9-17. The default behavior when you create the form library from within SharePoint is to open the forms in the browser. However, you can select the Open in the client application option and have the form opened by InfoPath Filler 2010.

FIGURE 9-17

Designing Your Form Template

With the Registrations form library complete, the next logical step is to build the Registration Form template. Adventure Works employees will fill out this form and save it to the form library you created in the previous section. One of the very first decisions you need to make here is how to design and lay out your form.

Start InfoPath Designer 2010. The best starting point is to select the type of form you want to design. When you choose a template as the basis of your form, descriptive text is displayed in the top-right corner of the dialog box, as shown in Figure 9-18. It is important to take a moment and review pre-built templates, their concepts, the matching color schemes, and the optimal layout used in each.

BEST PRACTICE #2

Using pre-built templates accelerates the form creation process and saves you a considerable amount of time if you are new to InfoPath 2010.

All available form templates are grouped into four main categories:

➤ **Popular Form Templates:** A wide range of popular form templates to start your design. When customizing SharePoint lists and document libraries, this is the category that you want to focus on.

➤ **Advanced Form Templates:** This category covers templates for more advanced scenarios, mostly for querying and submitting data to databases, web services, or other external data sources.

➤ **InfoPath 2007 Form Templates:** Form templates that also work in InfoPath 2007 in backward-compatible mode.

➤ **Templates Parts:** Contains three templates for building reusable components — also known as mini-form templates. Once built, mini-form templates can simplify the creation of more complex forms, much like splitting the page into user controls in classic ASP.NET.

From the Available Form Templates, choose the SharePoint Form Library template, and click Design this Form on the right side of the dialog box.

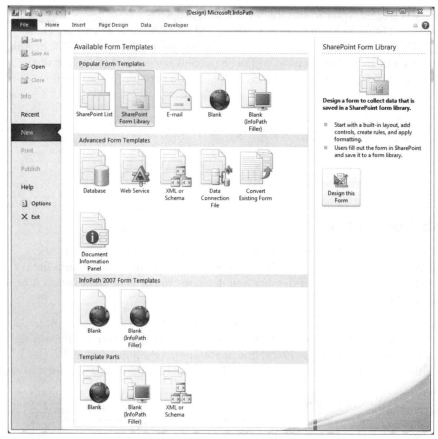

FIGURE 9-18

Right after you open InfoPath Designer 2010, you may notice that laying out your form to get a professional look and feel is now really easy. InfoPath uses page layouts as a framework to organize your form's content, including controls, graphics, and tables (also called section layouts).

First, you need to replace the page layout that InfoPath gives you by default with something that is more appropriate for the Training registration form. Just delete everything you see on the form (Ctrl+C/Delete). On the Page Design tab, select one of the five page layout templates, for example Color Bar. Add an appropriate title and adjust it so that it is centered. At this stage, your form contains only one page layout and a title, as shown in Figure 9-19.

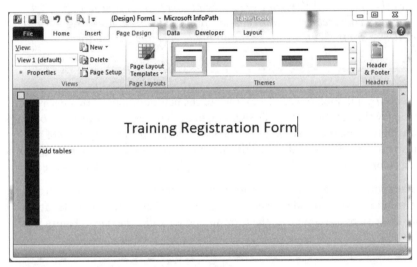

FIGURE 9-19

Next, you need to add a section layout to the form to create a logical grouping of information that you want to collect in your form. From the Insert tab under the Tables gallery, choose Single Column 4 – No heading, and insert it where it says "Add Tables," right underneath the title. The template adds three rows by default and you need to add three more rows so that the following controls can be placed on the form:

➤ **Event Name:** A required Drop-Down Listbox control linked to the Trainings list

➤ **Alternate Email:** A required textbox with validation rules

➤ **Emergency Contact Name:** A required textbox

➤ **Emergency Contact Phone Number:** A required textbox with validation rules

➤ **Short BIO:** An optional textbox

➤ **Manager:** An optional People/Group Picker control

From the new Controls galley in the Home tab, add the required controls to the main section layout on the design canvas. You can set the controls to be required by right-clicking on each control and selecting the Cannot be blank checkbox in the control's Properties dialog box (Validation section). Because each control on the form and its autogenerated field represent the data on the form, let's give them more descriptive names. To do this, name the controls and the fields (field1 to field6) as described in the bulleted list above.

> *It's a common misconception in InfoPath that fields, controls, and groups are interchangeable terms. A field represents the data that is collected by your form. All the fields available in your form can be accessed from Data tab ⇨ Show Fields ⇨ Fields task pane. A group is an element in the data source that can contain fields or other groups. A control can be bound to a field or a group. When bound, the data collected by a control is saved in the form's underlying XML file. However, a control can also be left unbound, meaning that it doesn't save any data.*

Now, you need to change the overall look of your form. One of the new additions to this release of InfoPath is the ability to apply themes. In the Page Design tab, in the Themes (also called Layout Styles) gallery, you can select an appropriate style that best describes your form's personality. One of the available groups is exclusive to SharePoint, and all the themes match out-of-the box SharePoint themes. Let's go ahead and pick a color scheme from that group, for example, SharePoint – Gray Scale.

If you still have your cursor within a table cell on your form, then in the Table Tools contextual tab, click on the borders button and make some adjustments to the form so that there is a border around the entire layout page. When these steps are complete, the form should look like the one in Figure 9-20.

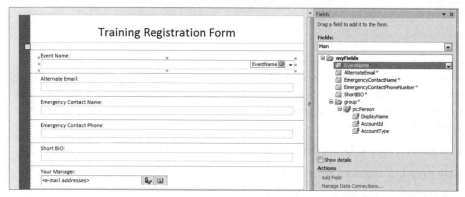

FIGURE 9-20

At this point, everything from the design perspective has been handled, and you can start adding the necessary business logics to your form.

Click on the emergency contact phone number textbox, and from the Controls Tools Properties tab, click the Manage Rules button to launch the Rules Manager. Here, you need to set a validation rule that fires when the emergency contact number doesn't match Phone number pattern.

As you can see in Figure 9-21, there are many ready-to-use data entry patterns that you can choose from. You can even customize each pattern's associated regular expressions and create your own customized pattern.

FIGURE 9-21

To validate the alternate email address field, copy the rule you just created for the Phone number field and paste it into the alternate email control's Rules task pane. You just need to change one thing: in the Data Entry Pattern dialog box, choose Email pattern instead of Phone number pattern.

 In InfoPath Designer 2010, one new improvement in the Rules task pane is the option to copy and paste rules. This helps you save time and work efficiently when designing your forms. Copying and pasting rules doesn't work across multiple forms.

Employees who fill out this form will be asked to specify their direct manager in the respective People/Group Picker control. Notice how, by adding this control to the design canvas, a group has been added in the Fields task pane containing three fields: DisplayName, AccountID, and AccountType.

First, go to the People Picker control's Properties dialog box, and in the SharePoint Server tab, specify the SharePoint site URL to query for people and groups. Notice in the General tab how you can narrow down the people/group picking query to choices like People Only, People and Groups, Allow multiple selection, or even a specific SharePoint group, as illustrated in Figure 9-22.

Note that if you added the People/Group Picker control to a customized SharePoint list form (such as Trainings list forms), then you wouldn't need to go through all these additional steps in order to set it up. The control is smart enough to pick the right context for you.

Querying SharePoint Lists in Forms

With the people picker properly configured, it's time to return to the Event Name Drop-Down Listbox control and wire it up to query the Trainings list you created earlier in this chapter.

From the Data tab, click on the From SharePoint List in the Get External Data gallery. In the first page of the Data Connection Wizard, type the full URL of the Trainings list, and click Next, as shown in Figure 9-23.

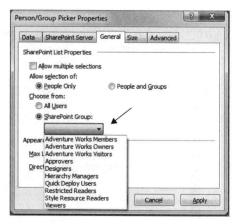

FIGURE 9-22

In the second screen, the Trainings list is already highlighted on the available list of libraries, so go ahead and click Next. Figure 9-24 illustrates the third screen of the wizard, where you should select the fields that must be included in the data source. Simply select all the columns you created in the Trainings list and click Next.

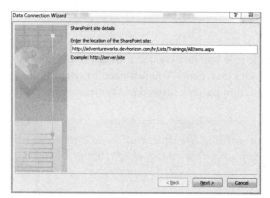

FIGURE 9-23

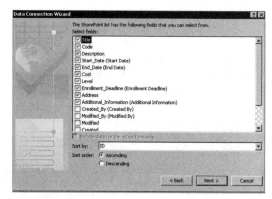

FIGURE 9-24

In the fourth step of the wizard, leave "Store a copy of data in the form template" unchecked, and click Next.

You're almost done. In the last step, type a proper name for the data source and check the "Automatically retrieve data when form is opened" option to create a secondary data source in your form, as shown in Figure 9-25. Finally, click Finish.

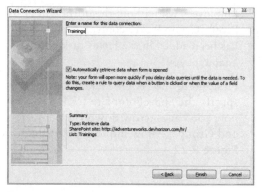

FIGURE 9-25

BEST PRACTICE #3

Before selecting "Automatically retrieve data when form is opened" when creating a data source with the Data Source Wizard, consider the following two tips: loading large data sources can significantly increase your form's initial rendering time and should be avoided if possible. You should postpone such queries to a later time during the form's lifecycle or make them on demand, based on user-initiated actions. One solution is to create wizards (using views) and have a splash screen in the default view that takes users' inputs and then queries a parameterized data source in the subsequent views. This option should not be selected if either the data source changes frequently or it contains sensitive information that must not be included in the form's schema (for offline use).

Note that, to keep the samples provided in this chapter relatively simple, querying external data sources in the form load event is not much of a concern. In general, this is not an ideal situation because it adds to the form's load time.

In the Event Name control's properties dialog box, select Get choices from an external data source, and in the Data source, select the secondary data source. Click the XPath image next to the Entries box, and choose the `ns2:SharePointListItem_RW` element. Set the Value and Display name to Code and Title fields, as shown in Figure 9-26, and click OK.

FIGURE 9-26

Last, but certainly not least, the data source must bring only a subset of data that's relevant to the users because, at present, it fetches all the training courses. As more training courses are created over time, there is a chance that employees will register for a training course that's already passed its registration due date. To address this issue, you can use a filter that enables employees to view only relevant trainings.

In InfoPath 2007, filters could be used only in form templates that were designed to be filled out in the InfoPath client and were not supported in browser-compatible form templates. There were workarounds, such as using conditional formatting or using web services, to overcome this limitation. For example, a proof of concept implementation of cascading filters in browser-enabled forms can be found in my blog at `www.devhorizon.com/go/14`. Thankfully, in InfoPath 2010, filtering functionality is fully supported in both client and browser-compatible form templates.

In the Trainings list, each training opportunity has an associated Enrollment Deadline column that indicates when the registration for the training is due. You will use this column to define the filter by following seven steps:

1. In the Event Name control's property dialog box, click the button next to the Entries box.

2. Select the `ns2:SharePointListItem_RW` group as the group to apply the filter to.

3. Click the Filter Data button to load the Filter Data dialog box.

4. Click the Add button to show the Specify Filter Conditions dialog box.

5. Select Enrollment Deadline as one the two operands participating in the filter condition.

6. Select "is greater than" as the operator of the filter.

7. For the second operand of the filter, select Use a formula and use the `now()` function.

Querying REST Web Services

In the previous section, you used the traditional technique for querying SharePoint lists, which has been around for a while. Alternatively, you can query the Trainings list using a new capability in SharePoint 2010, called WCF Data Services.

WCF Data Services is a framework that allows interactions with SharePoint data in a RESTful manner.

 WCF Data Services is not a one-way street for just browsing data; it provides full REST (Representational State Transfer) over HTTP support for browsing data, as well as manipulating it using regular HTTP verbs (GET, PUT, DELETE, and so on).

Everything starts with a URI, because REST is all about using URIs to identify resources, modify them, and transfer them using a representation of the resource. The most obvious advantage of using REST is simplicity. Anyone who can craft a URL can work with REST APIs, which makes REST even more powerful compared to other data access methodologies. Because InfoPath 2010 supports connecting to REST APIs, you can query the Trainings list (a resource in the REST context) using SharePoint's WCF Data Services.

 In order to use WCF Data Services in beta 1 of SharePoint 2010, the ADO.NET Data Services 1.5 runtime must be installed before you install SharePoint on your server. This prerequisite will likely be changed with the RTM release of SharePoint 2010.

Navigate to the Data tab in the Ribbon, and in the Get External Data gallery, click From Web Service, and then click From REST Web Service. Assuming that your SharePoint site is `http://adventureworks.devhorizon.com/hr`, your WCF Data Services endpoint can be accessed at: `http://adventureworks.devhorizon.com/hr/_vti_bin/ListData.svc/Trainings`

Type the URL in the Address textbox, and click Next in the wizard. In the next step, give the new data source a name, and check the "Automatically retrieve data when form is opened" option to create a secondary data source.

Before you consume this feed in your InfoPath form, step back and examine the XML output from the endpoint by typing the feed URL in the browser and pressing the Enter key. To see the returned raw XML, you may need to turn off the feed reader view in your browser. In Internet Explorer 8, this option can be turned off by unchecking the "Turn on feed reading view" option in Tools ⇨ Internet Options ⇨ Content Tab ⇨ Feed and Web Slices ⇨ Settings.

One great advantage of using REST data sources is that you can easily restrict the returned entities by applying the `$filter` expression to the entity set, identified in the last segment of a REST URI. In other words, you filter data right in the source as opposed to using form-level filtering.

On the Data tab, click Form Load from the Rules category. This will open the Rules task pane in which you can create rules that will run when the form is opened. Create a new rule and leave the condition section empty. This particular rule runs whenever your form loads and is not based on a specific condition — that's exactly what you want.

FIGURE 9-27

Next, click on the Add button and select Change REST URL (see Figure 9-27). Change REST URL is a new rule action that the InfoPath team has added to the product. It allows developers to change the REST URI dynamically when an event is triggered, such as form load or submit. This will bring up the Rule Details dialog box, which gives you more options for manipulating the URI you initially set for the data source, as shown in Figure 9-28.

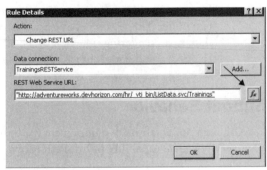

FIGURE 9-28

To implement the filter, click on the function (*fx*) button next to the URL and insert the following:

```
concat("http://adventureworks.devhorizon.com/hr/_vti_bin/ListData.svc/Trainings","?
$filter=EnrollmentDeadline gt datetime'", now(), "'")
```

Another rule action needs to be added to the Form Load that fires after the Change REST URL action runs. Again, click on the Add button in the Rules task pane, but this time, choose Query for the data rule action. As illustrated in Figure 9-29, in the Rule Details dialog box, you just need to click OK, because the Action and Data Connection values have already been set. Figure 9-30 shows both rules and their order in the Rules task pane for Form Load event.

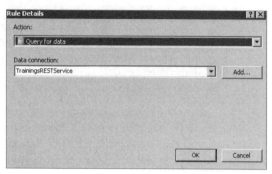

FIGURE 9-29

At this stage, the Event Name Drop-Down Listbox must be bound to the "atom:entry" element. In the Control's Properties dialog box, select "Get choices from an external data source," and in the Data source, select the secondary data source. Next, click on the XPath image next to the Entries box and choose the entry element. The entry atom element represents an individual list item in the returned feed and acts as a container for metadata and data associated with each list item. Set the Value and Display name to the Code and Title fields, and click OK.

That's it! Press F5 and preview the form. Your form should load only the trainings in which the enrollment deadline is greater than today. This example proves that it is quite easy to combine the power of REST data sources with formulas in InfoPath 2010 to create filters using absolutely no code.

FIGURE 9-30

BEST PRACTICE #4

Use query parameters to stop loading unnecessary data in your data sources. If you can't filter data at source, at least filter your data at form level if possible. Filtering data saves rendering time and boosts the overall performance of your form when the underlying data sources contain a lot of data.

Submit Behavior

Although not an absolute requirement for building the Training Management application, Submit is a very powerful capability of InfoPath forms.

Essentially, submitting provides the ability to control the behavior of the form and where the collected data ends up. Submitting an InfoPath form is different from saving it, and these two actions shouldn't be confused. The most obvious difference is that you cannot submit a form that has validation errors, but that's not the case when you save the form. Another difference is that, when you save an InfoPath form, the result is saved as XML in the form library. When you submit the form, not only do you have the option of saving the result as XML, but you also have plenty of other options, such as closing the form or running rules without writing any custom code. In many scenarios, the level of control you get out of the box for submitting your forms is what makes it a more appealing option than just saving the form.

If you go to the Data tab and select the Submit Options button, you will find several settings to define the submission behavior of the form. You can design your form to submit to a series of powerful connection points, such as the SharePoint form library, email, a web service, a web server, a DCL connection, or even a hosting environment. Finally, if you want to satisfy complex submission requirements, you can write custom code by selecting the appropriate option, as shown in Figure 9-31.

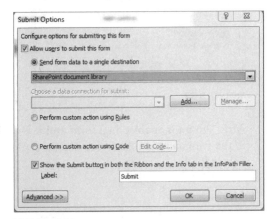

FIGURE 9-31

BEST PRACTICE #5

You should think about scalability when you are designing your forms, not when it becomes an issue. For example, if a form template is available on a publicly accessible website, chances are the form will be filled out and submitted (or saved) many times. Although lists and document libraries are much more scalable and can be throttled in SharePoint 2010, you should still consider bucketizing the form library and distributing the forms evenly in it; otherwise, you may experience performance degradation if more than 5000 forms exist per container (folder). Writing custom code to submit to multiple folders or libraries is one solution to address this capacity limitation of SharePoint and yet another reason that you may want to use Submit.

Also, you can define your own submit button. Simply add a regular button, and in the Control Properties tab, set its action to Submit, as shown in Figure 9-32. Alternatively, you can click on the button and choose submit Data from Add Rule in the Control Tools Properties contextual menu (see Figure 9-33). Both actions will result in the same behavior for the button.

FIGURE 9-32

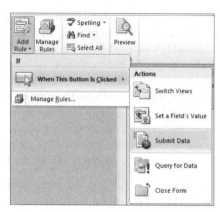

FIGURE 9-33

After submit is enabled in a form and it is determined what it does, a submit button appears in the Ribbon next to the Save and Save As options when the form is first opened, as shown in Figure 9-34.

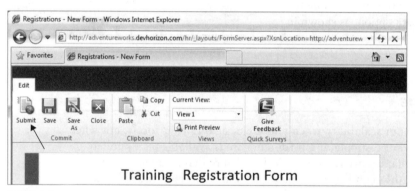

FIGURE 9-34

Some of the behaviors in the Ribbon are customizable from within the form template (Form Options ⇨ Web Browser). For example, you can hide the Save button and leave Submit as the only option to persist the form's data.

Form Programming

The requirements of the registration form dictate two more use cases to be implemented, so there is still some work to do before you can consider this form complete. First, employees at Adventure Works must be able to submit their registrations using their mobile devices. Second, when employees select a training course in the default view, training details should appear in a section control at the bottom of the form.

To implement a mobile-friendly registration form, you need to write custom code in the form's load event to detect whether the form is rendered in a mobile browser, and then switch the default view to a lighter view accordingly. There is guidance about this code below.

Nearly everything in the mobile view is identical to the default view with three exceptions. First, nobody enjoys writing a biography while being mobile, so the optional Short BIO control needs to be hidden. Second, because the People Picker Control is rendered as just a textbox in mobile web browsers (there is no search for a user capability), it should be hidden as well. Third, the mobile view doesn't have the training details section. Instead, the mobile view needs to store a value in a field to indicate that the form is being submitted using a mobile browser.

BEST PRACTICE #6

Unlike InfoPath 2007, where you could explicitly set "Enable rendering on a mobile device" in the form option, in InfoPath 2010 every form can be viewed on mobile devices by default. The key differences in rendering between desktop web browsers and browsers on handheld or mobile devices require taking into account special considerations when designing a form template for use on a mobile device. There are limitations on the behavior of some controls when rendered in mobile web browsers. There are unsupported controls and controls that are rendered as plain textboxes such as the Date/Time Picker and People/Group Picker.

To write custom code in your form and work with the InfoPath object model, the minimum requirements are:

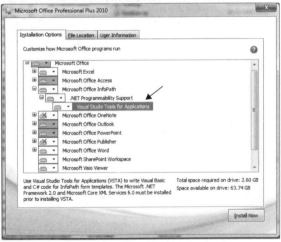

FIGURE 9-35

➤ Microsoft .Net Framework 2.0, Microsoft .Net Framework 2.0 SDK, and Microsoft Core XML Services 6.0.

➤ Visual Studio Tools for Applications (VSTA). By default, this is an optional component and is not selected in the InfoPath installation tree of the Microsoft Office setup application. You should explicitly set this component to Run from My Computer when you install InfoPath 2010, as shown in Figure 9-35.

➤ Selection of the default programming language (C# or VB.NET) to use when writing the code for a form. This can be set on the Developer ➪ Language. The programming language can be changed only before any code has been written for the form, so for example, you cannot mix and match VB.NET and C# code in one form.

BEST PRACTICE #7

In InfoPath 2010, you can write custom code in different versions of the
InfoPath object model and use C# or Visual Basic as the primary language.
It's a best practice to select your language and its compatibility mode based on
what you want to accomplish. For example, if you are writing custom code for
an InfoPath 2007–compatible form, then your options should be either Visual
Basic (InfoPath 2007–compatible) or C# (InfoPath 2007–compatible). In any other
situation, Visual Basic or C# (without the word "compatible" next to the language
name) must be selected as your preferred language.

To begin implementing the mobile view, you need to create the mobile field. In the Fields task pane,
click Add Field and define a field named `IsMobileField` of type `True/False(Boolean)`. Next,
follow the same steps outlined earlier to create a new view in the registration form named Mobile.
Simply copy and paste everything from the default view into the new view, and change the title
to something different to differentiate between views. In mobile view, delete the entire rows that
contain Short BIO and Manager controls to make the form more compact. Next, you need to select
Loading Event from the Developer tab. This will launch the code editor, and you're now ready to
begin developing in VSTA (Visual Studio Tools for Applications), as shown in Figure 9-36.

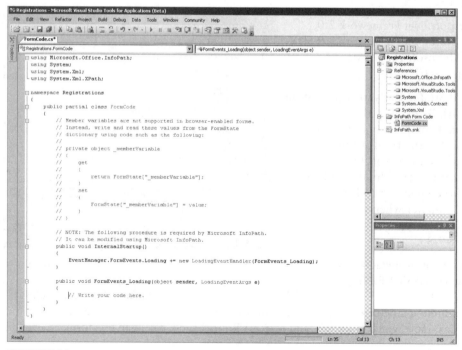

FIGURE 9-36

While it's entirely possible to write the code for event handlers beforehand and wire them up manually later by changing the form definition file (.xsf), the approach recommended by Microsoft is to create the event handlers in design mode — just as you did for the Form Load event. This way, InfoPath automatically creates the declarations of the event handlers in the code and makes the required modification to the form definition file that enables a form template to use those event handlers. The form definition file (.xsf) will be covered in greater detail later in this chapter.

The first step is to complete the `FormEvents_Loading` event handler, as shown in Listing 9-1. The event handler uses the `MainDataSource` property of the `XMLForm` class to call the `CreateNavigator` method to return an instance of the `XPathNavigator` class. The returned object defines a random and read-only access cursor model over the form's underlying XML data, which at this point is positioned at the root node.

Using the InfoPath object model, you can access and change pretty much everything in the form at runtime. You just need to know how to get a reference to the element you wish to change. Thankfully, the underlying data in InfoPath is all XML, so `XPathNavigator` and `XmlForm` classes can be easily used for interacting with the form's data. The `XmlForm` object is initialized in the form load, so you don't need to use the `this` keyword in C# (or the `Me` keyword in Visual Basic) to access its members, such as `MainDataSource` or `NamespaceManager`.

Next, the code uses the `Environment` object to determine which runtime environment and program was used to open the form. This class provides a property called `IsMobile`, which returns `true` if the form is viewed by a mobile browser.

Finally, the overloaded `SelectSingleNode` method is used to navigate to the `IsMobileField` field. Then, the code uses the `SetValue` method of the second `XPathNavigator` object to set the value of the field to `true`; otherwise, it is set to `false`. The `SelectSingleNode` method takes an XPath expression (string) and a resolver parameter for resolving namespace prefixes (via the `NamespaceManager` property of the `XmlForm` class). To determine the absolute XPath to the `IsMobileField` field in the `SelectSingleNode` method, right-click the field in the Fields task pane in InfoPath Designer, and from the context menu, click Copy XPath.

LIISTING 9-1: Code for Setting the IsMobileField Value

```
public void FormEvents_Loading(object sender, LoadingEventArgs e)
    {
        XPathNavigator rootNav = MainDataSource.CreateNavigator();
        if (Environment.IsMobile)
        {
            XPathNavigator mobileFieldNav = rootNav.SelectSingleNode(
"/my:myFields/my:IsMobileField", NamespaceManager);
            mobileFieldNav.SetValue("true");
        }
    }
```

Code Training Registration Form.xsn (FormCode.cs)

To fulfill the second business requirement of the registration form, there should be a section in the registration form that tracks the training details such as address, cost, start date, and so forth.

This section and all its contents will appear only in the default view, because the mobile view should be kept as light as possible. Additionally, this section appears only when an employee selects a training opportunity from the Event Name Drop-Down Listbox control; otherwise, it is hidden.

To implement this dynamic behavior, in the Fields task pane click Add Field and create a field named `HideEventDetailsField` of type `True/False(boolean)`. You will use this field to show/hide the Event Details section in the default view. Next, add a new row to the form's main table after the People Picker control, and insert a section (available in the Controls gallery on the Home tab) to the new row. Next, add a new table to the section and insert three textboxes in each row to host Start Date, Cost, and Address controls. Figure 9-37 shows the registration form with the changes applied.

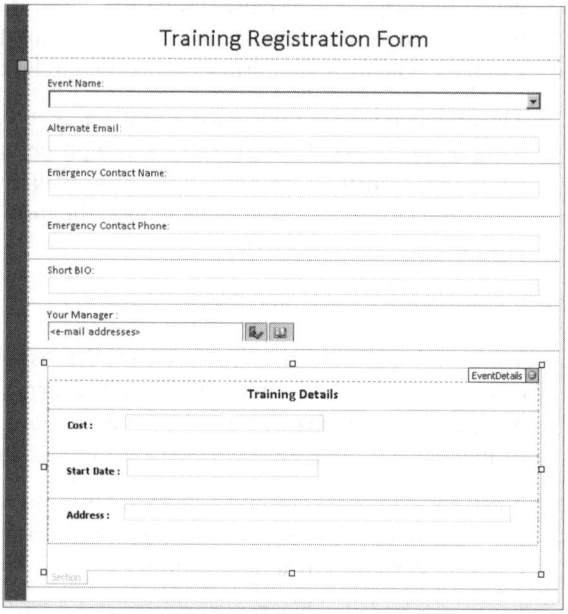

FIGURE 9-37

In InfoPath Designer, select the Event Details section, and then from the Rules task pane, add a new Conditional Formatting rule. With formatting rules in InfoPath 2010, you can apply text formatting and background shading to controls, and disable or highlight controls based on user input or a condition.

On the Conditional Formatting dialog box, click Add, and set up a formatting condition that says:

HideEventDetailsField is equal to TRUE

The last step to complete the formatting rule is to check the Hide this control check box, as shown in Figure 9-38.

At this point, the formatting rule you just created, in conjunction with the custom code in Listing 9-2, ensures that the Event Details section is hidden when the registration form loads in default view.

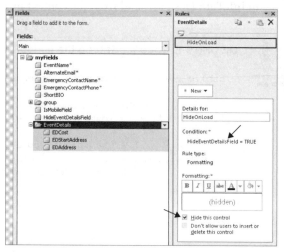

FIGURE 9-38

LISTING 9-2: Code for Setting the HideEventDetailsField Value

```
public void FormEvents_Loading(object sender, LoadingEventArgs e)
    {
        XPathNavigator rootNav = MainDataSource.CreateNavigator();
        if (Environment.IsMobile)
        {
            // Code Omitted for brevity
        }
        else
        {
            XPathNavigator hideEventDetailsFieldNav = rootNav.SelectSingleNode(
"/my:myFields/my:HideEventDetailsField", NamespaceManager);
            hideEventDetailsFieldNav.SetValue("true");
        }
    }
```

Training Registration Form.xsn (FormCode.cs)

With the Event Details section hidden at the form's startup, now you need to add the necessary logic to show this section and populate its content when the Event Name Drop-Down Listbox changes. First, save the form, and then right-click on the EventName field. From the context menu, select Programming ➪ Changed Event to launch VSTA, if it is not already open.

As you can see, the event binding code is placed in the InternalStartup() method of the FormCode.cs (or FormCode.vb) file in your form template project. The binding is done using the XmlChangedEventHandler delegate that represents the method that will handle the Changed event of the EventName field.

```
EventManager.XmlEvents["/my:myFields/my:EventName"].Changed +=
new XmlChangedEventHandler(EventName_Changed);
```

The Event_Changed event handler is autogenerated with no code in it. The code you write in this event handler will use the training code the employee selects from the Event Name drop-down listbox as a key to select the rest of the training's details. After the matching training is found, your code will populate the Event Details section with the rest of the details so that the employee can review the form before saving it, as shown in Listing 9-3.

The first three lines of the code are used to set the HideEventDetailsField field to false so that the formatting rule in the form kicks in and the Event Details section is toggled so that it is visible.

Notice the first bolded lines in the code, where a reference to the Trainings secondary data source is constructed, and an XPathNavigator object is created for accessing the data source. Next, the cursor is positioned at the root of data source and an iterator (of type XPathNodeIterator) over all of the Code nodes is returned. Because the returned XPathNodeIterator object is not pointing to the first node in a selected set of Code nodes, a call to the MoveNext method must be made to position the cursor on the first node in the selected set of nodes. This is done in the While expression.

The rest of the code is simply looping through the selected nodes and finding the one that matches the training code selected by the user. When the control flows into the while loop, two conditions are checked in the beginning:

➤ The training code in the current context node equals the training code selected by the user.

➤ User has not selected a blank value from the Event Name control.

If both of these conditions are met, this means that a node in data source with matching training code has been found. Notice the second bolded lines. The matching node is stored in the matchedTraining variable, and the corresponding XPathNavigator is moved to the parent node of the current Code node, which is the node that contains all the information about the training. The outerXML of the parent node is stored in the training object of type XMLDocument, and a navigator (detailsNav object) is created for it. Another navigator (domNav object) is created to access the fields in the Event Details section of the form.

The rest of the code is pretty straightforward. The controls in the Event details section are populated with information retrieved from the detailsNav navigator object.

LISTING 9-3: Code for EventName_Changed Event Handler

```
public void EventName_Changed(object sender, XmlEventArgs e)
    {
            XPathNavigator rootNav = MainDataSource.CreateNavigator();

            XPathNavigator hideEventDetailsFieldNav = rootNav.SelectSingleNode(
"/my:myFields/my:HideEventDetailsField", NamespaceManager);
            hideEventDetailsFieldNav.SetValue("false");
            XPathNavigator eventNameNav = rootNav.SelectSingleNode(
"/my:myFields/my:EventName", NamespaceManager);

            XPathNavigator trainingsNav = DataSources["Trainings"]
.CreateNavigator();
            trainingsNav.MoveToRoot();
            XPathNodeIterator codeSelectionIterator = trainingsNav.
Select("//*[local-name() = 'Code']");

            while (codeSelectionIterator.MoveNext())
                {
                if (codeSelectionIterator.Current.InnerXml.Equals(eventNameNav.
Value) && !codeSelectionIterator.Current.InnerXml.Equals(""))
                    {

                    XPathNavigator matchedTraining = codeSelectionIterator.
Current;
                    matchedTraining.MoveToParent();
                    XmlDocument training = new XmlDocument();
                    training.LoadXml(matchedTraining.OuterXml);
                    XPathNavigator detailsNav = training.CreateNavigator();
```

```
XPathNavigator domNav = MainDataSource.CreateNavigator();

                    // Populate the Start Date Field
                    XPathNavigator detailNav = detailsNav.
SelectSingleNode("//*[local-name() = 'Start_x0020_Date']");
                    XPathNavigator formNav =
                    domNav.SelectSingleNode(
"/my:myFields/my:EventDetails/my:EDStartAddress", NamespaceManager);
                    String eDate = detailNav.Value;
                    eDate = eDate.Substring(0, 10);
                    formNav.SetValue(eDate);

                    //Populate the Cost Field
                    detailNav = detailsNav.SelectSingleNode(
"//*[local-name() = 'Cost']");
                    formNav = domNav.SelectSingleNode(
"/my:myFields/my:EventDetails/my:EDCost", NamespaceManager);
                    formNav.SetValue(detailNav.Value);

                    // Populate the Address Field
                    detailNav = detailsNav.SelectSingleNode(
"//*[local-name() = 'Address']");
                    formNav = domNav.SelectSingleNode(
"/my:myFields/my:EventDetails/my:EDAddress", NamespaceManager);
                    formNav.SetValue(detailNav.Value);

                    break;
                }
            }

        }
```

Training Registration Form.xsn (FormCode.cs)

BEST PRACTICE #8

As demonstrated in this chapter, the code for an event handler associated with the Changed event that uses the XmlChangedEventHandler delegate should be auto-generated only from within InfoPath Designer 2010. Writing the event handlers beforehand and manually modifying the form definition file (.xsf) to wire them up is not a best practice. This is mainly because changes made to this file outside of InfoPath Designer 2010 might be lost if the form template is modified in InfoPath Designer 2010.

Now, the additional information section and all its contents show up only if an employee selects a training opportunity; otherwise, they are hidden. In general, showing and hiding parts of your forms help you design organized forms in which only relevant information is shown to the users.

Click the Preview button (From the Quick Access Toolbar) to test your form before publishing it. Typically, the Preview button is your friend when designing InfoPath forms; use it as much as possible.

Publishing an InfoPath Form

InfoPath is all about collecting, parsing, and validating data from multiple sources. The data that's collected in a form needs to be persisted somewhere. In the design phase of your forms, it's important to know where the form eventually ends up, because determining the final destination of your form defines your form's publishing model.

Again, just as with submitting a form versus saving it, publishing and saving a form template are not identical processes. Saving a form template is just saving it so that it can be reopened for further changes. However, publishing a form template refers to a process that prepares the form for distribution. If you do not publish a form template, you haven't distributed it properly and users will not be able to fill it out. Unlike list forms, form templates created by InfoPath Designer can be published to a variety of destinations. You can publish them to a SharePoint Server, a list of email recipients, a network location, or a shared folder on a computer, as listed in the Publish tab in the Backstage.

In the Training Management application, the registration forms are saved in a form library called Registrations, which was created earlier in this chapter. Before going any further into the actual process of publishing the Registration Form template, let's iterate through some of pros and cons of publishing to form libraries.

BEST PRACTICE #9

Although SharePoint 2010 makes it very easy to flip out-of-the-box SharePoint list forms to custom InfoPath forms, the traditional approach of publishing to form libraries is still the preferred method in many scenarios.

The most obvious advantage is that you can abstract complex logic in your form by using custom code. As discussed previously, SharePoint list forms do not support custom code.

Not every electronic form contains simple schemas like examples shown in this chapter. The second advantage of using a form library is that you can hide complex schema in your form, while every bit of data in the form's underlying data remains accessible through either InfoPath Designer or the InfoPath Object Model. A SharePoint list is just not sufficient to handle a form with complex schema, period.

Last, but not least, with form libraries, the possibilities are endless. If you know that, at some point in the future, you will need to take advantage of the functionalities that form libraries offer, just start off with a form library in the first place. You cannot convert a list form to a form library.

To publish your form to the Registrations form library, from the Backstage click Publish, and then click on the SharePoint Server button to launch the Publishing Wizard. The wizard is very similar to InfoPath 2007. First, you choose the location of the SharePoint site. Next, you select "Enable this form to be filled out by using a browser" and choose Form Library option, as shown in Figure 9-39.

In the next wizard, specify that the form template should be updated in an existing form library, and from the available libraries choose Registrations. Click Next to proceed to the next step.

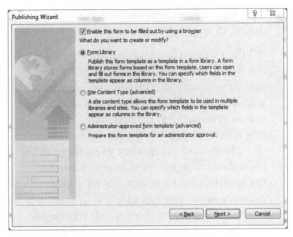

FIGURE 9-39

The next step of the wizard offers two important options:

1. **Property Promotion:** This option allows you to set specific fields in your form to be visible as columns in the SharePoint library, which can be used in SharePoint as metadata or workflow variables.

2. **Web Part Connection Parameter Promotion:** One of the new features in InfoPath 2010 is that forms can participate in web part connections. Unlike SharePoint list forms in which every field is, by default, available to participate in a web part connection scenario, when you publish a form to a SharePoint form library, you need to take explicit actions to determine what fields are available to be used in web part connections. You also need to specify whether a promoted field is used as a subscriber (Input), publisher (Output), or subscriber/publisher (Input/Output) parameter, as shown in Figure 9-40. Obviously, subscriber parameters can only receive data from other web parts but cannot send data. Publisher parameters can send data to other web parts but cannot receive data. More about forms with web part connection will be covered in the "Building Web Parts using InfoPath 2010" section later in this chapter.

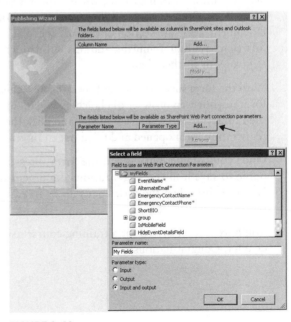

FIGURE 9-40

Both of these options are also available in the Property Promotion category in the Form Options dialog in the Backstage ➪ Info tab.

While it's entirely possible to promote all the fields inside the registration form and make them available as columns, in forms with complex schemas this technique may not be efficient. Again, remember that one reason to use a form library is to hide the schema and encapsulate everything in the form itself. The business requirement for the registration form dictates no property promotion, so you can safely skip this step to the last screen of the wizard, where you are presented with a summary of some of the information collected throughout the Publishing Wizard, as shown in Figure 9-41.

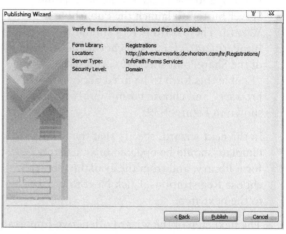

FIGURE 9-41

There are two things that need to be highlighted here. First, in InfoPath 2007, you had to go through the whole Publishing Wizard every time you made a minor change. In InfoPath 2010 and using the Quick Publish option (available in the Quick Access Toolbar), it's very convenient to just use One-Click Publish and have the form template updated in the destination. You only have to go through the Publishing Wizard for the first time or when you want to promote new properties.

Second, unlike with list forms, when a form is published to a form library it cannot be accessed using Form Options in the library settings page or from the Ribbon. Instead, it is configured in the Document Template section of the Advanced Settings option in the library setting page. Click the link that says Edit Template, and this will launch InfoPath Designer 2010 and download the form template for further changes.

With the form successfully published to the Registrations document library, you can now open the form in your web browser of choice. Navigate to the Registrations library, click Documents on the Library Tools contextual menu, and click the New Document button. Figure 9-42 shows the registration form opened and filled out in Internet Explorer 8.

Once you complete filling out the form, press the Save button and give the form a proper name to save it in the Registrations document library. Notice that the Event Details section is not visible when the form loads up or in editing mode, which is exactly what the business requirements call for.

You have just registered for a training course using the same form you developed throughout this chapter. Congratulations!

FIGURE 9-42

This form template can be found in the code download for this book, in the Chapter 9 .zip file. It is called Training Registration Form.xsn.

Publishing to a Form Library vs. Publishing to a Content Type

The form library is a perfect place to host forms, but you should also consider a couple of disadvantages. When you publish your form template directly to a form library, there are two major downsides:

1. One inconvenience of publishing a form template directly to a form library is that the publishing process strongly associates the form template with that particular library; therefore, this approach lacks reusability. If, at any point in the future, you decide to make the same template available in another form library, you need to go through the same publishing process, which can be painful!

2. Another major downside to this approach is that the publishing process creates a 1:1 relationship between the library and the template, which results in lack of support for the heterogeneous types of forms to be stored in the same library. This can quickly lead to chaos for site collection administrators who must deal with many standalone form libraries spread all over the site.

Thankfully, when publishing a form template to SharePoint, you have another option: publishing to a content type. Binding a form template to a content type opens up that template to be reused in other form libraries and essentially addresses all the issues mentioned above.

During the publishing wizard when you promote fields, always make sure that mappings between the promoted fields and the site columns are exactly what you expect them to be; otherwise you may end up causing duplicate site columns and making the previously published site columns orphaned. In the Publishing Wizard (see Figure 9-43), select each field name and click Modify to see the mapping with the site column. Typically, the first time you publish the form template to a server, you expect fields to be promoted to new site columns (see Figure 9-43). Select None: Create new site column in the Site column group drop down list. However, in subsequent republishing processes, you want to map to an existing site column (This Content Type) rather than creating another new column.

If you continue publishing to the same server, the association is remembered in the form's schema and you don't need to take any further action. The problem occurs when you publish a form template to multiple servers and then you come back, make some changes to the form template, and republish it again to the first server. In this case, your promoted site columns are recreated multiple times under the Microsoft Office InfoPath site column group with the same name but different IDs! Remember, always check the mappings before pressing the Publish button in the last step of Publishing Wizard.

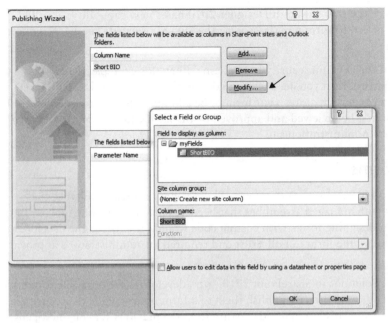

FIGURE 9-43

Form Security

Let's return to the last page of the Publishing Wizard, as shown earlier in Figure 9-41, to address a critical issue: security level. Each form template created in InfoPath 2010 should have one of the available three security levels:

1. Restricted

2. Domain

3. Full Trust

By default, InfoPath Designer 2010 adjusts the security level of your form according to the functionalities included in the form template, and that's the recommended option, as shown in

Figure 9-44. When you start out, all new blank form templates come with the Restricted security level, meaning that the form can only access content inside the form. As you complete your form and add functionality, such as querying SharePoint lists, scripts, or HTTP submit, the security level of the form will be automatically raised to Domain. The Domain security level is the maximum trust level that can be set automatically by InfoPath Designer 2010. This security model allows access outside of the form, but only within the domain in which the form

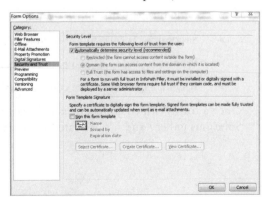

FIGURE 9-44

template physically resides. Note that InfoPath Designer 2010 has a new capability — called Sandbox Solutions — that is tied to form templates with the Domain security model. Sandboxing will be covered in the next section.

If you need to do things that the Domain security level doesn't allow (for example, deploying certificate-signed form templates), then you need to manually set the security level to Full Trust. Note that the Full Trust security level requires your form to be administrator-approved. This means that the form template must first be reviewed and approved by the farm's administrator and then deployed through the Central Administration site.

Sandboxing Your Forms

Like rules and formulas, writing custom code enables form developers to greatly enhance the functionality of their forms with managed assemblies that become part of the form template. In the previous release of InfoPath, designing forms with custom code would have forced the developer to manually set the security level of the form to Full Trust and required an administrator's approval to publish the form.

With the advent of Sandbox Solutions in SharePoint 2010, form developers are now able to sandbox their forms (with managed code) and directly publish them to a form library while the security level of the form is still set to Domain. This is a major departure from the previous version and opens a whole new world of opportunities in browser-enabled forms. If you are interested in knowing more about Sandbox Solutions, you should read chapter 3.

A unique characteristic of Sandbox Solutions is that they run in a partially trusted mode. So, using them doesn't conflict with the Domain security model. Moreover, this means that forms can be deployed using the site collection administrator privilege and right from within the InfoPath Designer, instead of through the Central Administration site.

The sandboxing infrastructure comes from the core platform and is widely used to limit the security vulnerabilities of the farm, while giving developers easy deployment of their code to any site collection.

Sandboxing your forms is a big time saver when developing and deploying electronic forms, but like anything else, it comes with its own limitations. The four major limitations related to electronic forms that have emerged as of this writing are:

➤ Only InfoPath 2010 forms can be sandboxed; there is absolutely no 2007 support.

➤ Sandboxed forms cannot submit to email data sources.

➤ Promoting fields as web part connection parameters is not allowed in Sandbox Solutions.

➤ Any managed metadata control on the form is not allowed in Sandbox Solutions.

Once a form with custom code is published to a SharePoint form library, it ends up in the Solutions gallery and it's activated, by default, as shown in Figure 9-45.

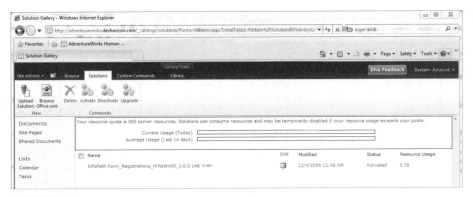

FIGURE 9-45

Essentially, the Solution gallery is a repository for all InfoPath and non-InfoPath Sandbox Solutions deployed to a given site collection. The Solution gallery can be accessed from the site collection's Administration panel (Site Actions ⇨ Site Settings ⇨ Galleries ⇨ Solutions). In addition to the repository at the site collection level, the sandboxing infrastructure uses a Windows service called SharePoint 2010 User Code Host, which is used to host sandboxed solutions within its process to control their behavior, as shown in Figure 9-46.

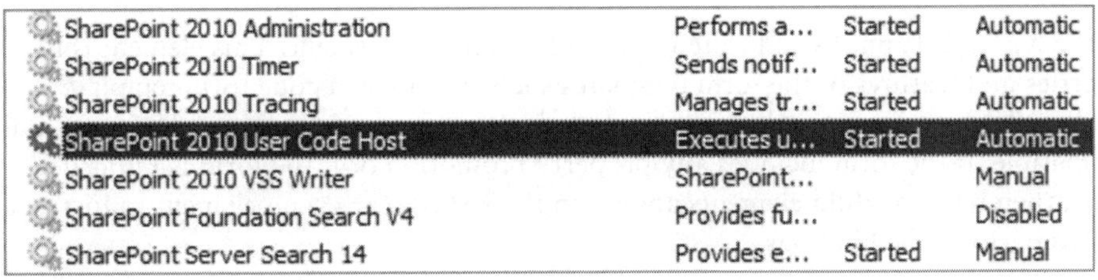

SharePoint 2010 Administration	Performs a...	Started	Automatic
SharePoint 2010 Timer	Sends notif...	Started	Automatic
SharePoint 2010 Tracing	Manages tr...	Started	Automatic
SharePoint 2010 User Code Host	Executes u...	Started	Automatic
SharePoint 2010 VSS Writer	SharePoint...		Manual
SharePoint Foundation Search V4	Provides fu...		Disabled
SharePoint Server Search 14	Provides e...	Started	Manual

FIGURE 9-46

Before you can publish your form to a form library as a Sandbox Solution, you should examine the service status in the Services MMC snap-in. Like other services in SharePoint 2010, this service should be managed only in the Central Administration ⇨ System Settings ⇨ Services on Server ⇨ Microsoft SharePoint Foundation Sandboxed Code Service.

Form Anatomy

The result of saving an InfoPath form template is a file with an .xsn extension. An XSN file is a kind of compressed CAB (cabinet) file that contains other XML files. If you change the extension to .CAB and double-click on the file, it will open the form template as an archive file. Alternatively, you can select Export Source Files from Publish tab in the Backstage to export the source files of a form template. Figure 9-47 shows the exported files for the Registration Form template.

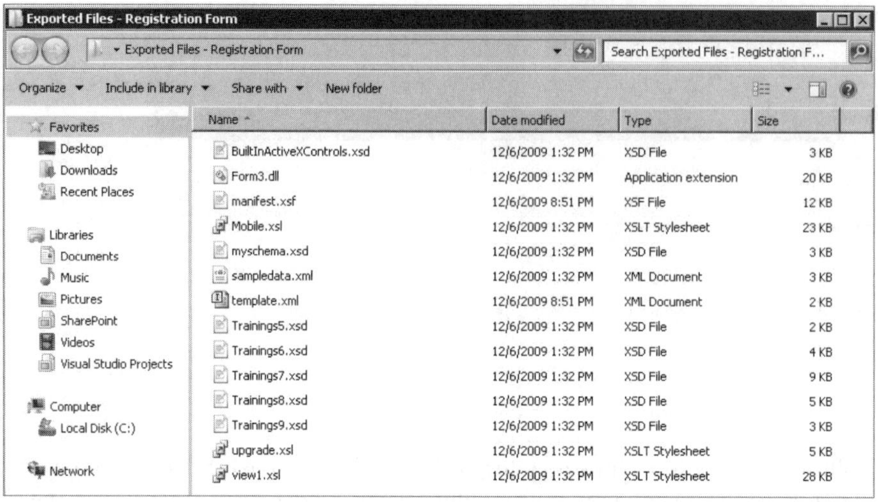

FIGURE 9-47

The form definition file (`manifest.xsf`) contains a listing of all other files that make up the template, as well as other information, including views used in the form, external data sources, and error messages. If you open this file in a text editor such as Notepad and scan it, you will soon realize why this file is considered the heart of the form template.

Scroll through the XML code until you locate the `xsf:extensions` element. This element is used to specify properties and features of the form templates such as managed code form template project settings for VSTA, settings for the views included in the form, and whether the form should be browser-compatible. If the form includes any property promotion or if the form is published to a content type, then relevant child elements appear in the `xsf:extensions` element to instruct SharePoint how to perform the bindings.

As you complete your form design, you should examine the content of `manifest.xsf` often to become familiar with the different parts of the form template and the underlying hooks to the form library.

Toward the end of the `manifest.xsf` file content, there is an `xsf:dataObjects` element that is used to define all the secondary data sources in the form. This element contains a collection of `xsf:dataObject` child elements.

Notice the bolded section in the code snippet below. Within the parent collection, each `xsf:dataObject` element is an in-memory representation (XML Document object model) of the associated external data source. The XML Document Object Model (DOM) programming interface enables form developers to traverse the secondary data source's tree-like structure and manipulate its nodes. The association between the `xsf:dataObject` element and the secondary data source is created via the `xsf:query` element. In this particular example, a SharePoint adaptor that points directly to the Trainings list is used to query for data. The `xsf:dataObject` element also has a `schema` attribute that references the schema file used for the data object — in this example, `Trainings.xsd`. The schema file is also part of the form template (See Figure 9-47).

```
<xsf:dataObjects>
<xsf:dataObject name="Trainings" schema="Trainings5.xsd" initOnLoad="yes">
 <xsf:query>
  <xsf:sharepointListAdapterRW queryAllowed="yes" submitAllowed="no" siteURL="
../../" sharePointListID="{37D0C58F-EA48-44A4-A30E-C26B4ABF6170}"
name="Trainings" contentTypeID="" sortBy="ID" sortAscending="yes"
relativeListUrl="../../Lists/Trainings/">
<xsf:field internalName="Title" required="yes" type="Text"></xsf:field>
<xsf:field internalName="Code" required="yes" type="Text"></xsf:field>
<xsf:field internalName="Description" required="yes" type="Text"></xsf:field>
<xsf:field internalName="Start_x0020_Date" required="yes" type="DateTime">
</xsf:field>
<xsf:field internalName="End_x0020_Date" required="yes" type="DateTime"></xsf:field>
<xsf:field internalName="Cose" required="yes" type="Currency"></xsf:field>
<xsf:field internalName="Level" required="yes" type="Number"></xsf:field>
<xsf:field internalName="Enrollment_x0020_Deadline" required="yes" type="DateTime">
</xsf:field>
<xsf:field internalName="Address" required="yes" type="Plain"></xsf:field>
<xsf:field internalName="Additional_x0020_Information" required="no" type="FullHTML">
</xsf:field>
<xsf:field internalName="ID" required="no" type="Counter"></xsf:field>
  </xsf:sharepointListAdapterRW>
</xsf:query>
</xsf:dataObject>
```

 Data connections inside the InfoPath form template are now relative URLs and are no longer hard-coded.

In addition to the schema files created for each secondary data source, the form template itself maintains a schema for the main XML data that it recognizes in a file named myschema.xsd. Listing 9-4 shows the schema file for the Registration Form template.

The schema file contains a set of predefined types such as boolean and string, as well as new types, for example, complexType and simpleType. In addition to the type declarations, the schema imposes some constraints on the structure and content of the form's data. For example, the my:requiredString type means the element cannot be blank, and the xsd:sequence element defines a specified sequence within the containing element, such as the myFields element.

Notice the first bolded line in Listing 9-4. This line identifies the http://schemas.microsoft. com/office/infopath/2007/PartnerControls namespace, whose schema components (inside the BuiltInActiveXControls.xsd file) are referenced in the myschema.xsd file. This is because of the Manager People Picker Control you placed on the registration form.

Also, notice the myFields bolded section in Listing 9-4, which appears to be the first element in the myschema.xsd file. This element references other elements that each represent a control in the Registration Form template.

While this isn't relevant now, it's important to note that the BuiltInActiveXControls.xsd file also contains the required schema for the External Item Picker control for selecting an instance of an external content type from BCS.

LISTING 9-4: Training Registration Form Schema

```
<?<?xml version="1.0" encoding="UTF-8" standalone="no"?>
<xsd:schema
targetNamespace="http://schemas.microsoft.com/office/infopath/2003/myXSD/2009-12-
02T01:21:42"
xmlns:xsi="http://www.w3.org/2001/XMLSchema-instance"
xmlns:pc="http://schemas.microsoft.com/office/infopath/2007/PartnerControls"
xmlns:my="http://schemas.microsoft.com/office/infopath/2003/myXSD/2009-12-02T01:21:42"
xmlns:xd="http://schemas.microsoft.com/office/infopath/2003"
xmlns:xsd="http://www.w3.org/2001/XMLSchema">
<xsd:import schemaLocation="BuiltInActiveXControls.xsd" namespace="
http://schemas.microsoft.com/office/infopath/2007/PartnerControls"/>
<xsd:element name="myFields">
 <xsd:complexType>
  <xsd:sequence>
    <xsd:element ref="my:EventName" minOccurs="0"/>
    <xsd:element ref="my:AlternateEmail" minOccurs="0"/>
    <xsd:element ref="my:EmergencyContactName" minOccurs="0"/>
    <xsd:element ref="my:EmergencyContactPhone" minOccurs="0"/>
    <xsd:element ref="my:ShortBIO" minOccurs="0"/>
    <xsd:element ref="my:group" minOccurs="0"/>
    <xsd:element ref="my:IsMobileField" minOccurs="0"/>
    <xsd:element ref="my:HideEventDetailsField" minOccurs="0"/>
    <xsd:element ref="my:EventDetails" minOccurs="0"/>
 </xsd:sequence>
<xsd:anyAttribute processContents="lax" namespace=
"http://www.w3.org/XML/1998/namespace"/>
</xsd:complexType>
 </xsd:element>
  <xsd:element name="EventName" type="my:requiredString"/>
  <xsd:element name="AlternateEmail" type="my:requiredString"/>
  <xsd:element name="EmergencyContactName" type="my:requiredString"/>
  <xsd:element name="EmergencyContactPhone" type="my:requiredString"/>
  <xsd:element name="ShortBIO" type="xsd:string"/>
  <xsd:element name="group">
  <xsd:complexType>
   <xsd:sequence>
    <xsd:element ref="pc:Person" minOccurs="0" maxOccurs="unbounded"/>
   </xsd:sequence>
  </xsd:complexType>
 </xsd:element>
  <xsd:element name="IsMobileField" nillable="true" type="xsd:boolean"/>
  <xsd:element name="HideEventDetailsField" nillable="true" type="xsd:boolean"/>
  <xsd:element name="EventDetails">
 <xsd:complexType>
  <xsd:sequence>
   <xsd:element ref="my:EDCost" minOccurs="0"/>
   <xsd:element ref="my:EDStartAddress" minOccurs="0"/>
   <xsd:element ref="my:EDAddress" minOccurs="0"/>
   </xsd:sequence>
  </xsd:complexType>
    </xsd:element>
    <xsd:element name="EDCost" type="xsd:string"/>
    <xsd:element name="EDStartAddress" type="xsd:string"/>
    <xsd:element name="EDAddress" type="xsd:string"/>
```

```
<xsd:simpleType name="requiredString">
<xsd:restriction base="xsd:string">
   <xsd:minLength value="1"/>
   </xsd:restriction>
   </xsd:simpleType>
   <xsd:simpleType name="requiredAnyURI">
   <xsd:restriction base="xsd:anyURI">
   <xsd:minLength value="1"/>
   </xsd:restriction>
   </xsd:simpleType>
   <xsd:simpleType name="requiredBase64Binary">
   <xsd:restriction base="xsd:base64Binary">
   <xsd:minLength value="1"/>
</xsd:restriction>
</xsd:simpleType>
</xsd:schema>
```

Training Registration Form.xsn

 The form's schema file provides a view of the underlying data that the form recognizes at a relatively high level of abstraction. By scanning the schema, you can quickly see that the data is structured in a hierarchy of data types exactly as they appear in the Fields task pane.

The next files to analyze in Figure 9-47 are the `view1.xsl` and `mobile.xsl` files. These two XSL-based files are the views that you created in the form template.

Most of the formatting rules or form-level filters you apply to data end up as XSL code and are placed in the respective view file. For instance, the following code snippet is taken from the view stylesheet for the `EventName` field of the registration form. In this file, you can find how XSL is used to filter the returned training courses in which Enrollment Deadline column contains a value greater than `now()` function.

Three more files in Figure 9-47 warrant some attention.

First, the `Form3.dll` file is the generated assembly for the code you added to `EventName_Changed` and `FormEvents_Loading` event handlers in the Form Programming section. Second, the `template.xml` file contains the actual XML data that is edited by InfoPath. By default, when debugging or previewing a form template, the data in `template.xml` file is used. Optionally, you can create your own data file and instruct InfoPath Designer 2010 to use it when previewing the form in InfoPath Designer 2010 or debugging it in VSTA. First, create a new XML file by copying and pasting the content of the `template.xml` file but with the sample data you want to use. Next, from Form Options, click Preview category. Under Sample Data, type the file location and press the OK button, as shown in Figure 9-48.

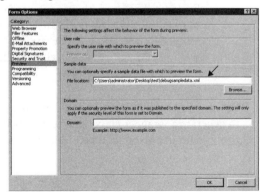

FIGURE 9-48

The third file is `sampledata.XML`. This file specifies the default values of the fields when the form opens in the client or browser application. This file is not used for previewing or debugging purposes, as the `template.xml` file is! In this file, you can only find the field definitions, type, and option to supply a default value and the actual value itself.

Extracting the Form's Data

The last use case to implement is the increment stat counter use case. In the Training Management application, there should be a way to see the total number of registrations for every training course, along with available seats when a registration is selected. To keep this information, you need to create a hidden SharePoint list named Stats, which contains one list item per training course. This list has four fields:

➤ A single line of text field named Code

➤ An integer field called Counter

➤ An integer field called Capacity (Default = 30)

➤ A Calculated field called Available Seats (Capacity – Counter)

The Counter field gets incremental updates every time a registration form is dropped in the Registration form library. One possible solution to implement this use case is to associate an event handler with the Registrations form library that extracts the form's data after the form is saved and updates the counter.

The XML data that is stored in the form library conforms to the form's schema (`myschema.xsd`), so technically any code that conforms to this schema can intercept the XML and interact with it. Recall from an earlier discussion that one of the primary reasons for creating the Registrations form library is to easily access all the data stored within the InfoPath form without having to promote any fields. One advantage of using an event handler over other solutions is that event handlers can run asynchronously with minimal overhead on the form itself.

BEST PRACTICE #10

Before overloading your form with extra functionality, always ask yourself: Does this logic change anything in the form itself? Does the form require this logic to function properly? If the answer is no, then you may need to consider other options. Remember, you develop solutions on top of a rich composite application development platform: SharePoint. The possibilities are endless!

Before you go any further in implementing the event handler, you should use the `XSD.EXE` utility to generate a wrapper class that represents the data elements. This class allows you to access the form's data in a strongly typed fashion instead of parsing the XML data by using XPath (like all the other samples so far). First, navigate to the location of the registration form's exported files (see the previous section) and run the following command:

```
Xsd.exe /c myschema.xsd  BuiltInActiveXControls.xsd
```

The XSD.exe utility is not following the imports and/or includes in myschma.xsd file, so you need to specify the BuiltInActiveXControls.xsd schema file directly on the command line, too. Otherwise, the utility will throw a missing element exception. The generated file is named after the schema files used in the command line, myschema_BuiltInActiveXControls.cs. Change the file name to RegitrationsSchema.cs instead. Note that the generated partial classes in this file are given the same name as the root elements, as shown in Listing 9-5.

LISTING 9-5: Partial myFields Class

```
namespace RegistrationsStatEventHandler {

    using System.Xml.Serialization;

    public partial class myFields {

        private string eventNameField;
        private string alternateEmailField;
        private string emergencyContactNameField;
        private string emergencyContactPhoneField;
        private string shortBIOField;
        private Person[] groupField;
        private System.Nullable<bool> isMobileFieldField;
        private bool isMobileFieldFieldSpecified;
        private System.Nullable<bool> hideEventDetailsFieldField;
        private bool hideEventDetailsFieldFieldSpecified;
        private EventDetails eventDetailsField;
        private System.Xml.XmlAttribute[] anyAttrField;


        public string EventName {
            get {
                return this.eventNameField;
            }
            set {
                this.eventNameField = value;
            }
        }

        public string AlternateEmail {
            get {
                return this.alternateEmailField;
            }
            set {
                this.alternateEmailField = value;
            }
```

```
        }
        public string EmergencyContactName {
            get {
                return this.emergencyContactNameField;
            }
            set {
                this.emergencyContactNameField = value;
            }
        }
        public string EmergencyContactPhone {
            get {
                return this.emergencyContactPhoneField;
            }
            set {
                this.emergencyContactPhoneField = value;
            }
        }
        public string ShortBIO {
            get {
                return this.shortBIOField;
            }
            set {
                this.shortBIOField = value;
            }
        }
        public Person[] group {
            get {
                return this.groupField;
            }
            set {
                this.groupField = value;
            }
        }
        public System.Nullable<bool> IsMobileField {
            get {
                return this.isMobileFieldField;
            }
            set {
                this.isMobileFieldField = value;
            }
        }
        public bool IsMobileFieldSpecified {
            get {
                return this.isMobileFieldFieldSpecified;
            }
            set {
                this.isMobileFieldFieldSpecified = value;
            }
        }
        public System.Nullable<bool> HideEventDetailsField {
            get {
                return this.hideEventDetailsFieldField;
            }
            set {
```

```
                    this.hideEventDetailsFieldField = value;
            }
        }
        public bool HideEventDetailsFieldSpecified {
            get {
                return this.hideEventDetailsFieldFieldSpecified;
            }
            set {
                this.hideEventDetailsFieldFieldSpecified = value;
            }
        }
        public EventDetails EventDetails {
            get {
                return this.eventDetailsField;
            }
            set {
                this.eventDetailsField = value;
            }
        }
        public System.Xml.XmlAttribute[] AnyAttr {
            get {
                return this.anyAttrField;
            }
            set {
                this.anyAttrField = value;
            }
        }
    }

    // Code Omitted For Brevity
}
```

RegistrationsStatEventHandler\ RegistrationsSchema.cs

With the wrapper class generated by the XSD.EXE tool, you can start coding the event handler. Start Visual Studio 2010, and create a new project using the Event Receiver template. Next, choose Deploy as a farm solution and click the Next button. Finally, select your event receiver type to be List Item Events, Form Library as the event source, and An item is being added for the event to hook up, as shown in Figure 9-49.

After you finish the wizard, Visual Studio will stub out all the necessary code and the Feature and Solution package necessary to deploy this event handler as a farm WSP solution.

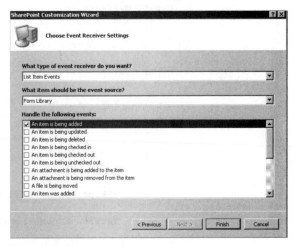

FIGURE 9-49

At this point, you can add to your project the wrapper class (RegitrationsSchema.cs) that the XSD.EXE utility generated.

If you ever make changes to the form's schema, you will need to rerun the XSD.EXE *utility against the new schema file, and then just delete the old wrapper class and add the new one to the project.*

When the package is deployed and the associated feature is activated, the callout code in Listing 9-6 is used to access and increment the counter value in the Stats list for a particular training. Next, you will want to rename EventReceiver1.cs to UpdateStatSink.cs and add the call out code within the class to override the ItemAdded method.

In the code, notice the first bolded section. In this section, the InfoPath form that was just added is retrieved and stored in a variable of type SPFile. Next, InfoPath's XML file is deserialized into a strongly typed C# object of type myFields. This is done via a call into a helper method called DeserializeFormData(SPFile,Type), which will be covered a bit later. If the returned object is not null, then a LINQ query is used to see if the selected training code exists in the Stats list.

The second bolded section indicates that if the Count function returns a number greater than zero, it means that the matching training code is found in the Stats list. Then, the code proceeds with incrementing its Counter field by one. This is all done through a call to a second helper method named IncrementCounter(SPListItem). On the opposite, if the matching training code is not found, a new list item is added to the Stats list and the Code and Counter columns are set accordingly.

LISTING 9-6: Overridden ItemAdded Method

```
public override void ItemAdded(SPItemEventProperties properties)
    {
        SPFile ifpFile = properties.ListItem.File;
        myFields fields = (myFields)DeserializeFormData(ifpFile,
        typeof(myFields));
        if (fields != null)
        {

            SPLinqDataContext cdc = new SPLinqDataContext(
"http://adventureworks.devhorizon.com/hr");

            var result = from trs in cdc.Stats
                    where trs.Code.Equals(fields.EventName)
                    select new { trs.Id };

            SPList statList = properties.Web.Lists["Stats"];
            if(result.Count() > 0)
            {
                SPListItem matched = statList.GetItemById((int) result.
First().Id);

                IncrementCounter(matched);
            }
            else
            {
                SPListItem newItem = statList.Items.Add();
```

```
                                    newItem["Code"] =fields.EventName;
                                    newItem["Counter"] = 1;
                                    newItem.Update();
                                }

                            }

                        }
```

Listing 9-7 demonstrates the `DeserializeFormData()` helper method, which was called from the `ItemAdded` method. This method starts with receiving two parameters of type `SPFile` and `Type`. In the code, the `SPFile` parameter is opened in binary format and the actual content is stored in a `byte` array, which is read it into a memory stream a bit later.

Notice the highlighted lines in the code. First, a new instance of the `XmlSerializer` class is initialized and an object of type `rootElementType` is serialized into it. The `rootElementType` parameter is of type `myFields`, because that's what passed in to it from the `ItemAdded` code. In the next line, a new `XmlReader` instance is created using the memory stream and, in the line after, it's deserialized into the `result` variable. Finally, the `result` variable is returned to the caller, which contains the actual content of the form data in a strongly typed object.

LISTING 9-7: DeserializeFormData Helper Method

Available for download on Wrox.com

```
private object DeserializeFormData(SPFile ipfFile, Type rootElementType)
        {
            byte[] xmlFormData = ipfFile.OpenBinary();
            object result = null;
            if (xmlFormData != null)
            {
                using (MemoryStream fileStream = new MemoryStream(xmlFormData))
                {
                    XmlSerializer serializer = new XmlSerializer(rootElementType);
                    XmlReader reader = XmlReader.Create(fileStream);
                    result = serializer.Deserialize(reader);
                    fileStream.Close();
                }
            }

            return result;
        }
```

Listing 9-8 demonstrates the second helper method used in the `ItemAdded` method. The only thing that needs to be highlighted about this method is the extra logic that is written to handle race condition when multiple instances of the event handler try to update the Counter column in the Stats list. This condition can occur when two or more registration forms are saved at the same time by different users.

Thankfully, the SharePoint object model automatically locks the list tem when retrieving and incrementing the Counter field's value, so all you need to do is to place your code in a try/catch block. If race condition occurs, the SharePoint object model throws an exception, meaning the existing counter value is dirty. If the value is considered dirty, there will be three attempts to retrieve and increment it. If all three attempts fail, the exception will be logged and the update won't happen.

LISTING 9-8: IncrementCounter Helper Method

```csharp
private void IncrementCounter(SPListItem item)
    {
        int retryUpdate = 0;

    doUpdate:
        try
        {
            int currentCounter = int.Parse(item["Counter"].ToString());
            item["Counter"] = currentCounter + 1;
            item.Update();
        }
        catch (Exception ex)
        {
            retryUpdate += 1;
            if (retryUpdate <= 3)
            {
                System.Threading.Thread.Sleep(3000);
                goto doUpdate;
            }
            else
            {
                // Log the exception
            }
        }
    }
```

RegistrationsStatEventHandler\UpdateStatSink\UpdateStatSink.cs

The last step to getting your event handler to work is to update the Class node in the Elements.xml to include the changes you have just made to the project. Listing 9-9 shows the Elements.xml file of the Feature that has been added to the project by Visual Studio 2010. This file identifies the assembly's fully qualified name, class (UpdateStatSink), and ItemAdded method to implement in the event handler.

In this particular example, the event handler is associated with all the form libraries of the site as specified by the ListTemplateId attribute in the bold line. In general, this is not an ideal situation. Instead, the event handler should be associated with a content type or a particular custom form library so that it is not kicked off every form library in the site.

LISTING 9-9: Elements.xml File

```xml
<<?xml version="1.0" encoding="utf-8"?>
<Elements xmlns="http://schemas.microsoft.com/sharepoint/">
  <Receivers ListTemplateId="115">
    <Receiver>
```

```
        <Name>RegistrationsStatEventHandlerItemAdding</Name>
        <Type>ItemAdded</Type>
        <Assembly>$SharePoint.Project.AssemblyFullName$</Assembly>
        <Class>RegistrationsStatEventHandler.UpdateStatSink</Class>
        <SequenceNumber>10000</SequenceNumber>
      </Receiver>
  </Receivers>
</Elements>
```

RegistrationsStatEventHandler\UpdateStatSink\Elements.xml

All you need to do is to press F5! Visual Studio will deploy the WSP package as a farm solution and activate the features, and the event handler will be associated with all the form libraries on the site. Navigate to Central Administration site ⇨ Solution Management and verify that the solution has been successfully deployed, as shown in Figure 9-50.

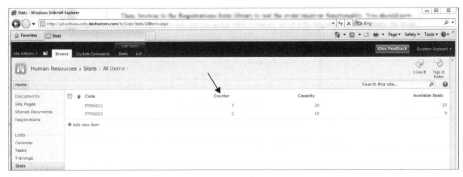

FIGURE 9-50

To prove this, browse to the Registrations library and create a new registration form. You should now have a fully functional solution so that when forms are saved to the Registrations form library, the event handler is kicked off to update the related counter in the Stats list, as shown in Figure 9-51.

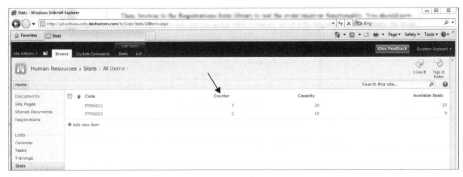

FIGURE 9-51

TOOLS FOR FORM DEVELOPERS

As you have seen so far, InfoPath 2010, along with Form Services 2010, provides a highly extensible platform on which you can build electronic forms that play an important role in various business processes across your organization.

Thankfully, a number of tools and utilities can make the form development journey much easier. Also, these tools can be used to investigate the issues that may arise during the lifecycle of your InfoPath projects. While it's entirely out of the scope of this book to evaluate all existing tools and utilities, let's have a quick look at a few of them that you will no doubt leverage when working with InfoPath forms.

The Rule Inspector

When adding declarative business logic or even custom code (imperative logic) to your form, it is often challenging to keep track of all fields and groups that invoke this logic or how this logic may affect other fields, groups, or logic in the form template.

To address this challenge, InfoPath Designer 2010 includes a tool called the Rule Inspector (formerly known as the Logic Inspector). When you access this tool, you initially see either the Overview pane alone or both the Overview pane and the Details pane, depending on how the tool is accessed, as shown in Figure 9-52.

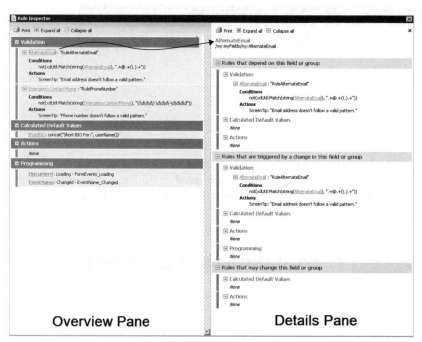

FIGURE 9-52

The overview pane on the left lists all of the business logic currently used in the form template, grouped into four categories: Validation, Calculated Default Values, Actions, and Programming. This grouping allows you to easily see what fields or groups contain the business logic, the type of the logic, and some information about each rule. If you click on any orange links in the overview pane, the details pane expands with more specific information, mostly about dependencies on other fields, groups, or rules in the form. Although the imperative logic in the Programming group is not disassembled, it is still helpful to see a high level view of the code behind, without having to launch VSTA.

For many form developers, when troubleshooting or reviewing an InfoPath form, the Rule Inspector is a helpful tool, and the first place they go after they open the form in the design mode.

The Design Checker

In InfoPath 2010, one of the driving forces behind browser-enabled forms was parity with the InfoPath client and parity with SharePoint. Although a lot of previously unsupported controls and scenarios are now supported in browser-enabled forms, before you publish your form to SharePoint, you should still run the Design Checker to identify incompatibility issues and to ensure that your form template works correctly. This tool can be found in the Info tab in the Backstage, as shown in Figure 9-53. The text in the middle indicates that the form template is currently compatible with Forms Services as a web browser form.

FIGURE 9-53

The compatibility mode of the form can be changed via the Form Options ➪ Compatibility category, as shown in Figure 9-54. Additionally, you have the option to specify the destination site's URL (or the URL for the Forms Services web service). The advantage of this is that during the design check process, the form is verified on the server without your having to walk through the full Publishing Wizard and later verify the form in the browser.

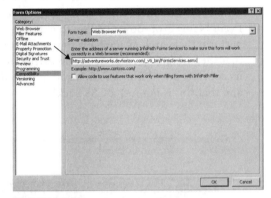

FIGURE 9-54

With the compatibility settings applied, you can click the Design Checker button in the Backstage to bring up the Design Checker task pane. At this point, all local and online checks are performed, and potential errors or warnings are revealed in the task pane, as shown in Figure 9-55.

Typically, errors will prevent the form template from being published as a browser-enabled form. However, warnings can be discarded, which may result in a dysfunctional browser-enabled form. Simply go through the list of issues, review them, and take appropriate actions to resolve them.

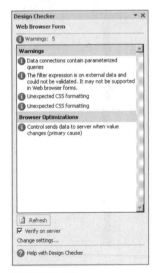

FIGURE 9-55

IE Developer Tools

Internet Explorer 8 ships with a powerful set of tools called Developer Tools, which you can access by pressing F12 or by selecting the Developer Tools from the Tools menu.

In browser-enabled forms, this tool can help form developers see what's going on underneath the HTTP request and simplifies the process of debugging their forms. In addition, IE8 Developer Tools provide visibility into IE's internal representation of the form and allow developers to switch between different document and browser modes (IE 7, IE 8, and IE8 Compatibility View) to ensure that the form renders properly when viewed across different versions of Internet Explorer.

Another interesting usage of IE Developer Tools is to learn how the underlying HTML is populated from the form's data elements, because there have been a lot of improvements in this area in the new release of InfoPath 2010.

For example, navigate to the Registrations form library and click on the New Document in the Ribbon to load the registration form. Do not select any training yet. Start the Developer Tools and search for the word "Cost" (one of the controls on the Event Details Section). As you can see, there is no HTML element that represents the Cost control yet. Now, select a training course from the Event Name drop-down listbox to make the details section visible. Press F5 to refresh the tool and perform the search again. This time the Cost control is found, as shown in Figure 9-56. This proves that the formatting rule you set up earlier in this chapter to make the Event Details section and all its controls invisible at form's loading, indeed, doesn't include them in the form's underlying HTML and that this is not just a CSS hack!

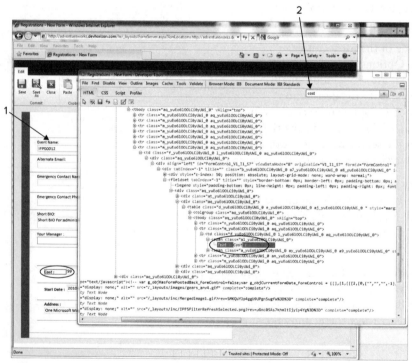

FIGURE 9-56

Fiddler Tool

When an InfoPath form is rendered in the browser, two types of transactions happen behind the scenes: initial load and postback. The initial load transaction occurs when first opening the form. It loads the form's HTML and the required resources (for example, JavaScript), so the form can be edited in the browser.

As the user interacts with the form, one or more postbacks to the server are made, so the State Service (a new service application used by Forms Services 2010) can store temporary data for user sessions in a SQL database. At this point, the conversation between the form and server is used to recreate the state of the form across related HTTP requests. The final postback occurs when the form is either submitted or saved and finally closed.

You can use Fiddler to watch all HTTP traffic between the form and server. One of the reasons that you may want to use this tool is to identify unnecessary postbacks and adjust your form design or logic to avoid them. For example, by using Fiddler and after monitoring the Trainings list custom InfoPath form (see the "Customizing SharePoint List Forms" section), it's obvious that having an Additional Information control in an optional section may cause a lot of unnecessary round trips to the server.

Figure 9-57 shows all the partial postbacks to the server (`/_layouts/Postback.FormServer.aspx`) as a result of adding and removing the Additional Information control several times. Do you really need this control to be in an optional section? Is it worth all these potential postbacks that users may cause? Truthfully, there is no definite answer to these types of questions, but one thing is crystal clear here, thanks to Fiddler: the optional section causes unnecessary postbacks. If you don't need it, just get rid of it.

 You can use Fiddler or Visual Studio's Web Test Recorder to record all HTTP requests between a browser-enabled InfoPath form and the server. The recorded information can be saved as web test files and added to Visual Studio Team Edition for Testers projects. For more information, see InfoPath Forms Services 2007 Web Testing Toolkit at `http://www.devhorizon.com/go/15`.

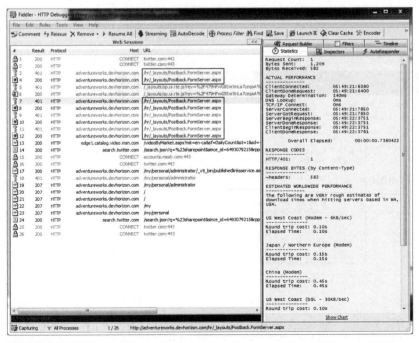

FIGURE 9-57

Tiny Inline Tools

In addition to the tools discussed so far, there are two more tools that can be executed right from within Internet Explorer when the form first loads:

1. `IP_DebugComplexity.ComposeSummary()`

2. `CurrentFormData_OptimizedForFirstRequest()`

As its name implies, the first tool provides a summary of the following counters in a browser-enabled form:

➤ View Data Tree Node

➤ Included Hidden Controls

➤ HTML InfoPath Controls

➤ HTML Elements

As shown in Figure 9-58, in order to run this tool, you should type the following JavaScript code into the address bar of the browser and press the Enter key.

```
javascript:alert(IP_DebugComplexity.ComposeSummary())
```

The Compose Summary tool doesn't fix anything in the form, nor does it give you guidelines on how to fix the issues. It just provides some facts that can be used to reduce the form's complexity. The total number of HTML elements that a form produces is an important factor in measuring the form's complexity.

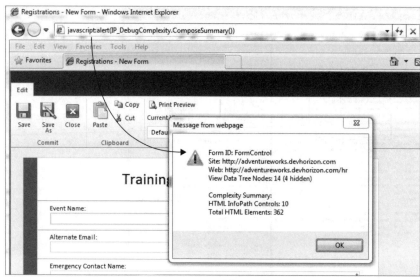

FIGURE 9-58

The second tool is used to see if the form is optimized for the initial load. As with the complexity tool, all you need to do is type the following JavaScript code into the address bar and press the Enter key:

```
javascript:alert(CurrentFormData_OptimizedForFirstRequest('FormControl'))
```

This tool spits out `true` or `false`. True means that the form is first-request optimized, and false means it's not. If the result is false, review your form design to find the potential issues and fix them.

BUILDING WEB PARTS USING INFOPATH

In Forms Service 2007, the out-of-the-box behavior for rendering browser-enabled forms is to use a call to the `FormServer.aspx` layout page and pass the `.XSN` location of the published form as a query string parameter (`?XsnLocation=|0`). Unfortunately, this technique presents a few challenges.

First, the displayed form occupies the entire page, and it does not reference either the application or system Master Pages. This limitation results in an inconsistent look and feel between the published InfoPath forms and the rest of the site's pages. The second issue is related to the first issue, because once the users visually lose the overall look and feel of the site, they think the form has opened in a brand new page. Therefore, they may close the browser once they have completed filling out the form. Obviously, closing the browser results in losing the state and context of the site — again, this is not ideal! The third issue is that, because the form is rendered on a completely different page from the one that was requested, it is not easy to establish a conversation with the form without passing additional query string parameters to the `FormServer.aspx` page and using custom coding in the form template to read those parameters.

Although there are a few solutions for embedding InfoPath forms in SharePoint pages, such as using the `XmlFormView` web part (in the `Microsoft.Office.InfoPath.Server` assembly) or boxing the `XmlFormView` ASP.NET control in your own web part, none of these solutions truly represent a tight integration between the form template and the rest of the functionalities on the page. Needless to say, they all require common SharePoint development techniques and configuration steps.

In this section, we will look at some of the ways Microsoft has improved the integration between InfoPath and SharePoint.

InfoPath Form Web Part

In SharePoint Server 2010, it's much easier than ever to host your forms on SharePoint pages using a brand new web part called the InfoPath Form web part. Assuming that you've already created a SharePoint web part page called the Trainings Dashboard, there are a couple easy steps for configuring the InfoPath Form web part on that page.

On the Trainings Dashboard page, click Add a Web Part in the left column Web Part zone. On the Page menu, select Office Client Applications category ⇨ InfoPath Form Web Part, and then click the Add button. Next, click on the link in the web part to open the Tool pane. Select the Registrations form library and Click OK, as shown in Figure 9-59. As you can see, the Content Type is set to Form, because that's the only content type currently available in the Registrations form library. If you have published your form to a content type, you need to specify it in the Content Type drop-down. Also, note that you have the option to exclude the InfoPath toolbar (also called the Ribbon), in case you have implemented custom submit behavior.

FIGURE 9-59

Using InfoPath to Create Connected Web Parts

In addition to InfoPath Form web part, another major improvement in browser-enabled forms is the addition of a new rule action called "Send data To Web Part." This rule can run anytime you can run an action in InfoPath, for example, on a form's loading or submission, on the click of a button, or on changing a field. This action allows users to build InfoPath forms that interact with other web parts on the same page or across two pages, all without a single line of code.

The web part connection scenario you build here enables Adventure Works employees to see the total number of available seats for a particular training course on their Trainings Dashboard. The registration form is used as a source that filters the Stats List View web part using a web part connection.

Recall from the "Publishing an InfoPath Form" section that one of the two promotion options you get in the Publishing Wizard is to promote fields as web part connection parameters.

On the registration form, add a Picture button next to the Event Name drop-down listbox. The Picture Button control (new in InfoPath 2010) supports all the actions that a standard button supports, but it allows you to use an image as a button, instead of the default ugly gray rectangular shape. Right-click on the control, and set an image to the control. The picture button can show a different picture when the user hovers over it.

Next, in the Rules task pane for the picture button, click Add and select "Send Data To Web Part," as shown in Figure 9-60. Selecting this option will bring up the Rule Details dialog box, where you need to specify which fields will be participating in the web part connection. Select the EventName field as an output parameter, and click OK to promote the field.

This action rule is enabled when two conditions are met. The first is when the condition in the rule is satisfied. By default, this condition is set to "None-Rule runs when button is clicked," but you can change the condition to satisfy your needs. The second condition is that a connection

FIGURE 9-60

has been established between InfoPath web part, containing the Registration Form template, and another web part.

With the picture button and "Send Data to Web Part" rule action in place, use the Quick Publish option and publish the form to the Registrations form library.

But the journey isn't over yet!

The Publishing Wizard errors out, referring you to the Design Checker for more information, as shown in Figure 9-61.

FIGURE 9-61

The error message is self-explanatory. You can't sandbox a form with promoted fields as web part connection parameters. Instead, you should switch the security model of your form to administrator-approved and publish it through the Central Administration site.

To begin the process of publishing your form as an administrator-approved form template, go to the Forms option, and under Security and Trust, select the Full Trust option. Next, from the Publish tab in the Backstage, choose SharePoint Server and go through the wizard one more time. Notice that in the second screen step (see Figure 9-62), the first two options are grayed out. In the next step, you will be asked to save the form template so that the farm administrator can review the form and take further action. You will also notice that the EventName field you just promoted as a web part connection parameter shows up in the property promotion step. Complete the Publishing Wizard and provide the farm administrator with the information in the last step of the Publishing Wizard.

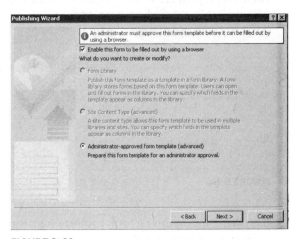

FIGURE 9-62

Switching hats here, let's suppose that you are the farm administrator and you have reviewed the form template and it looks harmless. Now, you want to deploy it. Navigate to the Central Administration site, and from the General Application Settings, click Upload form template under the InfoPath Forms Services category to upload the form and make it available on the farm, as shown in Figure 9-63.

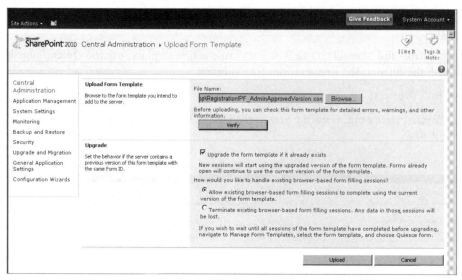

FIGURE 9-63

If everything has gone smoothly, you should be able to see the status of the uploaded form template change from Installing to Ready after a couple of seconds. At this point, select Activate to a Site Collection to activate the form as a feature on a specified site collection (see Figure 9-64). Alternatively, you can browse to any site collection and activate the feature yourself. Just remember, it is a site collection feature.

Type	Name		Version	Modified	Category	Status	Workflow Enabled
	RegistrationIPF_AdminApprovedVersion.xsn ▼		1.0.0.200	12/10/2009		Ready	No
	Coll	View Properties	14.0.0.0	11/19/2009	Workflow	Ready	Yes
	ddw	Activate to a Site Collection	14.0.0.0	11/19/2009	Workflow	Ready	Yes
	Exp	Deactivate from a Site Collection	14.0.0.0	11/19/2009	Workflow	Ready	Yes
	Xlat	Quiesce Form Template	14.0.0.0	11/19/2009	Workflow	Ready	Yes
		✕ Remove Form					

FIGURE 9-64

But what happens after a form template is activated on a site collection? This is a major point of confusion for many people who deploy an administrator-approved InfoPath form for the first time.

Essentially, activating an administrator-approved form adds a new content type to the site collection with the InfoPath form attached to it. Recall from the earlier discussion that attaching an InfoPath form to a content type makes it much more reusable and is a more compelling approach than strongly associating a form with a form library.

Figure 9-65 shows how you can add the new content type to the Registrations from library. It's no different from adding any content type to a document library.

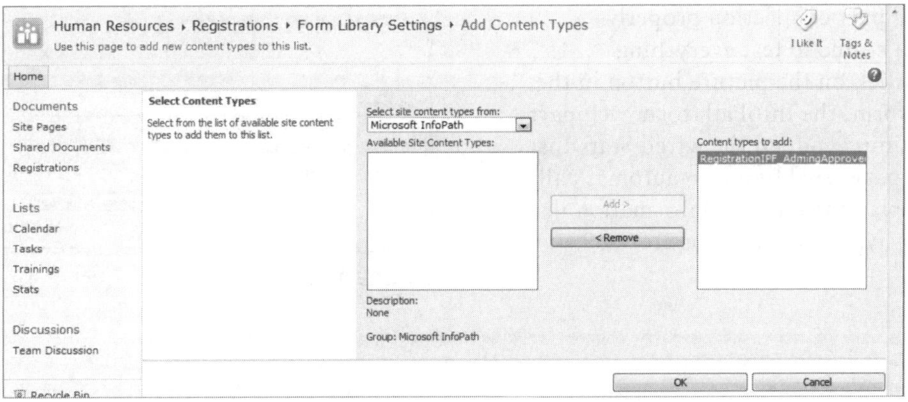

Human Resources › Registrations › Form Library Settings › Add Content Types

Use this page to add new content types to this list.

I Like It   Tags & Notes

Home

Documents
Site Pages
Shared Documents
Registrations

Lists
Calendar
Tasks
Trainings
Stats

Discussions
Team Discussion

Recycle Bin

Select Content Types

Select from the list of available site content types to add them to this list.

Select site content types from:
Microsoft InfoPath

Available Site Content Types:

Add >

< Remove

Content types to add:
RegistrationIPF_AdmingApprove

Description:
None

Group: Microsoft InfoPath

OK   Cancel

FIGURE 9-65

With the new content type added to the Registrations form library, you can start putting different pieces together and finalize the web part connection scenario. Go back to the Trainings Dashboard and delete the old InfoPath form web part and add a new one. Again, make it point to the Registrations library, but this time around, you have a new content type added to the form library that you can choose in the Content Type drop-down, as shown in Figure 9-66.

Now, add the Stats List View web part to the right column Web Part zone on the Trainings Dashboard and establish a web part connection, as shown in Figure 9-67. Next, a pop-up window called Configure Connection – Webpage Dialog asks about the provider and consumer fields used in the web part connection, as shown in Figure 9-68. In this example, the EventName field from the form template and the Code column from the Stats list are the publisher and the consumer, respectively.

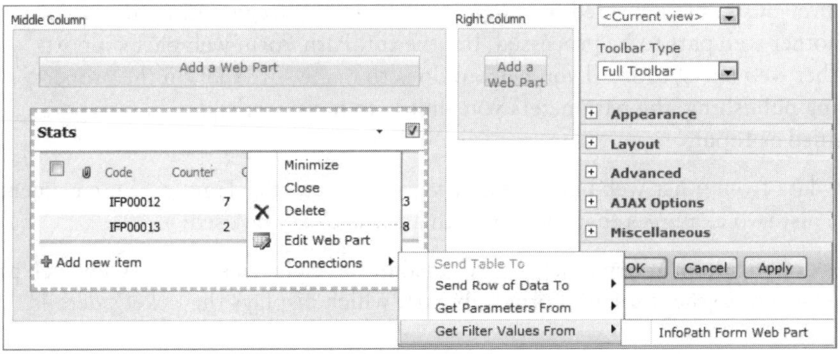

InfoPath Form Web Part

InfoPath Form

Use this Web Part to fill out an InfoPath form that has been published to a SharePoint list or document library.

List or Library:
Registrations

Content Type:
RegistrationIPF_AdminApprovedVersion

☐ Display a read-only form (lists only)

☑ Show InfoPath Ribbon or toolbar

FIGURE 9-66

Middle Column

Add a Web Part

Stats

☐ 📎 Code   Counter

IFP00012   7

IFP00013   2

➕ Add new item

Minimize
Close
✖ Delete
Edit Web Part
Connections

Right Column

Add a Web Part

<Current view>

Toolbar Type
Full Toolbar

⊞ **Appearance**
⊞ **Layout**
⊞ **Advanced**
⊞ **AJAX Options**
⊞ **Miscellaneous**

OK   Cancel   Apply

Send Table To
Send Row of Data To
Get Parameters From
Get Filter Values From   InfoPath Form Web Part

FIGURE 9-67

With the web part connection properly configured, it's time to test everything. When users click on the picture button in the registration form, the InfoPath form web part sends the training code to the wired Stats List View on the page, enabling it to automatically filter and display the relevant information in a customized way, as shown in Figure 9-69.

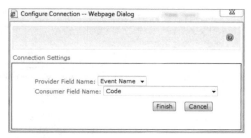

FIGURE 9-68

FIGURE 9-69

 If you are sending a single parameter, you can set the web part connection in the web part page. What if you are sending multiple parameters? You need to use SharePoint Designer 2010 to set up web part connections with multiple parameters.

Getting Data from Other Web Parts

The scenario in the previous section covered only inputting data in the registration form and sending it over to another web part to be processed, but the InfoPath Form web part supports getting data from other web parts, too. All you need to do is to make sure that, in the property promotion step during publishing, the parameters you choose to have participate in web part connection are specified as Input.

Even though getting data from other web parts is not a requirement in the Training Management application, here are just two examples that show how this feature may be used:

1. **In a help desk application:** When a ticket is selected in the Help Tickets List View web part, the Ticket ID is sent to the InfoPath Form web part, which displays the ticket's details.

2. **In a customer relationship management application:** When a customer is selected in the Customers List View web part, the Customer ID is sent to the InfoPath Form web part, which displays the customer requirement details.

Empowering Users with Mashups

In the web development lexicon, *mashup* is a buzzword, as mashups are fast becoming part of many web-based services offered across the Net. People have different perceptions about the term mashup and different images of it.

According to Wikipedia:

> *A mashup is a web page or application that combines data or functionality from two or more external sources to create a new service. The term mashup implies easy, fast integration, frequently using open APIs and data sources to produce results that were not the original reason for producing the raw source data.*

As for SharePoint, Wikipedia's definition helps describe that SharePoint is already a mashup! But why?

SharePoint is a composite application platform that can easily be integrated with various technologies without hardwired dependences. It provides the plumbing through which many services, such as BCS or Excel Services, can easily build solutions that combine data and functionalities from multiple external sources and surface them on a single SharePoint page.

Simplicity and modularity in the parts that participate in a mashup scenario are critical. SharePoint provides a set of rich web parts and the glue (web part connections) to build complex scenarios by using modular and simple pieces that can communicate with each other.

SharePoint empowers business users to have more influence and control over business applications, their day-to-day work tasks, and their participation in them. All of these reasons support that SharePoint is already an enterprise mashup.

In recent years, many customers have started to use InfoPath (or other Office Products) to provide a better presentation layer on top of their business processes. That's mainly because users who interact with these processes are much more familiar with a Microsoft-Office-style frontline than an entirely brand new interface. This not only motivates users to adopt it but also increases the productivity. In this way, forms drive business today.

As you saw throughout this chapter, InfoPath 2010 is a crucial building block in the mashup-friendly platform of SharePoint. The InfoPath Form web part and the ability to connect forms to other web parts on the page is a game changer in InfoPath 2010 and drastically extends the reach of electronic forms to a much broader set of users. Remember, SharePoint is all about empowering business users — with or without code!

The connectable web part scenario presented in this chapter is just proof of a concept of how the data inside an InfoPath form can relate to the data outside of the form. Using the techniques described in this chapter, you can quickly and easily create rich applications by using the InfoPath Form web part to host forms that take user input and send the values to other web parts on the page or the other way around.

SUMMARY

When you put together all the pieces presented in this chapter, you have a powerful array of options for designing and displaying your InfoPath forms in SharePoint. So what you have learned in this chapter?

This chapter began with customizing SharePoint list forms with InfoPath Designer 2010. List forms are great ways of interacting with SharePoint list data, but they are not always the best solutions. In the second part of the chapter, you learned how to design forms that are deployed to form libraries. Many aspects of an InfoPath form template were covered in the second part of the chapter, such as form programming and the files that make up a form template. Toward the end of the chapter, you learned how to use some of the existing tools to facilitate form development and troubleshooting.

At the end of this chapter, even though the presented web part connection scenario itself was a pretty simple one, you learned some very fundamental changes in the way that Microsoft is envisioning that SharePoint applications should be constructed, delivered, and experienced by end users.

10

ECM: Document Management

WHAT'S IN THIS CHAPTER?

➤ New Enterprise Content Management document management features

➤ Managing a taxonomy for your organization and publishing content types for site collections or SharePoint farms with the managed metadata store

➤ New features of the Document Center and document library

➤ Implementing the members of Microsoft.SharePoint.Taxonomy that allow developers to create custom solutions and extend the ECM framework

SharePoint Server 2010 provides many rich features that allow organizations to define an information architecture that is flexible yet powerful. With proper planning of content types, libraries, and managed metadata, you can secure manageability that will pay dividends as you accumulate content of all types, both structured and unstructured. Developers can make use of an extensive object model to then extend this capability to our existing applications, as well as create custom solutions hosted on SharePoint.

There is an explosion in the types of content that exist in organizations today. Examples include documents, digital assets, reports, web content, and social content. Enterprise Content Management (ECM) is the process of making sense of and bringing compliance to the massive amount of this electronic content that is stored on internal networks, external networks, the cloud, and SharePoint Server. In this chapter, the focus will be on managing documents; however, to do so, you will explore technologies and programming interfaces that can be used to manage other types of content as well.

In the past, the types of content developers managed have been relatively small. Examples of content include Microsoft Office documents, PDF files, AutoCAD Files, and the like. Today, there are many more types of content you are tasked to manage in an ECM system. Document management is a core part of the ECM features in SharePoint Server. Traditional document management can be defined as a subset of ECM, and it specifically deals with the technologies and features that allow us to control and manage documents from the beginning of the content creation process to the end.

A NEW ENTERPRISE CONTENT MINDSET

Much has changed with the user interface experience expected by consumers of content. Today, users access content on many types of devices, including PCs, tablets, netbooks, and mobile devices. To enhance the user experience, there is a need for rich search and contextual navigation. Allowing users to filter and navigate based on common terms and taxonomy provides an interface that is much more suitable to hosting large numbers of libraries and items.

Companies are being tasked with managing more content than ever before. Security, rules, and accountability requirements are getting more complex. This pattern will continue over the months and years ahead. As you prepare for an explosion of content, the new developer tools and features in SharePoint Server should ease this transition.

New ECM Features

SharePoint Server has a very rich set of features to support document management. However, in addition to managing traditional document artifacts, you can manage social content, including tacit updates from users, microblogging, wikis, blogs, and discussion forums. What makes SharePoint different than most other ECM systems is how it layers social technologies on top of the ECM features, while at the same time allowing us to manage this social content.

The new version of SharePoint Server provides additional features to make managing large numbers of complex content types easier. Some of these features include unique document IDs, document sets, and a global taxonomy. In this chapter, you will cover these welcome additions, while exploring how you can use new collaboration features in the context of document management.

Table 10-1 identifies the existing baseline document management features which were introduced in SharePoint 2007. Table 10-2 contains a list of the new features that are introduced in SharePoint Server 2010.

TABLE 10-1: Baseline ECM Features

FEATURE	DESCRIPTION
Document libraries	List definitions with features added to support document management.
Document Center	Site definition with structures in place to manage large amounts of documents.
Recycle Bin	Two-stage recycle bin allows for recovery of deleted documents without using backups.

FEATURE	DESCRIPTION
Versioning	Once versioning is enabled, drafts and major versions are stored as separate items in a library. The versions can be restored at any point in time.
Information policies	Farm-, site-collection-, site-, content-type-, and library-level information management policies. Built-in policy features include labels, bar codes, expiration, and auditing.
Records Center	Site definition used for retention and document routing.
Item-level permissions	Individual documents can be secured.
Content types	An abstraction layer fostering manageability of content and metadata. Settings, properties, and functionality can be defined for types of content rather than individual items.

These features have been carried over from Microsoft Office SharePoint Server 2007.

TABLE 10-2: New ECM Features in SharePoint Server 2010

FEATURE	DESCRIPTION
Managed Metadata Service application	Features that enable global metadata to be shared and managed across farms, site collections, sites, and libraries
Content type syndication	A subset of the Managed Metadata Service that allows content types to be published to and then disseminated from a hub
Unique Document ID Service	Creates a static URL for items
Content Organizer	Provides document routing within any site
Document sets	Provide compound document support
Metadata navigation and filtering	Filter and navigate based on predefined tags and taxonomy

Expanded ECM Object Model

The ECM programming model can be used to extend the functionality of the new ECM features and create custom solutions. The programming model includes support for three types of programming: the server-side object model for server-side programming, a client object model, and web services for client-side programming. The number of namespaces and types is vast; however, Table 10-3 illustrates some of the primary namespaces and some prominent types that are commonly used. In this chapter, there is sample code showing how some of the members might be used. The actual assembly files are located in the SharePoint root in the ISAPI folder.

TABLE 10-3: The ECM Object Model

NAMESPACE	DESCRIPTION
`Microsoft.Office.DocumentManagement`	Contains the API for the document ID and metadata navigation defaults
`Microsoft.Office.DocumentManagement.DocSite`	Contains the type that sets the document site feature receiver
`Microsoft.Office.DocumentManagement.DocumentSets`	Contains types that provide document sets' functionality
`Microsoft.Office.DocumentManagement.MetadataNavigation`	Contains types that provide metadata navigation defaults and filtering functionality
`Microsoft.Office.Server.WebControls`	Contains web controls for document IDs, document sets, metadata navigation, and large page libraries
`Microsoft.SharePoint.Taxonomy`	Provides the core pieces of the metadata and taxonomy API, including the building blocks of the managed metadata system, such as term, term set, group, and term management API
`Microsoft.SharePoint.Taxonomy.ContentTypeSync`	Provides the content type synchronization API, which publishes synchronized content types and reports on their status
`Microsoft.SharePoint.Taxonomy.Generic`	Provides generic dictionary objects and collection objects
`Microsoft.SharePoint.Taxonomy.Upgrade`	Provides SQL scripts for updating the metadata database
`Microsoft.SharePoint.Taxonomy.WebServices`	Provides web services that support term operations and term store operations such as matching, suggestion, and disambiguation information

SharePoint SDK

GETTING THE MOST OUT OF THE DOCUMENT CENTER

The Document Center in SharePoint Server is a site definition that can be used in combination with a content type hub to manage hundreds of millions of documents and act as a large archive. Of course, in a large system with hundreds of millions of items, many instances of a Document Center are provisioned, each with its own content database. When managing millions of documents, you store most of them in a finished state. Scale is achieved by using a distributed architecture.

While the constructs included in a Document Center are useful for large repositories, smaller teams can use a single Document Center instance to serve as a starting point for document management for smaller deployments. Typically, the documents stored in the Document Center are still being authored and consumed.

By design, the Document Center is meant to be easy to use, while also being easy to administer. Everyone can have access to its features, and everyone can see as much as they need to within the security defined by administrators and content stewards. It is worth noting that, while the Document Center is easy to use since it is preconfigured with the constructs needed to manage large sets of documents, you can also turn these features on in any team site.

The new Document Center in SharePoint 2010 is illustrated in Figure 10-1 and has been enhanced to include:

➤ Metadata navigation features and taxonomy capabilities

➤ A Document ID Service

➤ Integration with Office ClientNew, Open, and Save functions

➤ Multi-stage retention policies

➤ Folder-based information policies

➤ Location-based metadata defaults and metadata-driven navigation

➤ Integration with the Records Center site definition

➤ A configuration to act as a template that enables organizations to quickly start managing documents

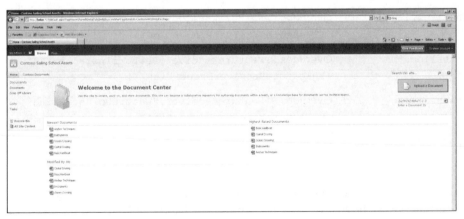

FIGURE 10-1

Note the Document ID search web part. Documents can be located using the unique ID assigned when they were created. In SharePoint 2010, all documents in site collection can automatically receive a unique ID. This feature can be enabled or disabled by the site administrator. This feature will be detailed later in the chapter.

When designing a document management strategy using SharePoint 2010, it is helpful to acknowledge that users will generally fall into three roles.

➤ Visitors are individuals who have read-only access to documents. Common tasks for visitors include browsing documents, searching, and reading documents.

➤ Contributors are individuals responsible for creating documents or document sets and participating in workflows.

➤ Content Stewards maintain document libraries and Document Centers and may be responsible for creating libraries, views, and subsites. They configure metadata, navigation, and security, and act as nontechnical administrators.

Visual Studio and the Document Center

Developers can use the `SetupDocSiteFeatureReceiver` class found in the `Microsoft.Office.DocumentManagement.DocSite` namespace and customize how the Document Center is created (see Table 10-4). The feature receiver is used like any other feature receiver. The feature events can make use of the object model to customize new Document Centers as they are created.

TABLE 10-4: SetupDocSiteFeatureReceiver Events

EVENT	DESCRIPTION
FeatureActivated	Overrides SPFeatureReceiver.FeatureActivated (SPFeatureReceiverProperties)
FeatureDeactivating	Overrides SPFeatureReceiver.FeatureDeactivating (SPFeatureReceiverProperties)
FeatureInstalled	Overrides SPFeatureReceiver.FeatureInstalled (SPFeatureReceiverProperties)
FeatureUninstalling	Overrides SPFeatureReceiver.FeatureUninstalling (SPFeatureReceiverProperties)
FeatureUpgrading	Inherited from SPFeatureReceiver

Developers can "round trip" site templates from SharePoint to Visual Studio and back to SharePoint. A custom site can be created using the browser or SharePoint Designer, then, saved as a template. The resulting template is a web solution package (.wsp file) stored in the site collection

Solution gallery. Once the template is saved, developers can import the .wsp file into Visual Studio. Modifications can be made, list definitions and columns added, and so forth. The resulting source code can be saved under source control, and represents a version of the Document Center and libraries. In addition, the .wsp file can be used to create additional subsites, or development or test environments.

In this next section, there is a step-by-step example of performing this "round trip" from SharePoint to Visual Studio and then back to SharePoint. In addition, there are details on adding document library list definitions and custom event handlers to assist with validation and business logic.

You will start by creating a Document Center with four document libraries. Later, you will export the template, import into Visual Studio, make changes, and then redeploy the changes. All of the source code is included with this book.

Creating and Customizing a Document Center

The Document Center is created with a configuration of lists, pages, and web parts that provide a starting point for content management. You may find the need to customize the site to meet your specific needs as you plan for managing your own content. The following steps demonstrate making a few simple changes to a Document Center.

1. Using Central Administration, create a site collection titled **Contoso Sailing Schools Assets** based on the enterprise Document Center site template.

2. Browse to the new Document Center, and create a Document Center titled **Contoso Documents**.

3. Open the new Document Center in the browser, and create a document library using the Site Actions menu of the new site. Name the document library **Class Descriptions**.

4. Create a second document library using the Site Actions menu of the new site. Name the document library **Instructor Resumes**.

5. Create a third document library using the Site Actions menu of the new site. Name the document library **Sail Plans**.

6. Create an asset library using the Site Actions menu of the new site. Name the asset library **Training Videos**.

Exporting the SharePoint Site

Next, create a SharePoint solution package that contains all of the elements contained in the Document Center. Once the site is saved as a solution in the Solution gallery, you can export the file and customize it in Visual Studio.

1. Using the `Contoso Documents` Document Center site created in the previous steps, navigate to the Site Actions and then Site Settings. Under the Site Actions column, select Save Site as a Template.

THE NEW SITE TEMPLATE FEATURE IN SHAREPOINT 2010

In the previous version of SharePoint, saving a site as a template created an
`.stp` template file that was stored in the template gallery. SharePoint 2010 creates
template files as solutions packages, which are stored in the Solution gallery as
shown in Figure 10-2.

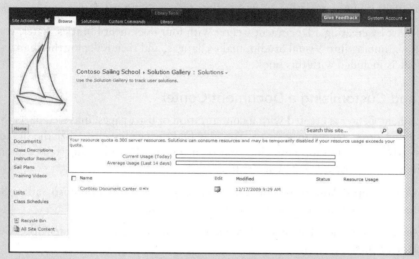

FIGURE 10-2

The files are in the standard `.wsp` format. Once these files are saved to the solution
gallery, they can be saved locally to your developer machine and imported into
Visual Studio 2010!

2. Name the site template file **contoso document center template**.

3. Name the site template name **Contoso Document Center Solution**.

4. For the description, enter **Contoso Document Center Solution**.

5. Click OK to create the template. Once the operation is completed, click on the link to the
Solution gallery in the resulting dialog box to view the saved solution.

6. In the Solution gallery, click the Contoso Document Center link to display the File
Download dialog box.

7. Click the Save button in the File Download dialog box and save the file on your desktop.

It is worth noting that, once the site is saved as a template in the Solution gallery, it can be activated and then used to create sites in the site collection. To activate the template, simply browse to the Solution gallery and select Activate while the `Contoso Document Center` solution is highlighted. You can see in Figure 10-3, when the template is activated, you will have the option of creating a new site based on the saved template.

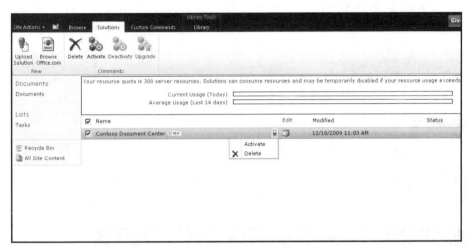

FIGURE 10-3

Importing the .wsp File

Once a `.wsp` file is saved, it can be imported into Visual Studio. It is best to create a site you can use for debugging before performing the import.

1. Using Central Administration, create a new web application.

2. Create a new top-level site using a blank site template. A blank site is created and used for debugging the site definition, as the template will reduce the likelihood of conflicts with existing libraries.

Now you need to import the Web Template from within Visual Studio.

1. Open Visual Studio 2010 and select New Project from the File menu. Under the Visual C# or Visual Basic node, select SharePoint and then click 2010. You can see the New Project types in Figure 10-4.

2. Select the Import SharePoint Solution Package project template on the right.

3. Name the project and directory **Contoso Document Center**, and click OK.

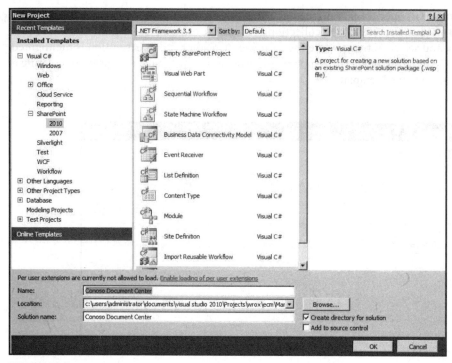

FIGURE 10-4

4. The next screen is the SharePoint Customization Wizard (see Figure 10-5). On the Specify the Site and Security Level for Debugging page, make sure to enter the URL for the debugging site you created above.

5. In the trust level section, change the default value from Deploy as a Sandboxed Solution to Deploy as a Farm Level Solution.

6. In the Specify a New Project source page, browse to the location where you saved the downloaded .wsp file, and then click Next.

7. Using the following dialog box, you can select which artifacts contained in the .wsp file you want to import. There are hundreds of items you can select. Use Ctrl+A to select all the items, and then click one of the checkboxes to deselect all the items.

8. Once the checkboxes are cleared, scroll down to the list instance section and select the three document libraries and the asset library you created earlier.

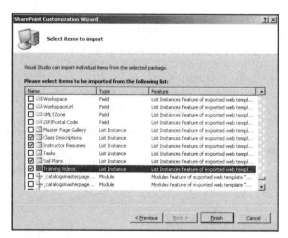

FIGURE 10-5

9. Click Finish to import the solution package and view the new site definition in Visual studio.

10. Note the following dialog box, shown in Figure 10-6, which lists the dependencies of the lists you selected. Visual Studio will cycle through each list instance and make sure that you have the required dependencies in your site definition!

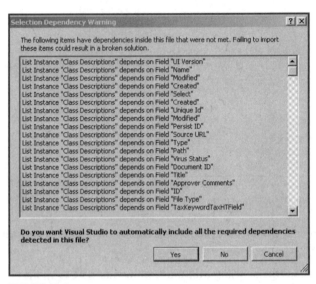

FIGURE 10-6

REPLACING THE FUNCTIONALITY OF THE SOLUTION GENERATOR

The Visual Studio extensions for Windows SharePoint Services 3.0 included a tool called the Solution Generator. Using the Solution Generator, one could create list and site definitions from existing sites. Note that this functionality is replaced in Visual Studio 2010 by the Import .wsp Project Template.

Debugging and Deploying the Project

Once you have the .wsp file imported, it can be customized and redeployed. First, the site definition should be deployed and debugged in your test environment. Using the following steps, the site definition can be deployed and debugged.

1. In Visual Studio, press F5 to deploy and run the .wsp import project.

2. Click the Documents link in the Quick Launch toolbar when the debugging site appears. You should see the libraries you created earlier. Your site should look like the one shown in Figure 10-7.

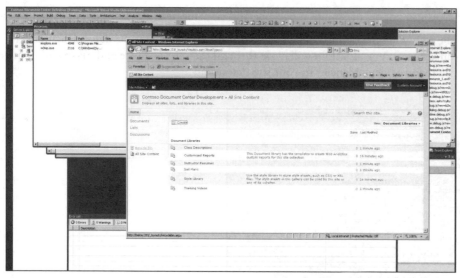

FIGURE 10-7

When you run your SharePoint project in debug mode, the SharePoint deployment process performs the following tasks:

1. Creates a web solution package (.wsp) file by using MSBuild commands. The .wsp file includes all of the necessary files and features for your site definition.

2. Since the SharePoint solution is a farm solution, the IIS application pool is recycled.

3. If a previous version of the package already exists, it will be removed. This step deactivates the features, uninstalls the solution package, and then deletes the solution package on the SharePoint server.

4. Installs the current version of the features and files in the .wsp file. This step installs the solution on the SharePoint server.

5. The Contoso Document Center and libraries are displayed in the web browser.

In this sample, a Document Center was created, libraries were created, and then the site was saved as a template. The saving process created a web solution package (.wsp file), which was then imported into Visual Studio. Once the file is imported into Visual Studio, you can add additional functionality and debug your new site definition.

CONTENT ROUTING

Architecting large repositories of documents requires advanced planning and possibly a team of content stewards. Uploading, navigation, and finding content becomes tricky when there is the potential for millions of items. SharePoint 2010 provides new features to assist content stewards in managing large repositories, as well as making repositories easier to use. One of these site-level features is the Content Organizer (CO).

Often, when users are adding content to a large repository, there is this sense that they are handing the content off to the content stewards. Much of the time, the content found in these larger repositories is in a finished state and ready for storage and consumption. One use of the Content Organizer is to route documents to specific site collections or folders based on rules and metadata.

Managing the Content Organizer

The CO is activated using the Site Features list. Once a feature is activated, you configure the Content Organizer using the Content Organizer Setting and Content Organizer Rules links found under Site Administration. The CO is the evolution of the Routing Table web part and document routing features found in the SharePoint 2007 Document Repositories site definition.

The Drop Off Library

When the Content Organizer (CO) feature is activated, a special document library, the Drop Off Library (see Figure 10-8), is created and added to the Quick Launch toolbar. Any content that derives from the document content type and is received by the Drop Off Library can be routed to alternate locations without user intervention. The location that the content is routed to is determined by rules that the content stewards create. Content can be routed to other site collections, libraries, or folders within libraries. The CO can be configured to force all content to be uploaded to the Drop Off Library. Once this is configured, it can act as a holding area for documents that do not have the required metadata needed for rule processing.

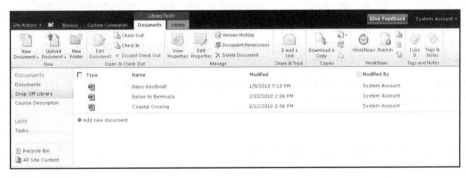

FIGURE 10-8

There are several different useful scenarios for using the Content Organizer, including:

➤ Mask upload complexities from contributors

➤ Deliver content flagged as confidential to secure locations

➤ Submit content to very large repositories

➤ Move content to folders with specific Document Information Policies

➤ Create new folders as needed and then move content to them

Documents may be sent to document libraries via different pipes. For example, you can use the context menu Send To pipe, manual uploads, workflows, and the object model. Since the Drop Off Library is a standard library, all of these submission pipes are supported.

Creating Rules

Typically, the content stewards are responsible for adding rules that will be used to route content around the organization. Before creating rules, the CO should be configured using Site Settings. There are several useful options available during configuration:

➤ The Redirect Users to the Drop Off library option redirects users' content to the Drop Off Library, if they try to upload content to a library that is associated with rules.

➤ When the Sending to Another Site option is enabled, content can be routed to other site collections. This is useful when the content stewards are responsible for lots of content that needs to be distributed across many site collections.

➤ Folder provisioning settings allow new folders to be created when certain thresholds are reached. This is another useful feature in repositories that contain a large number of documents. Folders can be provisioned, allowing you to maintain fewer than 5000 items in a given folder.

> *The List View Threshold is a new setting in SharePoint which represents the maximum number of items that can be retrieved in one request. The default value is 5000 and the minimum is 2000.*

➤ The Duplicate Submissions setting allows you to enable versioning or provide unique file names so that files are not overwritten.

➤ Role managers will be notified if files have been submitted to the Drop Off Library but have not been routed for various reasons.

Rules List

The content stewards add rules using the Content Organizer Rules link (see Figure 10-9), which can be accessed using the Site Settings. When content is received by the CO, rules are processed by priority and can assist the content stewards in making sure that content is stored in the appropriate place.

To create a new rule, you must provide the following information:

➤ **Rule name:** A user-friendly name, which may be exposed in the File Plan report.

➤ **Rule Status and Priority:** Set a value between 1 and 9 with 1 having the highest priority. Having a higher priority means the rule will execute before rules with a lower priority.

➤ **Submission's Content Type:** The selected content type properties will be exposed to condition logic. If the rules are met, the content will assume this content type.

➤ **Conditions:** Allows configuration of up to six logical comparisons of content type properties.

➤ **Target Location:** The location the content will be moved to if it matches all of the conditions defined. This location can be another site or site collection.

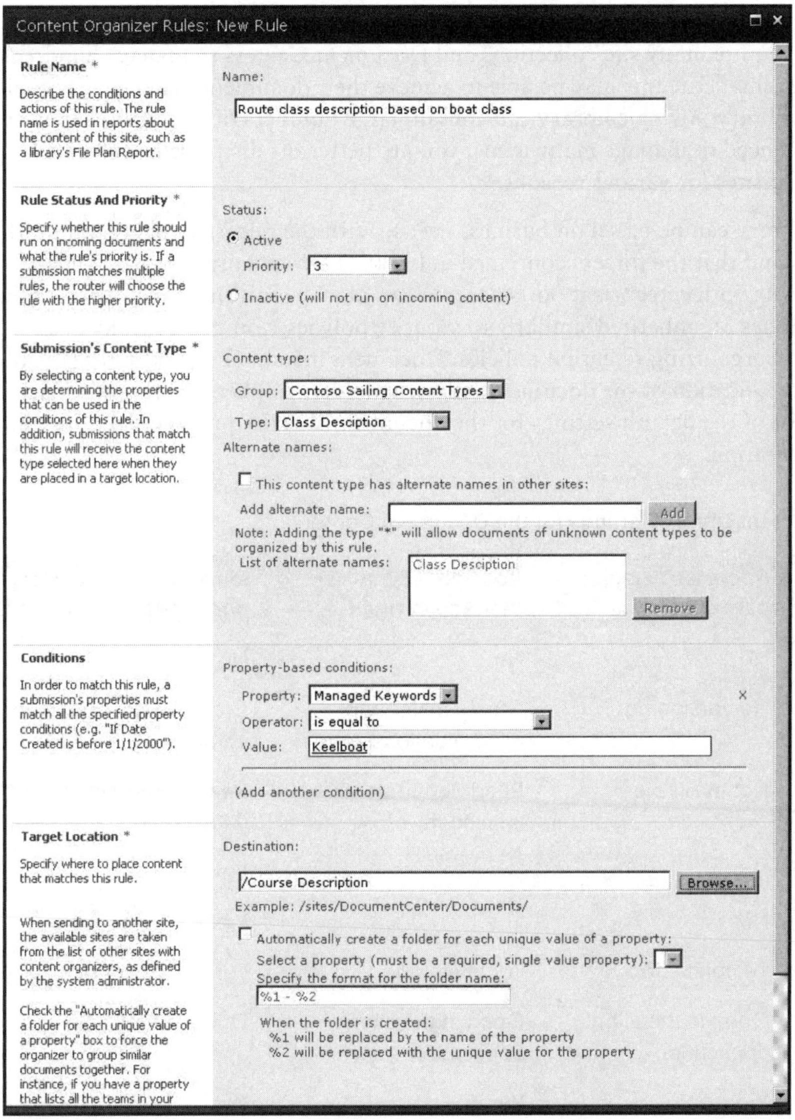

Content Organizer Rules: New Rule

Rule Name *

Describe the conditions and actions of this rule. The rule name is used in reports about the content of this site, such as a library's File Plan Report.

Name:

Route class description based on boat class

Rule Status And Priority *

Specify whether this rule should run on incoming documents and what the rule's priority is. If a submission matches multiple rules, the router will choose the rule with the higher priority.

Status:

⦿ Active

Priority: 3

○ Inactive (will not run on incoming content)

Submission's Content Type *

By selecting a content type, you are determining the properties that can be used in the conditions of this rule. In addition, submissions that match this rule will receive the content type selected here when they are placed in a target location.

Content type:

Group: Contoso Sailing Content Types

Type: Class Desciption

Alternate names:

☐ This content type has alternate names in other sites:

Add alternate name: [   ] Add

Note: Adding the type "*" will allow documents of unknown content types to be organized by this rule.

List of alternate names: Class Desciption

Remove

Conditions

In order to match this rule, a submission's properties must match all the specified property conditions (e.g. "If Date Created is before 1/1/2000").

Property-based conditions:

Property: Managed Keywords   X

Operator: is equal to

Value: Keelboat

(Add another condition)

Target Location *

Specify where to place content that matches this rule.

When sending to another site, the available sites are taken from the list of other sites with content organizers, as defined by the system administrator.

Check the "Automatically create a folder for each unique value of a property" box to force the organizer to group similar documents together. For instance, if you have a property that lists all the teams in your

Destination:

/Course Description   Browse...

Example: /sites/DocumentCenter/Documents/

☐ Automatically create a folder for each unique value of a property:

Select a property (must be a required, single value property): [ ]

Specify the format for the folder name:

%1 - %2

When the folder is created:
%1 will be replaced by the name of the property
%2 will be replaced with the unique value for the property

FIGURE 10-9

In summary, the Content Organizer is like the previous Record Router. You create rules that help the CO decide where the various types of content should be stored. This enables you to enforce security and information policies. The CO can route content based on properties as well as content type.

USING DOCUMENT LIBRARIES IN THE DOCUMENT CENTER

Like the previous version of the Document Center, there is one document library contained in newly provisioned Document Center sites. Of course, you can add additional libraries as needed. Many of the features explored in this chapter are managed at the document library level. While large organizations may require many site collections and Document Centers to manage hundreds of millions of documents, smaller teams may be able to achieve their document management goals using a single document library. A single library can contain large numbers of documents. However, generally speaking, if you need to manage many items, you are better off distributing the items across multiple libraries or sites for various reasons.

Folders in a document library can be based on business needs. With the release of SharePoint 2010, it is important to understand that the folders contained in libraries serve many purposes outside the traditional use, assisting with categorization. Since you can manage information policies at the folder level and these policies are inherited similarly to security policies, you can use folders as a means of maintaining and organizing retention policies. Document metadata can be automatically populated according to the location of the document, allowing folders to play a role in metadata as well. Table 10-5 is a list of the default settings for the document libraries provisioned using the Document Center site definition.

TABLE 10-5: Default Document Library Settings for the Document Center

LIST SETTING	DOCUMENT LIBRARY DEFAULT	MOSS 2007 DOCUMENT CENTER SETTING	SHAREPOINT SERVER "14" DOCUMENT CENTER SETTING
Content Approval	No	No	No
Version History	No versioning	Create major and minor versions	Create major and minor versions
Draft Item Security	Not available	Read Permissions (Minimum)	Read Permissions (Minimum)
Require Check Out	No	Yes	Yes
Content Types	No	Yes	Yes
Document Template	Template.doc	Template.doc	Template.doc
Browser-enabled Documents	Open in the client application	Open in the client application	Open in the client application
Folders	Yes	Yes	Yes
Big List	No	Not available	No
Search	Yes	Yes	Yes

Since the Document Center is designed to manage a large number of documents, the ability to quickly sort and filter, as well as navigate to, content is very important. SharePoint 2010 provides three different ways to quickly find the content needed: column-level filters, metadata navigation, and key filters.

Metadata Navigation and Filtering

Metadata-based navigation helps users find documents quickly and explore unstructured content that might span many folders in a library. Content stewards define navigation hierarchies based on content types, single-value choice fields, or managed metadata fields. The selected fields will appear on the Quick Launch toolbar and can be used to assist in navigating large amounts of documents.

Key filters can be defined (see Figure 10-10), allowing users to filter documents by terms entered in the Key Filters section of the Quick Launch toolbar. Both the navigation hierarchy and key filters are defined at the library level using Library Settings.

Field types that are available for key filters include:

➤ Content type

➤ Choice fields

➤ Managed Metadata fields

➤ Date and time fields

➤ Number fields

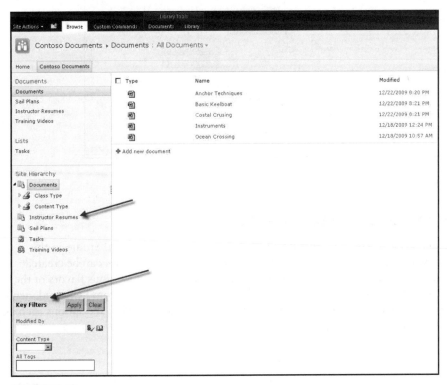

FIGURE 10-10

Queries and Indices

When defining columns used for navigation, SharePoint defaults to automatically creating and managing the column indices on the list. The indices are created using the data that will be used in queries, as the tree is navigated and nodes are selected. As new nodes are selected, SharePoint decides if it can reuse an index from the last query. If the previous index can't be used, a new query will be created using another available index. If the query fails because of too many results being returned, then a fallback query will be used to return top items from the list.

You manage metadata navigation and filtering using the Metadata Navigation Settings found under Site Settings (see Figure 10-11). Notice the default setting at the bottom, which allows SharePoint to automatically manage the column indices.

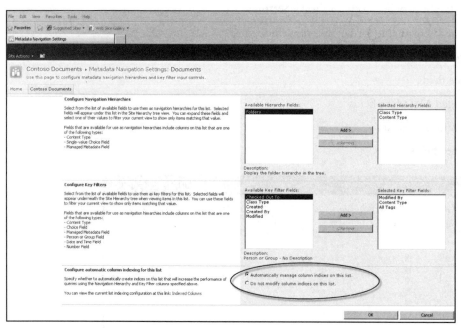

FIGURE 10-11

Visual Studio and Document Libraries

Much of what developers learned about document library definitions and Visual Studio in the previous version of SharePoint is still relevant today. Custom document libraries can be created using list definition templates found in Visual Studio 2010. You can use the various flavors of the object model to send and retrieve items to and from the document library. Custom fields and views can be added as part of any list definition. Listing 10-1 uses the object model to set options such as list throttling and synchronization properties.

LISTING 10-1: Document Library Manipulation Using the SharePoint Object Model

```csharp
using System;
using System.Collections.Generic;
using System.Linq;
using System.Text;
using Microsoft.SharePoint;
namespace DocumentLibraryManipulation
{
    class Program
    {
        static void Main(string[] args)
        {
            using (SPSite site = new SPSite("http://servername/docs"))
            {
                using (SPWeb spw = site.RootWeb)
                {
                    Guid ListId = spw.Lists.Add("Class Description", "Sailing Class
                    Descrition Documents", SPListTemplateType.DocumentLibrary);
                    SPList spdClassDesc = spw.Lists[ListId];

                    //indicate throttling status
                    spdClassDesc.EnableThrottling = false;

                    //indicates whether the list should be downloaded to the client
                     during offline synchronization
                    spdClassDesc.ExcludeFromOfflineClient = true;

                    // indicates whether the content of the list is included when
                    the list is saved as a list template
                    Boolean blCanbeSaved = spdClassDesc.ExcludeFromTemplate;

                    //Get related fields for the list as a collection
                    SPRelatedFieldCollection colRelated =
                    spdClassDesc.GetRelatedFields();

                    spdClassDesc.OnQuickLaunch = true;

                    spdClassDesc.Update();

                    Console.WriteLine("Library added...");

                    Console.ReadLine();
                }
            }
        }
    }
}
```

Create a Document Library List Definition in Visual Studio

You can create a list definition and list instance using the templates that are included in Visual Studio 2010. The list definitions are created using project templates included in Visual Studio.

To create a list definition and list instance:

1. To add a list definition to the Document Center site definition project created earlier, click the Project node in Solution Explorer and click Add New Item.

2. Expand the SharePoint node under Visual C#, and click 2010.

3. In the templates window, select List Definition and rename the default name from ListDefinition1 to **Sailing Charts,** as shown in Figure 10-12.

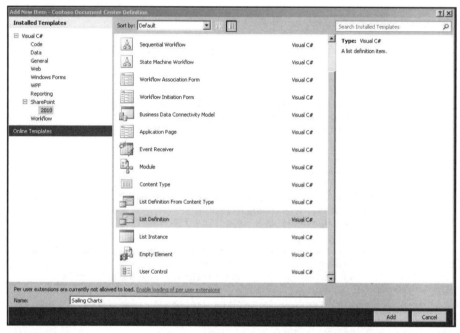

FIGURE 10-12

4. As shown in Figure 10-13, using the SharePoint Customization Wizard:

    ➤ The display name can be set.

    ➤ The base template for the list definition can be selected.

    ➤ A list instance can be generated.

After you click the Finished button, the new definition will be generated and a new folder will be created under the Solution Explorer. Once the list definition is generated, you can define custom fields as needed.

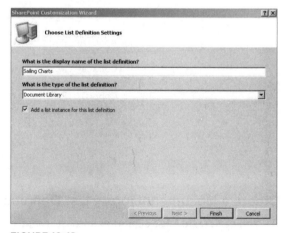

FIGURE 10-13

MANAGED METADATA

Metadata is structured information that describes or otherwise makes it easier to locate and manage content in the context that was intended. Metadata is often called data about data, or information about information.

An important reason for supplying an easy-to-use framework for creating descriptive metadata is to facilitate the discovery of relevant information. In addition to resource discovery, metadata can help organize social content and facilitate interoperability with external social networks. Administrative metadata about people objects can be used to create claims during authentication and then be forwarded to other systems.

Types of Metadata

There are several different types of metadata to consider here:

➤ Descriptive metadata describes an item for purposes such as search and identification. It can include basics such as title, subject, author, and keywords.

➤ Structural metadata indicates how compound items are put together; for example, what documents make up a contract or a proposal.

➤ Administrative metadata provides information to help manage a item, such as when and how it was created, file type and other technical information, and who can access it.

Social metadata is data added to content by people other than the content creator, such as tags, ratings, votes, and comments. Examples include ratings on `Amazon.com`, comments on `Expedia.com`, and tagging in `Dig.com`. In the past, how we found content was defined by search tools. Social metadata provides a more personalized way of organizing and finding content, where our network of colleagues and peers become our preferred source of information. You can use SharePoint Server to query ratings, comments, and other social metadata provided by our colleagues to determine what content is most relevant.

Tagging and Taxonomy

Tagging is the act of associating metadata with an item. You can separate tagging into two different categories. The first is authoritative tagging, and the second is social tagging. In authoritative tagging, the author of the item associates metadata with it, typically during the content creation process. In social tagging, other users add social metadata to content, usually after the content has been authored. Using SharePoint metadata, users can tag items in a web browser, office clients, or custom applications using the SharePoint metadata object model.

Taxonomy is formally defined as the practice of classification according to natural relationships. This chapter defines taxonomy as being a hierarchy of terms that includes synonyms, translations, and descriptions. The taxonomy can be thought of as a system of classification such as the Kingdom Phylum Class Order Genus Species you learned about in high school biology. When you associate authoritative tags with content, you use keywords. Keywords are stored throughout SharePoint in sites, lists, and libraries.

Terms are managed in the managed metadata store and represent a node in the taxonomy. Terms have a unique ID and contain text labels, which represent a keyword, synonym, abbreviation, or phrase.

Managed Metadata Service Application

The new metadata infrastructure in SharePoint Server consists of three major components:

1. Managed Metadata Services application
2. Term sets
3. Managed metadata column

The Managed Metadata Service application allows you to define content types and metadata and share them across lists, sites, site collections, web applications, and SharePoint farms. Content types are addressed later in this chapter. When an administrator configures the managed metadata store, a database is created to host the term store. There is one term store per shared service application. The term store consists of groups. Most often there will be many groups of terms, and the groups can be used as a security boundary. The groups contain term sets. There can be many term sets per group; however, there is a maximum of 1000 term sets per term store. Each term set can have 30k terms with a maximum of a million terms total. The terms contain synonyms, descriptions, translations, and custom properties. For example, you may track language of choice as a custom property.

Term Store Management Tool

When you click Term Store Management from the Site Settings page, you are taken to the Central Administration site. This is the global administration page for the term store. Changes made here affect the entire farm, as well as any farms that are consuming terms from the managed metadata store.

Create a Term Set Manually

The following steps can be used to create a new term set manually. Use the Document Center site you created earlier in the chapter.

1. From Site Settings, click Term Store Management.
2. Hover over the Managed Term Service in the pane on the left of the Term Management tool, and select New Group.
3. Name the group **Sailing**.
4. Using the resulting screen on the right, assign a Group Manager.
5. Click Save and refresh the page.
6. Hover over the new Sailing group, and select New Term Set.
7. Name the term set **Classes**; enter a description, owner, contact; and click Save.

8. Hover over the new Classes term set, and add the following terms:

> Cruising

> Keelboat

> Racing

> Yachting

You should see something like what is shown in Figure 10-14.

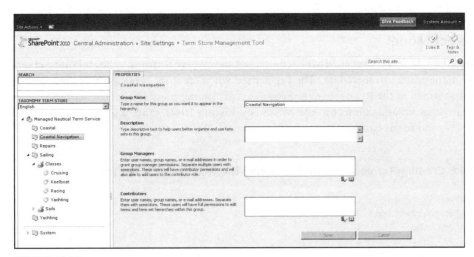

FIGURE 10-14

Once created, the new terms can be referenced by managed metadata columns and applied as metadata to documents. Users will be able to pick a term, type in a partial name, and see the type-ahead features.

Managed Metadata Columns

Managed metadata columns are single- or multi-value fields that map to an open or closed term set stored in the managed metadata store. The keyword and managed metadata controls both use a managed metadata column (see how one is populated in Figure 10-15).

The managed metadata columns support:

> Type-ahead

> Tree Picker

> Disambiguation

> Mutli-language support

> Synonyms

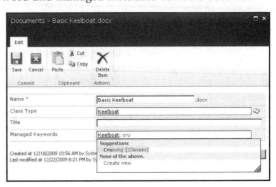

FIGURE 10-15

If the column is associated with an open term set, users will have the ability to create new terms as well. An open term set will most likely have less structure and governance associated with it. Generally, an open term set supports users by providing a means to create a *folksonomy*. A folksonomy is a collection of terms created by users to tag content. Think of it as a user driven approach to organizing content, as opposed to the taxonomy, which is more structured and defined ahead of time. The easiest way to learn how the managed metadata columns work is simply to create one. From any document library, you can create a new column and specify the column type as managed metadata. When creating a new column, if you select managed metadata as the type of information the column will hold, you will be presented with additional selection options to pick the term set used for the column.

Taxonomy Object Model

Enterprise Metadata Management (EMM) encompasses many new features in SharePoint Server that allow the management of metadata. The types used when creating applications to manage metadata are contained in the `Microsoft.SharePoint.Taxonomy` namespace. The namespace can be used to create sessions and connect to the MMS (see Listing 10-2). Once a session is established, groups, term sets, and terms can be managed programmatically.

LISTING 10-2: Creating Terms and Term Sets Using the Taxonomy Object Model

```
using System;
using System.Collections.Generic;
using System.Linq;
using System.Text;
using System.Web;
using Microsoft.SharePoint;
using Microsoft.SharePoint.Taxonomy;

namespace ManagedMetadataConnection
{
    class Program
    {
        static void Main(string[] args)
        {
            using (SPSite site = new SPSite("http://belize:777"))
            {
                //instantiate a new session to a site
                TaxonomySession sesssion = new TaxonomySession(site);

                //Get the term store
                TermStore NauticalStore = sesssion.TermStores["Managed Nautical
                 Term Service"];

                //Create a new term group
                Group Costal = NauticalStore.CreateGroup("Costal Sailing");

                //Create a new term set
```

```
TermSet termSetClasses = Costal.CreateTermSet("Class Types");

//Add terms
Term term1 = termSetClasses.CreateTerm("Sail Trimming", 1033);
Term term2 = termSetClasses.CreateTerm("Anchoring", 1033);
Term term3 = termSetClasses.CreateTerm("Cruising", 1033);
Term term4 = termSetClasses.CreateTerm("Deep Water", 1033);
Term term5 = termSetClasses.CreateTerm("Navigation", 1033);
Term term6 = termSetClasses.CreateTerm("GPS", 1033);
Term term7 = termSetClasses.CreateTerm("Sail Repairs", 1033);

//Commit changes to the store
NauticalStore.CommitAll();

//Delete a term
term1.Delete();

//set descriptions and labels
term2.SetDescription("Learn to Anchor Class", 1033);
term2.CreateLabel("Anchoring", 1033, false);

NauticalStore.CommitAll();

Console.WriteLine("Group added...");
Console.ReadLine();
            }
        }
    }
}
```

CONTENT TYPES

When implementing ECM solutions, the ability to manage content types across site collections is perhaps one of the most important new features in SharePoint. Certainly this release can be thought of as the release where SharePoint broke site collection and silo boundaries while facilitating manageability. The ability to create global content types that can be syndicated across SharePoint Farms and Site Collections eliminates boundaries you may have experienced in SharePoint 2007. No longer will you have to recreate the same content types for each site collection you manage.

Content types that can be shared ensure that users are using consistent templates and metadata. Since content types can have individual information policies, you have the ability to insist that content adhere to a policy, regardless of where it lives in the system. The ability to create, publish, and consume content types using a services-based model has many advantages. Companies with a global deployment can share content types across multiple farms spanning geographical locations.

Since metadata follows content type, companies can ensure consistent metadata across teams. When users create new content, you can ensure that they are using current templates and workflows to automate approval processes. In short, an organization truly purchases itself manageability of content by taking time to plan and publish content types.

Content Type Syndication

Content type syndication allows the publishing, consuming, and distributing of one or many content types to other farms, web applications, and site collections. Content type syndication requires a hub from which to publish. You create the content types the same way you did in the previous version, but now they can be syndicated through the hub to other site collections.

➤ **Hub:** A site collection designated as a source from which content types are shared throughout the enterprise

➤ **Content type syndication:** Publishing, sharing, or pushing one or more content types across site collections, web apps, and farm boundaries

Publishing

Published content types are no different from the standard content types you work with in SharePoint. The only difference is they are disseminated across the organization from the centralized hub. There is only one hub for each Metadata Shared Application Service. It is worth noting that you don't have to syndicate content types, even if you are using the Metadata Shared Application Service for term management and keywords. If a site collection is consuming metadata from a service application, it does not have to consume content types as well.

When a content type is selected to be published, the following components are published as well:

➤ Content type and all columns

➤ Column settings and defaults

➤ Information management policies

➤ Workflow associations

➤ Document Information panels

The Document Set

Conceptually, a document set can be thought of as a folder with enhanced functionality. From a technical standpoint, the document set is implemented as a folder content type inheriting from the folder parent content type. This allows for a compound document affect and the ability to attach multiple items to the set.

Often, there is a need to manage documents that should be treated as an interconnected unit but still allow individual settings and metadata for the documents that make up the set. To create and manage books using SharePoint, you might have to manage many files that make up a title. The text from various authors might be in several documents, one per chapter. Figures and code may be separate files. Document sets would allow you to manage the book as one unit, with workflows, metadata, and so forth. Each of the files that make up the various chapters could still have separate metadata and approval workflows.

To create a document set, select Create in the Content Type gallery page. Provide a descriptive name for the new content type, select Document Set Content Type as the parent content type, choose a group, and click OK. Creating the document set is that easy (see Figure 10-16). It truly is like creating any other content type.

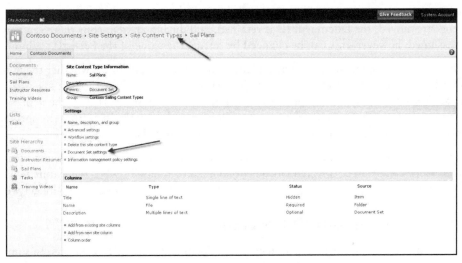

FIGURE 10-16

Examples of using document sets include automating content creation, providing process guidance, and assisting in managing related content. A document set can have a custom welcome page. The welcome page can contain verbiage describing the document set, as well as web parts and images.

Some features of a document set include:

➤ Welcome page

➤ Shared metadata

➤ Prepopulated templates or documents

➤ Versions

➤ Workflows

➤ Security boundary

➤ Unique document ID

DOCUMENT ID SERVICE

A content steward or administrator can activate the Document ID Service at the site collection level. Once the Document ID feature is activated, it can be managed using the Site Collection Settings page.

Document IDs will only be generated for the document and document set content type. Of course, your custom content types created using the Document content type or Document Set content type will generate IDs as well. Other content types will be ignored. Essentially what happens is that, as new documents are added to the list, the `item added` event is triggered and used to set the Document ID. The event receiver will generate Document IDs every time an item is added.

The default behavior is, if an existing ID is associated with the item, the ID is overwritten. When documents are moved, the Document ID is retained, and during an item copy there is a new Document ID assigned; however, this can be changed by setting the value of the PersistID column.

When a new document or document set is added, SharePoint Server checks to see whether the item has a document ID. If the item has a Document ID, the server checks to see whether the `PreserveID` attribute is set to True or False, and then sets it to False if it is currently set to True. If the item does not already have a Document ID, the server gets a Document ID for the item from the specified provider, writes it to metadata, and sets the `PreserveID` attribute to False.

Once a Document ID is generated, it can be used like any other piece of metadata. When configuring searches, a search scope can be used to search Document ID metadata. Finally, when the feature is deactivated, the setting links are removed and searching using Document ID scopes will no longer work.

Create a Custom Document ID Provider

A custom provider can be used to assign Document IDs to documents and document sets. In some organizations, business rules and metadata drive how IDs are created and assigned. Using a custom-generated Document ID gives you the ability to identify documents using existing numbering schemes that may already be present.

SharePoint Server supports the use of custom code to create Document IDs. Custom providers can be created by implementing a class that derives from the `IIDProvider` interface and then registering the provider in each site collection. Once the custom provider is deployed and registered, as new documents and document sets are added, the new custom provider will be used to assign the Document ID.

Create a Document ID Provider

Listing 10-3 illustrates how you can implement your own custom provider to generate unique IDs. This is useful in scenarios where you already have a document numbering system in place. First, execute the following steps:

1. Open Visual Studio 2010 and select New Project from the File menu. Under the Visual C# or Visual Basic node, select SharePoint, and then click 2010.

2. Select the Empty SharePoint Project template on the right.

3. Name the project name and the directory name **Custom Document ID Provider**, and click OK.

4. In the Solution Explorer right-click on the new project, and select Add New Item.

5. Select the Visual C# node and create a new Class item.

6. In the Solution Explorer right-click on the new Class.cs file, and rename it **CustomDocumentIDProvider.cs**. When prompted, make sure that you select Yes to rename the references.

7. Browse to the SharePoint root folder, and set a reference to the `Microsoft.Office` `.DocumentManagement` assembly.

8. Replace the code in `CustomDocumentIDProvider.cs` with the code in Listing 10-3.

LISTING 10-3: Implementing a Class that Derives from the IIDProvider Interface

```csharp
using System;
using System.Collections.Generic;
using System.Linq;
using System.Text;
using Microsoft.Office.DocumentManagement;

namespace CustomDocumentIDProvider
{
    class CustomDocumentIDProvider :
Microsoft.Office.DocumentManagement.DocumentIdProvider
    {
        public override bool DoCustomSearchBeforeDefaultSearch
        {
            //property used to trigger our custom search first.
            //If false then we will use the SharePoint search when retreiving
             Document IDs
            get
            {
                return false;
            }
        }

        //We implement our logic to generate an ID returned as a string
        public override string GenerateDocumentId(Microsoft.SharePoint.SPListItem
        listItem)
        {
            DateTime CurrTime = DateTime.Now;
            return CurrTime.ToString();
        }

        //Implement our own finder method.
        //Return empty if no results
        public override string[] GetDocumentUrlsById(Microsoft.SharePoint.SPSite
        site, string documentId)
        {
            string[] searchhits = new string[0];
            return new string[0];
        }

        //Sample text used in web parts and UI
        public override string GetSampleDocumentIdText(Microsoft.SharePoint.SPSite
        site)
        {

            return "Todays date please...";
        }
    }
}
```

Once the custom document ID provider has been created, it needs to be deployed and registered at the site collection level. Best practice is to use a feature and a feature event receiver to register the custom provider. During testing and development, you can do this using a console application or PowerShell (see Listing 10-4).

LISTING 10-4: Code to Deploy and Register Custom Document ID Provider within a Feature

```csharp
using System;
using System.Runtime.InteropServices;
using System.Security.Permissions;
using Microsoft.SharePoint;
using Microsoft.SharePoint.Security;
using Microsoft.Office.DocumentManagement;

namespace CustomDocumentIDProvider.Features.Feature1
{
    /// <summary>
    /// This class handles events raised during feature activation, deactivation,
     installation, uninstallation, and upgrade.
    /// </summary>
    /// <remarks>
    /// The GUID attached to this class may be used during packaging and should not
     be modified.
    /// </remarks>

    [Guid("07168ca9-ead3-427c-a1e6-939669a148fa")]
    public class Feature1EventReceiver : SPFeatureReceiver
    {

        public override void FeatureActivated(SPFeatureReceiverProperties properties)
          {
              SPSite sitecollection = (SPSite)properties.Feature.Parent;
              DocumentId.SetProvider(sitecollection,
              typeof(CustomDocumentIDProvider.CustomDocumentID));
          }


    }
}
```

SUMMARY

In this chapter, you learned how SharePoint can be used to manage documents and artifacts for small teams, as well as hundreds of millions of documents for large organizations. You discovered the importance of the Managed Metadata Service application that contains content type syndication features. Using the service application model, SharePoint helps you eliminate information silos by using constant metadata and terms across site collections and farms. Certainly there will be entire books written on this subject over time. As a developer, your next steps include regular visits to the online SDK to explore new developer documentation as it becomes available.

11

Business Connectivity Services

WHAT'S IN THIS CHAPTER?

➤ An overview of Business Connectivity Services

➤ How to create simple no-code BCS solutions

➤ How to administrate BCS

➤ How to enhance BCS solutions using SharePoint components

➤ How to create advanced BCS solutions in Visual Studio 2010

While Microsoft SharePoint Server 2010 is an excellent platform upon which to build information solutions, it will never be the only system in an organization. The simple fact is that organizations will always have additional systems — such as customer relationship management (CRM) and enterprise resource planning (ERP) systems — that target specific data sets and business processes. Additionally, organizations may have other custom applications, databases, and web services that are not part of the SharePoint infrastructure. These *external systems* (external to SharePoint that is) contain significant amounts of data and represent significant financial investments. As a consequence, these systems will not be replaced by any solution created solely in SharePoint.

The challenge, however, is that SharePoint solutions are often closely related to the data and processes contained in external systems. For example, a document library containing invoices may contain metadata also found in the ERP system or be addressed to a customer whose information is also in the CRM system. Without some way of utilizing data from the external systems, the SharePoint solution would be forced to duplicate the same information. This duplication would then lead to data maintenance issues between the external system and the SharePoint solution.

In addition to the data challenges presented within SharePoint itself, there are challenges when integrating external data with Office 2010 documents. When sales people create a quote, for example, they often look up customer contact information in a CRM system, copy it to the clipboard, and then paste it into the document. This duplication of effort obviously increases the time necessary to create documents. Furthermore, sales people must be connected to the network in order to access the CRM system; they cannot easily create a quote while offline.

Failure to sufficiently integrate external systems with SharePoint solutions can slow the adoption of SharePoint within an organization. After all, the most important data used by information workers is often in external systems. Therefore, your solutions must consider how to integrate external data and that is where Business Connectivity Services (BCS) comes into play. BCS is a broad and deep topic that cannot be completely covered in a single chapter. While this chapter provides significant technical information, readers interested in complete coverage should read the upcoming *Professional Business Connectivity Services* from Wiley in 2011.

INTRODUCING BUSINESS CONNECTIVITY SERVICES

BCS is an umbrella term for a set of technologies that brings data from external systems into SharePoint Server 2010 and Office 2010. If you have worked previously with the Microsoft Office SharePoint Server 2007 Business Data Catalog, then you might think of BCS as the evolution of the Business Data Catalog. If you have not previously worked with the Business Data Catalog, don't worry; no prior experience is required to understand or use BCS in SharePoint solutions. Figure 11-1 shows a diagram of the major functional blocks that make up BCS.

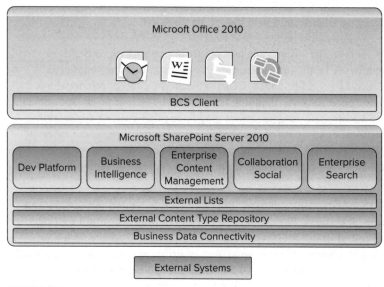

FIGURE 11-1

In the context of BCS, the term *external system* refers to any datasource that is outside of the SharePoint infrastructure. As previously noted, this can include third-party software, custom applications, databases, web services, and even cloud computing solutions. BCS communicates with external systems through the Business Data Connectivity (BDC) layer. The BDC layer contains the plumbing, runtime API, and connectivity functionality necessary to communicate with external systems.

While the BDC layer provides connectivity to the external system, it does not dictate what data is returned from the system. The operations and schema for the returned data is instead defined by an External Content Type (ECT). An ECT contains an entity definition that specifies the exact fields that should be returned from an external source. For example, a "Customer" ECT might specify that `CustomerID`, `FirstName`, and `LastName` fields be returned from the CRM system. Additionally, an ECT defines the operations that can be performed. The available operations include create, read, update, and delete (CRUD). Defining ECTs is one of the primary activities involved in creating a BCS solution and may be performed in either Microsoft SharePoint Designer 2010 (SPD) or Microsoft Visual Studio 2010 (VS2010). When completed, ECTs are stored in the External Content Type Catalog.

While it is possible to create many different custom solutions using BCS, the simplest way to surface external data in SharePoint is to use an External List. An External List is a SharePoint list that is based on an ECT. Just as standard lists (tasks, announcements, calendars, libraries, etc.) are based on content types, External Lists are based on External Content Types. External lists behave similarly to standard lists, support views, and item editing. External Lists can be used in support of any of the key functional areas within SharePoint Server.

In Office 2010, the BCS Client layer has the ability to use External Content Types to display external data in Office clients. This data may be displayed in Outlook using standard forms such as contact lists, or utilized in Word to support metadata and document creation. In all cases, you can make use of InfoPath to enhance the presentation of external data. Finally, External Lists may be taken offline with support from both Outlook and the SharePoint Workspace.

Creating Simple BCS Solutions

While BCS solutions can be complex, they can also be created with no code. Using the tools found in SharePoint Designer (SPD) and SharePoint, you can easily create an External Content Type and External List. This data may then be edited in SharePoint or Office clients. In this section, you'll walk through a simple BCS solution based on a SQL Server database. The database contains a single table of marketing campaign information, as shown in Figure 11-2. The goal of the walk-through is to create a list in SharePoint and a calendar in Outlook based on this data.

CampaignID	CampaignName	StartDate	EndDate
2	Contoso Celebrity Appearances	2010-05-01 00:00:00	2010-05-15 00:00:00
3	Summer Movie Tie-In	2010-07-04 00:00:00	2010-08-15 00:00:00
4	Holiday Sale	2010-11-01 00:00:00	2010-11-30 00:00:00
5	Vacation	2010-12-01 00:00:00	2011-02-01 00:00:00

FIGURE 11-2

Creating External Content Types

The solution begins with the definition of External Content Types to define the schema and operations to perform on the data. Whether your BCS solution ultimately uses code or not, you will almost always define the ECTs using the SharePoint Designer. The tooling in SPD for creating ECTs was designed to be sophisticated enough to be used by professional developers across all types of BCS solutions. To begin, you simply open a development site in SPD and click on the External Content Types object under the list of Site Objects, as shown in Figure 11-3.

Clicking on the New External Content Type button allows you to start defining basic ECT information. The basic ECT information consists of a Name, Display Name, Namespace, and Version. You may also select from a list of various Office Types, which determines what form will be used to render the information when it is displayed in Outlook. Figure 11-4 shows the basic ECT information for the walk-through with the Appointment Office Type selected.

FIGURE 11-3

Clicking on the Operations Design View button presents a form for defining connection information to an external system. Clicking the Add Connection button allows you to select from three types of connections: WCF, SQL, and .NET Type. Selecting WCF allows you to connect to a web service, SQL allows you to connect to a database, and .NET Type allows you to utilize a custom .NET Assembly Connector, which is covered later in the chapter. For this walk-through, the SQL connection type was used, and the information shown in Figure 11-5 was specified.

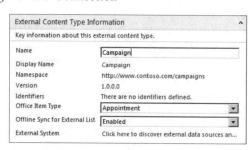

FIGURE 11-4

Once the datasource connection is made, SPD can create operations for the ECT. When using a SQL connection, SPD can infer a significant amount of information about the datasource and the operations, so it is easier to create the entire set of CRUD operations. In fact, all you have to do is right-click the table in the connection and select Create All Operations from the context menu, which will launch a wizard to collect the small amount of information required to complete the operation definitions. Figure 11-6 shows the context menu in SPD.

FIGURE 11-5

In order to complete the operation definitions, you must at least map fields from the ECT to fields in Outlook. This mapping determines how the ECT is displayed in the Outlook form. In the case of the walk-through, the Subject, Start, and End fields in Outlook must be mapped to the ECT. This is because Appointment was selected as the Office Type. For this walk-through, the `CampaignName` was mapped to `Subject`, `StartDate` to `Start`, and `EndDate` to `End`. When the wizard finishes, the ECT definition is complete and may be saved in SPD by clicking the Save button. The ECT is then visible in the list of ECTs for the site.

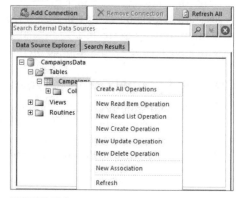

FIGURE 11-6

Creating External Lists

Once the ECT is created, it can be used as the basis for an External List. External Lists can be created directly in SPD or in the browser, using the Create menu in SharePoint. For this walk-through, a new External List was created by selecting the Lists and Libraries object from the list of Site Objects and then clicking the New External List button. When you create a new External List, the set of available ECTS is presented. Figure 11-7 shows the list of available ECTs with the new Campaign type visible.

Once the new External List is created, it may be viewed immediately in the browser. Because all of the CRUD operations were created, the list supports editing items, adding items, and deleting items. Figure 11-8 shows the new list in SharePoint Server 2010.

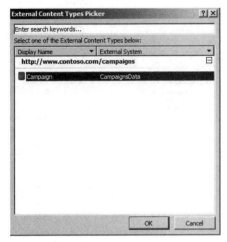

FIGURE 11-7

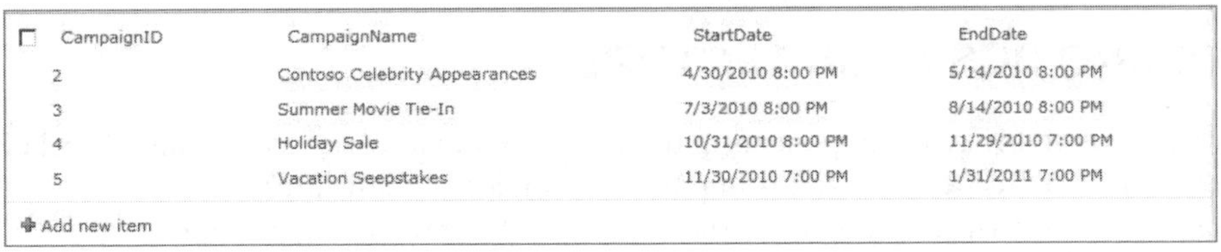

	CampaignID	CampaignName	StartDate	EndDate
	2	Contoso Celebrity Appearances	4/30/2010 8:00 PM	5/14/2010 8:00 PM
	3	Summer Movie Tie-In	7/3/2010 8:00 PM	8/14/2010 8:00 PM
	4	Holiday Sale	10/31/2010 8:00 PM	11/29/2010 7:00 PM
	5	Vacation Seepstakes	11/30/2010 7:00 PM	1/31/2011 7:00 PM

➕ Add new item

FIGURE 11-8

SharePoint Server 2010 supports taking lists offline through Microsoft Outlook. For this walk-through, the External List was defined as an Appointment Office Type, and it can be synchronized with Outlook by selecting the Connect to Outlook button in the List tab of the Ribbon within SharePoint. When this button is clicked, a Visual Studio Tools for Office (VSTO) package is accessed and an installation screen is presented. This VSTO package must be installed for synchronization to continue. Figure 11-9 shows the installation screen that is presented to the user.

FIGURE 11-9

In addition to taking the list offline through Outlook, you can also take it offline through the SharePoint Workspace. In this case, you click the Sync to SharePoint Workspace button on the list tab in the SharePoint Ribbon. In a fashion similar to Outlook, a VSTO package will be installed and then the list will be available in the SharePoint Workspace. Figure 11-10 shows the list in the SharePoint Workspace.

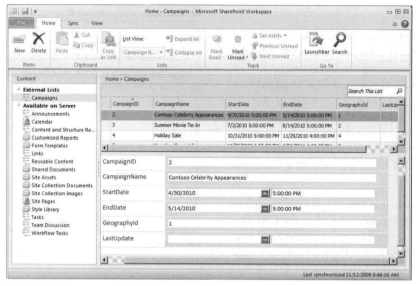

FIGURE 11-10

UNDERSTANDING BCS ARCHITECTURE

BCS is made up of several different components and interacts with many services within SharePoint. In order to create effective BCS solutions, it is important to understand the architecture, components, and service interfaces available to the developer. A detailed diagram of this architecture is presented in Figure 11-11.

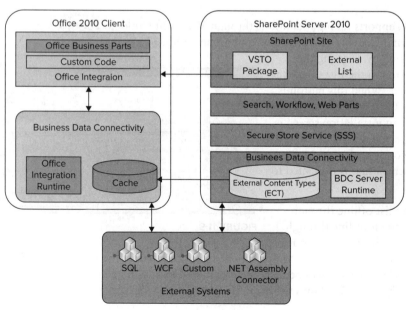

FIGURE 11-11

Understanding Connectors

As mentioned previously, BCS communicates with external systems using several different connectors. The simple solution presented earlier utilized the SQL connector to access a SQL Server database, but BCS also supports a WCF connector for accessing web services. Together, the SQL and WCF connector cover a significant number of datasources, but they can't cover all possible scenarios.

For systems that cannot be accessed as a database or a web service, a custom connector could be built. Custom connectors are intended to be built for a particular type of system. For example, you could build a custom connector for Microsoft Exchange. If you did this, then you would have options in SPD for connecting to SQL, WCF, and Exchange. Creating custom connectors is beyond the scope of this chapter.

In scenarios where you need more flexibility than is provided by the SQL and WCF connectors, you will likely build a .NET Assembly Connector instead. A .NET Assembly Connector is a project that you create in Visual Studio 2010 that contains the ECT definition and associated business logic for accessing a specific external system. The .NET Assembly Connector differs from the custom connector because it targets a specific instance of a system, as opposed to all instances of a specific system type. In other words, you can use a .NET Assembly Connector to access a specific folder in Exchange, while a custom connector could be used to access any folder in Exchange.

The .NET Assembly Connector is also useful for aggregating data from multiple sources into a single ECT, which cannot be accomplished using a custom connector. While accessing an external system, the .NET Assembly Connector can also apply business rules to data before it is made available in SharePoint, and facilitate search indexing of a specific external system. The .NET Assembly Connector is covered in detail later in the chapter.

Understanding Business Data Connectivity

As stated previously, BDC is the term that encompasses the plumbing and runtime components of BCS. Both the server and the client have BDC components. These components are complementary, so you can use a similar approach to creating BCS solutions whether you are focused on the server, client, or both. On the server, the BDC components consist of the ECT catalog and the server-side BDC runtime. On the client, the BDC components consist of a metadata cache and the client-side BDC runtime.

Managing the Business Data Connectivity Service

When you create ECTs in SPD and save them, they are stored in the ECT Catalog (also referred to as the metadata catalog). This catalog is a database that is accessed through the Business Data Connectivity service application. Figure 11-12 shows the basic architecture of the BDC service application.

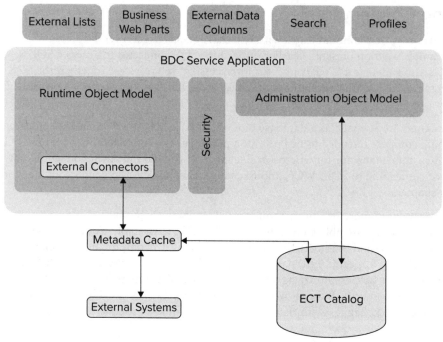

FIGURE 11-12

External Connectors and ECT metadata are used to access the external systems and retrieve data through the runtime object model. The BDC service application then provides that data for use inside of SharePoint. A metadata cache is maintained in the service so that ECT data is easily accessed without having to read it from the database. This metadata cache is updated every minute to ensure that the latest ECT data is available to the farm.

Along with caching metadata to improve performance, BCS also can limit the total number of connections made to the external system. Additionally, the BDC service application implements five different throttle settings to limit the connections made and data returned from external systems. Table 11-1 lists the throttles and the default settings.

TABLE 11-1: BDC Service Application Throttles

TYPE	DESCRIPTION	SCOPE	DEFAULT	MAXIMUM
Connections	Total number of connections allowed to external systems	Global	100	500
Items	Number of rows returned from a database query	Database	2000	25,000
Timeout	Database connection timeout	Database	60 sec	600 sec
Size	Size of returned data	WCF	3Mb	150Mb
Timeout	Web service connection timeout	WCF	60 sec	600 sec

Managing throttles is accomplished using PowerShell scripts. The following code displays the current throttle settings:

```
Add-PSSnapin Microsoft.SharePoint.PowerShell -ErrorAction SilentlyContinue
$bdc = Get-SPServiceApplicationProxy
        | Where {$_ -match "Business Data Connectivity"}

Get-SPBusinessDataCatalogThrottleConfig -ThrottleType Connections -Scope Global
                                        -ServiceApplicationProxy $bdc
Get-SPBusinessDataCatalogThrottleConfig -ThrottleType Items -Scope Database
                                        -ServiceApplicationProxy $bdc
Get-SPBusinessDataCatalogThrottleConfig -ThrottleType Timeout -Scope Database
                                        -ServiceApplicationProxy $bdc
Get-SPBusinessDataCatalogThrottleConfig -ThrottleType Size -Scope Wcf
                                        -ServiceApplicationProxy $bdc
Get-SPBusinessDataCatalogThrottleConfig -ThrottleType Timeout -Scope Wcf
                                        -ServiceApplicationProxy $bdc
```

List_Throttles.ps1

Each of the throttle settings may be modified using PowerShell. The following code shows how to change the number of items that can be returned from a database:

```
Add-PSSnapin Microsoft.SharePoint.PowerShell -ErrorAction SilentlyContinue
$bdc = Get-SPServiceApplicationProxy
        | Where {$_ -match "Business Data Connectivity"}

$throttle = Get-SPBusinessDataCatalogThrottleConfig
            -ThrottleType Items
            -Scope Database
            -ServiceApplicationProxy $bdc
Set-SPBusinessDataCatalogThrottleConfig
            -Maximum 3000
            -Default 1000
            -Identity $throttle
```

Alternately, you can simply disable any throttle. The following code shows how to disable the connections throttle:

```
Add-PSSnapin Microsoft.SharePoint.PowerShell -ErrorAction SilentlyContinue
$bdc = Get-SPServiceApplicationProxy
        | Where {$_ -match "Business Data Connectivity"}

$throttle = Get-SPBusinessDataCatalogThrottleConfig -ThrottleType Connections
            -Scope Global
            -ServiceApplicationProxy $bdc
Set-SPBusinessDataCatalogThrottleConfig -Enforced $false -Identity $throttle
```

The BDC service application is part of the service application framework in SharePoint. The management interface for the BDC service application is accessible through Central Administration by selecting Application Management ⇨ Manage Service Applications. Figure 11-13 shows the BDC service application in Central Administration.

From the Service Applications page, you can click the Properties button in the Ribbon and see the basic service properties for the BDC service application. In the Properties dialog, you will see the name of the database where the ECTs are stored. This database is set up when the BDC service application is first created

Campaign

CampaignID: 2
CampaignName: Contoso Celebrity Appearances
StartDate: 5/1/2010 12:00 AM
EndDate: 5/15/2010 12:00 AM

Campaigns

	CampaignID	CampaignName	StartDate	EndDate	GeographyId
☐	2	Contoso Celebrity Appearances	4/30/2010 8:00 PM	5/14/2010 8:00 PM	1
	3	Summer Movie Tie-In	7/3/2010 8:00 PM	8/14/2010 8:00 PM	2
	4	Holiday Sale	10/31/2010 8:00 PM	11/29/2010 7:00 PM	4
	5	Vacation Seepstakes	11/30/2010 7:00 PM	1/31/2011 7:00 PM	5

✦ Add new item

FIGURE 11-13

during farm installation and configuration. As with all services, you can also set administrative and connection permissions for the service so that it can be used by other servers in the SharePoint farm.

Clicking the Manage button on the Service Applications page will open the View External Content Types page. This page lists all of the ECTs that are currently stored in the catalog. Initially, the page is in Browse mode, but clicking the Edit tab in the Ribbon reveals administrative functionality for the ECTs. On the Edit tab, you can grant rights to manage the ECT catalog by clicking the Set Catalog Permissions button, and you can set rights for individual ECTs by clicking the Set Object Permissions button. This allows you to control the users that are able to use ECTs to access external systems.

On the Edit tab, there is also a drop-down list that determines how ECT information is presented on the page. Initially, the drop-down is set to External Content Types, which shows the ECTs in a list. Selecting External Datasources from the drop-down list will show all of the available connections that are defined. Selecting Application Models, on the other hand, will list the models, along with both connection and ECT information.

The list of Application Models is of special importance to the developer. This is because the Application Model contains the reference to the ECT, the connection information for the external systems, security information, and more. Furthermore, the model can be exported using the drop-down menu on the list item and then subsequently imported into another catalog. When a model is exported, it is saved as an XML file. Models can also be exported directly from SPD by right-clicking the ECT and selecting Export Application Model.

The following code shows part of a model based on the walk-through earlier in the chapter. Developers who have previous experience with the MOSS Business Data Catalog will immediately recognize many of the elements in the listing. Take special note of the highlighted code. In the `LobSystemInstance` properties, you can see the basic connection information for the external system. These values were all set when the external system connection was specified in SPD.

```xml
<?xml version="1.0" encoding="utf-16" standalone="yes"?>
<Model xmlns:xsi="http://www.w3.org/2001/XMLSchema-instance"
xsi:schemaLocation="http://schemas.microsoft.com/windows/2007/BusinessDataCatalog
BDCMetadata.xsd"
Name="SharePointDesigner-CampaignsData-Administrator"
 xmlns="http://schemas.microsoft.com/windows/2007/BusinessDataCatalog">
```

```
<Properties>
  <Property Name="Discovery" Type="System.String"></Property>
</Properties>
<LobSystems>
  <LobSystem Type="Database" Name="SharePointDesigner-CampaignsData">
    <Properties>
      <Property Name="DiscoveryVersion" Type="System.Int32">0</Property>
      <Property Name="WildcardCharacter" Type="System.String">%</Property>
      <Property Name="Discovery" Type="System.String"></Property>
    </Properties>
    <LobSystemInstances>
      <LobSystemInstance Name="SharePointDesigner-CampaignsData">
        <Properties>
          <Property Name="AuthenticationMode" Type="System.String">
            PassThrough
          </Property>
          <Property Name="DatabaseAccessProvider" Type="System.String">
            SqlServer
          </Property>
          <Property Name="RdbConnection Data Source" Type="System.String">
            Localhost
          </Property>
          <Property Name="RdbConnection Initial Catalog"
                    Type="System.String">ContosoAdvertising</Property>
          <Property Name="RdbConnection Integrated Security"
                    Type="System.String">SSPI</Property>
          <Property Name="RdbConnection Pooling" Type="System.Boolean">
            True
          </Property>
          <Property Name="Discovery" Type="System.String"></Property>
          <Property Name="ConnectionName" Type="System.String">
            CampaignsData
          </Property>
        </Properties>
      </LobSystemInstance>
    </LobSystemInstances>
  </LobSystem>
</LobSystems>
</Model>
```

Campaign.xml

The `AuthenticationMode` in the code sample is set to `PassThrough`. When set to this value, BCS will attempt to connect to the external system using the credentials of the current user. As you saw in the walk-through, options also exist to provide an explicit set of credentials or to map credentials using the Secure Store Service (SSS), which is covered later in the chapter.

Introducing the BDC Server Runtime

The BDC Server Runtime consists of the runtime object model, the administration object model, and the security infrastructure. The runtime object model provides access to ECTs, while the administration object model provides objects for managing the ECTs catalog. The security infrastructure facilitates authentication and authorization for ECT operations and external system access.

Understanding the Client Cache

When BCS solutions are taken to Office clients, a client cache is used to store external data for display with automatic synchronization between the client cache and the associated external system. The client cache is a SQL Server Compact Edition (SQLCE) database that is installed as part of the Office 2010 installation. There is no reason for developers to ever access the database directly, and doing so can damage the BCS installation.

A synchronization process (BCSSync.exe) runs on the client to synchronize the cache with the associated external systems. When CRUD operations are performed on data within the Office clients, the operations are queued inside the client cache and synchronized with the external system when it is available. The synchronization process will also attempt, at various intervals, to update data in the cache from the external system according to the user settings and availability of the external system. Conflicts between the cache and the external system are flagged for the end user so that they may be resolved.

Introducing the Office Integration Runtime

The Office Integration Runtime (OIR) is the set of components and the associated API that binds ECTs to the Office clients and your own custom solutions. The OIR loads whenever a host Office client is started. The OIR is installed on the client as part of the Office 2010 installation process.

Understanding the Secure Store Service

The Secure Store Service (SSS) is a service application that provides for the storage, mapping, and retrieval of credential information. Typically, the credentials stored by SSS are used to access external systems that do not support Windows authentication. This is accomplished by mapping the stored credentials to an existing Windows user or group.

In order to store credential sets for an external system, a new Target Application must be created in SSS. The Target Application acts as a container for credential sets mapped to an external system. The Target Application settings page contains a name for the application and a setting to specify whether each individual user will have a separate set of mapped credentials or whether every user will map to a single common set of credentials. Figure 11-14 shows application settings mapping a single set or credentials to an Active Directory group.

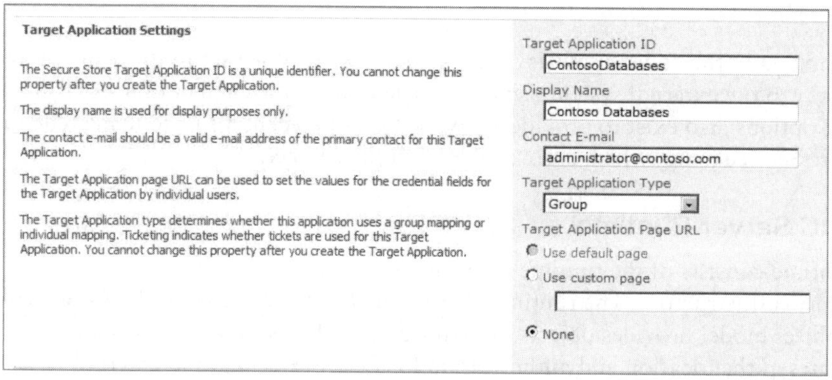

FIGURE 11-14

After the Target Application is defined, credential fields are defined. In most cases, the Target Application will save a username and password, but it is important to point out that SSS can save any text-based credential information. For example, a "domain" field could be added so that the credential sets consisted of username, password, and domain. Figure 11-15 shows typical username and password fields defined for an application.

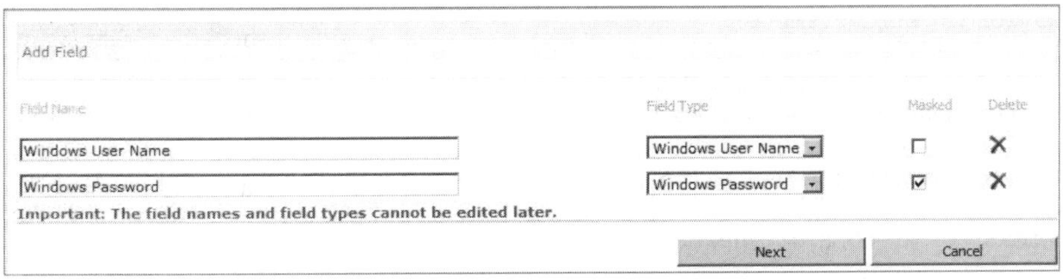

FIGURE 11-15

Once the application and credential fields are defined, you must enter the actual credential information. For each user or group that will access the external system, a set of credentials must be created using the field definitions for the application. Figure 11-16 shows credentials being entered for an application. Once the credentials are in place, the application can be used during the definition of an ECT to allow access to the external system using the credentials stored in the SSS. If an end user should attempt to access the system without proper credentials in SSS, then they will be directed to a login page so the credentials can be entered and stored.

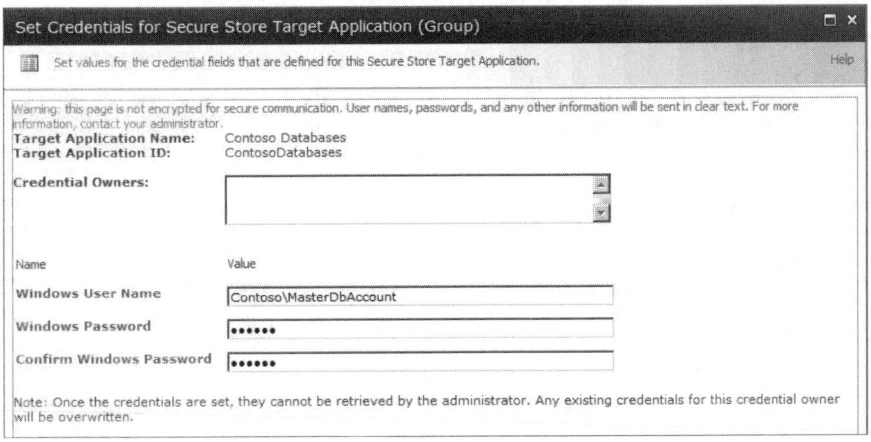

FIGURE 11-16

While BCS and SSS work well together to provide authentication in many scenarios, there will be times when you want to utilize SSS in custom solutions. In these cases, you can access SSS programmatically to retrieve credentials. These credentials are often used by connectors to access external systems that have proprietary security systems. Additionally, they can be used by web parts to access external systems directly without using BCS. The following code shows how to access the credentials in the default instance of SSS. Note that the credentials are stored as `SecureString` objects.

```
ISecureStoreProvider p = SecureStoreProviderFactory.Create();
string username = string.Empty;
string password = string.Empty;

using (SecureStoreCredentialCollection creds =
        p.GetCredentials("ContosoDatabases"))
{
    foreach (SecureStoreCredential c in creds)
    {
        switch (c.CredentialType)
        {
            case SecureStoreCredentialType.UserName:
                username = c.Credential.ToString();
                break;

            case SecureStoreCredentialType.Password:
                password = c.Credential.ToString();
                break;

            case SecureStoreCredentialType.WindowsUserName:
                username = c.Credential.ToString();
                break;

            case SecureStoreCredentialType.WindowsPassword:
                password = c.Credential.ToString();
                break;

            case SecureStoreCredentialType.Generic:
                //Generic credentials
                break;

            case SecureStoreCredentialType.Key:
                //Key
                break;

            case SecureStoreCredentialType.Pin:
                //Pin
                break;
        }
    }

    //Log in using the credentials
}
```

Credentials.sln

Understanding Package Deployment

When an end user elects to synchronize an external list with Outlook or the SharePoint Workspace, BCS creates a VSTO Click-Once deployment package that contains all of the elements necessary to work with the list on the client. The package is created by BCS just-in-time and stored under the list in a folder named `ClientSolution`. After the package is created, the deployment is started automatically.

The package contains the BDC Metadata Model defining the external system, ECTs, operations, and security information necessary to access and modify data. The package also contains subscription information, which tells the client cache what data to manage and how it should be refreshed. Finally, the package contains pre- and post-deployment steps that should be taken, such as creating custom forms in the client application to display the data.

Once deployed, the add-in can make use of *Office Business Parts* on the client to help render data. Office Business Parts are Windows form controls that display a single item or list of items in a task pane. These parts simplify the rendering process so that custom task panes do not have to be created for the client. In fact, BCS supports a special type of declarative solution for Outlook that makes use of Office Business Parts. This solution type is beyond the scope of this chapter.

UNDERSTANDING AUTHENTICATION SCENARIOS

When connecting to backend systems, BCS must deal with several different authentication scenarios. In the simplest case, BCS may be passing Windows credentials from the user through to the external system. However, most real-world applications have more complex requirements, for example, proprietary authentication mechanisms such as tokens or claims. For BCS solutions to be secure, they must gracefully deal with these situations.

Configuring Authentication Models

The most common BCS authentication scenario involves a database or web service as the external system. Most often, these systems are internal to the organization and use either Windows authentication or username/password authentication. In these scenarios, BCS supports two authentication models: *Trusted Subsystem* and *Impersonation and Delegation*. In the Trusted Subsystem model, BCS utilizes a single account to access the external system regardless of the end user's identity. Under Impersonation and Delegation, BCS attempts to impersonate the end user and access the external system. The `AuthenticationMode` element in the BDC Metadata Model determines how authentication is performed.

Understanding Passthrough Authentication

`Passthrough` authentication falls within the Impersonation and Delegation authentication model. Setting the value of the `AuthenticationMode` element to `Passthrough` causes BCS to use the credentials of the current user to access the external system. `Passthrough` is simple to set up by selecting "Connect with User's Identity" when configuring the external system connection in SPD, as was shown in the walk-through earlier in this chapter. However, `Passthrough` authentication is unlikely to be useful in many situations because of limitations inherent in Windows authentication.

Windows authentication takes two forms: *NTLM* and *Kerberos*. NTLM is the classic challenge-response protocol used to authenticate users. Kerberos is an advanced *ticket-based* protocol that is much more secure. While Kerberos authentication is considered to be a best practice for SharePoint deployment, it requires modification to Active Directory that many organizations avoid. As a result, the vast majority of networks still run under NTLM authentication.

The problem for BCS under NTLM authentication involves something known as the *double-hop issue*. The double-hop issue describes a scenario where the web server attempts to impersonate an end user through a series of "hops" involving authenticating to multiple servers. As a practical example, imagine that a BCS solution is created that connects to a web service using `Passthrough` authentication, which in turn wraps a secure datasource.

When an end user makes a request to view an external list based on the web service source, BCS attempts to impersonate the user when calling the web service. Because SharePoint itself is configured to impersonate end users, this first call will succeed. However, when the web service subsequently attempts to access the wrapped datasource, it will be prevented from continuing to impersonate the end user, and the account identity will change to that of the web service. At this point the original end-user identity is lost, and access to the datasource will be denied. This is the double-hop issue.

The double-hop issue is not a bug; it exists by design. The limitation is designed to prevent viruses from accessing network resources should credentials be compromised. Kerberos, however, does not suffer from this limitation because its ticketing-based protocol is more secure than challenge-response. So changing the network authentication mechanism from NTLM to Kerberos will solve the problem. Otherwise, you must use a different BCS authentication mechanism.

Understanding RevertToSelf

`RevertToSelf` falls within the Trusted Subsystem model of authentication. Setting the value of the `AuthenticationMode` element to `RevertToSelf` causes BCS to use the credentials of the application pool to access the external system. Configuring `RevertToSelf` is accomplished by editing the connection information to the external system after it is defined. In the SharePoint Designer, on the Summary View for the ECT, the connection information may be edited by clicking the hyperlink for the external system. Figure 11-17 shows the Connection Properties dialog. `RevertToSelf` is specified by selecting the option BDC Identity.

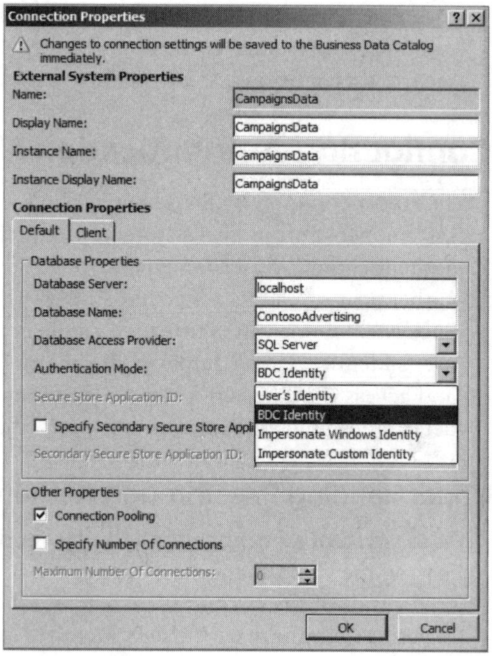

FIGURE 11-17

Using `RevertToSelf` authentication can help reduce double-hop problems. This is because BCS is no longer attempting to impersonate the end user all the way to the external system. The drawback, however, is that all access is accomplished by using the same account. Therefore, there is no mechanism to know who made changes to the external system.

Understanding Secure Store Options

Earlier in the chapter, you saw how to set up the SSS to map credentials from BCS to an external system. SSS is a flexible credential management service that supports both the Trusted Subsystem and Impersonation and Delegation authentication models. If you map all end-user credentials to a single group account in SSS, then you can support the Trusted Subsystem authentication model. If, on the other hand, you map end user credentials to a unique set of credentials per user, then SSS is supporting the Impersonation and Delegation authentication model.

Regardless of which authentication model you are implementing, SSS is capable of managing three different types of credentials: Windows, SQL, and username/password. These three credential types correspond to three different settings for the `AuthenticationMode` element: `WindowsCredentials`, `RdbCredentials`, and `Credentials`.

Setting the `AuthenticationMode` element to `WindowsCredentials` is done when the external system supports Windows authentication. Setting the `AuthenticationMode` to `RdbCredentials` is done when the external system is a database supporting SQL authentication. Setting the `AuthenticationMode` to `Credentials` is done when the external system supports simple username/password authentication. The `WindowsCredentials` and `RdbCredentials` settings work with both databases and web services when you select "Impersonate Windows Identity" or "Impersonate Custom Identity" in the Connection Properties dialog. The `Credentials` setting is used only with web services that do not support Windows authentication.

In addition to the primary SSS application, BCS supports a secondary SSS application that can be used for application-level authentication. This functionality exists to support special situations in which the external system requires credentials to be passed to the system as part of each operation. The credentials held in the secondary application can be configured as a filter to restrict the results returned from the external systems. Filters are discussed later in the chapter.

Accessing Claims-Based Systems

Because SharePoint 2010 supports claims authentication, BCS can also use claims to authenticate against external systems. Of course, to implement claims authentication, the external system must support claims and trust the claims provider used with SharePoint. At this writing, there are few systems that support claims authentication in most organizations, but the number will increase over time. A likely scenario today involves a custom Windows Communication Foundation (WCF) service that implements claims authentication.

In order to implement claims authentication, the `AuthenticationMode` should be set to `Passthrough`. As previously discussed, this will cause BCS to try to authenticate with the current user's credentials. However, when BCS attempts authentication, the WCF service will request a Security Assertion Markup Language (SAML) token, which is the currency used for authentication in a claims environment.

When BCS receives the request for a SAML token, it contacts the Secure Token Service (STS), a shared service running in the SharePoint farm. STS looks at the end user credentials and issues a SAML token. This SAML token is then used by the WCF connector to authenticate against the WCF service. For the most part, claims-based authentication happens automatically, provided that the external system accepts the SAML token provided by BCS.

Accessing Token-Based Systems

Today, many web-based applications utilize a token-based authentication system. These systems typically have a logon mechanism that is separate from the applications that they support. For example, Windows Live has a logon system that utilizes a Windows Live ID. This ID is used for many applications, including HotMail, SkyDrive, and Live Mesh. Regardless of the application, however, end users always use the same logon screen to authenticate themselves and receive a token that is trusted by the applications.

BCS can support authentication against token-based systems, but it requires the creation of a custom SSS provider designed to work with the particular token system. Additionally, a custom handler must be created to redirect users to the appropriate logon page for the system. Creating these customizations is beyond the scope of this chapter.

Managing Client Authentication

Generally, BCS clients have symmetry with the server-side functionality. The Application Model created in SPD is synchronized with clients when external lists are accessed through Office clients. However, some authentication settings, like those that use SSS, will not work correctly from the client because the client always accesses the external system directly without going through the server. In these cases, special consideration must be given to how the client handles authentication. Fortunately, the connection settings for the ECT allow you to specify different authentication values for client and server.

When the `AuthenticationMode` is set to `Passthrough`, the client will always try to connect to the external system using the Windows credentials of the current user. This means that the external system must support Windows authentication, and the current user must have rights to perform the requested operations. Otherwise, the call will fail.

When the `AuthenticationMode` is set to `RevertToSelf`, BCS is supposed to use the application pool account when accessing the external system. However, clients have no mechanism with which to use this account because they always access the external systems directly. In this case, authentication will fail.

Additional problems can occur when a Trusted Subsystem authentication model that maps to group credentials in SSS is used. This is because the BCS runtime on the client has no mechanism to determine whether the end user is in a particular Active Directory group. In this case, as well, authentication may fail.

Regardless of the authentication settings, the client will store its BCS credentials in the Credential Manager. The Credential Manager is a password store system that supports single sign-on (SSO) to a variety of systems, including websites and remote computers. Credential Manager is part of the operating system, so you can open it within Windows and view and manage your credentials. If authentication fails from the client, BCS automatically deletes the credentials from the Credential Manager store.

Managing Authorization

Authentication is only the first part of accessing data from external systems. Even after the user is authenticated, BCS must determine whether the user is authorized to call a particular operation on an ECT. BCS has four different permissions that may be assigned. These are Edit, Execute, Set Permissions, and Selectable in Clients. The Edit right grants the ability to create, delete, and update BCS metadata. The Execute right grants the ability to make a call to an external system. The Set Permissions right grants the ability to assign rights to other users, and the Selectable in Clients right provides access to utilities such as the entity picker. These rights can be assigned at the model, system, entity, and operation levels using the interface in Central Administration for the BDC shared service.

CREATING EXTERNAL CONTENT TYPES

External Content Types are at the heart of BCS; every BCS solution will have at least one ECT defined. The definition of an ECT includes all of the information schema, data operations, relationships, filters, actions, and security descriptors necessary to bring external system data into SharePoint. All of this information is defined inside of the Application Model, which centers on the definition of *entities*. The following code shows where entities are defined inside of the Application Model XML:

```xml
<?xml version="1.0" encoding="utf-16" standalone="yes"?>
<Model>
  <LobSystems>
    <LobSystem Type="Database" Name="CampaignsData">
      <LobSystemInstances>
        <LobSystemInstance Name="CampaignsData">
        </LobSystemInstance>
      </LobSystemInstances>
      <Entities>
        <Entity Namespace="http://www.contoso.com" Version="1.1.0.0"
        EstimatedInstanceCount="10000" Name="Campaign"
        DefaultDisplayName="Campaign">
        </Entity>
      </Entities>
    </LobSystem>
  </LobSystems>
</Model>
```

Campaign.xml

Creating Operations

BCS supports a wide variety of operations designed to facilitate accessing systems and performing CRUD functions. Generally, you will be concerned with basic reading and writing to external systems using `Finder` (Read List), `SpecificFinder` (Read Item), `Creator` (Create), `Updater` (Update), and `Deleter` (Delete), methods. These methods are also supported in SPD through menus in the Operations Design View. Methods that are not supported by SPD offer additional functionality and control, but must be created by hand-editing the BDC Metadata Model. Table 11-2 lists all of the supported BCS operations.

TABLE 11-2: Supported BCS Operations

NAME	DESCRIPTION
Finder	Returns multiple records from an external system based on a wildcard
SpecificFinder	Returns a single record from an external system based on a primary key
IdEnumerator	Returns all primary keys from an external system to support search indexing
Scalar	Returns a scalar value from an external system
AccessChecker	Checks to see what rights are allowed for a user
Creator	Creates a new record in an external system
Updater	Updates an existing record in an external system
Deleter	Deletes a record in an external system
ChangedIdEnumerator	Returns primary keys for records that have changed to support incremental search indexing
DeletedIdEnumerator	Returns primary keys for records that have been deleted to support incremental search indexing
AssociationNavigator	Navigates from one entity to a related entity
Associator	Associates an entity with another entity
Disassociator	Disassociates one entity from another
GenericInvoker	Used to perform operations not supported by any of the defined operations
StreamAccessor	Supports accessing BLOB data from an external system
BinarySecurityDescriptorAccessor	Returns a security descriptor
BulkSpecificFinder	Returns a set of records from the external system in a batch based on a set of primary keys
BulkAssociatedIdEnumerator	Returns a set of primary keys representing records associated with an entity
BulkAssociationNavigator	Supports navigation from one entity to many related entities
BulkIdEnumerator	Returns all primary keys in a batch from an external system to support search indexing

Finder methods are used to return a result set from the external system and are a requirement for creating external lists. You can create a Finder method in SPD by selecting to create a "New Read List" operation. The following code snippet shows the definition of a Finder method:

```xml
<Method Name="Read List" DefaultDisplayName="Campaign Read List">
  <Properties>
    <Property Name="RdbCommandType"
    Type="System.Data.CommandType, System.Data, Version=2.0.0.0, Culture=neutral,
    PublicKeyToken=b77a5c561934e089">Text</Property>
    <Property Name="RdbCommandText" Type="System.String">
    SELECT TOP(@CampaignID) [CampaignID] , [CampaignName] , [StartDate] ,
    [EndDate] , [GeographyId] , [LastUpdate]
    FROM [dbo].[Campaigns] ORDER BY [CampaignID]
    </Property>
    <Property Name="BackEndObjectType" Type="System.String">
      SqlServerTable
    </Property>
    <Property Name="BackEndObject" Type="System.String">Campaigns</Property>
    <Property Name="Schema" Type="System.String">dbo</Property>
  </Properties>
  <Parameters>
    <Parameter Direction="In" Name="@CampaignID">
      <TypeDescriptor TypeName="System.Int64" AssociatedFilter="Filter"
                      Name="CampaignID">
        <DefaultValues>
          <DefaultValue MethodInstanceName="Read List" Type="System.Int64">
            100
          </DefaultValue>
        </DefaultValues>
      </TypeDescriptor>
    </Parameter>
    <Parameter Direction="Return" Name="Read List">
      <TypeDescriptor TypeName="System.Data.IDataReader, System.Data,
      Version=2.0.0.0,
      Culture=neutral, PublicKeyToken=b77a5c561934e089" IsCollection="true"
      Name="Read List">
        <TypeDescriptors>
          <TypeDescriptor TypeName="System.Data.IDataRecord, System.Data,
          Version=2.0.0.0,
          Culture=neutral, PublicKeyToken=b77a5c561934e089"
          Name="Read ListElement">
            <TypeDescriptors>
              <TypeDescriptor TypeName="System.Int32" ReadOnly="true"
              IdentifierName="CampaignID" Name="CampaignID" />
              <TypeDescriptor TypeName="System.String" Name="CampaignName">
                <Properties>
                  <Property Name="Size" Type="System.Int32">50</Property>
                  <Property Name="RequiredInForms" Type="System.Boolean">
                    true
                  </Property>
                  <Property Name="ShowInPicker" Type="System.Boolean">
```

```
                        true
                    </Property>
                </Properties>
                    ...
        </Parameter>
    </Parameters>
    <MethodInstances>
        <MethodInstance Type="Finder" ReturnParameterName="Read List" Default="true"
        Name="Read List" DefaultDisplayName="Campaign Read List">
            <Properties>
                <Property Name="UseClientCachingForSearch" Type="System.String"></Property>
                <Property Name="RootFinder" Type="System.String"></Property>
                <Property Name="LastModifiedTimeStampField" Type="System.String">
                    LastUpdate
                </Property>
            </Properties>
        </MethodInstance>
    </MethodInstances>
</Method>
```

Campaign.xml

In the definition for the `Finder` method, SPD automatically generates a SQL query to retrieve items for display in the list. This is done when the methods are created in the wizard. Optionally, you could edit these entries to use stored procedures instead of dynamic SQL. Also, take note of how the return parameters are defined so that BCS understands the data returned from the external system. In particular, note the use of the `TypeDescriptor` element. The `TypeDescriptor` is used to map data types in the external system to .NET data types in BCS.

You can create multiple `Finder` methods, but one will always be designated as the default. The default `Finder` method forms the basis of the default view of an external list and provides support for crawling the external system so that it can be searched. SPD automatically adds a `RootFinder` property to the default `Finder` method. This property is used when crawling the external system to specify the records in the external system that should be indexed. Additionally, the method can be designated as a timestamp field to support incremental crawls. Designating a field as a timestamp is done in the Return Parameters section of the Operation Wizard and appears in the BDC Metadata Model as a `LastModifiedTimeStamp` property.

`SpecificFinder` methods are used to return a single item from the external system and are also required to support external lists. The `Creator`, `Updater`, and `Deleter` methods are optional for external lists. All of the methods have similar XML structures in the BDC Metadata Model.

Creating Relationships

BCS supports the definition of relationships between entities, which allows you to display one-to-many relationships and navigate between entities within SharePoint. In order to create a relationship, select New Association from the context menu in the Operations Design View.

This will start a wizard to help you define the new association. The wizard will ask you to select another ECT with which to make the association. If the ECTs are based on related tables in a database, SPD will infer the relationship using the foreign key. If not, you will have to specify the relationship manually by associating fields from the parent to child ECT. The following code shows a relationship between a Campaign entity and a Geography entity, where the relationship references the geography in which the campaign will occur.

```
<Method IsStatic="false" Name="GeographyAssociation">
  <Properties>
    ...
  </Properties>
  <Parameters>
    <Parameter Direction="In" Name="@GeographyId">
      <TypeDescriptor ... />
    </Parameter>
    <Parameter Direction="Return" Name="GeographyAssociation">
      <TypeDescriptor ...>
        <TypeDescriptors>
          ...
        </TypeDescriptors>
      </TypeDescriptor>
    </Parameter>
  </Parameters>
  <MethodInstances>
    <Association Name="GeographyAssociation" Type="AssociationNavigator"
     ReturnParameterName="GeographyAssociation"
     DefaultDisplayName="Geography Association">
      <Properties>
        <Property Name="ForeignFieldMappings" Type="System.String">
        ... ForeignFieldMapping ForeignIdentifierName="GeographyId" ...
        </Property>
      </Properties>
      <SourceEntity Namespace="http://www.contoso.com/marketing"
                    Name="Geography" />
      <DestinationEntity Namespace="http://www.contoso.com/marketing"
                    Name="Campaign" />
    </Association>
  </MethodInstances>
</Method>
```

Geography.xml

Defining Filters

When creating `Finder` and `SpecificFinder` methods, you quite often want to limit the information that is returned from the external system. You may want to limit the returned data simply to prevent a large amount of data from being requested, and support conditional queries or wildcards. Table 11-3 lists all of the filters supported in BCS along with a description.

TABLE 11-3: Supported BCS Filters

NAME	DESCRIPTION
Comparison	Filters the records returned based on a value compared to a specific field.
Limit	Limits the total number of records returned to a fixed amount. Not compatible with the PageNumber filter.
PageNumber	Limits the records returned using paging. Not compatible with the Limit filter.
Timestamp	Filters the records returned based on a specified DateTime field.
Wildcard	Filters the records returned based on "Starts With" or "Contains" values.

Whenever you are creating `Finder` and `SpecificFinder` methods, you should define either a `Limit` or `PageNumber` filter for the operation. These filters ensure that large result sets are not returned to an external list. While BCS does implement throttling, the ECT should implement its own tighter limits to ensure that query performance is maintained.

Defining filters in SPD is done in the Operation Wizard on the Filter Parameters Configuration page. On this page, you may click the Add Filter Parameter button to add a new filter. After adding a new filter, you must then click the Filter hyperlink to open the Filter Configuration dialog. Figure 11-18 shows the Filter Configuration dialog within the Operation Wizard.

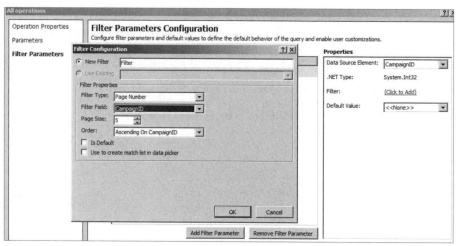

FIGURE 11-18

USING ECTS IN SHAREPOINT 2010

Once you have created ECTs, they can be used in SharePoint in a variety of ways. Initially, the external list is the simplest and most obvious way to surface external data. External lists, however, are only one way to use ECTs in SharePoint. SharePoint can also use ECTs to display data in web parts, support enhancements to other lists and facilities, and as a source for custom solutions. This section goes beyond the simple creation of an external list to show additional uses for ECTs.

Creating Custom Forms

External lists may be created from either SPD or from the Create page within SharePoint, and have many of the same capabilities as a standard list. When they are created from SPD, for example, you may also select to create an InfoPath form for editing items, by clicking the Create Lists and Form button. Creating an InfoPath form allows you to customize the appearance of the form as well as add validation logic.

Once you have created the InfoPath form, you can edit it by clicking the Design Forms in InfoPath button, which is available from the List Settings tab. Clicking this button will open the form in InfoPath, where you will have complete control over the appearance and functionality of the form. Figure 11-19 shows a simple item edit form that has been modified in InfoPath.

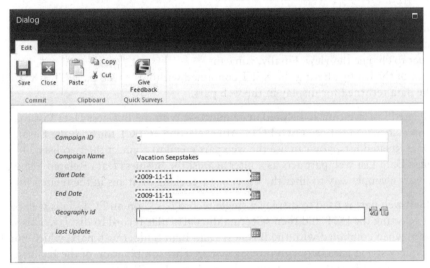

FIGURE 11-19

Using External Columns

Along with using an ECT as the basis for a list, you can also use an ECT as the source for a column in another list. This capability is known as creating an *external column*. When you create an external column for a list, you select the ECT to use as the basis for the column. You may then select one or more of the fields available in the ECT to display alongside the column you are creating.

These additional fields are known as *projected fields* because they project data from the ECT into the parent list. Figure 11-20 shows an external column definition.

Business Data Parts

Another way to use ECTs is through a set of web parts that ships with SharePoint Server 2010, known as *Business Data Parts*. Business Data Parts are designed specifically to display ECT data. The available parts include the Business Data List, Business Data Related List, and Business Data Item. These web parts display a list based on an ECT, a list based on an ECT association, or a single item, respectively.

The Business Data List part allows you to select an ECT and then displays a list of data based on a `Finder` method that you specify. In many ways, this web part is like an external list. You can, for example, modify the view by selecting which columns to display. If you have filters defined for the `Finder` method, these can be used to run simple queries against the list in order to change the view. Finally, you can

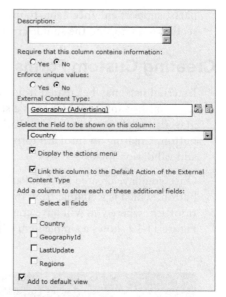

FIGURE 11-20

change the appearance of the list by altering the XSLT contained within the web part. This XSLT is used to transform the data returned for display in the web part.

The Business Data Related List is meant to be used in conjunction with the Business Data List to show data based on an association between two ECTs. After selecting an ECT for both the Business Data and Business Data Related lists, you can use the web part menu to connect the two lists. Once connected, the Business Data List web part acts as a filter against the Business Data Related List web part. This gives end users a simple way to filter the list view by clicking on items in the related list.

The Business Data Item web part is used to display a single record based on an ECT. This web part is configured by first selecting the ECT and then selecting the particular record to display. This web part is especially useful when combined with the Business Data Item Builder web part, which builds a business item from query string parameters in the page URL. This combination of the Business Data Item Builder web part and Business Data Item web part is used by BCS to create a *profile page* for an ECT. Profile pages are discussed in the next section. Figure 11-21 shows the Business Data List, Business Data Related List, and Business Data Item Builder web parts on a page.

Campaign List			Geography List
Actions ▾			Actions ▾
CampaignName	StartDate	EndDate	Regions
To display data in this web part, select an item in: Geography List			ᴿⱼ Northeast
			ᴿⱼ Southeast
Campaign			ᴿⱼ Midwest
CampaignName: Contoso Celebrity Appearances			ᴿⱼ Northwest
StartDate: 5/1/2010 12:00 AM			ᴿⱼ Southwest
EndDate: 5/15/2010 12:00 AM			

FIGURE 11-21

Creating a Profile Page

When SharePoint surfaces ECT data in lists and web parts, it does not necessarily show all of the available fields and associations. For example, when an ECT is used as the source for an external column, only a single field is required for display. When an end user sees partial ECT data, however, they are quite often interested in being able to drill into the data behind. This is where *profile pages* come into play. A profile page is a dedicated page that shows all of the ECT data for a specific record. This way, end users can jump from partial ECT data to a complete view of the record.

Profile pages are built using the Business Data Item Builder and Business Data Item web parts deployed onto a dedicated profile page. The profile page is typically accessed through an *action*. An action is defined as a hyperlink containing query string parameters that can be used by the Business Data Item Builder web part to construct the profile page. Actions are often surfaced as a drop-down menu associated with the displayed ECT data. Figure 11-22 shows an action menu associated with an external column.

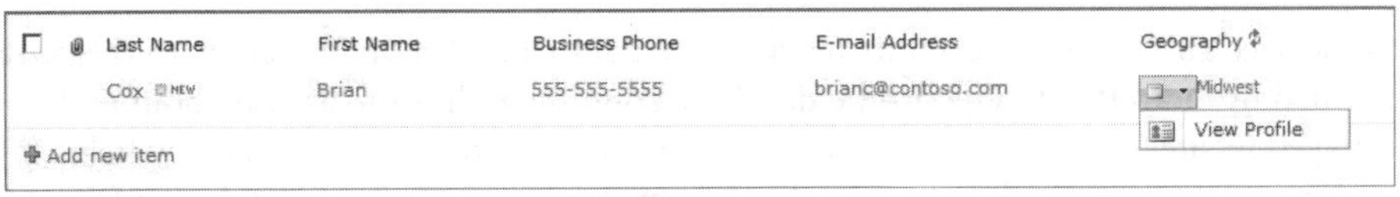

FIGURE 11-22

Before you can create profile pages, they must be enabled through the BDC service application. On the Edit tab for the BDC service application, you can click the Configure button in the Profile Pages group. In the dialog that opens, you must specify a SharePoint site where the profile pages can be created. After that, you can simply select ECTs and click the Create/Upgrade button to make profile pages for the ECTs you select. You can also make profile pages in SPD when you are designing your ECT.

Searching External Systems

As discussed earlier, ECTs created with SPD already support indexing by SharePoint Search. However, external systems will only be indexed if you explicitly set up a content source that includes the ECT. Content sources can be created within the Search service application, where you will have the option to create a content source associated with an external system.

When you select to create a new content source from an ECT, you will be presented with a drop-down list of the available BDC service applications. When you select a BDC service application, you will then have the option to index all external systems associated with the select service or to pick particular systems. Figure 11-23 shows the content source creation options.

After a content source is created and crawled, it may be used in the standard ways. This means that you may simply go to the Search Center, type a keyword, and return records from the external system. These results include a hyperlink to the profile page so that users can see the full details of the returned records. You may also set up search scopes and use them to search only the external system data.

Name	Name: *
Type a name to describe this content source.	Contoso Advertising

Content Source Type	Select the type of content to be crawled:
Select what type of content will be crawled. Note: This cannot be changed after this content source is created because other settings depend on it.	○ SharePoint Sites ○ Web Sites ○ File Shares ○ Exchange Public Folders ◉ Line of Business Data ○ Custom Repository

External Data Source	Select the Business Data Catalog Service Application:
A Line of Business Data content source crawls external data sources defined in an Application Model in a Business Data Catalog Service Application. Select whether to crawl all external data sources in the Business Data Catalog Service Application, or include only selected external data sources. Crawl Rule: To create a crawl rule for an external data source, use the following pattern: bdc3://*ExternalDataSourceName*	Business Data Connectivity ▼ ○ Crawl all external data sources in this Business Data Catalog Service Application ◉ Crawl selected external data source ☑ Advertising

FIGURE 11-23

Supplementing User Profiles

The User Profile service application is used to synchronize data from Active Directory to the profile database maintained by SharePoint. The profile database contains rich information about end users that can be displayed in sites. The User Profile service application maps Active Directory fields to fields in the user's profile. On a scheduled basis, this information is imported from Active Directory.

In much the same way that you can add search connections to external systems through ECTs, you can also add profile synchronization connections. Adding a new synchronization connection allows you to use data from external systems to supplement the data in the profile system. This is often useful in organizations that maintain a human resources (HR) system, but do not have rich data in their Active Directory system. In such cases, ECTs are designed against the HR system and mapped to fields in the profile database. Figure 11-24 shows a new connection being created in the User Profile service application.

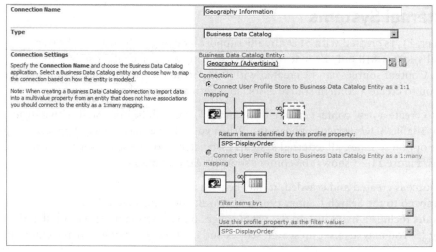

FIGURE 11-24

USING ECTS IN OFFICE 2010

Along with using ECTs on the SharePoint server, you can also utilize them in Office 2010 clients. With little effort, ECTs can be surfaced as lists in the SharePoint Workspace, items in Microsoft Outlook, or metadata columns in Microsoft Word. Furthermore, Office clients can sync with SharePoint to allow external lists to be managed offline.

Using the SharePoint Workspace

The SharePoint Workspace (SPW) is an Office 2010 client designed to be the central player in managing SharePoint data offline. Using SPW, end users can select to synchronize sites, lists, and libraries between their client and the SharePoint server.

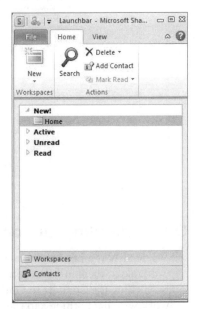

SPW has a simple interface that allows for synchronization to be initiated either through the browser or the SPW client. In the browser, end users can synchronize a single list or an entire site. Clicking the Sync to SharePoint Workspace button on the List tab causes SPW to synchronize a list. Clicking the same button on the Site Actions menu causes SPW to synchronize an entire site. The SPW client contains a *Launch Bar* that is accessible from an icon in the tray. The Launch Bar lists the available sites and allows you to specify new sites to synchronize by providing a URL. Figure 11-25 shows the Launch Bar.

SPW also contains a *Workspace Window* that can be opened to show all of the available lists and libraries in a site. In the walk-through earlier in the chapter, the Workspace Window was used to view an external list. The Workspace Window can be used to work with both lists and library documents, make

FIGURE 11-25

changes, and synchronize them with the server. When documents are added to the workspace, SPW will upload them to the server if it is online. If the client is offline, then documents are queued for upload in the *Upload Center*. The Upload Center presents the status of document upload and is accessible through an icon in the tray. Figure 11-26 shows the Upload Center.

Synchronization permissions can be managed through the SharePoint site. Site Collection administrators can use the standard permission settings to control who has access to the site. An additional option on the Site Settings page allows the administrator to set whether or not a particular site is available for offline use.

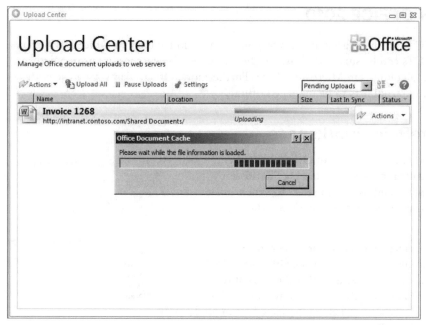

FIGURE 11-26

Understanding Outlook Integration

While SPW is a powerful client for managing SharePoint sites, many end users prefer to have data available to them in Microsoft Outlook as well. Lists can be synchronized with Microsoft Outlook by clicking the Connect to Outlook button on the List tab. Just like SPW, Outlook allows users to work with data offline and then synchronize it with SharePoint later.

When synchronizing external lists, ECTs can utilize Outlook forms by explicitly declaring that they should be displayed as an appointment, contact, task, or post when they are designed in SPD. Selecting the option to display an ECT as a particular type of Office item requires that external system fields be mapped to Outlook fields in the SPD wizard. Generally, the SPD wizards will prompt for the correct mapping through messages in the wizard. This mapping ensures that the data is correctly displayed inside of Outlook. Figure 11-27 shows sales campaign data from the earlier walkthrough displayed as a calendar in Outlook.

Synchronizing lists to Outlook brings along a VSTO solution for working with the items. While the synchronization behavior described in this section requires no customizations to work, you could choose to create your own VSTO solution to enhance the functionality of Outlook. This solution could be a full-blown custom VSTO solution created in Outlook or a special declarative solution unique to BCS. Creating custom VSTO solutions and declarative solutions is beyond the scope of this chapter but is worth investigating for more advanced needs.

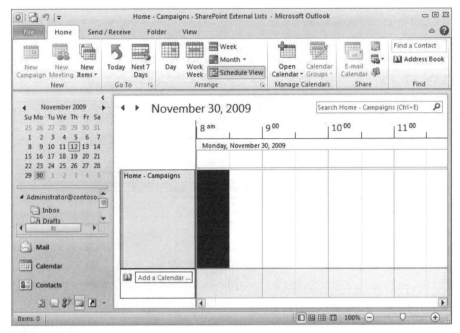

FIGURE 11-27

Using Word Quick Parts

When you choose to create an external column for a document library, this column will surface in Microsoft Word in the Document Information Pane (DIP) at the top of the document. The DIP is designed to present metadata information so that it can be filled in during the document creation process as opposed to prompting for metadata values when the document is saved.

In conjunction with viewing the metadata values in the DIP, document templates can also make use of *Quick Parts*. Quick Parts in Microsoft Word allow you to insert fields into the document template that are bound to the metadata fields of the document. When an end user fills in the field as part of the document creation process, the metadata values are set automatically. Adding Quick Parts to a document is done by selecting the appropriate metadata field from the Quick Parts list, which appears on the Insert tab in Microsoft Word.

While Quick Parts work well with all manner of document metadata, they work especially well with ECTs. This is because the Quick Parts will display a picker dialog for metadata that is based on an ECT. This makes it easy for end users to select valid values for the metadata, while improving the document creation experience. Figure 11-28 shows a document with a Quick Part based on the ECT created earlier in the walk-through. In the image, you can see the Quick Part field, the picker dialog, and the Quick Part list on the Insert tab.

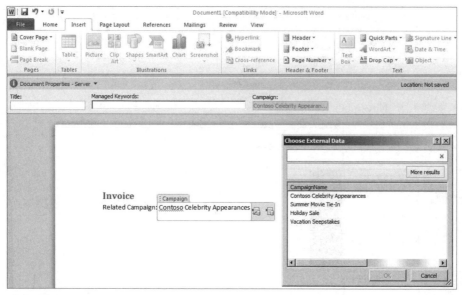

FIGURE 11-28

CREATING CUSTOM BCS SOLUTIONS

While BCS offers significant functionality without writing any code at all, there are advanced scenarios in which you will want to write custom BCS solutions. To support custom solutions, BCS has a complete set of object models for manipulating external data and managing ECT metadata. These models can be used on both the client and the server and have a high degree of symmetry between the two programming models.

Along with coding against the client and server model, you can also create your own external system connectors, as mentioned previously. These connectors are one of the most common BCS customizations because they give you a significant amount of control over the business logic applied to external data.

Using the Runtime Object Model

The Runtime Object Model is the API used for manipulating external data. Using the Runtime Object Model, you can perform full CRUD operations on external data through custom code. This is the programming interface used by external lists, which means that you can recreate the functionality of an external list in your own custom projects.

Using the Runtime Object Model requires you to set references in Visual Studio 2010 to the appropriate assemblies where the programming interface is defined. Selecting the correct assemblies is first a matter of deciding whether you are creating a server-side customization or a client-side customization. For server-side customizations, you will need to set references to the assemblies `Microsoft.BusinessData.dll` and `Microsoft.SharePoint.dll`. For client-side customizations,

you will need to set a reference to `Microsoft.BusinessData.dll` and `Microsoft.Office`
`.BusinessApplications.Runtime.dll`.

After you set a reference to the appropriate assemblies, the first challenge is to connect to the
appropriate catalog. If you are on the server, then you will connect with the metadata catalog
associated with the BDC service application. If you are on the client, then you will connect with the
client cache.

Connecting to the metadata catalog on the server can be done with or without a SharePoint
context, but the code will be different. In any case, you must get a reference to the
`BdcServiceApplicationProxy`. The `BdcServiceApplicationProxy` can then be used to connect
with the metadata catalog, which is represented by the `DatabaseBackedMetadataCatalog` object.
If your code is running with a SharePoint context, then the following code will connect to the
metadata catalog:

```
BdcServiceApplicationProxy p =
        (BdcServiceApplicationProxy)SPServiceContext.Current.GetDefaultProxy(
        typeof(BdcServiceApplicationProxy));
DatabaseBackedMetadataCatalog catalog = sap.GetDatabaseBackedMetadataCatalog();
```

HelloRuntimeOM.sln

If your code is running outside of a SharePoint context, then you will need additional code to
connect with the `BdcServiceApplicationProxy`. The following code shows how to create a LINQ
query to return the application proxy:

```
SPFarm farm = SPFarm.Local;
SPServiceProxyCollection spc = farm.ServiceProxies;
BdcServiceApplicationProxy sap = (BdcServiceApplicationProxy)((from sp in spc
                    where sp.TypeName.Equals("Business Data Connectivity")
                        select sp).First().ApplicationProxies.First());
DatabaseBackedMetadataCatalog catalog = sap.GetDatabaseBackedMetadataCatalog();
```

HelloRuntimeOM.sln

If your code is running on the client, then you will connect to the client cache instead of the metadata
catalog. The client cache is represented by the `RemoteSharedFileBackedMetadataCatalog`
object. The following code shows how to make the connection:

```
RemoteSharedFileBackedMetadataCatalog catalog =
    new RemoteSharedFileBackedMetadataCatalog();
```

HelloClientRuntimeOM.sln

Once you make a connection to the appropriate catalog, you can read or write to the entities it
contains. These changes will be reflected in the external system, as well as any external lists

based on the ECT. The following code shows how to retrieve an entity and print out the values of its fields:

```
IEntity ect = catalog.GetEntity("http://www.contoso.com/marketing", "Campaign");
ILobSystem lob = ect.GetLobSystem();
ILobSystemInstance lobi = lob.GetLobSystemInstances()["Advertising"];
IFilterCollection filter = ect.GetDefaultFinderFilters();
IEntityInstanceEnumerator ects = ect.FindFiltered(filter, lobi);
while (ects.MoveNext())
{
    Console.WriteLine(ects.Current["CampaignName"].ToString());
}
```

HelloRuntimeOM.sln

Along with reading or updating entities, you can also create new ones. As with other operations, these changes will flow all the way back to the external system. Of course, if you are writing to the client cache, the changes will only be made when the client is online. The following code shows how to add a new record to an external system through the ECT:

```
IView v = ect.GetCreatorView("Create");
IFieldValueDictionary dict = v.GetDefaultValues();
dict["CampaignName"] = "Fantastic Fall";
dict["StartDate"] = new DateTime(2009, 10, 15);
dict["EndDate"] = new DateTime(2009, 12, 1);
dict["GeographyId"] = 1;
dict["LastUpdate"] = DateTime.Today;
Identity id = ect.Create(dict, lobi);
```

HelloRuntimeOM.sln

Using the Administration Object Model

Along with the Runtime Object Model, BCS also has an Administration Object Model. The Administration Object Model allows you to manipulate the BDC Metadata Model. In order to work with the Administration Object Model, you must set a reference to `Microsoft.BusinessData.dll` and `Microsoft.SharePoint`.

As with the Runtime Object Model, you must first connect to the appropriate catalog before you can manipulate the data. In the case of the Administration Object Model, you must connect to the `AdministrationMetadataCatalog` object. Connecting to this catalog requires a reference to the `BdcServiceApplicationProxy` just as it did with the Runtime Object Model. The following code shows how to connect with the catalog if your code is running outside of a SharePoint context. Inside the context, you can use the `SPServiceContext` object, as shown previously.

```
SPFarm farm = SPFarm.Local;
SPServiceProxyCollection spc = farm.ServiceProxies;
BdcServiceApplicationProxy sap = (BdcServiceApplicationProxy)((from sp in spc
                    where sp.TypeName.Equals("Business Data Connectivity")
```

```
                                  select sp).First().ApplicationProxies.First());

    AdministrationMetadataCatalog catalog = sap.GetAdministrationMetadataCatalog();
```

MakeModel.sln

The Administration Object Model provides a set of objects that allow you to manipulate the Application Model XML. The names of the objects correspond closely to the names of the elements in the Application Model. The following code shows a complete example of creating a simple Application Model from code and saving it into the metadata catalog:

```
Model model = Model.Create("MiniCRM", true, catalog);
LobSystem lob = model.OwnedReferencedLobSystems.Create(
                "Customer", true, SystemType.Database);
LobSystemInstance lobi = lob.LobSystemInstances.Create("MiniCRM", true);

lobi.Properties.Add("AuthenticationMode", "PassThrough");
lobi.Properties.Add("DatabaseAccessProvider", "SqlServer");
lobi.Properties.Add("RdbConnection Data Source", "CONTOSOSERVER");
lobi.Properties.Add("RdbConnection Initial Catalog", "MiniCRM.Names");
lobi.Properties.Add("RdbConnection Integrated Security", "SSPI");
lobi.Properties.Add("RdbConnection Pooling", "true");

Entity ect = Entity.Create("Customer", "MiniCRM", true,
            new Version("1.0.0.0"), 10000,
            CacheUsage.Default, lob, model, catalog);

ect.Identifiers.Create("CustomerId", true, "System.Int32");

Method specificFinder = ect.Methods.Create(
"GetCustomer", true, false, "GetCustomer");

specificFinder.Properties.Add("RdbCommandText",
    "SELECT [CustomerId] ,[FullName] FROM MiniCRM.Names
    WHERE [CustomerId] = @CustomerId");
specificFinder.Properties.Add("RdbCommandType", "Text");

Parameter idParam = specificFinder.Parameters.Create(
                "@CustomerId", true, DirectionType.In);

idParam.CreateRootTypeDescriptor(
    "CustomerId", true, "System.Int32", "CustomerId",
    new IdentifierReference("CustomerId",
        new EntityReference("MiniCRM", "Customer", catalog), catalog),
    null, TypeDescriptorFlags.None, null, catalog);

Parameter custParam = specificFinder.Parameters.Create(
                "Customer", true, DirectionType.Return);

TypeDescriptor returnRootCollectionTypeDescriptor =
    custParam.CreateRootTypeDescriptor(
        "Customers", true,
        "System.Data.IDataReader, System.Data, Version=2.0.0.0, Culture=neutral,
```

```
            PublicKeyToken=b77a5c561934e089",
  "Customers", null, null, TypeDescriptorFlags.IsCollection, null, catalog);

TypeDescriptor returnRootElementTypeDescriptor =
    returnRootCollectionTypeDescriptor.ChildTypeDescriptors.Create(
        "Customer", true,
        "System.Data.IDataRecord, System.Data, Version=2.0.0.0, Culture=neutral,
         PublicKeyToken=b77a5c561934e089",
        "Customer", null, null, TypeDescriptorFlags.None, null);

returnRootElementTypeDescriptor.ChildTypeDescriptors.Create(
  "CustomerId", true, "System.Int32", "CustomerId",
        new IdentifierReference("CustomerId",
            new EntityReference("MiniCRM", "Customer", catalog), catalog),
        null, TypeDescriptorFlags.None, null);

returnRootElementTypeDescriptor.ChildTypeDescriptors.Create(
        "FirstName", true, "System.String", "FullName",
        null, null, TypeDescriptorFlags.None, null);


specificFinder.MethodInstances.Create(
"GetCustomer", true, returnRootElementTypeDescriptor,
    MethodInstanceType.SpecificFinder, true);

Method finder = ect.Methods.Create("GetCustomers", true, false, "GetCustomers");

finder.Properties.Add("RdbCommandText", "SELECT [CustomerId] ,
                      [FullName]FROM MiniCRM.Names");
finder.Properties.Add("RdbCommandType", "Text");

Parameter custsParam = finder.Parameters.Create(
        "Customer", true, DirectionType.Return);

TypeDescriptor returnRootCollectionTypeDescriptor2 =
    custsParam.CreateRootTypeDescriptor(
        "Customers", true,
        "System.Data.IDataReader, System.Data, Version=2.0.0.0, Culture=neutral,
         PublicKeyToken=b77a5c561934e089",
        "Customers", null, null, TypeDescriptorFlags.IsCollection, null, catalog);

TypeDescriptor returnRootElementTypeDescriptor2 =
    returnRootCollectionTypeDescriptor2.ChildTypeDescriptors.Create(
        "Customer", true,
        "System.Data.IDataRecord, System.Data, Version=2.0.0.0, Culture=neutral,
         PublicKeyToken=b77a5c561934e089",
        "Customer", null, null, TypeDescriptorFlags.None, null);

returnRootElementTypeDescriptor2.ChildTypeDescriptors.Create(
        "CustomerId", true, "System.Int32", "CustomerId",
        new IdentifierReference("CustomerId",
            new EntityReference("MiniCRM", "Customer", catalog), catalog),
        null, TypeDescriptorFlags.None, null);
```

```
returnRootElementTypeDescriptor2.ChildTypeDescriptors.Create(
      "FirstName", true, "System.String", "FullName",
      null, null, TypeDescriptorFlags.None, null);

finder.MethodInstances.Create(
"GetCustomers", true, returnRootCollectionTypeDescriptor2,
    MethodInstanceType.Finder, true);

ect.Activate();
```

MakeModel.sln

Creating .NET Assembly Connectors

A .NET Assembly Connector associates a custom assembly with an ECT so that you can precisely control how information is accessed, processed, and returned from external systems. Creating a .NET Assembly Connector is done using Visual Studio 2010, and starts by selecting the Business Data Connectivity Model project in the SharePoint 2010 group.

The new project template provides a simple entity definition to use as the starting point for your ECT. The starting entity is visible immediately on the design surface in the project. The design surface displays the identifier field and the methods for the entity. When the project is first created, the entity has an identifier field named `Identitfier1` and methods named `ReadList` and `ReadItem`. The identifier is essentially the primary key for the entity. The `ReadList` and `ReadItem` method represent the `Finder` and `SpecificFinder` methods for the entity. Figure 11-29 shows the starting entity.

FIGURE 11-29

One of the first tasks to perform in the project is to define any additional methods you need for the entity. Right-clicking the entity and selecting New Method will create a new method definition. When the new method definition is created, the Method Details pane will open so that you may further define the method. In particular, you must select the Method Instance type to use. Visual Studio supports all of the available method types described earlier in the chapter.

Along with the entity on the design surface, the template project provides two classes: `Entity1` and `Entity1Service`. The `Entity1` class contains the definitions for all of the fields in the entity, while the `Entity1Service` class contains the implementation for the methods.

The project template defines a simple entity with two fields: `Identifer1` and `Message`. `Identifier1` is the primary key for the entity and `Message` is a field that contains a text message. There is nothing special about these fields or methods — the project template simply creates them as an example to get you started. In fact, the project is complete as soon as it is created. You can run it directly from Visual Studio and create a new external list. So the project template functions as a starting point for your project as well as a sample application.

As a more practical example, this section will present a walk-through that creates a .NET Assembly Connector that returns data from an XML chunk. The XML chunk has product data that will be the basis for an external list. This XML chunk is accessible through a simple method, as shown in the following code.

```
private static string GetData()
{
    StringBuilder xml = new StringBuilder();
    xml.Append("<Products>");
    xml.Append("<Product ID=\"1\" Manufacturer=\"Microsoft\" Name=\"XBox-360\" />");
    xml.Append("<Product ID=\"2\" Manufacturer=\"Seagate\" Name=\"Harddrive\" />");
    xml.Append("<Product ID=\"3\" Manufacturer=\"Dell\" Name=\"Laptop\" />");
    xml.Append("<Product ID=\"4\" Manufacturer=\"Microsoft\" Name=\"Zune\" />");
    xml.Append("</Products>");

    return xml.ToString();
}
```

ProductConnector.sln

After creating a new Business Data Connectivity Model project, the entity was named `Product` and the model was updated to have an identifier named `ID`. The method definitions were also updated to return additional fields for `Name` and `Manufacturer`. The complete model can be seen by using the BDC Model Explorer, which is part of the project. Figure 11-30 shows the complete model for the `Product` entity.

After the methods are updated, the entity class itself must be updated to reflect the actual fields to be returned from the external system. In this example, `ID`, `Name`, and `Manufacturer` fields had to be added. The following code shows the final definition for the entity:

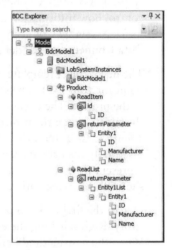

FIGURE 11-30

```
public partial class Product
{
    public string ID { get; set; }
    public string Manufacturer { get; set; }
    public string Name { get; set; }
}
```

ProductConnector.sln

Once the entity definition is complete, the method implementations must be coded. Each method in the entity corresponds to a method in code. For the example, this means coding a `ReadList` and `ReadItem` method. The following code shows the implementation for the methods:

```
public static Product ReadItem(string id)
{
    XDocument d = XDocument.Parse(GetData());

    var q = from c in d.Descendants("Product")
            where c.Attribute("ID").Equals(id)
            select new
            {
                ID = c.Attribute("ID").Value,
```

```
                Name = c.Attribute("Name").Value,
                Manufacturer = c.Attribute("Manufacturer").Value
            };

    Product product = new Product();
    product.ID = q.First().ID;
    product.Name = q.First().Name;
    product.Manufacturer = q.First().Manufacturer;

    return product;

}

public static IEnumerable<Product> ReadList()
{
    XDocument d = XDocument.Parse(GetData());

    var q = from c in d.Descendants("Product")
            select new
            {
                ID = c.Attribute("ID").Value,
                Name = c.Attribute("Name").Value,
                Manufacturer = c.Attribute("Manufacturer").Value
            };

    List<Product> products = new List<Product>();

    foreach (var p in q)
    {
        Entity1 product = new Product();
        product.ID = p.ID;
        product.Name = p.Name;
        product.Manufacturer = p.Manufacturer;
        products.Add(product);
    }

    return products;

}
```

ProductConnector.sln

Because the datasource is an XML chunk, it was simple to implement an XDocument to load the XML. LINQ queries were then used against the XML chunk to return the desired data. After the methods are implemented, the .NET Assembly Connector is complete. The project may be deployed directly to SharePoint, and an external list can be created against the Product ECT.

The key thing to note about the .NET Assembly Connector is that it gives complete control over the method implementations. This means you can easily implement additional business rules or security functions when retrieving data from external systems.

SUMMARY

Business Connectivity Services is a broad topic. The range of solutions includes simple no-code solutions all the way through fully customized Visual Studio projects. This chapter gave you a broad overview of the capabilities of BCS, including solutions and administration. However, there are several areas, such as declarative solutions and custom VSTO solutions, that simply cannot be covered in a single chapter. All-in-all, there are a lot of possibilities to consider. As you move forward with BCS, you should start with the simple solutions and add to them as you learn. This will help you grasp the more difficult technical details and incorporate them in your solutions.

12

Workflow

WHAT'S IN THIS CHAPTER?

➤ Prototyping workflows in Visio 2010

➤ Creating declarative workflows in SharePoint Designer 2010

➤ Developing custom actions in Visual Studio 2010

➤ Importing reusable workflows to Visual Studio 2010

➤ Using association, initiation, and task InfoPath forms in workflows

➤ Developing site workflows in Visual Studio 2010

➤ Building Pluggable Workflow Services

➤ Developing workflow event receivers

The SharePoint 2010 workflow platform is built on the engine that's provided by Microsoft .NET Framework 3.5. The improvements made to this platform will allow greater flexibility for creating powerful workflow scenarios.

Think of workflow in SharePoint 2010 in three primary scenarios:

➤ A workflow model is created as a draft or prototype by a business user in Visio or SharePoint Designer. The business user hands this model off to workflow developers at some point, and they take over in Visual Studio 2010. After the developers take over, they work to complete the workflow, add any required code, and modify it to match the business requirement and their server deployments. All further development on the workflow model is done in Visual Studio 2010.

➤ A developer builds activities in Visual Studio 2010 (known as SharePoint Designer Actions) for deployment to SharePoint. These activities can be used by a nontechnical person who owns the workflow business logic, and that person puts together the workflow in either SharePoint Designer or Visio.

➤ A developer builds and implements a workflow model in Visual Studio 2010 and packages it for deployment. In this scenario, all development on the workflow model is done in Visual Studio 2010.

These three scenarios will be the focus of the rest of this chapter.

TRAINING APPROVAL WORKFLOW

First, take a look at the scenario you are going to tackle. In this chapter, you'll continue on the example presented in Chapter 9 with one exception. You will create a content type named Training, and you'll add it as the default content type to the Trainings custom list. Following is a quick orientation about the use cases that will be discussed throughout this chapter.

The Human Resources (HR) department at the fictitious Adventure Works company uses SharePoint to implement a training-course-offering system. Figure 12-1 illustrates part of this application where an HR training coordinator can create trainings and add them to a SharePoint list named Trainings.

> *If you need a refresher on how to create the Human Resources site and the Trainings list, please refer to Chapter 9.*

The process starts when the training coordinator creates a training course and starts an instance of the Training Approval workflow. The running instance of the workflow adds a task to the Tasks list, which notifies the training manager that a new training course is waiting for his approval. The training manager interacts with the running instance of the workflow to complete the assigned task. This interaction requires approving the suggested training course, but the interaction could be other things such as rejecting it, reassigning the task, or requesting a change. If the approval decision is made, the workflow execution branches into one of the following two processes:

➤ If approved, a training site is created.

➤ If not approved, the suggested training is deleted from the Trainings list.

In either case, the workflow terminates in the final step.

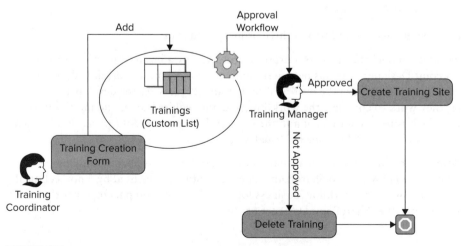

FIGURE 12-1

Creating the Training Content Type

Before diving into modeling the approval workflow, first you need to create the Training content type and add it to the Trainings list. Use the out-of-the-box Item content type as the parent and the following information to create the Training content type:

➤   **Title:** A title for the training opportunity (OOTB Site Column)

➤   **Code:** A code that uniquely identifies the training (unique eight-character fixed)

➤   **Description:** The description of the training (OOTB Site Column)

➤   **Start Date:** The training's start date (OOTB Site Column)

➤   **End Date:** The training's end date (OOTB Site Column)

➤   **Cost:** The cost of the training (American dollars)

➤   **Level:** The difficulty level associated with the training (a number from one to five)

➤   **Enrollment Deadline:** The date that enrollment ends

➤   **Address:** The address of the training facility (OOTB Site Column)

➤   **Additional Information:** Optional information about the training itself (enhanced rich text with pictures, tables, and hyperlinks)

 If some of the fields are not available in the available site columns pane, activate the SharePoint Server Publishing Infrastructure Feature.

With the Training content type, you should now be able to create a new custom list called Trainings, enable content type management in the list, and add the Training content type as the default content type to the list.

WORKFLOW DEVELOPMENT LIFECYCLE

If you have been doing workflow development or design for any amount of time, you have almost assuredly been engaged in some kind of communication and collaboration exercise with business stakeholders who own the process. Maybe you have been given a flowchart on a piece of paper, so you can look at it and come to a level of understanding on the business requirements or, even worse, maybe everything has been verbally communicated to you.

Furthermore, you may have had a lot of discussions with the business people to make sure that all stakeholders are clear on what is being implemented and that the development path is completely aligned with what they expect to see as the final product. The bottom line is that workflow development, just like any other development task, requires a two-way communication channel between the business people and the developer, and quite frankly, a channel that's always open! In practice, maybe this wasn't *that* hard, but the good news is, this process is a lot easier now. The new workflow lifecycle is one of the most exciting new features in SharePoint 2010 and is empowering the business user. All this has been made possible by introducing a series of new features along with a much tighter integration between Visio, SharePoint Designer, and Visual Studio 2010. Add to this many enhancements made to each tool for building workflows with the emphasis on developer experience, spending less time trying to solve challenges caused by each tool's specific shortcomings, and instead, spending more time on the business problem itself.

This section shows how these tools come together to help you model and implement a business process. You start by learning how to envision your workflow in Visio and then import it into SharePoint Designer and carry on working on it. Finally, you will learn how you can take things to the next level by extending the same workflow in Visual Studio 2010.

Prototyping in Visio

Visio has always been a wonderful tool for diagramming business processes, but for a long time it has suffered from having just a small number of people using it inside organizations for very limited use cases.

In the current wave of products with SharePoint 2010 and Office 2010, one of the new features is that business analysts can leverage Visio diagrams to model a workflow and draw its business process before it has gone through the implementation phase. Perhaps most important, business analysts who design and orchestrate a business process are already familiar with flowcharting in Visio and they don't necessarily need to know about the details of workflow implementation or SharePoint.

In this section, you will model the Training approval workflow in Visio 2010 and export it into an interchangeable file format so that it can be imported into SharePoint Designer in the next section.

And, with that, let's get started.

1. Launch Visio 2010 and, from the template categories, select the FlowChart template. Within the FlowChart template category, create a new file using the Microsoft SharePoint workflow drawing template, a brand-new template just for SharePoint workflows.

2. Once the new Visio file is created, notice that all workflow activities are divided into in three separate stencils, as follows:

    ➤ SharePoint Workflow Actions

    ➤ SharePoint Workflow Conditions

    ➤ SharePoint Workflow Terminators

Think of activities as building blocks of a workflow. It's important to understand that every workflow activity in Visio directly maps to an activity in SharePoint Designer and Visual Studio.

3. From the SharePoint Workflow Terminators stencil on the left-hand side of the window, find and add Start and Terminate shapes to the Drawing canvas. All the other shapes are going to go between these two shapes.

4. Open the SharePoint Workflow Conditions stencil and add a Compare Data Source shape to the Drawing canvas between the Start and Terminate Shapes. Then, change the name of the shape to "Manager Approved?"

5. Open the SharePoint Workflow Actions stencil and add Start Approval Process and Log to history list shapes between Start and Compare Data Source shapes. There are still three more shapes to add to the Drawing canvas after the Compare Data Source shape: one Delete Item shape and two Send an email shapes.

6. Add the process flow connections between the shapes, by hovering over each shape, clicking and dragging one of the arrows to the next shape. Use Figure 12-2 as an example. Finally, right-click the connection from the shape that says "Manager Approved?" to the one that says "Delete Item" and select No. Do the same thing for the other process flow, but this time around select Yes.

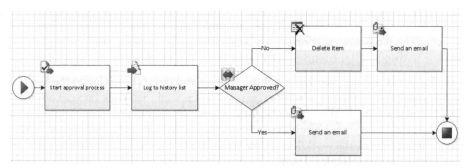

FIGURE 12-2

7. Save the process diagram to your local drive and name it `TrainingApproval WF_VisioModel.vsd`.

8. Lastly, you should export the workflow to a Workflow Visio Interchange (`.vwi`) file, which can then be used in the next section ("Customizing the Workflow in SharePoint Designer"). To export the workflow, click Export button in Process tab, and save the Visio diagram with a name such as `TrainingApprovalWF_VisioModel.vwi`.

In case you didn't notice, clicking the Export button does something before it actually lets you save the interchangeable file format. It validates the Visio diagram and stops you from saving it if the diagram has any issues, such as loose connectors. Sometimes validation happens quickly, so depending on the complexity of your diagram, you may or may not see it.

At any point during the modeling process, you can manually validate the diagram simply by clicking the Check Diagram button in the Process tab of the Ribbon.

Customizing the Workflow in SharePoint Designer

After a workflow is modeled in Visio, it can be handed off to IT professionals who are more technical and can extend the workflow using SharePoint Designer. This step of the workflow lifecycle starts out with importing the Visio workflow into SharePoint Designer and completing it in this tool. This includes defining initiation and association forms, variables, the parameters of each step, as well as adding some new steps. Finally, they will publish the complete workflow back to SharePoint. That was the short story.

When you opt to build your workflow using SharePoint Designer, there is one important thing to understand: Although SharePoint Designer 2010 offers many new improvements for building workflows, it doesn't replace Visual Studio under any circumstances. The primary purpose of SharePoint Designer is to build rules-based workflows in a declarative way, whereas Visual Studio is still the preferred tool for building powerful, enterprise-scale workflows, as you'll see later in this chapter.

To get started, follow these steps:

1. Browse to the Human Resources site where the Trainings list resides.

2. From Site Actions menu, click Edit in SharePoint Designer. This will open SharePoint Designer 2010 against the Human Resources site that you are currently in. As you can tell, SharePoint Designer is no longer constrained to a folder-based hierarchy, which means that you can click the Workflows section on the Navigation collections on the left-hand side of the window to display all the workflows scoped at the current site.

3. Click the Import from the Visio button in the Ribbon and point the dialog to the location where you saved `TrainingApprovalWF_VisioModel.vw`, and then click Next. This will take you to the next step of the Import Wizard, where you should give the workflow a name (e.g., Training Approval Workflow), choose Reusable Workflow option, and select the Training content type as the workflow target, as shown in Figure 12-3. You will learn about reusable workflows in the next section.

4. Click Finish to import the workflow. This will open the workflow design surface and display all activities defined in the Visio diagram with empty values, as shown in Figure 12-4.

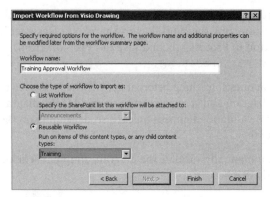

FIGURE 12-3

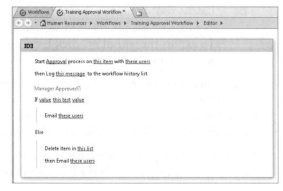

FIGURE 12-4

That's it. In just a short amount of time, you imported the workflow model created in Visio into SharePoint Designer and made it ready for further customization. Now the real fun begins!

One major item not covered in this chapter is the round trips between Visio and SharePoint Designer. What this means to you is that you can sync changes made to the workflow in SharePoint Designer with the original Visio diagram or vice versa. Perhaps most important, you can do this as many times as you wish.

Reusable Workflows

Before going any further in this chapter, let's shift gears and talk about a new feature called reusable workflows.

When you create a declarative workflow in SharePoint Designer 2010 against a SharePoint 2010 site, you don't need to strongly associate the workflow with a list; instead, you can point it to all content types or just a content type of your choice, as you did with the Training content type in the previous section.

The ability to make the workflow available for later attachment to any list across the site is referred to as "reusable workflow." In the previous version of SharePoint, a workflow could be reused only if it was developed in Visual Studio. Reusability has been a major request from customers who want to put the business logic modeling in the hands of those that are the most familiar with the business processes.

Reusable workflows offer more than just being loosely coupled from lists. Just keep this in mind as you read the rest of this section.

First of all, reusable workflows can be used as templates for creating other workflows. If you have worked with other workflow tools, such as K2, the notion of workflow templatization should be familiar to you. Much like these tools, SharePoint Designer 2010 now supports workflow templates and gives you the ability to use existing reusable workflows as a starting point for developing new ones. There are two ways you can use a reusable workflow as a template for building other workflows:

➤ Right-click a reusable workflow inside SharePoint Designer, and from the context menu select copy and modify.

➤ Save the workflow as a WSP solution file (aka a template) and then import it into Visual Studio 2010. This will be covered later in this chapter.

Not many people know this, but by default, when you create a reusable workflow, it's only reusable within the site in which it was created. If, however, you create a reusable workflow at the root web, you can convert your reusable workflow to a globally reusable workflow, which publishes a copy of the workflow to the global workflow catalog (the one that contains the out-the-box workflows). This process makes the workflow available to all sites in the current site collection. This can be done by clicking the Publish Globally button in the Ribbon next to our famous Import from Visio button. Needless to say, this option is dimmed if you are not in the root site.

 Globally reusable workflows cannot be directly imported to Visual Studio using the Import Reusable Workflow template.

So, the out-of-the-box workflows are reusable. Even though an OOTB workflow is read-only, you can unlock and drill through each one, see the At-a-Glance overview of the workflow, and further configure it using SharePoint Designer. Once again, for all practical purposes, this was almost impossible in the previous version of SharePoint.

With that understanding of when and why to use reusable workflows, let's get back to the Training approval workflow.

Association and Initiation Form Parameters

Workflows can collect data when they are initiated or associated. They can collect a number of different types of information in a number of different stages during their lifecycle.

Before you get into the workflow logic customization in SharePoint Designer, you must collect information from the person who associates the workflow with the Training content type. Additionally, you must collect information from the training coordinator when he or she initiates (starts) the workflows in order to allow the training course to go through the approval process.

For the example presented in this chapter, this includes:

➤ The training manager username (Association Form)

➤ A brief description on why the training coordinators think the training is important (Initiation Form)

Setting up the parameters for association and initiation forms is a simple matter of following a couple of steps. From the Workflow tab in the Ribbon, click Initiation Form Parameters and then click Add to set up the parameters as shown in Tables 12-1 and 12-2.

TABLE 12-1: Configuration Settings for the Why Important Parameter That Appears on the Initiation Form

ITEMS	VALUE
Field Name	Why Important
Information Type	Multiple lines of text
Collect form parameter during	Initiation (Starting the workflow)
Default value	Please describe why this training course is important.

TABLE 12-2: Configuration Settings for the Training Manager Parameter That Appears on the Association Form

ITEMS	VALUE
Field Name	Training Manager
Information Type	Person or Group
Collect form parameter during	Association (Attaching to the content type)
Show Field	User name
Allow selection of	People Only
SharePoint Group	Approvers
Allow blank Value	No

When you have set up the parameters, your workflow Association and Initiation Form Parameters should look like the ones shown in Figure 12-5.

Click OK to close the Association and Initiation Form Parameters window and return to the workflow design surface.

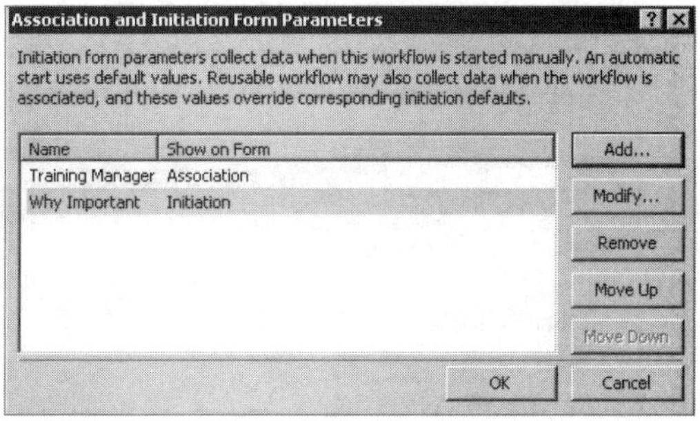

FIGURE 12-5

Customizing the Workflow Logic

With the Initiation and Association parameters created, you can now begin customizing the logic your workflow requires. As you saw in Figure 12-4, the imported workflow currently has one step marked "ID3." However, to make things cleaner, you will change the workflow so that it has two steps named as follows:

➤ On Approval Process

➤ After Approval Process

Step 1: On Approval Process

This step will start an approval process and notify the training manager that a training course needs to be approved. To accomplish this part of the example, follow these steps:

1. Position the insertion point (orange line), on the top of the step that says "ID3."

2. From the Ribbon, click Step to insert a new step.

3. Rename the step to On Approval Process.

4. Click the action that says "Start Approval process on this item with these users" to highlight it.

5. From the Ribbon, click Move up to move this action from the ID3 step to the Approval Process step.

6. With the focus on the Approval Process step, click the first link that says Approval or Approval (2), etc. This takes you to a page where you can customize the OOTB Approval action and its overall task process. A sample is shown in Figure 12-6.

In the Settings section, there are options to allow the training manager to reassign the approval task or to send the training back to the coordinator requesting that he or she make changes to the submitted training and send it back for approval. Notice also Task Outcomes, where you are given more options for interacting with the training approval process than just approving or rejecting it. For example, you can have a "To be Considered" outcome that stores the suggested training in another list for future use. Then, you can have your workflow treat these types of training courses completely differently than the rejected ones. Perhaps, if you want to see how powerful the OOTB Approval action really is, then you should click on one of the bottom three links in the Customization section. Each link leads you to a lot of configurations and options that are used for controlling the behavior of this action. For example, Figure 12-7 shows the Completion Conditions. Notice how the isItemApproved variable is set to Yes when the task is approved. You will use this variable later on to implement your own condition.

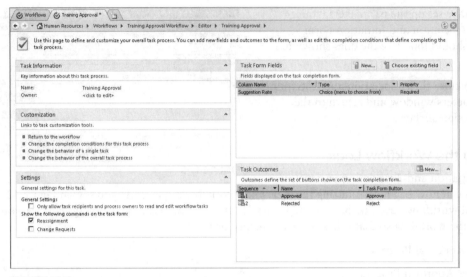

FIGURE 12-6

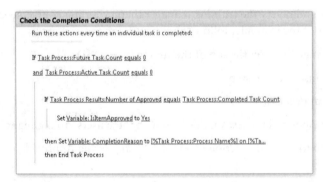

FIGURE 12-7

Leave everything else at its defaults in Figure 12-7 and click the left arrow on the workflow header (the breadcrumb) to go back to where you left off in Step 6. Resuming with step 7:

7. In the Task Information section, change Approval to Training Approval. Optionally, you can define who owns the approval process (if different from the training manager).

8. In the Task Form Fields section, click New to set up a task parameter as shown in Table 12-3. Essentially, a task parameter allows you to collect some information in the task form. For example, if the training is approved or rejected, you probably want the manager who is doing the approving or rejecting to rate the training suggestion.

TABLE 12-3: Configuration Settings for the Suggestion Rate Task Parameter That Appears on the Task Form

ITEM	VALUE
Field Name	Suggestion Rate
Information Type	Choice (menu to choose from)
Add to default view	Yes
Choices	Good, So-So, Poor (one per each line)
Default Value	Empty
Display as	Drop-down menu
Allow "Fill-in" choices	No
Allow blank Value	No

9. Click the "this item" link and select Current Item.

10. Click the "these users" link to open the Select Task Process Participants dialog box.

11. Configure the Participants parameter by clicking the lookup icon to the right of the field and selecting the participants.

➤ **Or select from existing Users or Groups:** Workflow Lookup for a User

➤ **Data Source:** Workflows Variables and Parameters

➤ **Field from source:** Parameter: Training Manager

➤ **Return field as:** Login Name

12. In Title parameter, type **Training Approval Required**.

13. For the body of the message, enter the information shown in Figure 12-8. The information in the bracket can be automatically generated by placing the cursor in the beginning of the instruction message and clicking the Add or Change Lookup button. Select the following Source and Field combinations:

➤ **Data source:** Current Item

➤ **Field from source:** Created By

➤ **Return field as:** Display Name

The first step in your workflow is now complete. The Workflow Designer surface should now look similar to Figure 12-9.

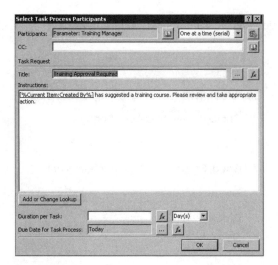

FIGURE 12-8

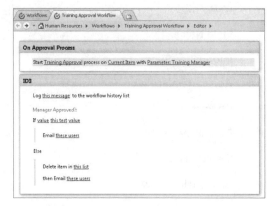

FIGURE 12-9

Before implementing the next step of the workflow, note three more things about the extra options that SharePoint Designer gives you for building workflows:

➤ Look back at Figure 12-6. Notice that, if you check the box to only allow task recipients and process owners to read and edit workflow tasks, then the training manager and the process owner are the only people who will see the task and perhaps the sensitive information residing in it. This means that the permission level for the task is broken, and it's created with a set of unique permissions. Previously this could be only accomplished programmatically by using the `CreateTask` and `CreateTaskWithContentType` activities and their `SpecialPermissions` property, as shown in Listing 12-1. For more information on creating tasks with custom permissions, see my blog post at `http://www.devhorizon .com/go/24`.

LISTING 12-1: Item-Level Permission in Workflow CreateTask Activity

```
private void createTask(object sender, EventArgs e)
  {
    //Code Omitted for brevity
    CreateTask task1 = sender as CreateTask;
    HybridDictionary permsCollection = new HybridDictionary();
    permsCollection.Add(taskProps.AssignedTo,
      SPRoleType.Administrator);
    task1.SpecialPermissions = permsCollection;
}
```

➤ Look back at Figure 12-8. In right top corner of the dialog there is a button with a plus sign on it that allows you to have multiple assignment stages with serial or parallel participants (the default is one serial assignment stage). So, technically, you can have multiple training managers reviewing approval tasks in serial or parallel.

➤ One more tip about Figure 12-8. In the scenario provided in this chapter, the person who creates the training course (the coordinator) is the person who initiates the workflow, so it's safe to use [%Current Item: Created By%] lookup in the body of the task instruction. However, if the training course is created by someone other than the coordinator, you can look up the initiator, too. Among the new data-binding enhancements made in SharePoint Designer 2010, there is a Workflow Lookup for the person who initiates the workflow. To look up the initiator, click the Lookup icon to the right of the Participants field and select the following:

> ➤ **Data source:** Workflow Context
>
> ➤ **Field from source:** Initiator
>
> ➤ **Return field as:** Display Name

Step 2: After Approval Process

Step 2 won't execute until the approval process in the previous step has been completed. To be technically accurate, after the approval action creates a task for the training manager, the workflow is serialized, or dehydrated, to the SharePoint database, waiting for the task to be approved or rejected. When the training manager approves or rejects the training course, the workflow wakes up (rehydrates, or is deserialized) and continues to the second step. To complete Step 2, follow these steps:

1. Rename the step from ID3 to After Approval Process.

2. Click on the "this message" link to define the message logged when the flow enters Step 2. Type **Inside After Approval Process** in the textbox.

3. Click the value link in the If statement, and then click the function (*fx*) button to define a workflow lookup, by selecting the following combinations:

   > ➤ **Data source:** Workflow Variables and Parameters
   >
   > ➤ **Field from source:** Variable:IsItemApproved

4. Click this test and select equals.

5. Click the second value link in the If statement, then select Yes.

6. Click on the "these users" link to open the Define Email Message dialog box. This is more or less just like it was in SharePoint Designer 2007.

7. In the To parameter, define the following lookup:

   > ➤ **Data Source:** Current Item
   >
   > ➤ **Field from source:** Created By
   >
   > ➤ **Return field as:** Email Address

8. In the Subject parameter, type **Your training suggestion is approved.**

9. For the body of the message, enter the information shown in Figure 12-10. The information in the bracket can be automatically generated by placing the cursor in the appropriate place and clicking the Add or Change Lookup button with the following Source and Field combinations:

> ➤ **Data source:** Current Item

> ➤ **Field from source:** Title

10. In the `Else` statement, click this list link and set it to Current Item.

11. Repeat Steps 6 through 9 for the second Email action with one exception: you need to compose a message to let the training coordinator know that the suggestion has been rejected.

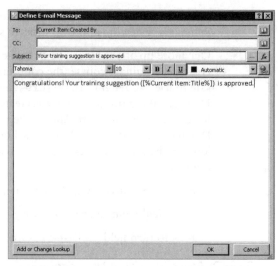

FIGURE 12-10

That takes care of the second step in your workflow. When you are done, the workflow designer surface should look like Figure 12-11.

All you need to do now is save and publish the workflow. First, click the Save button to save the workflow settings, and then click the Publish button in the Ribbon to publish the workflow back to the HR site.

At this point, the workflow has been published to the SharePoint site and is listed as a reusable workflow in the workflows home page in SharePoint Designer 2010. Unfortunately, there is still some cosmetic and plumbing work left before you can really say that you are done.

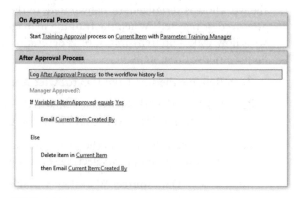

FIGURE 12-11

Workflow InfoPath Forms

If you recall, the training approval workflow needs some extra information passed into it to function properly. Specifically, it needs to know which user will be assigned the approval tasks (the training manager). In addition, it needs to collect some information from the person initiating the workflow (the training coordinator) about why he or she thinks the suggested training is important, so it can be displayed to the training manager.

To satisfy these requirements, it makes sense to have some forms within the workflow lifecycle. The training approval workflow requires three types of forms:

➤ **Association Form:** A form that collects some default settings used throughout the workflow lifecycle. This form is filled out once when an administrator configures the workflow and every time the default settings must be modified.

➤ **Initiation Form:** A form that collects information from the person who starts the workflow. If the workflow is configured to start automatically, this form can be omitted.

➤ **Task Form:** A form that collects information from people who are assigned a task by workflow.

Fortunately when you publish your workflow, SharePoint Designer generates all these three types of forms for you. To see how these forms look, click the Workflow Settings button in the Ribbon. This will take you to the training approval workflow home page, where all three forms are available in a section called Forms.

The word *three* is not a typo in the preceding paragraph, because there are really three forms there, even though there appear to be only two. The `Training Approval Workflow.xsn` file is a single InfoPath form that lumps the initiation and association forms together using two distinct views; one named Start (the default) is used for the initiation form and Associate is used for the association form. The `Approval.xsn` file represents the task form.

Go ahead and click on each form to open it in InfoPath Designer 2010. The process of customizing and publishing these forms back to SharePoint is covered in much greater detail in Chapter 9. Needless to say, you really don't need to make any changes except for applying some basic formatting and adding new titles to each form.

Figures 12-12 through 12-14 illustrate all three forms after your artworks are completed.

FIGURE 12-12

FIGURE 12-13

Note in the task form that, for each outcome, the Reassignment and Change Request options, you'll get a button. Notice also the Suggestion Rate field, which is used for rating the training suggestion, has a drop-down list and appears at the bottom of the form.

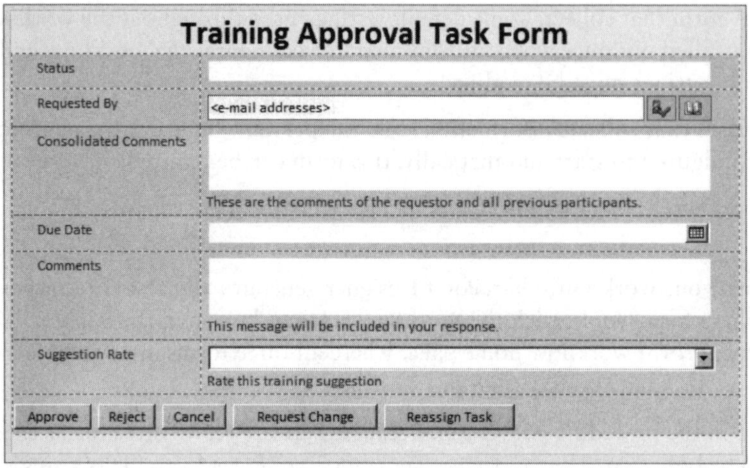

Training Approval Task Form

Status	
Requested By	`<e-mail addresses>`
Consolidated Comments	
	These are the comments of the requestor and all previous participants.
Due Date	
Comments	
	This message will be included in your response.
Suggestion Rate	
	Rate this training suggestion

Approve | Reject | Cancel | Request Change | Reassign Task

FIGURE 12-14

When you are done changing the look and feel of these forms, save them locally and then click Quick Publish, the big button in the Backstage, to sync your changes back to the original form templates in SharePoint. Additionally, you may need to save and publish the workflow again to see both form templates labeled as "custom form," as shown in Figure 12-15.

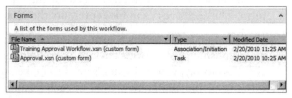

Forms

A list of the forms used by this workflow.

File Name	Type	Modified Date
Training Approval Workflow.xsn (custom form)	Association/Initiation	2/20/2010 11:25 AM
Approval.xsn (custom form)	Task	2/20/2010 10:25 AM

FIGURE 12-15

You have just created your first workflow in SharePoint Designer 2010 with three InfoPath forms. It's great that you have the workflow completed, but truth to be told, it doesn't *do* anything until it's glued to the Training content type.

Associating a Workflow to a Content Type

The last thing you need to do to wrap up your workflow customization foray in SharePoint Designer is to associate it with the Training content type. All you need to do is click the Association to Content Type button in the Ribbon and select Training. Essentially, what happens behind the scenes here is that SharePoint Designer attaches the workflow to the Training content type (not just the Training list).

The capability to attach declarative workflows to content types was the number-one feature request for SharePoint Designer 2010.

To do so, SharePoint Designer takes you directly to the workflow association page, where you should configure a few settings, such as workflow name, task list, and workflow history (standard stuff). You can leave pretty much everything in the first page set as their defaults and click Next to go to the page that contains your custom InfoPath association form, as shown in Figure 12-16. Enter the login name for the training manager (or look it up using the People Picker control), and then click Save when you are done.

This takes care of the workflow and the content type association and takes you to the final step: testing!

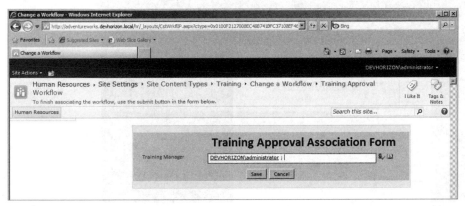

FIGURE 12-16

Testing the Workflow

With the workflow published and added to the Training content type, it can finally be tested. Navigate to the Trainings list and create a new training. Select the new training and, from the Ribbon, click Workflows.

This takes you to a page that shows all the workflows that are available for the Training content type. Go ahead and click your workflow's name to get it started. The first screen that you will see is the initiation form that SharePoint Designer created for you and that you customized using InfoPath Designer.

Fill in your comment for the Why Important field, and click start.

Your workflow will start, and you will be returned to the Trainings custom list. You'll also notice that a new column has been added to the list schema (and the current view) after your workflow name. It contains the current status of your workflow, In Progress, as shown in Figure 12-17.

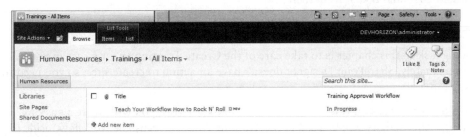

FIGURE 12-17

Back in the browser, if you check the Tasks list, you will see that a new task is created with the title of Training Approval Required. This task is assigned to the training manager you set up in the association form. Figure 12-18 demonstrates this task, as well as all the buttons that are provided to allow you to interact with the submitted training course. Go ahead and click the Approve button now.

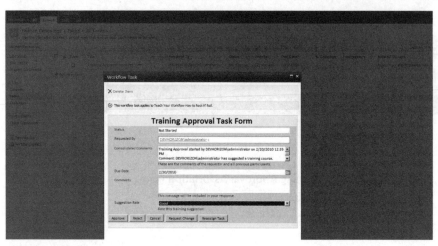

FIGURE 12-18

At this point, you should be able to see that the workflow's status is changed to Approved in the Trainings list, as well as see an email sent to the coordinator indicating that his training suggestion has been approved.

Creating Custom Actions with Visual Studio 2010

The workflow that you have built up to this point has a problem.

The problem is that it doesn't fully satisfy the business requirement of the Training Approval Workflow. Refer to Figure 12-1 again. Your workflow is missing the most important step of the process: Create Training Site.

In this section, you will learn how to build a custom workflow activity in Visual Studio 2010 that creates a training site. Then, you will learn how to use this activity in your SharePoint Designer reusable workflow (as a workflow action). Finally, you will learn how to import the whole workflow into Visual Studio 2010 and take it from there.

Setting Up the Visual Studio Project

Your first coding task in this chapter is to take care of the Create Training Site use case in your workflow. Unfortunately, SharePoint Designer doesn't have an action to create sites, so you need to code it yourself (finally!).

To make this process flexible so it can be reused in multiple scenarios, you will create a custom workflow activity. This activity will be used in the Training Approval reusable workflow inside the If statement of the "After Approval Process" step.

To get started, open Visual Studio 2010 and create an Empty SharePoint Project from the SharePoint 2010 template; name it AdventureWorksWFs.

When the SharePoint Customization Wizard dialog opens, go ahead and select Deploy as a farm solution, as shown in Figure 12-19.

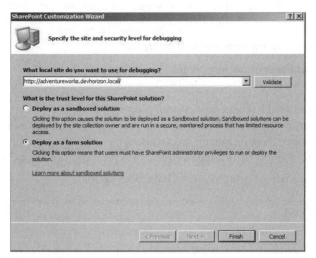

FIGURE 12-19

Before you begin, you need to add the following three references to your project:

➤ `Microsoft.SharePoint.dll`

➤ `Microsoft.Office.Workflow.Actions.dll`

➤ `System.Workflow.ComponentModel.dll`

Next, add a new Workflow Activity or just a C# class to the project and name it `CreateTrainingSite.cs`.

 In this chapter, we only cover custom activities that are deployed in a farm solution. For creating sandboxed custom activities that show up as actions in SharePoint Designer, see Microsoft Patterns and Practices SharePoint Guidance at www.microsoft.com/spg.

Replace the class declaration with the following line:

```
public class CreateTrainingSite : Activity
```

In addition, add the following three `using` statements:

```
using System.ComponentModel;
using System.Workflow.ComponentModel;
using Microsoft.SharePoint;
```

Coding the Activity

With the project now created, the next step you are going to tackle is creating the custom properties for your activity to capture some information. To make this activity work, you need two pieces of information at minimum:

➤ URL: This will be the location where the training site will be created.

➤ Site Name: This will be the name of the training site created by the activity. (In this example, it's the training code.)

To capture this information at design time, you need to create two custom properties of type DependencyProperty with appropriate setters and getters. Think of custom properties for an activity like custom properties on any other .NET component; there is nothing special about them. To create property dependencies, you can use the built-in workflow snippets. Just type wdp and then press the Tab key twice.

Listing 12-2 shows CreateTrainingSite.cs after both properties have been added.

LISTING 12-2: The CreateTrainingSite Class

```csharp
public class CreateTrainingSite : Activity
{
    public static DependencyProperty UrlProperty =
    DependencyProperty.Register("Url", typeof(string),
    typeof(CreateTrainingSite));

    [Description("Url of training site")]
    [Category("Chapter 12 Workflow")]
    [Browsable(true)]
    [DesignerSerializationVisibility
     (DesignerSerializationVisibility.Visible)]
    public string Url
      {
        get
          {
            return ((string)
              (base.GetValue(CreateTrainingSite.UrlProperty)));
          }
        set
          {
              base.SetValue(CreateTrainingSite.UrlProperty, value);
          }
      }
    public static DependencyProperty SiteNameProperty =
    DependencyProperty.Register("SiteName", typeof(string),
    typeof(CreateTrainingSite));

      [Description("Training site name")]
      [Category("Chapter 12 Workflow")]
      [Browsable(true)]
      [DesignerSerializationVisibility
       (DesignerSerializationVisibility.Visible)]
      public string SiteName
        {
          get
            {
```

```
            return ((string)
              (base.GetValue(CreateTrainingSite.SiteNameProperty)));
        }
    set
      {
          base.SetValue(CreateTrainingSite.SiteNameProperty, value);
      }
    }
  }
}
```

Each of the attributes decorating your dependency properties in Listing 12-2 means something different in Visual Studio and the SharePoint Designer workflow Designer surface. They are explained briefly in Table 12-4.

TABLE 12-4: Property Attributes

ATTRIBUTE	DESCRIPTION
Description	A description of what the property does.
Category	A category in which the property belongs within the Properties window of Visual Studio.
Browsable	Indicates whether or not the property is visible within the Properties window of Visual Studio. Possible values are True or False.
DesignerSerializationVisibility	Specifies the visibility of the property to the design-time serializer. Possible values are Visible, Hidden, and Content.

The next thing you need to take care of is overriding the Execute method in your activity, as shown in Listing 12-3. This code uses the dependency properties to retrieve the URL and the name for the training site and just creates it. The code for creating the site is relatively simple.

LISTING 12-3: Code to Create the Training Site

```
protected override ActivityExecutionStatus Execute(
ActivityExecutionContext executionContext)
  {
    using (SPSite siteCollection = new SPSite(Url))
      {
        using (SPWeb web = siteCollection.OpenWeb())
          {
            using (SPWeb trainingWeb = web.Webs.Add(SiteName))
              {
                trainingWeb.Description = "This site is
                created using the CreateTrainingSite activity.";
                 trainingWeb.Title = SiteName;
```

continues

LISTING 12-3: *(continued)*

```
            }
        }
    }
    return ActivityExecutionStatus.Closed;
}
```

AdventureWorksWFs\CreateTrainingSite.cs

With the Execute method created, the custom activity needs to be placed inside a WSP package so that it can be deployed to any SharePoint environment. That's what you will do in the next section.

Preparing the Activity for Deployment

Configure the AdventureWorksWFs project to be signed with a strong name key and then compile it. Next, right-click on the project and click Add ⇨ SharePoint Mapped Folder. Next, select the Template\1033\Workflow SharePoint location to map. This will add the Workflow mapped folder to AdventureWorksWFs project.

Right-click on the mapped Workflow folder, and select Add ⇨ New Item. From the list of available templates, select XML File and name it SPDCustomActivities.actions.

Replace the contents of the new XML file with the XML fragment in Listing 12-4.

> *Ensure that the PublicKeyToken within the* SPDCustomActivities.actions *file (24cb177bb81fb105) is updated with the public key token from the AdventureWorksWFs.dll assembly in your development machine.*

LISTING 12-4: Workflow Actions Schema File

```xml
<WorkflowInfo>
<Actions Sequential="then" Parallel="and">
    <Action Name="Create Training Site"
            ClassName="AdventureWorksWFs.CreateTrainingSite"
            Assembly="AdventureWorksWFs, Version=1.0.0.0,
            Culture=neutral,
            PublicKeyToken=24cb177bb81fb105"
            AppliesTo="all"
            Category="Adventure Works">
        <RuleDesigner Sentence="Create a training site using the name %1 at %2.">
          <FieldBind Field="SiteName" Text="The name of the
           training site (i.e. Code Field)"
             DesignerType="TextArea" Id="1"/>
          <FieldBind Field="Url" Text="Full url of the parent site" Id="2"
             DesignerType="TextArea"/>
        </RuleDesigner>
        <Parameters>
          <Parameter Name="SiteName" Type="System.String, mscorlib" Direction="In" />
          <Parameter Name="Url" Type="System.String, mscorlib" Direction="In" />
```

```
                </Parameters>
            </Action>
        </Actions>
    </WorkflowInfo>
```

AdventureWorksWFs\SPDCustomActivities.actions

In Listing 12-4, you define a custom workflow action with the code behind in the AdventureWorksWFs.dll assembly. RuleDesigner instructs the Workflow Designer about what needs to go where on the design surface.

 You can add a <Condition> *element to Listing 12-4 that points to a class containing a method to perform a specific condition check. For example, you can use this to check for the existence of a training site before it's created. The condition you define this way will appear in SharePoint Designer and you can reuse it when building declarative workflows. Refer to Microsoft Patterns and Practices SharePoint Guidance at* www.microsoft.com/spg *for instructions on how to implement conditions for your custom actions.*

It's obvious that when you add this activity to the workflow design surface, it's going to have two textboxes used in collecting the training site name and URL as input parameters (defined in the <Parameters> element). Note that these parameters are bound to the dependency properties you defined in Listing 12-2 using <FieldBind> elements.

Deploying the Activity

To see everything in action, you need to complete the last piece of your custom activity: deployment. So, to get started, simply follow these steps:

1. Right-click on the Features folder, and select Add Feature. This will open the Feature Designer.

2. Rename the new Feature file and its Title to AdventureWorksWFsFeature.

3. Change the Scope to Farm.

4. Right-click on the AdventureWorksWFsFeature file in Solution Explorer, and select Add Event Receiver.

5. Replace the contents of the FeatureReceiver class with the code shown in Listing 12-5.

6. Build and Deploy the AdventureWorksWFs.

LISTING 12-5: Adding the Custom Activity as authorizedType to the Web.config

```
public class AdventureWorksWFsFeatureEventReceiver : SPFeatureReceiver
{
    public override void FeatureActivated(
    SPFeatureReceiverProperties properties)
```

continues

LISTING 12-5: *(continued)*

```
    {
      SPWebService contentService = SPWebService.ContentService;
      contentService.WebConfigModifications.Add(GetConfigModification());
      contentService.Update();
      contentService.ApplyWebConfigModifications();
    }

  public override void FeatureDeactivating(
    SPFeatureReceiverProperties properties)
    {
      // Code Omitted for brevity
    }
  public SPWebConfigModification GetConfigModification()
    {
      string assemblyValue = typeof
        (CreateTrainingSite).Assembly.FullName;
      string namespaceValue =
        typeof(CreateTrainingSite).Namespace;
      SPWebConfigModification modification =
        new SPWebConfigModification(
        string.Format(CultureInfo.CurrentCulture,
        "authorizedType[@Assembly='{0}'][@Namespace='{1}']
        [@TypeName='*'][@Authorized='True']",
        assemblyValue, namespaceValue),
        "configuration/System.Workflow.ComponentModel.WorkflowCompiler
        /authorizedTypes");

      modification.Owner = "AdventureWorksWFs";
      modification.Sequence = 0;
      modification.Type = SPWebConfigModification.
      SPWebConfigModificationType.EnsureChildNode;
      modification.Value =
        string.Format(CultureInfo.CurrentCulture,
        "<authorizedType Assembly=\"{0}\"
        Namespace=\"{1}\"
        TypeName=\"*\" Authorized=\"True\" />",
        assemblyValue, namespaceValue);

      Trace.TraceInformation(
        "SPWebConfigModification value: {0}",
        modification.Value);

      return modification;
    }

}
```

AdventureWorksWFs\ AdventureWorksWFsFeatureEventReceiver.cs

There are a few last things to look at in Listing 12-5 before you move on to the next section. First of all, as you can tell, the code uses its own public key token. As always, update this key (24cb177bb81fb105) with the correct key from your own assembly. Second, the code uses the SPWebConfigModification class to programmatically add the custom activity declaration as an authorizedType to the web application's web.config file across your farm.

For more information about SPWebConfigModification *class, see my blog post at www.devhorizon.com/go/25.*

But, what's the authorizedType element, and why do you need it?

During the validation phase of workflow compilation, if this entry is not present in the web.config file, for reasons of security your request to access the CreateTrainingSite type will be rejected and you won't be able to add the action in SharePoint Designer. The authorizedType element indicates an Assembly, a Namespace, a TypeName, and an Authorized flag with possible values of True or False. Notice that, just as when you are adding a SafeControl element, wildcard characters are allowed, to include or exclude complete namespaces. For instance, using Type="*" indicates that all types within the AdventureWorksWFs namespace in the AdventureWorksWFs assembly are good to go (not any other namespaces).

When executed, the chunk of code in Listing 12-5 adds the following XML element to the web.config file of the content Web applications.

```
<authorizedType Assembly="AdventureWorksWFs, Version=1.0.0.0,
Culture=neutral, PublicKeyToken=24cb177bb81fb105" Namespace="AdventureWorksWFs"
TypeName="*"
Authorized="True"/>
```

The last step would be to build and deploy your solution. That wraps up your foray into custom activity development.

Completing SharePoint Designer Workflow

With the custom activity built and deployed to the SharePoint farm, you should now be able to go back to SharePoint Designer and finish where you left off before creating your custom activity.

Open SharePoint Designer and from the Workflows category, open the training approval workflow. Next, place the insertion point inside the If statement, just before the Email Current Item:Created By action. Click Action in the Ribbon and from the drop-down list click Create Training Site under the Adventure Works category, as shown in Figure 12-20.

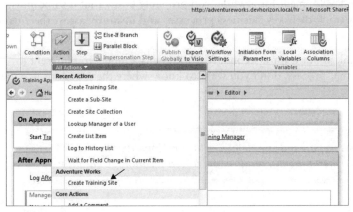

FIGURE 12-20

In the Name of the training site (i.e., Code field) link, define the following lookup:

➤ Data Source: Current Item

➤ Field from source: Code

In the full URL of the parent site link, type a fixed URL where the training sites will be created. You will end up with a surface that looks like Figure 12-21.

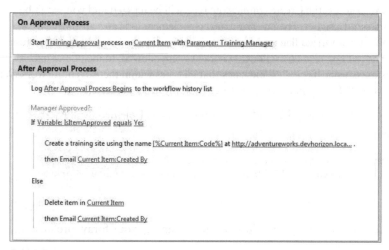

On Approval Process

Start <u>Training Approval</u> process on <u>Current Item</u> with <u>Parameter: Training Manager</u>

After Approval Process

Log <u>After Approval Process Begins</u> to the workflow history list

Manager Approved?:

If <u>Variable: IsItemApproved</u> <u>equals</u> <u>Yes</u>

    Create a training site using the name <u>[%Current Item:Code%]</u> at <u>http://adventureworks.devhorizon.loca...</u> .

    then Email <u>Current Item:Created By</u>

Else

    Delete item in <u>Current Item</u>

    then Email <u>Current Item:Created By</u>

FIGURE 12-21

For the sake of simplicity, the URL of the trainings' parent site is hard coded in the workflow action. When you are doing this for real, however, you will want to make the URL configurable either as an association parameter or persisted somewhere else such as in the SPSite or SPWeb property bags.

Before you take the new changes in the workflow and publish them back to SharePoint again, let's take a look at just one more setting to change: Workflow Visualization.

Workflow Visualization and Monitoring

If you have been doing workflow development for a while, you probably know that it's not unusual for companies to want to visually track their key business processes and instantly assess the current state of each process in real time.

Put yourself in their shoes and think about it for a second. A workflow is a model to represent a business process. As an owner of that process, don't you want to know where the process is at a given point in time?

It's easy to forget, but those small and simple pieces of functionality, such as business process updates, when missing, result in decreased technology adoption.

Unfortunately, in the previous versions of SharePoint this was not that easy to implement. Sure, you could provide an event system inside your workflow that raised events during the workflow lifecycle and persisted some information about the current stage of a workflow in a SharePoint list or database, and then build a nice UI based on the persisted information, but how easy would this be?

Thankfully, in SharePoint Server 2010, things are much clearer and easier. If you recall from earlier discussion in this chapter, you can use Visio 2010 to model your workflow. Well, that was just a warm-up and not the only way you can benefit from the Visio-Workflow love relationship in SharePoint Server 2010.

Similar to Excel Services in concept, a new service in SharePoint Server 2010 named Visio Services allows developers to build and publish data-driven visual diagrams to SharePoint. The underlying data for a data-bound Visio diagram can come from a variety of data sources, including the workflow tracking information. So, Visio Services has the ability to produce real-time visual diagrams of workflow steps and present them to process owners in the workflow status page.

To enable this functionality, simply go to the workflow settings page, and ensure that the checkbox "Show workflow visualization on status page" is checked. To render the workflow visualization component in the status page, you need to ensure that the following three pieces are in place:

➤ Activate the Visio Web Access farm feature.

➤ Activate the SharePoint Server Enterprise Site Collection features.

➤ Install Silverlight.

With the visualization option checked, you can push the workflow back into the HR site again by republishing it. At this point, you should be able to kick off another instance of the Approval Training process and see the visualization in action, as shown in the diagram in Figure 12-22.

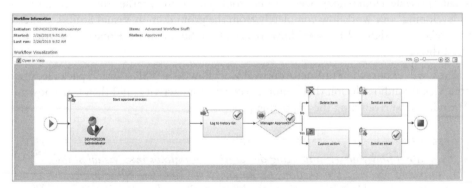

FIGURE 12-22

If everything goes smoothly and your workflow instance completes successfully, you can browse to the URL you specified for the training's parent site and see the custom team site that is created as part of the workflow execution.

Visualization aside, SharePoint workflows come with some reports to monitor how they are running based on the history information of their execution. Same as the visualization component, these reports are accessible in the Workflow Status page ➪ Workflow History section ➪ View workflow reports.

These reports are generated on-demand and they are in Excel format. You have the option to store the Excel file in a document library of the current site and either download it to Excel client or view it online using Office Web App, as shown in Figure 12-23.

➤ Cancellation & Error Report: As implied by the name, this report is used to record information about a workflow being cancelled or when it encounters errors before completion.

➤ Activity Duration Report: This report gives you information about the time taken by a workflow instance to complete as well as for each activity within the workflow.

List	Item	User	Date Occurred (GMT)	Event	Group	Outcome	Duration (Hours)	Description
Trainings	Advanced Workflow Stuff	DEVHORIZON\administrator	2010-02-26T21:37:42	Workflow Initiated	0		0	Training Approval was started
Trainings	Advanced Workflow Stuff	DEVHORIZON\administrator	2010-02-26T21:37:43	Task Created	0		0	Task created for DEVHORIZO
Trainings	Advanced Workflow Stuff	DEVHORIZON\administrator	2010-02-26T21:38:08	Task Completed	0	Approved by DEV	0	Task assigned to DEVHORIZO
Trainings	Advanced Workflow Stuff	DEVHORIZON\administrator	2010-02-26T21:38:08	Workflow Completed	0	Training Approval	0	Training Approval was comple

FIGURE 12-23

Importing to Visual Studio 2010

If you've made it this far in this chapter, you probably agree that, with the powerful combination of Visio and SharePoint Designer 2010, you have a nice, wizard-based approach to creating your custom workflows in your hands. You saw that extending the SharePoint Designer workflows using custom actions (developed in Visual Studio) was not that difficult either. Easy development aside, SharePoint Designer 2010 made it really easy to reuse your workflow in the site in which you created it or in the entire site collection.

What if you need to implement more sophisticated use cases? For this reason, and quite frankly many others, enterprise developers may need another tool. Thankfully, rather than using a third-party tool or developing your workflow completely from the ground up in Visual Studio, you can export your SharePoint Designer 2010 workflow to Visual Studio (every developer's best friend) and further extend it there.

In this section, you will export the Training Approval workflow to a WSP solution package, import it into the same Visual Studio solution that contains your custom activity, and then learn how to deal with a few nuances surrounding the importing process.

 Even if you don't find yourself importing declarative workflows into Visual Studio, I still recommend you read this section. An imported reusable workflow project is a fantastic example to learn how various workflow items, such as InfoPath forms, declarative rule conditions, and custom fields, are associated with and deployed alongside the workflow itself. This journey is quite an adventure!

To export your workflow to Visual Studio, first you need to save it as a template. To do so, click the Save as Template button in the Ribbon, as shown in Figure 12-24. One thing to keep in mind is that, in order to save a workflow as template, you need to publish it to SharePoint and then save it as template. Just saving a workflow to the site's workflows catalog won't cut it.

FIGURE 12-24

This would save the workflow as WSP file in the Site Assets library. In your site, browse to the Site Assets library (View All Site Content ➪ Site Assets) and the workflow should be there. Click the item that says Training Approval Workflow and, from the ECB (Edit Control Block) menu, click Send To ➪ Download a Copy. Next, save the `Training_Approval_Workflow.wsp` file to your local drive.

Now, go back to AdventureWorksWFs Visual Studio solution, right-click on the solution node, and select Add ➪ New Project. From the list of available SharePoint 2010 templates, select Import Reusable Workflow template. You also need to name the project something that's meaningful, such as TrainingApprovalWorkflow, and then click OK. On the SharePoint Customization Wizard dialog, ensure that the target site is the same as the site you deployed the custom activity project to earlier.

Select Deploy as farm solution, and click the Next button until you reach the step where you need to point the wizard to the location of the `Training_Approval_Workflow.wsp` file on your local drive. After you click Next, you should see the Training Approval workflow selected and ready to be converted to a sequential workflow. At this point, all you need to do is to click Finish.

 Visual Studio is the finish line in the marathon of the workflow development lifecycle. Once the workflow is imported into Visual Studio, it can't go back to SharePoint Designer or Visio.

Figure 12-25 shows the Visual Studio structure of the imported workflow project.

As you may notice, your workflow was imported to Visual Studio and converted to a code-separated workflow.

When you create a workflow in SharePoint Designer, it is an XOML-only workflow (aka a declarative workflow) with bunch of XML content and no code modules. Sure, you developed a custom action and used it in your workflow, but don't forget that the custom action was developed and kept in a separate assembly and you just referenced it in your workflow, again declaratively.

In code-separated workflows, the markup and the implementation logic of the workflow are kept in two separate files with different extensions, `.xoml` and `.xoml.cs` (or `xoml.vb`). They also compile differently than XOML-only

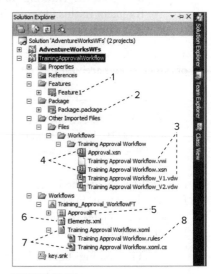

FIGURE 12-25

workflows. When you build your code-separated workflow, the markup file (.xoml.cs file) is compiled into a partial class. This partial class, along with the partial class from the code file (.xoml.cs file), is entered into the C# compiler and a .NET assembly is generated as the result of compilation. In XOML-only workflows, there is no code behind, so obviously the compilation process is different.

There is one more type of workflow that was not mentioned earlier because it had no relevancy to the discussion: code-only workflows. Typically, those are the workflows that most developers are familiar with. They just contain C# (VB.NET) code.

So with that understanding of different types of workflows, let's see what's available inside the imported project:

➤ **Feature1**: The feature used in adding the Approval Training workflow. This will be covered in more detail later.

➤ **Package.package**: This is the WSP package that contains the converted workflow feature.

➤ The .vwi and .vdw files: The Visio diagram and the interchangeable file you created in the "Prototyping in Visio section." These visualization files are only for XOML-only workflows that are created and they are of no use once they are ported over to the Visual Studio project.

➤ **The .xsn files**: Initiation, association, and task InfoPath forms.

➤ **ApprovalFT content type**: The Approval content type that's added to the Tasks list when Feature1 is activated. This will be explained later.

➤ **Element.xml**: The element manifest file for the Approval Training workflow. This will be covered in much greater detail later (See Listing 12-8).

➤ **The .xoml and .xoml.cs files**: The .xoml file contains the markup to declare various workflow activities (differentiated by the namespace). The .xoml.cs file is the code behind.

➤ **The .rules file**: This file contains RuleConditions associated with the workflow. As alluded to earlier, the Training Approval file doesn't have any custom conditions, so the XML fragment in this file contains only the OOTB conditions that are generated for the workflow by SharePoint Designer.

The .xoml file is the XML representation of your workflow (aka the markup), including all parameters and activities.

> *The XOML is like food for your body. If you don't feed the workflow engine with XOML, it won't function.*

Listing 12-6 shows the Feature definition file in the imported project. Note a few things about the Feature definition. First, the Feature's scope is set to site collection. This is required for adding workflow templates to SharePoint. Second, there are some element manifest files referenced in the Feature definition as follows:

➤ The first highlighted line is used to define a custom content type named ApprovalFT.

➤ The ApprovalFT content type references a custom field called Suggestion Rate, which is defined by the second highlighted element manifest. This file contains the actual field definition for suggestion rating. Note that this file is not shown in Figure 12-25, but it does exist under the ApprovalFT content type folder.

➤ The third highlighted line is the element manifest file for the workflow itself.

Available for download on Wrox.com

LISTING 12-6: Feature Definition for the Training Approval Workflow

```
<Feature xmlns="http://schemas.microsoft.com/sharepoint/"
Title="Converted workflows"
Id="2ee76467-59c3-4e7d-8321-19f6029c5ea5" Scope="Site">
<ElementManifests>
  <ElementManifest Location="ApprovalFT\Elements.xml" />
  <ElementManifest Location="Suggestion_Rate\Elements.xml" />
  <ElementManifest Location="Training_Approval_WorkflowFT\Elements.xml" />
</ElementManifests>
</Feature>
```

TrainingApprovalWorkflow\TrainingApprovalWorkflow.feature

The next element manifest to review is the one used for defining the ApprovalFT content type. Listing 12-7 shows this element manifest file.

Notice the first highlighted line in Listing 12-7. The ApprovalFT content type inherits the OOTB SharePoint Server Workflow Task content type and will be added to the Tasks list when Feature1 is activated. The Training Approval workflow creates task items based on this content type.

The second highlighted line references the Suggestion Rate custom filed. This field maps to the Task Parameter that you created with the same name when you customized the workflow earlier in this chapter. It is used to store the training coordinator's feedback (Good, So-So, or Bad) about a training. This field will show up as a custom site column when you deploy the workflow later to a desired site collection (Under the Custom Site Columns group).

Available for download on Wrox.com

LISTING 12-7: ApprovalFT Content Type

```
<?xml version="1.0" encoding="utf-8"?>
<Elements xmlns:xsi="http://www.w3.org/2001/XMLSchema-instance"
xmlsn:xsd="http://www.w3.org/2001/XMLSchema"
xmlsn="http://schemas.microsoft.com/sharepoint/">
<ContentType ID="0x010801004395428BE5AF4279A724EE6F59495385"
Name="ApprovalFT" Description="">
  <FieldRefs>
    <FieldRef Description="Rate this training suggestion"
    DisplayName="Suggestion Rate" ID="{92dfa913-154f-4531-87b7-5ed663631a17}"
    Name="FieldName_D59F504A_088C_4ADB_8947_3CE524791AF0_"
    Customization="" />
  </FieldRefs>
  <Forms xsi:nil="true" />
  <XmlDocuments>
```

continues

LISTING 12.7: *(continued)*

```
<XmlDocument NamespaceURI=
http://schemas.microsoft.com/sharepoint/v3/contenttype/forms/url">
  <FormUrls xmlns=
  "http://schemas.microsoft.com/sharepoint/v3/contenttype
  /forms/url">
    <Display>
      _layouts/TrainingApprovalWorkflow/ApprovalFT/
    </Display>
    <Edit>
    _layouts/TrainingApprovalWorkflow/ApprovalFT/
    </Edit>
  </FormUrls>
</XmlDocument>
</XmlDocuments>
</ContentType>
</Elements>
```

TrainingApprovalWorkflow\Training_Approval_WorkflowFT\ ApprovalFT\Elements.xml

Listing 12-8 shows the element manifest file for the Training Approval workflow. Note the following in Listing 12-8.

➤ The Name attribute of the Workflow element is the name of the workflow template that will appear in the list of available workflows when associating the workflow to the Training content type. You may want to rename the value to something shorter, for example ApprovalTrainingWorkflow.

➤ Leave the value of the InstantiationURL attribute at its default. When you start the workflow manually, SharePoint examines the InstantiationURL attribute to determine the proper .ASPX page. The default value points to an out-of-the-box page at _layouts/ IniWrkflIP.aspx. This page examines the value of the Instantiation_FormURN element, looking for an InfoPath form to load into an InfoPath form web part that's on the page. Yes, you guessed right! The Instantiation_FormURN attribute is currently missing. Don't worry; you will take care of this a bit later. When users start the form, IniWrkflIP.aspx passes the data it collects (i.e., the Why Important field) back to the SharePoint object model, which in turn starts the associated workflow and passes the information to the workflow instance.

➤ The same thing applies to the AssociationUrl attribute. It's pointing to a page at _layouts/CstWrkflIP.aspx that loads the association form specified in Instantiation_ FormURN attribute — which obviously has gone missing during the import process, too!

➤ The TaskListContentTypeId attribute refers to the ApprovalFT content type ID.

➤ The second and third highlighted lines are the association and initiation parameters you created when you customized the workflow in SharePoint Designer. They are just two custom fields used as the metadata of the workflow forms. Don't expect to see them in the site columns.

➤ The third highlighted line shows the StatusPageUrl attribute. This points to the workflow status page where you saw the Visio Silverlight visualization component along with other information about the workflow such as the workflow history data.

LISTING 12-8: Element Manifest for the Training Approval Workflow

```xml
<?xml version="1.0" encoding="utf-8"?>
<Elements xmlns:xsi="http://www.w3.org/2001/XMLSchema-instance" xmlns:xsd=
"http://www.w3.org/2001/XMLSchema"
 xmlsn="http://schemas.microsoft.com/sharepoint/">
  <Workflow Name="TrainingApprovalWorkflow - Training Approval    WorkflowFT"
  CodeBesideAssembly="$assemblyname$"
  CodeBesideClass="TrainingApprovalWorkflow.Training_Approval_WorkflowFT"
  Id="{3B395925-FA07-47CC-861E-62C28428E833}"
  AssociationUrl="_layouts/CstWrkflIP.aspx"
  InstantiationUrl="_layouts/IniWrkflIP.aspx"
  TaskListContentTypeId="0x010801004395428BE5AF4279A724EE6F59495385">

    <MetaData>
      <AssociationCategories>List</AssociationCategories>
      <Instantiation_FieldML>
        <Fields>
          <Field Name="TrainingManager" Required="TRUE"
          DisplayName="Training Manager"
          Description="" Direction="None"
          Type="User" Hidden="TRUE" ReadOnly="TRUE"
          FormType="Association" />

          <Field Name="WhyImportant" Required="TRUE"
          DisplayName="Why Important"
          Description="" Direction="None"
          Type="Note" Hidden="TRUE" ReadOnly="TRUE"
          FormType="Initiation">
            <Default>Please describe why this training course is
              important.
            </Default>
          </Field>
        </Fields>
      </Instantiation_FieldML>
      <Initiation_Parameters>
        <Parameters />
      </Initiation_Parameters>
      <StatusPageUrl>_layouts/WrkStat.aspx</StatusPageUrl>
    </MetaData>
  </Workflow>
</Elements>
```

TrainingApprovalWorkflow\Training_Approval_WorkflowFT\Elements.xml

With your tour of the imported project completed, it's now time to begin your investigation.

Identifying the Missing Pieces

Of course, the devil is always in the details. . . .

Although you may expect that you can just press F5 and expect the full-blown workflow to deploy and run in a SharePoint site, this is not the case in 99% of scenarios (I left 1% there just in case I missed something after testing 15 different importing scenarios).

The imported project is just a template. Don't expect it to be more than just a starting point to work from, as opposed to starting from scratch.

The following is the list of major issues related to the imported workflow project.

	WHAT ARE THE MISSING PIECES?
1	Two references are missing, so the project won't compile.
2	InfoPath forms are not packaged and deployed alongside the generated Feature definition and manifest files.
3	InfoPath forms are not specified in the element manifest file for the Training Approval workflow. Three `FormURN` elements are currently missing.
4	Initiation form is the default view in the imported `Training Approval Workflow` `.xsn` form template. When you deploy the form and try to associate the workflow to the Training content type, it's the initiation form that loads by default, and you won't be able to associate the workflow and define the Training Manager.
5	The tasks created by the workflow are not shown using the InfoPath task form.
6	The workflow is not associated with the Training content type. When you deploy the workflow, the Training Approval workflow won't show up in the list of the available workflows for the Training content type.

Let's address the missing items one at a time. First, the references.

Adding the Missing References

Figure 12-26 shows the `Training Approval Workflow.xoml` file. The XML fragment in this file is quite lengthy, but it's not very difficult to understand. To help you understand this file better, three line numbers have been added for the important parts.

Line #1 declares some CLR namespaces that contain the public types exposed as elements within the .xoml file. For example, `CreateTrainingSite` is a public type in AdventureWorksWFs.dll, so it's being declared at the beginning of this file and used as an attribute later on.

Line #2 is the declaration of your `CreateTrainingSite` activity. It's the child element of the `IfElseBranchActivity` element with the `ShapeText` attribute with the value of "Manager Approved?", as shown in Line #3.

When you import your workflow to Visual Studio, some of the required assemblies are not referenced correctly. To compile the project, you need to add the following references manually:

➤ Microsoft.Office.Workflow.Actions.dll: If you don't reference this assembly, the project doesn't compile. This assembly is located in the ISAPI folder under 14 hive.

➤ AdventureWorksWFs (from the Projects tab): If you don't add this reference, the project doesn't compile.

FIGURE 12-26

Compilation aside, if you don't add the AdventureWorksWFs project reference, you won't be able to see the Designer canvas for the workflow. To prove the point, delete the reference (if added), and then click on the `Training Approval Workflow.xoml` file. You should receive a very common error message like the one shown in Figure 12-27.

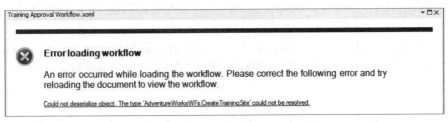

FIGURE 12-27

With the references in place, you should now be able to compile the project successfully (finally!).

Moving right along . . .

Packaging the InfoPath Forms

That brings us to the second item on the list of things to take care of.

At this point, if you attempt to build and deploy the workflow, it will deploy just fine, but the InfoPath forms won't be included in the WSP package. Obviously, if they are not in the package, they won't be available in the Feature folder when everything is deployed. If they are not deployed, then they won't be published and made available to your workflow either. Blame it on the Import Wizard; it's just a chain of problems it has caused for us.

Resolving this issue is a simple matter — just include the forms in the WSP package and modify the Feature definition file to include a Feature receiver that publishes the forms.

Start with the easy one: including the forms in the
WSP Package:

1. In the Workflows folder, right-click on
   the node that says "Training_Approval_
   WorkflowFT" and select Add ▷ New Item.

2. From the available SharePoint 2010
   templates, select Module and name it Forms.
   Note that if you choose a different name,
   you must modify the code snippets presented
   in the rest of this chapter and replace the
   word "Forms" with your own.

3. Drag the `Approval.xsn` and `Training
   Approval Workflow.xsn` files from Other
   Imported Files ▷ Files ▷ Workflows ▷
   Training Approval Workflow folder, and
   drop them in the Forms module. Your
   project looks something like Figure 12-28.

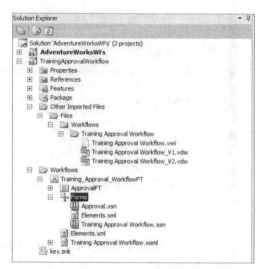

FIGURE 12-28

The next thing that you are going to tackle is to add a specific Feature receiver to the
ApprovalTrainingworkflow feature (formerly known as `Feature1`). You don't need to code this
Feature receiver, because it's is already shipped with the product. You will reuse it to publish the
InfoPath forms.

Go to the Feature Designer, and then click the Manifest button. This will bring up the Manifest
Editor dialog, where you can add the code in Listing 12-9 to the Edit Options textbox, as shown in
Figure 12-29.

LISTING 12-9: Feature Definition for the Training Approval Workflow

```xml
<?xml version="1.0" encoding="utf-8" ?>
<Feature
ReceiverAssembly="Microsoft.Office.Workflow.Feature,
Version=14.0.0.0, Culture=neutral,
PublicKeyToken=71e9bce111e9429c"
ReceiverClass= "Microsoft.Office.Workflow.Feature.WorkflowFeatureReceiver"
xmlns="http://schemas.microsoft.com/sharepoint/">
  <Properties>
    <Property Key="GloballyAvailable" Value="true" />
    <Property Key="RegisterForms" Value="Forms\*.xsn" />
  </Properties>
</Feature>
```

TrainingApprovalWorkflow\TrainingApprovalWorkflow.feature

Note three things about the Feature definition file shown in Listing 12-9:

➤ The Feature receiver is used when workflow contains InfoPath 2010 forms. It will publish the forms specified in the `<Properties>` element into InfoPath Forms Services 2010 when the Feature is installed. Note the version number, as it has been changed since the previous version (12.0.0.0). The public key is the same as before.

➤ The `Value` attribute for the `RegisterForms` key indicates the path to the InfoPath forms, which is relative to the Feature file location. This tells the Feature receiver where your forms are located.

➤ Leave the `GloballyAvailable` property set to `true`, so the forms are globally available across all site collections when they are published.

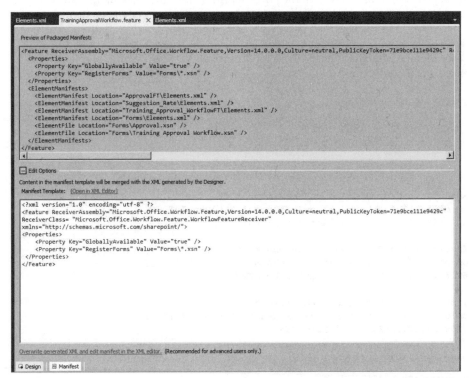

FIGURE 12-29

While you are in the Feature Designer, take a look at the Preview of Packaged Manifest textbox. Note the relative references to the forms within the `<ElementFile>` element that result from dragging and dropping the `.xsn` files to the `Forms` module folder.

Associating the Forms with the Workflow

As mentioned previously, the element manifest file for the Training Approval workflow is missing three `FormURN` elements that are used in specifying the workflow InfoPath forms for the workflow.

Listing 12-10 shows the changes that you need to make to the element manifest file for the Training Approval workflow to include the InfoPath forms.

Note the extra child elements in the `<MetaData/>`. Each element references an ID that points to a specific InfoPath form as follows:

➤ To specify the association form, the `Association_FormURN` element is used.

➤ To specify the initiation form, the `Instantiation_FormURN` element is used.

➤ To specify the task editing form, the `TaskID_FormURN` element is used.

Keep that in mind, though, the initiation and association forms are located within the same InfoPath form, and that's why they both have the same ID. URN is like GUID in the sense that's it's unique to the form. To find the unique ID, you need to open each form in InfoPath 2010 in Design mode. From the Backstage, click the Info tab, and then in the Form Statistics billboard, click on the button that says Form Template Properties. You'll see the URN in the ID textbox of the modal dialog that appears.

LISTING 12-10: Element Manifest for the Training Approval Workflow (some elements and attributes are not included for brevity)

```xml
<?xml version="1.0" encoding="utf-8"?>
<Elements xmlns:xsi="http://www.w3.org/2001/XMLSchema-instance" xmlns:xsd=
"http://www.w3.org/2001/XMLSchema"
xmlsn="http://schemas.microsoft.com/sharepoint/">

  <Workflow>
    <MetaData>
      <Association_FormURN>urn:schemas-microsoft-
      com:office:infopath:workflowInitAssoc:-AutoGen-2010-02-
      26T14:48:51:568Z</Association_FormURN>

      <Instantiation_FormURN>urn:schemas-microsoft-
      com:office:infopath:workflowInitAssoc:-AutoGen-2010-02-
      26T14:48:51:568Z</Instantiation_FormURN>

      <Task0_FormURN>urn:schemas-microsoft-
      com:office:infopath:workflowInitAssoc:-AutoGen-2010-02-
      20T09:36:06:585Z</Task0_FormURN>

      <AssociationCategories/>
      <Instantiation_FieldML>
        <Fields>
          </Fields>
      </Instantiation_FieldML>
      </Initiation_Parameters>
      </StatusPageUrl >
    </MetaData>
  </Workflow>
</Elements>
```

TrainingApprovalWorkflow\Training_Approval_WorkflowFT\Elements.xml

With the URNs properly referenced in the element manifest file, you can now move on to the fourth item in the list of things to take care of.

Switching to the Right InfoPath View Based on the Workflow Context

The fourth problem is that, when the `Training Approval Workflow.xsn` form is loaded, it always defaults to the Start view, which in turn loads the initiation form. This is great when users start the workflow, but it's certainly not the expected behavior when the workflow needs to be associated with the Training content type. To resolve this issue, you need to set up a rule that runs when the form loads, and changes the view to the right one based on the workflow context.

To prove the point, open `Training Approval Workflow.xsn` in InfoPath 2010 in Design mode and navigate to the Page Design tab in the Ribbon. In the Views drop-down list, notice how the Start view is set to default and the Associate view is set as the second view of the form, as shown in Figure 12-30.

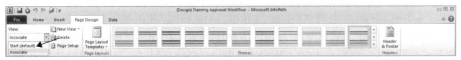

FIGURE 12-30

Navigate to the Data tab and go to the section called Rules. Click on the Form Load button to open the Rules pane for the Form Load event.

Click the New button and select Action. First, enter a meaningful name, such as `SwitchView`, in the textbox that says Details for.

 This chapter is on workflows. Creating declarative rules for use in an InfoPath form is covered in great detail in Chapter 9.

Second, you need to set the condition of the rule. The condition is clear: you want to switch the view to Associate when the workflow is in association mode. To do so, you will use the `isStartWorkflow` field from the form's secondary data source named `Context`, as shown in Figure 12-31.

Use the `isStartWorkflow` field as the left operand, "is equal to" as the operator, and the `string(false())` function as the right operand in the condition, as shown in Figure 12-32.

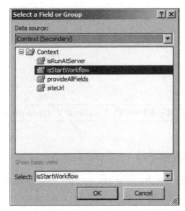

FIGURE 12-31

FIGURE 12-32

Third, click the Add button and select Switch views from the list of actions. Select Associate in the dialog box that appears and click OK.

That's it. Publish the form back to SharePoint using quick publish; you're done with it. Quick publish will also save the form locally in your Visual Studio project folder.

Displaying Tasks Using the WrkTaskIP.aspx Page

Listing 12-11 shows the changes that you need to make to the element manifest file for the ApprovalFT content type to display the tasks created by the workflow using the custom InfoPath task form.

Note the `<Display>` and `<Edit>` elements in Listing 12-11. The values point to an out-of-the-box page at _layouts/ WrkTaskIP.aspx. This page examines the value of the Task0_FormURN element, looking for an InfoPath form to load into an InfoPath form web part that's on the page. When users approve or reject an item, WrkTaskIP.aspx passes the data it collects (i.e., Suggestion Rate field) back to the workflow instance.

Available for download on Wrox.com

LISTING 12-11: ApprovalFT Content Type (Some elements and attributes are not included for brevity.)

```xml
<?xml version="1.0" encoding="utf-8"?>
<Elements xmlns:xsi="http://www.w3.org/2001/XMLSchema-instance"
xmlsn:xsd="http://www.w3.org/2001/XMLSchema"
xmlsn="http://schemas.microsoft.com/sharepoint/">
  <ContentType ID="0x01080100FA9090DE01D349CC8E81891FF66E43F2"
    Name="ApprovalFT" Description="">
    </FieldRefs>
    </Forms>
    <XmlDocuments>
      <XmlDocument NamespaceURI=
      "http://schemas.microsoft.com/sharepoint/v3/
      contenttype/forms/url">
        <FormUrls
        xmlns="http://schemas.microsoft.com/sharepoint/v3/
        contenttype/forms/url">
          <Display>_layouts/WrkTaskIP.aspx</Display>
          <Edit>_layouts/WrkTaskIP.aspx</Edit>
        </FormUrls>
      </XmlDocument>
    </XmlDocuments>
  </ContentType>
</Elements>
```

TrainingApprovalWorkflow\Training_Approval_WorkflowFT\ ApprovalFT\Elements.xml

Associating the Workflow with the Training Content Type

The last issue you need to fix is modifying the element manifest file for the workflow and associating it with the Training Approval workflow. SharePoint uses the value of the `<AssociationCategories>` element to display only the appropriate workflows for a list or content type.

To keep the focus on the workflow concept, this chapter assumes that the Training content type is already deployed and made available in the desired site collection where you will deploy the Training Approval workflow. You also need to know the Training's content type ID beforehand to specify it in the workflow element manifest file.

Optionally, you can add the necessary code to your project to create the Training content type declaratively or programmatically.

> *Another point worth emphasizing is that SharePoint 2010 allows developers to create content types programmatically and assign content type IDs. This is an improvement over the past when the only way a content type could be created and assigned an ID was declaratively.*
>
> *For more information about creating content types using the SharePoint 2010 object model, refer to Microsoft Patterns and Practices SharePoint Guidance at* `www.microsoft.com/spg`.

The values that goes inside the `<AssociationCategories>` element may include a character-delimited string, using the character ";" as the delimiter. This string can be up to 256 characters in length. Workflows associated with a specific list type and defined in a specified Feature have the following pattern:

Pattern: *"List;" + Feature ID + ";" + List ID*

Example:

```
<AssociationCategories>
    List; c3cce3c5-468c-4ad6-991c-c2d9936e409f;1300
</AssociationCategories>
```

Workflows that are associated with a content type, however, follow a different pattern.

Pattern: *"ContentType;" + Content Type ID*

Example:

```
<AssociationCategories>
    ContentType;0x0100E2C74F14CF94E2408485F68D42E58A1A
</AssociationCategories>
```

In contrast, a pattern defining a site workflow with no association to a list or content type has no delimiter. Site workflows will be covered in much greater detail later in this chapter.

Pattern: *"Site"*

Example:

```
<AssociationCategories>Site</AssociationCategories>
```

There are several ways to get the Training content type ID, but most likely the easiest way is through the browser. Browse to the Site Content Types gallery and click on Training content type. Highlight the value of the `ctype` query string parameter and copy it to the clipboard, as shown in Figure 12-33.

FIGURE 12-33

Listing 12-12 shows the element manifest file for the Training Approval workflow. Note the `<AssociationCategories>` element with the Training Content Type ID pasted from the clipboard.

LISTING 12-12: Element Manifest for the Training Approval Workflow (Some elements and attributes are not included for brevity.)

Available for download on Wrox.com

```xml
<?xml version="1.0" encoding="utf-8"?>
<Elements xmlns:xsi="http://www.w3.org/2001/XMLSchema-instance"
xmlsn:xsd="http://www.w3.org/2001/XMLSchema"
xmlsn="http://schemas.microsoft.com/sharepoint/">
  <Workflow>
    <MetaData>
        </Association_FormURN>
        </Instantiation_FormURN>
        </Task0_FormURN>
          <AssociationCategories>
            ContentType;0x0100E2C74F14CF94E2408485F68D42E58A1A
          </AssociationCategories>
        <Instantiation_FieldML>
          <Fields></Fields>
        </Instantiation_FieldML>
        </Initiation_Parameters>
        </StatusPageUrl >
    </MetaData>
  </Workflow>
</Elements>
```

TrainingApprovalWorkflow\Training_Approval_WorkflowFT\Elements.xml

Adding Some Code to the Workflow

Congratulations! Looks like your long list of things to take care of finally has come to an end. At this point, you can go ahead and add some code to the workflow.

Right-click the `Training Approval Workflow.xoml` file and select View Designer to open the workflow Designer canvas. In the Toolbox, in the Windows Workflow v3.0 section, drag a Code activity to the Designer and drop it directly below the `EmailActivity6` activity, as shown in Figure 12-34.

This will add an activity named `codeActivity1` to the workflow Designer canvas. Double-click the `CodeActivity1` activity to generate an event handler. Replace `codeActivity1_ExecuteCode` with the code in Listing 12-13.

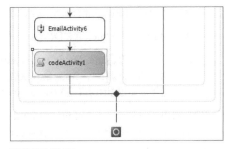

FIGURE 12-34

The code simply creates a sample announcement in the Announcements list in another site each time a training course is approved.

LISTING 12-13: Approval Training Workflow Partial Class

```
using Microsoft.SharePoint.WorkflowActions;
using Microsoft.SharePoint;
using System;

public partial class Training_Approval_WorkflowFT :
RootWorkflowActivityWithData
{
    protected override void Initialize(System.IServiceProvider provider){}

    private void codeActivity1_ExecuteCode(object sender,
     System.EventArgs e)
    {
        using (SPSite site = new SPSite("http://wf1/sites/clean"))
        {
            using (SPWeb web = site.OpenWeb())
            {
                SPList announcementsList = web.Lists["Announcements"];
                SPListItem aListItem = announcementsList.Items.Add();
                aListItem["Title"] = "Imported reusable workflow is up
                there!";
                aListItem.Update();
            }
        }
    }
}
```

TrainingApprovalWorkflow\Training Approval Workflow.xoml.cs

Putting It All Together

Now that you have all the plumbing work done, you should be able to package the workflow, with all its bells and whistles, and deploy it to a desired site collection. The business requirements of the Training Approval workflow dictate that everything must be deployed using a single package.

To satisfy this requirement, you need to take the following steps:

1. Go to the Package Designer for the `TrainingApprovalWorkflow` project.

2. In the Package Designer, select the `AdventureWorksWFs` Feature mapped folder and `Workflow(AdventureWorksWFs)` Feature from the Items in the Solution pane, and click the add button (>) to move them to Items in the Package pane.

This will cause these artifacts to be deployed with the WSP solution that you will build from the `TrainingApprovalWorkflow` project. The Package designer now should look as shown in Figure 12-35.

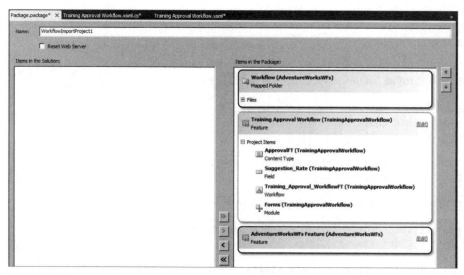

FIGURE 12-35

That's it. Save the Visual Studio solution, and you are ready to deploy it. Right-click on the `TrainingApprovalWorkflow` project in the Solution Explorer and select Deploy. Your workflow Feature should be successfully installed in all site collections.

Browse to a site collection other than the one used in SharePoint Designer and activate the Feature. Next, browse to Site Settings ⇨ Site Content Types ⇨ Training ⇨ Workflow Settings. Note that your workflow is assigned to the Training content type and shows up in the list of available workflows, as shown in Figure 12-36.

Figure 12-37 proves that the custom rule you added to the InfoPath form kicks in here and switches the form to the right view. Specify the training manager and click Save to associate the workflow to the Training content type.

Figure 12-38 shows the new Training Approval workflow started for a training suggestion.

FIGURE 12-36

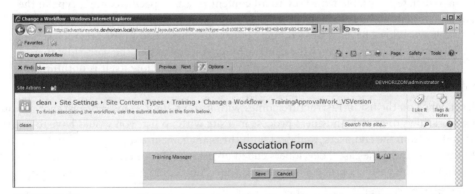

FIGURE 12-37

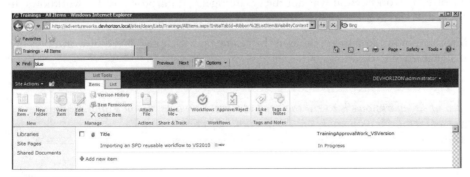

FIGURE 12-38

BUILDING WORKFLOWS WITH VISUAL STUDIO 2010

SharePoint Designer workflows are very powerful for modeling business processes, and the people who create them don't require any knowledge of code. However, the workflows lose their effectiveness in the broader spectrum of enterprise-scale applications, where more control over processes is key.

As mentioned previously, using Visual Studio is an extremely attractive option for workflow development. In Visual Studio 2010, there are four new areas for workflow developers that matter the most and, therefore, are the focus of the rest of this chapter:

➤ Site Workflows

➤ ASP.NET Association and Initiation Templates

➤ External Data Exchange Services (aka Pluggable Workflow Services)

➤ Workflow Events

Site Workflows

Still staying at a high level, let's have a refresher on reusable workflows again. You need it for this section.

In SharePoint 2010, workflows don't necessarily need to be strongly associated with a list instance. Instead, you can associate a reusable workflow to all content types, a specific content type in the current site, or across multiple sites in a given site collection, which makes it a globally reusable workflow. Reusable workflows have addressed many issues customers had in the previous versions of SharePoint. However, they are still very list-centric. Sure, you can assign the workflow to a content type, but unless that content type is attached to a list, the workflow itself is nothing more than just a bunch of code sitting around doing absolutely nothing.

Too much dependency on the list infrastructure comes with its own limitations. For instance, if you wanted to use workflows to model a business process in a site with no list, you would have to create a dummy list, hide it from the end users, and deal with the management issues and all kinds of other headaches. In the majority of the cases, developers ended up using other functionalities, such as event handlers, or even took the business process outside the SharePoint context and implemented it there.

Let's face it, although the previous version of SharePoint was an easy-to-use workflow host and got many people involved in workflows, it was not the greatest general-purpose host for workflows. In another words, SharePoint, as a workflow host, was not flexible enough.

Thankfully, Microsoft didn't stop there, though; they came up with a new breed of workflows in SharePoint 2010, named Site workflows.

 The idea of site workflows is to cut the dependency of a workflow on a SharePoint list item and let it run on literally any SharePoint object.

To give you some flavors of what you can accomplish using site workflows, let's jump right on few very common scenarios:

➤ **Scenario 1**: Accessing backend data sources — Picture this: every time a site workflow kicks off, a number of new customers are retrieved from a customer relationship management (CRM) application and added to the visitors group of the company's extranet site. The data access can be provided through Business Data Connectivity Services or a custom data access layer.

➤ **Scenario 2**: Managing site permissions — Imagine this: you want to automate the process of adding users to departmental sites and giving them permissions to the appropriate lists based on their job title. You can create a site workflow that runs in the portal site and let users start it directly from the View All Site Content page where there is a link to Site Workflows. Users are then routed through an approval process and finally given access or denied access to the requested site.

➤ **Scenario 3**: Implementing general business logic — Dream this: upon the creation of a project team site, a group work site is created along with it and added as a subsite.

➤ **Scenario 4**: Managing business process on folders — Love this: you want to create a workflow that runs on folders rather than individual items. When you start the workflow, it will assign a number of tasks to the owners of the documents within the folder. While the workflow instance is running, you can go to the workflow status page and find out about the outstanding tasks. Barbara Decker, who is one of the document's owners, receives an email, which includes a link pointing to the document that she's tasked to review. She opens the document in Word, reviews and modifies the document, and then completes her task from within the Word client without even visiting the site.

The scenario you are going to tackle in this section is similar to the one that was presented at the beginning of this chapter, with one exception: it breaks the dependency of the Training Approval workflow on the Trainings list context.

This means that training coordinators no longer need to go to the Training list, create a new training course, and kick off the workflow manually. Instead, they suggest the training course through an application page that starts a site workflow, as shown in Figure 12-39. The workflow routes the training suggestion through an approval process and finally creates the training site if necessary.

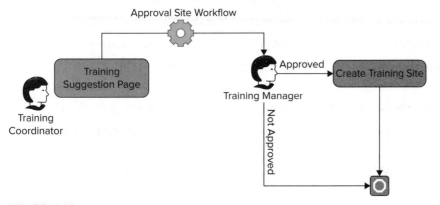

FIGURE 12-39

Building a Sequential Site Workflow

Now that you know what you are building, get started by creating a workflow project in Visual Studio. Select a Sequential Workflow template from the SharePoint ⇨ 2010 category, and name it `TrainingApprovalSiteWorkflow`.

In the SharePoint Customization Wizard, select the option to deploy the project as a farm solution, and click Next. In the second step, change the default name to `TrainingApprovalSiteWorkflow` and choose the second option, which says Site Workflow.

In the third step, you specify what lists to use for tasks created by the workflow and workflow history information. Leave everything at its default and click Next. The last step is about how to start the workflow. Again, leave the selected option (start manually) and click Finish.

 This is probably the best time to fill you in on two key tips. First, you cannot add workflow templates to Sandboxed Solutions. Second, unlike list-based workflows, site workflows cannot be started automatically.

After the project is created, rename the default `workflow1.cs` to `TrainingApprovalSWF.cs`. Make sure that you rename it in the code behind and the `Designer` class. The easiest way is to find the word `workflow1` and replace it with `TrainingApprovalSWF` in the entire project.

Next, add a reference to `AdventureWorksWFs` project where you created the `CreateTrainingSite` custom activity. This should immediately add the custom activity to the toolbox, as shown in Figure 12-40.

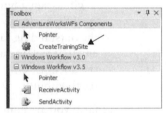

FIGURE 12-40

With the project now created, the next logical step is to model the workflow in the Designer canvas. Conceptually, this step is pretty similar to what you did in Visio 2010 when you built your declarative workflow earlier in this chapter.

Open the workflow in the Designer canvas and perform the following activities:

1. Add a `CreateTask` activity directly below the `OnWorkflowActivited1` activity.

2. Add a `logToHistoryListActivity` activity after the `CreateTask` activity.

3. Drag and drop an `OnTaskChanged` activity directly below the `logToHistoryListActivity` activity.

4. Add an `ifElseActivity` activity after the `OnTaskChanged` activity.

5. Add a `CreateTrainingSite` activity inside the `ifElseActivity` activity to the right branch.

6. Add a `SendEmail` activity inside the `ifElseActivity` activity to the left branch.

When you are done dropping activities into place, your Designer canvas should look like Figure 12-41. Notice that there are little red exclamation icons next to some of the activities. This is because they all failed in the design-time validation process. Don't worry about them; you will fix these errors next.

 Notice that the Visual Studio Workflow Designer is based on .NET 3.5 Framework, not .NET Framework 4.0.

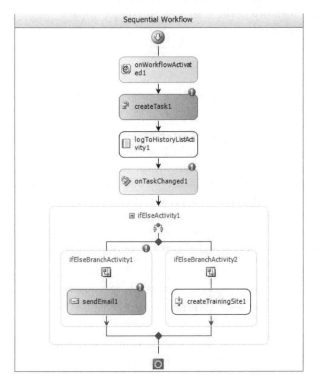

FIGURE 12-41

Click on `CreateTask1` and in the property windows, find the `Correlation Token` property. You need to type in "taskToken" as the value of this property. You also need to specify an owner for the `OwnerActivityName` subproperty. Select the value from the drop-down list and set it to the name of the workflow class (`TrainingApprovalSWF`). Repeat the same steps for the `OnTaskChanged1` activity to set the `Correlation Token` and `OwnerActivityName` properties. The correlation token of the `OnTaskChanged1` activity must match with the `CreateTask1` activity, so make sure that you select "taskToken" from the drop-down list. If this is not available, type it in again. With the correlation tokens properly set, the error icons should disappear from both activities.

ABOUT THE CORRELATION TOKEN

In the context of workflow tasks, a correlation token ensures that the related task activities are operating on the correct task. For example, the `CreateTask1` and `OnTaskChanged1` activities operate on the same task, so they get the same correlation token. If there were another set of `CreateTask` and `OnTaskChanged` activities that needed to create and work on a separate task, then they would get their own correlation token, too.

Correlation tokens are not only for task activities. They can be used anywhere in a workflow where message correlation is required. For example, a correlation token can be used to ensure that the correct instance of the workflow is resumed when a message is received, in response to a requested action.

Now you should be able to configure the `TaskId` and `TaskProperties` properties of the `CreateTask1` activity.

Go back to the property window for `CreateTask1` activity and find the `TaskId` property. Click the ellipse button to bring up the property binder dialog, then select the Bind To a new member tab. A member can be a field or a property of type "`System.Guid`". Type in `approvalTask_TaskId` as the member name, select the Create Field radio button, and click OK. The `TaskID` property ensures that each task gets its own GUID, which can be identified and used in the workflow later (you will see the usage in the `OnTaskChanged1` activity). Repeat the same steps for the `TaskProperties` property of the `CreateTask1` activity, and name it `approvalTask_TaskProperties`. This property represents the properties of a task created by the workflow and allows the workflow instance to set specific values in it.

The next activity to configure is the `LogToHistory` activity. There are two properties that you need to set: `HistoryOutcome` and `HistoryDescription`. Both properties are set the same way that `TaskId` was set in `CreateTask1`.

The review by the training manager introduces a natural delay where the workflow runtime engine is waiting for any change to the task item. While waiting for the training manager to complete his task, the workflow instance dehydrates and no longer remains in memory on the server it is running on. At this point, the state of the workflow instance is written to the SharePoint content database in such a way that it can be retrieved later.

Once the workflow wakes up (rehydrates), it continues on and the `OnTaskChanged1` activity is executed. To configure the `OnTaskChanged` activity, you need to wire up one more property: `TaskId`. This time, instead of creating a new field, bind it to `approvalTask_TaskId` field you created before.

Notice that the `OnTaskChanged1` activity has no `TaskProperties` property. This makes sense, because this activity doesn't create any task that the workflow needs to set values on it. Instead, it has two other properties: `BeforeTaskProperties` and `AfterTaskProperties`. In this example, you will only use the `AfterTaskProperties` property. To set this property, use the binding dialog box and create a new field named `onApprovalTaskChangedAfterProperties`.

Think of BeforeTaskProperties *and* AfterTaskProperties *like a "before and after" picture of someone who has had a hair transplant. The* BeforeTaskProperties *property contains a picture of the task before it's changed (pretty thin!). The* AfterTaskProperties *contains a picture of the task after it's changed. After a task is completed, it is thicker in terms of information, because it has the approval status, approver's comment, and probably some custom data. The bottom line: you should realize the difference!*

Configuring the SendEmail activity is very similar to other activities. The only point worth emphasizing here is the correlation token. In this activity, set the correlation token to workflowToken. The workflowToken token is the workflow's default correlation token, and it is generated automatically when you create a workflow project. Typically, this token is used in activities that do not correlate directly to workflow tasks. Using this token will automatically set the OwnerActivityName sub property. Type an email address in the From property and give the Subject property a meaningful value such as "Your training suggestion is rejected."

The last activity that you need to configure is your own activity. Setting up this activity is the simplest of all. It only exposes two properties: Url and SiteName. For both these properties, use the binding dialog box and create new fields of type "System.String" with proper names such as createTrainingSiteName and createTrainingSiteUrl. That's it for the CreateTrainingSite1 activity.

At this point, all of your activities are configured. Don't worry about the red little exclamation error in ifElseBrnachActivity1. This will be fixed later by code.

If you look at the code behind, you will see that Visual Studio has generated the following variable declarations and maybe some methods if you have double-clicked on any activity.

You are going to leave the workflow alone for a little while and come back to it after the next section. The next step is to create the initiation form.

Adding an ASPX Initiation Form

Your workflow needs an initiation form to be displayed to the training coordinators when they start it. This form allows the workflow to gather information about the training before it gets started. To keep things simple, this section only covers the initiation form creation, but nothing prevents you from following the same steps for creating the initiation form and creating association and task forms as well.

It's worth mentioning that the form that you will build is not an InfoPath form. It's an ASPX page that will be coded completely from scratch (for the most part, anyway. Read on.).

Thankfully, Visual Studio 2010 ships with new SPIs (SharePoint Project Items) for workflow forms. First, right-click on the TrainingApprovalSWF SPI in Solution Explorer and choose Add ➪ New Item. Select the Workflow Initiation Form template, name it start.aspx, and click OK. Next, change the namespace in the code behind, the HTML markup, and the Designer class from TrainingApprovalSiteWorkflow.TrainingApprovalSWF to TrainingApprovalSiteWorkflow.

This will fix some of the namespace conflicts that will occur later when you code the activities, so it is important that you take care of it here.

Notice how the new form is automatically associated with the workflow by the changes made to the element manifest file, as shown in Listing 12-14. If you need a refresher on the `InstantiationUrl` attribute, see the "Importing to Visual Studio" section earlier in this chapter.

LISTING 12-14: Training Approval Site Workflow Element Manifest File

```
<Elements xmlns="http://schemas.microsoft.com/sharepoint/">
  <Workflow
    Name="TrainingApprovalSiteWorkflow"
    Description="My SharePoint Workflow"
    Id="398fa8cf-ac70-4958-af59-a910da11bc9c"
    CodeBesideClass="TrainingApprovalSiteWorkflow.TrainingApprovalSWF"
    CodeBesideAssembly="$assemblyname$"
    InstantiationUrl=
    "_layouts/TrainingApprovalSiteWorkflow/TrainingApprovalSWF
    /start.aspx">
    <Categories/>
    <MetaData>
      <AssociationCategories>Site</AssociationCategories>
      <StatusPageUrl>_layouts/WrkStat.aspx</StatusPageUrl>
    </MetaData>
  </Workflow>
</Elements>
```

TrainingApprovalSiteWorkflow\ TrainingApprovalSWF\Elements.xml

The form you just added is an ASPX page with code behind and all the wiring already done. Open the code-behind file and take a peak. The `GetInitiationData` method sends the data from the initiation form to the workflow instance. The returned value of this method is what you reference in your workflow, using the `workflowProperties.InitiationData` property.

By default, this method returns an empty string, which is most likely not adequate in real-world solutions. Instead, you should use the XML serialization functionality included in the Microsoft .NET Framework to pass the form's data into the workflow. It is not enough to pass in the initialization form data to workflow; you also need to write the appropriate code in the workflow that pulls the XML data submitted by initiation form and deserializes it into an object. The deserialization part will be taken care of later when you code the activities.

The first step is to create a new C# class and add two references to the `System.IO` and `System.Xml` `.Serialization` assemblies. Next, add the code shown in Listing 12-15 to the class.

LISTING 12-15: Code to Serialize and Deserialize the Initiation Form Data

```
[Serializable()]
public class TrainingInfo
  {
```

```
          private string title = default(string);
          private string code = default(string);
          private string description = default(string);
          public string Title
            {
              get {return this.title;}
              set {this.title = value;}
            }
          public string Code
            {
              get { return this.code;}
              set { this.code = value;}
            }
          public string Description
            {
              get { return this.description;}
              set { this.description = value;}
            }
        }

    public class TrainingInitFormHelper
      {
          public static string SerializeTrainingForm(TrainingInfo training)
            {
              XmlSerializer serializer = new XmlSerializer(typeof(TrainingInfo));
              using (StringWriter writer = new StringWriter())
                {
                  serializer.Serialize(writer, training);
                  return writer.ToString();
                }
            }
      }
```

TrainingApprovalSiteWorkflow\TrainingApprovalSWF\start.aspx.cs

Listing 12-15 contains two classes: `TrainingInfo` and `TrainingInitFormHelper`. The `TrainingInfo` class represents a training object. For the sake of simplicity, the code only implements three fields, title, code, and description, with their getter and setter assessors. As implied by the name, the `TrainingInitFormHelper` class is a helper class to facilitate the process of persisting data collected by the workflow initiation form. There is nothing really special to this code; it just contains standard .NET code for serializing an object of type `TrainingInfo`.

The second step is to insert the following HTML markup inside the main content placeholder of the page:

```
          <asp:Label id="lblTitle" Text="Title:" runat="server"/>
          <asp:TextBox ID="txttitle" runat="server" />
          <br />
          <asp:Label id="lblCode" Text="Code:" runat="server"/>
          <asp:TextBox ID="txtTrainingCode" runat="server" />
          <br />
          <asp:Label id="lblDes" Text="Description:" runat="server"/>
          <asp:TextBox ID="txtDescription" runat="server"/>
          <br />
```

While you are in the HTML markup, you may also want to change the title of the page, button labels, and other elements. Next, go to the form's code behind and insert the following lines of code in the `GetInitiationData` method to collect and return the form's data:

```
TrainingInfo tInfo = new TrainingInfo();
tInfo.Title = txttitle.Text;
tInfo.Code = txtTrainingCode.Text;
tInfo.Description = txtDescription.Text;
string xmlString = TrainingInitFormHelper.SerializeTrainingForm(tInfo);
return xmlString;
```

Note one thing about the `start.aspx` code behind: the `StartSiteWorkflow()` method contains the code to programmatically start an instance of the Training Approval workflow, as shown in Listing 12-16.

The first line gets a collection of the workflow association object that represents the workflow that is associated with the initiation form. The second line starts a new instance of the workflow, passing in the association object and returned data from the `GetInitiationData` method, and tells the workflow to run synchronously. The other two possible values for running the workflow are `SynchronousAllowPostpone` and `Asynchronous`. The former is used to run the workflow instance synchronously, but switches to asynchronous if the synchronous execution fails. The latter enables the workflow to run synchronously.

The third line uses the `SPUtility.Redirect` method to redirect the user who starts the workflow back to a URL. This URL is the one that's specified in the `source` query string parameter of the original request. You will use this redirection later, but for now just keep in mind that, after starting the workflow, users don't have to stay in the initiation form or look at the boring workflow information in the status page. They can be redirected to anywhere you wish.

LISTING 12-16: Code Used in Starting the Site Workflow Programmatically

```
private void StartSiteWorkflow()
{
    SPWorkflowAssociation association =
        this.Web.WorkflowAssociations
        [new Guid(this.associationGuid)];
    this.Web.Site.WorkflowManager.StartWorkflow
        ((object)null, association, GetInitiationData(),
        SPWorkflowRunOptions.Synchronous);
    SPUtility.Redirect(this.Web.Url, SPRedirectFlags.UseSource,
        HttpContext.Current);
}
```

TrainingApprovalSiteWorkflow\TrainingApprovalSWF\start.aspx.cs

With the initiation form complete, the next step is to take care of the coding aspects of the workflow and go through the process of implementing the business logic.

Coding the Activities

With the workflow activities in place, properties bound to fields, and ASPX initiation form created, you can now start coding. Most of your coding here involves creating event handlers for the activities used in the workflow.

To avoid confusion, it's very important to understand that some of these event handlers are called during or after their associated activity is executed. For instance, the event handler for the sendEmail1 activity is run when the activity begins executing but before the email is sent out to the recipients. As another example, the event handler for the OnTaskChanged1 activity is called after the activity is executed. As mentioned previously, you can always access the values contained in the afterProperties property collection representing the changes made to the task.

And with that, let's begin coding.

The first activity you are going to implement is onWorkflowActivated1. In the Designer canvas, double-click the activity to generate the event handler. Click in the method body and insert the code shown in Listing 12-17. This code will deserialize an object of type TrainingInfo, passed by the ASPX initiation form, and store it in a class-scoped private variable named twInfo. The private variable is then used by other activities in the workflow to deliver the functionality they need. In this stage of the workflow, the name of the training site and its URL are also set using the fields created in the CreateTrainingSite1 activity.

LISTING 12-17: Coding the onWorkflowActivated1 Activity

```
private TrainingInfo twInfo = default(TrainingInfo);

private void onWorkflowActivated1_Invoked(object sender,
  ExternalDataEventArgs e)
  {
    XmlSerializer serializer = new XmlSerializer(typeof(TrainingInfo));
    XmlTextReader reader = new XmlTextReader(new
      System.IO.StringReader(workflowProperties.InitiationData));
    twInfo = (TrainingInfo)serializer.Deserialize(reader);
    createTrainingSiteName = twInfo.Code;
    createTrainingSiteUrl = workflowProperties.WebUrl;
  }
```

TrainingApprovalSiteWorkflow\TrainingApprovalSWF.cs

The next step is to create the task and assign it to the training manager. This task is created by the CreateTask1 activity. To set the initial attributes associated with the approval task, double-click the activity to generate the event handler and add the code shown in Listing 12-18. Most of the attributes represent the common fields in the task list of SharePoint.

Keep in mind that if you need to add custom data to the task, the SPWorkflowTaskProperties object contains a hash table to store extra information in the task in key-value pairs. You can set or get a specific custom property by using the property name as an index in the ExtendedProperties property. This mechanism really opens your hand to store information in the workflow task and use it later in the task form.

LISTING 12-18: Coding the createTask1 Activity

```
private void createTask1_MethodInvoking(object sender, EventArgs e)
    {
        createTask1.TaskId = Guid.NewGuid();
        approvalTask_TaskProperties = new
         Microsoft.SharePoint.Workflow.SPWorkflowTaskProperties();
        approvalTask_TaskProperties.AssignedTo =
         workflowProperties.Web.SiteAdministrators[0].LoginName;
        approvalTask_TaskProperties.DueDate = DateTime.Now.AddDays(1.0F);
        approvalTask_TaskProperties.Title = "Approval Required for " +
         twInfo.Title ;
        approvalTask_TaskProperties.Description =
         "Specify the approval result here.";
        createTask1.TaskProperties = approvalTask_TaskProperties;
    }
```

TrainingApprovalSiteWorkflow\TrainingApprovalSWF.cs

One warning on Listing 12-18: the `AssignedTo` property is set to the first administrator in the `SiteAdministrators` collection. In your production system, you want to read this value from the association data submitted to the workflow by the association form. The steps required to send and receive the association data are identical to those for the initiation form. Again, XML serialization is always your best friend; let it help you.

With the task created, the next step is to write an information entry in the workflow history list using the `logToHistoryListActivity1` activity. Right-click the activity and, from the context menu, click Generate Handler. Set the values of the `HistoryDescription` and `HistoryOutcome` properties, as shown in Listing 12-19.

LISTING 12-19: Coding the logToHistoryListActivity1 Activity

```
private void logToHistoryListActivity1_MethodInvoking(object sender,
    EventArgs e)
    {
        logToHistoryListActivityHistoryDescription =
         string.Format(" Training = {0}/{1} is waiting for
         approval",twInfo.Code,twInfo.Title);
        logToHistoryListActivityHistoryOutcome =
         string.Format(" A task is created for training {0}
         and assigned to the training manager ", twInfo.Title);
    }
```

TrainingApprovalSiteWorkflow\TrainingApprovalSWF.cs

Now, it's time to add the required logic to respond to the task changes. When the `OnTaskChanged1` activity is executed, you can access the values contained in the `beforeProperties` or `afterProperties` property collection objects. To access these properties, first add an event handler.

Before adding the necessary logic to the handler, create two additional local variables to help store the result of the task:

```
private bool bTrainingApproved = false;
private string strTrainingManagerComment =
 default(string);
```

Next, add the code in Listing 12-20 to the empty `onTaskChanged1_Invoked` method. The code determines whether the training manager has indicated that the task is complete and if the training course is approved. The Boolean evaluation of this condition is stored in a class-level variable named `bTrainingApproved`. For the sake of simplicity, the code assumes that when a workflow task is complete, it's either approved or rejected and the approval decision is specified in the description column of the task using the word "Approved" or "Rejected."

LISTING 12-20: Coding the onTaskChanged1 Activity

```
private void onTaskChanged1_Invoked(object sender, ExternalDataEventArgs e)
    {
      if (onApprovalTaskChangedAfterProperties.PercentComplete == 1.0F &&
      onApprovalTaskChangedAfterProperties.Description.Contains("Approved"))
        bTrainingApproved = true;
      else
        bTrainingApproved = false;
    }
```

TrainingApprovalSiteWorkflow\TrainingApprovalSWF.cs

For the `sendEmail1` activity, you have essentially three properties to set: `Subject`, `From`, and `Body`. However, because the former two properties are already configured, the process is much easier. Add the code in Listing 12-21 to the `sendEmail1_MethodInvoking` method that is created when you double-click the activity. The code creates some information about the suggested training course and includes it in the body of the email message.

LISTING 12-21: Coding the sendEmail1 Activity

```
private void sendEmail1_MethodInvoking(object sender, EventArgs e)
    {
      sendEmail1.Body = string.Format
       ("Sorry , but your suggestion {0}/{1}
       has been rejected by the training manager. ",
       twInfo.Code, twInfo.Title);
    }
```

TrainingApprovalSiteWorkflow\TrainingApprovalSWF.cs

At this point, all the activities are handled except for the final activity: `ifElseActivity1`. If you recall, the configuration of this activity was postponed, so it's now about time to get it coded, too.

In this activity, the workflow determines whether the training manager approved or rejected the training course subject to the workflow and takes a different path, depending on his decision.

The logic of branching is no different than in any IF ELSE statement. When the condition is evaluated, a `true` or `false` statement is returned and the workflow branches to one of the `ifelsebranchactivity` activities. There are two kinds of conditions that can be set for this activity:

➤ Declarative Rule Condition: This requires coding the logic in the workflow's built-in Condition Editor. The logic must always result in a Boolean evaluation.

➤ Code Condition: This requires an event handler just like all the other activities. The event handler must always result in a Boolean evaluation.

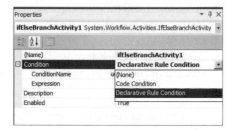

FIGURE 12-42

Select the branch that contains the `ifElseBranchActivity1` activity and set the `Condition` property to `Declarative Rule Condition`, as shown in Figure 12-42.

There are two more additional properties to set: `ConditionName` and `Expression`. Clicking in the textbox next to the `ConditionName` property will display the ellipses where you can click and launch the workflow's built-in Condition Editor. This dialog contains all of the declarative rule conditions in your workflow, and obviously it should be empty for now. Click the New button to launch the Rule Condition Editor dialog.

The Rule Condition Editor dialog is where you can type in the conditional expression. Notice that the editor comes with IntelliSense, which displays a list of properties, fields, and methods in the workflow class. Enter the following expression to determine whether the training course is rejected:

```
!this.bTrainingApproved
```

Clicking the OK button will return you to the Select Condition dialog, where you will rename the condition, giving it a more descriptive name. Repeat the same steps for the `ifElseBranchActivity2` branch, using the following expression:

```
this.bTrainingApproved
```

The conditions that you created above can be reused by other activities, too. Figure 12-43 shows the workflow's built-in Condition Editor after both conditions are created.

After all these button clicks, if you check the content of the `.rules` file, you will find the XML fragment of the condition you just wrote.

Compiling and Deploying

All of your activities are coded now. All you need to do is press F5 and wait for the workflow

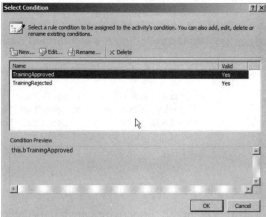

FIGURE 12-43

to compile and be deployed. The packaging process is no different from any other SPI, as everything will be bundled into a WSP solution.

 Depending on the changes you've made to the deployment configuration, you may need to go to the site collection Features gallery and activate the Feature manually. Workflow templates are defined at the site collection level.

Once the SharePoint site shows up, browse to the View All Site Content page and click Site Workflows. You should see all of the site workflows, as well as the workflow that was just deployed. Click on the workflow to start it. This redirects you to the workflow initiation form, as shown in Figure 12-44. Type in some information and click the Start Workflow button.

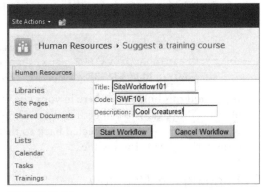

Go ahead and approve or reject the task. If the training suggestion is approved (include "Approved" in the description column), a site is created for the training. If not, the workflow simply terminates, but it sends an email to the training coordinator before doing so.

FIGURE 12-44

I will be the first one to admit that the initiation form is totally unstyled and looks horrible, quite literally. But, then again, this chapter is not meant to teach you branding 101!

Figure 12-45 shows the log entry created by the `logToHistoryListActivity1` activity.

FIGURE 12-45

Last, but certainly not least, there is one option available to direct users back to where they came originally from after starting a site workflow. If you have been using SharePoint for any amount of time, you probably know that URLs are everywhere and play an important role in many forms in SharePoint. On most SharePoint forms, you can simply add your own URL to the `Source` query string parameter and SharePoint will automatically redirect the user to that URL when the form is submitted. The same rule applies to site workflow initiation forms.

As mentioned previously, the initiation form code-behind file contains the redirection logic that redirects the workflow originator to the URL specified in the `Source` query string parameter. Take a look at the initiation form URL. It should be similar to the following URL, except that it contains your own site URL:

```
http://wfe1/hr/_layouts/TrainingApprovalSiteWorkflow/TrainingApprovalSWF/
TrainingApprovalSWF.aspx?TemplateID={a4a00127-4e88-47d2-9d0f-8388d70bb6e7}&
Source=http%3A%2F%2Fwf1%2Fhr%2F%5Flayouts%2Fworkflow%2Easpx
```

If you add this link somewhere in your site, by replacing the Source query string value with the URL of a specific page, you can get the users to the workflow initiation form. Then, when they start the workflow, they will be redirected back to that page. A very simple tip, but it makes a lot of people scratch their heads for a while.

Debugging the Workflow

As always, no application is complete without debugging, audit trails, logging, and testing. At a high level, workflow exceptions can be categorized in the following two distinctive groups:

➤ **Failed on start (retrying):** This usually means that the workflow assembly cannot be loaded or the assembly in the global assembly cache (GAC) does not match the information specified in the `<workflow>` element of the workflow manifest file.

➤ **Error Occurred:** This means that the workflow has started, but there was an error in one of the activities.

Debugging a workflow live is very similar to other types of debugging done with SharePoint projects created in Visual Studio 2010. You can set a few breakpoints in the code behind or on each activity in the Designer canvas and press F5. Behind the scenes, Visual Studio attaches to the right `W3WP.exe` process.

The SharePoint Unified Logging Service (ULS) also logs a large amount of information about each instance. Some of the core workflow exceptions are only caught by the ULS, which makes it a good place to refer to when debugging your workflows.

ULS logs and live debugging aside, there are three more options available when debugging workflows:

➤ **Fault handlers:** A developer uses the `FaultHandler` activity to capture a specific exception type and execute one or more activities in response to that exception when workflows fail.

➤ **Try-catch block:** As with any other application, a developer captures exceptions in the code using a `try-catch` block. This enables the developer to handle exceptions and take actions accordingly.

➤ **Workflow events:** A developer creates an event handler that listens to various workflow events and provides logging and error notifications to the site administrator. This will be covered later in this chapter.

Now that you have some idea of how you go about fault handling in your workflows, let's build a fault handler.

A `FaultHandler` activity can be associated with most of the activities in the workflow or the workflow itself. Obviously, when it's associated with the workflow, the handler acts at a global level as opposed to when it's local to a specific activity. Figure 12-46 shows how to associate a `FaultHandler` activity with the workflow.

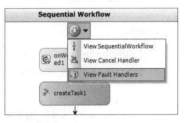

FIGURE 12-46

After selecting the View Fault Handlers option, the Designer canvas changes to the Workflow Exceptions mode. There is already a `FaultHandlersActivity` activity on the surface. This activity is a composite activity that can contain one or more `FaultHandler` activities. Drag a `FaultHandler` activity from the toolbox into the rectangular area directly below the icon that shows a folder with an exclamation mark next to it. Next, right-click the `FaultHandler` activity that you just added and select Properties from the context menu.

Find the `FaultType` property and then click the ellipsis button. From the list of available exceptions, select the `Microsoft .SharePoint.SPException`, as shown in Figure 12-47.

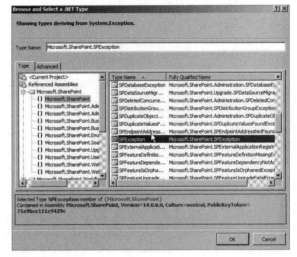

FIGURE 12-47

The `SPException` represents an exception in SharePoint. This exception is typically used when a violation of some kind happens. For example, attempting to delete one of the out-of-the-box galleries, such as Workflows, creates an `SPException` exception. Because attempting to create a site with the same name as an existing site is considered a violation, this exception suits the logic of your workflow very well.

Drag a `logToHistoryListActivity` activity from the toolbox and drop it directly above the termination step, where it says Drop Activities here. In the event of an exception of type `SPException`, this activity adds a log entry to the workflow history list associated with the workflow.

 Remember, the capability to copy and paste activities from one workflow Designer canvas to another Designer canvas is a great convenience. Let it help you.

For the `logToHistoryListActivity2` activity, there are two properties that you need to set: `HistoryOutcome` and `OtherData`. Both properties are set the same way that the properties of the `logToHistoryListActivity2` activity were set. The `OtherData` property is used to write additional information in the log entry written to the workflow history list. Unlike `HistoryOutcome` and `HistrotyDescription` properties, the `OtherData` property is not restricted to 255 characters in length.

Right-click the `logToHistoryListActivity2` activity, and then select the Generate Handlers option from the context menu. Add the code shown in Listing 12-22.

LISTING 12-22: Coding the logToHistoryListActivity2 Activity

```csharp
public String logToHistoryListActivity2HistoryOutcome =
  default(System.String);
public String logToHistoryListActivity2OtherData = default(System.String);

private void logToHistoryListActivity2_MethodInvoking
  (object sender, EventArgs e)
  {
    logToHistoryListActivity2HistoryOutcome =
    faultHandlerActivity1.Fault.ToString();
    logToHistoryListActivity2OtherData =
    faultHandlerActivity1.Fault.ToString();
  }
```

TrainingApprovalSiteWorkflow\TrainingApprovalSWF.cs

The `logToHistoryListActivity` activity writes the log entries to the workflow history list. The workflow history list is a hidden list and is not listed under View All Site Content link. You can find this list by clicking on the In Progress link in the workflow status page or by typing the following URL in the browser. Each workflow instance is uniquely identified by an ID of type `GUID`, which needs to be specified in the `WorkflowInstanceID` query string parameter. This ID is used to communicate with the instance.

```
http://wfe1 /_layouts/WrkStat.aspx?WorkflowInstanceID={00000000-0000-0000-
0000-000000000000}
```

The log entries are only kept for 60 days, by default. There is a timer job named Workflow Auto Cleanup that runs on a daily basis and removes log entries older than 60 days after the workflow is completed or canceled, as shown in Figure 12-48.

With the fault handler in place and the `logToHistoryListActivity` properties bound to fields and its event handler code, you can cause an intentional error to test the fault handler.

Start a workflow with "SWF01" as the training code. Once you verify that the training site is created, start the workflow one more time and use the same code. Because the `CreateTrainingSite` activity uses the training code as the title for the Web site, you should get the error message shown in Figure 12-49, in the workflow history list.

FIGURE 12-48

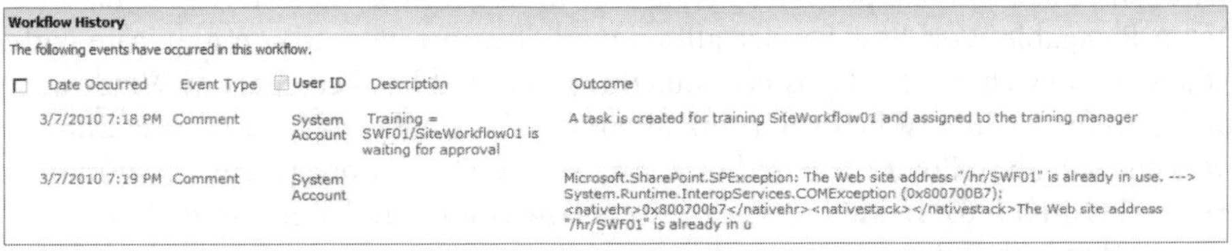

FIGURE 12-49

Pluggable Workflow Services

Previously, SharePoint-hosted workflows could only subscribe to a limited number of SharePoint core events such as `ISharePointService`, `ITaskService`, `IListItemService`, and `IModificationService`. However, many scenarios required workflow developers to interact with other internal or external events. Another issue was that workflow activities were intrinsically synchronous. So, running operations that take a long time to complete within the main workflow thread could potentially block other activities in the workflow from execution.

Imagine that you have created a workflow that interacts with a CRM web service and the service takes three seconds to respond to an action. There are 1000 instances of the workflow spawning every day. You certainly don't want to keep all those instances in the web frontend servers' memory for 3 seconds each just to complete a service call. Instead, you want to run the service call outside the workflow activity, so whenever the workflow gets the result back from the CRM service, the workflow wakes up and continues on, as shown in Figure 12-50.

In WSS 3.0, one solution to overcome this shortcoming was to use the combination of an event handler attached to the Tasks list and workflow tasks to send a request to CRM (using its native web services) and have CRM update the task with the result. Once the result is written to the task, you can always access it in the workflow channel by using the `OnTaskChanged` activity. Microsoft also had a pattern called business event, which was conceptually very similar to this solution.

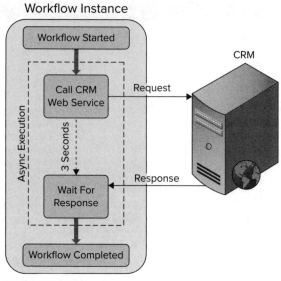

FIGURE 12-50

But, what if you want to get data into a workflow while it's running without getting tasks involved?

Thankfully, SharePoint 2010 now supports Pluggable Workflow Services via External Data Exchange (EDS). A Pluggable Workflow Service allows workflow instances to communicate with events outside the workflow channel. This is not something new and has been part of Windows Workflow Foundation for a while. When you think about it, all the dehydration and rehydration behaviors of workflows in SharePoint are based on the EDS communication system. So, Windows SharePoint Services 3.0 used it for modeling its own workflow communication system, but Microsoft just decided to lock it down and not allow SharePoint developers to directly benefit from it in their custom SharePoint-hosted workflows.

There are three primary uses for Pluggable Workflow Services:

1. Subscribing to internal and external events. Any event that dehydrates the workflow and rehydrates it when it's raised.

2. Handling long-running operations in an asynchronous manner, so the workflow can dehydrate and rehydrate the workflow while the operation is running.

3. Getting resource-intensive operations off the workflow thread so that it can switch back to other workflow activities; for example, if there are activities that have no dependency on the result of the operation or there are parallel activities that need to complete before the result is returned to the workflow.

There is nothing special about a Pluggable Workflow Service. Think of it as being like an event handler, feature receiver, or any other code that runs within the SharePoint. It's just some code that is registered with workflow runtime that runs in SharePoint and runs on the workflow host thread. This service can be implemented in such a way that it can interact with running instances of a workflow.

At a high level, creating a Pluggable Workflow Service involves several steps. To get started, add a C# class to your workflow project and name it `TrainingSiteCreationLocalService.cs`. Next, add the following using statements to the class:

```
using System.Workflow.Activities;
using System;
using Microsoft.SharePoint;
using System.Threading;
using System.Workflow.Runtime;
using Microsoft.SharePoint.Workflow;
```

Now, the class needs the logic required for the plumbing to work.

The first thing you need to create is the contract of the service. Listing 12-23 shows a service interface that's decorated with an `ExternalDataExchange` attribute. The interface definition contains an event and a method. The former provides the communication into the workflow, and the latter provides the communication into the service.

 From now on, the term "the service" refers to the Pluggable Workflow Service that you are implementing in this chapter.

An event called `MessageIn` is raised when the service needs to send a message into the workflow instance. When you insert this line, you get an error on the `CommunicationObjArgs` class. It's normal; you have defined an event handler, but you didn't specify the method that actually handles the event. Don't worry, you'll add this next. Keep in mind that you can have multiple events raised and more than one message pushed back into the workflow.

The interface also contains a method for the data that the workflow sends out to the service. Again, you can have the workflow communicate with the service to send more than one message.

LISTING 12-23: The Service Contract

```
[ExternalDataExchange]
public interface ITrainingSiteCreationService
{
    event EventHandler<CommunicationObjArgs> MessageIn;
    void CreateTrainingSite(string sitename, string url);
}
```

TrainingApprovalSiteWorkflow\PluggableWorkflowServices\TrainingSiteCreationLocalService.cs

With the service contact in place, the next step is to add the event class that inherits the `ExternalDataEventArgs` class, as shown in Listing 12-24. This class is the handler for the event you added to the interface definition. It represents a serializable message that needs to go into the workflow.

Two things must be implemented in this class. First, a constructor that uses the :base(Id) constructor. This ID uniquely identifies a workflow instance. As previously mentioned, without this ID, it's impossible to know which instance to correlate the message to. Second, the class must be marked as Serializable, so the message is serialized on the way into the workflow instance.

LISTING 12-24: Event Handler Implementation

```
[Serializable]
public class CommunicationObjArgs : ExternalDataEventArgs
  {
     public CommunicationObjArgs(Guid id) : base(id) { }
     public string webID;
  }
```

TrainingApprovalSiteWorkflow\PluggableWorkflowServices\TrainingSiteCreationLocalService.cs

The last piece of code you need to add is the actual service implementation, as shown in Listing 12-25. This class must derive from SPWorkflowExternalDataExchangeService and implement the service interface (the contract). At minimum, this class must implement two members:

➤   The method that's defined in the interface definition. In this example, it's called CreateTrainingSite().

➤   An inherited abstract member called SPWorkflowExternalDataExchangeService .CallEventHandler. This method will handle the callback to the workflow instance.

In addition to the member implementations, the service must declare a public event of type CommunicationObjArgs, so it can be used in the plumbing to route the event handler (see CallEventHandler method).

LISTING 12-25: Service Implementation

```
class StateObject
   {
     public SPWeb web;
     public Guid instanceId;
     public StateObject(Guid instanceId, SPWeb web)
       {
          this.instanceId = instanceId;
          this.web = web;
       }
   }

class TrainingSiteCreationService : SPWorkflowExternalDataExchangeService,
  ITrainingSiteCreationService
   {
     public event EventHandler<CommunicationObjArgs> MessageIn;
     public void CreateTrainingSite(string sitename, string url)
        {
          ThreadPool.QueueUserWorkItem(delegate(object state)
```

```
            {
                StateObject sObject = state as StateObject;
                string webID = string.Empty;
                using (SPSite siteCollection = new SPSite(url))
                    {
                        using (SPWeb web = siteCollection.OpenWeb())
                            {
                                using (SPWeb trainingWeb = web.Webs.Add(sitename))
                                    {
                                        trainingWeb.Description = "This site is created by a
                                         pluggable workflow service.";
                                        trainingWeb.Title = sitename;
                                        trainingWeb.Update();
                                        webID = trainingWeb.ID.ToString();
                                    }
                            }
                    }
                RaiseEvent(sObject.web, sObject.instanceId,
                 typeof(ITrainingSiteCreationService),
                 "MessageIn", new object[] { webID });
            }, new StateObject(WorkflowEnvironment.WorkflowInstanceId,
               this.CurrentWorkflow.ParentWeb));
        }

public override void CallEventHandler(Type eventType,
 string eventName,object[] eventData, SPWorkflow workflow,
 string identity,System.Workflow.Runtime.IPendingWork workHandler,
 object workItem)
    {
        var msg = new CommunicationObjArgs(workflow.InstanceId);
        msg.webID = eventData[0].ToString();
        msg.WorkHandler = workHandler;
        msg.WorkItem = workItem;
        msg.Identity = identity;
        this.MessageIn(null, msg);
    }

// Code omitted for brevity

    }
```

TrainingApprovalSiteWorkflow\PluggableWorkflowServices\TrainingSiteCreationLocalService.cs

Note a few things about Listing 12-25:

➤ ThreadPool.QueueUserWorkItem queues an anonymous method delegate for execution on a separate thread. This method will execute as soon as a thread pool thread becomes available.

➤ The QueueUserWorkItem method only takes two parameters. The first parameter is the code that the thread executes. Using an anonymous method delegate means that you do not need to create an additional method to execute the long-running code. The second parameter, which starts after the delegate (`new StateObject()`), is for an object containing data to be used inside the anonymous method delegate.

➤ `StateObject` is a class used to hold data to be used by the anonymous method delegate. This class contains two pieces of information: the workflow instance ID and the `SPWeb` object where the workflow is running.

➤ `RaiseEvent()` call raises a workflow event and sends an event back through `CallEventHandler()`.

➤ The `CallEventHandler()` method is the plumbing code that gets the returned message (`webID`) from the long-running code into the workflow instance. This is done by passing an instance of the `CommunicationObjArgs` to the workflow instance.

With the service implementation complete, the service needs to be registered with the SharePoint workflow runtime host. Open the `web.config` file and insert the following line into `<WorkflowServices>` element. As always, replace the public token key with your own.

```
<WorkflowService Assembly="TrainingApprovalSiteWorkflow,
Version=1.0.0.0, Culture=neutral, PublicKeyToken=b3dec5fc56831cdf"
Class="TrainingApprovalSiteWorkflow.TrainingSiteCreationService">
</WorkflowService>
```

While you are in the `web.config` file, notice how some EDS implementations that SharePoint Workflow communication systems uses are already registered.

Switch back to the workflow Designer canvas; you are done with the `TrainingSiteCreationLocalService.cs` file. Delete the `CreateTrainingSite1` activity in the right branch of the `ifElseActivity1` activity. Instead, drag and drop the following three activities into the workflow:

➤ `CallExternalMethodActivity`

➤ `HandleExternalEvent`

➤ `LogToHistoryListActivity`

These activities will be used for in and out communications with the service. Notice how one activity is blue and the other one is green. Blue in workflow activities denotes that the activity sends something out or does something. Green activities are those waiting for something to happen. The Designer canvas now should look like Figure 12-51.

The `CallExternalMethodActivity1` activity will call the `CreateTrainingSite` method in the service, and the `HandleExternalEvent1` activity will dehydrate the workflow and wait for the event `MessageIn` to be raised. After the event is raised (or if it was raised before the activity executes), the data that is passed into the workflow (`webId`) will be written to the workflow history list, using the `LogToHistoryListActivity3` activity.

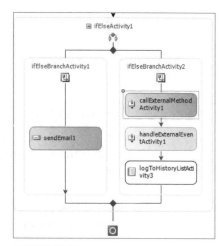

FIGURE 12-51

To provide a better designer experience, a command-line utility called wca.exe *can be executed against a compiled* ExternalDataExchange *interface to create strongly typed activities. These activities can be then dragged from toolbox just like any other activity and placed in workflow. If you opt to use this tool, I highly recommend that you run it only when the interface definition has been finalized and is no longer being actively developed. For more information about this tool, refer to the official documentation at* www.devhorizon.com/go/26.

The next step is to configure new activities to point to the service. For the CallExternalMethodActivity1 activity, there are four properties that must be set. Use the following combination as an example:

➤ **InterfaceType:** ITrainingSiteCreationService (see Figure 12-52)

➤ **MethodName:** CreateTrainingSite

➤ **sitename:** Bind it to a new field named callExternalMethodActivitysitename.

➤ **url:** Bind it to a new field named callExternalMethodActivityurl.

Just as with the CreateTrainingSite1 activity, the workflow must set the sitename and url properties of the CallExternalMethodActivity1 activity before the activity will execute. Insert the code shown in Listing 12-26 into the onWorkflowActivated1_Invoked method.

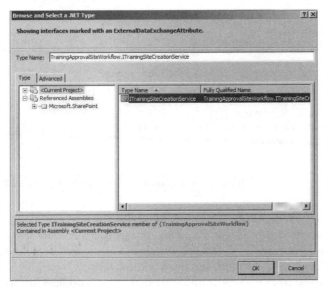

FIGURE 12-52

LISTING 12-26: Modifying the onWorkflowActivated1_Invoked Method

```
private void onWorkflowActivated1_Invoked(object sender,
  ExternalDataEventArgs e)
  {
    //Code Omitted for brevity
    callExternalMethodActivitysitename = twInfo.Code;
    callExternalMethodActivityurl = workflowProperties.WebUrl;
  }
```

TrainingApprovalSiteWorkflow\TrainingApprovalSWF.cs

To configure the `HandleExternalEvent` activity, you essentially have three properties to set. Use the following combination as an example:

➤ **InterfaceType:** `ITrainingSiteCreationService` (same as the `CallExternalMethodActivity` activity)

➤ **EventName:** `MessageIn`

➤ **e:** Bind it to a property (not a field) called `handleExternalEventActivity1_e1`.

The last activity that you need to configure is the `LogToHistoryListActivity3` activity. Setting up this activity is a piece of cake, because you have done this twice already. Bind the `HistoryOutcome` property to a field called `logToHistoryListActivity3HistoryOutcome`. Right-click the activity and, from the context menu, click Generate Handler. Set the value of the `HistoryOutcome` property, as shown in Listing 12-27. Notice how `webID` is used as a property of the `handleExternalEventActivity1_e1` property.

LISTING 12-27: Coding the logToHistoryListActivity3 Activity

```
private void logToHistoryListActivity3_MethodInvoking(object sender,
  EventArgs e)
  {
    logToHistoryListActivity3HistoryOutcome =
    string.Format("The ID of the training site created is {0}",
    handleExternalEventActivity1_e1.webID);
  }
```

TrainingApprovalSiteWorkflow\TrainingApprovalSWF.cs

That's it. The service is completed and everything's ready. Go ahead and deploy the new workflow. Run the workflow the same way as before and create a sample training. Ensure that you mark the task as 100% complete and type the word "Approved." The workflow should create the site using the Pluggable Workflow Service you created. Figure 12-53 illustrates the workflow history. Note how the `WebID` of the new training site is returned from the service and is written to the workflow history list. Basically, you got a message into the service (sitename and url) and a message out (`WebID`).

Congratulations on a job well done!

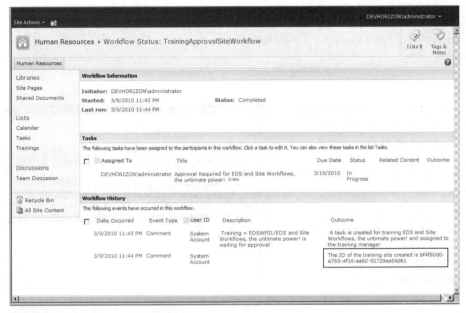

FIGURE 12-53

Tapping into Workflow Events

As indicated in the previous section, workflows in SharePoint 2010 have the ability to respond to events. SharePoint 2010 adds another new feature: workflow events. Essentially, workflows in SharePoint 2010 are structured to emit events that other event receivers can intercept and monitor. If workflows can listen to events and they can emit events, what does this tell you? The answer is that workflows can interact with each other. For example, imagine a series of chained workflows operating on the same list, with each starting after the previous one completes.

This new feature provides a number of key benefits for developers. The most obvious one is that it lends modularity to their workflow design, allowing them to break their workflows into smaller workflows and chain them together. This results in more reusable workflows. Consequently, this means that developers can create code to capture the events emitted by running instances of a workflow. For example, they can monitor and intercept out-of-the-box workflows for errors and handle them in an appropriate way, including custom error notification.

The event receivers have been dramatically improved in SharePoint 2010. The workflow events that ship with SharePoint 2010 are divided into the following four types:

➤   `WorkflowStarting`

➤   `WorkflowStarted`

➤   `WorkflowCompleted`

➤   `WorkflowPostponed`

It's important to understand that new workflow event receivers only fire on list workflows. They don't work for site workflows.

Consequently, Visual Studio 2010 has a new template and a new SPI for event receivers. When you create a new workflow event receiver, you can select the list and the desired workflow events to trap, as shown in Figure 12-54.

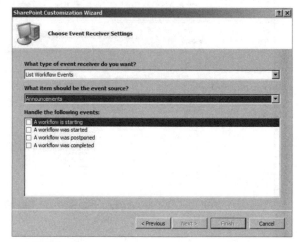

Once the project is created, the workflow event receiver is implemented in a class that inherits from the `SPWorkflowEventReceiver` class. Add the code shown in Listing 12-28 to the `WorkflowCompleted` method.

The code checks the workflow completion type and sends two types of notifications based on that. If the workflow completes successfully, a helper method is called and the email address of the person who started the workflow is passed into it. However, if the workflow errors out, the exception is retrieved and a notification error is sent to the administrator with the exception information included through another helper method.

FIGURE 12-54

Available for download on Wrox.com

LISTING 12-28: The WorkflowCompleted Method

```
public override void WorkflowCompleted(SPWorkflowEventProperties properties)
{
    switch (properties.CompletionType )
    {
        case SPWorkflowEventCompletionType.Completed:
            string orginUserEmail =
             properties.ActivationProperties.OriginatorEmail;
            SendSuccessNotification(orginUserEmail);
        break;
        case SPWorkflowEventCompletionType.Errored:
            Exception ex = properties.ErrorException;
            SendErrorNotification(ex);
        break;
        default:
        break;
    }
    base.WorkflowCompleted(properties);
..}
```

TappingintoWorkflowEvents\ChainWorkflows\ChainWorkflows.cs

SUMMARY

This chapter introduced a whole new landscape of workflow features in SharePoint 2010.

➤ Visio 2010 has two impacts on workflow development. It can be used to prototype a workflow as well as to visualize a running instance of a workflow.

➤ You can import that prototype into SharePoint Designer 2010. You can further customize the workflow by using the SharePoint Designer Workflow Designer.

➤ Reusable workflows are like templates. They can be used as a starting point for creating other workflows. If they are converted to globally reusable workflows, they can be shared across all sites within the same site collection.

➤ SharePoint Designer 2010 can create declarative workflows and associate them with content types, a functionality that was missing in the last version of the product.

➤ SharePoint Designer workflows come with all three types of workflow forms (association, initiation, and task). They all can be customized by InfoPath and published back to SharePoint.

➤ Developers can create workflow actions in Visual Studio 2010 for use in SharePoint Designer workflows. They can be sandboxed, too. In multi-tenant or hosting environments, this would be beneficial. Custom actions must be registered in the `web.config` file as an `authorizedType` element.

➤ A SharePoint Designer reusable workflow can be imported into Visual Studio, but it's just a template. It needs some touch-ups before it's a fully functional WSP package, ready for deployment to other site collections or web applications.

➤ Site workflows are a new type of workflow in SharePoint 2010. They can run on any SharePoint object, not only list items. Remember, site workflows cannot be saved as templates; neither can they be copied and modified. They are just not reusable.

➤ There are two SPIs in Visual Studio 2010 for creating ASPX association and initiation forms. These forms already have the code required to start and cancel a workflow programmatically.

➤ Starting with SharePoint 2010, workflows can listen to internal and external events through the implementation of a Pluggable Workflow Service. SharePoint workflow communication is accomplished through External Data Exchange.

➤ The `CallExternalMethodActivity` and `HandleExternalEvent` activities can be used to send and receive messages to and from a Pluggable Workflow Service asynchronously.

➤ Workflows in SharePoint 2010 can emit events that other event receivers can intercept and monitor.

13
Business Intelligence

WHAT'S IN THIS CHAPTER?

➤ Business intelligence concepts

➤ Doing business intelligence with Excel 2010 and Excel Services

➤ Building dashboards, KPIs, and scorecards using PerformancePoint

➤ Integrating SQL Server Reporting Services R2 with SharePoint 2010

➤ Reporting on SharePoint Data using Access 2010 and Access Service

Business intelligence (BI) is an umbrella term that refers to technologies, applications, and a number of exercises an organization may use to deploy shared business processes across multiple business units. Business Intelligence empowers users with the right insights and enables them to make better, faster, and more relevant decisions when they collaborate.

The focus of this chapter is on bringing SharePoint developers up to speed with the BI features of SharePoint Server 2010 through a series of step-by-step examples. This chapter also includes demonstrations of some of the new features shipped in the current wave of products with SharePoint Server 2010, Office Product 2010, and SQL Server 2008 R2.

CHALLENGES WITH TRADITIONAL BUSINESS INTELLIGENCE

Statistics in our industry state that the majority of people in organizations do not have proper access either to data or to the tools that they require to make effective business decisions. Think about it for a moment. With all the advancements happening so fast in the business intelligence sector, isn't this horrible?

When you look at the problem from different angles, it's obvious that part the problem lies in how we have been doing business intelligence over the past decade. This issue can be divided into three categories:

➤ Complexity in adoption

➤ Lack of must-have functionalities

➤ Hardware and software specifications

Until recently, the greatest challenge in many organizations was the fact that accessing data for the purpose of analysis was something historically restricted to certain groups of people using very specialized tools. With only a handful of staff members able to make use of the BI solutions, business users would come with ad hoc inquires for information resulting in highly qualified BI experts becoming a bunch of report writers, rather than people who look after the BI solutions and fulfill the ongoing corporate BI needs.

Furthermore, it was difficult to give the company leaders the ability to gauge the state of their business at a glance, so they could make agile decisions to keep the business moving forward. In many cases, delivering timely and accurate reports to key decision makers that summarized strategic and operational data has been done in unbelievably inefficient ways, such as through emails and file shares that could easily provide the out-of-date data.

This left the door open for developers and third-party vendors to build custom applications that delivered reports to key decision makers efficiently, which in turn translated into more costs and more hardwired dependencies. Let's not forget that the most compelling reason to do BI is to support decision making. So, the question is: Why must customers pay extra for something that should have been included in the technology to begin with?

From the hardware perspective, building a decent BI solution required assembling the right hardware, compression algorithms, and networking components that constitute the solution. The challenge for many organizations extending the reach of their BI solutions to broader sets of users was the storage and the computing power that was required to host decent BI solutions and make them available to the masses.

Business intelligence is not only for answering the questions that users may have in mind. The more important part of BI is to help users ask the right questions, and also to guide them through an often resource-intensive process to get the insights they need. The types of questions may not necessarily be anticipated or preaggregated into the BI solutions, so the hardware, software, and bandwidth specifications for hosting those solutions must be powerful enough to respond to such on-demand queries in a reasonably fast manner.

All these issues created quite a number of hurdles for the IT industry over the past decade. In the next section, you will look at the history of Microsoft BI, the integration of BI into SharePoint products and technologies, and how Microsoft has managed to address a major portion, if not all, of these issues.

INTEGRATION WITH SHAREPOINT: THE HISTORY

Like many other BI vendors at the time, Microsoft started its significant BI investment with the same limitations in adoption, lacking must-have functionalities and requirements for strong computing power. The problem was that most Microsoft BI solutions were strongly tied to SQL Server technology and SQL Enterprise Manager was the primary interface to interact with those solutions. Again, unless you knew how to work with SQL Server and to do BI, the chances that you were just a bystander in the whole BI world were very high!

Soon, Microsoft realized that the value of its BI platform would not become apparent until a paradigm shift occurred in its approach to doing traditional BI. Looking for a way to excel, Microsoft developed a new vision, which looked at things very differently than had been done before.

The new vision was based on taking BI to the masses, using it to connect people to each other and to connect people to data. The key area of focus was to take the BI out of the realm of specialty and niche tools and turning it into something that's mainstream. There were two primary justifications for the new vision. First, it would hide the difficulties of the underlying platform from the general public. Second, it would make the adoption of the platform much easier. Obviously, the more people that use a platform, the more valuable it becomes and the faster it grows.

Following the overall vision of "BI for everyone" and starting with SharePoint Portal Server 2003, Microsoft fostered this notion of integrating some aspects of their BI offering into their Information Portal technology. Theoretically, because SharePoint brings people together to work and make decisions collaboratively, it could have been the right starting point. However, this integration never extended beyond a couple of web parts natively rendering BI artifacts that are stored outside SharePoint content databases, in products such as Microsoft SQL Server Reporting Services 2000 and Microsoft Business Scorecard Manager 2005.

Okay, so what is wrong with storing BI artifacts outside SharePoint content databases? There are three obvious issues with this separation. First, you need to deal with a minimum of two separate products and repository frameworks to implement a single BI solution, which means more administrative effort. Second, users have to go through more than a hop to get to the backend datasource. For the environments without Kerberos delegation in place, this model can cause authentication issues — also known as double hops. The double-hop (one hop from the client browser to the SharePoint server and another hop to the BI server) problem is not a bug. It's an intentional security design to restrict identities from acting on behalf of other identities. Third, since the SQL Server based BI products and SharePoint Portal Server 2003 were using different security models, it was difficult to map SharePoint roles and permission-levels directly to the roles and permissions understandable by the BI product. In other words, it was difficult to apply a unified authorization model across the products.

In the spring of 2006, Microsoft acquired analytics vendor ProClarity, and soon Business Scorecard Manager 2005 and ProClarityAnalytics products were merged and formed a new product named Microsoft PerformancePoint Server 2007.

Later on, with the release of Microsoft Office SharePoint Server 2007, Microsoft's BI offering turned into something that was way more than just a couple of integration hooks, as is the case with SharePoint Portal Server 2003. In Microsoft Office SharePoint Server 2007 (MOSS 2007),

Microsoft made major improvements in four different areas: the Report Center template, full integration with SQL Server Reporting Services (SQL Server 2005 SP2), new Excel Services, and a Business Data Catalog for integration with line-of-business (LOB) applications.

Fortunately, Microsoft didn't stop there; they released more features that could change the way people used to build dashboard-style applications. Customers could use PerformancePoint Scorecard Builder 2007 and put together their own dashboards and publish them to the PerformancePoint monitoring server. Once the dashboards are published, customers could then use the Dashboard Viewer web part to integrate the dashboard into SharePoint pages. Again, the integration is just a web part that calls into PerformancePoint Server 2007 functioning as a standalone server. Both products were sold separately and they had different management environments and operations.

Even though the attempts Microsoft made to bring the best of both the SharePoint and BI worlds together in MOSS 2007 was great, it was still not enough to call it a full-fledged integration. In other words, the journey was not over yet! The next section is a sneak peek at some of the highlights of new BI features Microsoft has added to SharePoint Server 2010.

HIGHLIGHTS OF BUSINESS INTELLIGENCE IN SHAREPOINT SERVER 2010

The team that was building SharePoint Server 2010 made significant changes based on the customer feedback and the lessons learned in MOSS 2007. Starting with SharePoint Server 2010 Server, PerformancePoint is designed as a service application on top of the SharePoint 2010 Server platform. What is important about the new design is that PerformancePoint and SharePoint are no longer two separate products. Instead, both are finally offered as an integrated product on the Enterprise CAL. The biggest advantage of this move is that PerformancePoint contents are all stored and secured within SharePoint libraries, and they can benefit from the new features and enhancements made to the core SharePoint platform. PerformancePoint itself got many new features and enhancements.

There are many improvements in Excel Services 2010. Microsoft started with limited PivotTable and Excel Services integration in SharePoint 2007 and then expanded beyond that very dramatically in the newest version of SharePoint products and technologies. SharePoint Server 2010 can integrate with a specialized version of SQL Server Analysis Services (SSAS) engine, which allows business analysts to benefit from more sophisticated and high-performing interactive queries using PowerPivot.

In a nutshell, PowerPivot is a collaborative effort across several teams in Microsoft to make Excel, SharePoint, and SQL Server R2 work together to allow all users to discover and manage the right information, all done through the familiar environments such as an Excel client or a web browser.

On the API side, the enhanced Excel Services programmability model allows developers to interact with published Excel workbooks in several ways, such as through Enhanced Web Service APIs, the JavaScript object model, or the REST API. Last, but certainly not least, Excel workbooks work both in the enterprise and in the cloud across many popular browsers such as Internet Explorer, Firefox, and Safari on Mac.

Reporting Services integration with SharePoint Server 2010 is much tighter and cleaner than before. Reporting Services 2008 R2 not only supports native and connected mode (previously known as SharePoint integrated mode), but it also supports a new lightweight integration mode named local mode. In this mode, customers need to install SharePoint Server 2010 and the SQL Server 2008 R2 Reporting Services add-in, but no Reporting Services server is required. Local mode is a valuable out of-the-box feature that allows the viewing of SSRS reports with no SSRS server. Reporting Services has seen a number of improvements as well, which are discussed later in this chapter.

Access Services 2010 is probably one of the biggest service areas for customers, because now they can model their databases in the Access client application, publish everything to SharePoint, and keep the client and server models in sync. In Access 2007, customers could only move the tables up to SharePoint, but the rest of application was still living in an ACCDB inside the Access client application. In Access 2010, you can move the entire application to SharePoint and map it to a SharePoint team site. All the tables and data become standard SharePoint lists, and the forms are converted to standard ASPX pages stored in SharePoint document libraries. Finally, data macros become workflows, and reports inside the application are turned into `.rdl` files and are associated with the Reporting Services report execution engine.

Recall from the previous section that one of the barriers to extending the reach of BI to everyone was the required computer power. With the current wave of Microsoft products, many of the desktop and large-server scalability issues are addressed. On the sever side, 64-bit-only products allow customers to take advantage of greater addressable memory range, modern CPU architectures, and multicore technologies, which in turn translates into tremendous computer power and faster BI solutions. On the client side, in-memory cache and compression algorithms allow BI analysts to load millions of rows of data into a PowerPivot workbook and do BI faster than ever.

The rest of this chapter discusses some of these new features in more detail.

IMPORTANT TERMS AND CONCEPTS

As much as a BI developer may get confused when he or she first hears commonly used terms in SharePoint, such as "site" and "site collection," there are some BI terms that may sound a bit vague to a SharePoint developer with no BI background. Many BI techniques share terminology, and some terms are used interchangeably. In the interest of clarity, some of these terms are defined up front in this section and then referenced later on.

If you are a SharePoint developer, you are most likely very familiar with flat, table-style data structures, because lists in SharePoint mimic the exact same data storage format. Relational database management systems (RDBMSs), such as the SQL Server database engine, also use tables for storing data. Although storing data in tables has its own advantages, browsing through rows and columns rarely leads to useful analysis, especially when someone is looking for patterns and relationships that lie hidden in huge piles of data and information.

For instance, if you were analyzing Internet sales information of Adventure Works over the past few years, you would be more interested in the sums of sales per product, per country, and per quarter than in an analysis of the individual sales. Aggregating data at this level, although possible with most RDBMS engines, isn't the most optimized process.

Online Analytical Processing (OLAP) is a technology that tends to remove any granularity in the underlying data and focuses on enhanced data storage, faster data retrieval, and more intuitive navigational capabilities in large databases. Typically, OLAP's information comes from a database, referred to as a *data warehouse*. Compared to a relational database, a data warehouse requires much tighter design work up front for supporting analysis and data aggregation, such as summed totals and counts.

Because the storage unit used in OLAP is multidimensional, it's called a *cube* instead of a table. The interesting aspect of OLAP is its ability to store aggregated data hierarchically, and give users the ability to drill down or up aggregates by dimensional traits. *Dimensions* are a set of attributes representing an area of interest. For example, if you are looking at sales figures generally, you would be interested in geography, time, and product sales, as shown in Figure 13-1.

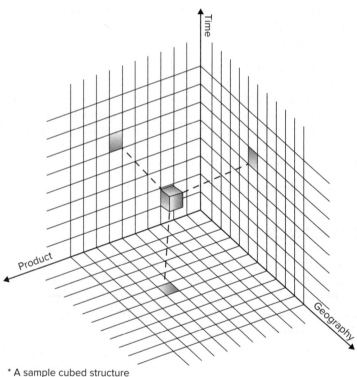

* A sample cubed structure

FIGURE 13-1

Dimensions give contextual information to the numerical figures, or **measures,** that you are aggregating on; for example, Internet sales amount, Internet gross profit, and Internet gross profit margin. OLAP calls each of these a measure. Because the measures are always preaggregated and anticipated by the cube, OLAP makes navigation through the data almost instantaneous.

If you want to look at a particular region that had a good quarter of sales, OLAP's navigational feature allows you to expand the quarterly view to see each month or day of the quarter. At the same time, you can also drill down into the region itself to find the cities with major increases in sales.

There are two more terms that need to be called out here:

➤ **Multidimensional Expressions (MDX):** MDX is the query language that lets you query cubes and return data.

➤ **Datasource:** A datasource is a stored set of information, such as tabular databases, OLAP cubes, Excel spreadsheets, SharePoint lists, or any other data object that contains the actual data.

USING THE ADVENTURE WORKS SAMPLE DATABASES

Your database source for examples provided in this chapter is the AdventureWorks database for SQL Server 2008 R2. You can download this sample database from CodePlex at `http://msftdbprodsamples.codeplex.com`. It's worth mentioning that the installation instructions are also available on CodePlex.

If the installation goes smoothly, you should be able to start SQL Server Management Studio, connect to the Database Engine, and see the new Adventure Works databases in your SQL Server 2008 R2 instance.

Unfortunately, the installation package does not automatically deploy the Analysis Services database, so you need to deploy it manually.

> *Before you can start the instructions below, ensure that the SSAS service account has permission to the SQL Server instance where the AdventureWorksDW2008R2 sample database exists. Additionally, ensure that the SSAS service account has permission to access the databases and is at least a member of the db_datareader role for the AdventureWorksDW2008R2 database.*

To deploy this database, you need to perform the following steps:

1. Start Business Intelligence Development Studio.

2. Click File ➪ Open ➪ Project ➪ Solution, and navigate to `Drive:\Program Files\ Microsoft SQL Server\100\Tools\Samples\AdventureWorks 2008R2 Analysis Services Project`. According to the version of your SQL Server, click on either the standard or the enterprise folder, and select `Adventure Works.sln`. As you can tell, SSAS databases are not supported in other editions of SQL Server.

3. Next, in the Solution Explorer double-click the `Adventure Works.ds` datasource. This will open the Data Source Designer Dialog box, as shown in Figure 13-2.

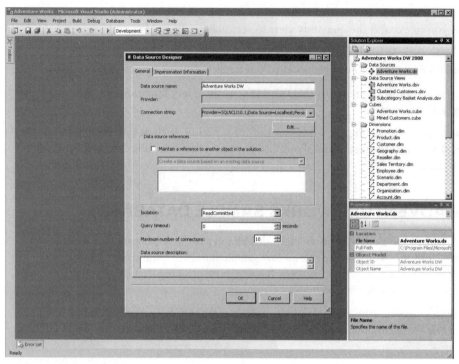

FIGURE 13-2

4. Click the Edit button, and in the Connection Manager, supply your SQL Server Database Engine connection information. Click the Test Connection button. If the test succeeds, click OK and OK to save the changes.

5. Right-click the solution in Solution Explorer, choose Properties. On the Adventure Works DW 2008 Property Pages dialog, change the Server property to your SSAS server name and database name.

6. In the Solution Explorer right-click on the solution, and click Deploy Solution.

At this point, you should be able to start SQL Server Management Studio, if it's not already open, connect to the Analysis Services, and see the new Adventure Works databases.

THE STARTING POINT: BUSINESS INTELLIGENCE CENTER

In SharePoint Server 2010, there are many different ways to manage and display BI assets. One of them is to use a site template called Business Intelligence Center, which is the enhanced version of the Report Center in MOSS 2007. This site template encompasses many of the BI capabilities that Microsoft has introduced in SharePoint Server 2010.

Although using Business Intelligence Center is not the only way to access SharePoint's BI features, this site template can provide a central location for teams and departments within your organization to store, retrieve, and modify shared reports.

To begin creating and using the Business Intelligence Center to its full capacity, you must first enable a few site collection scoped features. To enable these features, perform the following steps:

1. Click Site Actions menu ➪ Site Settings.

2. In the Site Collection Administration list, click the Site collection features link.

3. Activate the SharePoint Server Publishing Infrastructure feature. PerformancePoint Services uses this feature to perform dashboard publishing.

4. Activate the SharePoint Server Enterprise Site Collection Features feature. This feature enables Excel Services, Visio Services, and Access Services, included in the SharePoint Server Enterprise License.

5. Activate PerformancePoint Services Site Collection Features feature. This feature adds PerformancePoint content types and a Business Intelligence Center site template.

To properly examine the capabilities of the Business Intelligence Center in SharePoint Server 2010, create a new site with this template by clicking Site Actions ➪ New Site, and then choose Business Intelligence template, as shown in Figure 13-3.

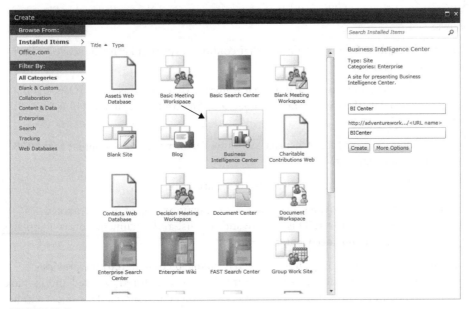

FIGURE 13-3

Next, fill out the title and the URL and press the Create button. Your new site should look like Figure 13-4.

Just like any other template, the Business Intelligence Center includes several features that can help you organize dashboards, reports, and the connections to external datasources in one centralized and standardized place.

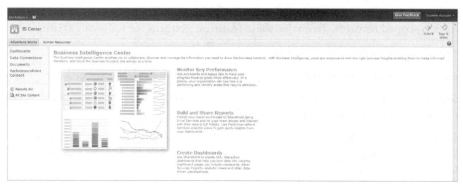

FIGURE 13-4

One obvious difference between Business Intelligence Center in this release and Report Center in the previous version of SharePoint is that lots of guidance and samples have been produced and placed into various pages of the site to assist users to start off with their BI implementation inside SharePoint as quickly as possible. And all samples just work!

Most of the BI functionalities available in this template are contained in two document libraries and one list as follows:

➤ Dashboards Document Library: A library that contains exported PerformancePoint dashboards organized in folders

➤ Data Connections Document Library (DCL): A library that contains ODC (Office Data connection) files, UDC (Universal Data Connection) files and PerformancePoint data connections

➤ PerformancePoint Content List: A list that contains PerformancePoint content and OOB views for organizing content.

There are two things about the new site that warrant more attention.

First, the BI Center automatically activates a site (not site collection) scoped feature named PerformancePoint Services Site Features. This feature adds the list and document library templates that are used in the Business Intelligence Center.

Second, PerformancePoint content storage has completely changed compared to the previous version. In SharePoint Server 2010, all PerformancePoint elements are stored, secured and managed in SharePoint lists and document libraries, not on the PerformancePoint server. This one, right here, is a huge game changer!

 Like other templates in SharePoint, the BI Center template can be further customized to meet your business requirement needs. The BI Center template already has all the content types, and list and document library definitions for your BI solutions, and is a great starting point.

EXCEL SERVICES

Excel has always been one of the most widely used data analysis tools, with which users take corporate data and bring it into workbooks and, for the purposes of analysis, combine it with other datasources that users can't track back to learn where they came from, such as XML data coming from a web service or data feed. Microsoft introduced a new server technology in MOSS 2007, named Excel Services, which has become an increasingly popular choice for sharing and collaborating on the data kept inside the Excel workbooks.

The primary driving force behind this technology was to make Excel and Excel Services the analysis tools of choice for users doing BI. This was done by changing Excel from being just a client-side application into an application that works both in the client and on the server. The server-side application model allows users to reuse the logic and content of their Excel workbooks in the browser, while easily protecting the IP behind them. Additionally, maintaining a single server-side version of the workbook gives everyone the right numbers and one version of the truth!

Excel 2010 picks up where Excel 2007 left off. There are two forms of Excel in SharePoint Server 2010: Excel Web App and Excel Services. Excel Web App is an extension of the Excel rich client that allows users to view and edit workbooks in the browser. Excel Services 2010 is the enhanced version of the same service that was offered back in MOSS 2007. Figure 13-5 illustrates what Microsoft has shipped in Excel Services 2010.

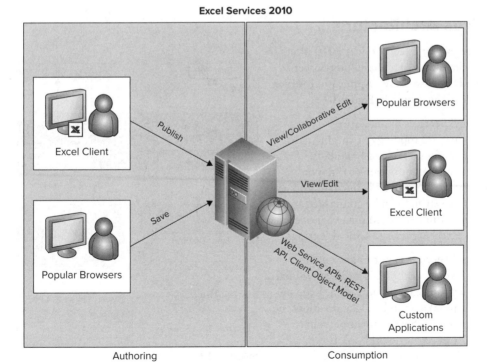

Excel Services 2010

Excel Client — Publish →
Popular Browsers — Save →
— View/Collaborative Edit → Popular Browsers
— View/Edit → Excel Client
— Web Service APIs, REST API, Client Object Model → Custom Applications

Authoring   Consumption

FIGURE 13-5

In the new architecture, an information worker uses the Office Excel 2010 rich client to author the Excel workbook and publish it to Excel Services 2010. Alternatively, he or she can save the workbook to a document library in Excel Services right on the server, where it is managed and secured by the site collections administrator. Once the workbook is published, it can be consumed and edited in three different ways:

1. Directly through the browser.

2. By downloading the workbook into the Excel rich client for further analysis as either a snapshot or an Excel workbook.

3. In custom applications through User Defined Functions (UDFs), the Web Services API, the Client object model, or the REST API.

What is important about Figure 13-5 is that the user experience in Excel Services 2010 is a major subset of the full Excel 2010 client on the desktop. For instance, with Excel Services 2010, users can:

➤ Collaborate on the whole or just parts of a workbook while performing distinct operations such as in-cell editing, sorting, filtering, pivoting, and entering parameters

➤ Work with connected or standalone external datasources in the workbook

➤ What if analysis — a use of underlying datasources in real time to model different data scenarios

➤ Build dashboard-style applications by using the web part connection framework between web parts on the same page or across pages

Excel Services Architecture

The functionalities that Excel Services 2010 offers are handled in three tiers of a SharePoint Server farm topology: Database Server, Application Server, and Web Frontend, as shown in Figure 13-6.

Because the Excel Services architecture is built on the SharePoint farm topology, it can be scaled up or out using configurable load-balancing scenarios and several other options to support large numbers of workbooks and concurrent requests. All these settings can be configured in Central Administration Site ⇨ Manage Service Applications ⇨ Excel Services ⇨ Global Settings.

Essentially, Excel Services is nothing without a workbook. An Excel workbook is a self-contained unit of an application that contains data, logic on the top of the data (aka a model), visualization and external assets such as those that connect up to the external datasources. A workbook is typically authored in the Excel client application and deployed to Excel Services, where it is stored and secured inside SharePoint content database.

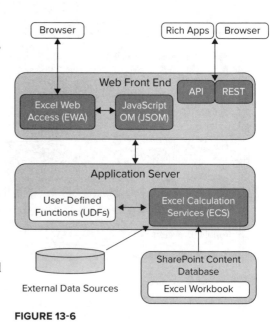

FIGURE 13-6

Next is the Application Server layer, which stands in the middle. A key component of Excel Services installed on the Application Server is Excel Calculation Services (ECS). This service application is responsible for loading the workbook, managing cache for concurrent access, and bringing data from external datasources. If a workbook contains custom logic implemented in UDFs, Excel Calculation Services combines that logic with the logic that was already placed in the workbook when it was authored.

The overall architecture of Excel Services limits interactions with the Application Server layer to being performed only through the Web Frontend layer, where three data access methods are exposed: the Excel Web Access (EWA) web part, the Web Services API, and the REST API.

EWA renders an Excel workbook in the browser with a high degree of fidelity with the Excel client. EWA is not new; it has been around since MOSS 2007, but what is new in Excel Services 2010 is a real JavaScript object model (JSOM) used to automate EWA. JSOM is typically JavaScript code that a developer inserts on a Web Part page that contains the EWA using a Content Editor web part or directly referenced in a custom ASPX page itself. JSOM is used to drive EWA and manipulate the rendered workbook inside. For example, you can use ISOM to capture the click event on a cell.

On the other hand, the Web Services API provides an interface to enable applications to access the workbooks through SOAP calls, while the REST API provides access to all aspects of a workbook, such as the visuals, the model, and the data, through simple URLs. All these middle-tier data access methods will be covered in more detail later in this chapter.

Office Data Connection

As with any other BI solution, when you start off with an Excel application, the first thing you may want to do is to go after data. In this section, you will create an Office Data Connection (.odc) file and store it in the Data Connections library of the Business Intelligence Center you created earlier in this chapter.

In order to connect to SQL Server Analysis Services and pull in some data, follow these steps:

1. Begin by opening Office Excel 2010.

2. From the Data tab in the Ribbon, click From Other Sources button.

3. For this particular example, select From Analysis Services.

4. Specify the Analysis Services instance you wish to connect to, and click Next.

5. Select the database and the cube you wish to connect to. For this example, you want to connect to the AdventureWorksDW2008R2 database and the AdventureWorks cube.

6. Change the file name and friendly name to AdventureWorksDW_ADCube.odc and AdventureWorksDW_ADCube, respectively. Also, make sure that you select Always attempt to use this file to refresh data, as shown in Figure 13-7.

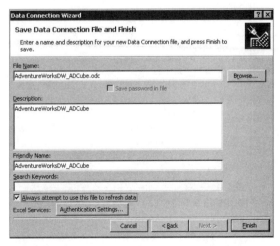

FIGURE 13-7

7. Click Authentication Settings, and select None as the method of authentication, as shown in Figure 13-8. This selection forces Excel Services to use the unattended service account to authenticate to SSAS. The unattended service account will be covered in detail in the next section.

8. Click Finish. When Excel 2010 displays the Import Data dialog box, select Only Create Connection, and then click OK.

9. Browse to `C:\Users\[Current User]\Documents\My Data Sources`, and upload the `AdventureWorksDW_ADCube.odc` file to the Data Connections Library in the Business Intelligence Center site you created earlier in this chapter.

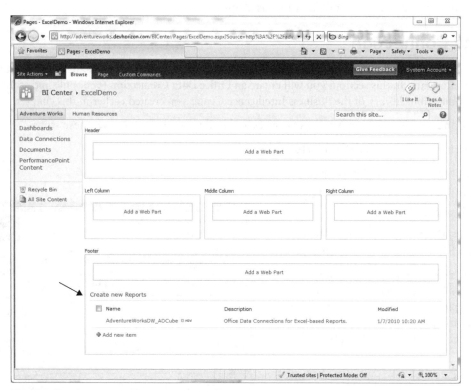

FIGURE 13-8

10. Edit the property of the file and change the Content Type to Office Data Connection file.

11. Next, create a new Web Part page called ExcelDemo and insert the Data Connections library in the Footer Web Part zone, as shown in Figure 13-9.

FIGURE 13-9

Creating the .odc files this way is a best practice because of two reasons. First, users don't need to know how to create the .odc files. Instead, they are created by IT and are made available to users. Second, this approach enables the users to access the data that they need quickly by clicking on the Office Data Connection file, which will open the Excel 2010 client, automatically send their credentials to the server, and authenticate them to the Analysis Services server. As a person who manages this connection string, if you ever want to adjust things or change them around, there is only one place you need to go to. Once the new settings are applied, they will be propagated into the workbooks in future connection requests.

The Unattended Service Account

As you saw in the previous section, there are three authentication options that Excel Services uses to authenticate to SSAS: Windows Authentication, SSS, and None.

The only case in which you would use Windows authentication is when SSAS accepts Windows authentication, and you want to let the identity of the workbook viewer delegate to the Analysis Services instance. This authentication method is known as Per-User identity and only Kerberos enables it. If you select Windows Authentication without implementing Kerberos, after the workbook is published to SharePoint, users will get the error shown in Figure 13-10 when viewing the workbook in the browser.

FIGURE 13-10

There are scenarios in which you want to have a single account act as a proxy for all your users when accessing the backend datasource. This account is referred to as an unattended service account, and it is widely used in the new service application infrastructure in SharePoint 2010.

 Note that "unattended service account" and "application pool identity" are not the same type of account. The unattended service account is a service application setting such as in Excel Services, Visio Services, Business Connectivity Services, and PerformancePoint Services. The unattended service account is stored in the service application's database and has nothing to do with IIS.

In MOSS 2007, the single sign-on (SSO) feature somehow implements the concept of the unattended service account, but not in a practical way. Unfortunately, the SSO feature introduced some serious limitations with non-Windows identity providers and anonymous users, so it was replaced with the Secure Store Service (SSS) in SharePoint Server 2010. The SSS works with all types of authentication providers, and it's not limited to Windows identities. It provides access to external datasources under the security context of a predefined set of credentials stored in the Service Application's database.

In Excel Services, each workbook can have its own unattended service account or they all can share a global unattended service account. If the workbook connection's authentication type is set to SSS, you need to reference a target application ID that stores the unattended service account credentials required for authenticating to SQL Server Analysis Services. This account may or may not be used by other BI applications that need to talk to the same backend datasource. Whether to use a single or different unattended service accounts really boils down to your business requirements, but keep one thing in mind: the more accounts you create, the more administrative effort is required to manage them.

If the workbook connection's authentication type is set to None, the global unattended service account is used. This account, along with many other Excel Services settings, can be configured in the Excel Services service application. Failure to define this account will cause the error in Figure 13-11 to be thrown.

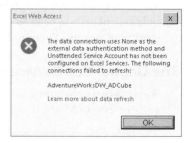

FIGURE 13-11

The process of creating the unattended service account is fairly straightforward. Before you start creating this account, you need to ensure that you are either the farm administrator or the service application administrator for the instance of the Secure Store Service.

In order to create this account, perform the following steps:

1. Browse to the Central Administration Site.

2. From the Application Management category, click Manage service applications.

3. From the list of existing service applications, click Secure Store Service application.

4. From the Ribbon, click the New button.

5. Figure 13-12 shows the settings for the new target application. In the Target Application ID box, type a name to identify this target application. In the Display Name box, type a friendly name that's shown in the user interface. In the Contact Email box, type the email address of the primary contact for this target application. Change the Target Application Type to Group for mapping all the members of one or more groups to a single set of credentials that can be authenticated to the SQL Server Analysis Services instance, and then click Next.

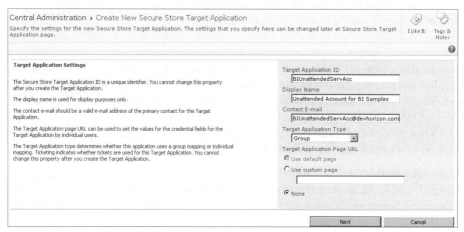

FIGURE 13-12

6. Since the target application type is Group, you can leave the default values in this page untouched and move on to the next step, by clicking Next.

7. In the Specify the membership settings page, in the Target Application Administrators field, specify all users who have access to manage the target application settings. Again, since the target application type is Group, in the Members field, specify a group or users to map to a set of credentials for this target application.

8. Click OK.

At this point, you should be able to see the new target application along with other target applications in the Manage Target Applications page, as shown in Figure 13-13.

FIGURE 13-13

After creating the target application, you should set credentials for it. To set credentials for the target application you've just created, follow these steps:

1. Select the target application you have just created, and then, in the menu, click Set credentials.

2. Fill out the fields for setting credentials (see Figure 13-14), and click OK. This is the account that is used to authenticate to SSAS, so you need to ensure that this account can authenticate to SSAS and is at least a member of the db_datareader role for the AdventureWorksDW2008R2 database.

FIGURE 13-14

You are almost there! The last step is to introduce the new target application to Excel Services. To do so, follow these steps:

1.   Browse to the Central Administration Site.

2.   From the Application Management category, choose Manage service applications.

3.   From the list of existing service applications, click Excel Services.

4.   From the Managed Excel Services page, click Global Settings.

5.   Browse all the way down to External Data section, and specify the new target application id (string text) in the Application ID textbox, as shown in Figure 13-15.

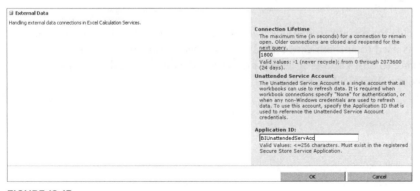

FIGURE 13-15

6.   Click OK when you are done.

Authoring Workbooks in Excel

AdventureWorks is a company that knows Business Intelligence gives them an edge over their competitors because when they make business decisions, those decisions are based on the latest and most up-to-date analysis of relevant business data Therefore, the BI team at AdventureWorks has created an OLAP cube to keep track of the Internet sales and has made it available to the business analysts to use for analysis.

The goal of this section is to perform a quick analysis of the data kept in that cube. The section starts out with a step-by-step procedure to create a simple PivotTable report and moves into some of the newest Excel 2010 features used for easier visualization and better insights into the key data values.

This section assumes that you already completed the following two tasks:

1. Created a site from the Business Intelligence Center template and named it BI Center (see the "Business Intelligence Center" section).

2. Properly set up an Office Data Connection to access the AdventureWorksDW2008R2 and the AdventureWorks cube and uploaded the `.odc` file to the Data Connections library (see the "Office Data Connection" section).

PivotTable and PivotCharts

Almost every spreadsheet application currently on the market ships with a feature that allows sorting and summarizing large tables of data independent of the original data layout kept in the spreadsheet itself. This feature has different names in products such as Microsoft Excel, OpenOffice.org Calc, Quantrix, and Google Docs, but the concept remains the same in all these products.

In Microsoft Excel, this capability is called a PivotTable. Essentially, a PivotTable is a powerful data summarization and cross-tabulation object that allows you to do free-form layout of your business data. For instance, when you use Microsoft Excel for cube browsing, you can import the cube's data into Excel and represent it as PivotChart or PivotTable report, connected to the same cube.

The following steps will help you create a new Excel workbook containing an OLAP PivotTable report based on data in the Analysis Services cube.

1. Browse to the ExcelDemo Web Part page in the BI Center, and click the `AdventureWorksDW_ADCube.odc` Office Data Connection file to open Excel.

2. At this point, you should see the PivotTable field list, and an empty PivotTable report is placed in the current worksheet at =$A$1.

3. To add some measures to the PivotTable, change Show Fields related to Internet Sales, and select the following three fields as measures:

   ➤ Internet Gross Profit

   ➤ Internet Gross Profit Margin

   ➤ Internet Sales Amount

4. Now, you need to add two dimensions to the PivotTable. Select Customer Geography and Source Currency Name from the PivotTable Tools tab, select the Design tab, and under PivotTable styles choose an appropriate style. Your workbook should look like Figure 13-16.

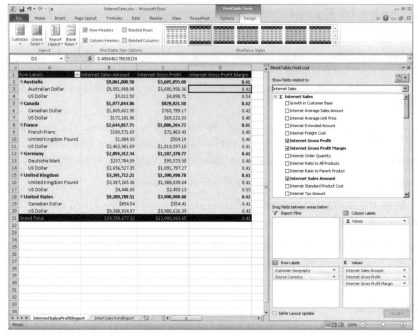

FIGURE 13-16

With the Internet Sales PivotTable inserted, make the report complete by adding a PivotChart to the worksheet. This chart will give focus to the sales data and make it easy to understand.

To add a PivotChart based on the data in the Internet Sales PivotTable, you need to perform two easy steps as follows:

1. From the PivotTable Tools Contextual menu, click Options, and then the PivotChart button to insert a PivotChart.

2. Select Clustered Column chart type, and press OK.

 PivotCharts are new in Excel 2010, and they are like normal Excel charts with one major difference. In PivotCharts, you can drill down into the hierarchies to identify the items you want to view, and this affects both the PivotChart and the associated PivotTable. In Excel 2007, you could only link charts to PivotTables and only navigate them through the PivotTable.

3. In the PivotChart you just inserted, click the Source Currency drop-down list and find US Dollar and Canadian Dollar, then click OK.

4. Click the Customer Geography drop-down and select Canada and United States. Your PivotTable should look like Figure 13-17.

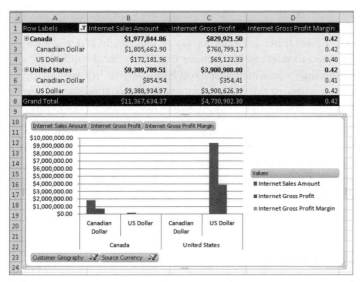

FIGURE 13-17

Two things need to be highlighted here. First, notice that when you apply filters to the PivotChart, a search box appears that allows you to look for a specific item in the hierarchy and find it, rather than having to browse all the way down or up in the hierarchy to find it. This is particularly important, because if a field contains lots of items, it's fairly difficult to find what you are looking for. Second, when you change the filters on the PivotTable, this affects the PivotTable and vice versa!

Label Filtering

In an Excel PivotTable, you can filter a column or row label by using the Label Filter or Value Filter options. In the Internet Sales PivotTable example, you can select the PivotTable to report on backend data only when Source Currency is equal to US Dollar, as shown in Figure 13-18.

To filter Source Category on US Dollars only, follow these steps:

1. In the PivotTable, click the arrow on right of the Row Labels heading.

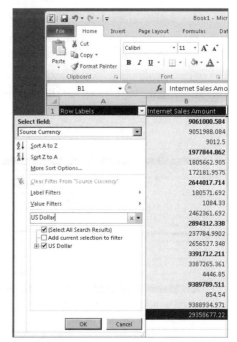

FIGURE 13-18

2. In the Select field drop-down, select Source Currency.

3. In the search box type US Dollar.

4. In the list of currencies, make sure that US Dollar is selected, and then click OK.

5. The PivotTable now shows results for work done on the selected currency, and you can focus your analysis on that data.

Visual Slicers

In Excel 2007, if you wanted to filter a PivotTable or PivotChart, you had to add it to the Report Filter section. Additionally, if you wanted to select multiple items in a filter, Excel would have shown you the tag "Multiple Items" without telling you which items you had selected. In Excel 2010, Visual Slicers are introduced to address issues of this kind. In nutshell, Slicers allow you to filter the data on PivotTables and PivotCharts with just a single click, which is much easier than before.

There are three characteristics about Slicers that make them a great navigation paradigm in Excel 2010. First, Slicers are rendered as buttons, making the filtering operations relatively easy. Second, you can select more than one item by holding the shift key and clicking on each item or by dragging mouse over a range. Third, the filters that produce no result from the backend datasource are grayed out, which is yet another good indicator when interacting with PivotTables and PivotCharts.

The following steps will help you add Category and Subcategory Slicers to the Internet Sales PivotTable.

1. In the PivotTable Tools, select Options tab.

2. In the Sort & Filter category, click Insert Slicer ⇨ Insert Slicers.

3. Select Internet Sales from the drop-down, and then select Product ⇨ Product Categories. Select both Category and Subcategory.

4. Resize and position the stacked version of both Slicers on the right side of the PivotTable. Also, using the Options menu, increase the columns in the Subcategory Slicer to 4.

5. Now, click on Bikes on the Category Slicer and notice how the related fields and the actual data are affected in the Subcategory Slicer PivotChart, and the PivotTable itself, as shown in Figure 13-19.

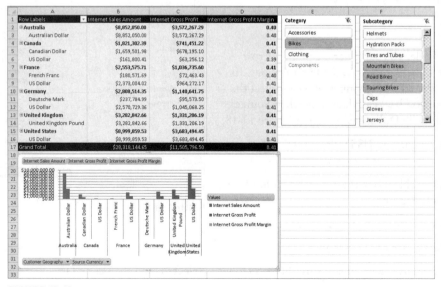

FIGURE 13-19

Sparklines

Another addition to Excel 2010 is the ability to add Sparklines to a set of data being reported on. A Sparkline is a powerful graphic that brings meaning and context to what it describes. Simply put, think of a Sparkline as a mini-chart without any fluff, such as tick marks, labels, axis lines, or a legend.

Excel 2010 ships with three distinct types of Sparklines:

➤ Line

➤ Columns

➤ Win/Loss

If you have worked with and loved the conditional formatting data bars introduced in Excel 2007, then you will find Sparklines even easier to use.

The following steps will help you add Sparklines to the Internet Sales report to highlight trends in the Internet sales report and identify Line values with special formatting.

1. Create a new sheet and name it **InternetSalesTrendReport**.

2. From the Insert tab, click PivotTable and add a new PivotTable to the existing sheet at =$A$1.

3. In the Create PivotTable dialog box, select Use an external data source and select AdventureWorksDW_ADCube from the Connections in this workbook section.

4. In the PivotTable Field List task pane, choose Internet Sales in the Show fields related to drop-down, and add a measure of Internet Sales Amount.

5. Now, select the `CustomerGeography` and `Date.Fiscal` as the attributes on which the Internet Sales Amount measure should be analyzed.

6. Place the cursor at cell =$G$3.

7. From the Insert tab, under the Sparklines group, click on Line Sparkline.

8. With the Create Sparkline dialog box open, select the cells from B3:E3, as shown in Figure 13-20.

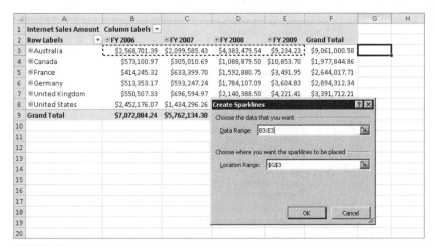

FIGURE 13-20

9. Click OK to create the Sparklines.

10. From the Design tab, update the formatting of the inserted Sparkline to highlight the min and max points.

11. The Sparkline object is like any other object placed in a cell, such as a formula, so it can be selected and dragged from cell G3 to G8 to insert the same line chart bound to other rows of the PivotTable, as shown in Figure 13-21.

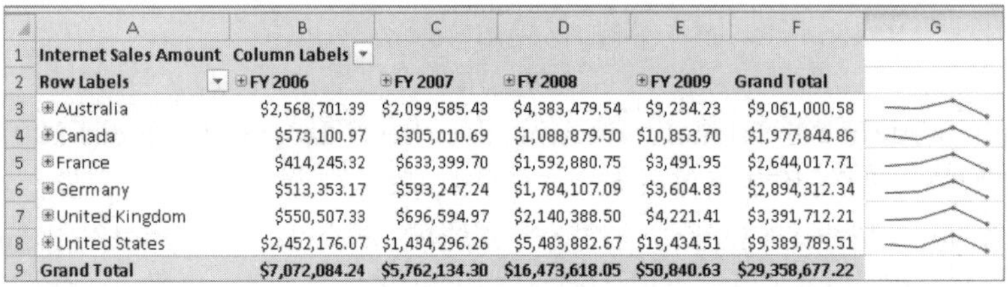

	A	B	C	D	E	F	G
1	Internet Sales Amount	Column Labels ▼					
2	Row Labels ▼	⊞ FY 2006	⊞ FY 2007	⊞ FY 2008	⊞ FY 2009	Grand Total	
3	⊞ Australia	$2,568,701.39	$2,099,585.43	$4,383,479.54	$9,234.23	$9,061,000.58	
4	⊞ Canada	$573,100.97	$305,010.69	$1,088,879.50	$10,853.70	$1,977,844.86	
5	⊞ France	$414,245.32	$633,399.70	$1,592,880.75	$3,491.95	$2,644,017.71	
6	⊞ Germany	$513,353.17	$593,247.24	$1,784,107.09	$3,604.83	$2,894,312.34	
7	⊞ United Kingdom	$550,507.33	$696,594.97	$2,140,388.50	$4,221.41	$3,391,712.21	
8	⊞ United States	$2,452,176.07	$1,434,296.26	$5,483,882.67	$19,434.51	$9,389,789.51	
9	Grand Total	$7,072,084.24	$5,762,134.30	$16,473,618.05	$50,840.63	$29,358,677.22	

FIGURE 13-21

Show Value As

In Excel 2007, if you wanted to perform certain types of calculations against a PivotTable for rows and columns, you would have to do this either outside of the PivotTable in your own function or turn them into a cube formula.

In Excel 2010, Microsoft has introduced a new feature named Show Value, which allows you change the way you view values, by selecting from a list of predefined calculations, as shown in Figure 13-22.

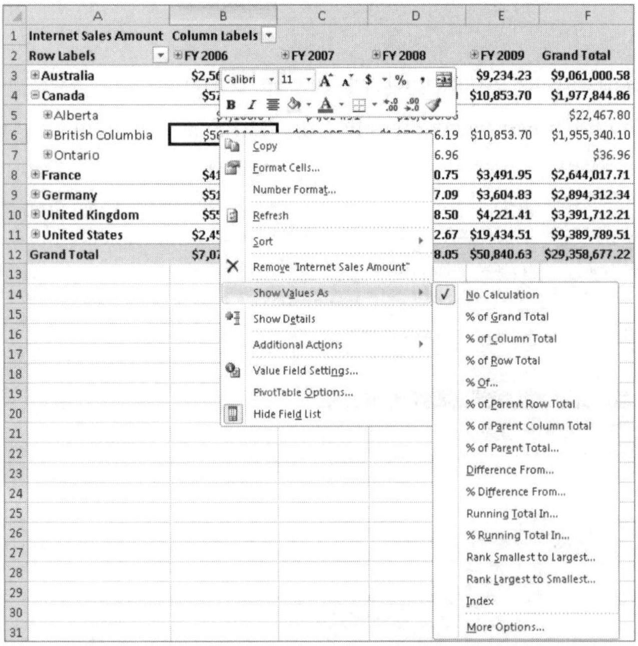

	A	B	C	D	E	F
1	Internet Sales Amount	Column Labels ▼				
2	Row Labels ▼	⊞ FY 2006	⊞ FY 2007	⊞ FY 2008	⊞ FY 2009	Grand Total
3	⊞ Australia	$2,56			$9,234.23	$9,061,000.58
4	⊟ Canada	$57			$10,853.70	$1,977,844.86
5	⊞ Alberta					$22,467.80
6	⊞ British Columbia	$56		6.19	$10,853.70	$1,955,340.10
7	⊞ Ontario			6.96		$36.96
8	⊞ France	$41		0.75	$3,491.95	$2,644,017.71
9	⊞ Germany	$51		7.09	$3,604.83	$2,894,312.34
10	⊞ United Kingdom	$55		8.50	$4,221.41	$3,391,712.21
11	⊞ United States	$2,45		2.67	$19,434.51	$9,389,789.51
12	Grand Total	$7,07		8.05	$50,840.63	$29,358,677.22

Show Values As menu options:

- No Calculation
- % of Grand Total
- % of Column Total
- % of Row Total
- % Of...
- % of Parent Row Total
- % of Parent Column Total
- % of Parent Total...
- Difference From...
- % Difference From...
- Running Total In...
- % Running Total In...
- Rank Smallest to Largest...
- Rank Largest to Smallest...
- Index
- More Options...

FIGURE 13-22

The following steps will help you calculate and display regional Internet sales as a percentage of the country sales.

1. Expand Canada node to show all the available regions.

2. Right-click on the value in any of the fiscal years, and from the context menu select % of Parent Total.

3. From the Base Field drop-down, select Country.

4. Click OK.

By looking at the PivotTable, you can quickly find out that in Canada for all year ends from 2002 to 2005, British Columbia has had the biggest percentage of sales among all provinces, as shown in Figure 13-23.

Canada	100.00%	100.00%	100.00%	100.00%	100.00%
Alberta	1.25%	1.52%	0.98%	0.00%	1.14%
British Columbia	98.75%	98.48%	99.02%	100.00%	98.86%
Ontario	0.00%	0.00%	0.00%	0.00%	0.00%

FIGURE 13-23

Named Sets

When working with OLAP PivotTables, there are scenarios where you want to work with the same logical group of items from the underlying data across multiple reports. For instance, most of the report layouts needed by Adventure Works need to show information about European countries. The problem is that this grouping doesn't exist in the cube, so you always end up applying the same filter to get reports for such countries over and over again.

A new feature in Excel 2010 that helps resolve issues of this kind is the ability to define Named Sets. This new feature allows you put common sets of items together and reuse them. This grouping can be done based on row items, column items, or your own MDX queries.

The following steps will help you add a Named Set to the Internet Sales PivotTable.

1. From the PivotTable Tools, click Options in the Ribbon.

2. Select Fields, Items, & Sets, and then select Create Set Based on Row Items.

3. Now, the Named Set creation UI will pop up, as shown in Figure 13-24. Note that Subtotals and Grand totals contain an All member. The UI contains all the tuple that currently define the row labels of the PivotTable.

4. Delete the countries that are not European.

5. Change the new Set name to something easier to remember in the future, such as "EU."

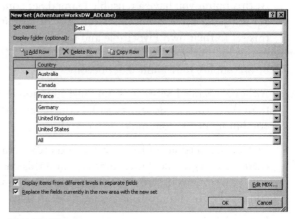

FIGURE 13-24

6. Click OK. Notice that the grouping has been created (without applying any filter), and the new Named Set is placed on the corresponding axis (Row Label), as shown in Figure 13-25.

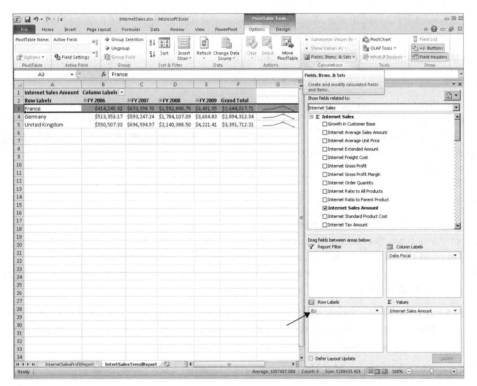

FIGURE 13-25

At this point, you have a reusable Named Set containing three European countries. The new Named Set is attached to the workbook and moves with it, so if anyone opens the workbook, they can reuse this set in their own PivotTable and focus on the rest of their analysis. Of course, the example used in this section was relatively simple, but the idea of reusability is pretty much the same, no matter how complex your Named Set becomes.

Although Named Sets may sound just like simple groupings of items, in reality they offer way more than that. You can do things with Named Sets that otherwise wouldn't be possible at all, such as combining items from multiple hierarchies.

In previous versions of Excel, you could create Named Sets with some limited functionalities, but there was no graphical user interface, and this could be only done through the Excel object model and by writing your own MDX queries. The Named Sets defined programmatically that way consisted only of items from a single hierarchy, and they could never be dynamic in nature.

In Excel 2010, you can make Named Sets based on your own custom MDX and use them in PivotTables to dynamically change their dimensionality. These types of Named Sets are called

Dynamic Sets. Dynamic Sets were first introduced in Analysis Services 2008, but unfortunately Excel 2007 couldn't fully benefit from them. For example, the Top 50 Selling Countries is one of the great examples in which Dynamic Sets can help a lot. Another example is when you want to see European countries when you're filtering on Source Currency by Euro and show North American countries when you're filtering by American dollar.

What-If Analysis

Like Dynamic Sets, Analysis Services has had writeback capability for a while, but it was not implemented in Excel out-of-the-box. In previous version of Excel, if you ever clicked on a cell in a PivotTable to edit its content, you would get an error message saying that PivotTables cannot be edited.

In Excel 2010, the ability to write back against a cube and change the underlying data is referred to as what-if analysis. This particular feature becomes extremely helpful when you use Excel and your existing data to plan something in future. In a nutshell, what-if analysis is all about clarifying what-if type questions you might have in your mind when looking at a PivotTable.

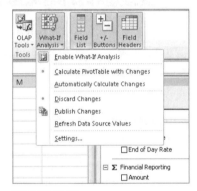

FIGURE 13-26

In order to use what-if analysis, you need to enable it from the PivotTable Tools ⇨ Options Tab.

Once the what-if analysis is enabled, you can edit any values and enter the value of your choice. At the end, you can atomically calculate the selected change or have the cube calculate it for you and commit the information back to the cube, as shown in Figure 13-26.

Publishing the Workbook

Now that you have a workbook created in Excel 2010, it's time to make this workbook available in SharePoint and examine the capabilities of Excel Services 2010. This process is known as publishing a workbook to Excel Services.

There are many configuration settings that can be applied to both the Excel Services application and the site that hosts your published workbook. Although diving into all these configuration settings is definitely out of the scope of this chapter, the rest of this section discusses some of these settings that can get you up and running.

Trusted Locations

A major consideration in deploying to Excel Services, and quite frankly the one you will want to plan carefully, is the file locations and connection document libraries that are considered trustworthy. The following steps walk you through defining these locations:

1. Browse to the Central Administration Site.

2. From the Application Management category, choose Manage service applications.

3. From the list of existing service applications, click Excel Services.

4. From the Manage Excel Services page, select Trusted File Locations.

5. If the location that you plan to publish your workbook is not in the list of trusted locations, click Add Trusted File Location and define that location.

6. Make sure you enable the workbook to make external connections by setting the Allow Data setting External to Trusted data connection libraries only or Trusted data connection libraries and embedded.

7. Click OK to go back to the Excel Services Trusted File Location page. At this point, the list of trusted file locations should look like Figure 13-27.

FIGURE 13-27

8. Browse back to the Manage Excel Services page, and this time around, select Trusted Data Connection Libraries.

9. From the Excel Services Trusted Data Connection Libraries page, specify the data connection library from which Excel workbooks opened in Excel Services are allowed to access the Office Data Connection files.

 Note that because service applications can be associated with multiple web applications, you should define multiple trusted locations for each web application that hosts your Excel workbooks. The same thing is true if you have assigned multiple Excel Services Service applications to one web application. You need to define the trusted locations for each service application.

Publishing to Excel Services

With the trusted locations properly configured, the next step is to publish the Internet Sales workbook to SharePoint and view it using Excel Services.

The following steps will help you publish the workbook:

1. From Excel 2010 Ribbon, click File to open the Backstage.

2. Switch to the Share tab.

3. From the Share billboard, click the Publish to Excel Services option, and then click Publish to Excel Services.

4. Click the Excel Services Options button that appears below Open in Excel Services option.

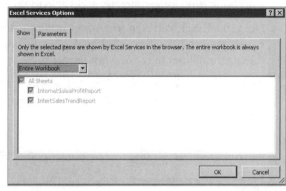

5. The Internet Sales workbook contains two worksheets, so you can decide if you want to publish the entire workbook or just portions of the workbook based on named cells, or parameters, defined within workbook. In this particular example, you will choose Entire Workbook, as shown in Figure 13-28.

FIGURE 13-28

6. Enter the path of the BI Center site you created earlier in this chapter, and click Save.

7. In Internet Explorer, navigate to the URL you specified in Step 6.

8. Click the link to `InternetSales.xlsx` to view it in the browser, as shown in Figure 13-29.

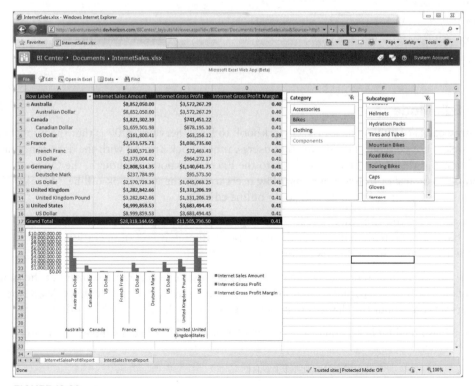

FIGURE 13-29

Once a workbook is published to SharePoint, Excel Services performs loading and calculations included within the workbook on the server, which means that whatever logic is behind the workbook is no longer directly accessible to the end users.

Next, the Excel Web App tries to open the workbook in view mode. Unlike the previous version, in Excel Services 2010 if the workbook contains unsupported features, it is still rendered, but some of the functionalities may not work properly.

As a final remark, the Excel Web App works in IE, Firefox, and Safari. Figure 13-30 shows `InternetSales.xlsx` opened in Safari browser in iPhone 3G.

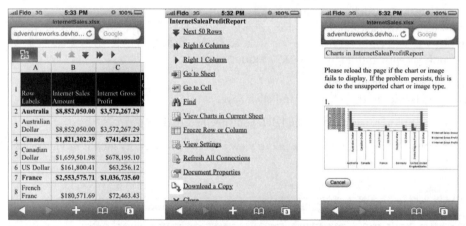

FIGURE 13-30

Switching to Edit Mode

One of the drawbacks of publishing an Excel workbook to Excel Services 2007 is that the published Excel workbook is not editable. This means that users cannot mock around with the data contained in the workbook and then save the changes back to the Excel workbook. Although, the Open In Excel and Open Snapshot In Excel options allow users to take the workbook offline and take further actions, most users prefer to be able to do online editing.

In Excel Services 2010, you can edit a workbook using Excel Web App. Edit mode offers only a subset of the Excel 2010 functionalities, but there is a fairly impressive set of operations that you can perform when editing the workbook online.

Edit mode also supports joint sessions, where more than one user can edit the document at the same time. This is done through a separate session for each user in Excel Web App. The Excel Web App keeps alerting everyone about the changes that have been made to the workbook by others.

Figure 13-31 shows an editable version of the Internet Sales workbook and a simple calculation at =$G$3.

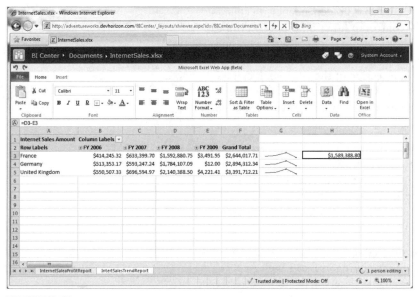

FIGURE 13-31

Excel Web Access Web Part

Another way to render and manipulate a published Excel workbook is through the Excel Web Access web part, also known as EWA. Figure 13-32 shows the entire Excel workbook displayed in a single EWA.

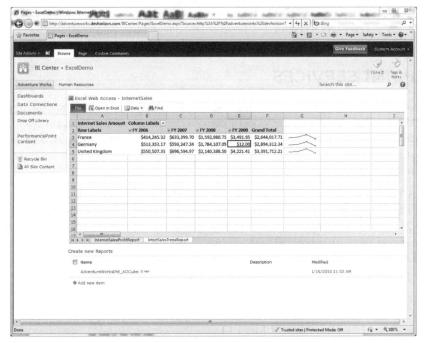

FIGURE 13-32

Unlike its predecessor, EWA has no dependency on client-side scripts or any ActiveX control to function properly. You can navigate through the sheets within the published workbook just as you would when using the Excel client. In addition to the entire workbook, a section of the workbook can be hosted and rendered in a EWA web part. This is done based on named parameters within the workbook, which should be created when authoring it.

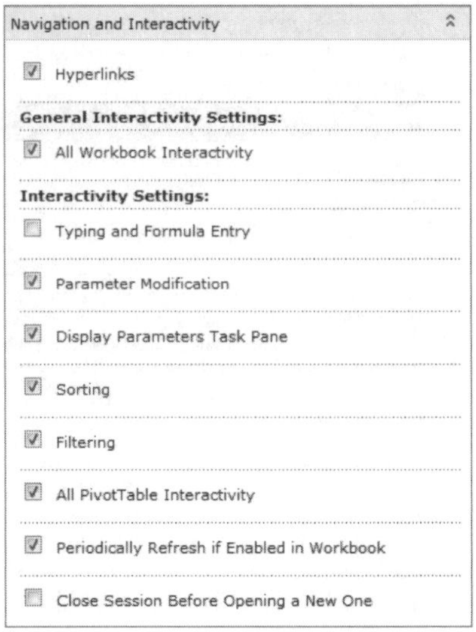

In Excel Services 2007, if you wanted to allow interaction with the workbook through the EWA, you had to list parameters on the left side in the Parameter pane. In the EWA web part's properties, you can control how much users can interact with the hosted workbook and for what features, as shown in Figure 13-33.

One thing needs to be highlighted here. Interactivity in EWA web parts is not the same as editing in Excel Web App. In the Excel Web App, the changes users make to the workbook are written back to the original workbook. When interacting with EWA, users can see changes in calculations and visualization objects, but the original workbook remains intact.

FIGURE 13-33

You can expose your Excel model in the Web Access web part and turn on the interactivity feature so that users can interact with the workbook without a need for listing parameters on the left side in the Parameter pane. Also, you have the option to specify whether changes made to the workbook need to be committed back or, in the case of a model, not committed back to the workbook.

Last, but certainly not least, EWA supports the Web Part Connection framework and can send data to or receive data from other web parts to create really powerful dashboards and mash-up scenarios.

PERFORMANCEPOINT SERVICES

Especially in today's tough economic times, dashboard-style applications that can present historical and real-time data to the decision makers in the form of metrics, reports, and data visualizations are becoming more and more popular. PerformancePoint Services is Microsoft's dashboard delivery tool, which now is part of the SharePoint Server 2010 Enterprise platform. But, why do you need PerformancePoint? Can't you build dashboards using SharePoint?

Yes, you certainly can! There are a lot of components in the SharePoint ecosystem that you can use to build out dashboard-style applications. SharePoint, right out of the box, offers some lightweight tools for hosting and displaying data, such as Web Part pages, status lists, and the Chart web part. You can combine these types of content with Visio diagrams, InfoPath forms, Reporting Services reports, or Excel workbooks to build dashboards. However, such dashboards may not present a level of sophistication people would like to see on their computer's screen every morning they come to work!

The good news is that PerformancePoint Services works with all these types of technologies to help you aggregate content and data to assemble richer and more interactive dashboards that suit any business requirements. The following sections discuss the out-of-the-box features in PerformancePoint Services and the techniques that you can use to create a PerformancePoint dashboard.

Dashboard vs. Scorecard

When it comes to business decision-making processes, sometimes there are terms with blurry lines between them, which makes things a bit difficult to understand. One example is the title of this section, dashboard versus scorecard, which is a very common point of confusion! We can look into clarifying this confusion from different angles.

Conceptually, a dashboard is a collection of real-time information that is used for evaluating performance and making sure that operational goals are met. However, a scorecard stays at a higher level than a dashboard and is more focused on monitoring the performance associated with organizational strategic objectives. So, the key difference here is short-term goals versus long-term success. In reality, making a distinction between a scorecard and a dashboard is absolutely unnecessary, as both are used to accomplish one thing: making sure that the business is on the right track to reach established goals in the future.

In the context of PerformancePoint Services, things are much simpler and less formal. A PerformancePoint dashboard is simply an .ASPX page that renders a bunch of heads-up displays, including a scorecard. Let's think about it this way for now!

PerformancePoint Services Architecture

The functionalities that PerformancePoint Services offer are handled in three tiers of a SharePoint Server farm topology: Database Server, Application Server, and Web Frontend, as shown in Figure 13-34.

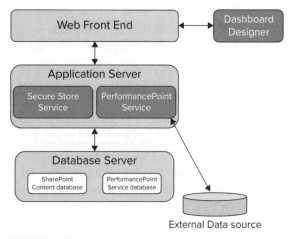

The Web Frontend server hosts the Dashboard Designer application, PerformancePoint web parts, PerformancePoint web services, and the service application proxy that is required to communicate with the PerformancePoint Services application installed on the application server. Like all other service application proxies, the PerformancePoint proxy talks to the PerformancePoint Services application using claims, so the environments with no Kerberos implementation are not affected by the double-hop security issue.

FIGURE 13-34

In the middle tier, there are two service applications that make the integration happen:

➤ Secure Store Service: This service application stores the password for the PerformancePoint Services unattended account. The unattended service account will be covered in the next section.

➤ PerformancePoint Services: This service application stores the settings needed for the instance. If you have ever worked with PerformancePoint 2007 and MOSS 2007 before, you probably recall that you had to go through many configuration settings to get the PerformancePoint dashboards to work. Thankfully, configuring PerformancePoint Services 2010 is much simpler than before, and it requires no changes in the SharePoint web application's web.config file anymore.

In the database layer, most of the configurations required for PerformancePoint service applications are stored in the PerformancePoint service database.

At the time of writing this book, PerformancePoint still doesn't support web applications with claims-based authentication, and that's because of how the click-once Dashboard Designer is structured. This limitation may be changed with the release of SharePoint Server 2010 SP1.

The Unattended Service Account

One of the challenging configuration steps in the previous version was to properly set up the authentication to the backend datasource. The problem was that the authentication option couldn't be defined per datasource; instead, PerformancePoint would use the application pool identity of the SharePoint Web application. From the security practice perspective, this was not recommended because users potentially could use PerformancePoint to access to the data that they shouldn't have access to at all, such as SharePoint content databases.

PerformancePoint Services 2010 implements per datasource authentication and has some new features that control how authentication to the datasource itself is configured. One of these new features is the unattended service account for PerformancePoint.

The unattended service account concept in PerformancePoint services 2010 is very similar to Excel Services' unattended account with two differences. As explained earlier in this chapter, in Excel Services you create the target application in the Secure Store Service application and then reference its Application ID in the Excel Services service application's settings. Thus, both the username and password are stored in the Secure Store Services application.

In PerformancePoint Services, however, you create the unattended account directly in the PerformancePoint Services application settings. In this case, the password is stored in Secure Store Service and the actual username is stored in the PerformancePoint Services database. If you look at a PerformancePoint target application, you will find that it only contains the password field and not the username field.

An unattended account can be created using the following steps:

1. Browse to the Central Administration Site.
2. From the Application Management category, choose Manage service applications.
3. From the list of existing service applications, click PerformancePoint Service Application.
4. Click the PerformancePoint Service Application Settings link.

5. Specify the unattended service account for PerformancePoint (see Figure 13-35), and click OK.

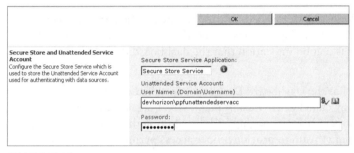

FIGURE 13-35

6. Browse to the Secure Store Service application's settings page and verify that the unattended account has been created.

Introducing Dashboard Designer

1. In Internet Explorer, navigate to the Business Intelligence Center site you created at the beginning of this chapter.

2. Click the Create Dashboards link, and then click Start using PerformancePoint Service link, as shown in Figure 13-36.

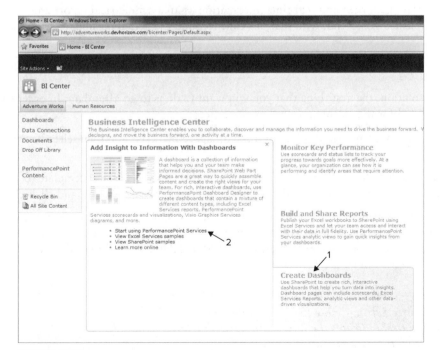

FIGURE 13-36

3. From the PerformancePoint Services page, click the big button that says Run Dashboard Designer. This will download and install the PerformancePoint Dashboard Designer to your workstation.

Once the executable file is downloaded and installed on your computer, the PerformancePoint Dashboard Designer appears. In the Data Connections folder, the Excel data connection file that you created earlier in this chapter is a good indication that the dashboard designer is live and connected to the BI Center site.

One thing that you may notice is that the Dashboard Designer is installed on the client machine using a web-based deployment technology called ClickOnce. A major advantage of this deployment model is that it frees the IT department from managing and distributing the application. All that's required is for the Dashboard Designer team to provide proper access permission to the BI Center site.

Once the Dashboard Designer is installed, you have an empty workspace. A workspace is a primary container for all of the elements that you can use to build your dashboard, and it keeps its content synched with the site from which it was launched.

Essentially, the workspace becomes an XML file (.ddwx) that encapsulates all the metadata required to describe a PerformancePoint dashboard. In the workspace, you can build new elements or you can import existing elements from a published dashboard such as scorecards, KPIs, reports, filters, indicators, and dashboards.

Creating Your First Dashboard

Now that you have created a PerformancePoint workspace, you are ready to create your first dashboard, which displays historical and real-time information as an asymmetrical report and compares it to an established goal. And, with that, it's time to build the actual dashboard from the ground up.

Dashboard Datasource

As with any other BI solution, the first thing that you will want to do is to go after data. In order to create the datasource used for this dashboard, follow these steps:

1. Right-click the Data Connections folder in the Workspace Browser, and then select New ➪ Data Source.

2. From the Select a Data Source Template menu, choose the Analysis Services template to create a datasource that connects to Microsoft SQL Server Analysis Services, and click OK.

3. In the Connection Settings, specify the Analysis Services instance you wish to connect to. In the next field, select the database and the cube you wish to connect to. For this example, you want to connect to the Adventure Works DW 2008R2 database and the Adventure Works cube, as shown in Figure 13-37.

In the Data Source Settings, note the Cache Lifetime setting. The value of this textbox (in minutes) indicates the interval of refreshing the dashboard information from the backend datasource.

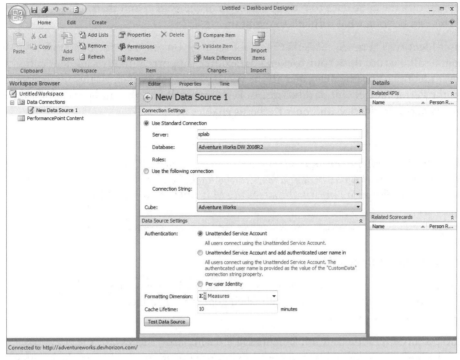

FIGURE 13-37

4. Click Test Data Source to make sure that your connection settings are correct.

5. Switch to the Properties tab and change the Name to AdventureWorksDW_ADCube_PerfPoint.

6. Save the new datasource by right-clicking it in the Workspace Browser, and then selecting Save.

At this point, you have successfully created the dashboard's main datasource and it's been uploaded already to the Data Connections document library by the Dashboard Designer.

Datasource Authentication Types

As you saw in Figure 13-36, there are three different authentication types available for the datasource you are building.

The unattended service account option has been discussed already, and by now you should know what it does, but the other two options deserve more attention:

➤ **Unattended Service Account and add authenticated user name in connection string:** If you select this option, supply the SharePoint authenticated provider and username (Forms, SAML, windows, etc.) as a string in the CustomData field in Analysis Services. You can then create a role (or set of roles) and write MDX queries using the CustomData string to dynamically restrict access to the cube data. The main challenge of this solution is that you need to modify the cube data to include the users of the system and their relationships to the data; this can be somewhat difficult to maintain.

➤ **Per-user Identity:** There are cases that may not require you to create the unattended service account at all. Picture this: Your backend datasource supports Windows authentication, and user identities must be delegated all the way down to the backend datasource when they access the PerformancePoint dashboards. In PerformancePoint, this authentication type is known as per-user identity, and only Kerberos enables it.

No matter what authentication type you choose for PerformancePoint Services, always make sure that it has proper access to the backend datasource that will be required. For more information, see my blog post at www.devhorizon .com/go/16.

Tracking Performance Using KPIs

Recall from the previous section that your goal for building the Internet Sales dashboard is to compare Internet sales information with an established goal, and then measure and monitor the success of the online business per country.

But what is success anyway? How is it implemented in a dashboard? Success (or the goal) in a certain area of the business is defined by someone in your organization who knows the business inside and out. In PerformancePoint, a primary metric used to implement and measure this success is something referred to as a key performance indicator (KPI). Once a KPI is defined and implemented, it can be used to monitor the organization's progress in a specific area, such as gross profit margin per product category earned from Internet sales.

In order to create a new KPI to track gross profit margin for Internet sales, you need to follow these steps:

1. Right-click the PerformancePoint Content folder and select New ⇨ KPI, as shown in Figure 13-38.

2. In the Select a KPI Template dialog, select Blank KPI, and then click OK.

3. Figure 13-39 shows the new KPI. Here, you can define your actual and Target values. You can also continue adding new actuals or targets to the current KPI. For example, if your organization has defined a minimum goal and stretched goal, you may want to bring them into the KPI by defining two Target values.

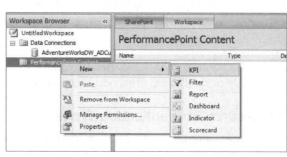

FIGURE 13-38

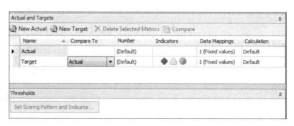

FIGURE 13-39

4. The current value for Actual is set to 1, which doesn't represent anything. Click the 1 (Fixed values) link in the Data Mappings column for Actual, and then in the Fixed Values Data Source Mapping dialog, click the Change Source button.

 In Analysis Services, you can build KPIs that have four values: Actual, Target, Status, and Trend. In PerformancePoint KPIs, you only have two values: Actual and Target. One interesting aspect about Actual and Target values in PerformancePoint is that they do not need to come from the same datasource. For example, you can define a KPI that gets the Actual Value from the cube and then have the Target value loaded from a SharePoint list. This makes PerformancePoint KPIs very flexible.

5. Select the AdventureWorksDW_ADCube_PerfPoint data connection, and click OK.

6. From the Select a measure drop-down, select Internet Gross Profit Margin.

7. Click OK to close the dialog.

8. Select the Target row, and click the Set Scoring Pattern and Indicator button in the Thresholds area, as shown in Figure 13-40.

9. In the first step of the Edit Binding Settings dialog (see Figure 13-41), you

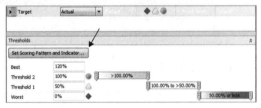

FIGURE 13-40

need to identify how the Actual value compares to a target. From the Scoring pattern, select the Increasing is Better option. Most of the time, you would use a normalized value where you take the Actual value and divide it by the Target value, so select the first option (Band by normalized value of Actual/Target) from the Banding method drop-down, and then click Next.

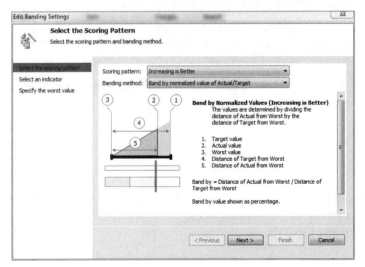

FIGURE 13-41

10. In the Select an Indicator step, select an indicator to use for the target that clearly shows whether the goal is met. You can choose from a collection of indicator templates available in PerformancePoint Dashboard Designer. Once you are done, click Next.

11. In the last step of the wizard, leave the worst value intact and click Finish. Now, you can see how Target values from 0% to beyond 100% are categorized by different colors. You can type in the ultimate values for each threshold or you can use the slider of each color to adjust the size of the percentage ranges.

12. You need to change the fixed value of the Target, which represents 100% gross profit margin. While 100% is an ideal percentage, you may want to adjust this value to something that's more realistic and makes more sense in your business, for example 40.65 % of the actual value. Click the 1 (Fixed Values) link and change the value from 1 to 0.4065.

> *The Adventure Works 2008 R2 cube does not have measures that can be used for the Target values of the sample KPI in this section. You need to use Fixed Values instead. Typically, Fixed Values are great when the measure doesn't change very often.*

13. Click OK.

14. Change the name of the KPI to Gross Profit Margin, by right-clicking it in the Workspace Browser and clicking Rename.

15. Save the KPI by right-clicking it in the Workspace Browser, and then selecting Save.

At this point, your new KPI should look like Figure 13-42. Notice on the Details pane that you have all available information about the KPI, such as related datasources.

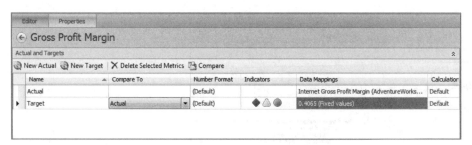

FIGURE 13-42

Building the Scorecard

With the dashboard's datasource and KPI complete, you have all the elements that you need to build the scorecard. This scorecard will contain the Gross Profit Margin KPI, and shows all sales across all years and is broken down by product category.

1. Right-click the PerformancePoint Content folder, and then click New ⇨ Scorecard. Change the name to Profit Margin SC.

2. From the Select a Scorecard Template dialog, select Standard Category. From the Template pane, select Blank Scorecard, and click Next.

3. Drag Gross Profit Margin KPI (Details KPIs ⇨ PerformancePoint Content) and drop it onto the first row where it says Drop Items here.

4. Click the Update button in the Edit tab.

5. From the Data Source drop-down, select AdventureWorksDW_ADCube_PerfPoint to make all the dimensions in the cube available for the scorecard, as shown in Figure 13-43.

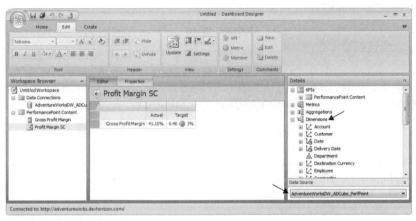

FIGURE 13-43

6. From the list of available dimensions, find and expand Product dimension.

7. Expand Product dimension and select Categories member.

8. Drag Categories to the left-hand side of the Gross Profit Margin cell, as shown in Figure 13-44.

9. From Select Members dialog, select All Products.

10. Click the Update button in the Edit tab. Notice how the KPI is nested in each category, as shown in Figure 13-45.

11. Save the scorecard by right-clicking it in the Workspace Browser and then selecting Save.

FIGURE 13-44

	Actual	Target	
⊟ All Products		△	
⊞ Accessories		●	
Gross Profit Margin	62.60%	0.4065 ● 54%	
⊞ Bikes		△	
Gross Profit Margin	40.63%	0.4065 △ 0%	
⊞ Clothing		◆	
Gross Profit Margin	40.15%	0.4065 ◆ -1%	
⊞ Components			
Gross Profit Margin		0.4065 ◇	

FIGURE 13-45

Native Reporting

In this section, you create a report that connects to the scorecard you created in the previous section and display Internet sales for all years grouped by product category.

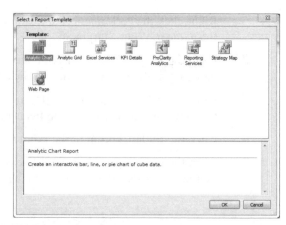

FIGURE 13-46

1. Right-click the PerformancePoint Content folder, and then click New ➪ Report.

2. From the Select a Report Template dialog, select Analytic Chart (see Figure 13-46), and then click OK.

 In addition to the native reports, PerformancePoint supports referencing the ProClarity Analytics Server page, a SQL Server Reporting Services report, an Excel Services workbook, and a Microsoft Office Visio strategy map in your dashboards.

3. From the Select a data connection dialog, select the datasource in the current workspace, and click Finish. Figure 13-47 shows what the workspace should look like when you build any type of report.

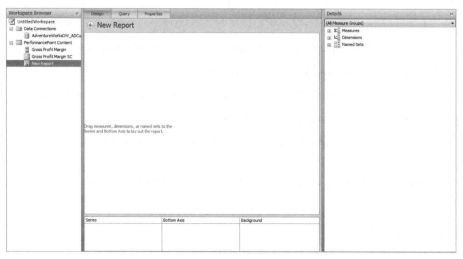

FIGURE 13-47

4. Switch to the Properties tab, and then change the name of the new report to Category Internet Sales by Year.

5. Switch back to the Design tab.

6. Expand the Measures node in the Details task pane on the right.

7. Drag the Internet Sales Amount item into the Bottom Axis box.

8. Expand the Dimensions and Product nodes, and drag Categories into the Background. Even if you will not show the actual categories in the chart, you still need to reference Categories in the Background, so that when you build the dashboard, the filter that connects categories from the scorecard to the chart knows where to filter. You will learn about the dashboard in the next section.

9. Expand Date Measure and Find Calendar.

10. Drag the Calendar Year into the Series section.

11. Change the name of the report to Complete Category Internet Sales By Year, by right-clicking it in the Workspace Browser and clicking Rename.

12. Right-click underneath the chart's legend, and from the context menu select Report Type ➪ Pie Chart. Your workspace should look like Figure 13-48.

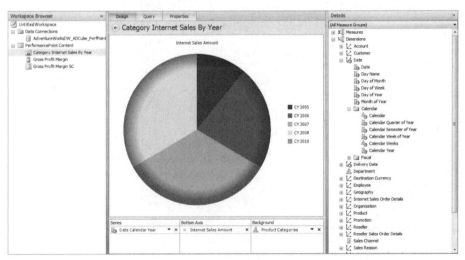

FIGURE 13-48

13. Save the report by right-clicking it in the Workspace Browser, and then selecting Save.

Putting Everything Together

Now that you have gone through all the steps of building different pieces of the dashboard, it's time to put all the pieces together. In this section, you will create a dashboard that displays the scorecard and the report and connect them. This connection will allow filtering of the report (the pie chart) using the currently selected category from the scorecard.

1. Right-click the PerformancePoint Content folder in the Workspace Browser, and then click New ⇨ Dashboard. Rename the new dashboard Internet Sales Dashboard.

2. From the Select a Dashboard Page template, select the 2 Columns page template and click OK.

3. From the Details pane, drag the Gross Profit Margin SC scorecard and drop it into the Left Column.

4. From the Details Pane, Drag the Category Internet Sales By Year report into the Right Column.

5. Drag the Row Member item from the scorecard column into the report column.

6. In the Connection dialog, change the Source value drop-down to Member Row: Member Unique Name. As mentioned in the previous section, the filter that connects the scorecard to the report will base this connection on the product category that exists in both elements.

7. Save the dashboard by right-clicking it in the Workspace Browser and then selecting Save. Figure 13-49 shows the finished dashboard.

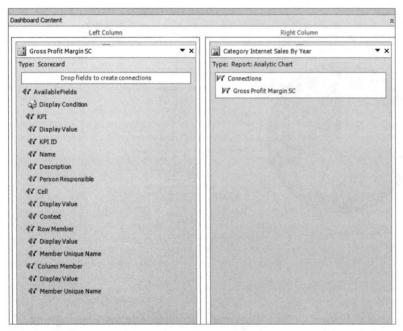

FIGURE 13-49

One-Click Publishing to SharePoint

With the dashboard layout completed, the next step is to make it available in SharePoint for online viewing. Remember, the dashboard contents are already stored in the BI Center site, so publishing here really means creating an instance of the dashboard definition and dumping it as an .ASPX page (aka an exported dashboard) in a dashboard's document library.

The distinction between a dashboard definition and the actual dashboard page still exists, as was the case in PerformancePoint 2007. If you take an exported dashboard (an `.ASPX` *file) and customize it using an HTML editor and replace the existing one with the customized version of the dashboard, next time the same dashboard is published to SharePoint, your changes will be overwritten. That's because you modified the instance, not the definition.*

You can publish your dashboard to any document as long as the following two conditions are met:

➤ The page is in a document library with PerformancePoint content types.

➤ The page has access to the dashboard elements in the BI Center.

Publishing the dashboard to SharePoint is relatively straightforward:

1. Right-click the dashboard in the Workspace Browser, and then select the Deploy to SharePoint menu item.

2. Select the Dashboards folder, and click OK.

3. From the Deploy To dialog, select the site and Dashboard document library and click OK. Optionally, you can select any of the available Master Pages in the current site collection for your dashboard. For example, if you want to see your dashboards with no chrome, you can develop a custom Master Page and select it to use when publishing your dashboard.

Once the deployment is completed, you will be redirected to a page (see Figure 13-50) where your dashboard is rendered with 100% fidelity to what you experienced in the authoring environment.

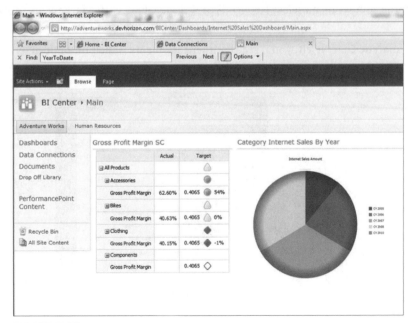

FIGURE 13-50

What Else Is in the Box?

The dashboard that you just published is nothing more than a Web Part page, two web parts, and a web part connection, which were all set up automatically as part of the dashboard-publishing process.

These connections are not exclusive to PerformancePoint web parts. Using the web part connection, you can take your dashboard design to the next level by adding more web parts to the page representing more complex analytical scenarios. You can examine the content of the dashboard by switching the page to edit mode, as shown in Figure 13-51.

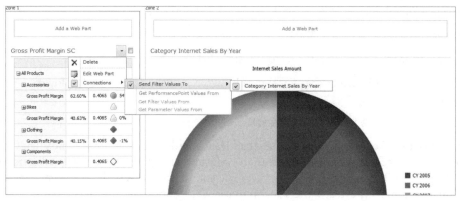

FIGURE 13-51

There are many more functionalities available on the chart itself. Let's suppose that, for the purpose of trend analysis, you need to change the type of the chart. To do so, right-click underneath the chart's legend, and from the context menu select Report Type ⇨ Line Chart with Markers, as shown in Figure 13-52.

If you right-click on the analytic chart itself, you'll see that there are plenty of helpful built-in functionalities at your fingertips, as shown in Figure 13-53.

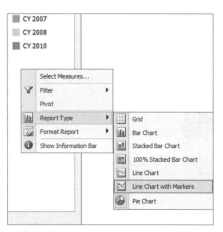

FIGURE 13-52

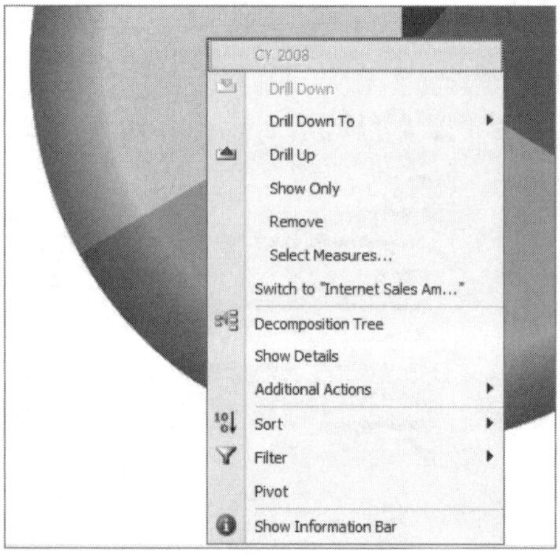

FIGURE 13-53

There are three options in this menu that need to be highlighted here:

➤ Drill Down or Drill Up: These options allow you to drill down or up to see different levels of detail presented by the chart element.

➤ Select Measures: If the measure that the report represents is not enough for your analysis, click Select Measures and select one or more items from the list of all measures that exist in the perspective.

➤ Decomposition Tree: This option offers another interactive way of navigating your dashboard. An advantage of using the Decomposition Tree is that it keeps the report sorted and it places insignificant contributors at the bottom of the hierarchy (see Figure 13-54). Of course, if you want to analyze negativity (i.e cities with worse sales amount), you can always flip the default sorting style using the drop-down menu on the top of each level. Decomposition Tree is a Silverlight application and requires the Microsoft Silverlight 3 framework to be installed on the client machine.

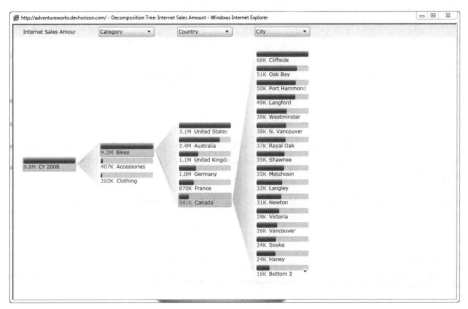

FIGURE 13-54

Last, but certainly not least, if you ever decide to show a dashboard element in a completely new page to have more real estate, from the web part that hosts the element, modify the properties, and select Open in New Window, as shown in Figure 13-55. You can also reset the view to the element's original state.

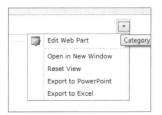

FIGURE 13-55

Time Intelligence Filtering

In your analysis, it's often required that you base all your time formulas and functions on a time dimension such as your company's fiscal year. In such scenarios, if your datasource is not aware of the time dimension you use, you will get the error that says the datasource has an invalid time intelligence configuration, as shown in Figure 13-56.

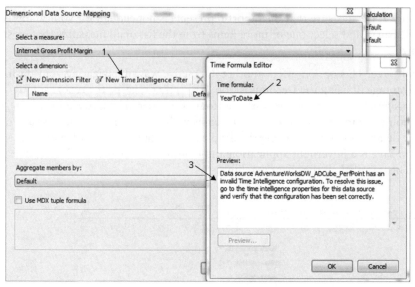

FIGURE 13-56

As suggested by the error message, setting the time intelligence configuration in your datasource prepares the groundwork for time intelligence. To configure the time intelligence in your datasource follow these steps:

1. Navigate to the Time tab in your datasource to select a time dimension, as shown in Figure 13-57.

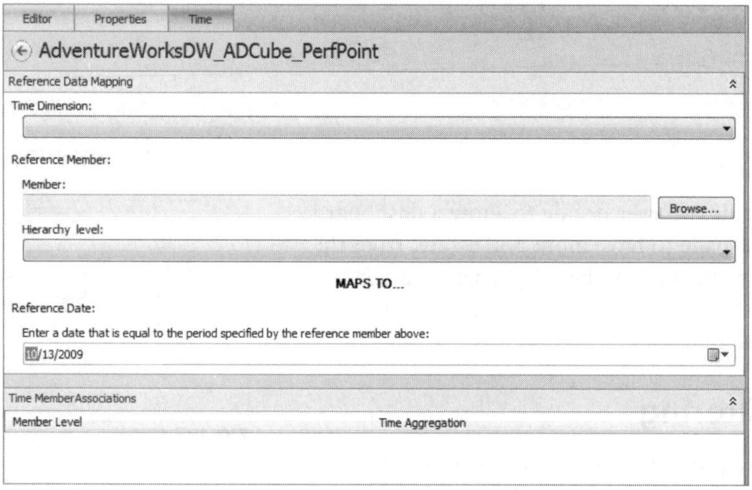

FIGURE 13-57

2. From the Time Dimension drop-down, select Data.Date.Fiscal, as shown in Figure 13-58.

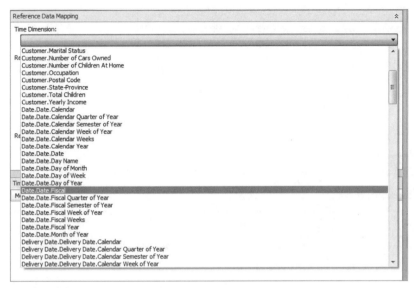

Reference Data Mapping

Time Dimension:

- Customer.Marital Status
- Customer.Number of Cars Owned
- Customer.Number of Children At Home
- Customer.Occupation
- Customer.Postal Code
- Customer.State-Province
- Customer.Total Children
- Customer.Yearly Income
- Date.Date.Calendar
- Date.Date.Calendar Quarter of Year
- Date.Date.Calendar Semester of Year
- Date.Date.Calendar Week of Year
- Date.Date.Calendar Weeks
- Date.Date.Calendar Year
- Date.Date.Date
- Date.Date.Day Name
- Date.Date.Day of Month
- Date.Date.Day of Week
- Date.Date.Day of Year
- Date.Date.Fiscal
- Date.Date.Fiscal Quarter of Year
- Date.Date.Fiscal Semester of Year
- Date.Date.Fiscal Week of Year
- Date.Date.Fiscal Weeks
- Date.Date.Fiscal Year
- Date.Date.Month of Year
- Delivery Date.Delivery Date.Calendar
- Delivery Date.Delivery Date.Calendar Quarter of Year
- Delivery Date.Delivery Date.Calendar Semester of Year
- Delivery Date.Delivery Date.Calendar Week of Year

FIGURE 13-58

3. Click Browse button in the Reference Member field and from the Select Members dialog, select July 1, 2005. Let's suppose that your company's fiscal year starts on July 1st each year. By selecting an reference of July 1st, you make the datasource aware that your time dimension has a starting point on the first day of July each year.

4. From the Hierarchy level drop-down, specify the granularity of the member you just referenced in the previous step. Since July first represents a day, you should select Day from the drop-down menu.

5. In the Date picker control, specify a data (i.e 11/1/2009) that is equal to the period specified by the reference member you chose in Step 2 (see Figure 13-59). PerformancePoint Services uses this date to associate the Reference Member to the traditional calendar.

6. In the Time Member Associations, map your time dimension hierarchies (on the left) to the defined Time Aggregations (on the right).

Now you can go ahead and create any formulas or filters that are based on this intelligent time dimension such as [Date.Fiscal].[FY 2006 to Date by Day].

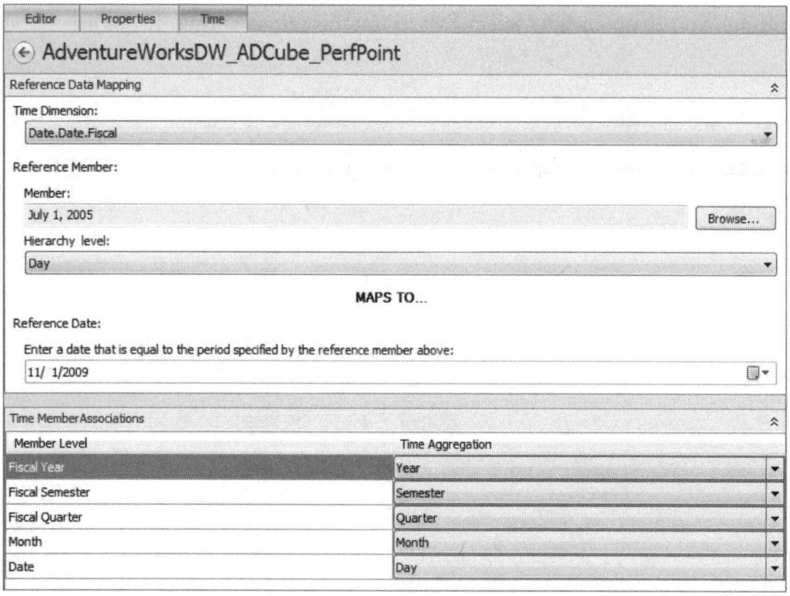

FIGURE 13-59

REPORTING SERVICES 2008 R2

Since the initial release of Reporting Service in 2004, there have been many improvements and shifts in the core architecture. Today, the latest version of the product is named SQL Server Reporting Services 2008 R2; a product that provides a variety of functionalities to help you develop your reports much more easily than before, and perhaps continue experiencing the satisfaction of the good old days!

Integration Modes

Unlike Excel Services or PerformancePoint Services, Reporting Services is not a native SharePoint service application. This means that an out-of-the-box SharePoint installation has no understanding of Reporting Services. So, the question is: What makes these two products aware of each other? The answer is a technique called Reporting Services integration with SharePoint.

Reporting Services 2008 R2 integration with SharePoint 2010 comes in two flavors:

1. Local mode

2. Connected mode

In order to integrate these two products, at a minimum, you need to download and install the SQL Server 2008 R2 Reporting Services add-in for Microsoft SharePoint Technologies 2010. This gives you the local mode, which is basically the lightest way you can integrate SSRS with SharePoint without any configuration steps. At the time of writing, the add-in is still up for Community Technical Preview (CTP) and can be downloaded at www.devhorizon.com/go/17.

It's worth noting that this particular CTP may expire by the time you are reading this chapter. If that's the case, you should either install the newer CTP or the RTM (Released to Manufacturing) version.

Connected mode, however, is where you get the most out of both products, and it involves more configuration steps both in the SQL Server Reporting Services configuration application and in the SharePoint Central Administration site.

> *If you are interested in learning more about the integration between these two products, I recommend the book* Wrox: Professional Microsoft SharePoint 2007 Reporting with SQL Server 2008 Reporting Services. *Although, this book may sound as if it's written for the older versions of both products, most of the information is still very applicable.*

Local Mode Architecture

In local mode, there is no Report Server and everything is installed on the web frontend server where SharePoint is installed. You can choose to install the add-in before or after the SharePoint installation. However, Microsoft's recommendation is to install it before, because there are fewer configuration steps involved. No additional configuration or replication out to servers in the farm will be necessary.

If you choose to install the add-in before installing SharePoint, the add-in creates SharePoint's 14 Hive folder structure and installs the required files, so when SharePoint is installed, the initial configuration of the local mode can be automatically configured.

The architecture of the local mode integration is pretty clean and straight forward, as shown in Figure 13-60.

When you install the add-in, three major components are included in the SharePoint web frontend:

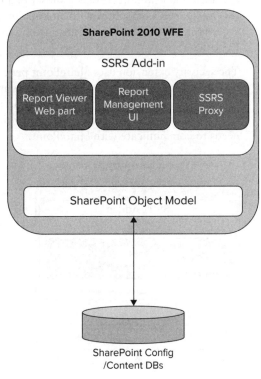

FIGURE 13-60

➤ **Report Viewer web part:** Installs an AJAX-enabled web part for rendering the Reporting Services report on a SharePoint page

➤ **Reporting Services proxy:** A SOAP endpoint that sets up the connection between both products (for full integration)

➤ **Report Management UI**: Adds all the Central Administration pages for configuring the integration, as well as application pages and ECB content menu options used for managing reports shared between all SharePoint web applications

Additionally, the add-in delivers the following new capabilities:

➤ Access Services reporting

➤ Reporting Services content types

➤ SharePoint list query support

➤ Ribbon user experience

➤ Support for logging in SharePoint Universal Logging Service (ULS)

Connected Mode Architecture

The local mode architecture is a subset of a larger architecture model named connected mode. In this mode, SSRS integrates with SharePoint at three different levels: farm, content databases, and security model. To make this integration possible, three additional components are installed on the Report Server, as shown in Figure 13-61.

The security extension uses SharePoint permissions levels to authorize access to report server operations such as reporting processing, snapshots, subscriptions, and the like. Data Management is responsible for doing SSRS native tasks and is the only component in the integration that has access to the Report Server database. The SharePoint Object Model is required, because Reporting Services needs to communicate with SharePoint.

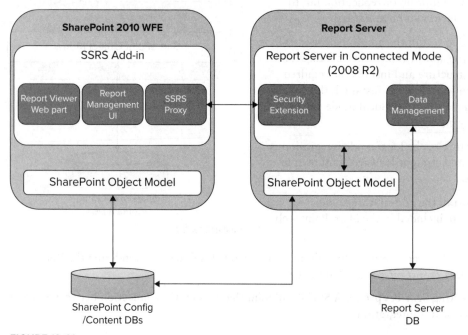

FIGURE 13-61

Authentication Mode

All the Reporting Services operations a user may perform in SharePoint application pages are routed, in the form of a request, to the Report Server for further processing. Depending on the authentication type of the connected mode integration, the request may or may not include the user's identity token in the header.

If you browse to the Reporting Services Integration page (Central Administration ➪ General Application Settings ➪ Reporting Services), you will find a group of settings that are considered to be the heart of the integration. What matters to our discussion here is authentication mode, as shown in Figure 13-62.

FIGURE 13-62

In this page you can select either of the following options:

➤ **Trusted Account:** In this particular mode of operation, the SharePoint user identity token flows from the WFE to the Report Server and is handed over to the security extension for further authorization actions. The actual connection between two servers is constructed and impersonated on behalf of the SharePoint application pool identity.

➤ **Windows Authentications:** This authentication mode is used only when you are in a single machine (standalone installation of both products) or when the Kerberos protocol is enabled. Obviously, the Windows integrated security only works for the web applications that are configured for Windows authentication.

Supporting Multiple Zones

Although the new claims-based authentication model in SharePoint 2010 allows you to plug multiple authentication providers into a single web application, there are still cases where you need to extend the web application and use multiple zones.

For example, let's suppose that Adventure Works requires some users to authenticate to the company's intranet sites using smart cards while others still enter their credentials to logon to the sites. The business requirements dictate that reports must work for both types of users regardless of their authentication method. To do so, the IT department has extended the intranet web application, created a new zone, and has set up the certificate mapping for that web application in IIS 7.0.

In the previous versions of Reporting Services, if you wanted to display SSRS reports to those users who authenticated themselves by using their smart cards, reports must have been published to the new zone configured for smart card; otherwise, reports would error out saying that SSRS reports don't support multi-zone scenarios. This was an issue because such reports were pretty useless in other zones.

Thankfully, Microsoft has addressed this issue in Reporting Services 2008 R2 by introducing multi-zone support in the connected mode. You can use the alternate access mapping functionality in SharePoint and set up access to Report Server items from one or more SharePoint zones (default, Internet, intranet, extranet, or custom). You will see an example of a report rendered in two different zones later on. Keep reading!

Anonymous Access to Reports

So far, you have learned that the multi-zone scenario is fully supported in SSRS 2008 R2 when it's configured in connected mode. Suppose that Adventure Works would like to allow access to the catalog of products report without forcing Internet users to log in.

Even though SharePoint supports anonymous access to a site and maps anonymous users to the Limited Access permission level, there is an issue in displaying SSRS reports to anonymous users in connected mode. Unfortunately, Reporting Services still requires a valid security context and doesn't support anonymous access to reports right out of the box. The issue is that Anonymous users do not represent a true security context in SharePoint; therefore, when they try to access reports, SSRS won't be able to authorize their access to Report Server.

 Obviously, you can always use custom development and wrap anonymous users in a valid security context (i.e., Guest) and resolve the issue. A proof-of-concept implementation of this technique can be found in my blog at www.devhorizon .com/go/18.

Reporting Services Execution Account

Report Server never allows its service account (configured in the Reporting Service Configuration Manager) and all its administrative privileges to be delegated when connecting to a resource on the network. So, if you are reporting against a datasource that does not require authentication or when you use a SQL account in your datasource, the question is how is the connection between Report Server and the datasource established? Under what security context? Remember, Report Server must use a valid Windows security context to access resources such as an XML file or a SQL instance that supports SQL authentication.

In the Reporting Services world, this liaison account is referred to as execution account and it's mainly used in the following two scenarios:

> **Scenario 1: Security context for network connection:** In this scenario, SSRS sends the connection requests over the network to connect to external datasources, such as an XML file or SQL Server when the report uses a SQL account to log in to the SQL Server instance. If the execution account is not specified, Report Server impersonates its service account but removes all administrator permissions when sending the connection request for security reasons.

> **Scenario 2: Access to external resource:** In this scenario, SSRS sends the connection requests to retrieve external resources used in a report that doesn't store credentials in its datasource.

For example, when you create a report that has a link to an external image stored in a remote server, in the preview mode your credentials as a developer will be used to display the image. However, when the report is deployed to production and viewed on a SharePoint site, Report Server uses its execution account to retrieve the image. If the execution account is not specified, the image is retrieved using no credentials (i.e., anonymous access). Obviously, if neither of these two accounts has sufficient rights to access the image, it won't show up in the report. This is very important to remember for deploying reports to SharePoint, because images used in your report may or may not be in the same site collection that the current report viewer has permission to access.

The Reporting Services execution account is totally different from the unattended account in Excel Services or PerformancePoint. The SSRS execution account must be used only for specific functions as described in this section. Microsoft has made it crystal clear that the execution account must not be used as a login account or for retrieving data from backend datasources. For more information, see the official statement in the "How to Use Unattended Report Processing Account" section in Book Online at www.devhorizon.com/go/19.

To set up an execution account you need to specify it in the Execution Account page in the Reporting Services Configuration tool, as shown in Figure 13-63.

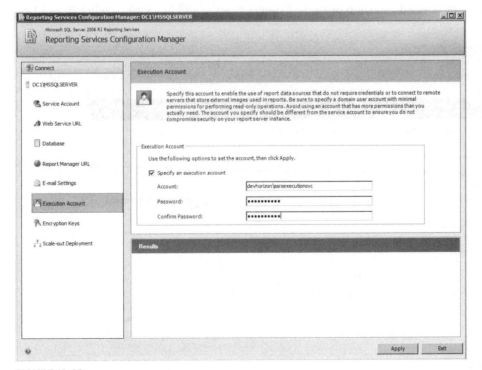

FIGURE 13-63

The execution account is encrypted and stored in the `RSReportServer.config` file.

If you have installed Reporting Services using a scale-out topology, you must run the configuration tool on each report server and use the same set of credentials for the execution account.

Configuring the BI Center

While Reporting Services reports can be deployed and managed in any site or document library, in this section you will continue using the BI Center site (which you built earlier) for housing Reporting Services reports.

To make a site such as the BI Center understand Reporting Services reports, models, and datasources, you need to add the required content types to the Data Connections and Documents libraries, because they are not added by default.

And, with that, let's get started:

1. Browse to the Data Connections library.

2. From the Ribbon, click on Library Tools ➪ Library Settings.

3. Under Content Types, click Add from existing site content types.

4. In the Select Content Types section, in Select site content types from, select Report Server Content Types from the drop-down list.

5. In the Available Site Content Types list, click Report Data Source, and then click Add to move the selected content type to the Content types to add list, as shown in Figure 13-64.

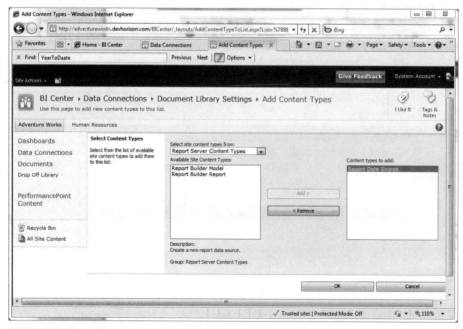

FIGURE 13-64

With the Data Connections library properly set up, next comes the Documents library. Follow the exact steps you took for the Data Connections library with one exception: from the list of available content types, only select Report Builder and Report this time.

The configuration steps you took in this section enable you to view and manage Reporting Services reports directly from the BI Center. Now, you can publish Reporting Services content to both document libraries and then view and manage those documents directly within the SharePoint context.

BIDS 2008 R2 or Report Builder 3.0?

Unlike Excel and PerformancePoint, in Reporting Services you have two options when it comes to the authoring tool: BIDS or Report Builder. What is BIDS and why should you care?

BIDS is short for Business Intelligence Development Studio. It's a development tool that allows you to build reports and deploy them to a SharePoint site. The latest version of BIDS ships with SQL Server 2008 R2 and is almost always referred to as BIDS 2008 R2.

BIDS 2008 R2 supports four operations of RDL (Report Definition Language) files: opening RDL files, building and previewing the RDL files, and deploying them to a SharePoint site that is configured with an instance of Report Server (2008 or 2008 R2), as shown in Figure 13-65.

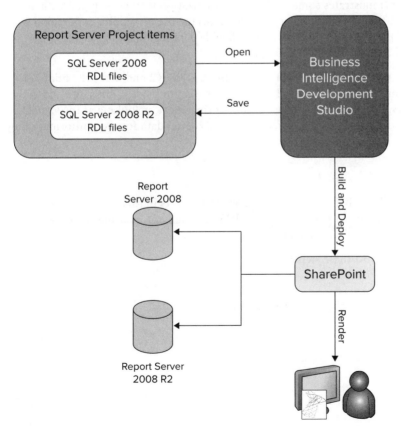

FIGURE 13-65

BIDS 2008 R2 works with both earlier and later versions of RDL files. Although BIDS may sound like an standalone product for report development only, in all reality BIDS is just a lightweight version of Microsoft Visual Studio 2008 with some BI project templates, such as Report Server project templates (for Reporting Services), Integration Services project templates, and Analysis Services project templates.

Although BIDS is the preferred tool for many report developers, it should be noted that that there is another option for developing reports: Microsoft Reporting Services Report Builder 3.0. You can download and install a small standalone MSI for this product (August 2009 CTP version) from the following URL: www.devhorizon.com/go/20. This product, also free, is an authoring tool to create reports. Report Builder is also a Click-Once application that has many of the same features in BIDS, but not all.

Since the audience of this book is mostly SharePoint developers, Reporting Builder 3.0 will not be used for creating reports, because it is mostly used by Information workers. The BIDS IDE is very similar to Visual Studio 2008, so it will be familiar to a lot of SharePoint developers.

Building and Deploying Reports

The report that you will build in this section shows the Adventure Works sales by quarter and product category. This report illustrates some of the new visualization features shipped with SQL Server Reporting Services 2008 R2. This report also illustrates the use of a tablix data region with nested row groups and column groups. Tablix is a very flexible data region and grouping report item which was first introduced in Reporting Services 2008.

Once you build the report, you can preview the report in BIDS 2008 R2 and make the final adjustment before publishing it. Finally, you will deploy this report to the BI Center site and make it available to the end users. Users can quickly get a sense of the report by looking at the visuals embedded in the report or drill down from summary data into detail data for more information by showing and hiding rows.

Authoring Reports

As mentioned before, you will use BIDS 2008 R2 to create the reports in this chapter. However, there are also two ways you can build your reports in BIDS: manually or by using the Report Wizard. In this section, you will use the manual process.

To author your first report, follow these steps:

1. Open BIDS 2008 R2.
2. Click Ctrl+Shift+N to open the New Project dialog.

3. From the available templates, select the Business Intelligence Projects types, and then click Report Server Project.

4. Name the project something descriptive such as Chapter13_SSRSReport, and click OK.

5. In the Solution Explorer, right-click the Shared Data Source and select Add New Data Source.

6. Point the new datasource to the AdventureWorks database, as shown in Figure 13-66.

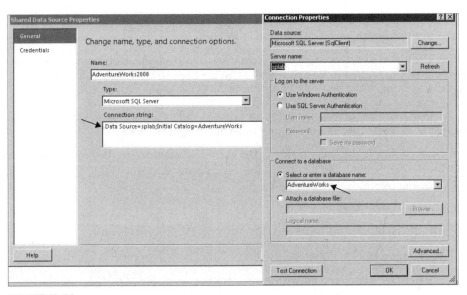

FIGURE 13-66

7. In the Solution Explorer, right-click the Reports folder and select Add ⇨ New Item, and then select Report template. Name the new report SalesByQtrAndProductCat.rdl. At this point, you should now have a blank canvas on which you can design your report layout.

8. In the Report Data tab, right-click the Datasets folder, and select Add Dataset to open the Dataset Properties dialog.

9. Change the name of the dataset to DSSales, and then select the Use a dataset embedded in my report option.

> *Starting in Reporting Services 2008 R2, datasets that you create in your reports can be stored externally from the report and shared between multiple reports. Like shared datasources, shared datasets can be created by IT or more senior developers and shared with information workers or other developers.*
>
> *Shared datasets can be created in two ways. Either right-click the Shared Datasets folder in the Solution Explorer and add a new dataset or simply right-click on a nonshared datasource and select Convert to Shared Dataset.*

10. Click the New button to open Data Source Properties.

11. Select the Use a shared datasource reference option, and from the drop-down list choose the datasource you created in Step 5. Click OK to get back to the Dataset Properties dialog.

12. Click the Query Designer button to open the Query Designer. Once the Query Designer dialog opens, click the Edit as Text button to switch to Query Mode.

13. Paste the query below in the query textbox. The query is a join between the ProductSubcategory, SalesOrderHeader, SalesOrderDetail, Product, and ProductCategory tables, and it's grouped on the following columns:

    a. Order date (only year)

    b. Category name

    c. Subcategory name

    d. The letter "Q" concatenated with `ProductCategoryID` (i.e., Q1, Q2, . .)

The query also takes two parameters, named `@StartDate` and `@EndDate`, to limit the calculation of the sales amount to a period of time specified by the parameters.

```
SELECT
    PC.Name AS Category, PS.Name AS Subcategory,
    DATEPART(yy, SOH.OrderDate) AS Year,
    'Q' + DATENAME(qq, SOH.OrderDate) AS Qtr,
    SUM(DET.UnitPrice * DET.OrderQty) AS Sales
FROM Production.ProductSubcategory PS INNER JOIN
    Sales.SalesOrderHeader SOH INNER JOIN
        Sales.SalesOrderDetail DET ON SOH.SalesOrderID = DET.SalesOrderID INNER JOIN
        Production.Product P ON DET.ProductID = P.ProductID
        ON PS.ProductSubcategoryID = P.ProductSubcategoryID INNER JOIN
    Production.ProductCategory PC ON PS.ProductCategoryID = PC.ProductCategoryID
WHERE (SOH.OrderDate BETWEEN (@StartDate) AND (@EndDate))
GROUP BY DATEPART(yy, SOH.OrderDate), PC.Name, PS.Name,
    'Q' + DATENAME(qq, SOH.OrderDate), PS.ProductSubcategoryID
```

You can examine the query result by clicking the button that has the exclamation mark on it and then entering a sample start date and end date such as 1/1/2003 and 12/31/2004. The returned result will appear in the grid below the query section, as shown in Figure 13-67. Once you are done, click OK to close the Query Designer.

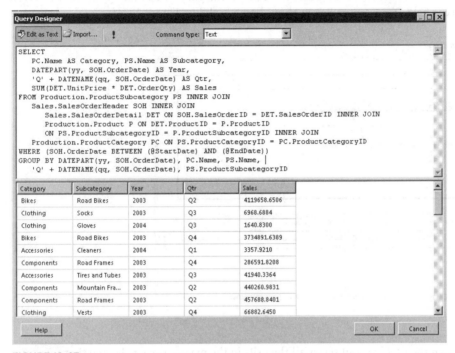

FIGURE 13-67

Step 14: Click OK again to close Dataset Properties dialog.

Laying Out Your Report

At this point, you should have a dataset with the following fields: Category, Subcategory, Year, Qtr, and Sales. The next logical step is to actually build the report display as outlined here:

1. Start by dragging a matrix from the toolbox to the Body section of the report.

2. From the Report Data tab, drag the following fields to the specified places on the design canvas:

   a. The Category field to the matrix cell where it says Rows

   b. The Year field to the matrix cell where it says Columns

   c. The Sales field to the matrix cell where it says Data

d. The Subcategory field to below the Category field in the grouping pane where it says Row Groups (bottom-left corner)

e. The Qtr field to below the Year field in the grouping pane where it says Column Groups (bottom-right corner)

3. Delete the column titles for the Category and Subcategory fields that appear on the left side of the Year field. Your report layout should now look like Figure 13-68.

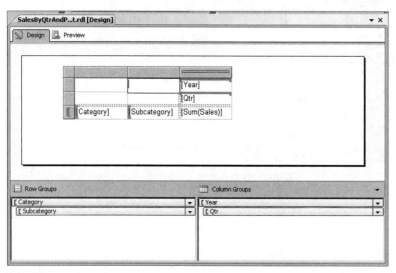

FIGURE 13-68

4. Hold down the Ctrl key and select all the cells in the matrix except the one that says Sum (Sales). From the properties window, change the following properties.

➤ BackgroundColor: SteelBlue

➤ Color: White

➤ FontWeight: Bold

5. Select the textbox that has [Sum(Sales)] in it. From the Properties windows, set '$'#,0;('$'#,0) as the value of the Format property (see Figure 13-69). This string is used to apply the currency format to each sales amount cell that appears in the final report.

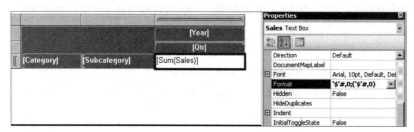

FIGURE 13-69

You are almost done with the initial formatting and clean up, but you still have to enable the drill-down, so the report allows users to look deeper in any area they choose. The goal is to show categories and years only when the report is first run and then allow users to see the subcategories and quarters by using the tree-style +/- controls that appear next to each category or year.

1. Click the subcategory group in Row Groups section to highlight it.

2. Click the down arrow that appears just to the right side of the group, and then select Group Properties.

3. Once the Group Properties window opens, go to the visibility section.

4. Select the Hide option and set the toggle item drop-down list to Category.

   This collapses and hides the subcategory when the report is first run. If you set the toggle item property to Category, when the report is run, a little plus sign appears next to each category, which allows users to drill down into each subcategory exactly like a tree view. You can repeat the exact same steps to toggle the Qtr field by Year.

That's everything you need to do to build a very basic report that shows the Adventure Works sales by quarter and product category. Finally, preview the report; it should appear like the one shown in Figure 13-70.

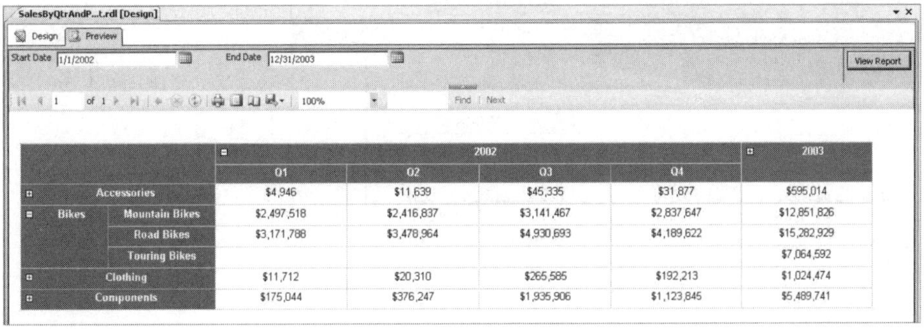

FIGURE 13-70

Data Visualizations

If you have been developing or designing reports for any amount of time, you probably know that no report is complete without some kind of visualization. Essentially, reports are there to allow end users to make fast business decisions, so if you can represent your report in such a way that they can intercept its data immediately and get the key points, your report would be of great value to them.

With SQL Server Reporting Services 2008, Microsoft introduced a useful data visualizations, named gauge. The gauge allows report developers to visually display aggregated data, and it's commonly used in digital dashboards. In SQL Server Reporting Services 2008 R2, more data visualizations are introduced. Sparklines, data bars, and indicators are additions to the SQL Server Reporting Services family, representing the same basic chart characteristics of values, categories, and series, but without any fluff such as axis lines, labels, or a legend.

➤ **Data bar:** A data bar is like a regular bar chart in which each bar can be scaled based on a given value to display one data point or more.

➤ **Sparkline:** Similar to Sparklines in Excel, a Sparkline in Reporting Services is just a mini-chart that trends over time. They are commonly used to display multiple data points.

➤ **Indicator:** An indicator is a small icon that is often used to display the status or trend over time for a specific value.

In the example in this section, you have a chance to work with a Sparkline chart, while continuing work from where you left off with the sales by quarter and product category report created in the previous section.

For a Sparkline chart, you need a value field like Sales and a group like Quarter for which to record the trend. To add this to your report, follow these steps:

1. Add a new column on the matrix by right-clicking the column that has the [Year], [Quarter] and [Sum(Sales)] fields, and select Inset Column ⇨ Right option, as shown in Figure 13-71. This creates a column to the right of the selected column, which is used to place your Sparkline.

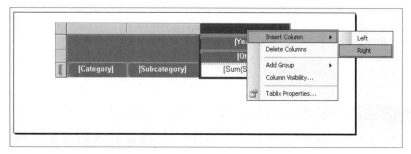

FIGURE 13-71

2. Add a Sparkline to the new column by dragging and dropping the Sparkline from the toolbox to the cell that appears to the right of the cell that has [Sum(Sales)]. Note that because Sparklines display aggregated data, they must be placed in a cell associated with a group.

3. From the Select Sparkline Type dialog, select Area and click OK. You should now have a Sparkline ready to be configured in the new column, as shown in Figure 13-72.

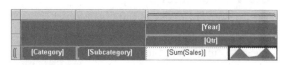

FIGURE 13-72

Click the Sparkline image. This will open the Chart Data dialog on the right. Click the yellow plus symbol to the right of the Values area, and select the Sales field from DSSales dataset.

4. Click the plus symbol to the right of the Category Groups area, and select Qtr field. Your report is now ready to preview. Switch to the preview window in BIDS, and your report should be like the one shown in Figure 13-73.

		2002		2003	
Accessories		$93,797		$595,014	
Bikes		$26,664,534		$35,199,346	
Clothing	Bib-Shorts	$102,183		$65,353	
	Caps	$9,467		$21,917	
	Gloves	$90,897		$118,132	
	Jerseys	$110,846		$363,284	
	Shorts	$49,384		$214,457	
	Socks	$3,173		$13,152	
	Tights	$123,871		$80,212	
	Vests		No Data Available	$147,968	
Components		$3,611,041		$5,489,741	

FIGURE 13-73

 This report can be found in the code download for this book, in the Chapter 13 .zip file. It is called `SalesByQtrAndProductCat.rdl`.

Tablix

Although you used a matrix in your report, you are really using a *tablix* data region under the covers. The tablix (table + matrix) data region was first introduced in Reporting Services 2008, and it offers the flexibility of the table combined with the crosstab reporting features of the matrix.

As you can see in your report, Product Category and Product Subcategory are sharing two different columns, and there is a considerable amount of horizontal spacing wasted in the first column. You can reduce this spacing and make both groups share the same column by using a new feature in tablix called stepped columns. If you have been doing crosstab reports, you probably know that this wasn't an easy thing to implement with the old matrix. For more information on stepped columns, refer to the official documentation at www.devhorizon.com/go/21.

Another feature in tablix that can help you improve your crosstab reports is something known as side-by-side crosstab sections. Your report is currently broken down by year at the top, but what if you wanted to have the same grouping (Product Category, Product subcategory) by territory side by side with the year section? What if you want to allow users to drill down into categories and subcategories and see the year breakdown and territory breakdown at the same time?

If you wanted to do this report in SSRS 2005, you had to do it using multiple matrices, but in SSRS 2008 and 2008 R2, you can use a tablix and its native support for side-by-side crosstab sections. All you need to do is to include the territory data in your return result set and add it as a parent column grouping in the same matrix you just used in your report. As matter of fact, you can have an unlimited number of side-by-side crosstab groups (correlated or uncorrelated) on rows and columns of a tablix data region.

The tablix feature of Reporting Services makes using asymmetric layouts in your report super easy.

Publishing Your Report to SharePoint

Now that you have prepared your report, you are ready to deploy it to SharePoint 2010. In BIDS, the terms *publish* and *deploy* are interchangeable. They both refer to a process that makes the report available in SharePoint for online viewing. Although the publishing process may seem simple at first glance, there is more to it than just moving the content from your local drive to a SharePoint site.

What happens during publishing that makes it a special process? First, BIDS validates the report before it is added to the destination libraries in SharePoint and if there are any problems you will be notified. As you may know, you can always go to a document library and upload documents yourself, but in this particular case, you should avoid direct uploads, because the validation check never occurs. This means that you never know if your reporting files are valid until either you manually access them or a background process such as snapshots, subscriptions, or a caching process references them.

Second, during the publishing process any shared datasource in the report project will be converted to an `.rsds` file name extension (originally, the file extension was `.rds`). Both `.rds` and `.rsds` files have the same content, but they come in different schemas. What's important to note is that it's only the `.rsds` file extension that is recognizable by SharePoint, and this is defined in the file extension mapping file (`Docicon.xml`) located at `Drive:\Program Files\Common Files\Microsoft Shared\Web Server Extensions\14\Template\XML` using the following entry:

```
<Mapping Key="rsds" Value="datasource.gif" OpenControl="SharePoint.OpenRsdsFiles"/>
```

The process of converting the `.rds` file extension to `.rsds` involves a web service call to the `CreateDataSource()` web method located at the `ReportService2006.asmx` endpoint, which makes the actual conversion. Note that you can perform the conversion programmatically by calling this web service and passing in an `.rds` file.

Finally, there is one more thing that the publishing process does for you. If you happen to publish a report that already exists in the destination document library, the report will be checked out, updated as a new version, and then checked back in for you. This is important because it illustrates that reports are treated like any other document content type for the purposes of versioning, permissions, and retention.

Publishing your report to SharePoint is relatively simple. Right-click the solution name and click Properties to open the Property dialog window, as shown in Figure 13-74.

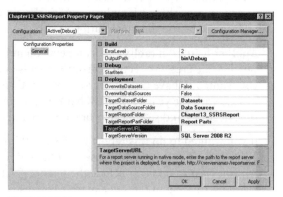

FIGURE 13-74

As you can tell, the Deployment Properties dialog has now changed to support new deployment settings related to shared datasets and the fact that BIDS 2008 R2 can open report definition files for both SSRS 2008 and SSRS 2008 R2.

Below, you will find all the properties and a brief explanation to help you understand what they are for and what you need to type in them to deploy your report to SharePoint.

➤ Boolean Properties: true or false:

➤ **OverwriteDatasets:** This setting specifies if the shared dataset definitions will be overwritten if they already exist in the TargetDatasetFolder in the target SharePoint site.

➤ **OverwriteDataSources:** This setting specifies if the shared datasource definitions will be overwritten if they already exist in the TargetDataSourceFolder in the target SharePoint site.

➤ URL Properties:

➤ **TargetDatasetFolder:** A folder relative to the URL you specify in the `TargetServerURL` property. This folder keeps all the shared dataset definition files.

➤ **TargetDataSourceFolder:** A folder relative to the URL you specify in the `TargetServerURL` property. This folder keeps all the shared datasource definition files (.rsds).

➤ **TargetReportFolder:** A folder relative to the URL you specify in `TargetServerURL` property. This folder keeps all the report definition files (.rdl).

➤ **TargetReportPartFolder:** A folder relative to the URL you specify in the `TargetServerURL` property. This folder keeps all the report part definition files (.rcs). Report parts will be covered in more detail later in this chapter.

➤ **TargetServerURL:** The URL of the target SharePoint site where you wish to deploy your report.

➤ **TargetServerVersion:** The expected version of SQL Server Reporting Services that is integrated with the target SharePoint site specified in the TargetServerURLproperty.

Set the value of the `TargetDatasetFolder`, `TargetReportFolder`, and `TargetReportPartFolder` properties to the fully qualified URL of the Documents document library in the BI Center (see the "Configuring the BI Center" section). Next, set `TargetDataSourceFolder` to the fully qualified URL of the Data Connections document library in the BI Center (see the "Configuring the BI Center" section). Finally, set the `TargetServerURL` property to the fully qualified URL of the BI Center and the `TargetServerVersion` property to SQL Server 2008 R2.

With the deployment properties completely configured, you are ready to deploy the report with all its items to SharePoint. Note that you need Full Control or Contribute permission in the site on which you are deploying your reports; otherwise, you will get the Reporting Services login when you attempt to build and deploy the reports. To deploy this report, all you have to do is right-click the solution and click Deploy.

At this point, you can browse to the document library and click the name of the report to render it in the browser (via `RSViewerPage.aspx`), as shown in Figure 13-75.

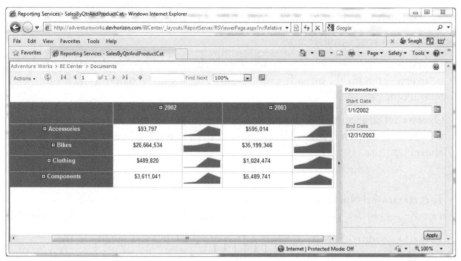

FIGURE 13-75

In case you didn't notice, there is a Cancel link on the page every time your report is run. This means that report processing is now completely asynchronous, and you have the option to cancel it while it's in progress.

Publishing Report Parts

By definition, report parts are individual items that make up an SSRS Report. They can be anything in a report from a parameter to a data region, such as a matrix. The idea is like splitting an ASPX page into smaller user controls, so they can be shared across multiple pages.

The good news is that these components can now be saved individually — without the rest of the report page. More precisely, however, report developers from either BIDS or Report Builder 3.0 publish report parts to a destination folder, and then other report developers or information workers can reuse the published parts and put together their own reports without having to build everything from the ground up.

Creating report parts in BIDS is for more experienced report developers, who will create these components and perhaps use source control, whereas Report Builder is for less experienced users, who should use the published report parts to build their own reports.

The report that you built in this section has only three items that can be published as report parts. To make these parts available on the SharePoint site, follow these steps:

1. From the Report menu, click Publish Report Parts.

2. This will open the Publish Report Items dialog, where you can select which items should be made available in the Report Parts library, as shown in Figure 13-76. Select all the items and click OK.

3. Redeploy your report by right-clicking the solution and click Deploy.

FIGURE 13-76

4. Browse to the Documents document library in SharePoint and verify that all the parts are successfully published to SharePoint, as shown in Figure 13-77.

Once the report parts are published to a site, they can be found and reused by information workers using Report Builder. To see a list of available report parts in Report Builder, browse to the View tab and select Report Part Gallery. You can search for a specific part by typing its name in the search box provided on the top of the pane.

FIGURE 13-77

Report Viewer Web Part

In addition to the `RSViewerPage.aspx`, there is another way of displaying your reports in SharePoint, through the use of the standalone Report Viewer web part. Adding a Report Viewer Web Part to a page is as easy as dragging and dropping it into a Web Part zone and then setting some simple properties.

To host your report in a Report Viewer web part, follow these steps:

1. Browse to Site Actions ⇨ View All Site Content.

2. In the All Site Content page, click the Create button.

3. In the Create dialog, select Page category and choose Web Part Page.

4. Click the Create button. This will take you to New Web Part page.

5. In the Name textbox, enter **SSRS Demo**.

6. Choose Header, Footer, 3 Columns from the available layout templates.

7. Click the Create button.

8. Add an instance of the Report Viewer web part to the Header Web Part zone.

9. Click the Web Part menu, and select Edit Web Part to open the Tool pane. Notice the extra tabs in the Tool pane, which provide custom properties specific to the Report Viewer web part, as illustrated in Figure 13-78.

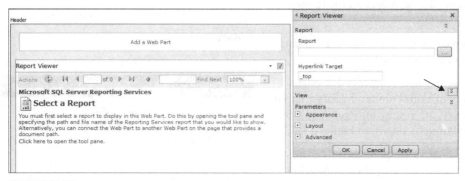

FIGURE 13-78

10. In the Report textbox, specify the relative path and file name of your report. In this example, it is /BICenter/Documents/SalesByQtrAndProductCat.rdl.

 Because current integration between Reporting Services and SharePoint supports multiples zones, the Reporting Services team has changed the Report Path to be relative. Previously, Report Path had to be a fully qualified URL.

11. Leave the default View settings.

12. In the Parameters tab, click the Load Parameters button. You can leave the report to use its default values, or you can override the report so that it is rendered with another value of your choice.

13. Click Apply, and then click OK to close the pane.

Figure 13-79 shows a rendered report in a Web Part page.

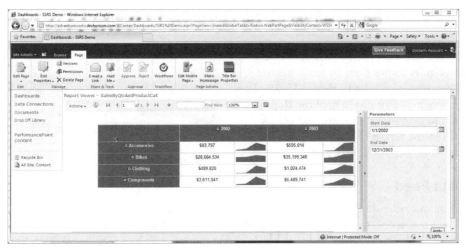

FIGURE 13-79

Now that you have a good understanding of the Report Viewer web part's capabilities, you should be aware of a few limitations with this web part.

First, you cannot have multiple reports in your site that point to different instances of Report Server. This is due to the fact that Reporting Services integration with SharePoint is implemented and configured at the farm level, and the Report Viewer web part and other integration operations simply follow the same model at each site collection level. Second, you cannot group multiple reports into a single instance of a Report Viewer web part. Third, you cannot open a saved report as an attachment to a list item. The Report Viewer web part can only respond to reports that are stored in a document library or are passed in via a connectable web part. Last, but certainly not least, the Report Viewer web part class is sealed and as such is not available for developers to leverage. If you need your own custom Report Viewer web part, you need to code it from scratch or put a wrapper around the Microsoft Report Viewer control.

Connectable Report Viewer Web Part

One of the great features of SharePoint is the Web Part Connection framework, which allows web parts to accept connections from other web parts. In a nutshell, a connection is an association between two web parts that enables them to share data.

As demonstrated throughout this chapter, building Dashboard pages where different types of web parts exist on the same page, each showing different content and data, is an important part of the BI capabilities of SharePoint 2010. In real-world scenarios, these web parts often communicate with each other and are very interactive.

In the previous section, it was mentioned that one of the limitations of the Report Viewer web part is its one-to-one association with a report definition file. A standalone Report Viewer web part is useful when visitors to a page are likely to be interested in a particular report. However, in dashboard-style scenarios, a standalone web part is less likely to be what you really want. You need a web part that's more interactive.

Thankfully, the Report Viewer web part acts as a subscriber in web part connections by implementing the required interfaces, as shown in Figure 13-80. This means that you can make an instance of the Report Viewer web part to communicate with, and get its parameters or even the report definition from another web part on the same page or across pages.

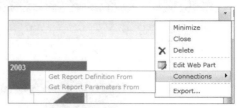

FIGURE 13-80

Report as a Data Feed

If you recall from an earlier discussion, one of the key factors to support the "BI for everyone" vision is to allow users access to the most up-to-date data for their day-to-day analysis. The problem is that, in many organizations, direct access to the backend datasources historically has been limited to a number of administrators and a few service accounts. That's mainly because directly accessing raw data without going through the business logic and security layers is not a best practice and can put organizational assets at much higher risk.

Starting with SQL Server 2008 R2, SSRS report data can be rendered as an Atom feed that follows WCF data services conventions. This means that you can get high-quality and refreshable data sourced from pretty much anywhere a report can get data from; whether that data is represented in a tablix, chart, or other form, really doesn't matter!

 To use your SSRS reports as data feeds, you need to install and configure Reporting Services and PowerPivot for SharePoint in the same farm. Also, on the client machine, the PowerPivot for Excel client must be installed. For more information, see the instructions at www.devhorizon.com/go/22.

Once you have found a report with backend data that you are interested in analyzing, you can pull it into your PowerPivot workbook by clicking the new orange Export to Data Feed button on the Report toolbar, as shown in Figure 13-81.

FIGURE 13-81

This will generate an .atomsvc file output and ask you if you want to open it locally.

If you already have an Excel workbook open, you will be prompted to either select an open workbook to add the data feed to, or create a new workbook for the feed.

Next, the Excel client is launched and it goes straight into the PowerPivot tab where the Table Import Wizard pops up.

If you click the Next button, the Table Import Wizard will show you a list of data regions in the report that you can import into your Gemini model and specify table names for. Optionally, you can preview data and select which columns from the data feed to add to your model, as shown in Figure 13-82.

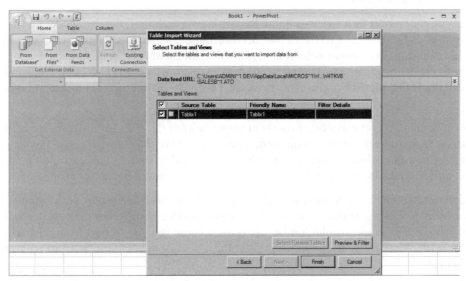

FIGURE 13-82

Now you should be able to consume the data feed and use the Tablix1 data region as a datasource in your PowerPivot workbook.

At the time of writing, SQL Server Reporting Services 2008 R2 is still in November CTP. In this version, the Export To Data Feed option only works for Tablix and Chart and not for Map. This will most likely change when the product is released to manufacturing (RTM).

Open with Report Builder

The Open with Report Builder option in SSRS 2008 R2 has received two major bug fixes. First, if you click the Actions menu and choose Open with Report Builder, Report Builder 3.0 now launches by default if it's installed on the server. This action points to the following URL to instruct Report Builder which report to open:

```
http://adventureworks.devhorizon.com/_vti_bin/ReportBuilder/ReportBuilder_3_0_0_0
.application?ReportPath=http://adventureworks.devhorizon.com/BICenter/Documents/
SalesByQtrAndProductCat.rdl
```

Prior to the SSRS 2008 R2 release, Report Builder 1.0 would be launched and it was almost impossible to make SharePoint open the Report Builder 2.0 instead.

A second issue that's been addressed in this release is the opening by Report Builder of published drill-through reports. Previously, this would result in an error by Report Builder, because Report Builder was trying to resolve the action locally. However, in Report Builder 3.0, the action is forwarded to SharePoint for further processing and no action is taken locally.

Caching and Snapshots

When a user clicks your report or it's viewed in the Report Viewer web part, the dataset defined in that report executes and returns data to the Report Server from the underlying datasource. Next, the report execution engine uses the report definition file stored in the SharePoint content database to determine how to create the report from the retrieved data, transform it into HTML, and finally push it down through the HTTP pipeline to the user's browser. This process is known as on-demand report execution.

Although the on-demand report execution process always results in the most up-to-date data being returned to users, each time the report is requested, a new instance of the report is created, which in turn results in a new query being issued against the underlying datasource. This can add up exponentially until it results in the utilization of all the resources in your SharePoint farm.

When users don't need on-demand report execution, and when you need fast report performance, there are some other processing options available to help you manage your report delivery needs in more efficient ways. For example, wouldn't it be nice if users could run your report from the cache or snapshots instead? What are your options to prevent the report from being run at arbitrary times during peak hours?

Thankfully, SSRS 2008 and 2008 R2 offer functionalities that can help you deliver your reports faster and more efficiently. These options are all available from the Edit Control Block (ECB) menu of the report definition file, as shown in Figure 13-83.

The goal of this chapter is to introduce techniques that can be used to improve the performance of your reports, which altogether result in a better user experience. Several operations that are discussed in this section require that you hard code the credentials in your report's datasource. That's because such operations do not represent a valid windows security context, and they can't access the backend datasources by themselves.

And, with that, let's start with storing credentials first!

FIGURE 13-83

Stored Credentials

Several operations that are discussed in this section require that you hard code the credentials in your report's datasource. That's because such operations do not represent a valid windows security context, and they can't access the backend datasources by themselves.

To store credentials in your datasource, browse to the Data Connections library where you published the datasource and just click on it. You will be taken directly to a page like the one shown in Figure 13-84. In this page, there are multiple options, but the one you will want to configure is the third one from the top, where it says Stored Credentials.

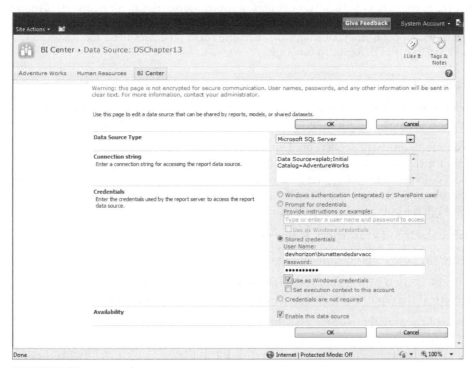

FIGURE 13-84

When you specify the stored credentials, there are two options you can select that determine how the stored credentials are authenticated.

➤ **Use as Windows credentials:** If you select Use as Windows credentials, the stored credentials should be a Windows user account, because it is passed to Windows for subsequent authentication. Thus, you can specify this option and then use a SQL login. Obviously, the account you use here must be granted read permission at minimum to access the resource.

There are two important tips to remember with regard to this option. First, do not check this box if your datasource is using database authentication only (for example, SQL Server authentication). Second, the Windows domain user account must also have permission to log on locally. This permission allows Report Server to impersonate the user on the Report Server box and send the connection request to the external datasource as that impersonated user.

➤ **Set execution context to this account:** You should select this option only if you want to set the execution context on the database server by impersonating the account that represents the stored credentials. Think of this option as the Transact-SQL SETUSER function in SQL Server.

There are two important tips to remember when selecting this check box. First, if your datasource is going after SQL Server databases, this option is not supported with Windows users; use SQL Server users instead. Second, do not use this option for reports initialized by subscriptions, report history, or snapshots, because these processes need a valid Windows user context (not a SQL login) to function.

Managing Parameters

In the real world, most of the reports you develop have one or more parameters, so before diving into evaluating other processing options, it makes sense to look at managing report parameters first.

Unlike when you run parameters' reports on-demand, end users won't get a chance to specify parameter values for reports delivered to them behind the scenes. As you saw, you can manage the default values configured for the report parameters when authoring reports in BIDS or Report Builder. You can also manage report parameters after they are published to SharePoint without having to go through the publishing process again.

To manage the parameters of your report, follow these steps:

1. Browse to the Documents document library.

2. Click the ECB menu, which appears to the right of the report title, and select Manage Parameters. If the report contains any parameters, they will be listed in order.

3. Click one of the available parameters, and you should see a page similar to the one shown in Figure 13-85.

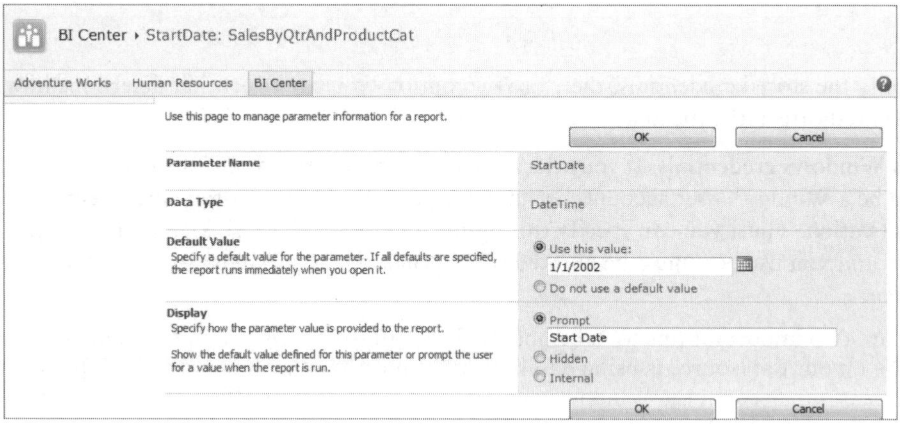

FIGURE 13-85

In this page, you can override the default value for the selected parameter as well as specify how the parameter value should be provided to the report. Available options are:

➤ **Prompt:** Parameter appears as a textbox (for single-valued parameters) or combobox (for multi-valued parameters) in the parameter input pane next to the rendered report. Users can specify a new value or select from the available options.

➤ **Hidden:** If you select this option, the parameter will be hidden in the Parameter Input pane, but its value can be set in background processes such as subscriptions, caching, and so on. You will learn about these processes a bit later.

➤ **Internal:** An internal parameter is not exposed to end users or background processes but is still available in the report definition file.

What's the Plan?

Reporting Services provides a powerful and easy-to-use caching mechanism that helps you keep a balance between having up-to-date data in your reports and having faster access to the reports.

 Like many other heavy-duty operations, caching a report is managed by Report Server, not SharePoint. A cached report does not utilize page output caching in SharePoint.

Of course, caching comes at a cost and can be destructive if used in inappropriate ways. So, before you jump right into the hassle of setting up your report for caching, you need to have a plan. The most important step is to figure out how your design can best utilize caching and what risks you need to be aware of.

When you configure a report for caching, the first time it is requested everything is identical to the on-demand report execution. In fact, the first user who hits the report turns the report into a cached instance and pays the price for everyone else who requests the same instance later on. A cached instance is tied to a combination of parameter values. For example, if you have a parameterized report that has two parameters A and B, then a cached instance of this report with parameter values of A1 and B1 is different from another cached instance that has A2 and B2 as parameter values.

Once the report is turned into a cached instance, it is stored in the Report Server temporary database as an intermediate format image until the cache is invalidated. At this point, if any user requests that report with the same combination of parameter values, the report server retrieves the image from the Report Server temporary database and translates it into a rendering format.

As you may notice, for a report that uses several parameters, there can be multiple cache instances in memory. So, this is something that you may want to consider right up front.

Another thing to consider in your cache planning is the cache refresh plan. The key question you should ask yourself in this step is: How frequently must the cache be invalidated? The answer to this surprisingly simple question reveals a lot about the schedule you need to associate with your cache refresh plan (see "Managing Cache Refresh Plans" later). Remember that, in a transactional database, underlying data may change often; keeping an in-memory representation of data for a long time can lead to inaccurate results and, obviously, wrong decisions.

You don't want to get demoted for just caching a report, right?

Caching Your Report

Now that you have a plan in place, the final piece of puzzle is the most obvious one, caching the report by following these steps:

1. Browse to the Documents document library.

2. Click the ECB menu, which appears to the right of the report title, and select Manage Processing Options.

3. From the Data Refresh Option section, select Use cached data option.

4. From the Cache Options section, select Elapsed time in minutes and leave it at 30 minutes until the cache is invalidated.

5. Click OK to enable caching for your report.

Managing Cache Refresh Plans

The way that you cached your report in the previous section is good, but you could use more control over how the report should be cached. In SSRS 2008 R2, Microsoft introduced cache refresh plans to address this issue.

To create a cache refresh plan, follow these steps:

1. Browse to the Documents document library.

2. Click the ECB menu, which appears to the right of the report title, and select Manage Cache Refresh Plans. You should be looking at a page like the one shown in Figure 13-86.

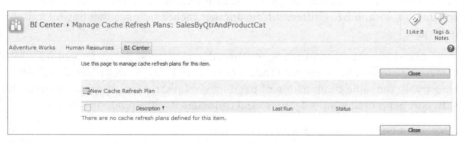

FIGURE 13-86

3. Click New Cache Refresh Plan. If you haven't enabled caching as described in the previous section, you will get the error message shown in Figure 13-87. When you click OK, caching will be automatically enabled for you.

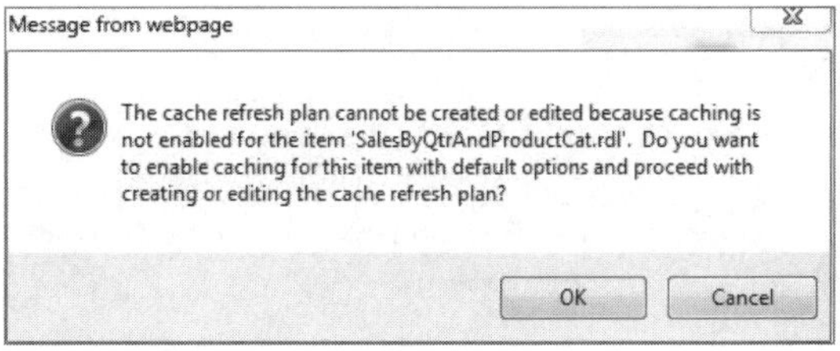

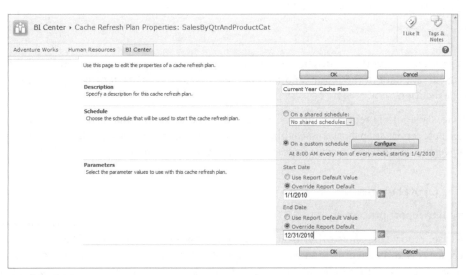

FIGURE 13-87

4. Create a cache plan for default parameter values (1/1/2002, 12/31/2003) and a custom schedule that caches this instance once only at 8 AM of 12/31/2009. Let's suppose that 12/31/2009 is the date on which this report is made available to the users.

5. Click OK to go back to Manage Cache Refresh Plans page.

6. Click New Cache Refresh Plan, to create a new cache plan.

7. Create a cache plan for overridden parameter values (1/1/2010, 12/31/2010) and a custom schedule that caches this instance at 8:00 AM every Monday of every week, starting 1/4/2010, as shown in Figure 13-88.

FIGURE 13-88

8. Click OK to go back to Manage Cache Refresh Plans page. Your cache plans should be like those shown in Figure 13-89.

FIGURE 13-89

With the two cache plans properly configured, now you have your report with the following caching policies:

➤ Your report with Start Date=1/1/2002 and End Date=12/31/2003 will be cached once at 8 AM on 12/31/2009 only.

➤ Your report with Start Date=1/1/2010 and End Date=12/31/2010 will be cached at 8:00 AM every Monday of every week, starting 1/4/2010.

➤ Any other combinations of parameter values follow the default caching schedule you set up in the previous section, which is 30 minutes.

Snapshots

As mentioned previously, caching your report is a great way to give end users a reasonable balance between having current data in the report and having them access reports faster than typical on-demand report execution.

Reporting Services also offers report snapshots that can be used as an alternative approach to caching. In concept, report snapshots and caching are used for a single purpose: delivering reports faster, while lowering on-demand execution costs. Report snapshots can be used for the following two purposes:

➤ Creating report histories

➤ Controlling report processing

Functionality-wise, report snapshots differ from a cached instance in several ways. The first, obvious, difference is that, in caching, you have full control over how often a cached instance should be invalidated (using an expiration schedule or cache refresh plan), but you certainly cannot control when the new cached instance kicks in. This is because cache refreshing depends on when the first request is received after a cached instance expires.

The report caching process lacks the ability to produce a persistent copy of the report from a specific point in time. Report snapshot can be run at a specified time regardless of user requests and can be placed into history without overwriting previous snapshots. Remember that when report execution is persisted, end users will have the ability to compare the report instances at various points in time. This is a very important feature and often a business requirement.

The following steps will walk you through creating a snapshot of your report:

1. Browse to the Documents document library.

2. Click the ECB menu, which appears to the right of the report title, and select Manage Parameters.

3. Change the default dates for the Start Date and End Date to be 1/1/2010 and 12/31/2010, then Click OK.

4. Again, click the ECB menu, and this time select Manage Processing Options.

5. From the Data Refresh Option section, select Use snapshot data option.

6. From Data Snapshot Options section, select Schedule Data Processing and then select On a custom schedule option.

7. Define a schedule that snapshots the report at 8:00 AM on day 30 of Mar, Jun, Sep, Dec, starting 3/1/2010 and ending 12/31/2010, as shown in Figure 13-90.

FIGURE 13-90

8.   Click OK to get back to the Manage Processing Options page.

9.   Click OK to enable snapshots for your report.

With the snapshot properly configured, on the specified dates an image of the report with the specified parameters is created and stored in the report history. You can see the snapshots taken by selecting View Report History from the same ECB menu.

Figure 13-91 shows the snapshot gallery for your report. As you can see, you can manually create snapshots too, by clicking on the New Snapshot button.

FIGURE 13-91

The schedule you defined in Step 7 is a bit different from the schedule you defined for cache refresh plans (see "Managing Cache Refresh Plans"). This schedule is for data processing, and it's independent from the report processing. The second difference between snapshots and caching is that in report caching you cache the data and report layout together. However, in snapshots, it's the data that can be retrieved in advance and stored as a snapshot, and when the report is actually viewed, everything is put together and returned to the end user. This makes snapshots a more lightweight report-processing option compared to caching.

The third difference is that rendering information is not tied to and stored with the snapshot. Instead, the final viewing format is adjusted based on what is appropriate for a user or an application requesting it. This functionality makes snapshots a much more portable solution. The fourth difference is that report snapshots offer less flexibility than report caching.

Snapshots are like pictures and lack interactivity to an extent. However, a cached report allows users to interact with the reports at the same level as on-demand report execution. For example, snapshots are always taken using the default parameter values (if applicable), and there is no way to change them afterward. This limitation forces you to create a different snapshot if you need to change the report parameters. Recall that, by using cache refresh plans, you can target multiple cached instances of the same report to different sets of parameters.

Figure 13-92 illustrates a snapshot report. Notice how the parameter input pane is disabled.

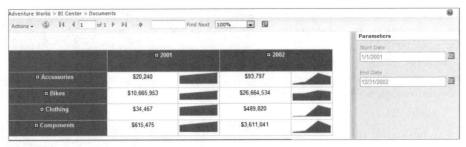

FIGURE 13-92

REPORTING ON SHAREPOINT DATA

SharePoint lists provide lots of functionalities that are already baked into the core SharePoint platform, such as UI elements for managing data, versioning, workflows, and so on. The increasing adoption of SharePoint, along with the great out-of-the-box functionality that SharePoint lists offer, make SharePoint lists a popular choice for storing data.

Whether it makes sense to store your data in SharePoint lists or not is a discussion for another time and place (it's not one solution fits all). In reality, however, organizations often have their data stored in various structured and unstructured data stores, including SharePoint lists.

With the advent of Business Connectivity Services and External Content Types in SharePoint 2010, the data in SharePoint lists comes from new places and no longer does all that data come in from users manually entering it. Instead you are accessing live business data through SharePoint.

No matter how that data is pumped into a SharePoint list, the raw data doesn't have any special meaning by itself. It has to be sliced and diced, sorted, filtered, aggregated, and ultimately formatted to make a point. In general, this is referred to as reporting.

In the previous version of SharePoint, you could create relationships between lists using the lookup field, but there is no easy way to enforce relationship behavior. Moreover, joining lists and aggregating, sorting, and formatting data can quickly become serious bottlenecks. Without the ability to perform such basic operations, reporting on SharePoint data has been challenging for quite a while.

Microsoft elected to take the relational behavior of lists to the next level in SharePoint 2010, by supporting referential integrity (Cascade Delete or Restrict Delete) in list schemas. The new model helps in maintaining the organized form of data and ensures that any reporting you do on such lists is accurate.

How About Querying Large Lists?

Limitations on queries against large SharePoint lists still do exist in SharePoint 2010, but this time around farm administrators have more control over how and when the queries can be executed. For example, administrators can set up query throttling to prevent queries from returning too many rows during peak business hours. If you browse to the Central Administration site and then click Application Management ⇨ Management Web Applications ⇨ General Settings ⇨ Resource Throttling, you will see that the default is set to 5000. For more information about Resource Throttling, refer to Chapter 4.

Sure enough, an administrator can set up happy hours in which large queries can be run, for example, starting 10 PM for 2 hours (see the second highlighted section of Figure 13-93).

But, what if you need a report during business hours and the query in that report exceeds the default list view threshold?

In the following sections, you will create two reports using Reporting Services 2008 R2 and Access 2010 against a sample SharePoint list. The goal is to learn how to report against SharePoint data, while minimizing the effect of list-throttling restrictions imposed by the farm settings.

Creating a Sample List

Before going any further on reporting against SharePoint list data, it makes sense to switch gears here and create a SharePoint list called "Sales Order Numbers" that stores some sales numbers. This is the sample list that will be used in the rest of this chapter.

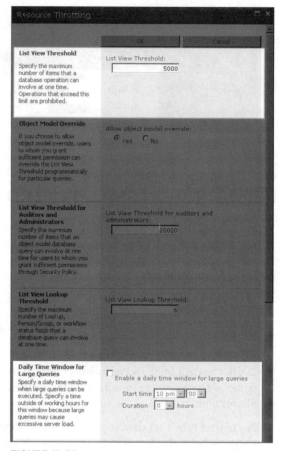

FIGURE 13-93

To create this list in the BI Center, follow these steps:

1. Browse to Site Actions ⇨ View All Site Content.

2. Click Create.

3. On the Create dialog, select List category, and then click Custom List template.

4. In the Title textbox, enter **SalesOrderNumbers**, and press the Create button.

5. Open the SQL Server Management Studio, and execute the following query in to get some sample sales numbers.

```
     SELECT TOP 10
     [SalesOrderNumber]
  FROM [AdventureWorks].[Sales].[SalesOrderHeader]
```

6. Select all the returned records and copy them to the clipboard, as shown in Figure 13-94.

7. Browse to the SalesOrderNumbers list, and click Datasheet View in the Ribbon, as shown in Figure 13-95.

8. Paste the content in the clipboard into the datasheet.

9. Switch back to the Standard View.

Using SQL Server Reporting Services 2008 R2

In SQL Server Reporting Services 2008 R2, Microsoft shipped a new SharePoint List data extension that allows querying against SharePoint list in both BIDS and Report Builder out of the box.

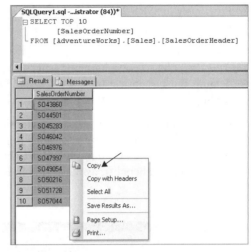

FIGURE 13-94

The process of creating SSRS reports against a SharePoint list is very similar to the process explained in the "Authoring Reports" section earlier in this chapter, and it won't be covered in this section. However, there are a few things that need to be highlighted here.

FIGURE 13-95

When creating your datasource, make sure that you specify the Type as Microsoft SharePoint List and set a fully qualified URL reference to the BI Center site that contains the SalesOrderNumbers list, as shown in Figure 13-96.

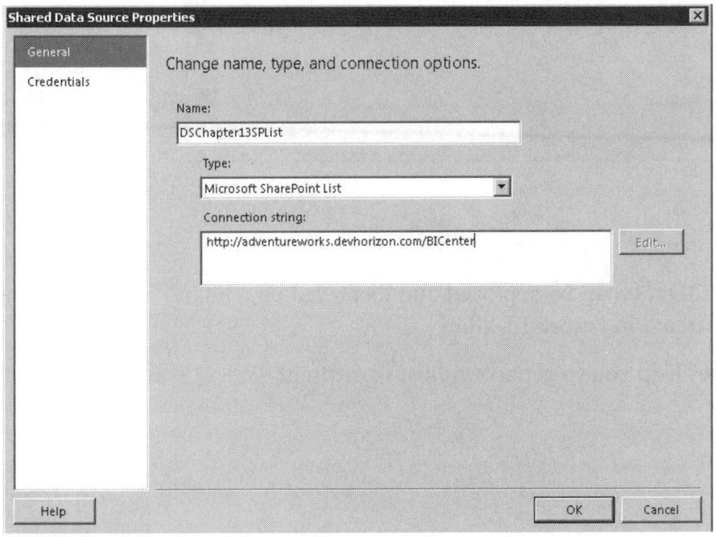

FIGURE 13-96

Previously in SSRS 2008, you needed to specify the Type as XML and set a web reference to the GetListItems method of the lists.asmx web service and pass in the name of the list as parameter.

Another point to consider here is specifying a valid authentication type in the Credentials tab. By default, the authentication is set to use the Do not use credentials option and this will cause an error when you create your dataset later if it's changed here.

In addition to SharePoint List data extension, SQL Server Reporting Services 2008 R2 ships with Query Designer support for both Report Builder and BIDS. Once the datasource is properly set up, you can create a dataset and use the Query Designer to extract the rows from the SalesOrderNumbers list, as illustrated in Figure 13-97.

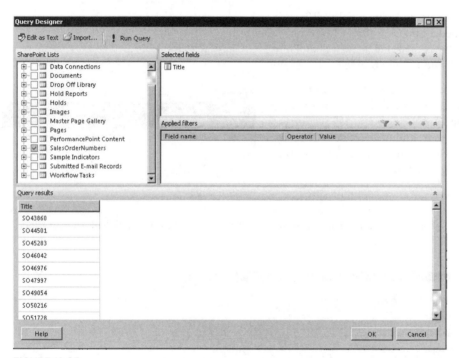

FIGURE 13-97

After the report is developed in BIDS, it can be deployed and displayed on a SharePoint page using a Report Viewer web part, as illustrated in Figure 13-98.

Now, how can Reporting Services help you to get around list throttling?

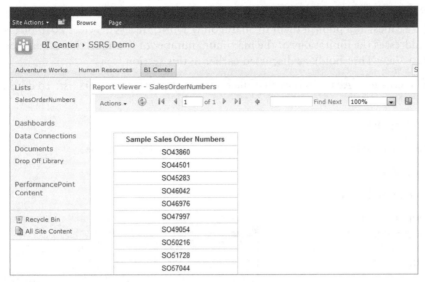

FIGURE 13-98

The list you set up in this section contains only 10 rows. In real-life scenarios where the list contains more records than the list view threshold, you can make a snapshot of the report during happy hours when the resource throttling restriction is not imposed, and render its snapshot in the Report Viewer web part during business hours. For more information, see the "Snapshots" section.

 This report can be found in the code download for this book, in the Chapter 13 .zip file. It is called SalesOrderNumbers.rdl.

Using Access 2010 and Access Services

Another way to report on SharePoint data is by using Access 2010 and Access Services. Access Services is a service application, and it's only available in the enterprise edition of SharePoint Server 2010. In addition to being an enterprise feature, Access Services uses Reporting Services 2008 R2 as its reporting engine. This means that a prerequisite for running Access Services reports in SharePoint is the installation of the Microsoft SQL Server 2008 R2 Reporting Services add-in and setting up the integration in local mode at a minimum.

Once you have installed the add-in and created a new Access Services service application in your farm, Access reports work in pretty much the same way they would in connected mode, as you have seen throughout this chapter.

There are three compelling reasons why you should be considering Access as a reporting solution for reporting on SharePoint data. First, the Access 2010 client application comes with a powerful query engine that can perform many different types of queries such as joins, filtering, aggregates, and master-child and parent-child relationships between SharePoint lists, that otherwise would be challenging to create and often require considerable custom coding. Second, the Access 2010 client has a flexible Report Designer environment that enables you to quickly and easily develop customized reports (.rdl files) and publish them to SharePoint. Third, Access Services 2010 offers a caching layer that addresses the limitations of the maximum number of list items that a query can return at one time (List View Threshold), as discussed earlier in this section.

In this section, you will create an Access report that queries the SalesOrderNumbers list. To do this, follow these steps:

1. Start Microsoft Access 2010.

2. From the available templates, select Blank database and name the database.

3. Click Create button.

4. Right-click Table1 and close it.

5. From the External Data tab, click More and select the SharePoint List option in the drop-down list, as shown in Figure 13-99.

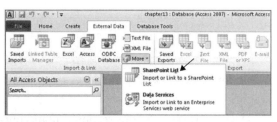

6. In the first screen of the wizard, enter the URL of the BI Center site and select Link to the datasource by creating a linked table option, as shown in Figure 13-100.

FIGURE 13-99

When you select this option, Access establishes a link to any lists that will be selected in the next section, instead of pulling their data into Access in one or more tables. The link goes both ways, meaning that if you modify the content in Access table, it will be synched up with the list and vice versa.

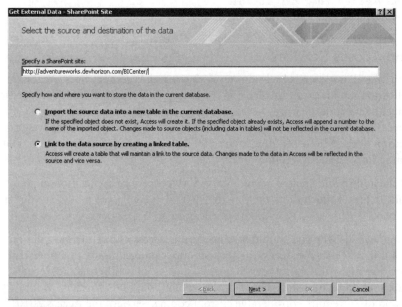

FIGURE 13-100

7. Select the SalesOrderNumbers custom list from which you want to pull data into Access and click OK. Note that if you want to construct joins between lists, you need to select them in this step of the wizard.

8. To create a query against the linked list, from the Create tab select Design Query.

9. In the Show Table dialog, click the Add button to add the SalesOrderNumbers table to the query design surface.

10. Double-click the Title field to include the selected fields for the query, as illustrated in Figure 13-101.

11. Right-click the Query tab, and select Datasheet View to preview the list data.

12. Click the Save button in the Quick Access toolbar. At this point, there should be two objects in your Access database.

Now that you have the list data all linked up to the Access, the next logical step would be to report on this data.

Creating the report from the SalesOrderNumbers table requires simply one button click. All you need to do is to go to the Create tab in the Ribbon and click Report to generate the report shown in Figure 13-102. Click Save to save the new report. Of course, you need to do some customization to make the report look more professional.

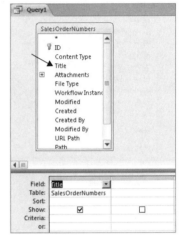

FIGURE 13-101

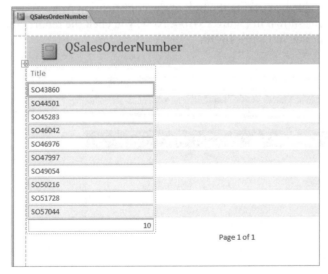

FIGURE 13-102

With the new report generated from the SharePoint list, you are now ready to publish the Access database to SharePoint and make the report available in the browser. To publish the Access database, go to the Backstage and from the File Types billboard select Publish to Access Services. Next, on the Access Services Overview pane, enter the URL of Access Services and the site on which you want this database to be made available. In this example, the site is a subsite of the BI Center, as shown in Figure 13-103.

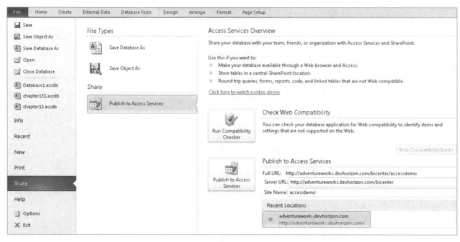

FIGURE 13-103

Once you are done, click Publish to Access Services; that's it!

Now you should be able to browse to the site by clicking the link in the confirmation page. Your Access workspace should look like the one shown in Figure 13-104. Now, you click the report, and you should get the exact same report you saw in Figure 13-98.

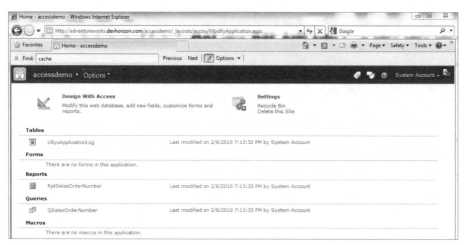

FIGURE 13-104

CLAIMS AND BI SOLUTIONS

In SharePoint Server 2010, there are some important developments related to authentication and authorization, which affect all the services running on the top of the new platform. These changes are particularly important for BI solutions deployed to SharePoint and when SharePoint plays the role of a middle man in accessing the backend data. Perhaps the most important impact is how claims-based identity has been plugged into the SharePoint authentication and authorization semantics through a new service called Security Token Service (STS).

In SharePoint 2010, when a user authenticates to a claims-aware web application, regardless of identity system or authentication type, a claims identity is issued by STS and then it's translated into an SPUser object. This identity is issued based on the standard protocols (SAML, WS-Trust, and WS-Federation) and works with any corporate identity system, such as Active Directory, WebSSO, Live ID, LDAP, SQL, or Custom. Without any special configuration, the claims identity flows along with the request through the server tiers (service applications) in a SharePoint farm.

In terms of the authorization semantics, things haven't changed much in SharePoint 2010, with one exception. Now you can authorize access to resources over a lot more attributes. Additionally, during the authentication process, you have a chance to call into the claim provider APIs and augment the existing claims for handling your own custom authorization scenarios. For more information, see the official documentation at www.devhorizon.com/go/23.

Now the question is does the new claims authentication in SharePoint 2010 mean that all the double hop issues are resolved? The answer is certainly no!

Service application infrastructure in SharePoint Server 2010 is claims-aware, but many external datasources are still not claims-aware. There are many scenarios where claims cannot be used. In the following list, you will find a number of them:

➤ **Scenario 1:** In this scenario, an Excel workbook or PerformancePoint scorecard is used against an Analysis Services cube which has role-based security (i.e., every role has its own view of the data). This will require Windows authentication for Analysis Services and, thus, a way to pass the identity for every user from SharePoint to Analysis Services. SQL Server Analysis Services is not claims-aware and has no idea who or what the SharePoint user is. In order to implement this, you either need to configure Kerberos or the unattended service account and add an authenticated username in the connection string.

➤ **Scenario 2:** Frontend web servers, the Excel Calculation Services application, and the SharePoint database servers run on different computers. In this scenario, if Excel Calculation Services are opening workbooks stored in SharePoint content databases, you should use Kerberos or the unattended account.

➤ **Scenario 3:** In this scenario, Excel Calculation Services is opening a workbook from non–Microsoft SharePoint Foundation trusted file locations, such as UNC shares or HTTP websites. The authentication method used in this scenario is either to use impersonation or process an account, as seen in Figure 13-105.

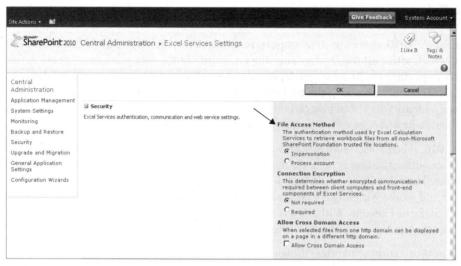

FIGURE 13-105

➤ **Scenario 4:** A very common scenario in which Kerberos is needed is when there are multiple machine hops from mid-tier to the last datasource, as shown in Figure 13-106. Remember, the minute an identity leaves the boundary of the Service Application tier, the claims identity may no longer be meaningful if a datasource doesn't understand the compliant SAML protocol.

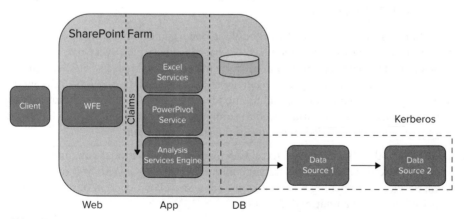

FIGURE 13-106

The scenario depicted in Figure 13-107 shows how the combination of claims and the unattended account can help you properly authenticate to the backend datasource. In this scenario, the claims identity flows between multiple service applications, and the Analysis Services engine impersonates the unattended account to connect to the external datasource.

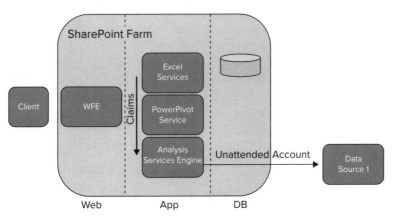

FIGURE 13-107

SUMMARY

In SharePoint Server 2010, BI is a very important topic and another area with significant enhancements. Even if you are a seasonal SharePoint developer, the chances are you are not very familiar with BI concepts, so the chapter started out by explaining some of the must-know BI terms and concepts.

The power of the BI template that ships out of the box with the Enterprise Edition of SharePoint 2010 hopefully came out in this chapter. The idea of using this template is to help you quickly and easily create a BI-focused SharePoint site that will make others think you spent hours putting it all together, so just use it!

This chapter introduced two of the most important BI service applications in SharePoint Server 2010: Excel Services and PerformancePoint Services. In the Excel Services section, you learned in particular how to import data into an Excel workbook, slice and dice it, and visualize and display it in a PivotTable and PivotChart. In the PerformancePoint section, you were introduced to a very common confusion in the BI world, that between the dashboard and scorecard. Hopefully, you walked away learning that, at the end of the day, they're all the same. Both scorecards and dashboards are used to monitor performance and make sure that the business is on the right track toward a set of predefined goals.

In the Reporting Services section, you learned not only how to build and deploy reports to a SharePoint site configured in connected mode, but also techniques such as caching and snapshots. These operations have the advantage of being scheduled and running in the background, giving you greater control over when and how report execution should occur. The goal is to enhance the performance of report execution and the user experience when viewing reports.

At the end of the chapter, you had a brief overview of two techniques used to query SharePoint lists: Reporting Services and Access Services. Although we didn't go into much detail, the core message was that both Reporting Services reports (with the snapshot feature) and Access reports can help you minimize the performance effects of reporting against large lists.

When you put together all the pieces presented in this chapter, you have a powerful array of options for building BI solutions that will address critical business needs.

14

SharePoint Online

WHAT'S IN THIS CHAPTER?

➤ An overview of SharePoint online

➤ Programming differences in the cloud

If you have not heard about public or private clouds, you must not be reading the news or blogs, or looking at what the different vendors are doing. Software as a service (SAAS) is all the rage in the computing world. While it has many merits, including ease of deployment, anywhere access, and quick upgrades, at the same time it has a number of obstacles, such as limited offline support, less mature development tools, and less control of customization. Regardless of these limitations, many people are looking to the cloud as the next major shift in the computing world. If you have not tried to build applications against a cloud service such as Microsoft Azure or SharePoint Online, get started today.

SHAREPOINT ONLINE OVERVIEW

There are two different versions of SharePoint Online: Standard and Dedicated. Table 14-1 provides an easy way to compare the different ways you can deploy SharePoint. This table compares SharePoint On-Premises, SharePoint Online Standard and SharePoint Online Dedicated.

TABLE 14-1: Different Deployment Options for SharePoint

AREA	ON-PREMISES	ONLINE STANDARD	ONLINE DEDICATED
Type of Hosting	Self-hosted and managed	Multi-tenant hosted by Microsoft	Dedicated hardware and hosting by Microsoft
Type of Physical Access	Direct access to physical machines	Shared Hardware with no physical access	Dedicated hardware with no physical access

continues

TABLE 14-1 *(continued)*

AREA	ON-PREMISES	ONLINE STANDARD	ONLINE DEDICATED
Administration Capabilities	Central Administration access supported	No Central Administration access but tenant administration access	Central Administration access supported
Customization	No limitations	No support for farm code but support for sandbox, SharePoint Designer (SPD), and client applications	Customizable, but some solutions require Microsoft Approval
Topology Support	Set by customer	No control but supports certificate- or forms-based authentication	Machine and process accounts in different AD forests
Size Limitations	No limits	Between 5 and 5000 users	5000 or more users

One of the major differences, as you can see in the table, is that SharePoint Online Standard does not support the full range of customizations like the other two deployments of SharePoint. Going even deeper, if you look at what constitutes a farm solution as opposed to a non-farm solution, the clarity of what will and won't work gets better. Table 14-2 shows examples of no-code solutions versus farm solutions.

TABLE 14-2: No-Code versus Farm Solutions

NO-CODE SOLUTION	FARM SOLUTION
Custom Markup (HTML, ASP.NET, XSLT)	Custom Server Components (coded workflows, timer jobs, Window Services)
SharePoint Designer solutions	Visual Studio Solutions (except for Sandbox Solutions)
Client-side code, such as Client OMs, including JavaScript and Silverlight	Application pages
Coding against SharePoint web services	Visual web parts

One other major difference between online and on-premises is that not all of the feature set of SharePoint is supported in the cloud. In particular, SharePoint Online does not support PerformancePoint or FAST in the cloud. Additionally, when dealing with search technologies, architecture and deployment become more critical when deploying in the cloud. For example, if you had a hybrid environment where you wanted to have one search index across both on-premises content and cloud content, where do you place your indexer — on-premises or online? The answer is that it depends, but either place that you decide to place it, you will be dealing with crawling across WANs. A solution may be to create two separate search deployments and use federated search. However, doing so results in the loss of the ability to have a single result set with integrated relevancy.

DEVELOPING IN THE CLOUD

As you can see by the summary above, some of the ways you are used to developing on-premises will not translate to the multi-tenant cloud. Using server-side code is a no-no when it comes to building applications where you are running SharePoint with other tenants on the server. When developing for online use, there are a number of different choices you have for development. You can use Sandbox Solutions, SPD, InfoPath, Access, or the SharePoint client object model in ASP.NET or Silverlight applications. Since many of these technologies have been covered already in this book, they will not be covered here again.

Instead, this chapter focuses on some of the best practices to use when developing in the cloud. These best practices can be used on-premises as well as on the cloud, but given the limitations of the cloud, you have more options on-premises.

Visual Sandbox Web Parts

One of the complaints about Sandbox Solutions is that you cannot create a visual web part as a Sandbox Solution. The reason for this is the way Visual Studio (VS) implements the visual web part and uses the `Page.LoadControl` method to load the user control that represents the web part. It requires access to the file system to get the ASCX file, then it compiles the ASCX file and returns a new type. There are a number of ways to resolve the problem of creating a visual web part, including compiling the ASCX yourself and referencing it in your Sandbox Solution.

However, there is an easier way than doing all this work yourself. There is a community effort to build tools for SharePoint on Codeplex. The tools available at Codeplex include a template for building visual web parts inside of a Sandbox Solution. You can download these tools from the following URLs: `http://sharepointdevtools.codeplex.com/` and `http://cksdev.codeplex.com/`.

Debugging Your Solutions

Depending on the technology you decide to use, there will be different techniques to debug your solutions. Unfortunately, many of the techniques you are used to will not work in an online development environment. For example, you cannot enable the Developer Dashboard in the online environment. Also, your Sandbox Solutions cannot write to the file system or over the network. For SharePoint debugging purposes, get comfortable writing debugging information as screen alerts or storing it within SharePoint lists. Furthermore, you will want to keep a SharePoint site just for development and then deploy your solutions to your online production site.

When it comes to Silverlight or client-side code, your choices for debugging are better, since you can use the tools built into Internet Explorer or Firefox to debug your solution.

The following Sandbox web part shows how to log on to a SharePoint list for debugging purposes:

```csharp
using System;
using System.ComponentModel;
using System.Runtime.InteropServices;
using System.Web.UI;
using System.Web.UI.WebControls;
using System.Web.UI.WebControls.WebParts;
using Microsoft.SharePoint;
using Microsoft.SharePoint.WebControls;

namespace SharePointOnlineLogging.WebPart1
{
    [ToolboxItemAttribute(false)]
    public class WebPart1 : WebPart
    {

        private Button logResultsButton = new Button() { Text = "Log Results" };
        private Label lbl = new Label();

        public WebPart1()
        {
        }

        protected override void CreateChildControls()
        {
            logResultsButton.Click += (object sender, EventArgs e) =>
            {

                SPContext context = SPContext.Current;

                SPWeb web = context.Web;

                SPList list = web.GetList("/Lists/
                  SharePointOnlineLogging-ListInstance1");

                string logResults = DateTime.Now.ToShortDateString() + " " +
                  DateTime.Now.ToShortTimeString()
                    + ": Logged from Sandbox Web Part!";

                SPListItem newItem = list.AddItem();


                newItem["Title"] = "New Log Result - " +
                DateTime.Now.ToShortTimeString();
                newItem["LoggingResult"] = logResults;

                newItem.Update();


                lbl.Text = "Logged Result: " + logResults;
            };
```

```
        Controls.Add(logResultsButton);

        Controls.Add(lbl);

        //base.CreateChildControls();
    }

    protected override void RenderContents(HtmlTextWriter writer)
    {
        base.RenderContents(writer);
    }
  }
}
```

WebPart1.cs

EXAMPLE CLOUD SCENARIOS

To help understand areas where using SharePoint in the cloud makes sense, the following scenarios describe where you can use the cloud and where you can't. As you will find, for out-of-the-box functionality, SharePoint Online is a very viable solution. The areas to watch out for include custom code and unsupported features in the cloud, or features that require administrative access to the server.

The first scenario is your typical team collaboration, wherein you are creating a team site, sharing documents, and performing simple customization of the site. Because this case does not require high-end development or administrative access, this scenario would be supported easily in the cloud. The only gotchas are to make sure that users who use Office on their desktop understand how to authenticate against SharePoint Online and how to determine the address for their sites, since they will be fully qualified domain names rather than Intranet style short names.

The next scenario is a company portal. This is where it gets more complex, because many portals require rich customization and publishing infrastructure. This is one scenario where you will have to evaluate your needs versus what SharePoint Online provides from a development standpoint. If you find that your existing portal makes use of a lot of custom code (such as custom field controls or complex worklows), you may not want to run your solution in SharePoint Online or rewrite these solutions to use Sandbox Solutions, which are supported in the Online environment.

SharePoint Online will have an offering for building Extranets since the security for Extranets is different than Intranet sites. Plus, sharing and invitations with external parties makes it easy for end users to invite their business partners from other companies. While this offer isn't complete at the time of the writing of this book, Extranets, depending on what the offer finally ships, may be the first scenario that you undertake with SharePoint Online as a complement to your on-premises deployment of SharePoint. You may get a quick win by making it easy to share information with your business partners without having to worry about access to your internal corporate networks. You will want to make sure that the Online service-level agreements for availability and recovery meet your corporate standards and that the security in place for SharePoint Online meets your security guidelines for your company.

The last scenario is Internet-facing sites. SharePoint Online will have an offer for anonymous Internet facing sites with SharePoint Online 2010; you will want to evaluate this offer for medium-sized websites. If you are running a large scale website that requires a lot of customizations, the Online offer will not meet your needs. You will want to run your Internet site on-premises until Online allows for complex customizations and support for technologies such as content deployment.

SUMMARY

In this chapter, you learned about the different versions of SharePoint Online. Also, you saw what is supported in an on-premises deployment, as opposed to an online deployment. With the 2010 release of SharePoint Online, there is better symmetry between the on-premises and online versions of SharePoint, but to a developer there are a significant number of differences. You will have to keep that in mind as you develop your code to make it portable from an on-premises solution to a SharePoint Online solution.

Additional Help and Resources

WHAT'S IN THIS APPENDIX?

➤ Included and additional help files

Developing for SharePoint involves bringing together a number of different technologies, including SharePoint, developer tools, and web development technologies. To be effective in developing in SharePoint, you need to understand the resources available to help you, both from Microsoft and the community. There are high-quality tools and documentation available from both resources.

HELP FILES FROM MICROSOFT

The key resource from Microsoft that every SharePoint developer should download is the SharePoint SDK. The SDK comes in two versions, one for SharePoint Foundation and another for SharePoint Server. You should download both sets of SDKs onto your development machine. You can find the SDKs at the Microsoft SharePoint Development Center at `http://msdn.microsoft.com/sharepoint`.

ONLINE HELP FROM MICROSOFT

One of the key resources available online for learning to develop with SharePoint is the MSDN Development Center for SharePoint at `http://msdn.microsoft.com/sharepoint`. Besides the Center, there are a number of other resources to look at, including the getting started website for SharePoint development at `http://www.mssharepointdeveloper.com`. In addition, Channel 9 from Microsoft has a number of videos available at `http://channel9.msdn.com/tags/sharepoint/` to help you get started developing with SharePoint.

One key resource to keep track of is the SharePoint team blog. On this blog, the SharePoint team posts relevant information about SharePoint that customers and partners would be interested in. The blog is located at `http://blogs.msdn.com/sharepoint`.

The last resource is the SharePoint Developer Documentation team blog. This blog is the location where the developer documentation team posts important information that may not be in the SDK or best practices for developing with SharePoint. You can find the blog at `http://blogs.msdn.com/sharepointdeveloperdocs/`.

HELP FROM THE COMMUNITY

SharePoint has a rich community when it comes to developing. Community-driven tools, such as the Community Kit for SharePoint: Development Tools Edition, are available at `http://cksdev.codeplex.com/`. In addition, there are a number of other online resources that you should review as you develop your SharePoint solutions. The following list shows some of the sites that might help you with your SharePoint development.

- ➤ **Paul Andrew's Blog:** `http://blogs.msdn.com/pandrew/`
- ➤ **Arpan Shah's Blog:** `http://blogs.msdn.com/arpans/`
- ➤ **Andrew Connell's Blog:** `http://www.andrewconnell.com/blog/`
- ➤ **SharePoint Dev Wiki:** `http://www.sharepointdevwiki.com`
- ➤ **Bamboo SharePoint Blog:** `http://community.bamboosolutions.com/blogs/sharepoint-2010/default.aspx`
- ➤ **Joel Oleson's SharePoint Blog:** `http://www.sharepointjoel.com/default.aspx`
- ➤ **Jeremy Thake's blog:** `http://wss.made4the.net/default.aspx`
- ➤ **Eric Harlan's blog:** `http://www.ericharlan.com/`
- ➤ **Fabian William's blog:** `http://fabiangwilliams.wordpress.com/`

INDEX

X